Principles and Practice of American Politics

Fifth Edition

Principles and Practice of American Politics

Classic and Contemporary Readings

Fifth Edition

Samuel Kernell
University of California, San Diego

Steven S. Smith
Washington University, St. Louis

Los Angeles | London | New Delhi
Singapore | Washington DC

Los Angeles | London | New Delhi
Singapore | Washington DC

FOR INFORMATION:

CQ Press
An Imprint of SAGE Publications, Inc.
2455 Teller Road
Thousand Oaks, California 91320
E-mail: order@sagepub.com

SAGE Publications Ltd.
1 Oliver's Yard
55 City Road
London EC1Y 1SP
United Kingdom

SAGE Publications India Pvt. Ltd.
B 1/I 1 Mohan Cooperative Industrial Area
Mathura Road, New Delhi 110 044
India

SAGE Publications Asia-Pacific Pte. Ltd.
3 Church Street
#10-04 Samsung Hub
Singapore 049483

Acquisitions Editor: Charisse Kiino
Editorial Assistant: Nancy Loh
Production Editor: Laureen Gleason
Copy Editor: Erin Livingston
Typesetter: C&M Digitals (P) Ltd.
Proofreader: Theresa Kay
Cover Designer: Stefan Killen Design
Marketing Manager: Jonathan Mason
Permissions Editor: Adele Hutchinson

Printed in the United States of America

Library of Congress Cataloging-in-Publication Data

Principles and practice of American politics : classic and contemporary readings / edited by Samuel Kernell, Steven S. Smith. — 5th ed.

p. cm.
ISBN 978-1-4522-2628-6 (pbk.)

1. United States—Politics and government. 2. Political culture—United States. I. Kernell, Samuel, 1945- II. Smith, Steven S., 1953-

JK21.P76 2013 320.973—dc23 2012016200

This book is printed on acid-free paper.

12 13 14 15 16 10 9 8 7 6 5 4 3 2 1

CONTENTS

Preface   xi

About the Editors   xiii

Chapter 1. Designing Institutions   1

1-1 MANCUR OLSON JR.   from *The Logic of Collective Action*   1

In an excerpt from his classic work of 1965, Mancur Olson Jr. explains why groups often have difficulty achieving their collective goals, even when agreement among their members is widespread.

1-2 GARRETT HARDIN   The Tragedy of the Commons   12

In another classic work, Garrett Hardin uses the idea of the *tragedy of the commons* to explain why public goods are so often misused.

1-3 BRUCE ACKERMAN   The Citizenship Agenda   25

The author criticizes the Constitution as overly attentive to fashioning republican institutions at the expense of democracy. He proposes several fundamental reforms to correct imbalance.

Chapter 2. The Constitutional Framework   34

2-1 JOHN P. ROCHE JR.   The Founding Fathers:
A Reform Caucus in Action   34

John P. Roche Jr. argues that the Framers were ultimately pragmatists who sought to satisfy constituents with often-conflicting goals.

2-2 BRUTUS   *Anti-Federalist* No. 3   59

In this essay, published early in the ratification debates, Brutus unveils the principal arguments against the Constitution.

2-3 JAMES MADISON   *Federalist* No. 10   64

James Madison argues that a large, diverse republic is not only capable of controlling the tyranny of faction but, when properly designed, the best means of doing so.

2-4 JAMES MADISON   *Federalist* No. 51   71

James Madison explains how the Constitution will employ checks and balances to prevent the people's representatives from exploiting their political power.

Chapter 3. Federalism   74

3-1 JAMES MADISON   *Federalist* No. 39   74

James Madison continues his exploration of the Constitution's salutary effects in this essay concentrating on federalism and republicanism.

**3-2 DONALD F. KETTL   Federalism: Sorting Out
Who Does What   80**

Donald F. Kettl explores the lessons of Hurricane Katrina for understanding the ever-evolving division of power and responsibility between the state and federal governments.

3-3 JONATHAN RAUCH   A Separate Peace   103

Jonathan Rauch states that federalism provides a "safety valve" to American democracy by allowing the various states to adopt different policies on issues on which differences of opinion run deep.

**3-4 THOMAS J. SARGENT   An American
History Lesson for Europe   107**

The author explores the lessons of American federalism for resolution of Europe's current debt crisis.

Chapter 4. Civil Rights   110

4-1 RICHARD THOMPSON FORD   from *The Race Card*   110

This essay argues that charges of racism are frequently made to gain political advantage. As a result, justifiable claims of racism tend to be discounted.

**4-2 KENNETH PREWITT   Immigrants and the
Changing Categories of Race   127**

This essay enlists census classifications of race and ethnicity to explore the evolution of racial identity.

Chapter 5. Civil Liberties   139

5-1 CASS R. SUNSTEIN   from *Republic.com 2.0*   139

The author applies established *freedom of speech* doctrines to novel forms of expression in the electronic age.

**5-2 WILLIAM N. ESKRIDGE JR.   A Liberal Vision of
U.S. Family Law in 2020   156**

After exploring how gay marriage will introduce new varieties of families, the author urges that revision of family law not be left exclusively to the courts.

5-3 SUPREME COURT OF THE UNITED STATES   *Roe v. Wade*   165

In this controversial decision, the Supreme Court considers whether the Constitution protects a woman's right to terminate her pregnancy against the objections of the State.

**5-4 GERALD N. ROSENBERG   The Real World of Constitutional
Rights: The Supreme Court and the Implementation
of the Abortion Decisions   174**

Gerald N. Rosenberg examines the political and legal environment surrounding abortion policy, which is still a source of conflict thirty years after *Roe v. Wade*.

Chapter 6. Congress   204

6-1 STEVEN S. SMITH   Congress, the Troubled Institution   204

Steven S. Smith describes Congress's struggles with partisanship, filibusters, and scandals as it tackles momentous issues.

6-2 SARAH A. BINDER   The Politics of Legislative Stalemate   220

Sarah A. Binder outlines the effects of divided party control of the institutions of government and partisan polarization on the policy-making process.

6-3 JOHN H. ALDRICH AND DAVID W. ROHDE   Congressional Committees in a Continuing Partisan Era   231

John H. Aldrich and David W. Rohde state that in an era of polarized parties, party leaders dominate standing committees in the policy-making process of the House of Representatives.

Chapter 7. The Presidency   254

7-1 RICHARD E. NEUSTADT   from *Presidential Power*   254

Richard E. Neustadt shows that successful presidential leadership depends on the ability to persuade.

7-2 JOHN P. BURKE   The Institutional Presidency   275

This essay examines the institutional ramifications of Congress's delegation of broad administrative authority.

7-3 SAMUEL KERNELL   from *Going Public*   300

Samuel Kernell observes that modern presidents, in their efforts to persuade other politicians to adopt their policy preferences, often "go public": a set of activities borrowed from presidential election campaigns.

Chapter 8. The Bureaucracy   318

8-1 TERRY M. MOE   The Politics of Bureaucratic Structure   318

Terry M. Moe argues that the federal bureaucracy is not structured on the basis of a theory of public administration but instead is the product of politics.

8-2 PAUL SINGER   Bush and the Bureaucracy: A Crusade for Control   333

Paul Singer argues that presidents pursue a variety of personnel, budget, and legal strategies to assert influence over policy decisions made in the federal bureaucracy.

8-3 DAVID E. LEWIS   from *The Politics of Presidential Appointments*   345

This essay states that presidents' strategies for controlling federal departments and agencies have evolved in important ways in recent decades.

8-4 MATHEW D. MCCUBBINS, ROGER G. NOLL, AND
BARRY R. WEINGAST **Administrative Procedures
as Instruments of Political Control** 369

Mathew D. McCubbins, Roger G. Noll, and Barry R. Weingast describe how oversight and
administrative procedures are used to induce compliance from government agencies to the
policy preferences of policy makers.

Chapter 9. The Judiciary 383

9-1 ANTONIN SCALIA from *A Matter of Interpretation:
Federal Courts and the Law* 383

In this lecture to law school students, Supreme Court Justice Antonin Scalia makes a strong
case for judges to limit their analysis to what laws say instead of exploring their intent.

9-2 STEPHEN BREYER from *Active Liberty* 401

Antonin Scalia's colleague, Supreme Court Justice Stephen Breyer, argues instead that
judges should weigh the implications of their decisions for advancing democracy.

9-3 ALEXANDER HAMILTON *Federalist* No. 78 414

While asserting that the unelected judiciary is the "least dangerous branch," Alexander
Hamilton assumes for the Supreme Court the important role of judicial review.

9-4 ROBERT A. CARP, KENNETH L. MANNING, AND
RONALD STIDHAM **The Voting Behavior of
Barack Obama's Judges: As Far Left as
Some Opponents Say or Just Mainstream Liberals?** 420

This essay argues that all presidents seek judges who share their policy views; the evidence
presented here shows that they have succeeded.

Chapter 10. Public Opinion 436

10-1 HERBERT ASHER **Analyzing and Interpreting Polls** 436

Herbert Asher explains the common ways that polls are misinterpreted and misused.

10-2 JAMES A. STIMSON, MICHAEL B. MACKUEN, AND
ROBERT S. ERIKSON **Dynamic Representation** 466

This essay explains how this important and creative study measures the correlation between
public preferences and government behavior.

10-3 MORRIS P. FIORINA from *Culture War? The
Myth of a Polarized America* 481

Morris P. Fiorina challenges the popular notion that Americans are becoming more deeply
divided on cultural issues.

10-4 JAMES Q. WILSON **How Divided Are We?** 492

James Q. Wilson argues that the ideological and partisan polarization of American politics is
real, has increased, and has spread to voters through political and media elites.

10-5 ROBERT D. PUTNAM AND DAVID E. CAMPBELL   Religion
     in American Politics   504

Robert D. Putnam and David E. Campbell explore the way religious values have come to influence attitudes about politics, the parties, and key social issues in the United States.

Chapter 11. Voting, Campaigns, and Elections   533

11-1 SAMUEL L. POPKIN   from *The Reasoning Voter*   533

Samuel L. Popkin argues that in a world of imperfect and incomplete information, voters rely on shortcuts to make decisions. His depiction of the decision-making processes of voters helps to explain the characteristics of campaigns and other features of American politics.

11-2 GARY C. JACOBSON   No Compromise: The Electoral
     Origins of Legislative Gridlock   541

Gary C. Jacobson describes the way that partisan polarization and gridlock in American policy making reflect the disparate electoral coalitions responsible for electing Democrats and Republicans to public office.

11-3 DARRELL M. WEST   from *Air Wars*   563

Darrell M. West describes the mechanics and strategies of modern television advertising in political campaigns.

11-4 MICHAEL SCHUDSON   America's Ignorant Voters   588

Michael Schudson observes that American voters are not becoming less knowledgeable about government (contrary to the conventional wisdom) and, even without all the facts about politics, are able to make reasonable judgments about candidates.

11-5 PAUL BLUMENTHAL   Super PACs and Secret Money   596

Paul Blumenthal describes the emergence of Super PACs and their surprising growth since the Supreme Court's Citizens United 2010 decision and a follow-up appeals court decision that certain kinds of organization can receive unlimited contributions from individuals, corporations, and unions.

Chapter 12. Political Parties   602

12-1 JOHN H. ALDRICH   from *Why Parties?*   602

John H. Aldrich describes the political problems that parties solve for candidates and voters.

12-2 LARRY M. BARTELS   Partisanship and Voting
     Behavior, 1952–1996   615

Larry M. Bartels describes trends in the party identification of Americans and explains the importance of these trends for voting behavior.

12-3 MORRIS P. FIORINA   Parties as Problem Solvers   626

According to Morris P. Fiorina, today's centralized, cohesive parties are no better at solving today's problems than the decentralized, disunited parties of a half century ago and may even make them worse.

Chapter 13. Interest Groups   640

13-1 E. E. SCHATTSCHNEIDER   The Scope and Bias of the Pressure System   640

In a still-relevant piece from the 1960s, E. E. Schattschneider argues that moneyed interests dominated midcentury politics by controlling the agenda and influencing policymakers.

13-2 JOHN R. WRIGHT   The Evolution of Interest Groups   649

John R. Wright surveys the development of interest groups in America, emphasizing the conflicting forces of collective action problems and societal disturbances.

13-3 RICHARD L. HALL AND FRANK W. WAYMAN   Buying Time: Moneyed Interests and the Mobilization of Bias in Congressional Committees   657

Legislators are more responsive to organized business interests than to unorganized voters, a responsiveness that is more evident in committee than on the floor and more evident in their commitment of time than in their votes.

Chapter 14. News Media   669

14-1 JAMES T. HAMILTON   The Market and the Media   669

News, James T. Hamilton reminds us, is a consumer product and as such changes with consumer demands and market competition.

14-2 MATTHEW A. BAUM AND TIM J. GROELING   from *War Stories*   685

Reporters and politicians engage each other with different goals in the news they jointly make. The authors assess the product of their interaction on foreign policy-making.

14-3 KRISTEN PURCELL, LEE RAINIE, AMY MITCHELL, TOM ROSENSTIEL, AND KENNY OLMSTEAD   Understanding the Participatory News Consumer   695

The Pew Research Center's report provides a detailed look at the effect of changes in information technology on the way Americans receive, use, and react to the news and news organizations.

Constitution of the United States   707

Credits   728

PREFACE

Assembling this set of readings for students of American politics has been a pleasure and a challenge. The pleasure has come in discovering so many articles that illuminate American politics. The challenge has come in finding far more than can be contained in a single volume. Consequently, despite its heft, *Principles and Practice of American Politics* represents a small sampling of the available literature.

Our shared perspective on politics has guided the selection of articles. Political actors pursue goals informed by self-interest. This perspective does not require abandoning all hope that politics can result in public policy that serves the common interests of the public today and for future generations. It says simply that to understand politics we need to understand what different political actors want and how this leads them to engage in various strategies to achieve their goals. For government actors, these goals will largely reflect the offices they hold, the constituents they represent, and the constitutional obligations and opportunities that define their roles. Other major actors—the public, the news media, and activists in political parties and interest groups—are similarly motivated by self-interest. They do not occupy government positions, and so their behavior is regulated by a different constellation of opportunities and limitations. Each chapter's readings introduce the interests, rules, and strategic contexts of political action in a major national political forum.

Conflict over social issues, polarization in Washington and the nation, legislative gridlock, and the tremendous challenges facing policymakers are among the subjects of the new selections for this edition. Our selections reflect the changing composition of the Supreme Court and the intensification of fights over Court nominations; the debates over the polarization of the American electorate and Congress; the place of parties, interest groups, and religion in our polity; the role of television and new media; and the ever-evolving state of civil rights and civil liberties.

We have chosen the readings to serve two audiences. Many instructors will employ *Principles and Practice of American Politics* as a supplement to an introductory American politics textbook. For others, this book may constitute the core reading material for a course. For the former, we selected readings that will animate the institutional processes described in the text. For the latter, we have sought readings that can stand alone and do not assume more than an elementary knowledge of American government and politics. In this edition, we have added essays that challenge students to think more carefully about alternative institutions and political arrangements. The essays present institutions of majority rule, the nature of racial discrimination, the development of same-sex unions, and the proper role of the Court as less settled issues that provide students an opportunity to think through (and discuss) their views on the future direction of American civic life.

Some of the selections are classics that all instructors will recognize; others, which may be less familiar, address contemporary political developments or proposals for reform. Each article adds emphasis and depth to textbook coverage and illustrates an important theme; most also introduce an important writer on American politics. We hope all of the articles enrich students' understanding of American politics.

We have taken care to include as much of each original source as possible. We have edited some of the pieces to make them appropriate for classroom use. Ellipses indicate where material has been excised, and brackets enclose editorial interpolations. Other changes are explained in the source note for the reading.

We wish to thank the editorial staff of CQ Press for its expertise, energy, and patience in helping us bring this project to completion. Brenda Carter and Charisse Kiino offered essential encouragement and guidance throughout the effort and provided superb editorial assistance, and Nancy Loh persisted in acquiring permission to reprint the selections. Several anonymous reviewers and the following political scientists provided very helpful comments on our plans for this edition: Scott Adler, University of Colorado; Craig Burnett, Appalachian State University; Marc J. Hetherington, Vanderbilt University; Kenneth L. Manning, University of Massachusetts–Dartmouth; Stephen Nicholson, University of California, Merced; Eric Schickler, University of California, Berkeley; John Shively, Longview Community College; John J. Theis, Lonestar College–Kingwood; and Lynn Vavreck, University of California, Los Angeles.

Samuel Kernell

Steven S. Smith

ABOUT THE EDITORS

Samuel Kernell is professor of political science at the University of California, San Diego, where he has taught since 1977. He taught previously at the University of Mississippi and the University of Minnesota and served as a senior fellow at the Brookings Institution. Kernell's research interests focus on the presidency, political communication, and American political history. His recent books include *Going Public: New Strategies of Presidential Leadership*; *James Madison: The Theory and Practice of Republican Government*, an edited collection of essays; and *The Logic of American Politics*, coauthored with Gary C. Jacobson and Thad Kousser. Kernell and Erik J. Engstrom are currently writing *Manufactured Responsiveness*, an analysis of the effects of nineteenth-century state electoral laws on national politics.

Steven S. Smith is professor of political science and director of the Weidenbaum Center at Washington University in St. Louis. He has taught at the University of Minnesota, Northwestern University, and George Washington University and has served as a senior fellow at the Brookings Institution. His research interests include American politics, congressional politics, Russian politics, positive theories of politics, and theories of institutional development. He is author or coauthor of the following: *Party Influence in Congress*; *Politics or Principle: Filibustering in the United States Senate*; *Committees in Congress*; *The American Congress*; *Call to Order: Floor Politics in the House and Senate*; *Managing Uncertainty in the House of Representatives*; and *The Politics of Institutional Choice: The Formation of the Russian State Duma*.

Chapter 1

Designing Institutions

———··———

1-1

from *The Logic of Collective Action*

Mancur Olson Jr.

With the publication of The Logic of Collective Action *in 1965, Mancur Olson Jr. introduced the fundamental dilemma of collective action to all who study politics. When members of a group agree to work together to achieve a collective goal, each member as an individual faces powerful disincentives, Olson showed, that can frustrate the efforts of the group as a whole. For example, when each can foresee that his or her relatively small contribution to a collective enterprise will not affect its overall success, many will fail to contribute—a phenomenon known as free riding—and leave to everyone else the burden of supplying the collective good. As a consequence, collective enterprises based on cooperation, and supported by the entire collectivity, nevertheless often fail.*

IT IS OFTEN taken for granted, at least where economic objectives are involved, that groups of individuals with common interests usually attempt to further those common interests. Groups of individuals with common interests are expected to act on behalf of their common interests much as single individuals are often expected to act on behalf of their personal interests. This opinion about group behavior is frequently found not only in popular discussions but also in scholarly writings. Many economists of diverse methodological and

Source: Mancur Olson Jr., *The Logic of Collective Action: Public Goods and the Theory of Groups* (Cambridge: Harvard University Press, 1971), 1–19.

ideological traditions have implicitly or explicitly accepted it. This view has, for example, been important in many theories of labor unions, in Marxian theories of class action, in concepts of "countervailing power," and in various discussions of economic institutions. It has, in addition, occupied a prominent place in political science, at least in the United States, where the study of pressure groups has been dominated by a celebrated "group theory" based on the idea that groups will act when necessary to further their common or group goals. Finally, it has played a significant role in many well-known sociological studies.

The view that groups act to serve their interests presumably is based upon the assumption that the individuals in groups act out of self-interest. If the individuals in a group altruistically disregarded their personal welfare, it would not be very likely that collectively they would seek some selfish common or group objective. Such altruism is, however, considered exceptional, and self-interested behavior is usually thought to be the rule, at least when economic issues are at stake; no one is surprised when individual businessmen seek higher profits, when individual workers seek higher wages, or when individual consumers seek lower prices. The idea that groups tend to act in support of their group interests is supposed to follow logically from this widely accepted premise of rational, self-interested behavior. In other words, if the members of some group have a common interest or objective, and if they would all be better off if that objective were achieved, it has been thought to follow logically that the individuals in that group would, if they were rational and self-interested, act to achieve that objective.

But it is *not* in fact true that the idea that groups will act in their self-interest follows logically from the premise of rational and self-interested behavior. It does *not* follow . . . that they would act to achieve that objective, even if they were all rational and self-interested. Indeed, unless the number of individuals in a group is quite small, or unless there is coercion or some other special device to make individuals act in their common interest, *rational, self-interested individuals will not act to achieve their common or group interests*. In other words, even if all of the individuals in a large group are rational and self-interested, and would gain if, as a group, they acted to achieve their common interest or objective, they will still not voluntarily act to achieve that common or group interest. The notion that groups of individuals will act to achieve their common or group interests, far from being a logical implication of the assumption that the individuals in a group will rationally further their individual interests, is in fact inconsistent with that assumption. . . .

A Theory of Groups and Organizations

The Purpose of Organization

Since most (though by no means all) of the action taken by or on behalf of groups of individuals is taken through organizations, it will be helpful to consider organizations in a general or theoretical way.[1] The logical place to begin any systematic study of organizations is with their purpose. But there are all types and shapes and sizes of organizations, even of economic organizations, and there is then some question whether there is any single purpose that would be characteristic of organizations generally. One purpose that is nonetheless characteristic of most organizations, and surely of practically all organizations with an important economic aspect, is the furtherance of the interests of their members. That would seem obvious, at least from the economist's perspective. To be sure, some organizations may out of ignorance fail to further their members' interests, and others may be enticed into serving only the ends of the leadership.[2] But organizations often perish if they do nothing to further the interests of their members, and this factor must severely limit the number of organizations that fail to serve their members.

The idea that organizations or associations exist to further the interests of their members is hardly novel, nor peculiar to economics; it goes back at least to Aristotle, who wrote, "Men journey together with a view to particular advantage, and by way of providing some particular thing needed for the purposes of life, and similarly the political association seems to have come together originally, and to continue in existence, for the sake of the *general* advantages it brings."[3] More recently Professor Leon Festinger, a social psychologist, pointed out that "the attraction of group membership is not so much in sheer belonging, but rather in attaining something by means of this membership."[4] The late Harold Laski, a political scientist, took it for granted that "associations exist to fulfill purposes which a group of men have in common."[5]

The kinds of organizations that are the focus of this study are *expected* to further the interests of their members.[6] Labor unions are expected to strive for higher wages and better working conditions for their members; farm organizations are expected to strive for favorable legislation for their members; cartels are expected to strive for higher prices for participating firms; the corporation is expected to further the interests of its stockholders;[7] and the state is expected to further the common interests of its citizens (though in this nationalistic age the state often has interests and ambitions apart from those of its citizens).

Notice that the interests that all of these diverse types of organizations are expected to further are for the most part *common* interests: the union members' common interest in higher wages, the farmers' common interest in favorable legislation, the cartel members' common interest in higher prices, the stockholders' common interest in higher dividends and stock prices, the citizens' common interest in good government. It is not an accident that the diverse types of organizations listed are all supposed to work primarily for the *common* interests of their members. Purely personal or individual interests can be advanced, and usually advanced most efficiently, by individual, unorganized action. There is obviously no purpose in having an organization when individual, unorganized action can serve the interests of the individual as well as or better than an organization; there would, for example, be no point in forming an organization simply to play solitaire. But when a number of individuals have a common or collective interest—when they share a single purpose or objective—individual, unorganized action (as we shall soon see) will either not be able to advance that common interest at all, or will not be able to advance that interest adequately. Organizations can therefore perform a function when there are common or group interests, and though organizations often also serve purely personal, individual interests, their characteristic and primary function is to advance the common interests of groups of individuals.

The assumption that organizations typically exist to further the common interests of groups of people is implicit in most of the literature about organizations, and two of the writers already cited make this assumption explicit: Harold Laski emphasized that organizations exist to achieve purposes or interests which "a group of men have in common," and Aristotle apparently had a similar notion in mind when he argued that political associations are created and maintained because of the "general advantages" they bring. . . . As Arthur Bentley, the founder of the "group theory" of modern political science, put it, "there is no group without its interest."[8] The social psychologist Raymond Cattell was equally explicit, and stated that "every group has its interest."[9] This is also the way the word "group" will be used here.

Just as those who belong to an organization or a group can be presumed to have a common interest,[10] so they obviously also have purely individual interests, different from those of the others in the organization or group. All of the members of a labor union, for example, have a common interest in higher wages, but at the same time each worker has a unique interest in his personal income, which depends not only on the rate of wages but also on the length of time that he works.

Public Goods and Large Groups

The combination of individual interests and common interests in an organization suggests an analogy with a competitive market. The firms in a perfectly competitive industry, for example, have a common interest in a higher price for the industry's product. Since a uniform price must prevail in such a market, a firm cannot expect a higher price for itself unless all of the other firms in the industry also have this higher price. But a firm in a competitive market also has an interest in selling as much as it can, until the cost of producing another unit exceeds the price of that unit. In this there is no common interest; each firm's interest is directly opposed to that of every other firm, for the more other firms sell, the lower the price and income for any given firm. In short, while all firms have a common interest in a higher price, they have antagonistic interests where output is concerned. . . .

For these reasons it is now generally understood that if the firms in an industry are maximizing profits, the profits for the industry as a whole will be less than they might otherwise be.[11] And almost everyone would agree that this theoretical conclusion fits the facts for markets characterized by pure competition. The important point is that this is true because, though all the firms have a common interest in a higher price for the industry's product, it is in the interest of each firm that the other firms pay the cost—in terms of the necessary reduction in output—needed to obtain a higher price.

About the only thing that keeps prices from falling in accordance with the process just described in perfectly competitive markets is outside intervention. Government price supports, tariffs, cartel agreements, and the like may keep the firms in a competitive market from acting contrary to their interests. Such aid or intervention is quite common. It is then important to ask how it comes about. How does a competitive industry obtain government assistance in maintaining the price of its product?

Consider a hypothetical, competitive industry, and suppose that most of the producers in that industry desire a tariff, a price-support program, or some other government intervention to increase the price for their product. To obtain any such assistance from the government, the producers in this industry will presumably have to organize a lobbying organization; they will have to become an active pressure group.[12] This lobbying organization may have to conduct a considerable campaign. If significant resistance is encountered, a great amount of money will be required.[13] Public relations experts will be needed to influence the newspapers, and some advertising may be necessary. Professional organizers will probably be needed to organize "spontaneous grass roots" meetings among the distressed producers in the industry, and to get those in the industry to write letters to their congressmen.[14] The campaign for the government assistance will take the time of some of the producers in the industry, as well as their money.

There is a striking parallel between the problem the perfectly competitive industry faces as it strives to obtain government assistance, and the problem it faces in the marketplace when the firms increase output and bring about a fall in price. *Just as it was not rational for a particular producer to restrict his output in order that there might be a higher price for the product of his industry, so it would not be rational for him to sacrifice his time and money to support a lobbying organization to obtain government*

assistance for the industry. In neither case would it be in the interest of the individual pro-
ducer to assume any of the costs himself. A lobbying organization, or indeed a labor union
or any other organization, working in the interest of a large group of firms or workers in
some industry, would get no assistance from the rational, self-interested individuals in that
industry. This would be true even if everyone in the industry were absolutely convinced that the proposed program was in their interest (though in fact some might think otherwise and make the organization's task yet more difficult).

Although the lobbying organization is only one example of the logical analogy between the organization and the market, it is of some practical importance. There are many powerful and well-financed lobbies with mass support in existence now, but these lobbying organizations do not get that support because of their legislative achievements. . . .

Some critics may argue that the rational person will, indeed, support a large organization, like a lobbying organization, that works in his interest, because he knows that if he does not, others will not do so either, and then the organization will fail, and he will be without the benefit that the organization could have provided. This argument shows the need for the analogy with the perfectly competitive market. For it would be quite as reasonable to argue that prices will never fall below the levels a monopoly would have charged in a perfectly competitive market, because if one firm increased its output, other firms would also, and the price would fall; but each firm could foresee this, so it would not start a chain of price-destroying increases in output. In fact, it does not work out this way in a competitive market; nor in a large organization. When the number of firms involved is large, no one will notice the effect on price if one firm increases its output, and so no one will change his plans because of it. Similarly, in a large organization, the loss of one dues payer will not noticeably increase the burden for any other one dues payer, and so a rational person would not believe that if he were to withdraw from an organization he would drive others to do so.

The foregoing argument must at the least have some relevance to economic organizations that are mainly means through which individuals attempt to obtain the same things they obtain through their activities in the market. Labor unions, for example, are organizations through which workers strive to get the same things they get with their individual efforts in the market—higher wages, better working conditions, and the like. It would be strange indeed if the workers did not confront some of the same problems in the union that they meet in the market, since their efforts in both places have some of the same purposes.

However similar the purposes may be, critics may object that attitudes in organizations are not at all like those in markets. In organizations, an emotional or ideological element is often also involved. Does this make the argument offered here practically irrelevant?

A most important type of organization—the national state—will serve to test this objection. Patriotism is probably the strongest non-economic motive for organizational allegiance in modern times. This age is sometimes called the age of nationalism. Many nations draw additional strength and unity from some powerful ideology, such as democracy or communism, as well as from a common religion, language, or cultural inheritance. The state not only has many such powerful sources of support; it also is very important economically. Almost any government is economically beneficial to its citizens, in that the law and order it provides is a prerequisite of all civilized economic activity. But despite the force of patriotism, the appeal of the national ideology, the bond of a common culture, and the indispensability of the system of law and order, no major state in modern history has been able to support itself through voluntary dues or contributions. Philanthropic contributions are not even a significant source of revenue for most countries. Taxes, *compulsory* payments by definition, are needed. Indeed, as the old saying indicates, their necessity is as certain as death itself.

If the state, with all of the emotional resources at its command, cannot finance its most basic and vital activities without resort to compulsion, it would seem that large private organizations might also have difficulty in getting the individuals in the groups whose interests they attempt to advance to make the necessary contributions voluntarily.[15]

The reason the state cannot survive on voluntary dues or payments, but must rely on taxation, is that the most fundamental services a nation-state provides are, in one important respect, like the higher price in a competitive market: they must be available to everyone if they are available to anyone. The basic and most elementary goods or services provided by government, like defense and police protection, and the system of law and order generally, are such that they go to everyone or practically everyone in the nation. It would obviously not be feasible, if indeed it were possible, to deny the protection provided by the military services, the police, and the courts to those who did not voluntarily pay their share of the costs of government, and taxation is accordingly necessary. The common or collective benefits provided by governments are usually called "public goods" by economists, and the concept of public goods is one of the oldest and most important ideas in the study of public finance. A common, collective, or public good is here defined as any good such that, if any person X_i in a group $X_1, \ldots, X_i, \ldots, X_n$ consumes it, it cannot feasibly be withheld from the others in that group.[16] In other words, those who do not purchase or pay for any of the public or collective good cannot be excluded or kept from sharing in the consumption of the good, as they can where noncollective goods are concerned.

Students of public finance have, however, neglected the fact that the achievement of any common goal or the satisfaction of any common interest means that a public or collective good has been provided for that group.[17] The very fact that a goal or purpose is common to a group means that no one in the group is excluded from the benefit or satisfaction brought about by its achievement. As the opening paragraphs of this chapter indicated, almost all groups and organizations have the purpose of serving the common interests of their members. As R. M. MacIver puts it, "Persons . . . have common interests in the degree to which they participate in a cause . . . which indivisibly embraces them all."[18] It is of the essence of an organization that it provides an inseparable, generalized benefit. It follows that the provision of public or collective goods is the fundamental function of organizations generally. A state is first of all an organization that provides public goods for its members, the citizens; and other types of organizations similarly provide collective goods for their members.

And just as a state cannot support itself by voluntary contributions, or by selling its basic services on the market, neither can other large organizations support themselves without providing some sanction, or some attraction distinct from the public good itself, that will lead individuals to help bear the burdens of maintaining the organization. The individual member of the typical large organization is in a position analogous to that of the firm in a perfectly competitive market, or the taxpayer in the state: his own efforts will not have a noticeable effect on the situation of his organization, and he can enjoy any improvements brought about by others whether or not he has worked in support of his organization.

There is no suggestion here that states or other organizations provide *only* public or collective goods. Governments often provide noncollective goods like electric power, for example, and they usually sell such goods on the market much as private firms would do. Moreover . . . large organizations that are not able to make membership compulsory *must also* provide some noncollective goods in order to give potential members an incentive to join. Still, collective goods are the characteristic organizational goods, for ordinary noncollective goods can always be provided by individual action, and only where common purposes or collective goods are concerned is organization or group action ever indispensable.[19]

NOTES

1. Economists have for the most part neglected to develop theories of organizations, but there are a few works from an economic point of view on the subject. See, for example, three papers by Jacob Marschak, "Elements for a Theory of Teams," *Management Science,* I (January 1955), 127–137, "Towards an Economic Theory of Organization and Information," in *Decision Processes,* ed. R. M. Thrall, C. H. Combs, and R. L. Davis (New York: John Wiley, 1954), pp. 187–220, and "Efficient and Viable Organization Forms," in *Modern Organization Theory,* ed. Mason Haire (New York: John Wiley, 1959), pp. 307–320; two papers by

R. Radner, "Application of Linear Programming to Team Decision Problems," *Management Science,* V (January 1959), 143–150, and "Team Decision Problems," *Annals of Mathematical Statistics,* XXXIII (September 1962), 857–881; C. B. McGuire, "Some Team Models of a Sales Organization," *Management Science,* VII (January 1961), 101–130; Oskar Morgenstern, *Prolegomena to a Theory of Organization* (Santa Monica, Calif.: RAND Research Memorandum 734, 1951); James G. March and Herbert A. Simon, *Organizations* (New York: John Wiley, 1958); Kenneth Boulding, *The Organizational Revolution* (New York: Harper, 1953).

2. Max Weber called attention to the case where an organization continues to exist for some time after it has become meaningless because some official is making a living out of it. See his *Theory of Social and Economic Organization,* trans. Talcott Parsons and A. M. Henderson (New York: Oxford University Press, 1947), p. 318.

3. *Ethics* viii.9.1160a.

4. Leon Festinger, "Group Attraction and Membership," in *Group Dynamics,* ed. Dorwin Cartwright and Alvin Zander (Evanston, Ill.: Row, Peterson, 1953), p. 93.

5. *A Grammar of Politics,* 4th ed. (London: George Allen & Unwin, 1939), p. 67.

6. Philanthropic and religious organizations are not necessarily expected to serve only the interests of their members; such organizations have other purposes that are considered more important, however much their members "need" to belong, or are improved or helped by belonging. But the complexity of such organizations need not be debated at length here, because this study will focus on organizations with a significant economic aspect. The emphasis here will have something in common with what Max Weber called the "associative group"; he called a group associative if "the orientation of social action with it rests on a rationally moti-vated agreement." Weber contrasted his "associative group" with the "communal group," which was centered on personal affection, erotic relationships, etc., like the family. (See Weber, pp. 136–139, and Grace Coyle, *Social Process in Organized Groups,* New York: Richard Smith, Inc., 1930, pp. 7–9.) The logic of the theory developed here can be extended to cover communal, religious, and philanthropic organizations, but the theory is not particularly useful in studying such groups. See Olson, pp. 61n17, 159–162.

7. That is, its members. This study does not follow the terminological usage of those organization theorists who describe employees as "members" of the organization for which they work. Here it is more convenient to follow the language of everyday usage instead, and to distinguish the members of, say, a union from the employees of that union. Similarly, the members of the union will be considered employees of the corporation for which they work.

8. Arthur Bentley, *The Process of Government* (Evanston, Ill.: Principia Press, 1949), p. 211. David B. Truman takes a similar approach; see his *The Governmental Process* (New York: Alfred A. Knopf, 1958), pp. 33–35. See also Sidney Verba, *Small Groups and Political Behavior* (Princeton, N.J.: Princeton University Press, 1961), pp. 12–13.

9. Raymond Cattell, "Concepts and Methods in the Measurement of Group Syntality," in *Small Groups,* eds. A. Paul Hare, Edgard F. Borgatta, and Robert F. Bales (New York: Alfred A. Knopf, 1955), p. 115.

10. Any organization or group will of course usually be divided into subgroups or factions that are opposed to one another. This fact does not weaken the assumption made here that organizations exist to serve the common interests of members, for the assumption does not imply that intragroup conflict is neglected. The opposing groups within an organization ordi-narily have some interest in common (if not, why would they maintain the organization?), and

the members of any subgroup or faction also have a separate common interest of their own. They will indeed often have a common purpose in defeating some other subgroup or faction. The approach used here does not neglect the conflict within groups and organizations, then, because it considers each organization as a unit only to the extent that it does in fact attempt to serve a common interest, and considers the various subgroups as the relevant units with common interests to analyze the factional strife.

11. For a fuller discussion of this question see Mancur Olson, Jr., and David McFarland, "The Restoration of Pure Monopoly and the Concept of the Industry," *Quarterly Journal of Economics,* LXXVI (November 1962), 613–631.

12. Robert Michels contends in his classic study that "democracy is inconceivable without organization," and that "the principle of organization is an absolutely essential condition for the political struggle of the masses." See his *Political Parties,* trans. Eden and Cedar Paul (New York: Dover Publications, 1959), pp. 21–22. See also Robert A. Brady, *Business as a System of Power* (New York: Columbia University Press, 1943), p. 193.

13. Alexander Heard, *The Costs of Democracy* (Chapel Hill: University of North Carolina Press, 1960), especially note 1, pp. 95–96. For example, in 1947 the National Association of Manufacturers spent over $4.6 million, and over a somewhat longer period the American Medical Association spent as much on a campaign against compulsory health insurance.

14. "If the full truth were ever known . . . lobbying, in all its ramifications, would prove to be a billion dollar industry." U.S. Congress, House, Select Committee on Lobbying Activities, *Report,* 81st Cong., 2nd Sess. (1950), as quoted in the *Congressional Quarterly Almanac,* 81st Cong., 2nd Sess., VI, 764–765.

15. Sociologists as well as economists have observed that ideological motives alone are not sufficient to bring forth the continuing effort of large masses of people. Max Weber provides a notable example:

All economic activity in a market economy is undertaken and carried through by individuals for their own ideal or material interests. This is naturally just as true when economic activity is oriented to the patterns of order of corporate groups. . . .

Even if an economic system were organized on a socialistic basis, there would be no fundamental difference in this respect. . . . The structure of interests and the relevant situation might change; there would be other means of pursuing interests, but this fundamental factor would remain just as relevant as before. It is of course true that economic action which is oriented on purely ideological grounds to the interest of others does exist. But it is even more certain that the mass of men do not act this way, and it is an induction from experience that they cannot do so and never will. . . .

In a market economy the interest in the maximization of income is necessarily the driving force of all economic activity (Weber, pp. 319–320). Talcott Parsons and Neil Smelser go even further in postulating that "performance" throughout society is proportional to the "rewards" and "sanctions" involved. See their *Economy and Society* (Glencoe, Ill.: Free Press, 1954), pp. 50–69.

16. This simple definition focuses upon two points that are important in the present context. The first point is that most collective goods can only be defined with respect to some specific group. One collective good goes to one group of people, another collective good to another group; one may benefit the whole world, another only two specific people. Moreover, some goods are collective goods to those in one group and at the same time private goods to

those in another, because some individuals can be kept from consuming them and others can't. Take for example the parade that is a collective good to all those who live in tall buildings overlooking the parade route, but which appears to be a private good to those who can see it only by buying tickets for a seat in the stands along the way. The second point is that once the relevant group has been defined, the definition used here, like Musgrave's, distinguishes collective good in terms of infeasibility of excluding potential consumers of the good. This approach is used because collective goods produced by organizations of all kinds seem to be such that exclusion is normally not feasible. To be sure, for some collective goods it is physically possible to practice exclusion. But, as Head has shown, it is not necessary that exclusion be technically impossible; it is only necessary that it be infeasible or uneconomic. Head has also shown most clearly that nonexcludability is only one of two basic elements in the traditional understanding of public goods. The other, he points out, is "jointness of supply." A good has "jointness" if making it available to one individual means that it can be easily or freely supplied to others as well. The polar case of jointness would be Samuelson's pure public good, which is a good such that additional consumption of it by one individual does not diminish the amount available to others. By the definition used here, jointness is not a necessary attribute of a public good. As later parts of this chapter will show, at least one type of collective good considered here exhibits no jointness whatever, and few if any would have the degree of jointness needed to qualify as pure public goods. Nonetheless, most of the collective goods to be studied here do display a large measure of jointness. On the definition and importance of public goods, see John G. Head, "Public Goods and Public Policy," *Public Finance*, vol. XVII, no. 3 (1962), 197–219; Richard Musgrave, *The Theory of Public Finance* (New York: McGraw-Hill, 1959); Paul A. Samuelson, "The Pure Theory of Public Expenditure," "Diagrammatic Exposition of A Theory of Public Expenditure," and "Aspects of Public Expenditure Theories," in *Review of Economics and Statistics*, XXXVI (November 1954), 387–390, XXXVII (November 1955), 350–356, and XL (November 1958), 332–338. For somewhat different opinions about the usefulness of the concept of public goods, see Julius Margolis, "A Comment on the Pure Theory of Public Expenditure," *Review of Economics and Statistics*, XXXVII (November 1955), 347–349, and Gerhard Colm, "Theory of Public Expenditures," *Annals of the American Academy of Political and Social Science*, CLXXXIII (January 1936), 1–11.

17.   There is no necessity that a public good to one group in a society is necessarily in the interest of the society as a whole. Just as a tariff could be a public good to the industry that sought it, so the removal of the tariff could be a public good to those who consumed the industry's product. This is equally true when the public-good concept is applied only to governments; for a military expenditure, or a tariff, or an immigration restriction that is a public good to one country could be a "public bad" to another country, and harmful to world society as a whole.

18.   R. M. MacIver in *Encyclopaedia of the Social Sciences*, VII (New York: Macmillan, 1932), 147.

19.   It does not, however, follow that organized or coordinated group action is *always* necessary to obtain a collective goal.

1-2

The Tragedy of the Commons

Garrett Hardin

In this seminal article, Garrett Hardin identifies another class of collective action problems, the "tragedy of the commons." The concept—a "tragedy" because of the inevitability with which public goods, or the "commons," will be exploited—is generally applied to study cases in which natural resources are being misused. Unlike the problems we have already encountered, which concern the production of public goods, the tragedy of the commons affects their conservation. Because public goods are freely available, members of the community will be tempted to overly consume them—to overfish, to overuse national parks, to pollute public water or air—even as they realize their behavior and that of their neighbors is destroying the goods. Hardin discusses social arrangements that can substitute for the commons, or public ownership of scarce resources, and argues that the tragedy of the commons is becoming a more pressing concern as the population increases. As with the problem of free riding described by Mancur Olson Jr., government authority offers one solution extricating participants from their bind.

AT THE END of a thoughtful article on the future of nuclear war, Wiesner and York concluded that: "Both sides in the arms race are . . . confronted by the dilemma of steadily increasing military power and steadily decreasing national security. *It is our considered professional judgment that this dilemma has no technical solution.* If the great powers continue to look for solutions in the area of science and technology only, the result will be to worsen the situation."[1]

I would like to focus your attention not on the subject of the article (national security in a nuclear world) but on the kind of conclusion they reached, namely that there is no technical solution to the problem. An implicit and almost universal assumption of discussions published in professional and semipopular scientific journals is that the problem under discussion has a technical solution. A technical solution may be defined as one that requires a change only in the techniques of the natural sciences, demanding little or nothing in the way of change in human values or ideas of morality.

Source: Garrett Hardin, "The Tragedy of the Commons," *Science,* December 3, 1968, 1243–1248.

In our day (though not in earlier times) technical solutions are always welcome. . . . [Yet of the] class of human problems which can be called "no technical solution problems" . . . [i]t is easy to show that [it] is not a null class. Recall the game of tick-tack-toe. Consider the problem, "How can I win the game of tick-tack-toe?" It is well known that I cannot, if I assume (in keeping with the conventions of game theory) that my opponent understands the game perfectly. Put another way, there is no "technical solution" to the problem. I can win only by giving a radical meaning to the word "win." I can hit my opponent over the head; or I can drug him; or I can falsify the records. Every way in which I "win" involves, in some sense, an abandonment of the game, as we intuitively understand it. (I can also, of course, openly abandon the game—refuse to play it. This is what most adults do.)

The class of "No technical solution problems" has members. My thesis is that the "population problem," as conventionally conceived, is a member of this class. How it is conventionally conceived needs some comment. It is fair to say that most people who anguish over the population problem are trying to find a way to avoid the evils of overpopulation without relinquishing any of the privileges they now enjoy. They think that farming the seas or developing new strains of wheat will solve the problem—technologically. I try to show here that the solution they seek cannot be found. The population problem cannot be solved in a technical way, any more than can the problem of winning the game of tick-tack-toe.

What Shall We Maximize?

Population, as Malthus said, naturally tends to grow "geometrically," or, as we would now say, exponentially. In a finite world this means that the per capita share of the world's goods must steadily decrease. Is ours a finite world?

A fair defense can be put forward for the view that the world is infinite; or that we do not know that it is not. But, in terms of the practical problems that we must face in the next few generations with the foreseeable technology, it is clear that we will greatly increase human misery if we do not, during the immediate future, assume that the world available to the terrestrial human population is finite. "Space" is no escape.[2]

A finite world can support only a finite population; therefore, population growth must eventually equal zero. . . . When this condition is met, what will be the situation of mankind? Specifically, can [Jeremy] Bentham's goal of "the greatest good for the greatest number" be realized? . . .

The . . . reason [why not] springs directly from biological facts. To live, any organism must have a source of energy (for example, food). This energy is utilized for two purposes: mere maintenance and work. For man, maintenance of life requires about 1600 kilocalories a day ("maintenance calories"). Anything that he does over and above merely staying alive will be defined as work, and is supported by "work calories" which he takes in. Work calories are used not only for what we call work in common speech; they are also required for all forms of enjoyment, from swimming and automobile racing to playing music and writing poetry. If our goal is to maximize population it is obvious what we must do: We must make the work calories per person approach as close to zero as possible. No gourmet meals, no vacations, no sports, no music, no literature, no art. . . . I think that everyone will grant, without argument or proof, that maximizing population does not maximize goods. Bentham's goal is impossible. . . .

The optimum population is, then, less than the maximum. The difficulty of defining the optimum is enormous; so far as I know, no one has seriously tackled this problem. Reaching an acceptable and stable solution will surely require more than one generation of hard analytical work—and much persuasion. . . .

We can make little progress in working toward optimum population size until we explicitly exorcize the spirit of Adam Smith in the field of practical demography. In economic affairs, *The Wealth of Nations* (1776) popularized the "invisible hand," the idea that an individual who "intends only his own gain," is, as it were, "led by an invisible hand to promote . . . the public interest."[3] Adam Smith did not assert that this was invariably true, and perhaps neither did any of his followers. But he contributed to a dominant tendency of thought that has ever since interfered with positive action based on rational analysis, namely, the tendency to assume that decisions reached individually will, in fact, be the best decisions for an entire society. If this assumption is correct it justifies the continuance of our present policy of laissez-faire in reproduction. If it is correct we can assume that men will control their individual fecundity so as to produce the optimum population. If the assumption is not correct, we need to reexamine our individual freedoms to see which ones are defensible.

Tragedy of Freedom in a Commons

The rebuttal to the invisible hand in population control is to be found in a scenario first sketched in a little-known pamphlet in 1833 by a mathematical amateur named William Forster Lloyd (1794–1852).[4] We may well call it "the tragedy of the commons," using the word "tragedy" as the philosopher Whitehead used it: "The essence of dramatic tragedy is not unhappiness. It resides in the solemnity of the remorseless working of things."[5] He then goes on to say, "This inevitableness of destiny can only be illustrated in terms of human life by incidents which in fact involve unhappiness. For it is only by them that the futility of escape can be made evident in the drama."

The tragedy of the commons develops in this way. Picture a pasture open to all. It is to be expected that each herdsman will try to keep as many cattle as possible on the commons. Such an arrangement may work reasonably satisfactorily for centuries because tribal wars, poaching, and disease keep the numbers of both man and beast well below the carrying capacity of the land. Finally, however, comes the day of reckoning, that is, the day when the long-desired goal of social stability becomes a reality. At this point, the inherent logic of the commons remorselessly generates tragedy.

As a rational being, each herdsman seeks to maximize his gain. Explicitly or implicitly, more or less consciously, he asks, "What is the utility *to me* of adding one more animal to my herd?" This utility has one negative and one positive component.

1. The positive component is a function of the increment of one animal. Since the herdsman receives all the proceeds from the sale of the additional animal, the positive utility is nearly +1.

2. The negative component is a function of the additional overgrazing created by one more animal. Since, however, the effects of overgrazing are shared by all the herdsmen, the negative utility for any particular decision-making herdsman is only a fraction of −1.

Adding together the component partial utilities, the rational herdsman concludes that the only sensible course for him to pursue is to add another animal to his herd. And another. . . . But this is the conclusion reached by each and every rational herdsman sharing a commons. Therein is the tragedy. Each man is locked into a system that compels him to increase his herd without limit—in a world that is limited. Ruin is the destination toward which all men rush, each pursuing his own best interest in a society that believes in the freedom of the commons. Freedom in a commons brings ruin to all.

Some would say that this is a platitude. Would that it were! In a sense, it was learned thousands of years ago, but natural selection favors the forces of psychological denial.[6] The individual benefits as an individual from his ability to deny the truth even though society as a whole, of which he is a part, suffers. Education can counteract the natural tendency to do the wrong thing, but the inexorable succession of generations requires that the basis for this knowledge be constantly refreshed.

A simple incident that occurred a few years ago in Leominster, Massachusetts, shows how perishable the knowledge is. During the Christmas shopping season the parking meters downtown were covered with plastic bags that bore tags reading: "Do not open until after Christmas. Free parking courtesy of the mayor and city council." In other words, facing the prospect of an increased demand for already scarce space, the city fathers reinstituted the system of the commons. (Cynically, we suspect that they gained more votes than they lost by this retrogressive act.)

In an approximate way, the logic of the commons has been understood for a long time, perhaps since the discovery of agriculture or the invention of private property in real estate. But it is understood mostly only in special cases which are not sufficiently generalized. Even at this late date, cattlemen leasing national land on the western ranges demonstrate no more than an ambivalent understanding, in constantly pressuring federal authorities to increase the head count to the point where overgrazing produces erosion and weed-dominance. Likewise, the oceans of the world continue to suffer from the survival of the philosophy of the commons. Maritime nations still respond automatically to the shibboleth of the "freedom of the seas." Professing to believe in the "inexhaustible resources of the oceans," they bring species after species of fish and whales closer to extinction.[7]

The National Parks present another instance of the working out of the tragedy of the commons. At present, they are open to all, without limit. The parks themselves are limited in extent—there is only one Yosemite Valley—whereas population seems to grow without limit. The values that visitors seek in the parks are steadily eroded. Plainly, we must soon cease to treat the parks as commons or they will be of no value to anyone.

What shall we do? We have several options. We might sell them off as private property. We might keep them as public property, but allocate the right to enter them. The allocation might be on the basis of wealth, by the use of an auction system. It might be on the basis of merit, as defined by some agreed-upon standards. It might be by lottery. Or it might be on a first-come, first-served basis, administered to long queues. These, I think, are all the reasonable possibilities. They are all objectionable. But we must choose—or acquiesce in the destruction of the commons that we call our National Parks.

Pollution

In a reverse way, the tragedy of the commons reappears in problems of pollution. Here it is not a question of taking something out of the commons, but of putting something in—sewage, or chemical, radioactive, and heat wastes into water; noxious and dangerous fumes into the air; and distracting and unpleasant advertising signs into the line of sight. The calculations of utility are much the same as before. The rational man finds that his share of the cost of the wastes he discharges into the commons is less than the cost of purifying his wastes before releasing them. Since this is true for everyone, we are locked into a system of "fouling our own nest," so long as we behave only as independent, rational, free-enterprisers.

The tragedy of the commons as a food basket is averted by private property, or something formally like it. But the air and waters surrounding us cannot readily be fenced, and so the tragedy of the commons as a cesspool must be prevented by different means, by coercive laws or taxing devices that make it cheaper for the polluter to treat his pollutants than to discharge them untreated. We have not progressed as far with the solution of this problem as we have with the first. Indeed, our particular concept of private property, which deters us from exhausting the positive resources of the earth, favors pollution. The owner of a factory on the bank of a stream—whose property extends to the middle of the stream—often has difficulty seeing why it is not his natural right to muddy the waters flowing past his door. The law, always behind the times, requires elaborate stitching and fitting to adapt it to this newly perceived aspect of the commons.

The pollution problem is a consequence of population. It did not much matter how a lonely American frontiersman disposed of his waste. "Flowing water purifies itself every 10 miles," my grandfather used to say, and the myth was near enough to the truth when he was a boy, for there were not too many people. But as population became denser, the natural chemical and biological recycling processes became overloaded, calling for a redefinition of property rights.

How to Legislate Temperance?

Analysis of the pollution problem as a function of population density uncovers a not generally recognized principle of morality, namely: *the morality of an act is a function of the state of the system at the time it is performed.*[8] Using the commons as a cesspool does not harm the general public under frontier conditions, because there is no public; the same behavior in a metropolis is unbearable. A hundred and fifty years ago a plainsman could kill an American bison, cut out only the tongue for his dinner, and discard the rest of the animal. He was not in any important sense being wasteful. Today, with only a few thousand bison left, we would be appalled at such behavior.

In passing, it is worth noting that the morality of an act cannot be determined from a photograph. One does not know whether a man killing an elephant or setting fire to the grassland is harming others until one knows the total system in which his act appears. "One picture is worth a thousand words," said an ancient Chinese; but it may take 10,000 words to validate it. It is as tempting to ecologists as it is to reformers in general to try to persuade others by way of the photographic shortcut. But the essence of an argument cannot be photographed: it must be presented rationally—in words.

That morality is system-sensitive escaped the attention of most codifiers of ethics in the past. "Thou shalt not . . ." is the form of traditional ethical directives which make no allowance for particular circumstances. The laws of our society follow the pattern of ancient ethics, and therefore are poorly suited to governing a complex, crowded, changeable world. Our epicyclic solution is to augment statutory law with administrative law. Since it is practically impossible to spell out all the conditions under which it is safe to burn trash in the back yard or to run an automobile without smog-control, by law we delegate the details to bureaus. The result is administrative law, which is rightly feared for an ancient reason—*Quis custodiet ipsos custodes?*—"Who shall watch the watchers themselves?" John Adams said that we must have "a government of laws and not men." Bureau administrators, trying to evaluate the morality of acts in the total system, are singularly liable to corruption, producing a government by men, not laws.

Prohibition is easy to legislate (though not necessarily to enforce); but how do we legislate temperance? Experience indicates that it can be accomplished best through the mediation of administrative law. We limit possibilities unnecessarily if we suppose that the sentiment of *Quis custodiet* denies us the use of administrative law. We should rather retain the phrase as a perpetual reminder of fearful dangers we cannot avoid. The great challenge facing us now is to invent the corrective feedbacks that are needed to keep custodians honest. We must find ways to legitimate the needed authority of both the custodians and the corrective feedbacks.

Freedom to Breed Is Intolerable

The tragedy of the commons is involved in population problems in another way. In a world governed solely by the principle of "dog eat dog"—if indeed there ever was such a world—how many children a family had would not be a matter of public concern. Parents who bred too exuberantly would leave fewer descendants, not more, because they would be unable to care adequately for their children. David Lack and others have found that such a negative feedback demonstrably controls the fecundity of birds.[9] But men are not birds, and have not acted like them for millenniums, at least.

If each human family were dependent only on its own resources; *if* the children of improvident parents starved to death; *if,* thus, overbreeding brought its own "punishment" to the germ line—*then* there would be no public interest in controlling the breeding of families. But our society is deeply committed to the welfare state,[10] and hence is confronted with another aspect of the tragedy of the commons.

In a welfare state, how shall we deal with the family, the religion, the race, or the class (or indeed any distinguishable and cohesive group) that adopts over-breeding as a policy to secure its own aggrandizement?[11] To couple the concept of freedom to breed with the belief that everyone born has an equal right to the commons is to lock the world into a tragic course of action.

Unfortunately this is just the course of action that is being pursued by the United Nations. In late 1967, some 30 nations agreed to the following: "The Universal Declaration of Human Rights describes the family as the natural and fundamental unit of society. It follows that any choice and decision with regard to the size of the family must irrevocably rest with the family itself, and cannot be made by anyone else."[12] It is painful to have to deny categorically the validity of this right; denying it, one feels as uncomfortable as a resident of Salem, Massachusetts, who denied the reality of witches in the 17th century. At the present time, in liberal quarters, something like a taboo acts to inhibit criticism of the United Nations. There is a feeling that the United Nations is "our last and best hope," that we shouldn't find fault with it; we shouldn't play into the hands of the archconservatives. However, let us not forget what Robert Louis Stevenson said: "The truth that is suppressed by friends is the readiest weapon of the enemy." If we love the truth we must openly deny the validity of the Universal Declaration of Human Rights, even though it is promoted by the United Nations. We should also join with Kingsley Davis in attempting to get Planned Parenthood–World Population to see the error of its ways in embracing the same tragic ideal.[13] . . .

The argument has here been stated in the context of the population problem, but it applies equally well to any instance in which society appeals to an individual exploiting a commons to restrain himself for the general good—by means of his conscience. To make such an appeal is to set up a selective system that works toward the elimination of conscience from the race.

Pathogenic Effects of Conscience

It is a mistake to think that we can control the breeding of mankind in the long run by an appeal to conscience. . . . If we ask a man who is exploiting a commons to desist "in the name of conscience," what are we saying to him? What does he hear?—not only at the moment but also in the wee small hours of the night when, half asleep, he remembers not merely the words we used but also the nonverbal communication cues we gave him unawares? Sooner or later, consciously or subconsciously, he senses that he has received two communications, and that they are contradictory: (i) (intended communication) "If you don't do as we ask, we will openly condemn you for not acting like a responsible citizen"; (ii) (the unintended communication) "If you *do* behave as we ask, we will secretly condemn you for a simpleton who can be shamed into standing aside while the rest of us exploit the commons." . . .

To conjure up a conscience in others is tempting to anyone who wishes to extend his control beyond the legal limits. Leaders at the highest level succumb to this temptation. Has any President during the past generation failed to call on labor unions to moderate voluntarily their demands for higher wages, or to steel companies to honor voluntary guidelines on prices? I can recall none. The rhetoric used on such occasions is designed to produce feelings of guilt in noncooperators.

For centuries it was assumed without proof that guilt was a valuable, perhaps even an indispensable, ingredient of the civilized life. Now, in this post-Freudian world, we doubt it.

Paul Goodman speaks from the modern point of view when he says: "No good has ever come from feeling guilty, neither intelligence, policy, nor compassion. The guilty do not pay attention to the object but only to themselves, and not even to their own interests, which might make sense, but to their anxieties."[14]

One does not have to be a professional psychiatrist to see the consequences of anxiety. We in the Western world are just emerging from a dreadful two-centuries-long Dark Ages of Eros that was sustained partly by prohibition laws, but perhaps more effectively by the anxiety-generating mechanisms of education. Alex Comfort has told the story well in *The Anxiety Makers;* it is not a pretty one.[15]

Since proof is difficult, we may even concede that the results of anxiety may sometimes, from certain points of view, be desirable. The larger question we should ask is whether, as a matter of policy, we should ever encourage the use of a technique the tendency (if not the intention) of which is psychologically pathogenic. We hear much talk these days of responsible parenthood; the coupled words are incorporated into the titles of some organizations devoted to birth control. Some people have proposed massive propaganda campaigns to instill responsibility into the nation's (or the world's) breeders. But what is the meaning of the word responsibility in this context? Is it not merely a synonym for the word conscience? When we use the word responsibility in the absence of substantial sanctions are we not trying to browbeat a free man in a commons into acting against his own interest? Responsibility is a verbal counterfeit for a substantial *quid pro quo*. It is an attempt to get something for nothing.

If the word responsibility is to be used at all, I suggest that it be in the sense Charles Frankel uses it.[16] "Responsibility," says this philosopher, "is the product of definite social arrangements." Notice that Frankel calls for social arrangements—not propaganda.

Mutual Coercion, Mutually Agreed Upon

The social arrangements that produce responsibility are arrangements that create coercion, of some sort. Consider bank-robbing. The man who takes money from a bank acts as if the bank were a commons. How do we prevent such action? Certainly not by trying to control his behavior solely by a verbal appeal to his sense of responsibility. Rather than rely on propaganda we follow Frankel's lead and insist that a bank is not a commons; we seek the definite social arrangements that will keep it from becoming a commons. That we thereby infringe on the freedom of would-be robbers we neither deny nor regret.

The morality of bank-robbing is particularly easy to understand because we accept complete prohibition of this activity. We are willing to say "Thou shalt not rob banks," without providing for exceptions. But temperance also can be created by coercion. Taxing is a good coercive device. To keep downtown shoppers temperate in their use of parking space we introduce parking meters for short periods, and traffic fines for longer ones. We need not actually forbid a citizen to park as long as he wants to; we need merely make it increasingly expensive for him to do so. Not prohibition, but carefully biased options are what we offer him. A Madison Avenue man might call this persuasion; I prefer the greater candor of the word coercion.

Coercion is a dirty word to most liberals now, but it need not forever be so. As with the four-letter words, its dirtiness can be cleansed away by exposure to the light, by saying it over and over without apology or embarrassment. To many, the word coercion implies arbitrary decisions of distant and irresponsible bureaucrats; but this is not a necessary part of its meaning. The only kind of coercion I recommend is mutual coercion, mutually agreed upon by the majority of the people affected.

To say that we mutually agree to coercion is not to say that we are required to enjoy it, or even to pretend we enjoy it. Who enjoys taxes? We all grumble about them. But we accept compulsory taxes because we recognize that voluntary taxes would favor the conscienceless. We institute and (grumblingly) support taxes and other coercive devices to escape the horror of the commons.

An alternative to the commons need not be perfectly just to be preferable. With real estate and other material goods, the alternative we have chosen is the institution of private property coupled with legal inheritance. Is this system perfectly just? As a genetically trained biologist I deny that it is. It seems to me that, if there are to be differences in individual inheritance, legal possession should be perfectly correlated with biological inheritance—that those who are biologically more fit to be the custodians of property and power should legally inherit more. But genetic recombination continually makes a mockery of the doctrine of "like father, like son" implicit in our laws of legal inheritance. An idiot can inherit millions, and a trust fund can keep his estate intact. We must admit that our legal system of private property plus inheritance is unjust—but we put up with it because we are not convinced, at the moment, that anyone has invented a better system. The alternative of the commons is too horrifying to contemplate. Injustice is preferable to total ruin.

It is one of the peculiarities of the warfare between reform and the status quo that it is thoughtlessly governed by a double standard. Whenever a reform measure is proposed it is often defeated when its opponents triumphantly discover a flaw in it. As Kingsley Davis has pointed out,[17] worshippers of the status quo sometimes imply that no reform is possible without unanimous agreement, an implication contrary to historical fact. As nearly as I can make out, automatic rejection of proposed reforms is based on one of two unconscious assumptions: (i) that the status quo is perfect; or (ii) that the choice we face is between reform and no action; if the proposed reform is imperfect, we presumably should take no action at all, while we wait for a perfect proposal.

But we can never do nothing. That which we have done for thousands of years is also action. It also produces evils. Once we are aware that the status quo is action, we can then compare its discoverable advantages and disadvantages with the predicted advantages and disadvantages of the proposed reform, discounting as best we can for our lack of experience. On the basis of such a comparison, we can make a rational decision which will not involve the unworkable assumption that only perfect systems are tolerable.

Recognition of Necessity

Perhaps the simplest summary of this analysis of man's population problems is this: the commons, if justifiable at all, is justifiable only under conditions of low-population density. As the human population has increased, the commons has had to be abandoned in one aspect after another.

First we abandoned the commons in food gathering, enclosing farm land and restricting pastures and hunting and fishing areas. These restrictions are still not complete throughout the world.

Somewhat later we saw that the commons as a place for waste disposal would also have to be abandoned. Restrictions on the disposal of domestic sewage are widely accepted in the Western world; we are still struggling to close the commons to pollution by automobiles, factories, insecticide sprayers, fertilizing operations, and atomic energy installations.

In a still more embryonic state is our recognition of the evils of the commons in matters of pleasure. There is almost no restriction on the propagation of sound waves in the public medium. The shopping public is assaulted with mindless music, without its consent. Our government is paying out billions of dollars to create supersonic transport which will disturb 50,000 people for every one person who is whisked from coast to coast 3 hours faster. Advertisers muddy the airwaves of radio and television and pollute the view of travelers. We are a long way from outlawing the commons in matters of pleasure. Is this because our Puritan inheritance makes us view pleasure as something of a sin, and pain (that is, the pollution of advertising) as the sign of virtue?

Every new enclosure of the commons involves the infringement of somebody's personal liberty. Infringements made in the distant past are accepted because no contemporary complains of a loss. It is the newly proposed infringements that we vigorously oppose; cries of "rights" and "freedom" fill the air. But what does "freedom" mean? When men mutually agreed to pass laws against robbing, mankind became more free, not less so. Individuals locked into the logic of the commons are free only to bring on universal ruin; once they see the necessity of mutual coercion, they become free to pursue other goals. I believe it was Hegel who said, "Freedom is the recognition of necessity."

The most important aspect of necessity that we must now recognize, is the necessity of abandoning the commons in breeding. No technical solution can rescue us from the misery of overpopulation. Freedom to breed will bring ruin to all. At the moment, to avoid hard decisions many of us are tempted to propagandize for conscience and responsible parenthood. The temptation must be resisted, because an appeal to independently acting consciences selects for the disappearance of all conscience in the long run, and an increase in anxiety in the short.

The only way we can preserve and nurture other and more precious freedoms is by relinquishing the freedom to breed, and that very soon. "Freedom is the recognition of necessity"—and it is the role of education to reveal to all the necessity of abandoning the freedom to breed. Only so, can we put an end to this aspect of the tragedy of the commons.

NOTES

1. J. B. Wiesner and H. F. York, *Sci. Amer.* 211 (No. 4), 27 (1964).

2. G. Hardin, *J. Hered.* 50, 68 (1959); S. von Hoernor, *Science* 137, 18 (1962).

3. A. Smith, *The Wealth of Nations* (Modern Library, New York, 1937), p. 423.

4. W. F. Lloyd, *Two Lectures on the Checks to Population* (Oxford Univ. Press, Oxford, England, 1833), reprinted (in part) in *Population, Evolution, and Birth Control,* G. Hardin, Ed. (Freeman, San Francisco, 1964), p. 37.

5. A. N. Whitehead, *Science and the Modern World* (Mentor, New York, 1948), p. 17.

6. G. Hardin, Ed. *Population, Evolution and Birth Control* (Freeman, San Francisco, 1964), p. 56.

7. S. McVay, *Sci. Amer.* 216 (No. 8), 13 (1966).

8. J. Fletcher, *Situation Ethics* (Westminster, Philadelphia, 1966).

9. D. Lack, *The Natural Regulation of Animal Numbers* (Clarendon Press, Oxford, 1954).

10. H. Girvetz, *From Wealth to Welfare* (Stanford Univ. Press, Stanford, Calif., 1950).

11. G. Hardin, *Perspec. Biol. Med.* 6, 366 (1963).

12. U. Thant, *Int. Planned Parenthood News,* No. 168 (February 1968), p. 3.

13. K. Davis, *Science* 158, 730 (1967).

14. P. Goodman, *New York Rev. Books* 10(8), 22 (23 May 1968).

15. A. Comfort, *The Anxiety Makers* (Nelson, London, 1967).

16. C. Frankel, *The Case for Modern Man* (Harper, New York, 1955), p. 203.

17. J. D. Roslansky, *Genetics and the Future of Man* (Appleton-Century-Crofts, New York, 1966), p. 177.

1-3

The Citizenship Agenda

Bruce Ackerman

Clearly, the author is unhappy with the conservative view with which the Supreme Court and conservatives in politics interpret the Constitution. He aspires for a set of institutions that empower citizens over special—generally, business—interests. What he really wants is more democracy—that is, individual citizens exerting more direct control over politicians. Ackerman senses, we suspect, that the real problem is not so much the people in government but the Constitution itself. He proposes three reforms that he sees would strengthen ordinary Americans' civic competence and force politicians to pay closer attention to their welfare. In the next section on the Constitution, we will find the framers more concerned with designing republican institutions to reign in democracy, or majority rule.

WHEN IT CAME to citizenship, the founders were full of paradox. Washington, Madison, and the rest were prepared to die for their vision of the union, but when it came to writing their commitment to American citizenship into the Constitution, they fell silent. They knew that most of their countrymen would not join them in giving federal citizenship priority over more local attachments, and so the original Constitution failed to mention, let alone define, one its key premises: The founders speak in the name of We the People, but never tell us who "we" are.

The question returned after four bloody years of the Civil War. And the Fourteenth Amendment answered it squarely: It explicitly established the primacy of national citizenship in the new constitutional order. Henceforth, state citizenship was derivative: Americans gained it by choosing to reside in whatever state they liked, and the amendment forbade the states from "abridg[ing] the privileges or immunities of citizens of United States." But then it fell silent, leaving the courts, and the rest of us, to figure out the precise contours of those privileges and immunities.

The open-ended character of this great guarantee was immediately reorganized. It was the Citizenship Clauses, not Due Process or Equal Protection, that

Source: Bruce Ackerman, "The Citizenship Agenda," in *The Constitution in 2020*, eds. Jack M. Balkin and Reva B. Siegel (New York: Oxford University Press, 2009), 109–118.

originally provoked a great debate over the rights guaranteed by the new nation emerging out of the bloody sacrifices of millions.

But then, another historical paradox. Precisely because the Citizenship Clauses were understood as most important, they were the centerpiece of the first great Supreme Court decision construing the Reconstruction amendments: the *Slaughterhouse Cases* of 1873. And precisely because the language of national citizenship was so new, the Supreme Court had trouble giving it legal meaning. By a 5–4 vote, the justices refused to believe that the American people had now put national citizenship at the core of their Constitution. They trivialized citizenship's "privileges," suggesting that they included little more than the right to move from state to state, to obtain a passport, and to claim diplomatic protection abroad. Anything more robust, the majority feared, would endanger familiar principles of federalism.

Over the next century, the Supreme Court reversed course, recognizing the Fourteenth Amendment as a source of a broad panoply of fundamental rights and requiring the states to comply with its commands. But it accomplished its nationalizing mission by promoting other clauses, most notably Due Process and Equal Protection, to central place. The Citizenship Clauses remain more or less a dead letter: Robert Bork was only exaggerating a bit when he said that they had as little legal meaning as an "inkblot." Despite his professed fidelity to the original understanding, Bork made this pronouncement[1] with supreme self-satisfaction as he cast this central Reconstruction text into the wilderness. But for the rest of us, the century-long silence should provoke a certain wonder.

We are in a curious situation. The Constitution assures us that "We the People of the United States" have created and reconstructed our supreme law over the generations. And yet the Court has refused to contribute to a robust constitutional discourse about the very citizenry that the Constitution celebrates.

The Court's silence contrasts with the eloquent efforts by twentieth-century Americans to expand and deepen the privileges of national citizenship. Women's suffrage during the Progressive Era, Social Security during the New Deal, the antidiscrimination laws of the civil rights era—all provide notable examples. All were initiated by political movements seeking to end second-class citizenship; but when they were received into our constitutional tradition, judges and lawyers dressed them up with other legal doctrines that belied their originating impulse. To this day, American politics revolves around efforts by one or another group to end second-class citizenship—but this phrase loses its resonance in our courts of law. This disjunction between law and politics is not inevitable. Despite centuries of silence, America's lawyers may yet reclaim the lost promise of national citizenship for the twenty-first century.

They won't be able to do it alone. The citizenship agenda will only become alive if Americans can once again affirm that their country isn't merely a vast free market zone, where individuals go their separate ways within a safe haven guarded by a mighty military. Lawyers have much to contribute to such a civic revival—but they won't get anywhere by trying to convince the current Supreme Court to restore the Citizenship Clauses to their central place. Despite professions of originalism, our right-wing judiciary will be in no rush to vindicate the privileges of citizenship against the economic forces threatening their effective exercise. In the run-up to 2020, the greatest legal contribution lies outside the courts. We must use our legal talents in a larger effort to reconstruct the institutional foundations of modern citizenship.

Many of our inherited civic institutions are dead or dying. Vietnam killed the citizen army. Television killed the political party as a popular institution. The citizen jury is on the fringe of everyday life. The only significant institution that still involves ordinary people is the public school, and it too is under attack.

Progressives have been fighting a rearguard battle in defense of the civic achievements of the twentieth century, including public education and progressive taxation, Social Security and Medicare, civil rights and environmental protection, union rights and workplace safety.

Many of these old progressive ideas deserve a central place in twenty-first-century life. But if the past is any guide, it won't be good enough to defend them against right-wing attack. From the American founding to the civil rights revolution, we have built our democracy through acts of bold institutional innovation—some more successful than others, but all pushing forward the movement to greater political inclusion, individual freedom, and social justice. If we are to move further down this path, there is an imperative need for large acts of institutional imagination.

This is the pressing task for the next generation of American lawyers. We should proceed in the distinctive spirit of realistic idealism. As realists, we should try to design institutional initiatives that will *actually work* in the real world, using all the tools of modern policy analysis for a hardheaded exploration of real-world options. Good intentions aren't enough. And yet we should also be unembarrassed idealists: We should not content ourselves with narrow variations on the status quo, but aim for practical frameworks that would enable ordinary Americans to take charge of their political and economic lives. We should seek to establish that the meaningful exercise of American citizenship is no pipe dream, but a practical project well worth a tough political struggle.

This has been the spirit of three collaborations with friends of mine that aim to kick off a new round of debate over the shape of the citizenship agenda: *Voting with Dollars*, with Ian Ayres; *Deliberation Day*, with Jim Fishkin; and *The Stakeholder Society*, with Anne Alston (all Yale University Press paperbacks). In setting out three planks for a new citizenship agenda, we tried to rediscover the art of talking about big ideas in ordinary English, staying clear of Beltway techno-babble. This is the only way to convince millions of Americans that meaningful citizenship is a real-world possibility—if they only will take the future into their own hands.

I won't mind if you find our proposals wrongheaded or counterproductive; nobody can please everybody, and you may be provoked to come up with better ideas than we have offered. But I will have utterly failed if you find my proposals obscure or pedantic.

Let's begin with the problem of big money in politics. Only one-third of 1 percent of American registered voters gave $200 or more to presidential candidates in the 2004 election cycle, but more than 65 percent of all contributors donated more than $200. Traditional forms of campaign reform won't change this reality. The 2002 McCain-Feingold law increased contribution limits from $1,000 to $2,000, making it likely that the balance of financial power will become more top-heavy in the future. To democratize the system, we need something new: Give all voters a special credit card account containing $50 that they can spend only on federal election campaigns. Armed with their cards, voters could go to local ATM machines whenever they liked and send their "patriot dollars" to favored candidates and political organizations. A little over 120 million Americans went to the polls in 2004. If they also had a chance to go to their ATMs, they would have injected more than 6.1 billion federally funded patriot dollars into the campaign—greatly diluting the power of the private $4 billion spent by all candidates for federal office in the 2004 electoral cycle.

Patriot dollars would invigorate the politics of ordinary citizenship. When each American voter has 50 patriot dollars in his or her pocket, candidates will have a powerful incentive to reach out and grab that money. Fund-raising will become a community affair; a box lunch for 100 could gross $5,000! These outreach efforts will provoke millions of conversations: Who should get the money? Who is a charlatan and who is really concerned about the country?

Patriot dollars have many merits, but one great limitation. Once citizens go to their ATMs to beam their patriot money onward, the candidates will continue to spend most of their money on sound-bite appeals on hot-button issues. Patriotic finance will redistribute the sound bites, emphasizing themes with greater resonance for ordinary citizens. But we will still be living in a sound-bite democracy, and this isn't good enough. The next challenge is to provide citizens with the tools they need to move beyond the media blitz and engage in thoughtful political discussion. An exemplary model is the American jury. Twelve men and women begin in total ignorance, but they learn a lot during the course of the trial. After hearing competing arguments, and reasoning together, they regularly—if not invariably—come up with perfectly sensible conclusions.

The task is to design a similar format for politics. Stanford political scientist Jim Fishkin and I have come up with a practical proposal based on a new technique, deliberative polling, which has been field-tested in thirty-five settings throughout the world—from Australia to Bulgaria, China to Denmark, Baton Rouge to Philadelphia.

Each poll invites a few hundred citizens to spend a weekend deliberating on major issues of public policy. Before they arrive, participants respond to a standard questionnaire that explores their knowledge about, and positions on, the issues. They then answer the same questionnaire after completing their deliberations. Comparing these before and after responses, social scientists have rigorously established that participants greatly increase their understanding of the issues and often change their minds on the best course of action. Ten percent swings are common. No less important, participants leave with a more confident sense of their capacities as citizens.

These experiments suggest a new way of thinking about democratic reform. Fishkin and I urge the creation of a new national holiday: Deliberation Day, which will be held two weeks before presidential elections. It will replace Presidents' Day as an official holiday; Americans will no longer honor Washington and Lincoln by searching for bargains at Presidents' Day sales. Instead, ordinary business will come to a halt, and citizens will be invited to gather at neighborhood centers to discuss the central issues raised by the leading candidates for the White House. Nobody will be forced to attend, but as with jury service, participants will be paid a stipend for the day's work of citizenship. DDay would begin with a nationally televised debate between the presidential candidates, who would discuss the leading issues in the traditional way. But then citizens would deliberate in small groups of 15 and later in larger plenary assemblies. The small groups begin where the televised debate leaves off. Each spends an hour defining questions that the national candidates left unanswered. Everybody then proceeds to a 500-citizen assembly to hear their questions answered by local representatives of the major parties. After lunch, participants repeat the morning procedure. By the end of the day, citizens will have moved beyond the top-down television debate by the leading candidates. They will have achieved a bottom-up understanding of the choices confronting the nation. Discussions begun on DDay will continue during the run-up to Election Day, drawing tens of millions of other citizens into the escalating national dialogue.

If Deliberation Day succeeds, sound-bite democracy would come to an end. Candidates would have powerful incentives to create longer and more substantive infomercials. Newscasts would be full of exit polls determining the extent to which citizen discussion had changed voting preferences—framing the intensifying debate that culminates on Election Day. While there will always be plenty of room for a politics of personality, the new system would put the focus where it belongs: on the crucial issues determining the future of the United States. Our initiative took an important step forward during the 2004 presidential elections, when seventeen PBS stations throughout the country assembled scientific samples of citizens from their regions to engage in a pilot Deliberation Day. Larger media efforts in the future will help to dramatize the proposal further, serving as a vital preliminary for the great leap forward to the new national holiday.

For now, it's more important to place the proposal into the larger context defined by the patriot dollar initiative. In our present sound-bite democracy, voters are bombarded by hot-button slogans generated by well-financed special interests. The point is to arouse knee-jerk reactions, not informed judgments. So it's no surprise that most Americans go to the polls with only the vaguest understanding of the issues. But once they are provided with new tools for engagement, Americans will be in a position to take their citizenship seriously. From the very beginning of the presidential campaign, candidates will be reaching out to them with great vigor—if only to pick their pockets and get at their patriot dollars. As citizens begin to "vote with their dollars," Deliberation Day will loom on the horizon. Candidates no longer will spend most of their money on ten-second sound bites. They will be beaming longer infomercials to enable partisans to state their case intelligently on DDay. By the time Election Day arrives, voters will be going to the polls with a far better sense of the stakes before the nation and of the nature of the rival responses proposed by the candidates.

I have no need to exaggerate. I am not conjuring some mythic version of Periclean Athens. I am not asking Americans to don togas, but to march with credit cards to their ATM machines and talk to their neighbors at local centers—this time acting as citizens, not consumers. I am not longing for some brave new world, but one where ordinary citizens can compete with big money on more equal terms.

Real reform in politics comes cheap. Patriot dollars will cost about $2 billion on an annualized basis ($6 billion during presidential elections, $2.5 billion during midterm elections). DDay will be even cheaper. Running the facilities will cost about $2 billion if 50–70 million Americans show up (plus a citizen stipend for those attending). Once again, this cost won't be incurred every year. Until DDay proves itself, let's start small and only schedule the holiday for presidential elections.

But once we move from political to economic citizenship, we confront big price tags. Only a large initiative has the chance to stop the spiraling inequalities that endanger the future of democratic life. There can be no disputing the basic facts: Since the 1970s, the average annual salary in the United States has only risen $4,250—from $32,500 in 1970 to $36,750 in 2002. That's about a 13 percent increase. But the pay of the top 100 chief executives went from $1.3 million to $18.5 million—from 39 times to more than 500 times that of an average worker. Such radical disparities in income have had a big impact on the distribution of wealth. Over the eighteen years from 1983 to 2001, the share of disposable wealth owned by the top 1 percent has moved up from 33 to 39 percent. The United States could be a poorly disguised oligarchy by 2020, with the top 1 percent controlling an enormous share of the disposable wealth, with more and more billionaires following the Bushes and Bloombergs into the public sphere.

Below the oligarchs, the United States has become a three-class society. About 30 percent of America's children will graduate from four-year colleges and move into the ranks of the symbol-using class. But the vast middle class, who graduate high school or a two-year college, will fail to share in the prosperity of the symbol users. To be sure, they won't confront the long-term unemployment that will threaten the bottom fifth who drop out of high school. But that is small consolation.

Over the last half century, progressive lawyers have fashioned one new legal tool to struggle against these forces of economic exclusion: civil rights law. They have spent numberless hours seeking to pry open more good jobs for blacks, women, and other subordinated groups. For all the half-steps, the result has been a great triumph for economic citizenship. But by itself, this does nothing to address the widening gap among the oligarchs, the minority of privileged symbol users, and the broad middle class in the United States.

If we don't do anything to confront these gaps, conservatives will continue to use them to generate middle-class hatred against a welfare state that seeks to help the bottom fifth of Americans sustain a minimal economic livelihood. There is a big hole here in the progressive vision of economic citizenship, and Anne Alstott and I have tried to fill it in *The Stakeholder Society*. Our idea is simple: As a birthright of citizenship, each American should be guaranteed a stake of $80,000 as he or she confronts the challenges of life as a young adult.

This stake will cover four years of tuition at a good private college, allowing the typical college graduate to start off life without a crippling debt burden.[2] But the initiative will yield even greater gains for the seven out of ten Americans who never gain the economic autonomy that a four-year degree provides. An $80,000 nest egg will provide middle-class Americans with a rough-and-ready sense of economic independence, permitting them to confront the labor market with their heads held high.

Stakeholding creates a new institution—citizenship inheritance—to compete with traditional family inheritance. In contrast to right-wing efforts to eliminate the "death tax" on the rich and super-rich, the citizenship agenda offers a more democratic vision. The nation's wealth, after all, is the product of generations of work by all Americans—the police officer on the beat and the teacher in the school, no less than the financial wizards on Wall Street. Stakeholding recognizes this basic point by granting all citizens a share of the nation's wealth as they start out in life, when they need it most.

In order to lay claim to their $80,000, Americans will have to complete high school. The 15 percent who drop out will only receive the interest on their stake, not the principal. But for the rest, there will be no strings attached. For the first time in a long time, ordinary Americans will have the real taste of economic freedom.

Some might throw away their $80,000 on frivolities. But the abuse of freedom by a few should not deprive the many of genuine opportunities to shape their lives while they are young. Thomas Jefferson's promise of the pursuit of happiness will no longer be reserved for Fourth of July declamations. It will describe the living truth of American life. The stakeholder society expands the progressive vision of economic citizenship. It gives a head start to the young and most vital elements of American society, while continuing to provide a safety net for the poor and elderly.

All this comes, of course, with a new tax, but one that gets to the heart of the problem, hitting only Americans in the top 10 or 15 percent in the wealth distribution and forcing the top 1 percent to pay about 40 percent of the total. Using data from 2001, Alstott and I show that an annual wealth tax of 2 percent, with a family exemption of $450,000, will finance our initiative—even assuming 30 percent tax evasion. The upshot is a new social contract, in which those who succeed in the market economy provide a citizen's inheritance for all Americans in the next generation.

Writing in the midst of the Republicans' ongoing campaign against the death tax, stakeholding may seem a pipe dream. But the idea is already taking off in Great Britain. Tony Blair made the citizen's inheritance into the "big idea" of his successful reelection campaign in 2001, and his Labour government followed through by enacting a variant of stakeholding into the law of the land.

As of September 1, 2002, all children born in Britain are provided with a bank account. Every child starts with £250, and kids get an extra £250 if their parents are in the lower third of the income distribution. This small stake accumulates with interest until the children reach eighteen, when the citizens receive their inheritance. The government plans to add additional amounts when children reach seven and perhaps at later ages as well. Starting in 2020, young Britons reaching eighteen each will be receiving a couple of thousand pounds—maybe more—as they start out in life.

To be sure, a few thousand pounds isn't $80,000. But the Blair example suggests that our vision of a citizenship agenda for 2020 shouldn't be entirely obscured by the darkness that has presently descended on the United States. We *will* recover from the politics of fear that the Bush administration has exploited with such great skill. Nothing lasts forever: The future will continue to be surprising; the day after tomorrow will bring new opportunities.

But will we be able to seize the moment by bringing dynamic new ideas to the table, or will we content ourselves with rehashing noble-but-tired variations on twentieth-century themes?

The year is 2020. Citizens have voted with their patriot dollars; they have debated stakeholding at Deliberation Day; and they have voted for a dynamic progressive president who has pledged to outdo the British in creating a substantial citizen's inheritance for every American. Or maybe progressive debate has left these initial proposals far behind, and we have come up with a more attractive and effective citizenship agenda to bring before the American people.

In any event, it is only within this context that we can expect the Supreme Court to get serious about the Citizenship Clauses. With a progressive president and Senate sending a new generation of justices onto the bench, the notion that citizenship has its privileges will no longer be derided, in Borkish terms, as constitutional nonsense. The unfulfilled promise of the Fourteenth Amendment will instead be viewed as a central challenge for interpretation of the twenty-first century; the "citizenship agenda" enacted by Congress may, over time, be understood as part of every American's constitutional birthright.[3]

But we have now moved far beyond 2020 to the next generation's struggle to redeem the promise of American life.

NOTES

1. Robert Bork, *The Tempting of America* 166 (New York: Free Press, 1990).

2. According to the College Board, the average, private, nonprofit, four-year college charged $21,235 in 2005–2006. Multiplied by four, that's $84,940. See http://www. collegeboard.com/press/releases/48884.html.

3. See Bruce Ackerman, "The Holmes Lectures: The Living Constitution," 120 Harv. L. Rev. 1737 (2007).

Chapter 2

The Constitutional Framework

—◦•◦—

2-1

The Founding Fathers: A Reform Caucus in Action

John P. Roche Jr.

Textbook consideration of the Constitution's Framers reverentially casts them as political philosophers conveying to future generations timeless laws of proper civic relations. Students of the era delve into arguments of The Federalist and other source materials to detect the intellectual roots of the Framers in the political theories of Locke, Montesquieu, Hume, and even Machiavelli. In this essay Roche reminds us that we should not forget that these were politicians charged with proposing a reform that had to win the endorsement of at least nine states before it became more than the collective ruminations of thirty-nine delegates. The Framers were certainly conversant with the leading political thought of their era—so conversant, indeed, that they exhibited great versatility in invoking these theorists in behalf of whatever scheme they were endorsing. Roche makes a persuasive case that the Constitution reflects the at times brilliant but always pragmatic choices of Framers ever mindful of the preferences of their constituents. Consequently, the Constitution was, in Roche's assessment, a "patch-work sewn together under the pressure of both time and events."

OVER THE LAST CENTURY and a half, the work of the Constitutional Convention and the motives of the Founding Fathers have . . . undergone miraculous

Source: John P. Roche, "The Founding Fathers: A Reform Caucus in Action," *American Political Science Review* 55, no. 4 (December 1961): 799–816. Some notes appearing in the original have been deleted.

metamorphoses: at one time acclaimed as liberals and bold social engineers, today they appear in the guise of sound Burkean conservatives. . . . The implicit assumption is that if James Madison were among us, he would be President of the Ford Foundation, while Alexander Hamilton would chair the Committee for Economic Development.

The "Fathers" have thus been admitted to our best circles; the revolutionary ferocity which confiscated all Tory property in reach and populated New Brunswick with outlaws has been converted by . . . American historians into a benign dedication to "consensus" and "prescriptive rights." The Daughters of the American Revolution have . . . at last found ancestors worthy of their descendants. It is not my purpose here to argue that the "Fathers" were, in fact, radical revolutionaries; that proposition has been brilliantly demonstrated by Robert R. Palmer in his *Age of the Democratic Revolution*. My concern is with the further position that not only were they revolutionaries, but also they were democrats. Indeed, . . . they were first and foremost superb democratic politicians. I suspect that in a contemporary setting, James Madison would be Speaker of the House of Representatives and Hamilton would be the *eminence grise* dominating . . . the Executive Office of the President. They were, with their colleagues, *political men* . . . and as recent research into the nature of American politics in the 1780s confirms,[1] they were committed (perhaps willy-nilly) to working within the democratic framework, within a universe of public approval. Charles Beard *and* the filiopietists to the contrary notwithstanding, the Philadelphia Convention was not a College of Cardinals or a council of Platonic guardians working within a manipulative, predemocratic framework; it was a *nationalist* reform caucus which had to operate with great delicacy and skill in a political cosmos full of enemies to achieve the one definitive goal-popular approbation.

Perhaps the time has come, to borrow Walton Hamilton's fine phrase, to raise the Framers from immortality to mortality, to give them credit for their magnificent demonstration of the art of democratic politics. The point must be reemphasized; they *made* history and did it within the limits of consensus. There was nothing inevitable about the future in 1787. . . . What they did was to hammer out a pragmatic compromise which would both bolster the "National interest" and be acceptable to the people. What inspiration they got came from their collective experience as professional politicians in a democratic society. As John Dickinson put it to his fellow delegates on August 13, "Experience must be our guide. Reason may mislead us."

In this context, let us examine the problems they confronted and the solutions they evolved. The Convention has been described picturesquely as a counter-revolutionary junta and the Constitution as a *coup d'état*,[2] but this has been accomplished by withdrawing the whole history of the movement for constitutional reform from its true context. No doubt the goals of the constitutional elite were "subversive" to the existing political order, but it is overlooked that their subversion could only have succeeded if the people of the United States endorsed it by regularized procedures. Indubitably they were "plotting" to establish a much stronger central government than existed under the Articles, but only in the sense in which one could argue equally well that John F. Kennedy was, from 1956 to 1960, "plotting" to become President. In short, on the fundamental *procedural* level, the Constitutionalists had to work according to the prevailing rules of the game. . . .

I

When the Constitutionalists went forth to subvert the Confederation, they utilized the mechanisms of political legitimacy. And the roadblocks which confronted them were formidable. At the same time, they were endowed with certain potent political assets. The history of the United States from 1786 to 1790 was largely one of a masterful employment of political expertise by the Constitutionalists as against bumbling, erratic behavior by the opponents of reform. Effectively, the Constitutionalists had to induce the states, by democratic techniques of coercion, to emasculate themselves. To be specific, if New York had refused to join the new Union, the project was doomed; yet before New York was safely in, the reluctant state legislature had *sua s'ponte* to take the following steps: (1) agree to send delegates to the Philadelphia Convention; (2) provide maintenance for these delegates (these were distinct stages: New Hampshire was early in naming delegates, but did not provide for their maintenance until July); (3) set up the special *ad hoc* convention to decide on ratification; and (4) concede to the decision of the *ad hoc* convention that New York should participate. New York admittedly was a tricky state, with a strong interest in a *status quo* which permitted her to exploit New Jersey and Connecticut, but the same legal hurdles existed in every state. And at the risk of becoming boring, it must be reiterated that the *only* weapon in the Constitutionalist arsenal was an effective mobilization of public opinion.

The group which undertook this struggle was an interesting amalgam of a few dedicated nationalists with the self-interested spokesmen of various parochial bailiwicks. The Georgians, for example, wanted a strong central authority to provide military protection for their huge, underpopulated state against the Creek Confederacy; Jerseymen and Connecticuters wanted to escape from economic bondage to New York; the Virginians hoped to establish a system which would give that great state its rightful place in the councils of the republic. The dominant figures in the politics of these states therefore cooperated in the call for the Convention. . . . There was, of course, a large element of personality in the affair: there is reason to suspect that Patrick Henry's opposition to the Convention and the Constitution was founded on his conviction that Jefferson was behind both, and a close study of local politics elsewhere would surely reveal that others supported the Constitution for the simple (and politically quite sufficient) reason that the "wrong" people were against it.

To say this is not to suggest that the Constitution rested on a foundation of impure or base motives. It is rather to argue that in politics there are no immaculate conceptions, and that in the drive for a stronger general government, motives of all sorts played a part. Few men in the history of mankind have espoused a view of the "common good" or "public interest" that militated against their private status; even Plato with all his reverence for disembodied reason managed to put philosophers on top of the pile. Thus it is not surprising that a number of diversified private interests joined to push the nationalist public interest; what would have been surprising was the absence of such a pragmatic united front. And the fact remains that, however motivated, these men did demonstrate a willingness to compromise their parochial interests in behalf of an ideal which took shape before their eyes and under their ministrations.

. . . [W]hat distinguished the leaders of the Constitutionalist caucus from their enemies was a "Continental" approach to political, economic and military issues. To the extent that they shared an institutional base of operations, it was the Continental Congress (thirty-nine of the delegates to the Federal Convention had served in Congress), and this was hardly a locale which inspired respect for the state governments. . . . [M]embership in the Congress under the Articles of Confederation worked to establish a continental frame of reference, that a Congressman from Pennsylvania and one from South Carolina would share a universe of discourse which provided them with a conceptual common denominator *vis-à-vis* their respective state legislatures. This was particularly true with respect to external affairs: the average state legislator was probably about as concerned with foreign policy then as he is today, but Congressmen were constantly forced to take the broad view of American prestige, were compelled to listen to the reports of Secretary John Jay and to the dispatches and pleas from their frustrated envoys in Britain, France and Spain. From considerations such as these, a "Continental" ideology developed which seems to have demanded a revision of our domestic institutions primarily on the ground that only by invigorating our general government could we assume our rightful place in the international arena. Indeed, an argument with great force—particularly since Washington was its incarnation—urged that our very survival in the Hobbesian jungle of world politics depended upon a reordering and strengthening of our national sovereignty.[3]

. . . [T]he great achievement of the Constitutionalists was their ultimate success in convincing the elected representatives of a majority of the white male population that change was imperative. A small group of political leaders with a Continental vision and essentially a consciousness of the United States' *international* impotence provided the matrix of the movement. To their standard other leaders rallied with their own parallel ambitions. Their great assets were (1) the presence in their caucus of the one authentic American "father figure," George Washington, whose prestige was enormous;[4] (2) the energy and talent of their leadership (in which one must include the towering intellectuals of the time, John Adams and Thomas Jefferson, despite their absence abroad), and their communications "network," which was far superior to anything on the opposition side;[5] (3) the preemptive skill which made "their" issue The Issue and kept the locally oriented opposition permanently on the defensive; and (4) the subjective consideration that these men were spokesmen of a new and compelling credo: *American* nationalism, that ill-defined but nonetheless potent sense of collective purpose that emerged from the American Revolution.

Despite great institutional handicaps, the Constitutionalists managed in the mid-1780s to mount an offensive which gained momentum as years went by. Their greatest problem was lethargy, and paradoxically, the number of barriers in their path may have proved an advantage in the long run. Beginning with the initial battle to get the Constitutional Convention called and delegates appointed, they could never relax, never let up the pressure. In practical terms, this meant that the local "organizations" created by the Constitutionalists were perpetually in movement building up their cadres for the next fight. (The word organization has to be used with great caution: a political organization in the United States— as in contemporary England—generally consisted of a magnate and his following, or a coalition of magnates. This did not necessarily mean that it was "undemocratic" or "aristocratic," in the Aristotelian sense of the word: while a few magnates such as the Livingstons could draft their followings, most exercised their leadership without coercion on the basis of popular endorsement. The absence of organized opposition did not imply the impossibility of competition any more than low public participation in elections necessarily indicated an undemocratic suffrage.)

The Constitutionalists got the jump on the "opposition" . . . at the outset with the demand for a Convention. Their opponents were caught in an old political trap: they were not being asked to approve any specific program of reform, but only to endorse a meeting to discuss and recommend needed reforms. If they took a hard line at the first stage, they were put in the position of glorifying the *status quo* and of denying the need for *any* changes. Moreover, the Constitutionalists could go to the people with a persuasive argument for "fair play"—"How can you condemn reform before you know precisely what is involved?" Since the state legislatures obviously would have the final say on any proposals that might emerge from the Convention, the Constitutionalists were merely reasonable men asking for a chance. Besides, since they did not make any concrete proposals at that stage, they were in a position to capitalize on every sort of generalized discontent with the Confederation.

Perhaps because of their poor intelligence system, perhaps because of over-confidence generated by the failure of all previous efforts to alter the Articles,[6] the opposition awoke too late to the dangers that confronted them in 1787. Not only did the Constitutionalists manage to get every state but Rhode Island . . . to appoint delegates to Philadelphia, but when the results were in, it appeared that they dominated the delegations. Given the apathy of the opposition, this was a natural phenomenon: in an ideologically nonpolarized political atmosphere those who get appointed to a special committee are likely to be the men who supported the movement for its creation. Even George Clinton, who seems to have been the first opposition leader to awake to the possibility of trouble, could not prevent the New York legislature from appointing Alexander Hamilton—though he did have the foresight to send two of his henchmen to dominate the delegation. Incidentally, much has been made of the fact that the delegates to Philadelphia were not elected by the people; some have adduced this fact as evidence of the "undemocratic" character of the gathering. But put in the context of the time, this argument is wholly specious: the central government under the Articles was considered a creature of the component states and in all the states but Rhode Island, Connecticut and New Hampshire, members of the national Congress were chosen by the state legislatures. This was not a consequence of elitism or fear of the mob; it was a logical extension of states'-rights doctrine to guarantee that the national institution did not end-run the state legislatures and make direct contact with the people.[7]

II

With delegations safely named, the focus shifted to Philadelphia. While waiting for a quorum to assemble, James Madison got busy and drafted the so-called Randolph or Virginia Plan with the aid of the Virginia delegation. This was a political master-stroke. Its consequence was that once business got underway, the framework of discussion was established on Madison's terms. There was no interminable argument over agenda; instead the delegates took the Virginia Resolutions—"just for purposes of discussion"—as their point of departure. And along with Madison's proposals, many of which were buried in the course of the summer, went his major premise: a new start on a Constitution rather than piece-meal amendment. This was not necessarily revolutionary—a little exegesis could demonstrate that a new Constitution might be formulated as "amendments" to the Articles of Confederation—but Madison's proposal that this "lump sum" amendment go into effect after approval by nine states (the Articles required unanimous state approval for any amendment) was thoroughly subversive.[8]

Standard treatments of the Convention divide the delegates into "nationalists" and "states'-righters" with various improvised shadings ("moderate national-ists," etc.), but these are *a posteriori* categories which obfuscate more than they clarify. What is striking to one who analyzes the Convention as a case-study in democratic politics is the lack of clear-cut ideological divisions in the Convention. Indeed, I submit that the evidence—Madison's *Notes,* the correspondence of the delegates, and debates on ratification—indicates that this was a remarkably homogeneous body on the ideological level. Yates and Lansing, Clinton's two chaperones for Hamilton, left in disgust on July 10. (Is there anything more tedious than sitting through endless disputes on matters one deems fundamen-tally misconceived? It takes an iron will to spend a hot summer as an ideological *agent provocateur.*) Luther Martin, Maryland's bibulous narcissist, left on September 4 in a huff when he discovered that others did not share his self-esteem; others went home for personal reasons. But the hard core of delegates accepted a grinding regimen throughout the attrition of a Philadelphia summer precisely because they shared the Constitutionalist goal.

Basic differences of opinion emerged, of course, but these were not ideologi-cal; they were *structural.* If the so-called "states'-rights" group had not accepted the fundamental purposes of the Convention, they could simply have pulled out and by doing so have aborted the whole enterprise. Instead of bolting, they returned day after day to argue and to compromise. An interesting symbol of this basic homogeneity was the initial agreement on secrecy: these professional poli-ticians did not want to become prisoners of publicity; they wanted to retain that freedom of maneuver which is only possible when men are not forced to take public stands in the preliminary stages of negotiation.[9] There was no legal means of binding the tongues of the delegates: at any stage in the game a delegate with basic principled objections to the emerging project could have taken the stump (as Luther Martin did after his exit) and denounced the convention to the skies. Yet Madison did not even inform Thomas Jefferson in Paris of the course of the deliberations[10] and available correspondence indicates that the delegates gener-ally observed the injunction. Secrecy is certainly uncharacteristic of any assem-bly marked by strong ideological polarization. This was noted at the time: the *New York Daily Advertiser,* August 14, 1787, commented that the " . . . profound secrecy hitherto observed by the Convention [we consider] a happy omen, as it demonstrates that the spirit of party on any great and essential point cannot have arisen to any height." [11]

Commentators on the Constitution who have read *The Federalist* in lieu of reading the actual debates have credited the Fathers with the invention of a sublime concept called "Federalism." Unfortunately *The Federalist* is probative evidence for only one proposition: that Hamilton and Madison were inspired propagandists with a genius for retrospective symmetry. Federalism, as the theory is generally defined, was an improvisation which was later promoted into a political theory. Experts on "federalism" should take to heart the advice of David Hume, who warned in his *Of the Rise and Progress of the Arts and Sciences* that "... there is no subject in which we must proceed with more caution than in [history], lest we assign causes which never existed and reduce what is merely contingent to stable and universal principles." In any event, the final balance in the Constitution between the states and the nation must have come as a great disappointment to Madison, while Hamilton's unitary views are too well known to need elucidation.

It is indeed astonishing how those who have glibly designated James Madison the "father" of Federalism have overlooked the solid body of fact which indicates that he shared Hamilton's quest for a unitary central government. To be specific, they have avoided examining the clear import of the Madison-Virginia Plan,[12] and have disregarded Madison's dogged inch-by-inch retreat from the bastions of centralization. The Virginia Plan envisioned a unitary national government effectively freed from and dominant over the states. The lower house of the national legislature was to be elected directly by the people of the states with membership proportional to population. The upper house was to be selected by the lower and the two chambers would elect the executive and choose the judges: The national government would be thus cut completely loose from the states.[13]

The structure of the general government was freed from state control in a truly radical fashion, but the scope of the authority of the national sovereign as Madison initially formulated it was breathtaking. ... The national legislature was to be empowered to disallow the acts of state legislatures, and the central government was vested, in addition to the powers of the nation under the Articles of Confederation, with plenary authority wherever "... the separate States are incompetent or in which the harmony of the United States may be interrupted by the exercise of individual legislation." [14] Finally, just to lock the door against state intrusion, the national Congress was to be given the power to use military force on recalcitrant states.[15] This was Madison's "model" of an ideal national government, though it later received little publicity in *The Federalist*.

The interesting thing was the reaction of the Convention to this militant program for a strong autonomous central government. Some delegates were startled, some obviously leery of so comprehensive a project of reform,[16] but nobody set off any fireworks and nobody walked out. Moreover, in the two weeks that followed, the Virginia Plan received substantial endorsement *en principe*; the initial temper of the gathering can be deduced from the approval "without debate or dissent," on May 31, of the Sixth Resolution which granted Congress the authority to disallow state legislation ". . . contravening *in its opinion* the Articles of Union." Indeed, an amendment was included to bar states from contravening national treaties.[17]

The Virginia Plan may therefore be considered, in ideological terms, as the delegates' Utopia, but as the discussions continued and became more specific, many of those present began to have second thoughts. After all, they were not residents of Utopia or guardians in Plato's Republic who could simply impose a philosophical ideal on subordinate strata of the population. They were practical politicians in a democratic society, and no matter what their private dreams might be, they had to take home an acceptable package and defend it—and their own political futures—against predictable attack. On June 14 the breaking point between dream and reality took place. Apparently realizing that under the Virginia Plan, Massachusetts, Virginia and Pennsylvania could virtually dominate the national government—and probably appreciating that to sell this program to "the folks back home" would be impossible—the delegates from the small states dug in their heels and demanded time for a consideration of alternatives. One gets a graphic sense of the inner politics from John Dickinson's reproach to Madison: "You see the consequences of pushing things too far. Some of the members from the small States wish for two branches in the General Legislature and are friends to a good National Government; but we would sooner submit to a foreign power than . . . be deprived of an equality of suffrage in both branches of the Legislature, and thereby be thrown under the domination of the large States." [18]

III

According to the standard script, at this point the "states'-rights" group intervened in force behind the New Jersey Plan, which has been characteristically portrayed as a reversion to the *status quo* under the Articles of Confederation with but minor modifications. A careful examination of the evidence indicates that only in a marginal sense is this an accurate description. It is true that the New Jersey Plan put the states back into the institutional picture, but one could argue that to do so was a recognition of political reality rather than an affirmation of states'-rights. A serious case can be made that the advocates of the New Jersey Plan, far from being ideological addicts of states'-rights, intended to substitute for the Virginia Plan a system which would both retain strong national power and have a chance of adoption in the states. The leading spokesman for the project asserted quite clearly that his views were based more on counsels of expediency than on principle; said Paterson on June 16: "I came here not to speak my own sentiments, but the sentiments of those who sent me. Our object is not such a Government as may be best in itself, but such a one as our Constituents have authorized us to prepare, and as they will approve." . . . With a shrewd eye, Paterson queried:

> Will the Operation and Force of the [central] Govt. depend upon the mode of Representn.—No—it will depend upon the Quantum of Power lodged in the leg. ex. and judy. Departments—Give [the existing] Congress the same Powers that you intend to give the two Branches, [under the Virginia Plan] and I apprehend they will act with as much Propriety and more Energy . . .[19]

In other words, the advocates of the New Jersey Plan concentrated their fire on what they held to be the *political liabilities* of the Virginia Plan—which were matters of institutional structure—rather than on the proposed scope of national authority. Indeed, the Supremacy Clause of the Constitution first saw the light of day in Paterson's Sixth Resolution; the New Jersey Plan contemplated the use of military force to secure compliance with national law; and finally Paterson made clear his view that under either the Virginia or the New Jersey systems, the general government would ". . . act on individuals and not on states." [20] From the states'-rights viewpoint, this was heresy: the fundament of that doctrine was the proposition that any central government had as its constituents the states, not the people, and could only reach the people through the agency of the state government.

Paterson then reopened the agenda of the Convention, but he did so within a distinctly nationalist framework. Paterson's position was one of favoring a strong central government in principle, but opposing one which in fact *put the big states in the saddle.* (The Virginia Plan, for all its abstract merits, did very well by Virginia.) As evidence for this speculation, there is a curious and intriguing proposal among Paterson's preliminary drafts of the New Jersey Plan:

> Whereas it is necessary in Order to form the People of the U. S. of America in to a Nation, that the States should be consolidated, by which means all the Citizens thereof will become equally intitled to and will equally participate in the same Privileges and Rights . . . it is therefore resolved, that all the Lands contained within the Limits of each state individually, and of the U. S. generally be considered as constituting one Body or Mass, and be divided into thirteen or more integral parts.
>
> Resolved, That such Divisions or integral Parts shall be styled Districts.[21]

This makes it sound as though Paterson was prepared to accept a strong unified central government along the lines of the Virginia Plan if the existing states were eliminated. He may have gotten the idea from his New Jersey colleague Judge David Brearley, who on June 9 had commented that the only remedy to the dilemma over representation was " . . . that a map of the U. S. be spread out, that all the existing boundaries be erased, and that a new partition of the whole be made into 13 equal parts." [22] According to Yates, Brearley added at this point " . . . then a government on the present [Virginia Plan] system will be just." [23]

This proposition was never pushed—it was patently unrealistic—but one can appreciate its purpose: it would have separated the men from the boys in the large-state delegations. How attached would the Virginians have been to their reform principles if Virginia were to disappear as a component geographical unit (the largest) for representational purposes? Up to this point, the Virginians had been in the happy position of supporting high ideals with that inner confidence born of knowledge that the "public interest" they endorsed would nourish their private interest. Worse, they had shown little willingness to compromise. Now the delegates from the small states announced that they were unprepared to be offered up as sacrificial victims to a "national interest" which reflected Virginia's parochial ambition. Caustic Charles Pinckney was not far off when he remarked sardonically that " . . . the whole [conflict] comes to this": "Give N. Jersey an equal vote, and she will dismiss her scruples, and concur in the Natil. system." [24] What he rather unfairly did not add was that the Jersey delegates were not free agents who could adhere to their private convictions; they had to take back, sponsor and risk their reputations on the reforms approved by the Convention— and in New Jersey, not in Virginia.

Paterson spoke on Saturday, and one can surmise that over the weekend there was a good deal of consultation, argument, and caucusing among the delegates. One member at least prepared a full length address: on Monday Alexander Hamilton, previously mute, rose and delivered a six-hour oration.[25] It was a remarkably apolitical speech; the gist of his position was that *both* the Virginia and New Jersey Plans were inadequately centralist, and he detailed a reform program which was reminiscent of the Protectorate under the Cromwellian *Instrument of Government* of 1653. It has been suggested that Hamilton did this in the best political tradition to emphasize the moderate character of the Virginia Plan,[26] to give the cautious delegates something *really* to worry about; but this interpretation seems somehow too clever. Particularly since the sentiments Hamilton expressed happened to be completely consistent with those he privately—and sometimes publicly—expressed throughout his life. He wanted, to take a striking phrase from a letter to George Washington, a "strong well mounted government";[27] in essence, the Hamilton Plan contemplated an elected life monarch, virtually free of public control, on the Hobbesian ground that only in this fashion could strength and stability be achieved. The other alternatives, he argued, would put policy-making at the mercy of the passions of the mob; only if the sovereign was beyond the reach of selfish influence would it be possible to have government in the interests of the whole community.[28]

From all accounts, this was a masterful and compelling speech, but (aside from furnishing John Lansing and Luther Martin with ammunition for later use against the Constitution) it made little impact. Hamilton was simply transmitting on a different wavelength from the rest of the delegates; the latter adjourned after his great effort, admired his rhetoric, and then returned to business.[29] It was rather as if they had taken a day off to attend the opera. Hamilton, never a particularly patient man or much of a negotiator, stayed for another ten days and then left, in considerable disgust, for New York.[30] Although he came back to Philadelphia sporadically and attended the last two weeks of the Convention, Hamilton played no part in the laborious task of hammering out the Constitution. . . .

IV

On Tuesday morning, June 19, the vacation was over. James Madison led off with a long, carefully reasoned speech analyzing the New Jersey Plan which, while intellectually vigorous in its criticisms, was quite conciliatory in mood. "The great difficulty," he observed, "lies in the affair of Representation; and if this could be adjusted, all others would be surmountable." [31] (As events were to demonstrate, this diagnosis was correct.) When he finished, a vote was taken on whether to continue with the Virginia Plan as the nucleus for a new constitution: seven states voted "Yes"; New York, New Jersey, and Delaware voted "No"; and Maryland, whose position often depended on which delegates happened to be on the floor, divided. Paterson, it seems, lost decisively; yet in a fundamental sense he and his allies had achieved their purpose: from that day onward, it could never be forgotten that the state governments loomed ominously in the background and that no verbal incantations could exorcise their power. Moreover, nobody bolted the convention: Paterson and his colleagues took their defeat in stride and set to work to modify the Virginia Plan, particularly with respect to its provisions on representation in the national legislature. Indeed, they won an immediate rhetorical bonus; when Oliver Ellsworth of Connecticut rose to move that the word "national" be expunged from the Third Virginia Resolution ("Resolved that a *national* Government ought to be established consisting of a *supreme* Legislative, Executive and Judiciary" [32]), Randolph agreed and the motion passed unanimously.[33] The process of compromise had begun.

For the next two weeks, the delegates circled around the problem of legislative representation. The Connecticut delegation appears to have evolved a possible compromise quite early in the debates, but the Virginians and particularly Madison (unaware that he would later be acclaimed as the prophet of "federalism") fought obdurately against providing for equal representation of states in the second chamber. There was a good deal of acrimony and at one point Benjamin Franklin—of all people—proposed the institution of a daily prayer; practical politicians in the gathering, however, were meditating more on the merits of a good committee than on the utility of Divine intervention. On July 2, the ice began to break when through a number of fortuitous events[34]—and one that seems deliberate[35]—the majority against equality of representation was converted into a dead tie. The Convention had reached the stage where it was "ripe" for a solution (presumably all the therapeutic speeches had been made), and the South Carolinians proposed a committee. Madison and James Wilson wanted none of it, but with only Pennsylvania dissenting, the body voted to establish a working party on the problem of representation.

The members of this committee, one from each state, were elected by the delegates—and a very interesting committee it was. Despite the fact that the Virginia Plan had held majority support up to that date, neither Madison nor Randolph was selected (Mason was the Virginian) and Baldwin of Georgia, whose shift in position had resulted in the tie, was chosen. From the composition, it was clear that this was not to be a "fighting" committee: the emphasis in membership was on what might be described as "second-level political entrepreneurs." On the basis of the discussions up to that time, only Luther Martin of Maryland could be described as a "bitter-ender." Admittedly, some divination enters into this sort of analysis, but one does get a sense of the mood of the delegates from these choices—including the interesting selection of Benjamin Franklin, despite his age and intellectual wobbliness, over the brilliant and incisive Wilson or the sharp, polemical Gouverneur Morris, to represent Pennsylvania. His passion for conciliation was more valuable at this juncture than Wilson's logical genius, or Morris' acerbic wit.

There is a common rumor that the Framers divided their time between philosophical discussions of government and reading the classics in political theory. Perhaps this is as good a time as any to note that their concerns were highly practical, that they spent little time canvassing abstractions. A number of them had some acquaintance with the history of political theory (probably gained from reading John Adams' monumental compilation *A Defense of the Constitutions of Government,*[36] the first volume of which appeared in 1786), and it was a poor rhetorician indeed who could not cite Locke, Montesquieu, or Harrington *in support* of a desired goal. Yet up to this point in the deliberations, no one had expounded a defense of states'-rights or the "separation of powers" on anything resembling a theoretical basis. It should be reiterated that the Madison model had no room either for the states or for the "separation of powers": effectively *all* governmental power was vested in the national legislature. The merits of Montesquieu did not turn up until *The Federalist;* and although a perverse argument could be made that Madison's ideal was truly in the tradition of John Locke's *Second Treatise of Government,*[37] the Locke whom the American rebels treated as an honorary president was a pluralistic defender of vested rights,[38] not of parliamentary supremacy.

It would be tedious to continue a blow-by-blow analysis of the work of the delegates; the critical fight was over representation of the states and once the Connecticut Compromise was adopted on July 17, the Convention was over the hump. Madison, James Wilson, and Gouverneur Morris of New York (who was there representing Pennsylvania!) fought the compromise all the way in a last-ditch effort to get a unitary state with parliamentary supremacy. But their allies deserted them and they demonstrated after their defeat the essentially opportunist character of their objections—using "opportunist" here in a non-pejorative sense, to indicate a willingness to swallow their objections and get on with the business. Moreover, once the compromise had carried (by five states to four, with one state divided), its advocates threw themselves vigorously into the job of strengthening the general government's substantive powers—as might have been predicted, indeed, from Paterson's early statements. It nourishes an increased respect for Madison's devotion to the art of politics, to realize that this dogged fighter could sit down six months later and prepare essays for *The Federalist* in contradiction to his basic convictions about the true course the Convention should have taken.

V

Two tricky issues will serve to illustrate the later process of accommodation. The first was the institutional position of the Executive. Madison argued for an executive chosen by the National Legislature and on May 29 this had been adopted with a provision that after his seven-year term was concluded, the chief magistrate should not be eligible for reelection. In late July this was reopened and for a week the matter was argued from several different points of view. A good deal of desultory speech-making ensued, but the gist of the problem was the opposition from two sources to election by the legislature. One group felt that the states should have a hand in the process; another small but influential circle urged direct election by the people. There were a number of proposals: election by the people, election by state governors, by electors chosen by state legislatures, by the National Legislature (James Wilson, perhaps ironically, proposed at one point that an Electoral College be chosen by lot from the National Legislature!), and there was some resemblance to three-dimensional chess in the dispute because of the presence of two other variables, length of tenure and reeligibility. Finally, after opening, reopening, and re-reopening the debate, the thorny problem was consigned to a committee for resolution.

The Brearley Committee on Postponed Matters was a superb aggregation of talent and its compromise on the Executive was a masterpiece of political improvisation. (The Electoral College, its creation, however, had little in its favor as an *institution*—as the delegates well appreciated.) The point of departure for all discussion about the presidency in the Convention was that in immediate terms, the problem was non-existent; in other words, everybody present knew that under any system devised, George Washington would be President. Thus they were dealing in the future tense and to a body of working politicians the merits of the Brearley proposal were obvious: everybody got a piece of cake. (Or to put it more academically, each viewpoint could leave the Convention and argue to its constituents that it had *really* won the day.) First, the state legislatures had the right to determine the mode of selection of the electors; second, the small states received a bonus in the Electoral College in the form of a guaranteed minimum of three votes while the big states got acceptance of the principle of proportional power; third, if the state legislatures agreed (as six did in the first presidential election), the people could be involved directly in the choice of electors; and finally, if no candidate received a majority in the College, the right of decision passed to the National Legislature with each state exercising equal strength. (In the Brearley recommendation, the election went to the Senate, but a motion from the floor substituted the House; this was accepted on the ground that the Senate already had enough authority over the executive in its treaty and appointment powers.)

This compromise was almost too good to be true, and the Framers snapped it up with little debate or controversy. No one seemed to think well of the College as an *institution;* indeed, what evidence there is suggests that there was an assumption that once Washington had finished his tenure as President, the electors would cease to produce majorities and the chief executive would usually be chosen in the House. George Mason observed casually that the selection would be made in the House nineteen times in twenty and no one seriously disputed this point. The vital aspect of the Electoral College was that it got the Convention over the hurdle and protected everybody's interests. The future was left to cope with the problem of what to do with this Rube Goldberg mechanism.

In short, the Framers did not in their wisdom endow the United States with a College of Cardinals—the Electoral College was neither an exercise in applied

Platonism nor an experiment in indirect government based on elitist distrust of the masses. It was merely a jerry-rigged improvisation which has subsequently been endowed with a high theoretical content. When an elector from Oklahoma in 1960 refused to cast his vote for Nixon (naming Byrd and Goldwater instead) on the ground that the Founding Fathers intended him to exercise his great independent wisdom, he was indulging in historical fantasy. If one were to indulge in counter-fantasy, he would be tempted to suggest that the Fathers would be startled to find the College still in operation—and perhaps even dismayed at their descendants' lack of judgment or inventiveness.[39]

The second issue on which some substantial practical bargaining took place was slavery. The morality of slavery was, by design, not at issue;[40] but in its other concrete aspects, slavery colored the arguments over taxation, commerce, and representation. The "Three-Fifths Compromise," that three-fifths of the slaves would be counted both for representation and for purposes of direct taxation (which was drawn from the past—it was a formula of Madison's utilized by Congress in 1783 to establish the basis of state contributions to the Confederation treasury) had allayed some Northern fears about Southern overrepresentation (no one then foresaw the trivial role that direct taxation would play in later federal financial policy), but doubts still remained. The Southerners, on the other hand, were afraid that Congressional control over commerce would lead to the exclusion of slaves or to their excessive taxation as imports. Moreover, the Southerners were disturbed over "navigation acts," *i.e.,* tariffs, or special legislation providing, for example, that exports be carried only in American ships; as a section depending upon exports, they wanted protection from the potential voracity of their commercial brethren of the Eastern states. To achieve this end, Mason and others urged that the Constitution include a proviso that navigation and commercial laws should require a two-thirds vote in Congress.

These problems came to a head in late August and, as usual, were handed to a committee in the hope that, in Gouverneur Morris' words, ". . . these things may form a bargain among the Northern and Southern states." [41] The Committee reported its measures of reconciliation on August 25, and on August 29 the package was wrapped up and delivered. What occurred can best be described in George Mason's dour version (he anticipated Calhoun in his conviction that permitting navigation acts to pass by majority vote would put the South in economic bondage to the North—it was mainly on this ground that he refused to sign the Constitution):

> The Constitution as agreed to till a fortnight before the Convention rose was such a one as he would have set his hand and heart to. . . . [Until that time] The 3 New England States were constantly with us in all questions . . . so that it was these three States with the 5 Southern ones against Pennsylvania, Jersey and Delaware. With respect to the importation of

slaves, [decision-making] was left to Congress. This disturbed the two Southernmost States who knew that Congress would immediately suppress the importation of slaves. Those two States therefore struck up a bargain with the three New England States. If they would join to admit slaves for some years, the two Southern-most States would join in changing the clause which required the 2/3 of the Legislature in any vote [on navigation acts]. It was done.[42]

On the floor of the Convention there was a virtual love-feast on this happy occasion. Charles Pinckney of South Carolina attempted to overturn the committee's decision, when the compromise was reported to the Convention, by insisting that the South needed protection from the imperialism of the Northern states. But his Southern colleagues were not prepared to rock the boat and General C. C. Pinckney arose to spread oil on the suddenly ruffled waters; he admitted that:

> It was in the true interest of the S[outhern] States to have no regulation of commerce; but considering the loss brought on the commerce of the Eastern States by the Revolution, their liberal conduct towards the views of South Carolina [on the regulation of the slave trade] and the interests the weak Southn. States had in being united with the strong Eastern states, he thought it proper that no fetters should be imposed on the power of making commercial regulations; *and that his constituents, though prejudiced against the Eastern States, would be reconciled to this liberality.* He had himself prejudices agst the Eastern States before he came here, but would acknowledge that he had found them as liberal and candid as any men whatever. (Italics added)[43]

Pierce Butler took the same tack, essentially arguing that he was not too happy about the possible consequences, but that a deal was a deal.[44] . . .

VI

Drawing on their vast collective political experience, utilizing every weapon in the politician's arsenal, looking constantly over their shoulders at their constituents, the delegates put together a Constitution. It was a makeshift affair; some sticky issues (for example, the qualification of voters) they ducked entirely; others they mastered with that ancient instrument of political sagacity, studied ambiguity (for example, citizenship), and some they just overlooked. In this last category, I suspect, fell the matter of the power of the federal courts to determine the constitutionality of acts of Congress. When the judicial article was formulated (Article III of the Constitution), deliberations were still in the stage where the legislature was endowed with broad power under the Randolph formulation, authority which by its own terms was scarcely amenable to judicial review. In essence, courts could hardly determine when " . . . the separate States are incompetent or . . . the harmony of the United States may be interrupted"; the National Legislature, as critics pointed out, was free to define its own jurisdiction. Later the definition of legislative authority was changed into the form we know, a series of stipulated powers, *but the delegates never seriously reexamined the jurisdiction of the judiciary under this new limited formulation.*[45] All arguments on the intention of the Framers in this matter are thus deductive and *a posteriori,* though some obviously make more sense than others.

The Framers were busy and distinguished men, anxious to get back to their families, their positions, and their constituents, not members of the French Academy devoting a lifetime to a dictionary. They were trying to do an important job, and do it in such a fashion that their handiwork would be acceptable to very diverse constituencies. No one was rhapsodic about the final document, but it was a beginning, a move in the right direction, and one they had reason to believe the people would endorse. In addition, since they had modified the impossible amendment provisions of the Articles (the requirement of unanimity which could always be frustrated by "Rogues Island") to one demanding approval by only three-quarters of the states, they seemed confident that gaps in the fabric which experience would reveal could be rewoven without undue difficulty. . . .

Madison, despite his reservations about the Constitution, was the campaign manager in ratification. His first task was to get the Congress in New York to light its own funeral pyre by approving the "amendments" to the Articles and sending them on to the state legislatures. Above all, momentum had to be maintained. The anti-Constitutionalists, now thoroughly alarmed and no novices in politics, realized that their best tactic was attrition rather than direct opposition. Thus they settled on a position expressing qualified approval but calling for a second Convention to remedy various defects (the one with the most demagogic appeal was the lack of a Bill of Rights). Madison knew that to accede to this demand would be equivalent to losing the battle, nor would he agree to conditional approval (despite wavering even by Hamilton). This was an all-or-nothing proposition: national salvation or national impotence with no intermediate positions possible. Unable to get congressional approval, he settled for second best: a unanimous resolution of Congress transmitting the Constitution to the states for whatever action they saw fit to take. The opponents then moved from New York and the Congress, where they had attempted to attach amendments and conditions, to the states for the final battle.

At first the campaign for ratification went beautifully: within eight months after the delegates set their names to the document, eight states had ratified. Only in Massachusetts had the result been close (187–168). Theoretically, a ratification by one more state convention would set the new government in motion, but in fact until Virginia and New York acceded to the new Union, the latter was a fiction. New Hampshire was the next to ratify; Rhode Island was involved in its characteristic political convulsions (the Legislature there sent the Constitution out to the towns for decision by popular vote and it got lost among a series of local issues); North Carolina's convention did not meet until July and then postponed a final decision. This is hardly the place for an extensive analysis of the conventions of New York and Virginia. Suffice it to say that the Constitutionalists clearly outmaneuvered their opponents, forced them into impossible political positions, and won both states narrowly. The Virginia Convention could serve as a classic study in effective floor management: Patrick Henry had to be contained, and a reading of the debates discloses a standard two-stage technique. Henry would give a four- or five-hour speech denouncing some section of the Constitution on every conceivable ground (the federal district, he averred at one point, would become a haven for convicts escaping from state authority!);[46] when Henry subsided, "Mr. Lee of Westmoreland" would rise and literally poleaxe him with sardonic invective (when Henry complained about the militia power, "Lighthorse Harry" really punched below the belt: observing that while the former Governor had been sitting in Richmond during the Revolution, *he* had been out in the trenches with the troops and thus felt better qualified to discuss military affairs).[47] Then the gentlemanly Constitutionalists (Madison, Pendleton and Marshall) would pick up the matters at issue and examine them in the light of reason.

Indeed, modern Americans who tend to think of James Madison as a rather desiccated character should spend some time with this transcript. Probably Madison put on his most spectacular demonstration of nimble rhetoric in what might be called "The Battle of the Absent Authorities." Patrick Henry in the course of one of his harangues alleged that Jefferson was known to be opposed to Virginia's approving the Constitution. This was clever: Henry hated Jefferson, but was prepared to use any weapon that came to hand. Madison's riposte was superb: First, he said that with all due respect to the great reputation of Jefferson, he was not in the country and therefore could not formulate an adequate judgment; second, no one should utilize the reputation of an outsider—the Virginia Convention was there to think for itself; third, if there were to be recourse to outsiders, the opinions of George Washington should certainly be taken into consideration; and finally, he knew from privileged personal communications from Jefferson that in fact the latter *strongly favored* the Constitution.[48] To devise an assault route into this rhetorical fortress was literally impossible.

VII

The fight was over; all that remained now was to establish the new frame of government in the spirit of its framers. And who were better qualified for this task than the Framers themselves? Thus victory for the Constitution meant simultaneous victory for the Constitutionalists; the anti-Constitutionalists either capitulated or vanished into limbo—soon Patrick Henry would be offered a seat on the Supreme Court[49] and Luther Martin would be known as the Federalist "bull-dog." [50] And irony of ironies, Alexander Hamilton and James Madison would shortly accumulate a reputation as the formulators of what is often alleged to be our political theory, the concept of "federalism." . . .

Thus we can ask what the Framers meant when they gave Congress the power to regulate interstate and foreign commerce, and we emerge, reluctantly perhaps, with the reply that . . . they may not have known what they meant, that there may not have been any semantic consensus. The Convention was not a seminar in analytic philosophy or linguistic analysis. Commerce was *commerce*— and if different interpretations of the word arose, later generations could worry about the problem of definition. The delegates were in a hurry to get a new government established; when definitional arguments arose, they characteristically took refuge in ambiguity. If different men voted for the same proposition for varying reasons, that was politics (and still is); if later generations were unsettled by this lack of precision, that would be their problem.

There was a good deal of definitional pluralism with respect to the problems the delegates did discuss, but when we move to the question of extrapolated intentions, we enter the realm of spiritualism. When men in our time, for instance, launch into elaborate talmudic exegesis to demonstrate that federal aid to parochial schools is (or is not) in accord with the intentions of the men who established the Republic and endorsed the Bill of Rights, they are engaging in historical Extra-Sensory Perception. (If one were to join this E. S. P. contingent for a minute, he might suggest that the hard-boiled politicians who wrote the Constitution and Bill of Rights would chuckle scornfully at such an invocation of authority: obviously a politician would chart his course on the intentions of the living, not of the dead, and count the number of Catholics in his constituency.)

The Constitution, then, was not an apotheosis of "constitutionalism," a triumph of architectonic genius; it was a patch-work sewn together under the pressure of both time and events by a group of extremely talented democratic politicians. They refused to attempt the establishment of a strong, centralized sovereignty on the principle of legislative supremacy for the excellent reason that the people would not accept it. They risked their political fortunes by opposing the established doctrines of state sovereignty because they were convinced that the existing system was leading to national impotence and probably foreign domination. For two years, they worked to get a convention established. For over three months, in what must have seemed to the faithful participants an endless process of give-and-take, they reasoned, cajoled, threatened, and bargained amongst themselves. The result was a Constitution which the people, in fact, by democratic processes, did accept, and a new and far better national government was established.

Beginning with the inspired propaganda of Hamilton, Madison and Jay, the ideological build-up got under way. *The Federalist* had little impact on the ratification of the Constitution, except perhaps in New York, but this volume had enormous influence on the image of the Constitution in the minds of future generations, particularly on historians and political scientists who have an innate fondness for theoretical symmetry. Yet, while the shades of Locke and Montesquieu *may* have been hovering in the background, and the delegates *may* have been unconscious instruments of a transcendent *telos,* the careful observer of the day-to-day work of the Convention finds no over-arching principles. The "separation of powers" to him seems to be a by-product of suspicion, and "federalism" he views as a *pis aller,* as the farthest point the delegates felt they could go in the destruction of state power without themselves inviting repudiation.

To conclude, the Constitution was neither a victory for abstract theory nor a great practical success. Well over half a million men had to die on the battlefields of the Civil War before certain constitutional principles could be defined—a baleful consideration which is somehow overlooked in our customary tributes to the farsighted genius of the Framers and to the supposed American talent for "constitutionalism." The Constitution was, however, a vivid demonstration of effective democratic political action, and of the forging of a national elite which literally persuaded its countrymen to hoist themselves by their own boot straps. American pro-consuls would be wise not to translate the Constitution into Japanese, or Swahili, or treat it as a work of semi-Divine origin; but when students of comparative politics examine the process of nation-building in countries newly freed from colonial rule, they may find the American experience instructive as a classic example of the potentialities of a democratic elite.

NOTES

1. The view that the right to vote in the states was severely circumscribed by property qualifications has been thoroughly discredited in recent years. See Chilton Williamson, *American Suffrage from Property to Democracy, 1760–1860* (Princeton, 1960). The contemporary position is that John Dickinson actually knew what he was talking about when he argued that there would be little opposition to vesting the right of suffrage in freeholders since "The great mass of our Citizens is composed at this time of freeholders, and will be pleased with it." Max

Farrand, *Records of the Federal Convention,* Vol. 2, p. 202 (New Haven, 1911). (Henceforth cited as *Farrand.*)

2. The classic statement of the *coup d'etat* theory is, of course, Charles A. Beard, *An Economic Interpretation of the Constitution of the United States* (New York, 1913).

3. "[T]he situation of the general government, if it can be called a government, is shaken to its foundation, and liable to be overturned by every blast. In a word, it is at an end; and, unless a remedy is soon applied, anarchy and confusion will inevitably ensue." Washington to Jefferson, May 30, 1787, *Farrand,* III, 31. See also Irving Brant, *James Madison, The Nationalist* (New York, 1948), ch. 25.

4. The story of James Madison's cultivation of Washington is told by Brant, *op. cit.,* pp. 394–97.

5. The "message center" being the Congress; nineteen members of Congress were simultaneously delegates to the Convention. One gets a sense of this coordination of effort from Broadus Mitchell, *Alexander Hamilton, Youth to Maturity* (New York, 1957), ch. 22.

6. The Annapolis Convention, called for the previous year, turned into a shambles: only five states sent commissioners, only three states were legally represented, and the instructions to delegates named varied quite widely from state to state. Clinton and others of his persuasion may have thought this disaster would put an end to the drive for reform. See Mitchell, *op. cit.,* pp. 362–67; Brant, *op. cit.,* pp. 375–87.

7. The terms "radical" and "conservative" have been bandied about a good deal in connection with the Constitution. This usage is nonsense if it is employed to distinguish between two economic "classes"—*e.g.,* radical debtors versus conservative creditors, radical farmers versus conservative capitalists, etc.—because there was no polarization along this line of division; the same types of people turned up on both sides. And many were hard to place in these terms: does one treat Robert Morris as a debtor or a creditor? or James Wilson? See Robert E. Brown, *Charles Beard and the Constitution* (Princeton, 1956), passim. The one line of division that holds up is between those deeply attached to states'-rights and those who felt that the Confederation was bankrupt. Thus, curiously, some of the most narrow-minded, parochial spokesmen of the time have earned the designation "radical" while those most willing to experiment and alter the *status quo* have been dubbed "conservative"! See Cecelia Kenyon, "Men of Little Faith," *William and Mary Quarterly,* Vol. 12, p. 3 (1955).

8. Yet, there was little objection to this crucial modification from any quarter—there almost seems to have been a gentlemen's agreement that Rhode Island's *liberum veto* had to be destroyed.

9. See Mason's letter to his son, May 27, 1787, in which he endorsed secrecy as "a proper precaution to prevent mistakes and misrepresentation until the business shall have been completed, when the whole may have a very different complexion from that in which the several crude and indigested parts might in their first shape appear if submitted to the public eye." *Farrand,* III, 28.

10. See Madison to Jefferson, June 6, 1787, *Farrand,* III, 35.

11. Cited in Charles Warren, *The Making of the Constitution* (Boston, 1928), p. 138.

12. "I hold it for a fundamental point, that an individual independence of the states is utterly irreconcilable with the idea of an aggregate sovereignty," Madison to Randolph, cited in Brant, *op. cit.,* p. 416.

13. The Randolph Plan was presented on May 29, see *Farrand,* I, 18–23; the state legislatures retained only the power to *nominate* candidates for the upper chamber. Madison's view of the

appropriate position of the states emerged even more strikingly in Yates' record of his speech on June 29: "Some contend that states are sovereign when in fact they are only political societies. There is a gradation of power in all societies, from the lowest corporation to the highest sovereign. The states never possessed the essential rights of sovereignty. . . . The states, at present, are only great corporations, having the power of making by-laws, and these are effectual only if they are not contradictory to the general confederation. The states ought to be placed under the control of the general government—at least as much so as they formerly were under the king and British parliament." *Farrand*, I, 471. Forty-six years later, after Yates' "Notes" had been published, Madison tried to explain this statement away as a misinterpretation: he did not flatly deny the authenticity of Yates' record, but attempted a defense that was half justification and half evasion. Madison to W. C. Rives, Oct. 21, 1833. *Farrand*, III, 521–24.

14. Resolution 6.

15. *Ibid.*

16. See the discussions on May 30 and 31. "Mr. Charles Pinkney wished to know of Mr. Randolph whether he meant to abolish the State Governts. Altogether . . . Mr. Butler said he had not made up his mind on the subject and was open to the light which discussion might throw on it . . . Genl. Pinkney expressed a doubt . . . Mr. Gerry seemed to entertain the same doubt." *Farrand*, I, 33–34. There were no denunciations—though it should perhaps be added that Luther Martin had not yet arrived.

17. *Farrand*, I, 54. (Italics added.)

18. *Ibid.*, p. 242. Delaware's delegates had been instructed by their general assembly to maintain in any new system the voting equality of the states. *Farrand*, III, 574.

19. *Ibid.*, pp. 275–76.

20. "But it is said that this national government is to act on individuals and not on states; and cannot a federal government be so framed as to operate in the same way? It surely may." *Ibid.*, pp. 182–83; also *ibid.* at p. 276.

21. *Farrand*, III, 613.

22. *Farrand*, I, 177.

23. *Ibid.*, p. 182.

24. *Ibid.*, p. 255.

25. J. C. Hamilton, cited *ibid.*, p. 293.

26. See, *e.g.*, Mitchell, *op. cit.*, p. 381.

27. Hamilton to Washington, July 3, 1787, *Farrand*, III, 53.

28. A reconstruction of the Hamilton Plan is found in *Farrand*, III, 617–30.

29. Said William Samuel Johnson on June 21: "A gentleman from New-York, with boldness and decision, proposed a system totally different from both [Virginia and New Jersey]; and though he has been praised by every body, he has been supported by none." *Farrand*, I, 363.

30. See his letter to Washington cited *supra* note 43.

31. *Farrand*, I, 321.

32. This formulation was voted into the Randolph Plan on May 30, 1787, by a vote of six states to none, with one divided. *Farrand*, I, 30.

33. *Farrand*, I, 335–36. In agreeing, Randolph stipulated his disagreement with Ellsworth's rationale, but said he did not object to merely changing an "expression." Those who subject the Constitution to minute semantic analysis might do well to keep this instance in mind; if Randolph could so concede the deletion of "national," one may wonder if any word changes can be given much weight.

34. According to Luther Martin, he was alone on the floor and cast Maryland's vote for equality of representation. Shortly thereafter, Jenifer came on the floor and "Mr. King, from Massachusetts, valuing himself on Mr. Jenifer to divide the State of Maryland on this question . . . requested of the President that the question might be put again; however, the motion was too extraordinary in its nature to meet with success." Cited from "The Genuine Information, . . ." *Farrand*, III, 188.

35. Namely Baldwin's vote *for* equality of representation which divided Georgia—with Few absent and Pierce in New York fighting a duel, Houston voted against equality and Baldwin shifted to tie the state. Baldwin was originally from Connecticut and attended and tutored at Yale, facts which have led to much speculation about the pressures the Connecticut delegation may have brought on him to save the day (Georgia was the last state to vote) and open the way to compromise. To employ a good Russian phrase, it was certainly not an accident that Baldwin voted the way he did. See *Warren*, p. 262.

36. For various contemporary comments, see *Warren*, pp. 814–18. On Adams' technique, see Zoltan Haraszti, "The Composition of Adams' *Defense*," in *John Adams and the Prophets of Progress* (Cambridge, 1952), ch. 9. In this connection it is interesting to check the Convention discussions for references to the authority of Locke, Montesquieu and Harrington, the theorists who have been assigned various degrees of paternal responsibility. There are no explicit references to James Harrington; one to John Locke (Luther Martin cited him on the state of nature, *Farrand*, I, 437); and seven to Montesquieu, only one of which related to the "separation of powers" (Madison in an odd speech, which he explained in a footnote was given to help a friend rather than advance his own views, cited Montesquieu on the separation of the executive and legislative branches, *Farrand*, II, 34). This, of course, does not prove that Locke and Co. were without influence; it shifts the burden of proof, however, to those who assert ideological causality. See Benjamin F. Wright, "The Origins of the Separation of Powers in America," *Economica*, Vol. 13 (1933), p. 184.

37. I share Willmoore Kendall's interpretation of Locke as a supporter of parliamentary supremacy and majoritarianism; see Kendall, *John Locke and the Doctrine of Majority Rule* (Urbana, 1941). Kendall's general position has recently received strong support in the definitive edition and commentary of Peter Laslett, *Locke's Two Treatises of Government* (Cambridge, 1960).

38. The American Locke is best delineated in Carl Becker, *The Declaration of Independence* (New York, 1948).

39. See John P. Roche, "The Electoral College: A Note on American Political Mythology," *Dissent* (Spring, 1961), pp. 197–99. The relevant debates took place July 19–26, 1787, *Farrand*, II, 50–128, and September 5–6, 1787, *ibid.*, pp. 505–31.

40. See the discussion on August 22, 1787, *Farrand*, II, 366–75; King seems to have expressed the sense of the Convention when he said, "the subject should be considered in a political light only." *Ibid.* at 373.

41. *Farrand*, II, 374. Randolph echoed his sentiment in different words.

42. Mason to Jefferson, cited in *Warren*, p. 584.

43. August 29, 1787, *Farrand*, II, 449–50.

44. *Ibid.*, p. 451. The plainest statement of the matter was put by the three North Carolina delegates (Blount, Spaight and Williamson) in their report to Governor Caswell, September 18, 1787. After noting that "no exertions have been wanting on our part to guard and promote the particular interest of North Carolina," they went on to explain the basis of the negotiations in cold-blooded fashion: "While we were taking so much care to guard ourselves against being

over reached and to form rules of Taxation that might operate in our favour, it is not to be supposed that our Northern Brethren were Inattentive to their particular Interest. A navigation Act or the power to regulate Commerce in the Hands of the National Government . . . is what the Southern States have given in Exchange for the advantages we Mentioned." They concluded by explaining that while the Constitution did deal with other matters besides taxes—"there are other Considerations of great Magnitude involved in the system"—they would not take up valuable time with boring details! *Farrand,* III, 83–84.

45. The Committee on Detail altered the general grant of legislative power envisioned by the Virginia Plan into a series of specific grants; these were examined closely between August 16 and August 23. One day only was devoted to the Judicial Article, August 27, and since no one raised the question of judicial review of *Federal* statutes, no light was cast on the matter. A number of random comments on the power of the judiciary were scattered throughout the discussions, but there was another variable which deprives them of much probative value: the proposed Council of Revision which would have joined the Executive with the judges in *legislative* review. Madison and Wilson, for example, favored this technique—which had nothing in common with what we think of as judicial review except that judges were involved in the task.

46. See *Elliot's Debates on the Federal Constitution* (Washington, 1836), Vol. 3, pp. 436–38.

47. This should be quoted to give the full flavor: "Without vanity, I may say I have had different experience of [militia] service from that of [Henry]. It was my fortune to be a soldier of my country. . . . I saw what the honorable gentleman did not see—our men fighting. . . ." *Ibid.,* p. 178.

48. *Ibid.,* p. 329.

49. Washington offered him the Chief Justiceship in 1796, but he declined; Charles Warren, *The Supreme Court in United States History* (Boston, 1947), Vol. 1, p. 139.

50. He was a zealous prosecutor of seditions in the period 1798–1800; with Justice Samuel Chase, like himself an alleged "radical" at the time of the Constitutional Convention, Martin hunted down Jeffersonian heretics. See James M. Smith, *Freedom's Fetters* (Ithaca, 1956), pp. 342–43.

2-2

Anti-Federalist No. 3

Brutus
November 15, 1787

After the Constitutional Convention, most of the delegates returned home to promote ratification by their states. Some, however, had opposed the final plan for the new government. They, along with allies who had boycotted the Convention, began lobbying their state legislatures to reject ratification. The two sides battled each other in the nation's newspapers. We celebrate the winners as the Framers, as contemporaries frequently called them.

Weeks after the Convention, Alexander Hamilton, James Madison, and John Jay launched a series of pro-ratification newspaper articles under the pen name Publius; collectively, they called themselves "Federalists," in order to allay misgivings about the creation of the new, more resourceful national government. After ratification, their eighty-five essays were published in book form as The Federalist, *and subsequently as* The Federalist Papers. *(Thomas Jefferson immediately added it to the required reading list of all University of Virginia undergraduates.)*

Their opponents, known as the "Anti-Federalists," were also capable political thinkers. While history has tended to denigrate them as "men of little faith," it is difficult to find fault with much of their reasoning. In the essay below—one of sixteen penned by Brutus (likely New York delegate Robert Yates)—the author highlights some serious issues with the new Constitution and its plan of "nominal" representation. How can the presence of a distant, national government advance democracy (popular control) over that presently provided by the smaller states' own assemblies? Why should a small, unelected, malapportioned Senate be permitted to veto any proposal arising in the more democratic institution, the House of Representatives? Both are serious problems which Madison grapples with in his famous "rebuttals" in the next readings.

To the citizens of the State of New-York. In the investigation of the constitution, under your consideration, great care should be taken, that you do not form your opinions respecting it, from unimportant provisions, or fallacious appearances.

On a careful examination, you will find, that many of its parts, of little moment, are well formed; in these it has a specious resemblance of a free government—but this is not sufficient to justify the adoption of it—the gilded pill, is often found to contain the most deadly poison.

You are not however to expect, a perfect form of government, any more than to meet with perfection in man: your views therefore, ought to be directed to the main pillars upon which a free government is to rest. . . . Under these impressions, it has been my object to turn your attention to the principal defects in this system. . . . I shall now [in this third essay] proceed . . . to examine its parts more minutely, and show that the powers are not properly deposited, for the security of public liberty.

The first important object that presents itself in the organization of this government, is the legislature. This is to be composed of two branches; the first to be called the general assembly [the House of Representatives], and is to be chosen by the people of the respective states, in proportion to the number of their inhabitants, and is to consist of sixty five members, with powers in the legislature to increase the number, not to exceed one for every thirty thousand inhabitants. The second branch is to be called the senate, and is to consist of twenty-six members, two of which are to be chosen by the legislatures of each of the states.

In the former of these there is an appearance of justice, in the appointment of its members—but if the clause, which provides for this branch, be stripped of its ambiguity, it will be found that there is really no equality of representation, even in this house.

The words are "representatives and direct taxes, shall be apportioned among the several states, which may be included in this union, according to their respective numbers, which shall be determined by adding to the whole number of free persons, including those bound to service for a term of years, and excluding Indians not taxed, three fifths of all other persons."—What a strange and unnecessary accumulation of words are here used to conceal from the public eye what might have been expressed in the following concise manner. Representatives are to be proportioned among the states respectively, according to the number of freemen and slaves inhabiting them, counting five slaves for three free men.

"In a free state," says the celebrated Montesquieu, "every man who is supposed to be a free agent, ought to be concerned in his own government. Therefore the legislature should reside in the whole body of the people, or their representatives." But it has never been alleged that those who are not free agents, can, upon any rational principle, have any thing to do in government, either by themselves or others. If they have no share in government, why is the number of members in the assembly, to be increased on their account? Is it because in some of the states, a considerable part of the property of the inhabitants consists in a number of their fellow men, who are held in bondage, in defiance of every idea of benevolence, justice, and religion, and contrary to all the principles of liberty, which have been publicly avowed in the late glorious revolution? If this be a just ground for representation, the horses in some of the states, and the oxen in others, ought to be represented—for a great share of property in some of them consists in these animals; and they have as much control over their own actions, as these poor unhappy creatures, who are intended to be described in the above recited clause, by the words, "all other persons." By this mode of apportionment, the representatives of the different parts of the union will be extremely unequal. . . .

There appears at the first view a manifest inconsistency in the apportionment of representatives in the senate, upon the plan of a consolidated government. On every principle of equity, and propriety, representation in a government should be in exact proportion to the numbers, or the aids afforded by the persons represented. How unreasonable and unjust then is it that Delaware should have a representation in the senate, equal to Massachusetts, or Virginia, the latter of which contains ten times her numbers . . . ? This article of the constitution will appear the more objectionable, if it is considered, that the powers vested in this branch of the legislature are very extensive, and greatly surpass those lodged in the assembly [House of Representatives], not only for general purposes, but in many instances, for the internal police of the states. The Other branch of the legislature, in which, if in either, a faint spark of democracy is to be found, should have been properly organized and established—but upon examination you will find, that this branch does not possess the qualities of a just representation, and that there is no kind of security, imperfect as it is for its remaining in the hands of the people. . . .

The very term, representative, implies, that the person or body chosen for this purpose, should resemble those who appoint them. A representation of the people of America, if it be a true one, must be like the people. It ought to be so constituted, that a person, who is a stranger to the country, might be able to form a just idea of their character, by knowing that of their representatives. . . . Society instituted government to promote the happiness of the whole, and this is the great end always in view in the delegation of powers. It must then have been intended, that those who are placed instead of the people, should possess their sentiments and feelings, and be governed by their interests, or, in other words, should bear the strongest resemblance of those in whose room they are substituted. It is obvious, that for an assembly to be a true likeness of the people of any country, they must be considerably numerous. One man or a few men cannot possibly represent the feelings, opinions, and characters of a great multitude. In this respect, the new constitution is radically defective. The house of assembly, which is intended as a representation of the people of America, will not, nor cannot, in the nature of things, be a proper one. Sixty-five men cannot be found in the United States, who hold the sentiments, possess the feelings, or are acquainted with the wants and interests of this vast country. This extensive continent is made up of a number of different classes of people; and to have a proper representation of them each class ought to have an opportunity of choosing their best informed men for the purpose; but this cannot possibly be the case in so small a number. The state of New York, on the present apportionment, will send six members to the assembly: I will venture to affirm, that number cannot be found in the state, who will bear a just resemblance to the several classes of people who compose it. In this assembly, the farmer, merchant, mechanic and other various orders of people, ought to be represented according to their respective weight and numbers; and the representatives ought to be intimately acquainted with the wants, understand the interests of the several orders in the society, and feel a proper sense and becoming zeal to promote their prosperity.

I cannot conceive that any six men in this state can be found properly qualified in these respects to discharge such important duties: but supposing it possible to find them, is there the least degree of probability that the choice of the people will fall upon such men? According to the common course of human affairs, the natural aristocracy of the country will be elected. Wealth always creates influence, and this is generally much increased by large family connections: this class in society will for ever have a great number of dependents; besides, they will always favor each other—it is their interest to combine—they will therefore constantly unite their efforts to procure men of their own rank to be elected—they will concentrate all their force in every part of the state into one point, and by acting together, will most generally carry their election. It is probable, that but few of the merchants, and those most opulent and ambitious, will have a representation from their body. Few of them are characters sufficiently conspicuous to attract the notice of the electors of the state in so limited a representation. The great body of the yeomen of the country cannot expect any of their order in this assembly. The station will be too elevated for them to aspire to. The distance between the people and their representatives will be so very great that there is no probability that a farmer, however respectable, will be chosen. The mechanics of every branch, must expect to be excluded from a seat in this Body. It will and must be esteemed a station too high and exalted to be filled by any but the first men in the state, in point of fortune; so that in reality there will be no part of the people represented, but the rich, even in that branch of the legislature, which is called the democratic. The well born, and highest orders in life, as they term themselves, will be ignorant of the sentiments of the middling class of citizens, strangers to their ability, wants, and difficulties, and void of sympathy, and fellow feeling. This branch of the legislature will not only be an imperfect representation, but there will be no security in so small a body, against bribery, and corruption. It will consist at first, of sixty-five, and can never exceed one for every thirty thousand inhabitants; a majority of these, that is, thirty-three, are a quorum, and a majority of which, or seventeen, may pass any law—so that twenty-five men, will have the power to give away all the property of the citizens of these states. What security therefore can there be for the people, where their liberties and property are at the disposal of so few men? It will literally be a government in the hands of the few to oppress and plunder the many. . . . The rulers of this country must be composed of very different materials . . . if the majority of the legislature are not, before many years, entirely at the devotion of the executive. . . .

The more I reflect on this subject, the more firmly am I persuaded, that the representation is merely nominal—a mere burlesque; and that no security is provided against corruption and undue influence. No free people on earth, who have elected persons to legislate for them, ever reposed that confidence in so small a number. The British house of commons consists of five hundred and fifty-eight members; the number of inhabitants in Great Britain is computed at eight millions. This gives one member for a little more than fourteen thousand, which exceeds double the proportion this country can ever have: and yet we require a larger representation in proportion to our numbers, than Great Britain, because this country is much more extensive, and differs more in its productions, interests, manners, and habits. The democratic branch of the legislatures of the several states in the union consists, I believe at present, of near two thousand; and this number was not thought too large for the security of liberty by the framers of our state constitutions: some of the states may have erred in this respect, but the difference between two thousand, and sixty-five, is so very great, that it will bear no comparison.

Other objections offer themselves against this part of the constitution. I shall reserve them for a future paper, when I shall show, defective as this representation is, no security is provided that even this shadow of the right will remain with the people.

2-3

Federalist No. 10

James Madison
November 22, 1787

When one reads this tightly reasoned, highly conceptual essay, it is easy to forget that it was published in a New York newspaper with the purpose of persuading that state's ratification convention to endorse the Constitution. Although after ratification this essay went unnoticed for more than a century, today it stands atop virtually every scholar's ranking of The Federalist *essays. Written in November 1787, it was James Madison's first contribution to the ratification debate. In responding to Brutus's claim that only small democracies are viable, Madison develops a persuasive rationale for a large, diverse republic—one that he had employed several times in debates at the Convention and that his pro-ratification allies had popularized. The modern reader can appreciate how it resonates with the nation's diversity of interests in the twenty-first century. And everyone, then and now, can admire the solid logic employed by this intelligent man, who begins with a few unobjectionable assumptions and derives from them the counterintuitive conclusion that the surest way to avoid the tyranny of faction is to design a political system in which factions are numerous and none can dominate. This essay repays careful reading.*

AMONG THE NUMEROUS advantages promised by a well-constructed Union, none deserves to be more accurately developed than its tendency to break and control the violence of faction. The friend of popular governments never finds himself so much alarmed for their character and fate, as when he contemplates their propensity to this dangerous vice. He will not fail, therefore, to set a due value on any plan which, without violating the principles to which he is attached, provides a proper cure for it. The instability, injustice, and confusion introduced into the public councils, have, in truth, been the mortal diseases under which popular governments have everywhere perished; as they continue to be the favorite and fruitful topics from which the adversaries to liberty derive their most specious declamations. The valuable improvements made by the American constitutions on the popular models, both ancient and modern, cannot certainly be too much admired; but it would be an unwarrantable partiality, to contend that they have as effectually obviated the danger on this side, as was wished and expected. Complaints are everywhere heard from our most considerate and virtuous citizens, equally the friends of public and private faith, and of public and personal liberty, that our governments are too unstable, that the public good is disregarded in the conflicts of rival parties, and that measures are too often decided, not according to the rules of justice and the rights of the minor party, but by the superior force of an interested and overbearing majority. However anxiously we may wish that these complaints had no foundation, the evidence, of known facts will not permit us to deny that they are in some degree true. It will be found, indeed, on a candid review of our situation, that some of the distresses under which we labor have been erroneously charged on the operation of our governments; but it will be found, at the same time, that other causes will not alone account for many of our heaviest misfortunes; and, particularly, for that prevailing and increasing distrust of public engagements, and alarm for private rights, which are echoed from one end of the continent to the other. These must be chiefly, if not wholly, effects of the unsteadiness and injustice with which a factious spirit has tainted our public administrations.

By a faction, I understand a number of citizens, whether amounting to a majority or a minority of the whole, who are united and actuated by some common impulse of passion, or of interest, adversed to the rights of other citizens, or to the permanent and aggregate interests of the community.

There are two methods of curing the mischiefs of faction: the one, by removing its causes; the other, by controlling its effects. There are again two methods of removing the causes of faction: the one, by destroying the liberty which is essential to its existence; the other, by giving to every citizen the same opinions, the same passions, and the same interests.

It could never be more truly said than of the first remedy, that it was worse than the disease. Liberty is to faction what air is to fire, an aliment without which it instantly expires. But it could not be less folly to abolish liberty, which is essential to political life, because it nourishes faction, than it would be to wish the annihilation of air, which is essential to animal life, because it imparts to fire its destructive agency.

The second expedient is as impracticable as the first would be unwise. As long as the reason of man continues fallible, and he is at liberty to exercise it, different opinions will be formed. As long as the connection subsists between his reason and his self-love, his opinions and his passions will have a reciprocal influence on each other; and the former will be objects to which the latter will attach themselves. The diversity in the faculties of men, from which the rights of property originate, is not less an insuperable obstacle to a uniformity of interests. The protection of these faculties is the first object of government. From the protection of different and unequal faculties of acquiring property, the possession of different degrees and kinds of property immediately results; and from the influence of these on the sentiments and views of the respective proprietors, ensues a division of the society into different interests and parties.

The latent causes of faction are thus sown in the nature of man; and we see them everywhere brought into different degrees of activity, according to the different circumstances of civil society. A zeal for different opinions concerning religion, concerning government, and many other points, as well of speculation as of practice; an attachment to different leaders ambitiously contending for pre-eminence and power; or to persons of other descriptions whose fortunes have been interesting to the human passions, have, in turn, divided mankind into parties, inflamed them with mutual animosity, and rendered them much more disposed to vex and oppress each other than to co-operate for their common good. So strong is this propensity of mankind to fall into mutual animosities, that where no substantial occasion presents itself, the most frivolous and fanciful distinctions have been sufficient to kindle their unfriendly passions and excite their most violent conflicts. But the most common and durable source of factions has been the various and unequal distribution of property. Those who hold and those who are without property have ever formed distinct interests in society. Those who are creditors, and those who are debtors, fall under a like discrimination. A landed interest, a manufacturing interest, a mercantile interest, a moneyed interest, with many lesser interests, grow up of necessity in civilized nations, and divide them into different classes, actuated by different sentiments and views. The regulation of these various and interfering interests forms the principal task of modern legislation, and involves the spirit of party and faction in the necessary and ordinary operations of the government.

No man is allowed to be a judge in his own cause, because his interest would certainly bias his judgment, and, not improbably, corrupt his integrity. With equal, nay with greater reason, a body of men are unfit to be both judges and parties at the same time; yet what are many of the most important acts of legislation, but so many judicial determinations, not indeed concerning the rights of single persons, but concerning the rights of large bodies of citizens? And what are the different classes of legislators but advocates and parties to the causes which they determine? Is a law proposed concerning private debts? It is a question to which the creditors are parties on one side and the debtors on the other. Justice ought to hold the balance between them. Yet the parties are, and must be, themselves the judges; and the most numerous party, or, in other words, the most powerful faction must be expected to prevail. Shall domestic manufactures be encouraged, and in what degree, by restrictions on foreign manufactures? are questions which would be differently decided by the landed and the manufacturing classes, and probably by neither with a sole regard to justice and the public good. The apportionment of taxes on the various descriptions of property is an act which seems to require the most exact impartiality; yet there is, perhaps, no legislative act in which greater opportunity and temptation are given to a predominant party to trample on the rules of justice. Every shilling with which they overburden the inferior number, is a shilling saved to their own pockets.

It is in vain to say that enlightened statesmen will be able to adjust these clashing interests, and render them all subservient to the public good. Enlightened statesmen will not always be at the helm. Nor, in many cases, can such an adjustment be made at all without taking into view indirect and remote considerations, which will rarely prevail over the immediate interest which one party may find in disregarding the rights of another or the good of the whole. The inference to which we are brought is, that the causes of faction cannot be removed, and that relief is only to be sought in the means of controlling its effects.

If a faction consists of less than a majority, relief is supplied by the republican principle, which enables the majority to defeat its sinister views by regular vote. It may clog the administration, it may convulse the society; but it will be unable to execute and mask its violence under the forms of the Constitution. When a majority is included in a faction, the form of popular government, on the other hand, enables it to sacrifice to its ruling passion or interest both the public good and the rights of other citizens. To secure the public good and private rights against the danger of such a faction, and at the same time to preserve the spirit and the form of popular government, is then the great object to which our inquiries are directed. Let me add that it is the great desideratum by which this form of government can be rescued from the opprobrium under which it has so long labored, and be recommended to the esteem and adoption of mankind.

By what means is this object attainable? Evidently by one of two only. Either the existence of the same passion or interest in a majority at the same time must be prevented, or the majority, having such coexistent passion or interest, must be rendered, by their number and local situation, unable to concert and carry into effect schemes of oppression. If the impulse and the opportunity be suffered to coincide, we well know that neither moral nor religious motives can be relied on as an adequate control. They are not found to be such on the injustice and violence of individuals, and lose their efficacy in proportion to the number combined together, that is, in proportion as their efficacy becomes needful.

From this view of the subject it may be concluded that a pure democracy, by which I mean a society consisting of a small number of citizens, who assemble and administer the government in person, can admit of no cure for the mischiefs of faction. A common passion or interest will, in almost every case, be felt by a majority of the whole; a communication and concert result from the form of government itself; and there is nothing to check the inducements to sacrifice the weaker party or an obnoxious individual. Hence it is that such democracies have ever been spectacles of turbulence and contention; have ever been found incompatible with personal security or the rights of property; and have in general been as short in their lives as they have been violent in their deaths. Theoretic politicians, who have patronized this species of government, have erroneously supposed that by reducing mankind to a perfect equality in their political rights, they would, at the same time, be perfectly equalized and assimilated in their possessions, their opinions, and their passions.

A republic, by which I mean a government in which the scheme of representation takes place, opens a different prospect, and promises the cure for which we are seeking. Let us examine the points in which it varies from pure democracy, and we shall comprehend both the nature of the cure and the efficacy which it must derive from the Union.

The two great points of difference between a democracy and a republic are: first, the delegation of the government, in the latter, to a small number of citizens elected by the rest; secondly, the greater number of citizens, and greater sphere of country, over which the latter may be extended. The effect of the first difference is, on the one hand, to refine and enlarge the public views, by passing them through the medium of a chosen body of citizens, whose wisdom may best discern the true interest of their country, and whose patriotism and love of justice will be least likely to sacrifice it to temporary or partial considerations. Under such a regulation, it may well happen that the public voice, pronounced by the representatives of the people, will be more consonant to the public good than if pronounced by the people themselves, convened for the purpose. On the other hand, the effect may be inverted. Men of factious tempers, of local prejudices, or of sinister designs, may, by intrigue, by corruption, or by other means, first obtain the suffrages, and then betray the interests, of the people. The question resulting is, whether small or extensive republics are more favorable to the election of proper guardians of the public weal; and it is clearly decided in favor of the latter by two obvious considerations.

In the first place, it is to be remarked that, however small the republic may be, the representatives must be raised to a certain number, in order to guard against the cabals of a few; and that, however large it may be, they must be limited to a certain number, in order to guard against the confusion of a multitude. Hence, the number of representatives in the two cases not being in proportion to that of the two constituents, and being proportionally greater in the small republic, it follows that, if the proportion of fit characters be not less in the large than in the small republic, the former will present a greater option, and consequently a greater probability of a fit choice.

In the next place, as each representative will be chosen by a greater number of citizens in the large than in the small republic, it will be more difficult for unworthy candidates to practice with success the vicious arts by which elections are too often carried; and the suffrages of the people being more free, will be more likely to centre in men who possess the most attractive merit and the most diffusive and established characters.

It must be confessed that in this, as in most other cases, there is a mean, on both sides of which inconveniences will be found to lie. By enlarging too much the number of electors, you render the representatives too little acquainted with all their local circumstances and lesser interests; as by reducing it too much, you render him unduly attached to these, and too little fit to comprehend and pursue great and national objects. The federal Constitution forms a happy combination in this respect; the great and aggregate interests being referred to the national, the local and particular to the State legislatures.

The other point of difference is, the greater number of citizens and extent of territory which may be brought within the compass of republican than of democratic government; and it is this circumstance principally which renders factious combinations less to be dreaded in the former than in the latter. The smaller the society, the fewer probably will be the distinct parties and interests composing it; the fewer the distinct parties and interests, the more frequently will a majority be found of the same party; and the smaller the number of individuals composing a majority, and the smaller the compass within which they are placed, the more easily will they concert and execute their plans of oppression. Extend the sphere, and you take in a greater variety of parties and interests; you make it less probable that a majority of the whole will have a common motive to invade the rights of other citizens; or if such a common motive exists, it will be more difficult for all who feel it to discover their own strength, and to act in unison with each other. Besides other impediments, it may be remarked that, where there is a consciousness of unjust or dishonorable purposes, communication is always checked by distrust in proportion to the number whose concurrence is necessary.

Hence, it clearly appears, that the same advantage which a republic has over a democracy, in controlling the effects of faction, is enjoyed by a large over a small republic,—is enjoyed by the Union over the States composing it. Does the advantage consist in the substitution of representatives whose enlightened views and virtuous sentiments render them superior to local prejudices and schemes of injustice? It will not be denied that the representation of the Union will be most likely to possess these requisite endowments. Does it consist in the greater security afforded by a greater variety of parties, against the event of any one party being able to outnumber and oppress the rest? In an equal degree does the increased variety of parties comprised within the Union, increase this security. Does it, in fine, consist in the greater obstacles opposed to the concert and accomplishment of the secret wishes of an unjust and interested majority? Here, again, the extent of the Union gives it the most palpable advantage.

The influence of factious leaders may kindle a flame within their particular States, but will be unable to spread a general conflagration through the other States. A religious sect may degenerate into a political faction in a part of the Confederacy; but the variety of sects dispersed over the entire face of it must secure the national councils against any danger from that source. A rage for paper money, for an abolition of debts, for an equal division of property, or for any other improper or wicked project, will be less apt to pervade the whole body of the Union than a particular member of it; in the same proportion as such a malady is more likely to taint a particular county or district, than an entire State.

In the extent and proper structure of the Union, therefore, we behold a republican remedy for the diseases most incident to republican government. And according to the degree of pleasure and pride we feel in being republicans, ought to be our zeal in cherishing the spirit and supporting the character of Federalists.

2-4

Federalist No. 51

James Madison
February 8, 1788

*Where Federalist No. 10 finds solution to tyranny in the way society is orga-
nized, No. 51 turns its attention to the Constitution. In a representative
democracy citizens must delegate authority to their representatives. But what
is to prevent these ambitious politicians from feathering their own nests or
usurping power altogether at their constituencies' expense? The solution,
according to James Madison, is to be found in "pitting ambition against ambition," just as the solution in No. 10 lay in pitting interest against interest. In
this essay, Madison explains how the Constitution's system of checks and
balances will accomplish this goal. Note that he does not try to refute Brutus
directly by defending the design of the Senate, which would have been a tough
argument. Rather he assumes a different premise—namely, the popularly
elected House of Representatives will push the envelope of its authority. He
then avers that the Senate and the executive may find the House irresistible,
requiring some future Convention to strengthen these institutions to buttress
separation of powers.*

To what expedient, then, shall we finally resort, for maintaining in practice the
necessary partition of power among the several departments, as laid down in the
Constitution? The only answer that can be given is, that as all these exterior
provisions are found to be inadequate, the defect must be supplied, by so contriv-
ing the interior structure of the government as that its several constituent parts
may, by their mutual relations, be the means of keeping each other in their
proper places. Without presuming to undertake a full development of this
important idea, I will hazard a few general observations, which may perhaps
place it in a clearer light, and enable us to form a more correct judgment of the
principles and structure of the government planned by the convention.

In order to lay a due foundation for that separate and distinct exercise of the
different powers of government, which to a certain extent is admitted on all
hands to be essential to the preservation of liberty, it is evident that each department should have a will of its own; and consequently should be so constituted
that the members of each should have as little agency as possible in the appointment of the members of the others. Were this principle rigorously adhered to, it

would require that all the appointments for the supreme executive, legislative, and judiciary magistracies should be drawn from the same fountain of authority, the people, through channels having no communication whatever with one another. Perhaps such a plan of constructing the several departments would be less difficult in practice than it may in contemplation appear. Some difficulties, however, and some additional expense would attend the execution of it. Some deviations, therefore, from the principle must be admitted. In the constitution of the judiciary department in particular, it might be inexpedient to insist rigorously on the principle: first, because peculiar qualifications being essential in the members, the primary consideration ought to be to select that mode of choice which best secures these qualifications; secondly, because the permanent tenure by which the appointments are held in that department, must soon destroy all sense of dependence on the authority conferring them.

It is equally evident, that the members of each department should be as little dependent as possible on those of the others, for the emoluments annexed to their offices. Were the executive magistrate, or the judges, not independent of the legislature in this particular, their independence in every other would be merely nominal.

But the great security against a gradual concentration of the several powers in the same department, consists in giving to those who administer each department the necessary constitutional means and personal motives to resist encroachments of the others. The provision for defense must in this, as in all other cases, be made commensurate to the danger of attack. Ambition must be made to counteract ambition. The interest of the man must be connected with the constitutional rights of the place. It may be a reflection on human nature, that such devices should be necessary to control the abuses of government. But what is government itself, but the greatest of all reflections on human nature? If men were angels, no government would be necessary. If angels were to govern men, neither external nor internal controls on government would be necessary. In framing a government which is to be administered by men over men, the great difficulty lies in this: you must first enable the government to control the governed; and in the next place oblige it to control itself. A dependence on the people is, no doubt, the primary control on the government; but experience has taught mankind the necessity of auxiliary precautions.

This policy of supplying, by opposite and rival interests, the defect of better motives, might be traced through the whole system of human affairs, private as well as public. We see it particularly displayed in all the subordinate distributions of power, where the constant aim is to divide and arrange the several offices in such a manner as that each may be a check on the other; that the private interest of every individual may be a sentinel over the public rights. These inventions of prudence cannot be less requisite in the distribution of the supreme powers of the State.

But it is not possible to give to each department an equal power of self-defense. In republican government, the legislative authority necessarily predominates. The remedy for this inconveniency is to divide the legislature into different branches; and to render them, by different modes of election and different principles of action, as little connected with each other as the nature of their common functions and their common dependence on the society will admit. It may even be necessary to guard against dangerous encroachments by still further precautions. As the weight of the legislative authority requires that it should be thus divided, the weakness of the executive may require, on the other hand, that it should be fortified. An absolute negative on the legislature appears, at first view, to be the natural defense with which the executive magistrate should be armed. But perhaps it would be neither altogether safe nor alone sufficient. On ordinary occasions it might not be exerted with the requisite firmness, and on extraordinary occasions it might be perfidiously abused. May not this defect of an absolute negative be supplied by some qualified connection between this weaker department and the weaker branch of the stronger department, by which the latter may be led to support the constitutional rights of the former, without being too much detached from the rights of its own department? . . .

Chapter 3

Federalism

———•———

3-1

Federalist No. 39

James Madison
Independent Journal
January 16, 1788

Unlike Madison's arguments in Nos. 10 and 51, this essay presents a simpler, more straightforward defense of the Constitution. In it, Madison develops the principles of a republic and a federal system. One of the chief arguments against ratification was the claim that Constitution was undemocratic. Except for members of the House of Representatives, the officeholders in these new, still-hypothetical institutions would not be directly elected by the people. In response, Madison casts a republican form of government as the apotheosis of moderation. He does not abandon democracy, however. Indirectly, he argues, all officeholders, other than judges, will remain tethered to the public.

The spectre of a distant, powerful national government was another favorite anti-federalist issue. Here Madison goes to great links to distinguish a federal system from the all-powerful national government of the opposition's rhetoric. Over the years, the distinction that was important to Madison has become blurred. We use federal and national government interchangeably, which in the first instance is a misnomer, since federal refers to shared powers between states and the national government.

To the People of the State of New York: The last paper having concluded the observations which were meant to introduce a candid survey of the plan of government reported by the convention, we now proceed to the execution of that part of our undertaking.

The first question that offers itself is, whether the general form and aspect of the government be strictly republican. It is evident that no other form would be reconcilable with the genius of the people of America; with the fundamental principles of the Revolution; or with that honorable determination which animates every votary of freedom, to rest all our political experiments on the capacity of mankind for self-government. If the plan of the convention, therefore, be found to depart from the republican character, its advocates must abandon it as no longer defensible.

What, then, are the distinctive characters of the republican form? Were an answer to this question to be sought, not by recurring to principles, but in the application of the term by political writers, to the constitution of different States, no satisfactory one would ever be found. Holland, in which no particle of the supreme authority is derived from the people, has passed almost universally under the denomination of a republic. The same title has been bestowed on Venice, where absolute power over the great body of the people is exercised, in the most absolute manner, by a small body of hereditary nobles. Poland, which is a mixture of aristocracy and of monarchy in their worst forms, has been dignified with the same appellation. The government of England, which has one republican branch only, combined with an hereditary aristocracy and monarchy, has, with equal impropriety, been frequently placed on the list of republics. These examples, which are nearly as dissimilar to each other as to a genuine republic, show the extreme inaccuracy with which the term has been used in political disquisitions.

If we resort for a criterion to the different principles on which different forms of government are established, we may define a republic to be, or at least may bestow that name on, a government which derives all its powers directly or indirectly from the great body of the people, and is administered by persons holding their offices during pleasure, for a limited period, or during good behavior. It is *essential* to such a government that it be derived from the great body of the society, not from an inconsiderable proportion, or a favored class of it; otherwise a handful of tyrannical nobles, exercising their oppressions by a delegation of their powers, might aspire to the rank of republicans, and claim for their government the honorable title of republic. It is *sufficient* for such a government that the persons administering it be appointed, either directly or indirectly, by the people; and that they hold their appointments by either of the tenures just specified; otherwise every government in the United States, as well as every other popular government that has been or can be well organized or well executed, would be degraded from the republican character. According to the constitution of every State in the Union, some or other of the officers of government are appointed indirectly only by the people. According to most of them, the chief magistrate himself is so appointed. And according to one, this mode of appointment is extended to one of the co-ordinate branches of the legislature. According to all the constitutions, also, the tenure of the highest offices is extended to a definite period, and in many instances, both within the legislative and executive departments, to a period of years. According to the provisions of most of the constitutions, again, as well as according to the most respectable and received opinions on the subject, the members of the judiciary department are to retain their offices by the firm tenure of good behavior.

On comparing the Constitution planned by the convention with the standard here fixed, we perceive at once that it is, in the most rigid sense, conformable to it. The House of Representatives, like that of one branch at least of all the State legislatures, is elected immediately by the great body of the people. The Senate, like the present Congress, and the Senate of Maryland, derives its appointment indirectly from the people. The President is indirectly derived from the choice of the people, according to the example in most of the States. Even the judges, with all other officers of the Union, will, as in the several States, be the choice, though a remote choice, of the people themselves, the duration of the appointments is equally conformable to the republican standard, and to the model of State constitutions. The House of Representatives is periodically elective, as in all the States; and for the period of two years, as in the State of South Carolina. The Senate is elective, for the period of six years; which is but one year more than the period of the Senate of Maryland, and but two more than that of the Senates of New York and Virginia. The President is to continue in office for the period of four years; as in New York and Delaware, the chief magistrate is elected for three years, and in South Carolina for two years. In the other States the election is annual. In several of the States, however, no constitutional provision is made for the impeachment of the chief magistrate. And in Delaware and Virginia he is not impeachable till out of office. The President of the United States is impeachable at any time during his continuance in office. The tenure by which the judges are to hold their places, is, as it unquestionably ought to be, that of good behavior. The tenure of the ministerial offices generally, will be a subject of legal regulation, conformably to the reason of the case and the example of the State constitutions.

Could any further proof be required of the republican complexion of this system, the most decisive one might be found in its absolute prohibition of titles of nobility, both under the federal and the State governments; and in its express guaranty of the republican form to each of the latter.

"But it was not sufficient," say the adversaries of the proposed Constitution, "for the convention to adhere to the republican form. They ought, with equal care, to have preserved the *federal* form, which regards the Union as a *Confederacy* of sovereign states; instead of which, they have framed a *national* government, which regards the Union as a *consolidation* of the States." And it is asked by what authority this bold and radical innovation was undertaken? The handle which has been made of this objection requires that it should be examined with some precision.

Without inquiring into the accuracy of the distinction on which the objection is founded, it will be necessary to a just estimate of its force, first, to ascertain the real character of the government in question; secondly, to inquire how far the convention were authorized to propose such a government; and thirdly, how far the duty they owed to their country could supply any defect of regular authority.

First. In order to ascertain the real character of the government, it may be considered in relation to the foundation on which it is to be established; to the sources from which its ordinary powers are to be drawn; to the operation of those powers; to the extent of them; and to the authority by which future changes in the government are to be introduced.

On examining the first relation, it appears, on one hand, that the Constitution is to be founded on the assent and ratification of the people of America, given by deputies elected for the special purpose; but, on the other, that this assent and ratification is to be given by the people, not as individuals composing one entire nation, but as composing the distinct and independent States to which they respectively belong. It is to be the assent and ratification of the several States, derived from the supreme authority in each State, the authority of the people themselves. The act, therefore, establishing the Constitution, will not be a *national*, but a *federal* act.

That it will be a federal and not a national act, as these terms are understood by the objectors; the act of the people, as forming so many independent States, not as forming one aggregate nation, is obvious from this single consideration, that it is to result neither from the decision of a *majority* of the people of the Union, nor from that of a *majority* of the States. It must result from the *unanimous* assent of the several States that are parties to it, differing no otherwise from their ordinary assent than in its being expressed, not by the legislative authority, but by that of the people themselves. Were the people regarded in this transaction as forming one nation, the will of the majority of the whole people of the United States would bind the minority, in the same manner as the majority in each State must bind the minority; and the will of the majority must be determined either by a comparison of the individual votes, or by considering the will of the majority of the States as evidence of the will of a majority of the people of the United States. Neither of these rules have been adopted. Each State, in ratifying the

Constitution, is considered as a sovereign body, independent of all others, and only to be bound by its own voluntary act. In this relation, then, the new Constitution will, if established, be a *federal*, and not a *national* constitution.

The next relation is, to the sources from which the ordinary powers of government are to be derived. The House of Representatives will derive its powers from the people of America; and the people will be represented in the same proportion, and on the same principle, as they are in the legislature of a particular State. So far the government is *national*, not *federal*. The Senate, on the other hand, will derive its powers from the States, as political and coequal societies; and these will be represented on the principle of equality in the Senate, as they now are in the existing Congress. So far the government is *federal*, not *national*. The executive power will be derived from a very compound source. The immediate election of the President is to be made by the States in their political characters. The votes allotted to them are in a compound ratio, which considers them partly as distinct and coequal societies, partly as unequal members of the same society. The eventual election, again, is to be made by that branch of the legislature which consists of the national representatives; but in this particular act they are to be thrown into the form of individual delegations, from so many distinct and coequal bodies politic. From this aspect of the government it appears to be of a mixed character, presenting at least as many *federal* as *national* features.

The difference between a federal and national government, as it relates to the *operation of the government*, is supposed to consist in this, that in the former the powers operate on the political bodies composing the Confederacy, in their political capacities; in the latter, on the individual citizens composing the nation, in their individual capacities. On trying the Constitution by this criterion, it falls under the *national*, not the *federal* character; though perhaps not so completely as has been understood. In several cases, and particularly in the trial of controversies to which States may be parties, they must be viewed and proceeded against in their collective and political capacities only. So far the national countenance of the government on this side seems to be disfigured by a few federal features. But this blemish is perhaps unavoidable in any plan; and the operation of the government on the people, in their individual capacities, in its ordinary and most essential proceedings, may, on the whole, designate it, in this relation, a *national* government.

But if the government be national with regard to the *operation* of its powers, it changes its aspect again when we contemplate it in relation to the *extent* of its powers. The idea of a national government involves in it, not only an authority over the individual citizens, but an indefinite supremacy over all persons and things, so far as they are objects of lawful government. Among a people consolidated into one nation, this supremacy is completely vested in the national legislature. Among communities united for particular purposes, it is vested partly in the general and partly in the municipal legislatures. In the former case, all local authorities are subordinate to the supreme; and may be controlled, directed, or abolished by it at pleasure. In the latter, the local or municipal authorities form distinct and independent portions of the supremacy, no more subject, within their respective spheres, to the general authority, than the general authority is subject to them, within its own sphere. In this relation, then, the proposed government cannot be deemed a *national* one; since its jurisdiction extends to certain enumerated objects only, and leaves to the several States a residuary and inviolable sovereignty over all other objects. It is true that in controversies relating to the boundary between the two jurisdictions, the tribunal which is ultimately to decide, is to be established under the general government. But this does not change the principle of the case. The decision is to be impartially made, according to the rules of the Constitution; and all the usual and most effectual precautions are taken to secure this impartiality. Some such tribunal is clearly essential to prevent an appeal to the sword and a dissolution of the compact; and that it ought to be established under the general rather than under the local governments, or, to speak more properly, that it could be safely established under the first alone, is a position not likely to be combated.

If we try the Constitution by its last relation to the authority by which amendments are to be made, we find it neither wholly *national* nor wholly *federal*. Were it wholly national, the supreme and ultimate authority would reside in the *majority* of the people of the Union; and this authority would be competent at all times, like that of a majority of every national society, to alter or abolish its established government. Were it wholly federal, on the other hand, the concurrence of each State in the Union would be essential to every alteration that would be binding on all. The mode provided by the plan of the convention is not founded on either of these principles. In requiring more than a majority, and particularly in computing the proportion by *States*, not by *citizens*, it departs from the *national* and advances towards the *federal* character; in rendering the concurrence of less than the whole number of States sufficient, it loses again the *federal* and partakes of the *national* character.

The proposed Constitution, therefore, even when tested by the rules laid down by its antagonists, is, in strictness, neither a national nor a federal Constitution, but a composition of both. In its foundation it is federal, not national; in the sources from which the ordinary powers of the government are drawn, it is partly federal and partly national; in the operation of these powers, it is national, not federal; in the extent of them, again, it is federal, not national; and, finally, in the authoritative mode of introducing amendments, it is neither wholly federal nor wholly national.

PUBLIUS

3-2

Federalism: Sorting Out Who Does What

Donald F. Kettl

The phrase "separation of powers" refers to the division of authority across the institutions of the national government; "federalism" refers to the vertical division of authority and responsibility between Washington and the states. The Constitution keeps state authority separate and distinct, but its Framers did not build walls separating these governments into exclusive domains of policy. Instead, American federalism, like separation of powers, is a system of shared powers. During the twentieth century, power and responsibility have undoubtedly shifted to the national (or, as it is commonly called, "federal") government. Yet the states remain key participants, meaning that successful programs involve continuous coordination across these levels of government. Mostly the arrangement works reasonably well. But as Hurricane Katrina taught us in 2005, America's federalism is anything but a finely tuned machine. In the following essay, Donald Kettl, one of the nation's authorities on the subject, finds the difficult lessons this disaster taught the public and policymakers.

As HE WAS driving down the highway near Tampa's airport in late 2009, Erich Campbell spotted two cruisers from the Florida Highway Patrol. To warn drivers heading toward the speed trap, he did what drivers have done for decades: he flashed his headlights. Almost immediately, another trooper pulled him over and gave him a $115 ticket for improperly using his high-beam lights. Campbell struck back with a class action lawsuit that alleged the trooper's actions deprived him of the free-speech rights promised in the First Amendment of the U.S. Constitution. "The flashing of lights to communicate with another driver is clearly free speech," his attorney contended. The suit not only challenged Campbell's fine but also asked the state courts to force the state to refund the fines levied against 2,400 other motorists who had flashed their lights as warnings, to add civil damages, and to forbid officers in the state from pulling over drivers for flashing their lights.

Source: This piece is an original essay commissioned for this volume. Some of the material in this reading first appeared in the author's "Potomac Chronicle" column, which is featured every other month in *Governing* magazine, a publication for state and local governments.

State officials tried to defend the troopers' actions, pointing to rules prohibiting flashing lights, though a spokesperson for the International Union of Police Associations said the law was aimed at strobes and other rapidly flashing lights that drivers could use to impersonate police officers. Another section of the law explicitly allows drivers to "blink" their headlights to signal they are ready to pass another vehicle. Scholars of the First Amendment struggled to sort out all the complex issues, including whether nonverbal conduct (like flashing lights or honking horns) is protected speech and whether a class-action challenge was valid. The Panama City *News Herald* published an editorial entitled "Keep Flashing Legal." Under the barrage, the state highway patrol decided that pulling motorists over for flashing their headlights was not worth the hassle. A memo from headquarters told troopers simply, "You are directed to suspend enforcement action for this type of driver behavior."[1]

In the complex world of American politics, it never takes long for the powers and responsibilities and obligations of different levels of government to collide. In this case, a 38-year-old driver created a sensation by using the federal Constitution to challenge the enforcement actions of a state official. Arizona and Mississippi have challenged federal immigration policy by passing tougher laws than the federal standard. The Obama administration bypassed wildly disparate state policies by pushing through Congress a health reform law that required all citizens to get health insurance and all states to create health exchanges to help their citizens buy policies—against which opponents promptly filed a vigorous challenge that went all the way to the U.S. Supreme Court. The Tenth Amendment to the U.S. Constitution is pretty clear: "The powers not delegated to the United States by the Constitution, nor prohibited by it to the States, are reserved to the States respectively, or to the people." Put simply, if the Constitution does not allow the federal government to take action, power rests with the states and their citizens. But that has scarcely prohibited an enormous expansion of federal power since the ratification of the Tenth Amendment in 1791. In fact, it has created battle lines over sorting out who does what, and these lines have been the trenches for unending conflict in American federalism.

The nation's founders, of course, did not set out to create an eternal struggle. They were pragmatic leaders trying to find a delicate balance between large and small states and between maritime and agricultural states, with many other struggles playing out as well. They agree on one thing, captured in the name they chose for the nation. They could have called the emerging nation any number of things, but they made the states the centerpiece, united in a new continent called America. The choice of the United States of America not only provides identity but defines the conflict. We are located in America, but few problems are purely America-based any longer. We are a collection of states, uneasily united in a single nation. The Founders could have pushed harder to resolve the issue, but that would have produced disunited states and no nation. So they finessed the issue, creating rough divisions without sharp definitions. Throughout the nation's history, that's led to debates about the Louisiana Purchase, slavery, the Civil War, the nation's currency, civil rights, health care—and Erich Campbell's driving habits.

These issues continue to play themselves out in problems large and small. Few have been larger in recent memory than Hurricane Katrina's assault on the Gulf Coast over Labor Day weekend 2005. The storm—and the government's response to it—was not only a stunning reminder of just how far the nation still must go to resolve deep racial and class divisions in American society. It also marked a collapse—both political and administrative—of American federalism. Thousands of New Orleans residents found themselves marooned at the tattered Superdome. CNN got its cameras there, but neither the city, nor the state, nor the federal government could seem to get food, water, or medicine to the trapped residents. The military and an armada of buses finally arrived to take the trapped refugees to safety but not before people died in the chaos.

Standing in front of the St. Louis Cathedral in New Orleans just days after the Superdome evacuation, President Bush applauded the work of government officials. Nevertheless, he admitted, "the system, at every level of government, was not well coordinated and was overwhelmed in the first few days." He stunned state and local officials with what came next. "It is now clear," he said, "that a challenge on this scale requires greater federal authority and a broader role for the armed forces—the institution of our government most capable of massive logistical operations on a moment's notice."[2] The glaring headlines and searing pictures had painted a portrait of the failure of federalism. The initial chaos quickly gave way to finger-pointing, with federal officials saying they were awaiting clear requests, submitted in the proper form, from state and local officials. Louisiana Governor Kathleen Blanco, in her first phone call to the president, asked for "all federal firepower." She continued, "I meant everything. Just send it. Give me planes, give me boats. . . ."[3]

New Orleans Mayor Ray Nagin sent out his own plea: "I need everything." He criticized federal officials and said, "They're thinking small, man. And this is a major, major, major deal. And I can't emphasize it enough, man. This is crazy." When top federal officials told them help was on the way, Nagin countered, "They're not here." Frustrated, he added, "Now get off your asses and do something, and let's fix the biggest goddamn crisis in the history of this country." [4] But help was painfully slow in coming.

Challenging Federalism

Mayor Nagin was stuck for four days in the battered Hyatt Hotel, with no air conditioning in the sweltering late summer heat. The mayor and his staff found their temporary headquarters in shambles. Not only had the storm isolated them, but it spun off a tornado that ripped away part of the hotel. For the first two days, Nagin had no communication with the outside world except through press releases to CNN reporters. One of his technology aides then remembered that he had established an Internet phone account. The mayor's technology aides eventually found a working Internet connection in one of the hotel's conference rooms and managed to get eight lines hooked up just in time to get a call from President Bush in Air Force One. Conditions were brutal. When a gang tried to break into the hotel and steal their small supply of food, the mayor and his small party had to evacuate from the fourth to the 27th floor. The phones they were using worked only if the caller leaned over the balcony into the indoor atrium. "This was when the last parts of the government were about to come undone," explained Greg Meffert, New Orleans's chief technology officer. "It felt like the Alamo—we were surrounded and had only short bursts of communication." [5]

It was little wonder that the president considered a larger role for the military in disaster response. Katrina literally and figuratively swamped the ability of state and local governments to respond. But although the nation's governors saw an important federal role, they rejected the idea of federal control. A month after the storm hit, *USA Today* published a survey of the governors. A total of thirty-eight governors had responded. Only two supported the president's plan. Mississippi Governor Haley Barbour, a Republican who had once headed the party and whose state took a direct hit from Katrina, said the states might need some federal help. "But we don't need them coming and running things," said the governor's spokesperson. Michigan Governor Jennifer Granholm, a Democrat, was blunter. "Whether a governor is a Republican or Democrat, I would expect the response would be, 'Hell no,'" she said.[6] Lurking behind the terrible difficulty in marshaling an effective response to Katrina's devastation was a more subtle political battle over how to manage the inevitable political fallout. Shortly after the storm overwhelmed news coverage on television sets around the nation, the Pew Research Center for the People and the Press surveyed Americans about how they viewed government's response to the storm. The survey revealed an enormous gulf with huge implications for federalism: When asked whether President Bush had done all he could, 53 percent of Republicans agreed. However, 85 percent of Democrats and 71 percent of independents believed he could have done more. When asked about the response of state and local governments, there was little partisan difference in the answers. Among Republicans, 54 percent rated the response of state and local governments as only "fair" or "poor." For Democrats the figure was 51 percent, and for independents, 52 percent.[7]

There were big partisan divisions in Americans' assessment of the federal government's response to the disaster. Top Republicans quickly calculated that conversations about what went wrong at the federal level—whether the Federal Emergency Management Agency (FEMA) could or should have acted differently, for example—could only go in the wrong direction, from President Bush's point of view. So they resisted calls for a national commission to examine the government's response and instead relied on the polls to point to a different interpretation: that state and local governments should have responded better and had failed their citizens. In part, that explains President Bush's suggestion about a stronger military role in responding to disasters. His underlying argument was that when the crisis occurred, state and local governments could not rise to the challenge. Only the federal government—at least, the federal military—could respond effectively. Coming from a former governor, the argument might have seemed strange. But for a president facing devastating performance by his own emergency response agency and equally devastating findings in public opinion polls, it made sense to deflect blame to state and local governments and to rely on the military's response to deflect criticism of his actions.

Since then, federal officials have quietly looked at the overall strategy, and the conclusion has been "Hell yes"—if a Katrina-like event recurs, many federal officials are ready to come fast and push with a big effort, even if state and local officials say they do not need or want federal assistance. They looked at the disastrous political fallout for federal officials from what they view as failures of state and local officials—and the great toll on human health and safety from the early local struggles to deal with the overwhelming disaster. Lurking behind the assessment is an even more fundamental question: When bad things happen, from natural disasters to terrorist attacks, who is ultimately responsible for "life, liberty and the pursuit of happiness," as the Declaration of Independence puts it?

Wilma's Test

Soon after Katrina's floodwaters subsided, another enormous storm, Hurricane Wilma, flared up in the Gulf of Mexico. This time the storm struck at southern Florida. Although the devastation was not nearly as brutal as that from Katrina's blow at New Orleans and southern Mississippi, Wilma left hundreds of thousands of residents without food, water, or electric power for days.

The storm got much less attention from the news media, but government officials and administrators put planning and response under a microscope. Before Wilma hit, Florida Governor Jeb Bush firmly told members of Congress, "I can say with certainty that federalizing emergency response to catastrophic events would be a disaster as bad as Hurricane Katrina." In fact, he concluded, "If you federalize, all the innovation, creativity, and knowledge at the local level would subside." [8] If the storm did its worst, the state's Division of Emergency Management promised, residents would have ice, food, and water within twenty-four hours. The storm hit hard, but it stopped short of Category 5. Six million residents found themselves without ice, food, water, or electricity. Long lines snaked around the few operating gasoline pumps. A three-star army general called state officials to say he wanted to fly in and take command. According to later reports, Governor Bush told federal Department of Homeland Security officials that the federal takeover effort was "insulting" to him personally.

Florida officials launched a clever countercoup. Craig Fugate, Florida's emergency manager, seized the Department of Homeland Security's National Incident Management System. In principle, every incident must have a single commander to prevent battles over who is in charge of what. "I'd now like to introduce the incident commander," Fugate told federal officials during a video-conference. To the stunned surprise of the feds from the Department of Homeland Security, he pulled in Governor Bush. Under the federal government's own rules, federal officials were required to support the incident commander, and Fugate's maneuver had outflanked them. One of Fugate's first acts was to seize control of 300 satellite phones that the federal department had sent to Florida for the use of its officials and give them to local emergency workers instead. FEMA sent in a large team of workers, but its employees ended up working under the overall authority of state officials.

Governor Bush said the state was responsible for the problems that developed, but everyone had basic supplies within seventy-two hours. And if state officials did not meet their twenty-four-hour response target, they nevertheless retained control of the operation—and overall command of the federal response. When big storms hit, Fugate—a rabid University of Florida fan—puts on a weather-beaten, orange Gators cap. When the crisis ebbs, he switches to a clean blue one. Within days of Wilma's assault on southern Florida, Fugate was wearing his blue Gators cap again.

Federalism's Arenas

In the storms, federalism played itself out in a host of complex ways. In part, the issue was a political one: With so many different players at all levels involved in the difficult process, finger-pointing and blame-shifting became inevitable. In part, it was fiscal: Given the enormity of the damage, who ought to pay for—and control decisions about—rebuilding the region? And in part, it was administrative: Why did the federal, state, and local governments find it so difficult to provide a coordinated, effective response?

And as with everything else in federalism, complicated issues became entangled with each other. In mid-2005, America's governors had pushed hard for fundamental changes in the Medicaid program, the nation's most important program for providing medical and nursing home care for the poor, including the poor elderly. From 1998 to 2003, Medicaid spending increased 62 percent, compared with a 36 percent increase for Medicare, the federal program that pays doctor and hospital bills for seniors. Experts estimated that over the next fifteen years, Medicaid's cost would grow 145 percent, an annual growth rate of 8.2 percent for the states.[9] For most governors, Medicaid was the fastest-growing item in the budget, and they looked for help in funding a program that, after all, was mostly federal. "Governors believe that Medicaid reform must be driven by good public policy and not by the federal budget process," the National Governors Association concluded in a 2005 report.[10] That is going to be hard to avoid, however. Analysts at the Centers for Medicare and Medicaid Services estimate that by 2020, the federal government will account for half of all health care spending. Medicaid alone is projected to grow from 15 percent of all health care spending in 2009 to 20 percent in 2020.[11]

The George W. Bush administration's secretary of the federal Department of Health and Human Services, Michael Leavitt, created a special commission to study Medicaid and strategies for putting it on a sounder financial footing. The commission proposed giving states more flexibility in managing the program, including new options for reducing the cost of prescription drugs. It also argued for making it harder for individuals to transfer their assets to others so as to qualify sooner for Medicaid benefits (which have strict limits on recipients' income, savings, and other assets). The commission, however, did not solve the biggest problems: dealing with the rising cost of long-term care, especially in nursing homes, and as the commission put it, "expanding the number of people covered with quality care while recognizing budget constraints." [12]

The governors hoped that their work, coupled with the special commission's work, would build momentum for fundamental reform. The two projects, they thought, could come together in President Bush's budget address early in 2006 and set the stage for sweeping changes. But the rising costs of the war in Iraq, coupled with the enormous, uncounted costs of federal assistance for the Gulf Coast, torpedoed that plan. Thus, in addition to the administrative, financial, and political implications of the hurricanes, the states had to reckon with significant collateral damage: The storms blew away what governors hoped would be their best chance for Medicaid reform. No one in Washington had the resources or the energy for a major assault on such a difficult set of questions, so the states concluded they might well end up having to attack the problems piecemeal and on their own.

Federalism behaved, at once, exactly as the Founders designed it—and precisely as some of them feared it would stumble in crisis. However, the Founders never intended this American invention of "federalism" to be a bold, sweeping innovation. They were supremely practical men (women were not invited to Philadelphia to help frame the new nation) with a supremely practical problem. Northern states did not trust southern states. Farmers did not trust merchants. Most of all, larger states did not trust smaller states and vice versa. The fledgling nation's army had won independence from Great Britain, but the notables gathered in Philadelphia in 1787 needed to find some glue to hold the new country together. If they had failed, the individual states would have been too small to endure—and would surely have proved easy pickings for European nations eager to expand.

The system of federalism that the Founders created had few rules and fewer fixed boundaries. As federalism has developed over the centuries, however, two important facts about the system have become clear. First, federalism's very strength comes from its enormous flexibility—its ability to adapt to new problems and political cross-pressures. Second, it creates alternative venues for political action. Interests that fight and lose at the state level have been able to find clever ways of taking their battles to the national government. Losers at the national level have been able to refight their wars in the states.

Throughout American history, we have frequently looked on federalism as a rather sterile scheme for determining who is in charge of what in our governmental system. But that misses most of what makes federalism important and exciting. It makes far more sense to view federalism as an ever-evolving, flexible system for creating arenas for political action. Americans have long celebrated their basic document of government as a "living Constitution." No part of it has lived more—indeed, changed more—than that involving the relationship between the national and the state governments and the relationships among the states. This can be seen clearly in the rich variations on the three themes that Katrina highlighted: political, fiscal, and administrative federalism.

Political Federalism

In the 1990s, some South Carolina business owners launched the *Tropic Sea* as a casino boat for "cruises to nowhere." However, the enterprise soon became a cruise to a very important somewhere by raising the question: Just how far can—and should—federal power intrude on the prerogatives of the states?

This balance-of-power question is as old as the American republic and in fact predates the Constitution. When the colonies declared their independence from King George III, they formed a loose confederation. It proved barely strong enough to win the war and not nearly strong enough to help govern the new nation. Problems with the country's Articles of Confederation led the nation's leaders to gather in Philadelphia to draft a new constitution. At the core of their debate was the question of how much power to give the national government and how much to reserve to the states. The Founders followed a time-honored tradition in resolving such tough issues—they sidestepped it. The Constitution is silent on the question, and the Tenth Amendment simply reinforces the obvious: The national government has only the powers that the Constitution gives it. By leaving the details vague, the authors of the Constitution avoided a wrenching political battle. They also ensured that generations of Americans after them would refight the same battles—most often with legal stratagems in the nation's courts but sometimes, as in the Civil War, with blood.

A Cruise to Somewhere?

The *Tropic Sea* sailed into an ongoing struggle in South Carolina politics. Although developers loved gambling ships such as the *Tropic Sea,* which lured tourists to the state, several legislators and local officials did not, and they had been actively campaigning against the ships. As a result, when the *Tropic Sea* asked permission to dock at Charleston's State Ports Authority (SPA) Pier, the SPA said no. The boat ended up at anchor in the harbor while its owners sought help from the Federal Maritime Commission (FMC). The FMC sided with the boat owners but was overturned by a federal appeals court. The case eventually ended up in the U.S. Supreme Court.

South Carolina argued that, as a state government, it wasn't subject to the FMC's jurisdiction, and in a bitter five-to-four decision at the end of its 2002 term, the Supreme Court agreed. Writing for the majority, Justice Clarence Thomas looked past the usual foundation of political struggles over state power, the Tenth Amendment, and instead built his argument on the little-noticed Eleventh Amendment, ratified in 1798, which specifies that the judicial power of the United State[s] does not extend to the states. This amendment supported the notion of *dual federalism*—separate spheres of federal and state action. In the decades after its ratification, however, the dual federalism argument gradually eroded, especially after 1868, under the weight of the "equal protection" clause of the Fourteenth Amendment. That amendment asserts that all citizens have the right to equal treatment under the law. In establishing a national standard, the Fourteenth Amendment gave the courts power to enforce national policy over state objections. That pushed away the dual federalism concept and helped shift the balance of power to the national government. After William Rehnquist became chief justice in 1986, however, dual federalism resurfaced and surged ahead again.

In ruling for South Carolina, Justice Thomas admitted that there was little textual evidence to support his position. Rather, he said, dual federalism was "embedded in our constitutional structure." The concept helped uphold the "dignity" of the states as dual sovereigns. That, he said, was the core of the decision.[13]

Asserting the dignity of the states is a new constitutional standard. The Eleventh Amendment explicitly applies to federal courts, not federal administrators, such as employees of the FMC. Conservatives, of course, had long criticized liberals for making law from the bench. In this case, however, it was the conservatives on the Court who crafted a new principle, which they used to push back the scope of the national government's power.

Federalism Means War

The Supreme Court under Rehnquist gradually chipped away at national power and aggressively worked to strengthen the role of the states. The major federalism decisions have all been by votes of five to four, built on the conservative bloc of William Rehnquist, Clarence Thomas, Anthony Kennedy, Sandra Day O'Connor, and Antonin Scalia. The disputes, on the Court as well as off, have become increasingly intense. As *New York Times* reporter Linda Greenhouse put it, "These days, federalism means war." [14]

The battles became so sharp that candidates' views on federalism were critical in the battles over new appointments to the Supreme Court, especially those of Chief Justice John Roberts and Justice Samuel Alito. Given the ages of several other justices, more appointment battles are certain—and so are questions about the Court's role in reframing federalism. Will the Court remain on its dual federalism course? Staying that course raises two very difficult questions.

First, just how far is the Court prepared to go in pursuing dual federalism? In the past it has ruled that workers cannot sue states for discrimination under federal age and disability standards. It has also protected states from suits by people who claimed unfair competition from state activities in the marketplace, such as photocopying by state universities. Bit by bit the Court has extended state power at the expense of the national government's jurisdiction.

At some point, however, the pursuit of state "dignity" will collide with national standards for equal protection. At some point, state protection against national labor standards will crash into national protection of civil rights and civil liberties. That point might come in debates over family leave or prescription drugs, over voting rights or transportation of nuclear waste. But a collision is certain. From the Fourteenth Amendment, there is a long tradition of asserting national power over the states. From the Rehnquist court, there is a new legal argument for reasserting state power. In the Roberts court, the fundamental questions about the federal government's power to shape state health policy is likely to cast a very long shadow over the power balance in American federalism.

Neither argument is an absolute. In some issues (such as civil rights), there is a strong case for national preeminence. In other issues (such as the states' own systems of law), there is a strong case for state preeminence. Still other issues (such as gambling boats) rest squarely in the middle. And in some issues (like headlight-flashing), federal issues are dragged in to push changes in state and local policy. The nation then has to determine how best to balance competing policy goals and constitutional principles. Sometimes those battles are fought out in the legislative and executive branches, but most often, they are contested in the courts.

Since the dawn of Roosevelt's New Deal in the 1930s, national power has grown at the expense of the states. Now, with an uncommon purpose, the conservatives on the Supreme Court are pushing that line back. The Roberts Court can continue the campaign to reassert the power of the states, but clearly, at some point, it will have to hold national interests paramount. What is less clear is where and how the Court will draw that line.

The second question that the Court's pro-dual federalism course raises is even tougher: How far can the Court advance state-centered federalism without running headlong into the new campaign for homeland security, which demands a strong national role? It is one thing for the Court to pursue the principles of state sovereignty and dignity. But beefing up homeland security inevitably means strengthening federal power. There is a vital national interest in ensuring that state and local governments protect critical infrastructure, such as water systems and harbors. The nation needs not only a strong intelligence apparatus but also a powerful emergency response system.

Federalism and the Living Constitution

It may be that relatively few Americans care about whether a gambling boat can dock at a South Carolina port, and the author's personal observation is that flashing headlights to warn about speed traps is on the decline as police tactics have become more sophisticated. But the basic issue—where to draw the line between national and state power and who ought to draw it—is an issue that all Americans care about, even if they spend little time thinking about it in those terms. It has been the stuff of bloody battles and endless debate. As political scientist Howard Gillman told the *New York Times,* federalism has become "the biggest and deepest disagreement about the nature of our constitutional system." [15] The equal protection and homeland security issues will only intensify that disagreement as we wade deeper into the real meaning of the states' "dignity."

These issues are scarcely ones that the Founders could have anticipated when they wrote the Constitution and the Bill of Rights. Few present-day Americans, after all, had heard the phrase "homeland security" before September 11, 2001. Few Americans stop to think about the relative roles of the federal, state, and local governments—as well as the private and nonprofit sectors—in providing their health care. That, however, is an enormous financial and political issue, as a senior citizen with heart pains calls the local 911 number, talks with a county dispatcher, is transported in a municipal ambulance, perhaps to a state university hospital where the care is funded by the federal government's Medicare program. The genius of the Founders was that they recognized the importance of federalism, that they put broad boundaries around it, but did not try to resolve it for all time. They created a mechanism for Americans in subsequent generations to adjust the balance, subtly—sometimes loudly—and continually.

It was no easy matter to recognize the key questions out of thousands that engaged the members of the Constitutional Convention in Philadelphia. It was even tougher to resolve the questions just sufficiently to win the Constitution's adoption without pushing so hard as to deepen the divisions. And it was quite remarkable to do so in a way that has allowed us to reshape the balance in our time.

Fiscal Federalism

These grand debates are what most Americans think of when they think of "federalism." They are the stuff of high school civics classes and the enduring classics of American history. For national, state, and local policymakers, however, the soft underbelly of federalism is much more often the question of who pays for what.

That has not always been the case. But in the 1950s, as the nation—and the national government—became much more ambitious about domestic policy, fiscal federalism became increasingly important. During that period, citizens and national policymakers wanted the country to undertake new, large-scale projects, such as building a national network of highways and tearing down decaying slums. State and local governments could not, or would not, move ahead on such matters. Often they simply did not have the funds to do so; sometimes local political forces opposed the policies. Even without those impediments, state and local governments almost always lacked the ability to coordinate the creation of such complex systems as effective high-speed highways with other jurisdictions. (Who would want to drive on a modern, four-lane road only to hit a two-lane gravel path at the state line? As it is, drivers often complain that snow plowing some-times stops at municipal boundaries.) Therefore citizens and national policymak-ers pressed to empower the national government to undertake the projects.

National Goals through Intergovernmental Grants

The national government tackled the problem of getting local and state govern-ments to do what it wanted done by offering them grants. If local governments lacked the resources to tear down dilapidated housing, the national government could create an "urban renewal" program and provide the money, thus avoiding the constitutional problem that would have come with national coercion. The national government did not *make* local governments accept the money or tear down the slums. But few local officials could resist a national program that helped them do what they, too—or at least many of their constituents—wanted done.

The same was true at the state level. In the 1950s, Americans were buying cars in record numbers, but they found the roads increasingly clogged. Long-distance driving often proved a special chore, because road systems did not connect well and the quality of the roads fell far below the performance ability of the cars driv-ing on them. During the Eisenhower administration, the national government decided to tackle that problem by creating a new program—the interstate high-way system—and inducing states to join it by funding 90 percent of the construc-tion costs. With motorists demanding better roads, the offer was too good to refuse. Since this was occurring amid the hottest moments of the cold war, President Dwight D. Eisenhower reinforced the idea of a national interest by arguing that the system served both transportation and defense goals—it would allow troops to move quickly to wherever they might be needed. (Wags have since joked that the system could best serve the national defense by luring Russian tanks onto the Beltway around Washington, D.C., and challenging them to cope with the traffic and find the right exit.)

The strategy continued to be used through the 1960s. When Lyndon B. Johnson announced his War on Poverty, he decided to fight it primarily through national grants to state and local governments. He created the Model Cities pro-gram, which provided aid to local communities trying to uproot poverty and rebuild urban neighborhoods and established other programs to provide better housing for poor Americans. He founded Medicaid, which provided grants to state governments so that they, in turn, could provide health care to the poor. More grants followed to support job training, criminal justice, public health, and a host of other national goals.

It was a clever strategy in a number of ways. For one, it sidestepped constitu-tional limitations on national interference in state and local issues: The national government did not force state and local governments to join the programs; it simply made them financially irresistible. No state or local officials wanted to have to explain to constituents why they left cheap money on the table, especially when their neighbors were benefiting from the programs.

This approach sidestepped another tough constitutional problem as well: the national government's dealing directly with local governments. Through long-standing constitutional interpretation and practice, local governments are considered creatures of the states, not the national government. The states created the national government, so constitutionally the national government must deal with the states. Hence the states alone have the power to control what local governments can—and cannot—do. Before Johnson's program, local governments struggled with increasing problems of poverty, substandard housing, and other human needs. They often found themselves without power or enough money to attack the problems. Few state governments themselves had adequate resources to address these serious issues, and in many states, political forces prevented the creation of new programs that might have helped. As Figure 1 shows,

Figure 1. Federal Aid to State and Local Governments

Source: U.S. Office of Management and Budget, *Budget of the United States Government, Fiscal Year 2013: Historical Tables* (Table 12.1), http://www.whitehouse.gov/omb/budget/Historicals. Figures for 2012 through 2017 are estimates.

federal grants to state and local governments remained relatively flat since the early 1990s, until the Great Recession of the late 2000s led the federal government to create a big stimulus program to assist state and local governments. With the end of the stimulus program, however, federal aid as a share of the federal government began sagging again.

Many analysts concluded that the only solution was to create a direct link between the national and local governments—a link that bypassed the states. But given both constitutional limits and political conflicts, how could such a link be established? Federal grants to local governments proved the answer. Across the nation, state governments gave permission for local governments to receive the money. If the national government agreed to take on the problems and keep state officials out of the process, the programs seemed an attractive proposition to state and local officials alike.

From the 1950s through the 1970s, these intergovernmental aid programs became increasingly popular and important. They not only grew in size but also became ever more vital elements of state and local government financing. In 1938, federal aid had amounted to just 8.7 percent of state and local revenue. It surged to 22 percent—more than one out of every five dollars raised by state and local governments—in 1978, at the high-water mark of federal aid.

As the national government used its funds to support state and local governments and to induce them to do things they might not have done otherwise, federal aid became not only an increasingly important part of the policy system but also something on which those governments became ever more dependent. When the national government began tightening its fiscal belt in the late 1970s, state and local governments felt the effects keenly. In 1980, federal aid was 40 percent of all spending by state and local governments from their own sources. A decade later, it dropped to 25 percent. Federal aid bounced back to 37 percent of state and local government spending from their own sources in 2010, but that was the product of big budget cuts by state and local governments because of the recession and the federal government's stimulus program to boost the economy. With the stimulus ending in 2011, however, tough budget times for state and local governments remained with little sign of more help from the feds.[16]

Few federal programs were abolished. Rather, the national government simply cut back support—leaving state and local governments to deal with ongoing commitments and, in many cases, powerful supporters who fought hard to keep the programs alive. In the federal highway program, federal support mostly provided aid for construction, not maintenance. As highways aged, state governments found themselves with huge bills for repairing crumbling bridges and old roadbeds. Similar problems rippled throughout state and local government budgets. The Government Accountability Office concluded in 2012 that state and

local governments face big challenges—and that they will only grow in the coming decades.[17] That left many state and local officials wondering if they were on
their own—and when they could count on the feds for help.

No News Was Bad News

When recession hit in 2002, state and local governments looked expectantly to
Washington for some hope—and help. The nation's governors, in particular,
were hoping for good news when President George W. Bush began 2003 by
announcing his plans for a $670 billion tax cut. They hoped the speech would
contain at least some help for their ailing budgets. Except for a modest proposal
on unemployment insurance, however, they found themselves left out in the
January cold.

With their budgets in the biggest crisis since World War II, governors had
been lobbying hard for national help. They hoped for a short-term resuscitation
of revenue sharing, the federal government's program of distributing broad
grants to state and local governments to use as they wished. The program ended
in 1982, but they wanted to bring it back. Failing that, they pressed for at least
some tinkering with the formula for reimbursing Medicaid spending, the fastest-
growing program in many state budgets and one, as noted earlier, that was originally launched through the incentive of national grants. Changes in the Medicaid
formulas, the governors hoped, would ease their budget worries.

Ignoring most of the states' pleas, Bush instead advanced a bold stroke to
restructure the national tax system. The administration did suggest some changes
to Medicaid, but the changes proposed would have reduced aid (or increased
costs) for the poor, and they immediately incited opposition from groups struggling to protect the program. The states were left on their own with a $90 billion
budget shortfall that threatened to soak up all of the short-term economic stimulus Bush was proposing, and more. The net effect promised to be an economic
wash surrounded by political conflict.

Who is at fault here? The feds, for failing to extend a helping hand when the states
needed it most? Or the states, for digging themselves into the hole and whining when
Bush refused to help them out? As with most questions of fault, the answer is, both.

If Bush truly had been interested in jump-starting the economy, pumping
money through the states would quickly have done just that. But the president
was concerned more with long-term revision of the tax code than with short-
term economic stimulus, especially through the states. As for the states, their
fault lies in having hitched their spending to the booming economy of the
1990s. They forgot "Stein's Law," derived by the late Herbert Stein, once
chair of the president's Council of Economic Advisers: "Things that can't go on

forever—won't."[18] When the boom collapsed, the states found themselves hooked on spending increases they could not support.

Exploding Health Care Costs

In the 1990s, national aid to state and local governments had actually resumed its upward course (see Figure 1, p. 93) but not because the national government had decided to resume its generosity to state and local governments. Rather, the reason was that national aid for payments to individuals—mostly through Medicaid—suddenly accelerated, as the benefits became more generous and health care costs began to grow rapidly. Grants for all other purposes had leveled off or shrunk, but national aid for health care had swung quickly upward, as had state governments' own spending for their matching share of the costs. In 1960, federal grants for payments to individuals amounted to 31 percent of all grants. By 2017, the federal government experts estimate that the figure will swell to 75 percent (see Figure 2). There will be little federal aid for anything but payments to individuals, most of which will be Medicaid.

As the new century began, health care costs (particularly under Medicaid) exploded at precisely the same moment that state revenues collapsed. Spending for doctor visits, hospital care, and especially prescription drugs swelled at the highest rate in a decade, growing to 30 percent of state spending, and it could not have come at a worse time for state governments. It has swamped the states' efforts to control the rest of their budgets and aggravated their financial hemorrhage. The monster in the states' budgetary basement has become health care: treating the uninsured, providing long-term care for the elderly, and buying prescription drugs. With the baby boomers reaching retirement age, the budgetary problem promises to get worse.

State spending pegged to unsustainable revenue growth and the sudden increase in health care costs threaten a continuing, profound crisis for state policymakers. Aggravating it is the projection by most economists that economic growth will not proceed fast enough to bail out the states any time soon. It's little wonder that in some states, Democrats were quietly rooting for Republican governors to make the hard budgetary decisions and vice versa. If the states are the laboratories of democracy, the lurching of budgetary Frankensteins could litter broken test tubes across the floor. This is a long way from the 1960s and early 1970s, when the feds then saw state and local problems as their own and invested substantial federal money to fix them. Democrats and Republicans joined together to provide national funds to leverage state and local action. The partnership might have been paternalistic, but it shaped policy for decades. When budget cuts hit in the late 1970s and early 1980s, national-state ties became increasingly frayed. They unraveled further with the Bush administration's 2002 loosening of air pollution regulations, which complicated the job many states

Figure 2. Grants for Payments to Individuals as a Share of All Grants

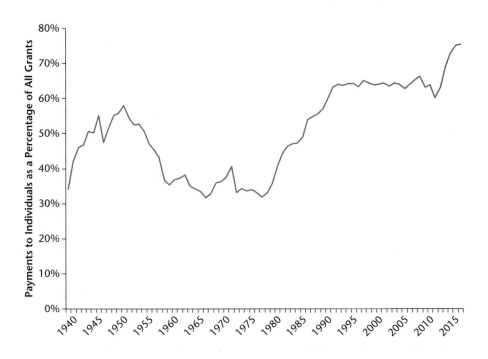

Source: U.S. Office of Management and Budget, ***Budget of the United States Government, Fiscal Year 2013: Historical Tables*** (Table 12.1), http://www.whitehouse.gov/omb/budget/Historicals. Figures for 2012 through 2017 are estimates.

faced in meeting pollution standards and frayed some more with the administration's capital gains tax plan. During the Obama administration, officials first announced tougher rules and then rolled them back following loud protests.

The states can—indeed, they have to—deal with some of these problems by putting their spending back into balance with a realistic view of their revenues. They need to update their revenue systems. But they cannot solve their fundamental fiscal problems without a new partnership between the states and the federal system. And that will be hard to realize as long as the two groups move in such different orbits that the fundamental problems they share never come together.

Administrative Federalism

A close corollary of the rise of fiscal federalism has been the growing importance of state and local governments as administrative agents of national programs. As close observers of Washington politics know, the national government has increased its spending without increasing the number of bureaucrats. How has it been able to do

so? The national government has leveraged the activity of state and local governments as agents to do much of its work. As is the case in fiscal federalism, the states
usually have discretion about whether to enlist as national agents, but the construction of programs typically leaves them little choice. Consider, for example, the case
of environmental policy. Under national environmental laws, state governments
have substantial responsibility for issuing permits and monitoring emissions.

The Environmental Protection Agency (EPA) relies heavily on state governments for much of the frontline work. In the process, however, some states have
used that role to set their own policies, which often have been far broader than
those of the EPA. In a peculiar, an up-from-the-bottom style of federalism has
meant that some states have, in practice, set policy for the entire nation.

Policymaking for the Nation—in Sacramento

Top officials in the capital have been increasingly consumed by a war about the air,
and there is a good chance that a decade from now, the EPA administrator will not
be setting much environmental policy. Recent agency administrators, both
Republican and Democratic, have been pinned down in a fierce guerrilla battle
between some congressional members who are trying to lighten the burden of environmental regulations and others who are trying to toughen pollution standards and
reduce global warming. The administrator's job increasingly has been to chart the
EPA's course through the political crossfire. As the melee has raged in Washington,
the policy initiative has shifted to the states and to foreign governments.

It is little wonder that California has been so aggressive in campaigning to
reduce air pollution. Pollution problems in the Los Angeles basin are legendary.
Medical research has shown that kids growing up in the area suffer a 10 percent
to 15 percent decrease in lung function and suffer more from asthma and respira-
tory infections than their counterparts elsewhere in the country. Autopsies of
152 young people who died suddenly from crime or health problems revealed
that all of them had inflamed airways and 27 percent had severe lung damage.

The state has set tougher standards than federal regulations required, and in the
past twenty-five years, the results have been remarkable. The number of health
advisories for high levels of ozone shrank from 166 in 1976 to just 15 in 2001.

In July 2002, California took another tough step. The legislature passed a bill
requiring that all cars sold in California after 2009 meet tough standards for
greenhouse gases, the carbon-based emissions scientists believe promote global
warming. In signing the bill, Governor Gray Davis chided the national government for "failing to ratify the Kyoto treaty on global warming." They "missed
their opportunity to do the right thing," Davis said. "So it is left to California, the
nation's most populous state and the world's fifth largest economy, to take the

lead." California was proud to "join the long-standing and successful effort of European nations against global warming." [19]

With its legislation, California rendered moot President Bush's March 2001 decision to withdraw the United States from the Kyoto treaty, at least with respect to carbon dioxide pollution from cars. Carmakers had waged a fierce battle against the California bill, but in the end, they could not beat the forces of environmentalists and citizens worried about public health. They found themselves trooping off to Sacramento to haggle over the details of the new regulations.

No automaker can afford to ignore California and its huge market, as was clear after the state's earlier decision to mandate cleaner gas and catalytic converters. When California mandated catalytic converters to scrub auto exhaust, it soon became impossible to buy cars in Wisconsin or Texas that did not contain the device as well. As California goes, at least in air pollution, so goes the nation.

For California regulators, the aggressive antipollution campaign has not been a one-way street. The new California law requires regulators to reduce not only smog but also greenhouse gases, such as carbon dioxide. New-generation diesel engines are more fuel efficient than many gasoline-powered engines. That means less fuel and fewer carbon dioxide emissions. And that, in turn, has brought California regulators into close negotiations with automakers about encouraging production of diesel-powered cars.

For those who have long seen diesels as blue-smoke-belching behemoths, the idea that diesel power might be a pollution-reducing strategy may seem preposterous. It may seem even more unlikely that government would be encouraging a shift to diesel engines or that government regulators would be in conversations with automakers hammering out deals to do so. Above all, it may seem incredible that the government taking the action would be a state government. But that is exactly what is happening in California.

All this, in turn, has led to budding ties between state regulators and the European Union (EU). European nations have been working as hard and as long on global warming as anyone. The EU's aggressive efforts to reduce greenhouse gases have stimulated new diesel technologies. So California regulators find themselves steering in the same direction as their counterparts abroad. Put together, this means that American policy for auto emissions is subtly shifting course, driven by activities at the state and international levels.

State governments have long prided themselves on being the nation's policy laboratories, and healthy competition among them might produce new breakthroughs. But there is also a profound risk that the nation could find its policy strategies increasingly evolving through accidental bits and bumps, without a national debate about what is truly in the national interest. The trend is already briskly under way. General Electric chief executive Jeffrey Immelt has said that 99 percent of all new regulations the company faces are, over time, coming not from the national government but from the European Union.[20] The states are vigorously developing new pollution standards. Meanwhile, as Washington policymakers focus on the interest group battles that constantly consume them, they risk fighting more and more about less and less.

Conclusion

If James Madison today rode his horse to Washington, down the interstate from an exit near his Virginia estate at Montpelier, would he recognize the system of federalism he helped to craft? (And would Americans remember that he, more than any of the other Founders, was the architect of the system of federalism we have today?) He would undoubtedly be stunned at the very idea of using federalism to work out problems of ship-based gambling, health care for the poor, headlights as free speech, or climate change. However, on a few moments' reflection—and perhaps after a bit of conversation to get up to speed on the stunning policy predicaments of the twenty-first century and to get his smartphone activated—he would see in these puzzles echoes of the issues he and his colleagues dealt with at the end of the eighteenth century. He would surely recognize the tough battles that raged in the days after the fierce hurricanes of 2005. They were little different in tone from the ones he and his colleagues waged in Philadelphia. And he might quietly smile that the Founders' deliberate strategy of constructive tension along the fault lines of American politics—and American federalism—had proven so resilient over the centuries.

The glue holding together America's special—and peculiar—democratic system comes from a unique blending of federal, state, and local responsibilities. Early Americans faced a fundamental, dramatic choice: to assign those responsibilities clearly to different levels of government and then write rules for governments to coordinate their inevitable differences or to allow governments to share responsibilities and then to negotiate their differences through a political process. The latter is the cornerstone of American federalism.

Thus Federalism is a much-revered constitutional principle, rooted deeply in the American tradition, which draws its life from political bargaining. It is tempting to read the Constitution, think of the stirring rhetoric of the Founders, and celebrate federalism as a set of rules. In reality, federalism is a set of political action arenas. It is far less an institution than a living organism, one that breathes, grows, shrinks, and changes in response to the forces pressing upon it.

Federalism has helped Americans survive the pressures that led to the Civil War, and it has often made possible programs and policies that might not otherwise have existed. It would be hard, for example, to imagine the national government itself taking on the job of building the massive interstate highway system. Only through federalism did this crucial system come into being, as federalism introduced the possibility of a political, fiscal, and administrative partnership that made possible a program no one government alone could have produced. By the same means, federalism has transformed American cities (for better or worse) through urban renewal, launched a war on poverty, helped clean the environment, and produced a health care program for the nation's poor.

Of course, this partnership has not always been a happy or peaceful one. Governors are never convinced that the national government provides enough money, and national policymakers constantly find it difficult to corral fifty different states—and tens of thousands of local governments—into a coherent policy system. When Hurricane Katrina devastated the Gulf Coast, federalism created a series of roadblocks that vastly complicated the job of getting critical relief to suffering citizens. New Orleans's mayor blamed Louisiana's governor. The governor called on the federal government to send everything it had, but the feds said that the governor had not requested the information in the right way. When the process of rebuilding began, New Orleans residents complained that the feds were slow in providing everything from new maps of the flood plain to trailers for displaced residents. Louisiana residents complained that citizens in Mississippi, the state next door, received more money per capita.

In the storm's wake, study after study pointed to failures of leadership and coordination. It is no exaggeration to conclude that the struggle to coordinate the intergovernmental system cost some people their lives. When quick, coordinated governmental response is needed, federalism has sometimes proved slow and disjointed. It is a system far better equipped to broaden participation in the political process than to produce efficient government.

Of course, if we had wanted that kind of government, we would long ago have sided with Alexander Hamilton in his effort to bring energy to the executive, to strengthen presidential power, and to centralize power in Washington. Other Founders rejected his argument, and the resulting political system has proved remarkably resilient. The system's flexibility and constructive tension has not only made it possible to work out accommodations for the tough issues. It has also created arenas in which Americans with many different points of view can continue to contest the future of the nation's public policy. But the new challenges of homeland security, Katrina-like disasters, health reform, and climate change all raise tough questions about how to ensure that the quest for responsiveness does not prove administratively chaotic.

NOTES

1. See Rick Neale, "Headlight Flashing Faces Test as Free Speech in Florida," *USA Today,* September 19, 2011, http://www.usatoday.com/news/nation/story/2011-09-18/flashing-headlights-free-speech-Florida-lawsuit/50458176/1; Steve Bosquet, "Man Sues Florida for

Right to Flash Headlights," *Tampa Bay Times,* September 9, 2011, http://www.tampabay.com/news/courts/civil/article1190703.ece; and "Keep Flashing Legal," Panama City *News Herald,* August 31, 2011, http://www.newsherald.com/articles/flashing-96518-law-one.html.

2. George W. Bush, "Address to the Nation," September 15, 2005, www.whitehouse.gov/news/releases/2005/09/2005915-8.html (accessed January 19, 2006).

3. CNN.com, "American Morning: Interview With Governor Kathleen Blanco; State of Emergency in New Orleans," September 2, 2005, http://transcripts.cnn.com/TRANSCRIPTS/0509/02/ltm.03.html (accessed January 19, 2006).

4. CNN.com, "Transcript of Radio Interview with Mayor Nagin," September 2, 2005, www.cnn.com/2005/US/09/02/nagin.transcript/ (accessed January 19, 2006).

5. Christopher Rhoads and Peter Grant, "City Officials Struggled to Keep Order with Crisis," *Wall Street Journal,* September 9, 2005, A1.

6. Bill Nichols and Richard Benedetto, "Govs to Bush: Relief Our Job," *USA Today,* October 2, 2005, www.usatoday.com/news/washington/2005-10-02-gov-survey_x.htm (accessed January 19, 2006).

7. Pew Research Center for the People and the Press, "Two-in-Three Critical of Bush's Relief Efforts," September 8, 2005, http://people-press.org/reports/display.php3?ReportID=255 (accessed January 20, 2006).

8. The facts and quotations in this discussion come from Robert Block and Amy Schatz, "Local and Federal Authorities Battle to Control Disaster Relief," *Wall Street Journal,* December 8, 2005, A1.

9. Bipartisan Commission on Medicaid Reform, "The Medicaid Commission," September 1, 2005, p. 8.

10. National Governors Association, "Medicaid Reform: A Preliminary Report," June 15, 2005, 1, www.nga.org/Files/pdf/0506medicaid.pdf (accessed January 21, 2006).

11. Centers for Medicare and Medicaid Services, "National Health Expenditure Projections 2010-2020," https://www.cms.gov/NationalHealthExpendData/03_National HealthAccountsProjected.asp.

12. Ibid., 14. http://aspe.hhs.gov/medicaid/oct/guiding.pdf.

13. *Federal Maritime Commission v. South Carolina Ports Authority,* No. 01-46. See Linda Greenhouse, "Justices Expand States' Immunity in Federalism Case," *New York Times,* May 29, 2002, sec. A.

14. Linda Greenhouse, "The Nation: 5-to-4, Now and Forever; At the Court, Dissent over States' Rights Is Now War," *New York Times,* June 9, 2002, sec. 4.

15. Ibid.

16. U.S. Census Bureau, *Statistical Abstract of the United States, 2012* (Washington, DC: Government Printing Office), Table 431.

17. U.S. Government Accountability Office, *State and Local Governments Fiscal Outlook: April 2012 Update* (April 2012), at http://www.gao.gov/assets/590/589908.pdf (accessed April 21, 2012).

18. Herbert Stein, interview with the author.

19. Gray Davis, "California Takes on Air Pollution," *Washington Post,* July 22, 2002, sec. A.

20. Brandon Mitchener, "Increasingly, Rules of Global Economy Are Set in Brussels," *Wall Street Journal,* April 23, 2002, sec. A.

3-3

A Separate Peace

Jonathan Rauch

The previous essay presents American federalism the way it is typically portrayed—as an amalgam of state and federal responsibilities whose separate administration challenges effective coordination. Disaster policy, for example, has gravitated from the states to the federal government. Secondary education has witnessed an expanded federal role, but primary responsibility remains with the states. Both areas, however, exhibit serious friction between these levels of government. Jonathan Rauch considers in this essay another commonly expressed virtue of federalism: the states' capacity to act independently allows many different policy approaches to be tested simultaneously. Successes tend to be copied by other states and frequently serve as models for national policy. Rauch finds an additional virtue in independent state action: it moderates easily inflamed cultural issues. In the case of abortion, the issue became highly contentious after the Supreme Court proclaimed in Roe v. Wade *the right to an abortion to be a national privacy right. But with gay marriage, the national government has stayed clear. As states pass their own laws, mostly banning gay marriage, the issue has remained defused.*

Mitt Romney, the former governor of Massachusetts and a 2008 Republican presidential candidate, is a thoughtful politician, for a politician. So it was not surprising to find him recently debating one of the country's core conundrums. It was a little surprising, though, to find him debating himself.

Romney believes abortion is wrong, but he thinks the decision on whether to allow it should be left to the states. In February, *National Journal* asked him if he favored a constitutional amendment banning abortion. No, he replied:

> What I've indicated is that I am pro-life and that my hope is that the Supreme Court will give to the states . . . their own ability to make their own decisions with regard to their own abortion law. . . . My view is not to impose a single federal rule on the entire nation, a one-size fits all approach, but instead allow states to make their own decisions in this regard.

Romney also believes gay marriage is wrong, but he thinks the decision on whether to allow it should *not* be left to the states. Last year, he poured scorn on

Source: Jonathan Rauch, "A Separate Peace," *The Atlantic Monthly,* April 2007.

Senator John McCain, who (like Romney) opposes gay marriage, but who (unlike Romney) opposes a U.S. constitutional amendment banning it. "Look," Romney said, "if somebody says they're in favor of gay marriage, I respect that view. If someone says—like I do—that I oppose same-sex marriage, I respect that view. But those who try and pretend to have it both ways, I find it to be disingenuous."

Taking the two quotations side by side, one could be excused for supposing Romney was trying to have it both ways. However, in fairness to him, now is not the first time Republicans have argued with themselves over moral federalism—or, what may be a better term, moral pluralism: leaving states free to go their separate ways when a national moral consensus is lacking.

In 1973, when the Supreme Court (in *Roe v. Wade*) declared abortion to be a constitutional right, conservatives were outraged. But what to do? Republicans were divided. Abortion opponents wanted the practice banned by a constitutional amendment, and supporters of Ronald Reagan soon took up the cause. Reagan, of course, was preparing a conservative primary challenge to the politically vulnerable and ideologically moderate Republican president, Gerald Ford—and Ford was in a bind, because his wife, Betty, had already endorsed Roe ("a great, great decision").

Ford's response was also to call for a constitutional amendment—but one that would return authority over abortion to the states, not impose a federal ban. In the end, Ford won the presidential nomination but lost the struggle within his party: The 1976 Republican platform called for "enactment of a constitutional amendment to restore protection of the right to life for unborn children."

The more things change, the more they stay the same: In this decade, Vice President Cheney—a Ford administration alumnus, as it happens—has called for the gay-marriage issue to be left to the states. But his party's cultural right has insisted on a national ban: not one gay marriage on U.S. soil! When President [George W.] Bush sided with the right, he effectively cast the deciding vote, and moral pluralism lost.

Who was right, Cheney or Bush? Ford or Reagan? Romney or Romney? A priori, the answer isn't obvious, but the country has recently run, in effect, a laboratory experiment. On abortion, it went with a uniform national rule. On gay marriage, it has gone the other way.

Abortion started in the state legislatures, where it was sometimes contentious but hardly the stuff of a nationwide culture war. Neither party's national political platform had an abortion plank until 1976. In the late 1960s and early 1970s, some liberal-minded states began easing restrictive abortion laws. When the Supreme Court nationalized the issue, in 1973, it short-circuited a debate that was only just getting started.

By doing that, it moved abortion out of the realm of normal politics, which cuts deals and develops consensus, and into the realm of protest politics, which rejects compromise and fosters radicalism. Outraged abortion opponents mobilized; alarmed abortion-rights advocates countermobilized; the political parties migrated to extreme positions and entrenched themselves there; the Supreme Court became a punching bag; and abortion became an indigestible mass in the pit of the country's political stomach.

Gay marriage started out looking similarly intractable and inflammable. As with abortion, a few liberal states began breaking with tradition, thereby initiating a broader moral debate; and, as with abortion, purists on both extremes denounced the middle as unsustainable or intolerable, saying that gay marriage (like abortion) must be illegal (or legal) everywhere in order to be effectively illegal (or legal) anywhere. The purists got help when two important actors preemptively rejected compromise. The Massachusetts Supreme Judicial Court ordered same-sex marriage in 2003, and then refused even to consider civil unions. That decision provoked President Bush's equally provocative endorsement of a constitutional ban on gay marriage. The battle lines appeared to have been drawn for a national culture war, waged by extremes of left and right over the heads of a marginalized center.

But the political system, and the public, refused to be hustled. Congress rejected a federal constitutional ban. The federal courts stayed out of the argument (and Bush's appointment of two conservative Supreme Court justices who look favorably on states' rights probably ensures that the Court will keep its distance). With the federal government standing aside, the states got busy. All but a handful passed bans on gay marriage. Several adopted civil unions instead of gay marriage. One, Massachusetts, is tussling over efforts to revoke gay marriage.

The result is a diversity of practice that mirrors the diversity of opinion. And gay marriage, not incidentally, is moving out of the realm of protest politics and into the realm of normal politics; in the 2006 elections, the issue was distinctly less inflammatory than two years earlier. It is also moving out of the courts. According to Carrie Evans, the state legislative director of the Human Rights Campaign (a gay-rights organization), most gay-marriage litigation has already passed through the judicial pipeline; only four states have cases under way, and few other plausible venues remain. "It's all going to shift to the state legislatures," she says. "The state and national groups will have to go there."

Barring the unexpected, then, same-sex marriage began in the courts and will wind up in the state legislatures and on state ballots: the abortion tape runs backward. The issue will remain controversial, producing its share of flare-ups and fireworks; but it will become more tractable over time, as the country works its way toward a consensus. As a political issue, gay marriage will be around for years, but as a catalyst for culture war, it has already peaked.

Although I bow to no one in my support for gay marriage—society needs more marriages, not fewer, and gay couples need the protections and obligations of marriage, and gay individuals need the hope and promise of marriage—the last few years have provided a potent demonstration of the power of moral pluralism to act as a political shock absorber. Even moral absolutists—people who believe gay marriage is a basic human right or, for that matter, people who believe abortion is murder—should grudgingly support pluralism, because it makes the world safe for their moral activism by keeping the cultural peace. Someone should tell Mitt Romney. Maybe Mitt Romney could tell him.

3-4

An American History Lesson for Europe

Thomas J. Sargent

Not long ago, Europe appeared to be heading down an easy path toward a kind of United States of Europe. Just as the Constitution integrated the economies of the separate states, Europe launched its movement by dismantling national trade barriers and adopting a common currency.

In this essay, Thomas Sargent, a professor of economics and 2011 winner of the Nobel Prize, explains that the problem posed for the European Union when some of its members fail to exercise economic discipline has close parallels in America's early experience. In the 1820s and 1830s, some states overspent on public works, teetered on bankruptcy, and asked the federal government to bail them out. The federal government had three choices: bail out the profligate state and in doing so, unwittingly invite others to do the same; make demands on the prodigal states, forcing them to live more frugally; or do nothing and let them go bankrupt. The government selected the last option. The European Union today, Sargent explains, faces precisely the same situation with Greece.

IN 1789, THE political price for our federal constitution included a bailout of the 13 indebted states. But it was by refusing to bail out the states a second time in the 1840s that the United States preserved its federal system, with substantial fiscal independence for state governments. Facing a similar moment, Europe might learn from our experience.

The 1789 bailout was part of a grand bargain designed by Alexander Hamilton to convert the creditors of the 13 states into advocates of a stronger federal government—one having the ability to raise all revenues required to service the large debts that the Continental Congress and the 13 states had both accumulated to finance that "Glorious Cause," our war of independence.

Hamilton and George Washington wanted those debts to be paid. They had to engineer institutional changes to achieve that goal. Under our first constitution, the Articles of Confederation, the continental government had virtually no power to tax. For revenues it depended on voluntary contributions from the 13 states.

Source: Thomas J. Sargent, "An American History Lesson for Europe," *The Wall Street Journal*, February 3, 2012.

About two-thirds of our total debts were owed by the continental government, the other third by the 13 states. If they had been valued at par, federal and state debts together would have constituted about 40% of gross domestic product. But because tax revenues were not big enough to service them, both federal and state debts traded at very deep discounts, deeper than those we see in Europe today. From the point of view of the creditors of the states and the United States, if not our taxpayers, there was a fiscal crisis in the 1780s. Fiscal crises often end in rearrangements of political institutions designed to sort out which old promises will be broken and which sustained.

Hamilton's Report on Public Credit from 1790 describes the grand bargain and his reasons for advocating it. The Articles were replaced by the new U.S. Constitution, which shifted exclusive authority to levy tariffs from the states to the federal government. In return, the Congress assumed the states' debts in August 1790. The federal government immediately imposed a tariff, and it used about half of the ample revenues that soon rolled in to service its debts. State and federal debts went from trading at deep discounts to par in the early 1790s.

Why did Hamilton and Washington want to honor our debts? Because they wanted the U.S. government to build a good reputation vis-à-vis its creditors. Hamilton reasoned that honoring the existing debts would allow the government to borrow on good terms in the future. That ability to borrow would generate fiscal flexibility by creating a prospective source of revenues beyond current taxes, one that might be used to finance surges in government expenditures associated with wars and other future difficulties and opportunities.

Why did Hamilton and Washington want the federal government to bail out the 13 states? Because they wanted to realign interests in a way that would induce voters to support a federal government with ample ability to tax.

They thus built a good reputation for the U.S. by creating another, potentially troublesome, reputation with the states—the perception that the federal government would bail them out. Although the trade-off was made mainly for political reasons, one of Hamilton's stated reasons for bailing out the states was that most of their debts had been incurred for their contributions to a national public good: acquiring independence from Great Britain. Was that reason authentic or was it just a convenient cover, a rationalization for Hamilton's real goal, which was to convert the creditors of the state governments into advocates of the central government's ability to tax?

Now fast-forward into the next century. To finance canals and railroads, many state governments incurred large debts in the 1820s and 1830s. A financial crisis in the late 1830s pushed many of those state debts into default.

Appealing to the precedent set by the 1789 bailout, state creditors asked the federal government to bail out the states once again. After an enlightening debate, in the early 1840s Congress declined, so many states repudiated their debts.

In the aftermath of those repudiations, many states rewrote their constitutions to require year-by-year balanced budgets, something they had never done before. As noted, fiscal crises, like the one in Europe today, often produce political rearrangements—at best peaceful ones like these.

Did the federal government do the right thing in refusing to bail out the states in the early 1840s? By doing so, the federal government reset its reputation vis-à-vis the states, telling them in effect not to expect it to underwrite their profligacy. In the short run, that cost the federal government substantially in terms of its reputation with its own creditors. Federal credit abroad suffered along with state credit. But in the long run, the decision exposed state governments to continuing market discipline, making future crises and requests for federal bailouts less likely.

If the federal government had chosen to bail out the states a second time, it probably would have taken greater control over state taxes and revenues in order to prevent yet another bailout situation. Refusal to bail out the states was thus a pivot point in sustaining a federal system in the United States. It led the states to discipline themselves by rearranging their constitutions in ways designed to allow them to retain freedom and responsibility for taxing and spending within their borders.

Europeans today might be tempted to say "yes" to bailouts. Or they might also recall a time when Americans preserved their own federal system by saying "no."

Chapter 4

Civil Rights

————

4-1

from *The Race Card*

Richard Thompson Ford

This chapter of Ford's provocative, widely discussed book The Race Card *tackles overuse of charges of racism. Such charges are so serious, they often are employed by one side to gain the upper hand in conflicts that are not based on prejudice. The race card's overuse, this Stanford law professor (who happens to be African American) argues, has undermined its credibility even in those cases where prejudice is present.*

... THE YEAR 1991 marked the end of an era in American civil rights. Thurgood Marshall—the first black Supreme Court justice, the lead attorney for the NAACP [National Association for the Advancement of Colored People] in the historic racial desegregation case *Brown v. Board of Education*—announced his intention to retire from the bench. Immediately the speculation and maneuvering concerning Marshall's replacement began. It was widely expected that another African American would be—indeed, *would have to* be—appointed. Liberals and civil rights groups began a predictable campaign directed at the Republican president— George H. W. Bush—who would nominate Marshall's successor. It was crucial, they insisted, that the nation's highest court include a person of color. The Bush

Source: Richard Thompson Ford, "Introduction: Playing the Race Card," in *The Race Card: How Bluffing about Bias Makes Race Relations Worse* (New York: Farrar, Straus and Giroux, 2008), 9–36. Notes appearing in the original have been deleted.

administration would demonstrate the racial insensitivity—indeed bigotry—that its enemies had long suspected if it appointed a white person to fill this vacancy. Partisan politics and ideological litmus tests surely should be put aside in this instance. Marshall's vacancy should be filled by a person who could understand and express the unique experience of racial minorities in this country.

If it had its druthers, the Bush administration would certainly appoint a conservative. And the most prominent conservative judges were white. But Republicans couldn't afford to ignore the race issue. Part of the GOP's long-term strategy involved improving its dismal level of support among minorities. But the party couldn't shake its reputation as racially insensitive or downright racist. Its long-lived "Southern strategy" relied on race-baiting to deliver white votes to GOP candidates. Bush had been elected, in part, on the strength of a notorious ad campaign that many felt exploited racial bigotry. The ad pilloried Democratic candidate Michael Dukakis for supporting a program that allowed prison inmates to take "furloughs" from incarceration. The ad informed the public that a convicted murderer, Willie Horton, beat a man and raped his fiancée after failing to return from furlough. The ad prominently featured Horton's menacing black face, complete with shaggy Black Panther Afro and beard. Bush's campaign manager, Lee Atwater, crowed, "By the time this election is over, Willie Horton will be a household name." Atwater did not exaggerate. By the end of the campaign, one might have thought Horton was Dukakis's running mate. The ad may have helped Bush win the election, but it didn't help Bush or the Republicans improve their standing with African Americans.

Bush faced a dilemma. If he nominated a white conservative to the Supreme Court, it would reinforce the perception that he and the Republicans were insensitive to racial injustice, hostile to civil rights, even closet racists. But the black judges with the stature and experience for the position were civil rights liberals.

Beltway conservatives must have bristled at this bind. The liberals were using a blatant racial quota—something conservatives vehemently opposed on principle—to push the president to a more liberal nominee. Many of the "New Right" became conservatives in reaction to this kind of identity politics. They had seen their neighborhood schools forcibly integrated through racial busing imposed by liberal judges. They felt that their cherished family alma maters had succumbed to the cheap thrills of radical chic and caved in to the pressures of black nationalist mau-mauing and feminist hectoring. "Disadvantaged minorities" displaced their sons in the entering classes of Ivy League universities; militant feminists demanded integration, disrupting the comfortable esprit de corps of campus men's clubs. The traditional liberal arts curriculum had been watered down with overtly political ethnic and feminist authors, a concession to a misguided and trendy pluralism. The grande dame of classical education—Western Civilization—had been raped by radicals and begat such bastardizations as "World Civilizations" and "Cultures, Ideas, and Values." In the newly hyper-liberal colleges, they had been forced to sit through what they felt were self-righteous screeds about "white male oppression," and they were browbeaten by pious professors and students alike, each competing to be more sensitive and tolerant than thou.

And were the people who got into college through race and gender quotas grateful to be there? Hardly. Instead, they harangued and harassed, complained and cajoled for ethnic studies, feminist studies, special theme houses, "sensitivity" days, mandatory tolerance workshops. They held marches, sit-ins, and rallies for every conceivable left-wing cause.

And it wasn't enough for them to have their special self-segregated programs (the rationale of *integration* was conveniently forgotten once they had bullied their way in). They also wanted to piss on everyone else's fun. The only silver lining in all this cloudy "social progress" was that the introduction of large numbers of women made it easier to get lucky. But the feminists were quick to put a stop to that: they pressed for sex harassment codes, turned dorm counselors into antisex police, and proposed fraternization rules so strict that you had to get a signed and notarized consent form before you could so much as ask a coed out on a date. They bullied the universities—successfully in many cases—to kill off the Greek system just because a party or two got a little bit out of hand.

When graduation finally came, these same malcontents followed the conservatives right into government and private industry, making the same demands there. So everyone had to sit through race and gender "sensitivity training" at work. There were new rules everywhere to make sure no one's delicate sensibilities were ever "offended." And now they were doing it again, playing the race card to force the president of the United States to choose a left-wing affirmative action nominee for the Supreme Court.

But conservatives had an ace up their sleeves. A black conservative with just enough experience to be a plausible candidate but not so much as to have left a long paper trail of controversial published opinions. One can imagine the number of champagne corks that popped the night someone—maybe a young, up-and-coming member of the Federalist Society—made his career in conservative politics with the suggestion "Clarence Thomas." Imagine the strategy meeting of some unknown conservative think tank. The jowly old guard grumbling; the fresh-faced Young Turks scowling. Marshall's getting up in years; what to do if he retires while our team is in the White House? How do we deal with the race issue? Then someone says it: "Clarence Thomas." It was racial politics jujitsu: use the enemy's strength against him. *We have to pick a black nominee? Fine. We'll give you a black nominee so conservative he makes Edmund Burke look like Che Guevara. So what that he's just barely been appointed to the federal bench? Are the quota-crazy affirmative action liberals going to say that a black candidate is unqualified?*

Clarence Thomas hit the liberals right between the eyes. Liberals had pressed so forcefully, so righteously, so sincerely on the importance of racial diversity on the Court. They had carefully honed all of the moves in support of affirmative action. They had perfected the subtle and not so subtle insinuation that anyone who suggested that an affirmative action candidate wasn't qualified was a closet racist. Now all of these finely tuned arguments would be redeployed in support of the most conservative jurist since Hammurabi. The liberals would have to swallow hard and accept Thomas or confront their own best arguments and the charge of hypocrisy to boot.

Liberals were suddenly on the run. They had defeated other ultraconservative candidates, such as Ronald Reagan's nominee Robert Bork, focusing on their published opinions, public statements, and scholarship to demonstrate that the nominees' views on hot-button issues such as abortion and civil rights were outside the political mainstream. They tried to do the same with Thomas. Prominent black law professors testified, expressing concern about Thomas's hostility to school desegregation and affirmative action, but Thomas had no scholarly career and hence no scholarship. He had made few public statements and, since he had served as a judge for only two years, had published few controversial opinions. When asked about his views on abortion, Thomas stonewalled, insisting that he had not considered one of the few legal issues about which almost everyone— lawyer, Beltway warrior, and civilian alike—had an opinion. The Harvard Law School professor Christopher Edley pointed out that "when applied to fundamental matters, this [answer] is almost disqualifying. A well-qualified nominee should at least be able to suggest. . . . the framework for his or her analysis. How else can you discern someone's constitutional vision, which is the key question before you?" But Edley's plea for a tough look at Thomas's qualifications fell on deaf ears. Because his race subtly but effectively insulated him from criticism about his qualifications, Thomas's inexperience was proving to be an advantage. He didn't need to impress the Senate; he just had to avoid giving them ammunition against him. Thomas was able to deflect hard questions by demurring.

Conservatives were buying confetti and chilling bottles of Krug when Anita Hill turned up in the District. Hill was a prim young black woman who had worked with Thomas on the Equal Employment Opportunity Commission (EEOC). She claimed that Thomas had sexually harassed her, following a classic pattern: he asked her out, she declined, he started hassling her with off-color jokes and references to porn. Hill was a believable accuser, in large part because it was hard to imagine that this proper woman could have invented a story that included a porn star named Long Dong Silver and references to pubic hair on a can of Diet Coke. *Someone* had to have exposed her to these ideas. Not that Thomas was an obvious suspect, this tightly wound man, impeccably sexless in Beltway-standard gray flannel and blue serge. But look closely enough and you could almost see it: the leer, the gleam in the eyes, the licking of the lips. Could he be Willie Horton's kith and kin after all—a sexual predator dressed up for Court?

The Senate confirmation hearings began as a duller than average legal theory symposium involving issues such as "fidelity to the Constitution" and the meaning of "penumbral rights." After Hill's accusations they morphed into a *Jerry Springer* episode that had put on airs. The nation witnessed a parade of disgruntled former coworkers, jilted ex-lovers, and other "character witnesses" testifying to the integrity or duplicity of Thomas and Hill. *The Clarence 'n Anita Show* offered the viewing public that most comfortable scene of American pop theater, wherein the vain and cocky black man gets taken down a notch or two by the headstrong black woman. Hill played a demure Sapphire Stevens to Thomas's somber Amos Jones, with EEOC colleague and Thomas supporter John Doggett making a cameo as Kingfish Stevens.

The daytime drama came to a head when a beleaguered Thomas described the hearings as a "high-tech lynching for uppity blacks." Although race had thus far served as a silent inoculation against critique, here it was deployed openly as a full-strength antibiotic. Thomas sought to link his struggle to sit on the highest Court in the United States to the struggles of African Americans to avoid physical mutilation, torture, and death. He implicitly evoked the experience of blacks such as Emmett Till, a young black man from Chicago who was tortured and killed by whites after teasing a white woman in Mississippi. He compared milquetoast Democrats on the Senate Judiciary Committee to an angry mob armed with firearms and strong rope.

No one dared openly scoff, but many found the analogy harder to swallow than a diet cola of dubious purity. The irony of the moment was striking, even in this, a political drama that Oscar Wilde could have written: Thomas—a corrosive skeptic of accusations of racism during his tenure at the EEOC—cried racism the moment his nomination was in real jeopardy. When the chips were down and the stakes were high, this staunch defender of color blindness shamelessly played the race card.

Irony notwithstanding, it's possible that race *did* play a role in validating Hill's accusations. Clarence Thomas was about to enjoy the highest honor the legal profession can bestow—an appointment to the Supreme Court of the United States—when Democrats introduced the nation to Anita Hill. At the very moment when Thomas should have been basking in the admiration of his peers, he was forced to address charges of a most embarrassing and sordid nature. Nothing could be less consistent with the esteem in which members of the federal judiciary were typically held. Nothing could have more effectively undermined the judge's persona of cool rationality, objectivity, and cerebral detachment than the image of the sex fiend so enslaved to bodily passions that he abused his authority and preyed on his employees. Thomas must have been furious. *Attack me for my record, for my reasoning, for my ideology if you must. But this? This is (literally) hitting below the belt.*

Worse yet, these charges had an ugly racial overtone, intended or not: the black man as sexual predator. That's how many of Thomas's colleagues and much of the nation would receive them. The people who advanced the charges and pressed the issue had to have known this. These charges were probably more believable to many people and certainly much more damaging psychologically to Thomas because of his race. In this light, the claim that the hearings were a "high-tech lynching" isn't quite so far-fetched. Even those disinclined to support Thomas on his merits might worry that the stereotype of the oversexed black man colored, so to speak, the proceedings, making the charges seem more plausible. Veteran anti-racists, well acquainted with theories of illicit and unconscious racism, might doubt that it was mere coincidence that the first Supreme Court nominee to face such resistance—based not on his record or his competence, but on his *sexual* predilections—was a black man.

"I believe Anita Hill" became a slogan of left liberals during the confirmation hearings. But like most slogans, it stood for more and less than its literal denotation. It stood for a feminist conviction that sex harassment demanded attention and condemnation. It stood for opposition to Thomas and his ideological views generally. It stood for solidarity with a brave woman who faced the full brunt of the right-wing public opinion machine. It stood for all of these things, almost to the exclusion of a sober and objective evaluation of her story and its plausibility. Mightn't an embattled Thomas reasonably have suspected that part of the reason so many believed her and not him, part of the reason her story, tarnished by the passage of time, gained the luster of plausibility and for many the gleam of Truth, was that her account confirmed one of the most pernicious of racial stereotypes?

What Is the Race Card?

In 1903 the black sociologist W.E.B. Du Bois opined that "the problem of the twentieth century is the color line." In the twenty-first century, will the problem be that everyone talks a good line about color?

Playing the race card is not new. Tom Wolfe called it "mau-mauing" back in 1970. Ever since the civil rights movement convinced the majority of Americans that racial prejudice is petty and contemptible, people have complained of racism loud and long, for good reasons and, sometimes, for bad ones. But when Wolfe coined the term, mau-mauing was the exclusive tactic of underprivileged minorities: people with legitimate complaints of discrimination, if occasionally excessive modes of expressing those complaints. Today the rhetoric of racism is a national patois, spoken fluently by ghetto hustlers and Wall Street stockbrokers, civil rights agitators and Republican Party hacks, criminal defense attorneys and Supreme Court nominees. Lawyers and judges and parishioners and priests have mastered the sleight of hand required to play the race card.

Superstar entertainers complain of racism when negotiating, renewing, or breaching their multimillion-dollar contracts; liberal and conservative politicians alike play subtle race politics to win elections or secure the confirmation of nominees: wealth and privilege are no impediments to deploying the race card. Nor, for that matter, is race. Upper-class WASPs complain of "reverse racism"—a melodramatic description of integrationist policies that no one believes are motivated by racial animus or bigotry. And if race isn't directly involved, you can always insist that whatever's eating you is like racism. Opponents of same-sex marriage aren't just narrow-minded religious zealots; they're the moral equivalent of the KKK. A rule that requires obese passengers to buy the number of seats they occupy—which in crowded coach class may be *two*—isn't a way to ensure that other customers get their share of scarce elbow room; it's like making Rosa Parks stand in the back of the bus. A dress code against tattoos, body piercings, funky haircuts, or cutoff shorts isn't just uptight; it's a new Jim Crow. Smoking bans consign nicotine addicts to "ghettos" or "concentration camps." Gripes are as common as face cards in a pinochle deck. The race card may turn yours into a winning hand.

Playing the race card is wrong and troubling for several reasons. Most obviously, it's dishonest. When people transgress or just screw up, they should take their lumps—not try to wriggle out of them with tactics of distraction or blame shifting. When people face disappointments, they should forbear graciously, not try to wheedle a more favorable outcome through false accusation. Playing the race card is also dangerous and shortsighted. Like the boy who cried wolf, people who too frequently cry racism are unlikely to be taken seriously when a predator actually emerges from the woods. Playing the race card places all claims of racism—valid and phony—under a cloud of suspicion. Finally, playing the race card is mean-spirited. Racism is a serious charge—it ruins careers and destroys reputations. When warranted, it should. But when trumped up, the charge of racism is a particularly vicious slander.

But the race card is not a simple matter of opportunism and deception. It is a by-product of deep ideological conflict in our society over how to describe and deal with questions of social justice. When bigotry was openly tolerated, people often announced it or did nothing to conceal it. Therefore, many of the earliest struggles for civil rights aimed at some conspicuous targets: Jim Crow laws, blatantly discriminatory practices, out-and-out race-based exclusion. But today most people try to hide their prejudices. As a result, a lot of time and energy must be spent just trying to determine whether bigotry is in play or not. Everyone involved—accuser and accused alike—has an incentive to lie and dissemble, to downplay or to exaggerate. And as overt prejudice has receded, we've developed new theories of prejudice designed to tease out hidden or repressed motivations and to identify inadvertent forms of wrongful discrimination.

This has given rise to a great deal of conflict over how to define bigotry and how to decide whether it's at work. Some of this conflict is necessary and healthy. We should refine and revisit our understanding of wrongful discrimination as part of an ongoing struggle for social justice. And we should debate and argue over civil rights, which reflect some of our society's most profound moral commitments. If no one ever pressed novel or controversial civil rights claims, we could never expand our conception of justice.

But there are also costs to more ambitious applications of civil rights. The extraordinary social and legal condemnation of racism and other social prejudices encourages people to recast what are basically run-of-the-mill social conflicts as cases of bigotry. Overuse and abuse of the claim of bias is bad for society and bad for social justice. When a conflict really does involve hatred or deepseated irrational prejudice, dialogue is pointless and condemnation is appropriate. But the emotionally charged accusation of bigotry is counterproductive when a conflict involves questions on which reasonable people can differ. Playing the race card makes it too easy to dismiss rather than address the legitimate concerns of others. And the accusation of bigotry inevitably provokes defensiveness and resentment rather than thoughtful reaction. The resulting interactions usually don't qualify as speech, much less dialogue. They're generally closer to mud wrestling. No one gets away clean.

When does a grievance deserve the special and unequivocal condemnation reserved for racism? Despite more than a century of litigation under the Constitution and federal civil rights laws, we still don't have a straightforward answer to that question. In fact, in some ways the answer is getting more convoluted and confusing, and the resulting conflicts more numerous and frustrating.

Some people are convinced that most accusations of bias are disingenuous. There are plenty of pundits, politicians, and bloggers ready to dismiss any accusation of bias as calculating and self-serving. One Internet blog posted this parody: "Is the society not giving you what you think it owes you? Then it's time to get yourself the Race Card. . . . It's like a 'Get Out of Jail Free' card, but much, much more. Losing an argument in a debate? Throw down your Race Card and quickly hush your opponent . . ." Clever, but this perspective suffers from a toxic cynicism and a blissed-out naïveté all at once. On the one hand, it implies that racism is not a real social problem, that less than a generation after federal troops were required to integrate schools and court orders were needed to integrate lunch counters, there's no racial bias left. Anyone who suggests otherwise is playing the race card. On the other hand, it presumes that racial minorities are so devious as to consistently make claims they know to be false, and that many people are credulous enough to believe them, despite the fact that racism has long since gone the way of wooden shoes.

At the same time, many people—and not only the credulous and the opportunistic—believe such accusations as Clarence Thomas's shrill complaint of a high-tech lynching and Brawley/Sharpton's apparently staged and obviously managed racial assault, and they rally to the causes of some unlikely victims. Major black organizations such as the Los Angeles branch of the NAACP rallied to Clarence Thomas after his notorious exclamation. Law professor Patricia Williams, one of academia's more nuanced and astute commentators on issues of race and gender, struggled to find in Tawana Brawley's story evidence of her victimization rather than her duplicity: "Even if she did it to herself . . . her condition was. . . . the expression of some crime against her, some tremendous violence, some great violation that challenges comprehension."

Indeed, some people object to the idea that anyone might ever "play the race card." For instance, Professor Michael Eric Dyson argues, "There's no such thing as a race card being played by black people not already dealing with the race deck that white America has put on the table." This is true enough as far as it goes. Playing the race card is an effective tactic because accusations of racism are plausible, and they're plausible because there are in fact a lot of instances of racism. But don't some people take advantage of this real social evil for unearned advantage? And don't people, even with good intentions, occasionally misapprehend their plight, complaining of prejudice when other factors are to blame? What accounts for such disagreements? Why do some reasonable people see evidence of racism where others see only the smirking one-eyed jack of the race card?

Post-racism

In the summer of 2006, *The Economist* magazine informed the hoi polloi that "serious champagne drinkers sip only the prestige cuvées produced by a handful of winemakers." The article quoted Jean-Claude Rouzaud, the former manager of the Louis Roederer house, who opined that a three-hundred-dollar bottle of Roederer's Cristal Champagne was intended for "that 3–5% of consumers who really know wine, and who take the time to taste it correctly." Under the subheading "Unwelcome Attention" (the editor's phrase, not Rouzaud's), the article went on to note what any moderately attentive student of American pop culture already knows: the most conspicuous consumers of high-end champagne—Cristal in particular—are not oenophiles of highly refined sensibilities, but rather "rap artists, whose taste for swigging bubbly in clubs is less a sign of a refined palate than a passion for a 'bling-bling' lifestyle that includes ten-carat diamond studs, chunky gold jewelry, pimped up Caddies and sensuous women." When asked how the venerable house of Roederer feels about this, the new director, Frédéric Rouzaud, took the bait: "What can we do? We can't forbid people from buying it. I'm sure Dom Pérignon or Krug would be delighted to have their business."

Days after the publication of the article, hip-hop artist Jay-Z announced a boycott: "It has come to my attention that the managing director of Cristal. . . . views the 'hip-hop' culture as 'unwelcome attention.' I view his comments as racist and will no longer support any of his products."

What are we to make of a boycott—the time-honored tactic of the struggle for basic civil rights—of prestige cuvée champagne? Why, when black unemployment, poverty, rates of incarceration, and life expectancy remain severe and unaddressed problems, did anyone pay a moment's attention to the offhand comment of the representative of a vintner with roots in prerevolutionary France? Jay-Z talked the line of a scrappy civil rights activist, but with the inflections of a jilted socialite: "Jay-Z . . . will now be serving only Krug and Dom Pérignon," sniffed the press release. When a young, black, self-described "hustler" from Brooklyn seems as precious as a Park Avenue debutante, we've turned some sort of corner in race relations. But where are we headed? Is M. Rouzaud's wary, though not overtly hostile or contemptuous, reaction to hip-hop—an art form that often explicitly extols a life of violence and crime—racist, as Jay-Z insists? Rouzaud's comments *might* have reflected racism—*we don't want blacks drinking our wine*—but they might have reflected concern over the association of the brand with an ostentatious subculture that extols violence and crime. Do we think the reaction would have been much different had, say, the notorious British punk band the Sex Pistols embraced Cristal Champagne during the band's heyday in the 1970s? (Unlikely, I admit.) It would have been fair enough for Jay-Z to boycott Cristal because Rouzaud insulted the *hip-hop* culture, of which he is a part, but that wouldn't have made headlines or garnered much sympathy. After all, a lot of people, including some prominent blacks, have disparaging things to say about hip-hop. By contrast, *racism* from the director of a well-known international company *is* news, and it guarantees the instinctive condemnation of millions of people. Because Rouzaud's statement was subject to multiple interpretations, one had a choice as to whether to fame the insult narrowly, in terms of hip-hop, or broadly, in terms of race. It's not surprising that the personally affronted Jay-Z chose the latter.

Having done so, he triggered a chain of predictable—indeed, reflexive—reactions. Contemporary racial politics make it a virtue to assume the worst when confronted with such ambiguous circumstances. The person who assumes the best of others and offers plausible alternatives to the verdict of racism is typically dismissed as naive or even complicit in racial injustice. This presumption of guilt leads people to play the race card, and it effectively silences those who would call their bluff.

At the same time, presuming the worst is understandable in a society in which racism persists but is rarely expressed openly. If Rouzaud is a racist, he certainly wouldn't announce it. But he might inadvertently reveal his prejudice in the context of an interview about a bunch of black nouveaux riches who guzzle his finest cuvée as if it were cheap malt liquor. People who are regularly at risk of suffering from concealed racism can't afford to take Pollyanna's perspective. A marked man had better always look for hidden assassins; a black person—marked by race for social contempt—had better always look for hidden bigotry.

A 2006 article in the arts and culture magazine *Black Book* announced the rise of a "post-racist" culture. The term is too clever by half, but still evocative and compelling. Like "postmodern" or "postcolonial," the prefix in post-racist doesn't suggest the demise of what it modifies—in this case racism. Instead, "post" suggests a sort of supernova late stage of racism in which its contradictions and excesses both cancel out and amplify its original functions.

The post-racist has absorbed the values of the civil rights movement—she is perfectly comfortable with black authority figures, black classmates, black neighbors. He thinks it's unremarkable that the secretary of state is a black woman. She says that she doesn't really think of her black friends as "black," and she means it. She also freely indulges in the black stereotypes our culture has on offer: hip-hop's image of the black thug, the black pimp, the black drug dealer, the black crack whore, the black hustler. The post-racist is free to be explicitly and crudely bigoted because he does so with tongue planted firmly in cheek. The post-racist parodies racism, but she doesn't exactly repudiate it. Instead, she revels in its excesses with almost a kind of nostalgia, just as the film *Austin Powers: International Man of Mystery* archly mocks the 1960s spy movies and swinging London but also yearns for them with an almost heartbreaking sincerity.

One of the intriguing characteristics of post-racism is that it is practiced by all races on an almost egalitarian basis. A black bartender quoted in the *Black Book* article quipped, "This is the best time in history to be a black man in America because it's easier than ever to sleep with white women." This crass assessment of racial justice is characteristically post-racist. It manages to say something profoundly humanist (it's a better world today because erotic attachments no longer need observe the color line), but at the same time vaguely racist (black men so obsessively long for sex with white women that they define their quality of life largely by the availability of such opportunities).

Perhaps Jay-Z's exquisitely constructed public image and Rouzaud's reaction to it are examples of post-racism. Jay-Z's image would be incomprehensible without a shared backdrop of racial stereotypes. The hip-hop persona is both a reaction to racist stereotypes and also—let's face it—a performance of them. Given this, Rouzaud's ill-considered comments are all the more ambiguous. Was his apparent distaste for hip-hop culture a reflection of a racist distaste for *blacks* or a less-objectionable distaste for the antisocial behavior stereotypically attributed to blacks by racists? When we're dealing with such ambiguities, one person's righteous accusation of prejudice will look to another like a cheap shot at playing the race card.

The civil rights reforms of the 1960s codified a remarkable transformation in social attitudes and norms. In less than a generation, racial bias was demoted from legally enforced common sense to legally prohibited nonsense. Racism became unlawful, immoral, and, perhaps more important, déclassé. In 1942 only 32 percent of whites believed that the races should attend the same schools; 68 percent favored segregation. By 1964 those figures had almost flipped: 63 percent favored integrated schools while 37 percent preferred segregation. In 1944, 55 percent of whites believed the best jobs should be reserved for whites; by 1970, only 12 percent did.

Today antiracism has been incorporated into the dominant institutions of society. Schools once accepted racial integration only under court order, the armed forces only under executive order, private enterprise only under congressional mandate. Now universities, the military, and private business combine forces to defend integration and race-conscious affirmative action. Officially sanctioned racist propaganda has been replaced by multicultural sensitivity training. Once antiestablishment, antiracism is now part of the establishment. This change in social norms, as much as the legal liability attached to racial discrimination in housing, employment, and public accommodation, is the invaluable legacy of the civil rights movement. Civil rights legislation and the change in social attitudes that accompanied it have dramatically reduced the severity and extent of deliberate and overt race discrimination. Racism persists, but contrary to the claims of some racial demagogues, it hasn't simply changed form or become subtler. It is also not as prevalent or as severe as it was in the era of Jim Crow.

The black civil rights movement is now as much a part of American nationalist lore as the Boston Tea Party or Paul Revere's midnight ride. Like the colonists who tipped the East India Company's heavily taxed orange pekoe into Boston Harbor, the soon-to-be leaders of the civil rights movement were long-suffering solid citizens, pushed to rebellion by manifest oppression. Popular history (after a scant forty years already slipping into legend and cliché) has it that Rosa Parks refused to yield her seat on a Montgomery, Alabama, public bus simply because she was tired. No political activist she: just a simple working-woman who had had enough (in fact, Parks *was* a committed civil rights activist). According to legends informed by poetry and song, the tea boycott in New England and the bus boycott in the Old South both involved reluctant revolutionaries, ordinary people inspired to extraordinary actions by a reflexive hostility to injustice. They were people who wanted to tend their own gardens but got fed up with being treated like manure. Once they were roused to action, these reluctant revolutionaries were fierce partisans. They faced the bayonets and rifles of the world's strongest and most disciplined army. They faced fire hoses, firebombings, billy clubs, and rottweilers. They risked injury, imprisonment, and even death. They exhibited the classical American virtues of proud courage and grim determination—true grit.

They prevailed because of their commitment, but also because of their savvy. The minutemen combined the modern weapons of Europe with the supple tactics of the Native American warrior. They used the terrain to their advantage. Clothed to blend in with the landscape, they attacked the conspicuous files of redcoats from behind the cover of brush. They mounted perhaps the world's first guerrilla war against an imperial regime. The freedom riders combined the non-violence of Gandhi with the oratory charisma of Winston Churchill and the media sense of Edward R. Murrow. They knew they couldn't win by force, and they didn't try. Instead they prevailed through persuasion and moral example. They understood that they needed to convince not Bull Connor and George Wallace, but Hubert Humphrey and Lyndon Johnson. Both the freedom fighters and the freedom riders had a gift for practical problem solving, an outsider's disdain for conventions, a maverick's ability to think outside the box—the paradigmatic Yankee virtues of pragmatism and ingenuity.

And perhaps most important, both revolutions are stories of progress, examples of American idealism and industriousness shaping a society where continual improvement can almost be taken for granted. American history is, from this popular perspective, a story of uninterrupted technological, economic, and moral progress. At least since the Jacksonians advanced the doctrine of Manifest Destiny, Americans have taken comfort in the belief that our position in the world and in history is preordained. An indispensable part of this confidence is the belief that we as a nation are getting not only stronger but also better: wiser, nobler, more beneficent, and more just. Our institutions and customs are superior not only because they contain timeless principles and reflect unshakable truths but also because they possess the capacity to adapt and improve. Just as the cotton gin replaced manual cleaning of the raw crop, so too American moral ingenuity eventually developed superior replacements for slavery, sharecropping, and Jim Crow segregation. The civil rights movement—once a marginal and suspect political radicalism—has been neatly woven into this tale of inexorable national progress. Now racial justice is among the most touted achievements of American society. Like assembly-line production, the tungsten filament, and jazz, it is a source of national pride and a valuable international export. It builds morale at home and helps in the symbolic balance of trade abroad.

As a result, the accusation of bias—racial bias and any other kind of bias analogous to it—is a potent weapon. Racism is not only unfair and irrational, it is unpatriotic and anti-American. And, according to this story, racism is also deviant: deviant in the literal sense that it is rare, and deviant in the colloquial and pejorative sense that it is twisted, sick, and repellent. Here nationalism meets popular psychology. The racist is a fossil of an ancient régime of blood privilege and also a pathetic and potentially dangerous psychopath; a fetishist of skin, hair, and lips; a moral pervert.

Obviously there's a lot to like here. Antiracist causes acquire authority as a result of their conscription into the vanguard of nationalistic pride, and they enjoy legitimacy as a result of their induction into the popular cult of psychotherapy. But along with these advantages come the characteristic drawbacks of patriotic nationalism and pop psychology: on the one hand, jingoism and fanaticism; on the other, sentimentalism and magical thinking. Like patriotic movements generally, antiracism now attracts yahoos and opportunists: "It's a Black Thing; you wouldn't understand" is as insipid and dangerous a slogan as "My country right or wrong." Just as hack politicians wrap themselves in the flag, they now also seek cover in the mantle of racial justice. And like the formulaic 12-step programs of dime-store psychotherapy, antiracism has spawned an industry where the narcissistic confessional substitutes for introspection, cheap theatricality stands in for valuable insight, and simplistic dogma masquerades as analysis.

Playing the race card is a symptom of this crisis of partial success. In dealing with overt racism, the antiracist has the full coercive power of government and the weight of popular consensus behind her. This access to power and influence attracts the unscrupulous opportunist along with the sincere victim and the honest petitioner. And as in any exclusive club, there's not only the problem of gatecrashers, there's also that of inappropriate demeanor. For most of American history, antiracism was a movement of resistance and critique. Antiracists fought against the dominant institutions of society, seeking reform or fomenting rebellion. Because obvious racial injustices persist—and simply out of custom and habit—antiracist rhetoric retains the belligerent, confrontational tone appropriate to a marginal protest movement. But today's antiracists often must defend, enforce, and strengthen dominant norms, using the influence of large and powerful bureaucracies and the coercive power of government. The fiery style of the revolutionary mixes badly with the cool professional technique of an authoritative bureaucracy. Speaking truth to power is an anachronism when the person speaking also has the power. So as charlatans cry "racism" to finagle undeserved advantages, the bad fit between rhetoric and reality, between adopted pose and social position can make even sensible claims sound like grandstanding.

. . . When are complaints of prejudice valid and appropriate and when are they exaggerated, paranoid, or simply dishonest?

. . . When people complain of racism, it is typical to assume that there must be a blameworthy racist who should be made to pay. But many of today's racial injustices are not caused by simple prejudice; instead, they are the legacies of the racial caste system of our recent past, entrenched by the inertia of class hierarchy and reinforced by the unforgiving competition of capitalist markets. As a result, many people have legitimate grievances, but no racist to blame for them. The victims of the injustices will correctly blame racism, but too often they will incorrectly try to find someone to label a racist. Skeptical observers who see no racists will conclude that the complaint is unreasonable and perhaps dishonest. I call this the problem of *racism without racists*.

. . . Was Hurricane Katrina a racial justice issue? When a Yellow Cab ignores a black man's hail, is it racism? If a store clerk is surly to a black customer, can we conclude that she's a bigot?

The success of the civil rights movement inspired many others to frame their struggles in similar terms. Feminists, gays and lesbians, the disabled, and the elderly are just a few of the groups who have successfully made explicit analogies to the cause of racial justice. Conservatives attack affirmative action as reverse racism. Multiculturalism redefined racism as discrimination based not only on skin color or heredity, but also on "culture." And a host of interest groups, such as dog owners, the obese, and cigarette smokers, have implausibly but insistently compared their causes to the struggle against racism. At best, these claims seek to extend the principles underlying civil rights to new situations. But at worst, these claims seem to define "bigotry" so broadly that the losing side of almost any social or political conflict can claim to be the victims of racelike bias. Today almost anyone can play the race card by making claims of what I'll call *racism by analogy*.

. . . Is discrimination on the basis of culture, weight, or appearance as bad as discrimination on the basis of race? Should the law prohibit these, as well as a growing list of arguably analogous biases? How can we distinguish those types of discrimination that demand legal sanction from reasonable distinctions, defensible preferences, and sensible generalizations? Because the law often offers little or no redress for garden-variety unfairness, many people are tempted to recast their grievances in terms that the law will recognize: in other words, to play the race card.

Although there is widespread agreement that racism and analogous prejudices are wrong, there is no agreement as to what counts as racism. The success of the civil rights movement encouraged more ambitious claims, and the phenomenon of racism without racists led activists to apply the civil rights model to subtler forms of racial injustice. Today, there is greater disagreement as to what counts as racism. There are several reasonable definitions available, each of which will yield a different conclusion given the same set of facts. The difficulty in figuring out who is and is not a racist begins with the problem of *defining discrimination*.

. . . Sometimes the law offers a valuable alternative to the jumble of ideas about discrimination used by social critics and social scientists; sometimes it just adds to the confusion. Is it racism if an employer adopts a policy that incidentally excludes a disproportionate percentage of minorities, or is it so only if he adopts it *because* it excludes them? Is it sex discrimination if a company fires a female employee for a combination of good reasons and sex stereotypes? Is racial profiling always a form of racism—even when the profile is accurate and used in good faith? Can a police department round up every black man in town as a part of a manhunt for a criminal at large? Is affirmative action really "reverse racism"? The law has answers to these questions—some that may surprise or even anger you.

The practical goals of civil rights are contested. During the Jim Crow era, antiracists agreed that the goal was to dismantle explicitly discriminatory practices and formal segregation. But it wasn't clear whether the ultimate goal was formal legal equality, or economic equality, or whether there was a substantive commitment to social integration. With blatant discrimination on the wane, it has become obvious that antiracists don't agree on the ultimate goal: mainstream liberals favor social integration, but black nationalists and some multiculturalists reject integration in favor of racial solidarity and cultural autonomy. When the ultimate goal is contested, it can be hard to tell what furthers racial justice and what hinders it. For instance, affirmative action is inconsistent with formal equality, but it furthers economic equality and integration; separate ethnic and racial organizations and clubs promote solidarity and cultural autonomy but violate norms of equality and hinder social integration. This can produce a catch-22, where any course of action will be "racist" according to someone. I call this problem the *clash of ends*. . . . Should we still strive for integration, or can we now conclude that segregation is a result of innocent preferences for solidarity and community?

. . . We can and should refine the legal and cultural definition of discrimination to make it more precise and less subject to abuse. Although no simple definition of "racism" is available, an understanding of the history of American racial injustice—and of the potential and the limits of legal intervention—suggests practical and intuitively compelling limits to the law's application.

Not only can we do better; we must. Ever since the acquittal of O.J. Simpson, the idea that race is a "card" to be played for selfish advantage has become commonplace. The Simpson trial and the popular reactions to it are prime examples of the risks playing the race card poses to racial harmony and social justice. The race card threatens to undermine public support for civil rights and other policies that promote social justice. It breeds and exacerbates distrust between the races, making genuine claims of racism less credible. It helps to fracture society into mutually suspicious and antagonistic social groups, eroding the political solidarity that could underwrite social harmony and egalitarianism. And it distracts attention from the real issues involved in conflicts that are mislabeled as instances of bigotry. The unforgiving social and economic conditions that remain unaddressed, in part as a result of playing the race card, entrench the social disadvantage of the most vulnerable—disproportionately racial minorities—and thereby fuel another round of increasingly desperate uses of the race card.

4-2

Immigrants and the Changing Categories of Race

Kenneth Prewitt

Racial classification has always been included in the Census. This former director of the Census Bureau points out that throughout history interest in counting people according to racial classifications has involved more than casual curiosity. Policies are at stake. During the slavery era, the Constitution provided that in allocating congressional seats according to population, slaves were to be counted as 3/5 a citizen. During the civil rights era policies led to increased differentiation of racial and ethnic categories. And in today's environment, emphasizing diversity and multiracialism, the number of categories (and combinations) has proliferated.

Since this essay was written, the results of the 2010 Census have been released. As Prewitt forecasted, the number of Americans identifying themselves to be multiracial has grown sharply—nearly 3 percent of the total population—and it will continue to grow. Half of all births in America are minorities and five percent are listed as multiracial.

THE STUDY OF immigration has its distinct vocabulary—incorporation, assimilation, mobilization, coalitions, conflict, identity, and so forth. The terms in play touch on the broad question of whether ethnic and racial boundaries are being hardened or blurred, and to what extent the recent immigrant flows contribute to some mixture of these outcomes. The small contribution I offer is the reminder that the boundaries themselves, or at least their accessibility to research, rest on the way in which official statistics label population groups—starting even with the labels foreign born and native born.

Subdividing the population is as old as census taking itself. Numbers, the fourth book of the Hebrew Bible, has Yahweh instructing Moses: "Take ye the sum of all the congregation of the children of Israel, after their families, with the number of their names, every male . . . from twenty years old and upward." Here the key categories are male/female and under/over twenty. The intent, of course, was to know how many of the Israelites are "able to go forth to war."

Source: Kenneth Prewitt, "Immigrants and the Changing Categories of Race," in Taeku Lee, S. Karthick Ramakrishnan, and Ricardo Ramírez, eds., *Transforming Politics, Transforming America: The Political and Civic Incorporation of Immigrants in the United States* (Charlottesville, VA: University of Virginia Press, 2006), 19–31. Some notes and bibliographic references appearing in the original have been deleted.

A census is never just a count; it is always also a series of classifications selected to serve policy decisions.

America's earliest national census in 1790 rested, first, on a geographical classification—needed, of course, to allocate seats in the new Congress proportionate to population size. This census also divided the population by civil status: taxed and untaxed, free and slave. These civil status categories generated a racial classification that separated those of European descent from those of African descent and from Native Americans. The earliest censuses did not even bother to distinguish between native born and foreign born.

The nation's first racial classification carried a lot of policy and political weight. Including slaves in the census counts, even at three-fifths, rewarded the South with approximately a dozen more congressional seats and votes in the Electoral College than a count limited to its white population would have provided. This population bonus was among the several compromises struck with the slave-owning states to secure ratification of the new federal constitution. It had immense consequences. Known by historians as the "slave power," the bonus in the Electoral College put Thomas Jefferson in the White House, and then his Virginian compatriots, James Madison and James Monroe. As Gary Wills documents in detail, a steady stream of proslavery (and anti-Indian) acts by Congress can be traced to the "extra" congressional seats awarded to the Southern states by the three-fifths clause (Wills 2003).

It is instructive to compare the ease with which a racial classification was introduced into our statistical system with the resistance resulting from an occupational classification. In preparing for the nation's first decennial census, James Madison proposed a question to classify America's working population into agriculture, commerce, or manufacturing. The new Congress rebuffed his initiative, registering both a technical and a philosophical objection. Technically, said the congressional opponents, the categories were imprecise, because, after all, the same person could fall into all three sectors—being a farmer who manufactured nails on the side and traded those he did not need to a neighboring farmer who made ax handles. More philosophically, Madison's critics held that an occupational classification would admit to, and perhaps even excite, differing economic interests. This very possibility challenged eighteenth-century thought that took society to be a harmonious whole, and viewed the task of governing as that of divining a common good rather than that of managing conflicting interests. The harmonious whole that was blind to occupational differences was not, of course, color-blind. In the color-coded language that becomes prominent in the nineteenth century, the earliest census separates the black, red, and white population groups.

I take from the 1790 census a larger lesson. To divide the population into its several race groups was unquestioned. The categories could change, but not the need for the classification itself. In 1820 "free colored persons" was added to the census form (as, by the way, was Madison's occupation question). After the Civil War, interest in shades of color led the census to classify people as mulatto, quadroon, and octoroon, motivated by a race science that viewed race mixing as detrimental to the moral fiber of the nation itself. New immigrant groups began to appear in census categories around the same time. Chinese and Japanese were counted in 1890. Later, in 1920, Filipinos, Koreans, and Hindus appeared on the census form. Before 1930, Mexicans were counted as white, but in 1930 were separately counted as a race. This was quickly dropped when the government of Mexico complained, and Mexicans remained "white" until the category Hispanic origin appeared in the 1980 census (and has remained in every census since), though as I note in more detail below, labeled an ethnic rather than racial group. Following statehood for Hawaii, Hawaiian and part-Hawaiian appear on the 1960 census form, though statehood for Alaska did not generate a specific category for Aleut and Eskimo until 1980.

America's changing demography is traced to both immigration and imperialism, the latter resting on purchase as well as conquest. The Louisiana Purchase brought Creoles into America's population. The purchase of the Russian colony of Alaska in 1867 added the Inuit, the Kodiak, and other Alaskan natives. The Mexican-American War in midcentury added the nation's first large Mexican population. The Spanish-American War later in the century added Puerto Rico, other Caribbean islands, and their peoples, as well as Guam and the Philippines. When Hawaii was annexed in 1898, its native Pacific Islander population fell under American rule. Although population increases that resulted from conquest and purchase were relatively small, they added substantially to the country's racial diversity, completing David Hollinger's "racial pentagon" (1995) by adding brown and yellow to the eighteenth-century population base of white, black, and red.

The nineteenth- and early twentieth-century immigration story is less about race than about national origin and religion, though these traits were often "racialized" as in the swarthy southern Europeans or the Jewish race. The well-known story is how a permissive immigration policy that brought workers to a growing economy was combined with civic exclusion, denial of citizenship, and limited rights. And when people with nativist tendencies in American political life worried that the internal borders were not holding, permissive immigration was brought to a sharp and sudden halt. The restrictive 1924 legislation drew specifically on the census to set limits that effectively denied entry to those national origin groups that had dominated immigration flows for the previous half century.

From the founding period through the Second World War, racial classification in our official statistical system interacted with two politically related policy narratives. One, the three-fifths clause, entrenched slaveholding interests until the Civil War, and then, even as three-fifths gave way to a full count of African Americans, entrenched a Jim Crow society and continued disproportionate power for the South in Congress and the Electoral College. The census made room for Southern blacks, but voting rolls and polling booths did not. The second policy narrative is the racially constructed policy that excluded Asians, Mexicans, Hawaiians, Puerto Ricans, and other minorities from civic life, and then, with the Immigration Act of 1924, sought to wind the demographic clock back to Anglo dominance. These policy narratives eventually gave way to a liberalization of immigration and a reopening of America's gates with the Immigration and Nationality (McCarran-Walter) Act of 1952—which lifted the ban on immigration set by the 1924 Act, but kept stringent quotas on immigrants from particular sending countries (e.g., the limit on Japanese immigrants was set at 128 persons per year)—and the 1965 Hart-Cellar Act amendments to the 1952 legislation, which effectively ended the discriminatory national origin-based quota system.

If state-sanctioned discrimination is the central policy narrative linked to racial classification for more than a century and a half, the 1960s ended it only in part. Discrimination was to end, but not classification itself or its tight coupling to national policy. That is, the long period that precedes the civil rights legislation of the 1960s and the shorter period that immediately follows it rest on two propositions: First, that there should be a racial classification system that assigns every American to one and only one of a small number of discrete ethnoracial groups. The second proposition is that this racial classification system should be designed to serve public policy purposes. Where earlier policies had been discriminatory, new civil rights policies were intended to right those wrongs and benefit groups that had been "historically discriminated against." Belonging to a racial minority becomes a basis from which to assert civic rights. In this task, statistical proportionality became a much-deployed legal and administrative tool. Soon, the nation was enmeshed in a new form of politics. Equal opportunity becomes proportional representation. Disparate impact gains an important place in legal reasoning. Institutional racism enters the political vocabulary. Individual rights came to share political space with group rights.

Accompanying this shift in vocabulary and focus was a broadened understanding of civil rights, which was quickly adjudged to be about more than redressing the legacy of slavery. It was about all "groups historically discriminated against"— including, especially, Native Americans, Hispanics, and Asians. Civil rights became minority rights, and references to black-white were supplanted by references to people of color. Even this was too narrow a construction. The minority rights revolution came to encompass other groups historically discriminated against, in particular, women and the disabled.

Statistical proportionality was central to this steady broadening of the civil rights agenda. Through legislation like the Civil Rights Act of 1964 and the Voting Rights Act of 1965 and the subsequent Supreme Court interpretations of these laws, the discriminatory and exclusionary nature of society came to be determined by examining whether certain groups were statistically underrepresented in colleges and universities, in the better jobs, in winning government contracts, in home mortgages, and in elected office. Underrepresentation was accepted as an indicator of denied social justice.

The census racial classification system that gave rise to concepts of underrepresentation and to statistical proportionality as a juridical and administrative tool had a small number of discrete categories—white, black, Indian, Asian and, as an ethnic category, Hispanic. But with the census classification scheme steadily accumulating more policy weight, the categories themselves could hardly be left to chance. The "politics of classification" changed, drawing fresh energy from multicultural identity politics. These politics brought many advocacy groups to issues that had generally been the preserve of statistical agencies.

Fueling these politics is a broad public question. Why do we have an official ethnoracial classification? For much of American history, the answer was self-evident: the classification helped in the design and implementation of discriminatory and exclusionist policies. When these policies were radically challenged and eventually dismantled, the policy use of classification remained in place. Except now it was historical wrongs and ongoing discrimination that were made tractable to policy intervention.

Recent developments have begun to confuse this basic understanding of the policy function of ethnoracial classification. Today the country has a less sure or agreed-upon answer to why we preserve the racial classification system, at least in its current broad outline, which essentially carries forward race categories that date to the seventeenth century. There are many reasons for why we are on shakier grounds at present. Here I take up two: immigration and multiracialism.

Immigration

It should be stressed at the outset that at various moments in American history, new immigrant groups fit uneasily into the prevailing color-denominated racial classification. In the late nineteenth century, Southern European Catholics and Central European Jews, though in different ways, fiercely resisted being "racialized" and thereby prevented from joining the dominant white group. Our attention, however, is with the present period, starting with the Hart-Cellar Act in 1965 that removed national origin-based quotas and introduced, instead, family reunification, political refugee status, and skill-based criteria as the controlling factors in immigration policy. The late twentieth-century immigration surge led to shifts in the regions of the world sending immigrants to the United States. Asians and Latinos arrived in large numbers, patterns that show no signs of reversal. The current immigration flows—to the United States and elsewhere—bring immigrants who are culturally, linguistically, ethnically, and religiously unlike the populations of the receiving countries.

The post-1965 wave of immigration challenges an ethnoracial classification designed for the midcentury demographic makeup of the country. Policymakers and statisticians are today being pressed by ethnic lobbies, demographers, and indeed common sense to provide data that allow for meaningful generalization about America's much more diverse population. There is now an active, self-conscious politics of how the country should sort and classify.

For example, the Census Bureau presently has five racial and ethnic advisory committees, representing groups historically discriminated against: African Americans, Asians, Hispanics, Native Hawaiians and Pacific Islanders, and Native Americans. Do immigrants from the Middle East, Central Asia, and Islamic Africa have to find their way into this preexisting structure or argue for their own committees? If the latter, how many such committees should the Census Bureau appoint? Today's immigrants, or their leaders, take for granted that categories will not be determined by distant government agencies but will result from advocacy and agitation.

We got a taste of this in the period leading up to the 2000 census, when the government initiated a review of the standards for collecting information on race and ethnicity announced in 1977. Those standards, issued by the Office of Management and Budget (OMB) as Statistical Policy Directive No. 15, instructed all federal agencies to collect and report race and ethnic data in five categories: American Indian or Alaskan Native; Asian or Pacific Islander; black; white; and Hispanic, with the first four called races and Hispanic called an ethnic group.

These standards were examined again in the 1990s. Two major changes were made. First, responding to research that documented differences between Native Hawaiian/Pacific Islanders and the Asian category to which they had been assigned, as well as to advocacy by a persuasive senator from Hawaii, the federal office responsible for statistical policy allowed Native Hawaiian/Pacific Islanders to become a separate racial group. Other groups—Arabs, Creoles, and Cape Verdeans, particularly—presented arguments for why they, too, should get their own category. Though none of these efforts were eventually successful, the Arab case was the one most closely considered. The inability of this group to decide whether Arab or Middle Easterner was the best label, and how geographically to define the Middle East, made it difficult for OMB to be responsive. Advocacy groups indicated at the time that they would continue to press for a separate category, but the aftermath of 9/11 and the subsequent stereotyping of Arab Americans may complicate these efforts. The new standard also made it clearer that the population was to have two primary "ethnic" groups: "Hispanic or Latino" and "Not Hispanic or Latino."

The changes introduced in 1997 did not, however, resolve the larger issue: how well do the present race categories accommodate the great demographic diversity introduced by four decades of immigrants coming to the United States from every world region. Consider recent immigrants from Africa. The cultural, linguistic, religious, and even color differences between, for example, Islamic Somalis and sixth-generation descendants of Bantu slaves from Africa's Gold Coast are great indeed. Yet these Somalis, as well as Ethiopians, Sudanese, Senegalese, and others, have no place in official statistics to go except to the black African American category. Similar points can be made about Northern Africans, except in this case they are treated as white in the official statistics. If in the 1990s, Arabs, Creoles and Cape Verdeans complained of a mismatch with official statistical categories, diasporic Africans are likely to offer similar complaints in the decades ahead. We return below to the complications that late twentieth-century immigration introduces into our classification system, but first we turn to the second major change introduced in 1997.

Multiracialism

The most noticed change in the 2000 census was, of course, the multiple-race option. The revision of OMB Directive 15 that was announced in the October 1997 *Federal Register* introduced the "Mark one or more" provision in connection with the race categories. This change allows respondents to indicate their heritage as they select one or more of the five primary race groupings. As a result, rather than the previous scheme of five racial categories and two ethnic categories, there were now 63 possible combinations of "Mark one or more" among the race categories and 126 possible combinations when race is cross-tabulated with the Hispanic/non-Hispanic distinction.

The multiple-race option was not heavily used in the 2000 census (2.4 percent of the population), and agencies that enforce nondiscriminatory laws accommodated the expanding number of racial categories by devising collapsing rules. No major disruptions in political/administrative conditions occurred. The short-term public and political response to the multiple-race option does not, I suggest, adequately predict what is in store for the United States. Self-identification as multiracial will increase, partly as a result of social legitimation, especially among the young, but also resulting from increasing rates of marriage across racial lines. Beyond this, there will be continuing pressure to expand the number of primary groups in the classification system.

I suggested earlier that there was a generally agreed-upon answer to the basic question: Why does the nation classify by race and ethnicity? Because the classification facilitates policymaking. Since the 1960s, the policies that have drawn most heavily on racial classification have, of course, been those associated with voting rights, affirmative action, and related social justice measures.

Those who advocated for the multiple-race option, and for expanding ethnoracial categories more generally, start from a different place. For them, the categories are less about social justice than social identity. If this makes the classification less useful, or perhaps even useless, for race-sensitive policies, that is the price to pay for the right to be recognized for who one is.

In 1997 congressional hearings reviewing whether to introduce a multirace option, the opposing positions were clear. Traditional civil rights organizations argued against a multirace option, stressing the responsibility of government to police discrimination. The NAACP held that the "creation of a separate multiracial classification might disaggregate the apparent numbers of members of discrete minority groups, diluting benefits to which they are entitled as a protected class under civil rights laws and under the Constitution itself." A Latino spokesperson noted that, though identity claims "resonate with the Latino community, we understand that the purpose of the census is both to enforce and implement the law, and inform lawmakers about the distinct needs of special historically disadvantaged populations."

The advocates for multiracialism countered that to force them into a box that did not reflect their true identity was to deny them their civil rights. The counterargument, as voiced by the Association of Multiethnic Americans, was explicit: "We want choice in the matter. We want choice in the matter of who we are, just like any other community. We are not saying that we are a solution to civil rights laws or civil rights injustices of the past." It is ironic, the testimony continued, that "our people are being asked to correct by virtue of how we define ourselves all of the past injustices [toward] other groups of people." In this testimony, and the advocacy movement it represented, the purpose of ethnoracial classification extends beyond its use in the enforcement of public policies. Official statistics are a site for choice, expression, and identity. As Jennifer Hochschild observes, it is ironic that the Census Bureau, widely perceived to be a stodgy data collection agency, is acting as a leading force for deconstruction (Hochschild 2002).

We begin to see ways in which the immigrant flows and the new multirace option might combine to further destabilize the current classification system. Much will depend on how different immigrant groups position themselves in the arguments that opposed "enforcement of antidiscrimination laws" against "expression of social identity." On the one hand, immigrants are likely to experience discrimination. President Bill Clinton's "Initiative on Race" offers the following argument: New immigrants from Southeast Asia "continue to feel the legacy of discriminatory laws against Asian Pacific Americans because they continue to be perceived and treated as foreigners." If discrimination is the issue, we might expect new immigrant groups to side with those African Americans and Hispanics who believe, reasonably so, that a small number of discrete categories in the classification system is needed for enforcement purposes.

On the other hand, some new immigrant groups, Asians in particular, are marrying across racial lines at rates that far exceed those of African Americans and Hispanics. This will likely draw them, or their children, to the "mark one or more" option, and will align them with the advocates insisting that the purpose of categories is to offer choice and expression.

Hispanics present yet a further complication. As an officially designated ethnic group, they can be of any race—when race, in the statistical system, is limited to the five primary groups noted above. What actually happened in the 2000 census strongly suggests that a large number of Hispanics, as many as fifteen million, do not see themselves as fitting into one of those five groups. The census form allowed for "Other" as a sixth option in the race question. Hispanic respondents account for 97 percent of those who used the "Other" option, and the proportion of all Hispanics who selected it was 47 percent in 2000. This group essentially opted out of choices presented by the primary race classification and declared themselves to be their own race group. That these patterns cannot be attributed to confusion on the part of Hispanics is suggested by independent survey data. When 3000 Hispanics were asked in a 2002 survey what race they considered themselves to be, 46 percent responded that they were Hispanic or Latino—even though this was not one of the options presented.

What we have, then, is a far-from-settled classification system, at least from the perspective of the fastest growing segment of America's population—its recent immigrants. There are two other, perhaps smaller, perhaps not, chapters to the story—the political movement to end racial classification altogether and the arrival of the diversity rhetoric. I discuss each briefly.

End Racial Measurement

A statewide California ballot initiative, Proposition 54 (officially termed the "Classification by Race, Ethnicity, Color, and National Origin" initiative, but popularly known as the "Racial Privacy Initiative"), in the fall of 2004, declared that "[t]he state [including all political subdivisions or governmental instrumentalities] shall not classify any individual by race, ethnicity, color or national origin in the operation of public education, public contracting, or public employment." Spearheaded by University of California regent Ward Connerly (who also led the successful effort to eliminate affirmative action programs in public-sector employment and education with Proposition 209), Proposition 54 met with significant opposition, and despite drawing three million voters, was easily defeated. Its supporters have promised to push ahead, perhaps next in Michigan.

Our interest here is less the fate of this particular referendum than in the sentiment it reflects. Many Americans, and not just those who would end racial measurement in order to end affirmative action or other race-sensitive practices, are uncomfortable with ethnoracial classification. They would like it to go away, or, at least, play a less-prominent role in American life. It is difficult to gauge how widespread or deep this sentiment is, particularly among recent immigrant groups—though, at least in California, racial minorities voted strongly against the Racial Privacy Initiative.

The Diversity Agenda

The diversity vocabulary, now widespread in higher education and corporate America, can be viewed as the end point of a half-century process that steadily broadened the civil rights language, which, as noted, starts with a focus on slave descendents, is broadened to encompass people of color, and then again to all groups historically discriminated against, and on to any group experiencing discrimination, and finally to the generalized notion of any group underserved or underrepresented. Diversity is the natural next step.

Consider first how the term "diversity" is used in higher education. Claims to diversity invariably start with reference to groups historically discriminated against. But higher education does not stop at this point. The diversity initiative is about much more than compensating for patterns of historic discrimination.

Universities claim they are diverse because they attract students from every state in the nation and, even better, from many foreign countries. Claims to diversity reference multiple religions on campus or students of differing social class backgrounds. Diversity statements often take note of lifestyles and sexual orientation. Many move beyond demographic traits altogether and stress how different intellectual persuasions can be (or should be) found on campus. At Rutgers, to take only one example, diversity "encompasses race, ethnicity, culture, social class, national origin, gender, age, religious beliefs, sexual orientation, mental ability and physical ability." The rationale for diversity is less focused on social justice than on the pedagogic argument that it improves the educational experience for all students on campus. At Harvard, for example, diversity "develops the kind of understanding that can only come when we are willing to test our ideas and arguments in the company of people with very different perspectives."

Diversity is broadly construed by corporate America as well. General Motors notes that "diversity includes race and gender as well as the broader aspects of age, education level, family status, language, military status, physical abilities, religion, sexual orientation, union representation, and years of service." At DuPont, "When employees offer their own diverse insights and cultural sensitivities, they open new customer bases and market opportunities." Here the rationale is gains in profit or productivity.

The diversity language interests here for what it says about the statistical underpinnings of affirmative action efforts. In 2004 the Supreme Court ruled in *Grutter v. Bollinger* (123 S. Ct. 2325, 2341 [2003]) that universities can apply various criteria in constituting their student bodies. But this ruling left little room for the application of statistics in determining how many of which groups will constitute diversity. This is probably a good thing. Taking the term diversity at face value—which would imply measuring, perhaps, the dozens if not hundreds of different cultures, language groups, and nationalities represented in American society—runs into the small "n" problem rather quickly. The University of Michigan lawyers defending diversity before the Supreme Court emphasized the importance of "critical mass," but they were careful not to put a numeric value to it. Diversity, they suggested, is a matter of judgment rather than measurement—a "know it when you see it" defense.

If this position can be sustained, applying a diversity rationale when assembling an entering college class or a workforce or an army will simply sidestep measurement and will not seriously impact racial classification. If, however, there were an attempt to bring statistics to diversity arguments, categories would proliferate well beyond the capacity of measurement. The effort would collapse, with unforeseeable consequences for racial classification. It is simply too early to know how diversity considerations will work their way through the institutions of America and whether immigrant groups will latch onto the diversity rhetoric as a way to claim places in education or the job market.

Conclusions

The ethnoracial classification system that currently underpins official statistics in the United States is unstable and will undergo additional changes. Elsewhere I have argued that the distinction between race and ethnicity as used in official statistics is itself suspect (Prewitt 2005). This argument gains even more force when considering the great diversity of national origin, linguistic, and religious groups that have made their way to American shores since immigration policy was liberalized in 1965. Certainly the presumption that there are only two ethnic groups in the United States—Hispanic and Non/Hispanic—makes little sense. Nor should we expect every recently arrived group to feel comfortable in one of the preexisting five primary race groups. So what gets added, by what criteria, and in response to what political pressure? Hovering over these issues is the broader question of the purpose to be served by the classification system: enforcement or affirmation? Perhaps there is a way to realize both of these functions. I have suggested elsewhere a way to preserve the enforcement purpose with one question on the census form, and yet respond to the demands for affirmation and identity expression through another question on the form (Prewitt 2005). Whether that is practical remains to be tested.

The only certainty I see in the future of racial classification is a politics that includes a much more active role by recent immigrants, especially by Hispanics and Asians, than has historically been the case. This is not to say that how to incorporate immigrants into preexisting classification is a new consideration in statistical policy. It is not, but compared to the nineteenth and early twentieth century, the politics today are much more open. Who "owns" the racial classification system? No one and everyone is probably the answer, and immigration scholars will need to be attentive to how different groups politically position themselves as the classification system again comes under review.

REFERENCES

Hochschild, Jennifer L. 2002. *Multiple Racial Identifiers in the 2000 Census, and Then What? The New Race Question: How the Census Counts Multiracial Individuals.* New York: Russell Sage Foundation, 340–353.

Hollinger, David. 1995. *Postethnic America: Beyond Multiculturalism.* New York: Basic Books.

Prewitt, Kenneth. 2002. *Race in the 2000 Census: A Turning Point.* New York: Russell Sage Foundation.

Prewitt, Kenneth. 2005. "Racial Classification in America: Where Do We Go from Here?" *Daedalus* (Winter): 5–17.

Wills, Gary. 2003. *Negro President: Jefferson and the Slave Power.* New York: Houghton Mifflin.

Chapter 5

Civil Liberties

———

5-1

from *Republic.com 2.0*

Cass R. Sunstein

It is difficult to think of more universal and absolute language concerning free speech than the First Amendment's provision: "Congress shall make no law . . . abridging the freedom of speech." Yet, jurists have long noted that it cannot be absolute. Justice Oliver Wendell Holmes famously observed that the amendment does not allow a person to yell "Fire!" in a crowded theater. In this essay, Cass Sunstein cites numerous circumstances—many involving new communications technologies—that appear equally problematic. Where and how should the line be drawn between speech that is protected and speech that is not? He presents and assesses two competing principles of free speech. One is a kind of libertarian, "consumerist" principle that individuals and organizations invoke to protect whatever speech they want to say or sponsor. The alternative, favored by Sunstein, is the democratic principle that holds some speech to be more sacrosanct than other speech. In this scheme, the most protected speech is that which affects democratic control of government; government is allowed to regulate other forms of speech, such as statements that are patently harmful.

WERE THOSE RESPONSIBLE for the ILOVEYOU virus protected by the free-speech principle? It would be silly to say that they are. But if this form of speech may be regulated, what are the limits on government's power?

Source: Cass R. Sunstein, from "Freedom of Speech," in *Republic.com 2.0*, by Cass R. Sunstein (Princeton, N.J.: Princeton University Press, 2007), 165–189.

139

Consider a case involving not email but a website—a case that may, in some ways, turn out to be emblematic of the future. The site in question had a dramatic name: "The Nuremberg Files." It began, "A coalition of concerned citizens throughout the USA is cooperating in collecting dossiers on abortionists in anticipation that one day we may be able to hold them on trial for crimes against humanity." The site contained a long list of "Alleged Abortionists and Their Accomplices," with the explicit goal of recording "the name of every person working in the baby slaughter business in the United States of America." The list included the names, home addresses, and license-plate numbers of many doctors who performed abortions, and also included the names of their spouses and children.

So far, perhaps, so good. But three of these doctors had been killed. Whenever a doctor was killed, the website showed a line drawn through his name. The site also included a set of "wanted posters," Old West–style, with photographs of doctors with the word "Wanted" under each one. A group of doctors brought suit, contending the practices of which this site was a part amounted in practice to "a hit list" with death threats and intimidation. The jury awarded them over $100 million in damages; the verdict was upheld on appeal, though the dollar award was reduced substantially (it remained in the millions of dollars).

Should the free-speech principle have protected the Nuremberg Files? Maybe it should have. But if you think so, would you allow a website to post names and addresses of doctors who performed abortions, with explicit instructions about how and where to kill them? Would you allow a website to post bomb-making instructions? To post such instructions alongside advice about how and where to use the bombs? To show terrorists exactly where and how to strike? As we have seen, there is nothing fanciful about these questions. Dozens of sites now contain instructions about how to make bombs—though to my knowledge, none of them tells people how and where to use them. If you have no problem with bomb-making instructions on websites, you might consider some other questions. Does your understanding of free speech allow people to work together at a site called pricefixing.com, through which competitors can agree to set prices and engage in other anticompetitive practices? (I made that one up.) Does your understanding of free speech allow people to make unauthorized copies of movies, music, and books, and to give or sell those copies to dozens, thousands, or millions of others? (I didn't make that one up.)

My basic argument here is that the free-speech principle, properly understood, is not an absolute and that it allows government to undertake a wide range of restrictions on what people want to say on the Internet. However the hardest questions should be resolved, the government can regulate computer viruses, criminal conspiracy, and explicit incitement to engage in criminal acts, at least if the incitement is likely to be effective. In my view, it would also be acceptable for government to require broadcasters to provide educational programming for children on television, as in fact it now does; to mandate free air time for candidates for public office; and to regulate contributions to and expenditures on political campaigns, at least within certain boundaries.

This is not the place for a full discussion of constitutional doctrines relating to freedom of expression. But in the process of showing the democratic roots of the system of free expression, I attempt to provide an outline of the basic constitutional principles.[1]

Emerging Wisdom? Televisions as Toasters

An emerging view is that the First Amendment to the Constitution requires government to respect consumer sovereignty. Indeed, the First Amendment is often treated as if it incorporates the economic ideal—as if it is based on the view that consumer choice is what the system of communications is all about. Although it is foreign to the original conception of the free-speech principle, this view can be found in many places in current law.

For one thing, it helps to explain the constitutional protection given to commercial advertising. This protection is exceedingly recent. Until 1976,[2] the consensus within the Supreme Court and the legal culture in general was that the First Amendment did not protect commercial speech at all. Since that time, commercial speech has come to be treated more and more like ordinary speech, to the point where Justice Thomas has even doubted whether the law should distinguish at all between commercial and political speech.[3] To date, Justice Thomas has not prevailed on this count. But the Court's commercial-speech decisions often strike down restrictions on advertising, and for that reason, those decisions are best seen as a way of connecting the idea of consumer sovereignty with the First Amendment itself.

Belonging in the same category is the frequent constitutional hostility to campaign-finance regulation. The Supreme Court has held that financial expenditures on behalf of political candidates are generally protected by the free-speech principle—and in what seems to me an act of considerable hubris, the Court has also held that it is illegitimate for government to try to promote political equality by imposing ceilings on permissible expenditures.[4] The inequality that comes from divergences in wealth is not, [i]n the Court's view, a proper subject for democratic control. According to the Court, campaign-finance restrictions cannot be justified by reference to equality at all. It is for this reason that candidate *expenditures* from candidates' personal funds may not be regulated. It is also for this reason that restrictions on campaign *contributions* from one person to a candidate can be regulated only as a way of preventing the reality or appearance of corruption.

The constitutional debate over campaign-finance regulation remains complex and unresolved, and the members of the Supreme Court are badly divided.[5] Some of the justices would further reduce the government's existing authority to regulate campaign contributions, on the theory that such contributions lie at the heart of what the free-speech principle protects. Here too an idea of consumer sovereignty seems to be at work. In many of the debates over campaign expenditures and contributions, the political process itself is being treated as a kind of market in which citizens are seen as consumers, expressing their will not only through votes and statements but also through money. I do not mean to suggest that the government should be able to impose whatever restrictions it wishes. I mean only to notice, and to question, the idea that the political domain should be seen as a market and the influential claim that government is entirely disabled from responding to the translation of economic inequality into political equality.

Even more relevant for present purposes is the widespread suggestion, with some support in current constitutional law, that the free-speech principle forbids government from interfering with the communications market by, for example, attempting to draw people's attention to serious issues or regulating the content of what appears on television networks.[6] To be sure, everyone agrees that the government is permitted to create and protect property rights, even if this means that speech will be regulated as a result. We have seen that the government may give property rights to websites and broadcasters; there is no constitutional problem with that. Everyone also agrees that the government is permitted to control monopolistic behavior and thus to enforce antitrust law, which is designed to ensure genuinely free markets in communications. Structural regulation, not involving direct control of speech but intended to make sure that the market works well, is usually unobjectionable. Hence government can create copyright law and, at least within limits, forbid unauthorized copying. (There is, however, an extremely important and active debate about how to reconcile copyright law and the free-speech principle.)[7] But if government attempts to require television broadcasters to cover public issues, or to provide free air time for candidates, or to ensure a certain level of high-quality programming for children, many people will claim that the First Amendment is being violated. What lies beneath the surface of these debates?

Two Free-Speech Principles

We might distinguish here between the free-speech principle as it operates in courts and the free-speech principle as it operates in public debate. As far as courts are concerned, there is as yet no clear answer to many of the constitutional questions that would be raised by government efforts to make the speech market work better. For example, we do not really know, as a matter of constitutional law, whether government can require educational and public-affairs programming on television. The Court allowed such regulation when three or four television stations dominated the scene, but it has left open the question of whether such regulation would be legitimate today.[8] As a matter of prediction, the most that can be said is that there is a reasonable chance that the Court would permit government to adopt modest initiatives, so long as it was promoting goals associated with deliberative democracy.

Indeed the Court has been very cautious, and self-consciously so, about laying down firm rules governing the role of the free-speech principle on new technologies. The Court is aware that things are changing rapidly and that there is much that it does not know. Because issues of fact and value are in a state of flux, it has tended to offer narrow, case-specific rulings that offer little guidance, and constraint, for the future.[9]

But the free-speech principle has an independent life outside of the courtroom. It is often invoked, sometimes strategically though sometimes as a matter of principle, in such a way as to discourage government initiatives that might make the communications market serve democratic goals. Outside of the law, and inside the offices of lobbyists, newspapers, radio stations, and recording studios, as well as even in ordinary households, the First Amendment has a large *cultural* presence. This is no less important than its technical role in courts. Here the identification of the free-speech principle with consumer sovereignty is becoming all the tighter. Worst of all, the emerging cultural understanding severs the link between the First Amendment and democratic self-rule.

Recall here Bill Gates's words: "It's already getting a little unwieldy. When you turn on DirectTV and you step through every channel—well, there's three minutes of your life. When you walk into your living room six years from now, you'll be able to just say what you're interested in, and have the screen help you pick out a video that you care about. It's not going to be 'Let's look at channels 4, 5, and 7.'" Taken to its logical extreme, the emerging wisdom would identify the First Amendment with the dream of unlimited consumer sovereignty with respect to speech. It would see the First Amendment in precisely Gates's terms. It would transform the First Amendment into a constitutional guarantee of consumer sovereignty in the domain of communications.

I have had some experience with the conception of the First Amendment as an embodiment of consumer sovereignty, and it may be useful to offer a brief account of that experience. From 1997 to 1998, I served on the President's Advisory Committee on the Public Interest Obligations of Digital Television Broadcasters. Our task was to consider whether and how television broadcasters should be required to promote public-interest goals—through, for example, closed captioning for the hearing-impaired, emergency warnings, educational programming for children, and free air time for candidates. About half of the committee's members were broadcasters, and most of them were entirely happy to challenge proposed government regulation as intrusive and indefensible. One of the two co-chairs was the redoubtable Leslie Moonves, president of CBS. Moonves is an obviously intelligent, public-spirited man but also the furthest thing from a shrinking violet, and he is, to say the least, attuned to the economic interests of the television networks. Because of its composition, this group was not about to recommend anything dramatic. On the contrary, it was bound to be highly respectful of the prerogatives of television broadcasters. In any case the Advisory Committee was just that—an advisory committee—and we had power only to write a report, and no authority to impose any duties on anyone at all.

Nonetheless, the committee was subject to a sustained, intense, high-profile, and evidently well-funded lobbying effort by economic interests, generally associated with the broadcasting industry, seeking to invoke the First Amendment to suggest that any and all public-interest obligations should and would be found unconstitutional. An elegantly dressed and high-priced Washington lawyer testified before us for an endless hour, making quite outlandish claims about the meaning of the First Amendment. A long stream of legal documents was generated and sent to all of us, most of them arguing that (for example) a requirement of free air time for candidates would offend the Constitution. At our meetings, the most obvious (omni) presence was Jack Goodman, the lawyer for the National Association of Broadcasters (NAB), the lobbying and litigating arm of the broadcast industry, which wields the First Amendment as a kind of protectionist weapon against almost everything that government tries to do. To say that Goodman and the NAB would invoke the free-speech principle at the drop of a hat, or the faintest step of a Federal Communications Commission official in the distance, is only a slight exaggeration.

Of course all this was an entirely legitimate exercise of free speech. But when the President's Advisory Committee on the Public Interest Obligations of Digital Television Broadcasters already consists, in large part, of broadcasters, and when that very committee is besieged with tendentious and implausible interpretations of the First Amendment, something does seem amiss. There is a more general point. The National Association of Broadcasters and others with similar economic interests typically use the First Amendment in precisely the same way that the National Rifle Association uses the Second Amendment. We should think of the two camps as jurisprudential twins. The National Association of Broadcasters is prepared to make self-serving and outlandish claims about the First Amendment before the public and before courts, and to pay lawyers and publicists a lot of money to help establish those claims. (Perhaps they will ultimately succeed.) The National Rifle Association does the same thing with the Second Amendment. In both cases, those whose social and economic interests are at stake are prepared to use the Constitution, however implausibly invoked, in order to give a veneer of principle and respectability to arguments that would otherwise seem hopelessly partisan and self-interested.

Indeed our advisory committee heard a great deal about the First Amendment, and about marginally relevant Supreme Court decisions, and about footnotes in lower-court opinions, but exceedingly little, in fact close to nothing, about the pragmatic and empirical issues on which many of our inquiries should have turned. If educational programming for children is required on CBS, NBC, and ABC, how many children will end up watching? What would they watch, or do, instead? Would educational programming help them? When educational programming is required, how much do the networks lose in dollars, and who pays the tab—advertisers, consumers, network employees, or someone else? What would be the real-world effects, on citizens and fund-raising alike, of free air time for candidates? Would such a requirement produce more substantial attention to serious issues? Would it reduce current pressures to raise money? What are the consequences of violence on television for both children and adults? Does television violence actually increase violence in the real world? Does it make children anxious in a way that creates genuine psychological harm? How, exactly, are the hard-of-hearing affected when captions are absent?

We can go further still. In the early part of the twentieth century, the due process clause of the Fourteenth Amendment was used to forbid government from regulating the labor market through, for example, minimum-wage and maximum-hour legislation.[10] The Court thought that the Constitution allowed workers and employers to set wages and hours as they "choose," without regulatory constraints. This is one of the most notorious periods in the entire history of the Supreme Court. Judicial use of the Fourteenth Amendment for these purposes is now almost universally agreed to have been a grotesque abuse of power. Nearly everyone now sees that the underlying questions were democratic ones, not ones for the judiciary. The Court should not have forbidden democratic experimentation that would, plausibly at least, have done considerable good.

In fact a central animating idea, in these now-discredited decisions, was that of consumer sovereignty—ensuring that government would not "interfere" with the terms produced by workers, employers, and consumers. (The word "interfere" has to be in quotation marks because the government was there already; the law of property, contract, and torts helps account for how much workers receive, how long they work, and how much consumers pay.) But in the early part of the twenty-first century, the First Amendment is serving a similar purpose in popular debate and sometimes in courts as well. All too often, it is being invoked on behalf of consumer sovereignty in a way that prevents the democratic process from resolving complex questions that turn on issues of fact and value that are ill-suited to judicial resolution.

To say this is not to say that the First Amendment should play no role at all. On the contrary, it imposes serious limits on what might be done. But some imaginable initiatives, responding to the problems I have discussed thus far, are fully consistent with the free-speech guarantee. Indeed, they would promote its highest aspirations.

Free Speech Is Not an Absolute

We can identify some flaws in the emerging view of the First Amendment by investigating the idea that the free-speech guarantee is "an absolute" in the specific sense that government may not regulate speech at all. This view plays a large role in public debate, and in some ways it is a salutary myth. Certainly the idea that the First Amendment is an absolute helps to discourage government from doing things that it ought not to do. At the same time it gives greater rhetorical power to critics of illegitimate government censorship. But a myth, even if in some ways salutary, remains a myth; and any publicly influential myth is likely to create many problems.

There should be no ambiguity on the point: free speech is not an absolute. We have seen that the government is allowed to regulate speech by imposing neutral rules of property law, telling would-be speakers that they may not have access to certain speech outlets. But this is only the beginning. Government is permitted to regulate computer viruses; unlicensed medical advice; attempted bribery; perjury; criminal conspiracies ("let's fix prices!"); threats to assassinate the president; blackmail ("I'll tell everyone the truth about your private life unless you give me $100"); criminal solicitation ("might you help me rob this bank?"); child pornography; violations of the copyright law; false advertising; purely verbal fraud ("this stock is worth $100,000"); and much more. Many of these forms of speech will not be especially harmful. A fruitless and doomed attempt to solicit someone to commit a crime, for example, is still criminal solicitation; a pitifully executed attempt at fraud is still fraud; sending a computer virus that doesn't actually work is still against the law.

Perhaps you disagree with the view, settled as a matter of current American law (and so settled in most other nations as well), that *all* of these forms of speech are unprotected by the free-speech principle. There is certainly a good argument that some current uses of the copyright law impose unnecessary and unjustifiable restrictions on free speech—and that these restrictions are especially troublesome in the era of the Internet.[11] But you are not a free-speech absolutist unless you believe that *each* of these forms of speech should be protected by that principle. And if this is your belief, you are a most unusual person (and you will have a lot of explaining to do).

This is not the place for a full account of the reach of the First Amendment of the American Constitution.[12] But it is plain that some distinctions must be made among different kinds of speech. It is important, for example, to distinguish between speech that can be shown to be quite harmful and speech that is relatively harmless. As a general rule, the government should not be able to regulate the latter. We might also distinguish between speech that bears on democratic self-government and speech that does not; certainly an especially severe burden should be placed on any government efforts to regulate political speech. Less simply, we might want to distinguish among the *kinds of lines* that government is drawing in terms of the likelihood that government is acting on the basis of illegitimate reasons (a point to which I will return).

These ideas could be combined in various ways, and indeed the fabric of modern free-speech law in America reflects one such combination. Despite the increasing prominence of the idea that the free-speech principle requires unrestricted choices by individual consumers, the Court continues to say that political speech receives the highest protection and that government may regulate (for example) commercial advertising, obscenity, and libel of ordinary people without meeting the especially stringent burden of justification required for political speech. But for present purposes, all that is necessary is to say that no one really believes that the free-speech principle, or the First Amendment, is an absolute. We should be very thankful for that.

The First Amendment and Democratic Deliberation

The fundamental concern of this book is to see how unlimited consumer options might compromise the preconditions of a system of freedom of expression, which include unchosen exposures and shared experiences. To understand the nature of this concern, we will make most progress if we insist that the free-speech principle should be read in light of the commitment to democratic deliberation. In other words, a central point of the free-speech principle is to carry out that commitment.

There are profound differences between those who emphasize consumer sovereignty and those who stress the democratic roots of the free-speech principle. For the latter, government efforts to regulate commercial advertising need not be objectionable. Certainly false and misleading commercial advertising is more readily subject to government control than false and misleading political speech. For those who believe that the free-speech principle has democratic foundations and is not fundamentally about consumer sovereignty, government regulation of television, radio, and the Internet is not always objectionable, at least so long as it is reasonably taken as an effort to promote democratic goals.

Suppose, for example, that government proposes to require television broadcasters (as indeed it now does) to provide three hours per week of educational programming for children. Or suppose that government decides to require television broadcasters to provide a certain amount of free air time for candidates for public office, or a certain amount of time on coverage of elections. For those who believe in consumer sovereignty, these requirements are quite troublesome, indeed they seem like a core violation of the free-speech guarantee. For those who associate the free-speech principle with democratic goals, these requirements are fully consistent with its highest aspirations. Indeed in many democracies— including, for example, Germany and Italy—it is well understood that the mass media can be regulated in the interest of improving democratic self-government.[13]

There is nothing novel or iconoclastic in the democratic conception of free speech. On the contrary, this conception lay at the heart of the original understanding of freedom of speech in America. In attacking the Alien and Sedition Acts, for example, James Madison claimed that they were inconsistent with the free-speech principle, which he linked explicitly to the American transformation of the concept of political sovereignty. In England, Madison noted, sovereignty was vested in the King. But "in the United States, the case is altogether different. The People, not the Government, possess the absolute sovereignty." It was on this foundation that any "Sedition Act" must be judged illegitimate. "[T]he right of electing the members of the Government constitutes . . . the essence of a free and responsible government," and "the value and efficacy of this right depends on the knowledge of the comparative merits and demerits of the candidates for the public trust."[14] It was for this reason that the power represented by a Sedition Act ought, "more than any other, to produce universal alarm; because it is levelled against that right of freely examining public characters and measures, and of free communication among the people thereon, which has ever been justly deemed the only effectual guardian of every other right."

In this way Madison saw "free communication among the people" not as an exercise in consumer sovereignty, in which speech was treated as a kind of commodity, but instead as a central part of self-government, the "only effectual guardian of every other right." Here Madison's conception of free speech was a close cousin of that of Justice Louis Brandeis, who . . . saw public discussion as a "political duty" and believed that the greatest menace to liberty would be "an inert people." A central part of the American constitutional tradition, then, places a high premium on speech that is critical to democratic processes, and centers the First Amendment on the goal of self-government. If history is our guide, it follows that government efforts to promote a well-functioning system of free expression, as through extensions of the public-forum idea, may well be acceptable. It also follows that government faces special burdens when it attempts to regulate political speech, burdens that are somewhat more severe than those it faces when it attempts to regulate other forms of speech.

American history is not the only basis for seeing the First Amendment in light of the commitment to democratic deliberation. The argument can be justified by basic principle as well.[15]

Consider the question whether the free-speech principle should be taken to forbid efforts to make communications markets work better from the democratic point of view. Return to our standard examples: educational programming for children, free air time for candidates for public office, closed-captioning for the hearing-impaired. (I am putting the Internet to one side for now because it raises distinctive questions.) Perhaps some of these proposals would do little or no good, or even harm; but from what standpoint should they be judged inconsistent with the free-speech guarantee?

If we believe that the Constitution gives all owners of speech outlets an unbridgeable right to decide what appears on "their" outlets, the answer is clear: government could require none of these things. But why should we believe that? If government is not favoring any point of view, and if it is really improving the operation of democratic processes, it is hard to find a legitimate basis for complaint. Indeed, the Supreme Court has expressly held that the owner of shopping centers—areas where a great deal of speech occurs—may be required to keep their property open for expressive activity.[16] Shopping centers are not television broadcasters; but if a democratic government is attempting to build on the idea of a public forum so as to increase the likelihood of exposure to and debate about diverse views, is there really a reasonable objection from the standpoint of free speech itself?

In a similar vein, it makes sense to say that speech that is political in character, in the sense that it relates to democratic self-government, cannot be regulated without an especially strong showing of government justification—and that commercial advertising, obscenity, and other speech that is not political in that sense can be regulated on the basis of a somewhat weaker government justification. I will not attempt here to offer a full defense of this idea, which of course raises some hard line-drawing problems. But in light of the importance of the question to imaginable government regulation of new technologies, there are three points that deserve brief mention.

First, an insistence that government's burden is greatest when it is regulating political speech emerges from a sensible understanding of government's own incentives. It is here that government is most likely to be acting on the basis of illegitimate considerations, such as self-protection, or giving assistance to powerful private groups. Government is least trustworthy when it is attempting to control speech that might harm its own interests; and when speech is political, government's own interests are almost certainly at stake. This is not to deny that government is often untrustworthy when it is regulating commercial speech, art, or other speech that does not relate to democratic self-government. But we have the strongest reasons to distrust government regulation when political issues are involved.

Second, an emphasis on democratic deliberation protects speech not only when regulation is most likely to be biased, but also when regulation is most likely to be harmful. If government regulates child pornography on the Internet or requires educational programming for children on television, it remains possible to invoke the normal democratic channels to protest these forms of regulation as ineffectual, intrusive, or worse. But when government forbids criticism of an ongoing war effort, the normal channels are foreclosed, in an important sense, by the very regulation at issue. Controls on public debate are uniquely damaging because they impair the process of deliberation that is a precondition for political legitimacy.

Third, an emphasis on democratic deliberation is likely to fit, far better than any alternative, with the most reasonable views about particular free-speech problems. However much we disagree about the most difficult speech problems, we are likely to believe that at a minimum, the free-speech principle protects political expression unless government has exceedingly strong grounds for regulating it. On the other hand, forms of speech such as perjury, attempted bribery, threats, unlicensed medical advice, and criminal solicitation are not likely to seem to be at the heart of the free-speech guarantee.

An understanding of this kind certainly does not answer all constitutional questions. It does not provide a clear test for distinguishing between political and nonpolitical speech, a predictably vexing question.[17] (To those who believe that the absence of a clear test is decisive against the distinction itself, the best response is that any alternative test will lead to line-drawing problems of its own. Because everyone agrees that some forms of speech are regulable, line drawing is literally inevitable. If you're skeptical, try to think of a test that eliminates problems of this kind.) It does not say whether and when government may regulate art or literature, sexually explicit speech, or libelous speech. In all cases, government is required to have a strong justification for regulating speech, political or not. But the approach I am defending does help to orient inquiry. When government is regulating false or fraudulent commercial advertising, libel of private persons, or child pornography, it is likely to be on firm ground. When government is attempting to control criminal conspiracy or speech that contains direct threats of violence aimed at particular people, it need not meet the stringent standards required for regulation of political dissent. What I have suggested here, without fully defending the point, is that a conception of the First Amendment that is rooted in democratic deliberation is an exceedingly good place to start.

Forms of Neutrality

None of this means that the government is permitted to regulate the emerging communications market however it wishes. To know whether to object to what government is doing, it is important to know what *kind* of line it is drawing.[18] There are three possibilities here.

- The government might be regulating speech in a way that is *neutral with respect to the content of the speech at issue*. This is the least objectionable way of regulating speech. For example, government is permitted to say that people may not use loudspeakers on the public streets after midnight or that speakers cannot have access to the front lawn immediately in front of the White House. A regulation of this kind imposes no controls on speech of any particular content. An Internet example: if government says that no one may use the website of CNN unless CNN gives permission, it is acting in a way that is entirely neutral with respect to speech content. So too with restrictions on sending computer viruses. The government bans the ILOVEYOU virus, but it also bans the IHATEYOU virus and the IAMINDIFFERENTTOYOU virus. What is against the law is sending viruses; their content is irrelevant.

- The government might regulate speech in a way that depends on the content of what is said, but without discriminating against any particular point of view. Suppose, for example, that government bans commercial speech on the subways but allows all other forms of speech on the subways. In the technical language of First Amendment law, this form of regulation is "content-based" but "viewpoint-neutral." Consider the old fairness doctrine, which required broadcasters to cover public issues and to allow speech by those with opposing views. Here the content of speech is highly relevant to what government is requiring, but no specific point of view is benefited or punished. The same can be said for the damages award against the Nuremburg Trials website; the content of the speech definitely mattered, but no particular point of view was being punished. The same award would be given against a website that treated pro-life people in the same way that the Nuremburg Trials treated doctors. In the same category would be a regulation saying that in certain areas, sexually explicit speech must be made inaccessible to children. In these cases, no lines are being drawn directly on the basis of point of view.

- The government might regulate a point of view that it fears or dislikes. This form of regulation is often called "viewpoint discrimination." Government might say, for example, that no one may criticize a decision to go to war, or that no one may claim that one racial group is inferior to another, or that no one may advocate violent overthrow of government. Here the government is singling out a point of view that it wants to ban, perhaps because it believes that the particular point of view is especially dangerous.

It makes sense to say that these three kinds of regulations should be treated differently, on the Internet as elsewhere. Viewpoint discrimination is the most objectionable. Content-neutral regulation is the least objectionable. If officials are regulating speech because of the point of view that it contains, their action is almost certainly unconstitutional. Government should not be allowed to censor arguments and positions merely because it fears or disapproves of them. If officials are banning a disfavored viewpoint, they ought to be required to show, at the very least, that the viewpoint really creates serious risks that cannot be adequately combated with more speech. Officials ought also be required to explain, in altogether convincing terms, why they are punishing one point of view and not its opposite.

A content-neutral regulation is at the opposite extreme, and such regulations are often legitimate. If the government has acted in a content-neutral way, courts usually do not and should not intervene, at least if the basic channels of communications remain open, and if government has a solid reason for the regulation. Of course a gratuitous or purposeless regulation must be struck down even if it is content-neutral. Suppose that government says that the public streets—or for that matter the Internet—may be used for expressive activity, but only between 8 p.m. and 8:30 p.m. If so, the neutrality of the regulation is no defense. But content-neutral regulations are frequently easy to justify; their very neutrality, and hence breadth, ensures that there is a good reason for them. The government is unlikely to ban expressive activity from 8:30 p.m. until 7:59 a.m. because so many people would resist the ban. The more likely regulation prohibits noisy demonstrations when people are trying to sleep, and there is nothing wrong with such prohibitions.

Now consider the intermediate case. When government is regulating in a way that is based on content but neutral with respect to point of view, there are two issues. The first is whether the particular line being drawn suggests lurking viewpoint discrimination—a hidden but detectable desire to ban a certain point of view. When it does, the law should probably be struck down. If government says that the most recent war, or abortion, may not be discussed on television, it is, as a technical matter, discriminating against a whole topic, not against any particular point of view; but there is pretty good reason to suspect government's motivations. A ban on discussion of the most recent war is probably an effort to protect the government from criticism.

The second and perhaps more fundamental issue is whether government is able to invoke strong, content-neutral grounds for engaging in this form of regulation. A ban on televised discussion of the most recent war should be struck down for this reason. The ban seems to have no real point, aside from forbidding certain points of view from being expressed. But the government has a stronger argument if, for example, it is requiring broadcasters to offer three hours of educational programming for children. In that case, it is trying to ensure that television serves children, an entirely legitimate interest.

Of course some cases may test the line between discrimination on the basis of content and discrimination on the basis of viewpoint. If government is regulating sexually explicit speech when that speech offends contemporary community standards, is it regulating on the basis of viewpoint or merely content? This is not an easy question, and many people have argued over the right answer. But an understanding of the three categories discussed here should be sufficient to make sense out of the bulk of imaginable free-speech challenges—and should provide some help in approaching the rest of them as well.

Penalties and Subsidies

Of course government can do a range of things to improve the system of free speech. Here it is important to make a further distinction, between "subsidies" on the one hand and "penalties" on the other. Government is likely to have a great deal of trouble when it is imposing penalties on speech. Such penalties are the model of what a system of free expression avoids. Government will have more room to maneuver if it is giving out selective subsidies. Public officials are not required to give money out to all speakers, and if they are giving money to some people but not to others, they may well be on firm ground. But the distinction between the penalties and subsidies is not always obvious.

The most conspicuous penalties are criminal and civil punishments. If government makes it a crime to libel people over the Internet or imposes civil fines on television broadcasters who do not provide free air time for candidates for office, it is punishing speech. The analysis of these penalties should depend on the considerations discussed thus far—whether political speech is involved, what kind of line the government is drawing, and so forth.

Somewhat trickier, but belonging in the same category, are cases in which government is *withdrawing a benefit to which people would otherwise be entitled* when the reason for the withdrawal is the government's view about the appropriate content of speech. Suppose, for example, that government gives an annual cash subsidy to all speakers of a certain kind—say, those networks that agree to provide educational programming for children. But suppose that government withdraws the subsidy from those networks that provide speech of which the government disapproves. Imagine, for example, that the government withdraws the subsidy from networks whose news shows are critical of the president. For the most part, these sorts of penalties should be analyzed in exactly the same way as criminal or civil punishment. When benefits are being withdrawn, just as when ordinary punishment is being imposed, government is depriving people of goods to which they would otherwise be entitled, and we probably have excellent reason to distrust its motives. If government responds to dissenters by taking away benefits that they would otherwise receive, it is violating the free-speech principle.

But a quite different issue is posed when government gives out selective subsidies to speakers. It often does this by, for example, funding some museums and artists but not others, and generally through the National Endowment for the Arts and the Public Broadcasting System. Imagine a situation in which government is willing to fund educational programming for children and pays a station to air that programming on Saturday morning—without also funding situation comedies or game shows. Or imagine that government funds a series of historical exhibits on the Civil War without also funding exhibits on the Vietnam War, or on World War II, or on the history of sex equality in America. What is most important here can be stated very simply: *under current law in the United States (and generally elsewhere), government is permitted to subsidize speech however it wishes.*[19]

Government often is a speaker, and as such, it is permitted to say whatever it likes. No one thinks that there is a problem if officials endorse one view and reject another. And if government seeks to use taxpayer funds to subsidize certain projects and enterprises, there is usually no basis for constitutional complaint. The only exception to this principle is that if government is allocating funds to private speakers in a way that discriminates on the basis of viewpoint, there might be a First Amendment problem.[20] The precise nature of this exception remains unclear. But it would certainly be possible to challenge, on constitutional grounds, a decision by government to fund the Republican Party website without also funding the Democratic Party website.

Of course this kind of discrimination goes far beyond anything that I shall be suggesting here. What is important, then, is that government has a great deal of room to maneuver insofar as it is not penalizing speech but instead subsidizing it.

A Restrained, Prudent First Amendment

This chapter has dealt with a range of free-speech issues, some of them briskly, and it is important not to lose the forest for the trees. My basic claims have been that the First Amendment in large part embodies a democratic ideal, that it should not be identified with the notion of consumer sovereignty, and that it is not an absolute. The core requirement of the free-speech principle is that with respect to politics, government must remain neutral among points of view. Content regulation is disfavored; viewpoint discrimination is almost always out of bounds. A key task is to ensure compliance with these requirements in the contemporary environment.

NOTES

1. For more detailed treatments, see Cass R. Sunstein, *Democracy and the Problem of Free Speech* (New York: Free Press, 1993); Alexander Meiklejohn, *Free Speech and its Relation to Self-Government* (New York: Harper, 1948); and C. Edwin Baker, *Human Liberty and Freedom of Speech* (New York: Oxford University Press, 1995).

2. *Virginia State Bd. of Pharmacy v. Virginia Citizens Consumer Council,* 425 U.S. 748 (1976).

3. *44 Liquormart, Inc. v. Rhode Island,* 517 U.S. 484 (1996).

4. See *Buckley v. Valeo,* 424 U.S. 1 (1979).

5. See, e.g., *Randall v. Sorrell,* 126 S. Ct. 2479 (2006); *McConnell v. FEC,* 540 U.S. 93 (2003).

6. See, e.g., Thomas Krattenmaker and L. A. Powe, "Converging First Amendment Principles for Converging Communications Media," *Yale LJ* 104 (1995): 1719, 1725.

7. For discussion, see Lessig, *Free Culture*; Benkler, *Wealth of Networks.*

8. The old case, allowing government action, is *Red Lion Broadcasting v. FCC,* 395 U.S. 367 (1969).

9. See, e.g., *Denver Area Educational Telecommunications Consortium, Inc. v. FCC,* 518 U.S. 727 (1996). The Court's caution is defended in Cass R. Sunstein, *One Case at a Time* (Cambridge, Mass.: Harvard University Press, 1999).

10. See *Lochner v. New York,* 198 U.S. 45 (1905).

11. See Lessig, *Free Culture*; Benkler, *Wealth of Networks.*

12. For an effort in this direction, see Sunstein, *Democracy and the Problem of Free Speech.*

13. See ibid., 77–81, for an overview.

14. James Madison, "Report on the Virginia Resolution, January 1800," in *Writings of James Madison* vol. 6, ed. Gaillard Hunt (New York: Putnam, 1906), 385–401.

15. I draw here on Sunstein, *Democracy and the Problem of Free Speech,* 132–36.

16. *Pruneyard Shopping Center v. Robins,* 447 U.S. 74 (1980).

17. I attempt to answer it in Sunstein, *Democracy and the Problem of Free Speech,* 121–65.

18. The best discussion is Geoffrey Stone, "Content Regulation and the First Amendment," *Wm. & Mary L. Rev.* 25 (1983): 189.

19. See *Rumsfeld v. Forum for Academic and Institutional Rights,* 126 S. Ct. 1297 (2006).

20. The murkiness of current law is illustrated by the Court's decisions in ibid., in which the Court unanimously upheld the Solomon Amendment, withdrawing federal funding from educational institutions that refused to provide equal access to the United States military; and in *National Endowment for the Arts v. Finley,* 524 U.S. 569 (1998), in which a sharply divided Court upheld a statute directing the NEA, when making funding decisions, to consider "general standards of decency and respect for the diverse beliefs and values of the American public." In the NEA case, the Court suggested that it would have ruled differently if the statute had discriminated on the basis of viewpoint.

5-2

A Liberal Vision of U.S. Family Law in 2020

William N. Eskridge, Jr.

*States and other western countries are adopting multiple variations of part-
ner commitments. Eskridge identifies six different kinds of "marriage" and
considers their implications for family law. Specifically, each creates specific
issues that remain to be resolved when it comes to adoption and separation.
In this thoughtful essay, Yale law professor William Eskridge cautions policy
to go slowly and not rely wholly on the courts to define the responsibilities
these new forms of unions involve.*

FAMILY LAW IN the United States underwent a revolution in the twentieth century. Before the revolution, family law focused on marriage as the only legitimate situs for love, sex, and children, while at the same time it defined marital
eligibility narrowly and its inescapable duties broadly. In 1900, for example, it
was illegal almost everywhere in the United States for two adults to enjoy sexual
intercourse or to cohabit sexually unless they were married to one another; children born outside of marriage were legal as well as social bastards.

To enjoy the advantages of marriage, Americans were required to accept
obligations of support and sexual fidelity, as well as other duties that could not
be waived as a matter of law; these obligations were usually for life, as divorce
was difficult in 1900. Ironically, adults wanting to legitimate their sexual activities or children by marrying were often not permitted to do so; the law prohibited the marriage of many disabled people, persons of different races, and
same-sex couples.[1]

American family life and its norms changed in the twentieth century. Family
law has, on the whole, liberalized, offering adults a lot more choices. First,
Americans now enjoy the freedom to find love, sex, and family outside of marriage. Not only do states allow adults to have nonmarital sex, but they provide
legal methods for regulating cohabiting relationships and protecting children
born outside of marriage. Second, Americans can create families of choice. Most
adults in this country enjoy substantial freedom to marry the person they choose,
freely adopt children, and even engage third parties to assist in childbearing.

Source: William N. Eskridge, Jr., "A Liberal Vision of U.S. Family Law in 2020," in *The Constitution in 2020*,
eds. Jack M. Balkin and Reva B. Siegel (New York: Oxford University Press, 2009), 245–254.

Third, Americans unhappy with their marriages have escape options. The old rule of marriage-for-life has been supplanted by essentially no-fault divorce across the United States.[2]

What connection does the Constitution have with the legal revolution in U.S. family law? Surprisingly little. State legislatures and judges have accomplished most of the liberalization of U.S. family law, with the Supreme Court playing mostly a cleaning-up role. The most salient principles have been *autonomy* (pro-choice) and *equality* (inclusion). While these principles have taken the positive law quite far, they are now under siege in debates about lesbian and gay families. Embodying both autonomy and equality principles, same-sex marriage has been a piñata for cultural conservatives. Liberals should respond with a third principle supporting lesbian and gay, as well as straight, households: responsible commitment. This principle should become the third leg of a liberal constitutionalism that offers couples of all orientations a menu of relationship choices, while at the same time encouraging committed relationships, including adults' responsibility toward children.

Liberal Principles: Autonomy, Equal Treatment, Responsible Commitment

The autonomy and equality principles have worked together to liberalize U.S. family law. Women's equality as partners in relationships, rather than their roles as mothers and homemakers under the governance of husbands, was a prerequisite to a conception of the family as entailing the partnership of autonomous adults. Once policymakers viewed the family this way, the autonomy principle has supported expanded eligibility rules, greater sexual freedom within and outside of marriage, and broader exit options. Equality was front and center for the momentous struggle to recognize different-race marriages.

Liberals should recognize the limits of these principles as traditionally applied. For example, the autonomy principle supports the freedom of infertile couples to have resort to alternative reproductive technologies and of same-sex couples to raise children within their households, but it does not help society decide how to resolve disputes when those households dissolve. As the Supreme Court has ruled, the autonomy principle assures priority for the blood parent, but that often runs athwart the best interests of the child. In many cases, say social psychologists, the child suffers if wrenched from his not-related caregiver. Shouldn't those interests be important?

When the autonomy principle imposes third-party costs, especially upon children, it loses much of its moral authority. This critique applies to some liberalizations that have already been accomplished, like no-fault divorce. From case studies and preliminary empirical examinations, scholars argue that parental divorce has terrible effects upon children. Feminists criticize easy divorce on equality grounds, as it typically leaves wives worse off than before, but the effect-on-children criticism cuts more deeply. The most vulnerable persons, with no direct say in the parental decision to divorce, bear sometimes devastating consequences. Those consequences are primarily psychic, although they also include the economic hardships following many divorces.[3]

Another criticism is that the liberalization of family law has altered the nature of intimate relationships. Marriage is a treasured institution because its committed-for-life culture is a training ground for altruism; mutually committed adults sacrifice temporary pleasures for one another and for the welfare of the family. A society which validates cohabiting relationships, tolerates adultery, and permits no-fault divorce is a society that has moved away from a traditionalist philosophy— demanding self-sacrifice, permanent mutual commitment, and the family as a collective unity—toward a consumerist philosophy of self-satisfaction, mutual cooperation, and the family as a collection of pleasure-seeking individuals. Ours is a society where sex, relationships, and even children are morphing into hedonic goods, that is, sources of pleasure and sites of consumer choice.

This critique has come out of the closet during the same-sex marriage debate. Same-sex marriage is a liberal gimme. If two women love each other and want to commit to one another for life, both the autonomy and equality premises suggest that the state should recognize their relationship as a marriage—yet this obvious resolution is not the one that U.S. law has thus far taken. Why not? Although much opposition to same-sex marriage is inspired by antihomosexual prejudice and irrational stereotyping, not all of it is. Many cultural conservatives argue that same-sex marriage will be a fatal tipping point for the institution, its Maginot Line. Once that line is crossed, choice will be all that's left in marriage; it will lose its ability to inspire partners to make sacrifices for one another and the children they are raising.[4]

In most of the United States, conservative arguments like this have sent liberals running for cover, but same-sex marriage offers liberals a third principle that complements the ones that swept the field in the twentieth century. Lesbian and gay couples who have been leading the same-sex marriage parade in the last decade are not hedonistic home wreckers. Rather, they are responsible adults committed to one another and to the children that about one-fourth of the couples are raising. Same-sex marriage is not about selfish choices, for Americans today can enjoy sex outside of marriage with no legal worries and few social sanctions. Same-sex marriage is all about *responsible commitment*. The state should be encouraging that norm for same-sex as well as different-sex couples, at the same time that it should allow considerable choice in family recognition.

What is most distinctive about civil marriage is the legal duties it entails. Couples do not receive most of the benefits of marriage unless they accept its obligations. Civil marriage reinforces the long-term nature of the couple's interpersonal commitment. Deciding to get married requires conversations between the partners about that commitment, and marriage is a public signal to family, friends, and coworkers that the partners have undertaken these commitments. Liberals should value the commitment feature of marriage and childrearing. The mutual altruism it entails enriches the lives of the partners, is beneficial for their children, and bears significant social insurance and other benefits for the larger community. The case for same-sex marriage then becomes a synthesis of three liberal principles: Like different-sex couples (equality), same-sex couples ought to have the choice (autonomy) to accept the duties as well as the rights of marriage and, increasingly for lesbian and gay couples, childrearing (responsible commitment).

In same-sex marriage, the gay rights movement offers progress constitutionalism a cutting-edge issue where it can again prove the worthiness of liberal values *and* offers liberalism an opportunity to deepen its values. To be sure, public opinion remains unpersuaded of the case for same-sex marriage. Popular hostility to a norm often triggers a race by progressives to the U.S. Supreme Court to constitutionalize their norm. Progressives should *not* follow such a strategy for same-sex marriage. What we have learned from family law evolution in the United States and the same-sex marriage experience all over the world is the best way to proceed is incrementally, legislatively, and locally.[5]

In the near future, the main audience for constitutional argument will be state judges in jurisdictions (mainly in the Northeast and on the Pacific Coast now) where grassroots movements have prepared citizens to accept the legitimacy of lesbian and gay families. In such states, judges can place equal marriage rights on the public agenda, can reverse the burden of legislative inertia, and can sometimes (as the Massachusetts Supreme Court did in 2003–2004) create conditions under which irresponsible predictions made by gay rights opponents can be falsified. By 2020, the U.S. Constitution ought to be ripe for a national constitutional requirement that states must provide some legal structure for same-sex relationships (e.g., marriages, civil unions, domestic partnerships).

Toward a Menu of Equally Available Relationship Options

In most states, by 2020, marriage will no longer be the only option for different-sex as well as same-sex couples. Adults in Western countries have demanded more choices within their romantic relationships. Responding to this demand, postindustrial Western nations have already legalized sexual cohabitation outside of marriage, and most grant some legal rights and duties to cohabiting couples.

The same-sex marriage debate has generated yet more new legal institutions, which are noted below. What is emerging is a regime where the state will offer a menu of options for couples desiring state recognition of their relationships.

I do not know what the menu will look like in 2020, and the options will vary by nation or state. Here is a stylized list of options, ordered from least to most like "traditional" marriage:[6]

1. *Domestic partnership.* By signing a form identifying a significant other (of any sex), many corporate and municipal employees can add that person to the health care, life insurance, and other benefits provided by the employer to married employees. Being someone's domestic partner typically signals a level of commitment only slightly greater than being a close friend.

2. *Cohabitation.* Sexual cohabitation suggests greater commitment and interdependence, which the state both rewards and obligates. Thus, a cohabitation regime will generally impose duties of support on the couple, especially if there is specialization within the household. European and Canadian laws also provide legal presumptions of joint property ownership and tenancy, family and bereavement leave, and sometimes wrongful death claims for cohabiting partners.

3. *Cohabitation-plus regimes, reciprocal beneficiaries* and *pactes civils* respectively. These new forms presume a greater level of commitment but allow dissolution through a summary process. In addition to duties of mutual support, the state provides a wider array of unitive rights, namely, rules treating the partners as coupled and granting them financial and other benefits that reflect their unity as to matters like health care decisions when one partner is incapacitated.

4. *Registered partnerships (Scandinavia) or civil unions (New England).* Under these new legal forms, the state provides most of the legal rights and duties of marriage, but without the name and its interjurisdictional portability. In addition to mutual support and fidelity and with the added difficulty of legal divorce proceedings in the event of a breakup, the state will reinforce family ties by giving the partners mutual rights over their adopted or biological children.

5. *Marriage.* The state provides all the traditional rights and benefits, but with exit easier (albeit not costless) through no-fault divorce. In addition to the cultural and religious significance the name carries with it, "marriage" is much more likely to be recognized in other jurisdictions.

6. *Covenant marriage.* Some U.S. jurisdictions offer an option that; is more like traditional marriage, because it is harder to exit. Louisiana's covenant marriage law requires husbands and wives in unhappy marriages to go through compulsory mediation and longer waiting period before they can divorce. This is the closest any state now comes to "traditional" marriage-for-life.

No U.S. state or European nation offers this complete menu of options, and only a handful of jurisdictions offers same-sex couples the same menu as that available to different-sex couples. The menu tells us where we are going. Its main normative virtue is that it respects people's autonomy. Couples choose among an array of state regulatory regimes keyed to the level of commitment they want to signal or create. So couples uncertain if they want to live together permanently might choose domestic partnership or cohabitation regimes, which are easy to exit. Committed couples will choose civil union or marriage, which is harder to exit but offers a larger array of legal rights and benefits. Couples rearing children will also often choose either marriage or civil union. In my view, the menu regime must also be equally accessible to same-sex perhaps slowly, for the reasons suggested earlier.

An objection to the emerging menu is that it might derogate from the principle of responsible commitment. A menu that includes cohabitation-plus and civil union options will siphon more couples away from marriage, a signal that some would take to be an abandonment of altruistic, committed relationships. Indeed, increasing numbers of scholars argue that the state should get out of the marriage business entirely and just offer couples civil unions or domestic partnerships.[7]

The effect of such a menu on committed relationships remains to be seen. A menu that offers civil union *and* marriage to lesbian, gay, and straight couples is in some respects more in line with responsible commitment than a regime that excludes loving same-sex couples as well as couples suspicious of the patriarchal, exclusionary, and sectarian features of marriage. Moreover, a menu that also includes covenant marriage is a move toward *greater* commitment, not less. Relatedly, something like the menu sketched above might facilitate communication about the precise expectations in a relationship. A person deciding how much to invest in a relationship receives valuable information when her romantic partner tells her that she or he is willing to cohabit but not marry. *Responsible* commitment means not rushing into marriage thoughtlessly, and commitment itself might flourish in a regime that allows couples to experiment.

The Challenges of the New World of Mix-and-Match Parenting

With no-fault divorce, nonmarital children, and adoption commonplace rather than exceptional, the typical family is no longer one where two spouses owe marital duties to one another, and both owe parental duties to the children. Person A, for example, may be the cohabiting partner or spouse of person B, with whom he is raising child C, conceived with the aid of person D, a surrogate or a sperm donor; A may also be the stepparent (with B) of child E, have joint custody (with former spouse F) of child G, and have support obligations for child H, conceived in a nonmarital relationship with person I. This fracturing of responsibilities is a consequence of freedom of choice (overwhelmingly pre-ferred by straight Americans), but the costs of it are borne primarily by depen-dent partners and children. Those costs include insufficient nurturing and financial support for those partners and children. What I call *mix-and match par-enting* also may be exacting psychological and other costs on nondependent part-ners, some of whom may feel regret, confusion, or role overload because of their multiple and fractured responsibilities.[8]

The decline of the nuclear (mom, dad, and biological kids) family generates understandable anxiety among Americans, for they see that their own desired regime may be having a lamentable effect not only on children's tangible wel-fare, but upon the family as a refuge of altruism and mutual support. Liberal constitutionalism should be responsive to this anxiety, but not in ways that dis-respect choice and equality norms without evidence that particular choices actu-ally undermine responsible commitment.

On the one hand, liberal constitutionalism should support rights of lesbian and gay couples to adopt children and to bear children within their relationships, typically through artificial insemination (for lesbian couples) and surrogacy (for gay couples). State discriminations against lesbian and gay families should be subject to skeptical scrutiny, for they typically reflect prejudice and stereotypes rather than the genuine needs of children. Generally, liberal constitutionalism should be open to new reproductive technologies, though liberals should be attentive to issues of free choice and inequality that present themselves in sur-rogacy. Indeed, a liberal approach to surrogacy would provide useful informa-tion to the participants, create contract default rules, and perhaps insist upon mandatory rules, such as waiting periods, to minimize regret.

On the other hand, the evidence is strong that children suffer when their par-ents break up. This is certainly a cost of no-fault divorce, and perhaps of cohabi-tation regimes as well. Liberal constitutionalism should emphasize the creation and strict (interstate) enforcement of fair support formulas, especially as they relate to the support of children. The liberal agenda might also borrow some ideas from covenant marriage: Without making divorce substantively harder to achieve, the state should require family counseling and perhaps waiting periods before spouses with children end their marriages.

Anxiety about nonmarital children fuels opposition to same-sex marriage. Opponents correctly perceive that there is a correlation between high rates of nonmarital children in a society and its willingness to recognize same-sex unions, but incorrectly claim that same-sex marriage then correlates with *and causes* the family instability that harms children. The data from Scandinavia refute the lat-ter claim. Moreover, because approximately one-fourth of U.S. lesbian and gay couples are rearing children within their households, state recognition of their committed unions (including divorce requirements that make it harder to split up) could benefit rather than harm their children.[9]

Liberals should support Martha Fineman's suggestion that family law devote more resources to support parent-child relationships. The Family Medical Leave Act of 1993 requires employers to give parents time off from their jobs for child care and other family responsibilities. Liberals should consider nationalizing the California approach, which requires that such leaves be paid. This is a start. A liberal family law should consider other ways to support working-class and poor parents and to educate their children more effectively.[10]

Like same-sex marriage, little of the positive liberal agenda for children can or should be imposed by judges interpreting the U.S. Constitution. (State judges interpreting state constitutions, on the other hand, are more likely to insist on same-sex marriage, civil unions, and nondiscriminatory adoption rights.) The primary role for federal judges is cleaning up clearly outdated discrimination that remains from earlier eras. A prime candidate is Florida's blanket exclusion of lesbians, gay men, and bisexuals from adoption. This exclusion originated in the political hysteria accompanying Anita Bryant's antihomosexual Dade County campaign in 1977, rests upon no serious evidence regarding lesbian and gay capabilities, and in practice operates *against* children's interests, as revealed in 2004 litigation.[11] No other state has an adoption restriction that explicitly targets lesbian and gay parents, and it is likely that the Florida exclusion will not survive, in its present from, in 2020. Nor will presumptions survive against lesbian and gay parents involved in child custody disputes with former spouses. Found mainly in the southern states that long discriminated against different-race couples, these antigay discriminations are objectionable mainly because they violate the responsible commitment features of the liberal agenda for the Constitution in 2020.[12]

NOTES

1. See generally Nancy F. Cott, *Public Vows: A History of Marriage and the Nation* (2000).

2. See generally Jana B. Singer, *The Privatization of Family Law,* 1992 Wis. L. Rev. 1443–1568.

3. See, e.g., Sara McLanahan and Gary D. Sandefur, *Growing Up with a Single Parent: What Hurts, What Helps* (1994); Judith Wallerstein et al., *The Unexpected Legacy of Divorce: A 25 Year Landmark Study* (2000).

4. See, e.g., Maggie Gallagher, "A Reality Waiting to Happen," in Lynn D. Wardle et al., eds., *Marriage and Same-Sex Unions: A Debate* 11-12 (2003).

5. On the incremental process by which states have come to recognize same-sex marriages and unions, see William N. Eskridge, Jr., *Equality Practice: Civil Unions and the Future of Gay Rights* (2002); Robert Wintemute and Mads Andenaes, eds., *Legal Recognition of Same-Sex Partnerships: A Study of National, European, and International Law* (2001); Kees Waaldijk, *More or*

Less Together: Levels of Legal Consequences of Marriage, Cohabitation, and Registered Partnership for Different-Sex and Same-Sex Partners: A Comparative Study of Nine European Countries (2005).

6. The menu of options is drawn from Eskridge, *Equality Practice*, 121–26.

7. E.g., Brenda Cossman and Bruce Ryder, *The Legal Regulation of Adult Personal Relationships: Evaluating Policy Objectives and Legal Options in Federal Legislation* (May 2000), available at www.lcc.gc.ca/research_project/oo_regulations_i-en.asp.

8. See Katharine Bartlett, *Rethinking Parenthood as an Exclusive Status*, 70 Va. L. Rev. (1984).

9. On the evidence that the recognition of same-sex marriages or unions has no depressive effect upon different-sex marriages, see William N. Eskridge, Jr., and Darren R. Spedale, *Gay Marriage: For Better or for Worse? What We've Learned from the Evidence*, chap. 5 (2006).

10. See Martha Albertson Fineman, *The Neutered Mother, the Sexual Family, and Other Twentieth Century Tragedies* (1995).

11. *Lofton v. Secretary Dep't of Children & Social Services*, 377 F. 3d 1275 (11th Cir. 2004) (Barkett, J., dissenting from denial of rehearing en banc)

12. See *Bottoms v. Bottoms*, 457 S.E. 2d 102 (1995) (Keenan, J., dissenting) (powerfully arguing against the validity of antilesbian presumption in custody cases).

5-3

Roe v. Wade

Supreme Court of the United States

To what extent can rights perceived by the people, but not explicitly protected by the Constitution, be recognized as constitutional principles by the courts? Judges often disagree on where the lines should be drawn. This question arose in Roe v. Wade, *the Supreme Court's 1973 decision on abortion. The specific issue was, does the Constitution embrace a woman's right to terminate her pregnancy by abortion? A 5–4 majority on the Supreme Court held that a woman's right to an abortion fell within the right to privacy protected by the Fourteenth Amendment. The decision gave a woman autonomy over the pregnancy during the first trimester and defined different levels of state interest for the second and third trimesters. The Court's ruling affected the laws of forty-six states. Justice Harry Blackmun, arguing for the majority, insisted that the Court had recognized such a right in a long series of cases and that it was appropriate to extend the right to a woman's decision to terminate a pregnancy. In a dissenting opinion, Justice William Rehnquist, who later became chief justice, argued that because abortion was not considered an implicit right at the time the Fourteenth Amendment, states must be allowed to regulate it.*

ROE ET AL. V. WADE, DISTRICT ATTORNEY OF DALLAS COUNTY

410 U.S. 113

APPEAL FROM THE UNITED STATES DISTRICT COURT FOR THE NORTHERN DISTRICT OF TEXAS.

Decided January 22, 1973.

MR. JUSTICE BLACKMUN delivered the opinion of the Court.

This Texas federal appeal and its Georgia companion, *Doe v. Bolton, post,* . . . present constitutional challenges to state criminal abortion legislation. The Texas statutes under attack here are typical of those that have been in effect in many States for approximately a century. . . .

We forthwith acknowledge our awareness of the sensitive and emotional nature of the abortion controversy, of the vigorous opposing views, even among physicians, and of the deep and seemingly absolute convictions that the subject inspires. One's philosophy, one's experiences, one's exposure to the raw edges of human existence, one's religious training, one's attitudes toward life and family and their values, and the moral standards one establishes and seeks to observe, are all likely to influence and to color one's thinking and conclusions about abortion. . . .

Our task, of course, is to resolve the issue by constitutional measurement, free of emotion and of predilection. We seek earnestly to do this, and, because we do, we have inquired into, and in this opinion place some emphasis upon, medical and medical-legal history and what that history reveals about man's attitudes toward the abortion procedure over the centuries. We bear in mind, too, Mr. Justice Holmes' admonition in his now-vindicated dissent in *Lochner v. New York,* 198 U. S. 45, 76 (1905):

> [The Constitution] is made for people of fundamentally differing views, and the accident of our finding certain opinions natural and familiar or novel and even shocking ought not to conclude our judgment upon the question whether statutes embodying them conflict with the Constitution of the United States.

. . . Jane Roe [a pseudonym used to protect the identity of the woman], a single woman who was residing in Dallas County, Texas, instituted this federal action in March 1970 against the District Attorney of the county. She sought a declaratory judgment that the Texas criminal abortion statutes were unconstitutional on their face, and an injunction restraining the defendant from enforcing the statutes.

Roe alleged that she was unmarried and pregnant; that she wished to terminate her pregnancy by an abortion "performed by a competent, licensed physician, under safe clinical conditions"; that she was unable to get a "legal" abortion in Texas because her life did not appear to be threatened by the continuation of her pregnancy; and that she could not afford to travel to another jurisdiction in order to secure a legal abortion under safe conditions. She claimed that the Texas statutes were unconstitutionally vague and that they abridged her right of personal privacy, protected by the First, Fourth, Fifth, Ninth, and Fourteenth Amendments. By an amendment to her complaint Roe purported to sue "on behalf of herself and all other women" similarly situated. . . .

The principal thrust of appellant's attack on the Texas statutes is that they improperly invade a right, said to be possessed by the pregnant woman, to choose to terminate her pregnancy. Appellant would discover this right in the concept of personal "liberty" embodied in the Fourteenth Amendment's Due Process Clause; or in personal, marital, familial, and sexual privacy said to be protected by the Bill of Rights or its penumbras, . . . or among those rights reserved to the people by the Ninth Amendment. . . .

It perhaps is not generally appreciated that the restrictive criminal abortion laws in effect in a majority of States today are of relatively recent vintage. Those laws, generally proscribing abortion or its attempt at any time during pregnancy except when necessary to preserve the pregnant woman's life, are not of ancient or even of common-law origin. Instead, they derive from statutory changes effected, for the most part, in the latter half of the 19th century. . . .

It is thus apparent that at common law, at the time of the adoption of our Constitution, and throughout the major portion of the 19th century, abortion was viewed with less disfavor than under most American statutes currently in effect. Phrasing it another way, a woman enjoyed a substantially broader right to terminate a pregnancy than she does in most States today. At least with respect to the early stage of pregnancy, and very possibly without such a limitation, the opportunity to make this choice was present in this country well into the 19th century. Even later, the law continued for some time to treat less punitively an abortion procured in early pregnancy. . . .

The Constitution does not explicitly mention any right of privacy. In a line of decisions, however, going back perhaps as far as *Union Pacific R. Co. v. Botsford* . . . (1891), the Court has recognized that a right of personal privacy, or a guarantee of certain areas or zones of privacy, does exist under the Constitution. In varying contexts, the Court or individual Justices have, indeed, found at least the roots of that right in the First Amendment . . . ; in the Fourth and Fifth Amendments . . . ; in the penumbras of the Bill of Rights . . . ; in the Ninth Amendment . . . ; or in the concept of liberty guaranteed by the first section of the Fourteenth Amendment. . . . These decisions make it clear that only personal rights that can be deemed "fundamental" or "implicit in the concept of ordered liberty," . . . are included in this guarantee of personal privacy. They also make it clear that the right has some extension to activities relating to marriage . . . ; procreation . . . ; contraception . . . ; family relationships . . . ; and child rearing and education. . . .

This right of privacy, whether it be founded in the Fourteenth Amendment's concept of personal liberty and restrictions upon state action, as we feel it is, or, as the District Court determined, in the Ninth Amendment's reservation of rights to the people, is broad enough to encompass a woman's decision whether or not to terminate her pregnancy. The detriment that the State would impose upon the pregnant woman by denying this choice altogether is apparent. Specific and direct harm medically diagnosable even in early pregnancy may be involved.

Maternity, or additional offspring, may force upon the woman a distressful life and future. Psychological harm may be imminent. Mental and physical health may be taxed by child care. There is also the distress, for all concerned, associated with the unwanted child, and there is the problem of bringing a child into a family already unable, psychologically and otherwise, to care for it. In other cases, as in this one, the additional difficulties and continuing stigma of unwed motherhood may be involved. All these are factors the woman and her responsible physician necessarily will consider in consultation.

On the basis of elements such as these, appellant and some *amici* argue that the woman's right is absolute and that she is entitled to terminate her pregnancy at whatever time, in whatever way, and for whatever reason she alone chooses. With this we do not agree. Appellant's arguments that Texas either has no valid interest at all in regulating the abortion decision, or no interest strong enough to support any limitation upon the woman's sole determination, are unpersuasive. The Court's decisions recognizing a right of privacy also acknowledge that some state regulation in areas protected by that right is appropriate. As noted above, a State may properly assert important interests in safeguarding health, in maintaining medical standards, and in protecting potential life. At some point in pregnancy, these respective interests become sufficiently compelling to sustain regulation of the factors that govern the abortion decision. The privacy right involved, therefore, cannot be said to be absolute. . . .

We, therefore, conclude that the right of personal privacy includes the abortion decision, but that this right is not unqualified and must be considered against important state interests in regulation. . . .

Where certain "fundamental rights" are involved, the Court has held that regulation limiting these rights may be justified only by a "compelling state interest," . . . and that legislative enactments must be narrowly drawn to express only the legitimate state interests at stake. . . .

In the recent abortion cases . . . courts have recognized these principles. Those striking down state laws have generally scrutinized the State's interests in protecting health and potential life, and have concluded that neither interest justified broad limitations on the reasons for which a physician and his pregnant patient might decide that she should have an abortion in the early stages of pregnancy. Courts sustaining state laws have held that the State's determinations to protect health or prenatal life are dominant and constitutionally justifiable. . . .

The District Court held that the appellee [the district attorney, defending the Texas law] failed to meet his burden of demonstrating that the Texas statute's infringement upon Roe's rights was necessary to support a compelling state interest, and that, although the appellee presented "several compelling justifications for state presence in the area of abortions," the statutes outstripped these justifications and swept "far beyond any areas of compelling state interest." 314 F. Supp., at 1222–1223. Appellant and appellee both contest that holding. Appellant, as has been indicated, claims an absolute right that bars any state imposition of criminal penalties in the area. Appellee argues that the State's determination to recognize and protect prenatal life from and after conception constitutes a compelling state interest. As noted above, we do not agree fully with either formulation.

A. The appellee and certain *amici* argue that the fetus is a "person" within the language and meaning of the Fourteenth Amendment. In support of this, they outline at length and in detail the well-known facts of fetal development. If this suggestion of personhood is established, the appellant's case, of course, collapses, for the fetus' right to life would then be guaranteed specifically by the Amendment. The appellant conceded as much on reargument. On the other hand, the appellee conceded on reargument that no case could be cited that holds that a fetus is a person within the meaning of the Fourteenth Amendment.

The Constitution does not define "person" in so many words. Section 1 of the Fourteenth Amendment contains three references to "person." The first, in defining "citizens," speaks of "persons born or naturalized in the United States." The word also appears both in the Due Process Clause and in the Equal Protection Clause. "Person" is used in other places in the Constitution: in the listing of qualifications for Representatives and Senators, Art. I, § 2, cl. 2, and § 3, cl. 3; in the Apportionment Clause, Art. I, § 2, cl. 3; in the Migration and Importation provision, Art. I, § 9, cl. 1; in the Emolument Clause, Art. I, § 9, cl. 8; in the Electors provisions, Art. II, § 1, cl. 2, and the superseded cl. 3; in the provision outlining qualifications for the office of President, Art. II, § 1, cl. 5; in the Extradition provisions, Art. IV, § 2, cl. 2, and the superseded Fugitive Slave Clause 3; and in the Fifth, Twelfth, and Twenty-second Amendments, as well as in §§ 2 and 3 of the Fourteenth Amendment. But in nearly all these instances, the use of the word is such that it has application only postnatally. None indicates, with any assurance, that it has any possible pre-natal application.

All this, together with our observation, *supra,* that throughout the major portion of the 19th century prevailing legal abortion practices were far freer than they are today, persuades us that the word "person," as used in the Fourteenth Amendment, does not include the unborn. This is in accord with the results reached in those few cases where the issue has been squarely presented. . . . Indeed, our decision in *United States v. Vuitch,* 402 U. S. 62 (1971), inferentially is to the same effect, for we there would not have indulged in statutory interpretation favorable to abortion in specified circumstances if the necessary consequence was the termination of life entitled to Fourteenth Amendment protection.

This conclusion, however, does not of itself fully answer the contentions raised by Texas, and we pass on to other considerations.

B. The pregnant woman cannot be isolated in her privacy. She carries an embryo and, later, a fetus, if one accepts the medical definitions of the developing young in the human uterus. . . . As we have intimated above, it is reasonable and appropriate for a State to decide that at some point in time another interest, that of health of the mother or that of potential human life, becomes significantly involved. The woman's privacy is no longer sole and any right of privacy she possesses must be measured accordingly.

Texas urges that, apart from the Fourteenth Amendment, life begins at conception and is present throughout pregnancy, and that, therefore, the State has a compelling interest in protecting that life from and after conception. We need not resolve the difficult question of when life begins. When those trained in the respective disciplines of medicine, philosophy, and theology are unable to arrive at any consensus, the judiciary, at this point in the development of man's knowledge, is not in a position to speculate as to the answer.

It should be sufficient to note briefly the wide divergence of thinking on this most sensitive and difficult question. There has always been strong support for the view that life does not begin until live birth. This was the belief of the Stoics. It appears to be the predominant, though not the unanimous, attitude of the Jewish faith. It may be taken to represent also the position of a large segment of the Protestant community, insofar as that can be ascertained; organized groups that have taken a formal position on the abortion issue have generally regarded abortion as a matter for the conscience of the individual and her family. As we have noted, the common law found greater significance in quickening. Physicians and their scientific colleagues have regarded that event with less interest and have tended to focus either upon conception, upon live birth, or upon the interim point at which the fetus becomes "viable," that is, potentially able to live outside the mother's womb, albeit with artificial aid. Viability is usually placed at about seven months (28 weeks) but may occur earlier, even at 24 weeks. The Aristotelian theory of "mediate animation," that held sway throughout the Middle Ages and the Renaissance in Europe, continued to be official Roman Catholic dogma until the 19th century, despite opposition to this "ensoulment" theory from those in the Church who would recognize the existence of life from the moment of conception. The latter is now, of course, the official belief of the Catholic Church. As one brief *amicus* discloses, this is a view strongly held by many non-Catholics as well, and by many physicians. Substantial problems for precise definition of this view are posed, however, by new embryological data that purport to indicate that conception is a "process" over time, rather than an event, and by new medical techniques such as menstrual extraction, the "morning-after" pill, implantation of embryos, artificial insemination, and even artificial wombs. . . .

In view of all this, we do not agree that, by adopting one theory of life, Texas may override the rights of the pregnant woman that are at stake. We repeat, however, that the State does have an important and legitimate interest in preserving and protecting the health of the pregnant woman, whether she be a resident of the State or a nonresident who seeks medical consultation and treatment there, and that it has still *another* important and legitimate interest in protecting the potentiality of human life. These interests are separate and distinct. Each grows in substantiality as the woman approaches term and, at a point during pregnancy, each becomes "compelling." . . .

The judgment of the District Court as to intervenor Hallford is reversed, and Dr. Hallford's complaint in intervention is dismissed. In all other respects, the judgment of the District Court is affirmed. Costs are allowed to the appellee.

It is so ordered.

MR. JUSTICE REHNQUIST, dissenting.

The Court's opinion brings to the decision of this troubling question both extensive historical fact and a wealth of legal scholarship. While the opinion thus commands my respect, I find myself nonetheless in fundamental disagreement with those parts of it that invalidate the Texas statute in question, and therefore dissent. . . .

. . . I have difficulty in concluding, as the Court does, that the right of "privacy" is involved in this case. Texas, by the statute here challenged, bars the performance of a medical abortion by a licensed physician on a plaintiff such as Roe. A transaction resulting in an operation such as this is not "private" in the ordinary usage of that word. Nor is the "privacy" that the Court finds here even a distant relative of the freedom from searches and seizures protected by the Fourth Amendment to the Constitution, which the Court has referred to as embodying a right to privacy. *Katz v. United States*, 389 U. S. 347 (1967).

If the Court means by the term "privacy" no more than that the claim of a person to be free from unwanted state regulation of consensual transactions may be a form of "liberty" protected by the Fourteenth Amendment, there is no doubt that similar claims have been upheld in our earlier decisions on the basis of that liberty. I agree with the statement of MR. JUSTICE STEWART in his concurring opinion that the "liberty," against deprivation of which without due process the Fourteenth Amendment protects, embraces more than the rights found in the Bill of Rights. But that liberty is not guaranteed absolutely against deprivation, only against deprivation without due process of law. The test traditionally applied in the area of social and economic legislation is whether or not a law such as that challenged has a rational relation to a valid state objective. . . . The

Due Process Clause of the Fourteenth Amendment undoubtedly does place a limit, albeit a broad one, on legislative power to enact laws such as this. If the Texas statute were to prohibit an abortion even where the mother's life is in jeopardy, I have little doubt that such a statute would lack a rational relation to a valid state objective under the test stated in *Williamson, supra*. But the Court's sweeping invalidation of any restrictions on abortion during the first trimester is impossible to justify under that standard, and the conscious weighing of competing factors that the Court's opinion apparently substitutes for the established test is far more appropriate to a legislative judgment than to a judicial one.

The Court eschews the history of the Fourteenth Amendment in its reliance on the "compelling state interest" test. . . . But the Court adds a new wrinkle to this test by transposing it from the legal considerations associated with the Equal Protection Clause of the Fourteenth Amendment to this case arising under the Due Process Clause of the Fourteenth Amendment. Unless I misapprehend the consequences of this transplanting of the "compelling state interest test," the Court's opinion will accomplish the seemingly impossible feat of leaving this area of the law more confused than it found it.

While the Court's opinion quotes from the dissent of Mr. Justice Holmes in *Lochner v. New York* . . . (1905), the result it reaches is more closely attuned to the majority opinion of Mr. Justice Peckham in that case. As in *Lochner* and similar cases applying substantive due process standards to economic and social welfare legislation, the adoption of the compelling state interest standard will inevitably require this Court to examine the legislative policies and pass on the wisdom of these policies in the very process of deciding whether a particular state interest put forward may or may not be "compelling." The decision here to break pregnancy into three distinct terms and to outline the permissible restrictions the State may impose in each one, for example, partakes more of judicial legislation than it does of a determination of the intent of the drafters of the Fourteenth Amendment.

The fact that a majority of the States reflecting, after all, the majority sentiment in those States, have had restrictions on abortions for at least a century is a strong indication, it seems to me, that the asserted right to an abortion is not "so rooted in the traditions and conscience of our people as to be ranked as fundamental," *Snyder v. Massachusetts* . . . (1934). Even today, when society's views on abortion are changing, the very existence of the debate is evidence that the "right" to an abortion is not so universally accepted as the appellant would have us believe.

To reach its result the Court necessarily has had to find within the scope of the Fourteenth Amendment a right that was apparently completely unknown to the drafters of the Amendment. As early as 1821, the first state law dealing directly with abortion was enacted by the Connecticut Legislature . . . . By the time of the adoption of the Fourteenth Amendment in 1868, there were at least 36 laws enacted by state or territorial legislatures limiting abortion. While many States have amended or updated their laws, 21 of the laws on the books in 1868 remain in effect today. Indeed, the Texas statute struck down today was, as the majority notes, first enacted in 1857 and "has remained substantially unchanged to the present time." . . .

There apparently was no question concerning the validity of this provision or of any of the other state statutes when the Fourteenth Amendment was adopted. The only conclusion possible from this history is that the drafters did not intend to have the Fourteenth Amendment withdraw from the States the power to legislate with respect to this matter . . . .

For all of the foregoing reasons, I respectfully dissent.

5-4

The Real World of Constitutional Rights: The Supreme Court and the Implementation of the Abortion Decisions

Gerald N. Rosenberg

When one considers how exposed the Constitution's "religious establish-ment" clause is to continuous revision, it is not surprising to find other, less established rights deeply enmeshed in politics as well. The next essay exam-ines the right to an abortion, a controversial aspect of civil liberties policy that has been defended as an application of the "right to privacy."

The Supreme Court began asserting the right to privacy in earnest with Griswold v. Connecticut *in 1965, when it ruled that a married couple's decision to use birth control lay beyond the purview of the government. The 1973* Roe v. Wade *decision establishing a woman's right to an abortion— the best known and most controversial privacy right—has further established privacy as a class of rights implicit in the Bill of Rights. But, as Gerald N. Rosenberg explains,* Roe v. Wade *left many aspects of abortion rights unre-solved, and a lively public debate on the subject continues today.*

IN *ROE V. WADE* and *Doe v. Bolton* (1973) the Supreme Court held unconstitutional Texas and Georgia laws prohibiting abortions except for "the purpose of saving the life of the mother" (Texas) and where "pregnancy would endanger the life of the pregnant mother or would seriously and permanently injure her health" (Georgia). The Court asserted that women had a fundamental right of privacy to decide whether or not to bear a child. Dividing pregnancy roughly into three trimesters, the Court held that in the first trimester the choice of abortion was a woman's alone, in consultation with a physician. During the second trimester, states could regulate abortion for the preservation and protection of women's health, and in approximately the third trimester, after fetal viability, could ban abortions outright, except where necessary to preserve a woman's life or health. Although responding specifically to the laws of Texas and Georgia, the broad

Source: Gerald N. Rosenberg, "The Real World of Constitutional Rights: The Supreme Court and the Implementation of the Abortion Decisions," in *Contemplating Courts,* ed. Lee Epstein (Washington, D.C.: CQ Press, 1995), 390–419. Some notes and bibliographic references appearing in the original have been deleted.

scope of the Court's constitutional interpretation invalidated the abortion laws of almost every state and the District of Columbia.[1] According to one critic, *Roe* and *Doe* "may stand as the most radical decisions ever issued by the Supreme Court" (Noonan 1973, 261).

Roe and *Doe* are generally considered leading examples of judicial action in support of relatively powerless groups unable to win legislative victories. In these cases, women were that politically disadvantaged group; indeed, it has been claimed, "No victory for women's rights since enactment of the 19th Amendment has been greater than the one achieved" in *Roe* and *Doe* ("A Woman's Right" 1973, A4). But women are not the only disadvantaged interests who have attempted to use litigation to achieve policy ends. Starting with the famous cases brought by civil rights groups, and spreading to issues raised by environmental groups, consumer groups, and others, reformers have over the past decades looked to the courts as important producers of political and social change. Yet, during the same period, students of judicial politics have learned that court opinions are not always implemented with the speed and directness that rule by law assumes. This is particularly the case with decisions that touch on controversial, emotional issues or deeply held beliefs, such as abortion.

This chapter contains an exploration of the effect of the Court's abortion decisions, both *Roe* and *Doe,* and the key decisions based on them. How did the public, politicians, medical professionals, and interest groups react to them? Were the decisions implemented? Did they bring safe and legal abortions to all American women? To some American women? If the answer turns out to be only some, then I want to know why. What are the factors that have led a constitutional right to be unevenly available? More generally, are there conditions under which Court decisions on behalf of relatively powerless groups are more or less likely to be implemented.[2]

The analysis presented here shows that the effect and implementation of the Court's abortion decisions have been neither straightforward nor simple. Political response has varied and access to legal and safe abortion has increased, but in an uneven and nonuniform way. These findings are best explained by two related factors. First, at the time of the initial decisions there was widespread support for legal abortion from several sets of actors, including relevant political and professional elites on both the national and local level, the public at large, and activists. Second, the Court's decisions, by allowing clinics to perform abortions, made it possible for women to obtain abortions in some places where hospitals refused to provide them. Implementation by private clinics, however, has led to uneven availability of abortion services and has encouraged local political opposition.

The Abortion Cases

Roe and *Doe* were the Court's first major abortion decisions, but they were not its last.[3] In response to these decisions, many states rewrote their abortion laws, ostensibly to conform with the Court's constitutional mandate but actually with the goal of restricting the newly created right. Cases quickly arose, and continue to arise, challenging state laws as inconsistent with the Court's ruling, if not openly and clearly hostile to it. In general, the Court's response has been to preserve the core holding of *Roe* and *Doe* that a woman has a virtually unfettered constitutional right to an abortion before fetal viability, but to defer to legislation in areas not explicitly dealt with in those decisions. These cases require brief mention.

Areas of Litigation

Since *Roe* and *Doe,* the Court has heard three kinds of cases on abortion. One type involves state and federal funding for abortion. Here, the Court has consistently upheld the right of government not to fund abortion services and to prohibit the provision of abortions in public hospitals, unless the abortion is medically necessary. In perhaps the most important case, *Harris v. McRae* (1980), the Court upheld the most restrictive version of the so-called Hyde Amendment, which barred the use of federal funds for even medically necessary abortions, including those involving pregnancies due to rape or incest.

A second area that has provoked a great deal of litigation is the degree of participation in the abortion decision constitutionally allowed to the spouse of a pregnant married woman or the parents of a pregnant single minor. The Court has consistently struck down laws requiring spousal involvement but has upheld laws requiring parental notification or consent, as long as there is a "judicial bypass" option allowing minors to bypass their parents and obtain permission from a court.

A third area generating litigation involves the procedural requirements that states can impose for abortions. Most of these cases have arisen from state attempts to make abortion as difficult as possible to obtain. Regulations include requiring all post-first trimester abortions to be performed in hospitals; the informed, written consent of a woman before an abortion can be performed; a twenty-four-hour waiting period before an abortion can be performed; a pathology report for each abortion and the presence of a second physician at abortions occurring after potential viability; the preservation by physicians of the life of viable fetuses; and restrictions on the disposal of fetal remains. The Court's most recent pronouncement on these issues, *Planned Parenthood of Southeastern Pennsylvania v. Casey* (1992), found informed consent, a twenty-four-hour waiting period, and certain reporting requirements constitutional.

Trends in Court Treatment of Abortion Cases

Since the late 1980s, as *Casey* suggests, the Court has upheld more restrictions on the abortion right. In *Webster v. Reproductive Health Services* (1989), the Court upheld a 1986 restrictive Missouri law, and in 1991, in *Rust v. Sullivan,* it upheld government regulations prohibiting family-planning organizations that receive federal funds from counseling patients about abortion or providing abortion referrals. Most important, in *Casey* the Court abandoned the trimester frame-work of *Roe.* Although the justices did not agree on the proper constitutional standard for assessing state restrictions on abortion, Justices Sandra Day O'Connor, Anthony M. Kennedy, and David H. Souter adopted an "undue bur-den" standard. Under this standard, states may regulate abortion but may not place an undue burden on women seeking an abortion of a nonviable fetus.

Many commentators expected *Casey* to generate an avalanche of litigation centering directly on the abortion rights. Given the ambiguity of the undue bur-den standard, they expected expanded state activity to limit abortion. These expectations may yet be fulfilled, but, interestingly, Court cases since *Casey* have not specifically focused on the abortion right per se. Rather, in recent litigation the Court has been asked to resolve questions concerning access to abortion; namely, what steps can courts take to prevent antiabortion advocates from inter-fering with public access to family-planning and abortion clinics. The reason these kinds of questions arose is not difficult to discern; the 1990s has seen the rise of militant tactics—ranging from boisterous protests to harassment of clinic workers and even to the murder of physicians performing abortions—by certain segments of the antiabortion movement.

These "access" cases have generated mixed Court rulings. In *Bray v. Alexandria Women's Health Clinic* (1993), the Court rejected an attempt by pro-choice groups to use the 1871 Ku Klux Klan Act as a way to bring federal courts into this area. But, in *Madsen v. Women's Health Center* (1994), the Court upheld parts of a Florida trial court injunction permanently enjoining antiabortion protesters from block-ing access to an abortion clinic and from physically harassing persons leaving or entering it. With the enactment by Congress of the Freedom of Access to Clinic Entrances Act in 1994, and the immediate filing of a legal challenge, it is likely that the Court will have another opportunity to address this issue.

Implementing Constitutional Rights

How have the public, politicians, medical professionals, and interest groups reacted to the Court decisions since *Roe* and *Doe*? How has access to legal and safe abortion changed in the wake of these decisions? In other words, when the Supreme Court announces a new constitutional right, what happens?

Legal Abortions: The Numbers

An obvious way to consider this question, at least in the abortion realm, is to look at the number of legal abortions performed before and after the 1973 decisions. For, if the Court has had an important effect on society in this area, we might expect to find dramatic increases in the number of legal abortions obtained after 1973. Collecting statistics on legal abortion, however, is not an easy task. Record keeping is not as precise and complete as one would hope. Two organizations, the public Centers for Disease Control and Prevention in Atlanta and the private Alan Guttmacher Institute in New York, are the most thorough and reliable collectors of the information. The data they have collected on the number of legal abortions performed between 1966 and 1992 and the yearly percentage change are shown in Figure 1.

Interestingly, these data present a mixed picture of the effect of the abortion decisions. On the one hand, they suggest that after *Roe* the number of legal abortions increased at a strong pace throughout the 1970s (the solid line in Figure 1).

Figure 1. Legal Abortions, 1966–1992

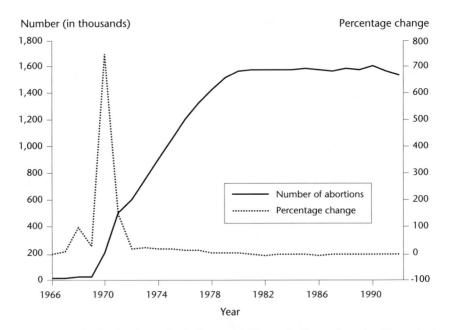

Sources: Estimates by the Alan Guttmacher Institute and the Centers for Disease Control and Prevention in Henshaw and Van Vort 1994, 100–106, 112; Lader 1973, 209; U.S. Congress 1974, 1976; Weinstock et al. 1975, 23. When sources differed, I have relied on data from the Alan Guttmacher Institute since its estimates are based on surveys of all known abortion providers and are generally more complete. Data points for 1983, 1986, and 1990 are estimates based on interpolations made by the Alan Guttmacher Institute.

On the other hand, they reveal that the changes after 1973 were part of a trend that started in 1970, three years before the Court acted. Strikingly, the largest increase in the number of legal abortions occurs between 1970 and 1971, two years before *Roe*! In raw numerical terms, the increase between 1972 and 1973 is 157,800, a full 134,500 fewer than the pre-*Roe* increase in 1970–1971. It is possible, of course, that the effect of *Roe* was not felt in 1973. Even though the decision was handed down in January, perhaps the 1973–1974 comparison gives a more accurate picture. If this is the case, the increase, 154,000, is still substantially smaller than the change during 1970–1971. And while the number of legal abortions continued to increase in the years immediately after 1974, that rate eventually stabilized and by the 1990s had actually declined. The dotted line in Figure 1 (representing the percentage change in the number of legal abortions performed from one year to the next) shows, too, that the largest increases in the number of legal abortions occurred in the years prior to *Roe* . . . .

The data presented above show that the largest numerical increases in legal abortions occurred in the years prior to initial Supreme Court action . . . . There was no steep or unusual increase in the number of legal abortions following *Roe*. To be sure, it is possible that without constitutional protection for abortion no more states would have liberalized or repealed their laws and those that had done so might have overturned their previous efforts. And the fact that the number of legal abortions continued to increase after 1973 suggests that the Court was effective in easing access to safe and legal abortion. But those increases, while large, were smaller than those of previous years. Hence, the growth in the number of legal abortions can be only partially attributed to the Court; it might even be the case that the increases would have continued without the Court's 1973 decisions.

What Happened?

Particularly interesting about the data presented above is that they suggest that *Roe* itself failed to generate major changes in the number of legal abortions. This finding is compatible with political science literature, in which it is argued that Supreme Court decisions, particularly ones dealing with emotional and controversial issues, are not automatically and completely implemented. It also appears to fit nicely with an argument I have made elsewhere (Rosenberg 1991), which suggests that several factors must be present for new constitutional rights to be implemented. These include widespread support from political and professional elites on both the national and local level, from the public at large, and from activists and a willingness on the part of those called on to implement the decision to act accordingly. This is true, as Alexander Hamilton pointed out two centuries ago, because courts lack the power of "either the sword or the purse." To a greater extent than other government institutions, courts are dependent on both elite and popular support for their decisions to be implemented.

To fill out my argument in greater detail, I examine both pre- and post-1973 actions as they relate to the implementation of the abortion right. In so doing, I reach two important conclusions. First, by the time the Court reached its decisions in 1973, little political opposition to abortion existed on the federal level, relevant professional elites and social activists gave it widespread support, it was practiced on a large scale (see Figure 1), and public support for it was growing. These positions placed abortion reform in the American mainstream. Second, in the years after 1973, opposition to abortion strengthened and grew.

Pre-*Roe* Support

In the decade or so prior to *Roe,* there was a sea change in the public position of abortion in American life. At the start of the 1960s, abortion was not a political issue. Abortions, illegal as they were, were performed clandestinely, and women who underwent the procedure did not talk about it.[4] By 1972, however, abortion had become a public and political issue. While little legislative or administrative action was taken on the federal level, a social movement, organized in the mid- and late 1960s, to reform and repeal prohibitions on abortion met with some success at the state level, and public opinion swung dramatically from opposition to abortion in most cases to substantial support.

Elites and Social Activists

Although abortions have always been performed, public discussion did not surface until the 1950s. In 1962 the American Law Institute (ALI) published its Model Penal Code on abortion, permitting abortion if continuing the pregnancy would adversely affect the physical or mental health of the woman, if there was risk of birth defects, or if the pregnancy resulted from rape or incest. Publicity about birth defects caused by Thalidomide, a drug prescribed in the 1960s to cure infertility, and a German measles epidemic in the years 1962–1965 kept the issue prominent. By November 1965 the American Medical Association Board of Trustees approved a report urging adoption of the ALI law.

In 1966, reform activists began making numerous radio and television appearances.[5] By then there were several pro-choice groups, including the Society for Humane Abortion in California; the Association for the Study of Abortion in New York, a prestigious board of doctors and lawyers; and the Illinois Committee for Medical Control of Abortion, which advocated repeal of all abortion laws.

Abortion referral services were also started. Previously, pro-choice activists had made private referrals to competent doctors in the United States and Mexico, who performed illegal but safe abortions. But by the late 1960s, abortion referral groups operated publicly. In New York City, in 1967, twenty-two clergy announced the formation of their group, gaining front-page coverage in the *New York Times* (Fiske 1967). The Chicago referral service took out a full page ad in the *Sun-Times* announcing its services. In Los Angeles, the referral service was serving more than a thousand women per month. By the late 1960s pro-choice organizations, including abortion-referral services, were operating in many major U.S. cities. And by 1971, the clergy referral service operated publicly in eighteen states with a staff of about 700 clergy and lay people (Hole and Levine 1971, 299).

In order to tap this emerging support, the National Association for the Repeal of Abortion Laws (NARAL) was founded.[6] Protesting in the streets, lecturing, and organizing "days of anger" began to have an effect. Women who had undergone illegal abortions wrote and spoke openly about them. Seventy-five leading national groups endorsed the repeal of all abortion laws between 1967 and the end of 1972, including twenty-eight religious and twenty-one medical groups. Among the religious groups, support ranged from the American Jewish Congress to the American Baptist Convention. Medical groups included the American Public Health Association, the American Psychiatric Association, the American Medical Association, the National Council of Obstetrics-Gynecology, and the American College of Obstetricians and Gynecologists. Among other groups, support included the American Bar Association and a host of liberal organizations. Even the YWCA supported repeal (U.S. Congress 1976, 4:53–91).

The Federal Government

In the late 1960s, while the abortion law reform battle was being fought in the states, the federal arena was quiet. For example, although states with less restrictive laws received Medicaid funds that paid for some abortions, for "six years after 1967, not a single bill was introduced, much less considered, in Congress to curtail the use of federal funds for abortion" (Rosoff 1975, 13). The pace momentarily quickened in 1968 when the Presidential Advisory Council on the Status of Women, appointed by President Lyndon Johnson, recommended the repeal of all abortion laws (Lader 1973, 81–82).

Still, abortion was not a major issue in the 1968 presidential campaign. Despite his personal beliefs, the newly elected president, Richard M. Nixon, did not take active steps to limit abortion, and the U.S. government did not enter *Roe* nor, after the decision, did it give support to congressional efforts to limit abortion.[7] Although it is true that in 1973 and 1974 President Nixon was occupied with other matters, his administration essentially avoided the abortion issue.

In Congress there was virtually no abortion activity prior to 1973. In April 1970, Sen. Bob Packwood (R-Ore.) introduced a National Abortion Act designed to "guarantee and protect" the "fundamental constitutional right" of a woman "to control her own fertility" (U.S. Congress 1970a). He also introduced a bill to liberalize the District of Columbia's abortion law (U.S. Congress 1970b). Otherwise, Congress remained essentially inactive on the abortion issue.

The States

It is not at all surprising that the president and Congress did not involve themselves in the abortion reform movement of the 1960s. Laws banning abortion were state laws, so most of the early abortion law reform activity was directed at state governments. In the early and middle parts of the decade there was some legislative discussion in California, New Hampshire, and New York. By 1967, reform bills were introduced in twenty-eight states, including California, Colorado, Delaware, Florida, Georgia, Maryland, Oklahoma, New Jersey, New York, North Carolina, and Pennsylvania (Rubin 1982). The first successful liberalization drive was in Colorado, which adopted a reform bill, modeled on the ALI's Model Penal Code. Interestingly, another early reform state was California, where Gov. Ronald Reagan, despite intense opposition, signed a reform bill.

These victories further propelled the reform movement, and in 1968, abortion legislation was pending in some thirty states. During 1968–1969 seven states— Arkansas, Delaware, Georgia, Kansas, Maryland, New Mexico, and Oregon— enacted reform laws based on or similar to the ALI model (Lader 1973, 84). In 1970, four states went even further. In chronological order, Hawaii, New York, Alaska, and Washington essentially repealed prohibitions on abortions in the first two trimesters.

To sum up, in the five or so years prior to the Supreme Court's decisions, reform and repeal bills had been debated in most states, and seventeen plus the District of Columbia acted to liberalize their laws (Craig and O'Brien 1993, 75). State action had removed some obstacles to abortion, and safe and legal abortions were thus available in scattered states. And, as indicated in Figure 1, in 1972, nearly 600,000 legal abortions were performed. Activity was widespread, vocal, and effective.

Public Opinion

Another important element in the effectiveness of the Court is the amount of support from the population at large. By the eve of the Court's decision in 1973, public opinion had dramatically shifted from opposition to abortion in most cases to substantial, if not majority, support. Indeed, in the decades that have followed, opinion on abortion has remained remarkably stable.[8]

Looking at the 1960s as a whole, Blake (1971, 543, 544) found that opinions on discretionary abortion were "changing rapidly over time" and polls were recording "rapidly growing support." For example, relying on data from Gallup polls, Blake (1977b, 49) found that support for elective abortion increased approximately two and one-half times from 1968 to 1972. One set of Gallup polls recorded a fifteen-point drop in the percentage of respondents disapproving of abortions for financial reasons in the eight months between October 1969 and June 1970 (Blake 1977a, 58). . . . In 1971, a national poll taken for the Commission on Population Growth and the American Future found 50 percent of its respondents agreeing with the statement that the abortion "decision should be left up to persons involved and their doctor" (Rosenthal 1971, 22). Thus, in the words of one study, "[b]y the time the Supreme Court made its ruling, there was strong public support behind the legalization of abortion" (Ebaugh and Haney 1980, 493).

Much of the reason for the growth in support for the repeal of the laws on abortion, both from the public and from organizations, may have come from changes in opinion by the professional elite. Polls throughout the late 1960s reported that important subgroups of the American population were increasingly supportive of abortion law reform and repeal. Several nonscientific polls of doctors, for example, suggested a great deal of support for abortion reform. A scientific poll of nearly thirteen thousand respondents in nursing, medical, and social work schools in the autumn and winter of 1971 showed strong support for repeal. The poll found split opinions among nursing students and faculty but found that 69 percent of medical students, 71 percent of medical faculty, 76 percent of social work students, and 75 percent of social work faculty supported "freely accessible abortion" (Rosen et al. 1974, 165). And a poll by the American Council of Education of 180,000 college freshmen in 1970 found that 83 percent favored the legalization of abortion (Currivan 1970). It is clear that in the late 1960s and early 1970s, the public was becoming increasingly supportive of legal abortion.

Post-*Roe* Activity

The relative quiet of the early 1960s has yet to return to the abortion arena. Rather than settling the issue, the Court's decisions added even more controversy. On the federal level, legislative and administrative action dealing with abortion has swung back and forth, from more or less benign neglect prior to 1973 to open antipathy to modest support. State action has followed a different course. Legislative efforts in the 1960s and early 1970s to reform and repeal abortion laws gave way to efforts to limit access to abortions. Public opinion remained stable until the *Webster* decision, after which there was a noticeable shift toward the pro-choice position. Finally, the antiabortion movement grew both more vocal and more violent.

The Federal Government: The President

On the presidential level, little changed in the years immediately after *Roe*. Nixon, as noted, took no action, and Gerald R. Ford, during his short term, said little about abortion until the presidential campaign in 1976, when he took a middle-of-the-road, antiabortion position, supporting local option, the law before *Roe,* and opposing federal funding of abortion (Craig and O'Brien 1993, 160–161). His Justice Department, however, did not enter the case of *Planned Parenthood of Central Missouri v. Danforth,* in which numerous state restrictions on the provision of abortion were challenged, and the Ford administration took no major steps to help the antiabortion forces.[9]

The Carter administration, unlike its Republican predecessors, did act to limit access to abortion. As a presidential candidate Carter opposed federal spending for abortion, and as president, during a press conference in June 1977, he stated his support for the Supreme Court's decisions allowing states to refuse Medicaid funding for abortions (Rubin 1982, 107). The Carter administration also sent its solicitor general into the Supreme Court to defend the Hyde Amendment.

Ronald Reagan was publicly committed to ending legal abortion. Opposition to *Roe* was said to be a litmus test for federal judicial appointments, and Reagan repeatedly used his formidable rhetorical skills in support of antiabortion activists. Under his presidency, antiabortion laws enacted included prohibiting fetal tissue research by federal scientists, banning most abortions at military hospitals, and denying funding to organizations that counseled or provided abortion services abroad. His administration submitted amicus curiae cases in all the Court's abortion cases, and in two (*Thornburgh v. American College of Obstetricians and Gynecologists,* 1986, and *Webster*) urged that *Roe* be overturned. Yet, despite the rhetoric and the symbolism, these actions had little effect on the abortion rate. As Craig and O'Brien (1993, 190) put it, "in spite of almost eight years of antiabortion rhetoric, Reagan had accomplished little in curbing abortion."

The administration of George Bush was as, if not more, hostile to the constitutional right to abortion as its predecessor. It filed antiabortion briefs in several abortion cases and urged that *Roe* be overturned. During Bush's presidency, the Food and Drug Administration placed RU-486, a French abortion drug, on the list of unapproved drugs, making it ineligible to be imported for personal use. And, in the administration's most celebrated antiabortion action, the secretary of the Health and Human Services Department, Louis W. Sullivan, issued regulations prohibiting family-planning organizations that received federal funds from counseling patients about abortion or providing referrals (the "gag rule" upheld in *Rust*).

President Bill Clinton brought a sea change to the abortion issue. As the first pro-choice president since *Roe,* he acted quickly to reverse decisions of his predecessors. In particular, on the third day of his administration, and the twentieth anniversary of *Roe,* Clinton issued five abortion-related memos.

1. He rescinded the ban on abortion counseling at federally financed clinics (negating *Rust*).

2. He rescinded restrictions on federal financing of fetal tissue research.

3. He eased U.S. policy on abortions in military hospitals.

4. He reversed Reagan policy on aid to international family planning programs involved in abortion-related activities.

5. He called for review of the ban on RU-486, the French abortion pill (Toner 1993).

In addition, in late May 1994, he signed the Freedom of Access to Clinic Entrances Act, giving federal protection to facilities and personnel providing abortion services. And, in early August 1994, the U.S. Justice Department sent U.S. marshals to help guard abortion clinics in at least twelve communities around the country (Thomas 1994). Furthermore, his two Supreme Court appointees as of 1994, Ruth Bader Ginsburg and Stephen Breyer, are apparently both pro-choice.

The Federal Government: Congress

In contrast to the executive branch, Congress engaged in a great deal of antiabortion activity after 1973, although almost none of it was successful, and some supportive activity actually occurred in the late 1980s and early 1990s. By means of legislation designed to overturn *Roe,* riders to various spending bills, and constitutional amendments, many members of Congress made their opposition to abortion clear. Perhaps the most important congressional action was the passage of the Hyde Amendment, which restricted federal funding of abortion: First passed in 1976, and then in subsequent years, the amendment prohibited the use of federal funds for abortion except in extremely limited circumstances. Although the wording varied in some years, the least limited version allowed funding only to save the life of the woman, when rape or incest had occurred, or when some long-lasting health damage, certified by two physicians, would result from the pregnancy. The amendment has been effective and the number of federally funded abortions fell from 294,600 in 1977 to 267 in 1992 (Daley and Gold 1994, 250).

Despite the amount of congressional activity, the Hyde Amendment was the only serious piece of antiabortion legislation enacted.[10] And, in 1994, Congress actually enacted legislation granting federal protection to abortion clinics. Thus, Congress was hostile in words but cautious in action with abortion. While not supporting the Court and the right to abortion, congressional action did not bar legal abortion.[11]

The States

Prior to 1973 the states had been the main arena for the abortion battle, and Court action did not do much to change that. In the wake of the Court decisions, all but a few states had to rewrite their abortion laws to conform to the Court's constitutional mandate. Their reactions, like those on the federal level, varied enormously. Some states acted to bring their laws into conformity with the Court's ruling, while others reenacted their former restrictive laws or enacted regulations designed to impede access to abortion. Since abortion is a state matter, the potential for state action affecting the availability of legal abortion was high.

At the outset, a national survey reported that state governments "moved with extreme caution in implementing the Supreme Court's ruling" (Brody 1973, A1). By the end of 1973, Blake (1977b, 46) reports, 260 abortion-related bills had been introduced in state legislatures and 39 enacted. In 1974, 189 bills were introduced and 19 enacted. In total, in the two years immediately following the Court decisions, 62 laws relating to abortion were enacted by 32 states. And state activity continued, with more abortion laws enacted in 1977 than in any year since 1973 (Rubin 1982, 126, 136).

Many of these laws were hostile to abortion. "Perhaps the major share," Blake (1977b, 61 n. 2) believes, was "obstructive and unconstitutional." They included spousal and parental consent requirements, tedious written-consent forms describing the "horrors" of abortion, funding limitations, waiting periods, hospitalization requirements, elaborate statistical reporting requirements, and burdensome medical procedures. Other action undertaken by states was simple and directly to the point. North Dakota and Rhode Island, for example, responded to the Court's decisions by enacting laws allowing abortion only to preserve the life of the woman (Weinstock et al. 1975, 28; "Rhode Island" 1973). Virginia rejected a bill bringing its statutes into conformity with the Court's order (Brody 1973, 46). Arkansas enforced a state law allowing abortion only if the pregnancy threatened the life or health of the woman ("Abortions Legal for Year" 1973, A14). In Louisiana, the attorney general threatened to take away the license of any physician performing an abortion, and the state medical society declared that any physician who performed an abortion, except to save the woman's life, violated the ethical principles of medicine (Weinstock et al. 1975, 28). The Louisiana State Board of Medical Examiners also pledged to prevent physicians from performing abortions (Brody 1973). In Pennsylvania, the state medical society announced that it did "not condone abortion on demand" and retained its strict standards (King 1973, 35). And in Saint Louis, the city attorney threatened to arrest any physician who performed an abortion (King 1973). Given this kind of activity, it can be concluded that in many states the Court's intent was "widely and purposively frustrated" (Blake 1977b, 60–61).

Variation in state response to the constitutional right to an abortion continues to this day. Although legal abortions are performed in all states, the availability of abortion services varies enormously. As noted, a variety of restrictions on abortion have been enacted across the country. In the wake of the Court's decision in *Webster* (1989), which upheld a restrictive Missouri law, a new round of state restrictions on abortion was generally expected. Indeed, within two years of the decision nine states and Guam enacted restrictions. Nevertheless, four states enacted legislation protecting a woman's right to abortion (Craig and O'Brien 1993, 280). The Pennsylvania enactments were challenged in *Casey* (1992), in which the "undue burden" standard was announced. The lack of clarity in this standard virtually ensures that restrictions will continue to be enacted.

Public Opinion

As shown in Figure 2, public opinion changed little from the early 1970s (pre-*Roe*) until the *Webster* decision in 1989, after which a small but important growth in pro-choice support occurred. Although differently worded questions produce different results, it is clear that the American public remains strongly supportive of abortion when the woman's health is endangered by continuing the pregnancy, when there is a strong chance of a serious fetal defect, and when the pregnancy is the result of rape or incest. The public is more divided when abortion is sought for economic reasons, by single unmarried women unwilling to marry, and by married women who do not want more children. "The overall picture that emerges is that a majority supports leaving abortion legal and available to women unfortunate enough to need it, though many in the majority remain concerned about the moral implications" (Craig and O'Brien 1993, 269). . . .

Figure 2. Public Opinion and Abortion, Selected Years, 1975–1992

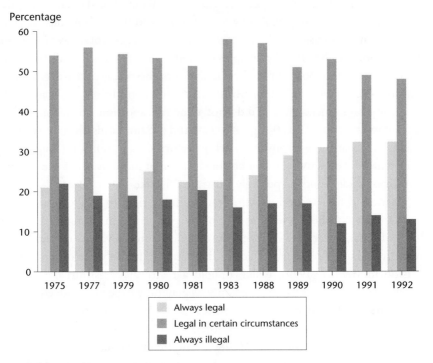

Percentage

Always legal
Legal in certain circumstances
Always illegal

Source: Newport and McAneny 1992, 51–52.
Note: "No opinion" omitted.

Anti-Abortion Activity

Organized opposition to abortion increased dramatically in the years following the Court's initial decisions. National groups such as the American Life Lobby, Americans United for Life, the National Right to Life Committee, the Pro-Life Action League, and Operation Rescue and numerous local groups have adopted some of the tactics of the reformers. They have marched, lobbied, and protested, urging that abortion be made illegal in most or all circumstances. In addition, in the 1980s, groups like Operation Rescue began to adopt more violent tactics. And, since 1982, the U.S. Bureau of Alcohol, Tobacco and Firearms has reported 146 incidents of bombing, arson, or attempts against clinics and related sites in thirty states, causing more than $12 million in damages (Thomas 1994). The high level of harassment of abortion clinics is shown in Table 1.

The level of harassment appears to have increased over time. In just 1992 and 1993 the U.S. Bureau of Alcohol, Tobacco and Firearms recorded thirty-six incidents, which resulted in an estimated $3.8 million in damages (Thomas 1994). The National Abortion Federation, representing roughly half of the nation's

Table 1. Abortion Clinics Reporting Harassment, 1985 and 1988 (in percentage)

Activity	1985	1988
Picketing	80	81
Picketing with physical contact or blocking	47	46
Demonstrations resulting in arrests	—	38
Bomb threats	48	36
Vandalism	28	34
Picketing homes of staff members	16	17

Source: Surveys of all abortion providers taken by the Alan Guttmacher Institute in Henshaw (1991, 246–252, 263).

Note: Dash = question not asked.

clinics, noted that incidents of reported vandalism at its clinics more than doubled from 1991 to 1992 (Barringer 1993). From May 1992 to August 1993 the U.S. Bureau of Alcohol, Tobacco and Firearms reported that 123 family-planning clinics were bombed or burned (Baum 1993). In 1992 more than forty clinics were attacked with butyric acid (a chemical injected through key holes, under doors, or into ventilation shafts) forcing clinic closures and requiring costly repairs (Anderson and Binstein 1993, C27). One of the aims of this violence appears to be to raise the cost of operating abortion clinics to such an extent as to force their closure. In 1992 and 1993, for example, arson destroyed clinics in Missoula and Helena, Montana, and in Boise, Idaho. The clinics have either been unable to reopen or have had great difficulty in doing so because of the difficulty of finding owners willing to rent to them and obtaining insurance coverage. In 1990, in the wake of such violence, one major insurer, Traveler's Insurance Company, decided not to insure any abortion-related concerns (Baum 1993).

Another tactic aimed at shutting down abortion clinics is to conduct large, sustained protests. During the summer of 1991, for example, Operation Rescue staged forty-six days of protest in Wichita, Kansas, resulting in the arrest of approximately 2,700 people. During the summer of 1993, Operation Rescue launched a seven-city campaign with similar aims. In addition, there have been individual acts of violence against abortion providers. Dr. David Gunn was murdered in March 1993 outside an abortion clinic in Pensacola, Florida; Dr. George Tiller was shot in August 1993 in Wichita, Kansas; and Dr. John Britton and his escort, James Barrett, a retired air force lieutenant colonel, were murdered in late July 1994, also in Pensacola. Commenting on the murders of Dr. Britton and James Barrett, Don Treshman, director of the antiabortion group Rescue America, issued an ominous warning: "Up to now, the killings have been on one side, with 30 million dead babies and hundreds of dead and maimed mothers. On the other side, there are two dead doctors. Maybe the balance is going to shift" (quoted in Lewin 1994, A7).[12] In sum, as Forrest and Henshaw (1987, 13) concluded, "anti-abortion harassment in the United States is widespread and frequent."

Two important facts can be gleaned from the foregoing discussion. First, at the time of the 1973 abortion decisions, large segments of the political and professional elite were either indifferent to or supported abortion reform. Second, after the decisions, many political leaders vociferously opposed abortion. Congress enacted antiabortion legislation as did some of the states. In addition, activist opposition was growing. How this opposition affected the implementation of the decisions is the focus of the next section.

The Effect of Opposition on the Implementation of Abortion Rights

On the eve of the abortion decisions, there was widespread support from critical professional elites, growing public support, successful reform in many states, and indifference from most national politicians. Is this sufficient for the implementation of constitutional rights?

Constitutional rights are not self-implementing. That is, to make a right a reality, the behavior of individuals and the policies of the institutions in which they work must change. Because abortion is a medical procedure, and because safe abortion requires trained personnel, the implementation of abortion rights depends on the medical profession to provide abortion services. When done properly, first-term and most second-term abortions can be performed on an outpatient basis, and there is less risk of death in the procedure than there is in childbirth or in such routine operations as tonsillectomies. Thus, no medical or technical reasons stand in the way of the provision of abortion services. Following Supreme Court action, however, the medical profession moved with "extreme caution" in making abortion available (Brody 1973, 1). Coupled with the hostility of some state legislatures, barriers to legal abortion remained.

These barriers have proved to be strong. Perhaps the strongest barrier has been opposition from hospitals. In Table 2, I track the response of hospitals to the Court's decisions. The results are staggering. Despite the relative ease and safety of the abortion procedure, and the unambiguous holding of the Court, both public and private hospitals throughout America have refused to perform abortions. *The vast majority of public and private hospitals have never performed an abortion!* In 1973 and the first quarter of 1974, for example, slightly more than three-quarters of public and private non-Catholic general care short-term hospitals did not perform a single abortion (Weinstock et al. 1975, 31). As illustrated in the table, the passage of time has not improved the situation. By 1976, three years after the decision, at least 70 percent of hospitals provided no abortion services. By 1992 the situation had further deteriorated: only 18 percent of private non-Catholic general care short-term hospitals and only 13 percent of public hospitals provided abortions. As Stanley Henshaw (1986, 253, emphasis added) concluded, reviewing the data in 1986, "most hospitals have *never* performed abortions."

These figures mask the fact that even the limited availability of hospital abortions detailed here varies widely across states. In 1973, for example, only 4 percent of all abortions were performed in the eight states that make up the East South Central and West South Central census divisions (Weinstock et al. 1975, 25).[13] Two states, on the other hand, New York and California (which are home to about 20 percent of all U.S. women), accounted for 37 percent of all abortions

Table 2. Hospitals Providing Abortions, Selected Years, 1973–1992 (percentage)

Year	Private, short-term, non-Catholic, general	Public
1973	24	—
1974	27	17
1975	30	—
1976	31	20
1977	31	21
1978	29	—
1979	28	—
1980	27	17
1982	26	16
1985	23	17
1988	21	15
1992	18	13

Sources: Forrest, Sullivan, and Tietze 1978, table 5; Henshaw 1986, 253; Henshaw et al. 1982, table 7; Henshaw, Forrest, and Van Vort 1987, 68; Henshaw and Van Vort 1990, 102–108, 142; Henshaw and Van Vort 1994, 100–106, 122; Rubin 1982, 154; Sullivan, Tietze, and Dryfoos, 1977, figure 10; Weinstock et al. 1975, 32.

Note: Dash = unavailable.

in 1974 (Alan Guttmacher Institute 1976). In eleven states, "not a single public hospital reported performance of a single abortion for any purpose whatsoever in all of 1973" (Weinstock et al. 1975, 31). By 1976, three years after Court action, no hospitals, public or private, in Louisiana, North Dakota, and South Dakota performed abortions. The Dakotas alone had thirty public and sixty-two private hospitals. In five other states, which had a total of eighty-two public hospitals, not one performed an abortion. In thirteen additional states, less than 10 percent of each state's public hospitals reported performing any abortions (Forrest, Sullivan, and Tietze 1979, 46). Only in the states of California, Hawaii, New York, and North Carolina and in the District of Columbia did more than half the public hospitals perform any abortions during 1974–1975 (Alan Guttmacher Institute 1976, 30). By 1992, the situation was little better, with five states (California, New York, Texas, Florida, and Illinois) accounting for 49 percent of all legal abortions (Henshaw and Van Vort 1994, 102).

This refusal of hospitals to perform abortions means that women seeking them, particularly from rural areas, have to travel, often a great distance, to exercise their constitutional rights. In 1973, for example, 150,000 women traveled out of their state of residence to obtain abortions. By 1982 the numbers had dropped, but more than 100,000 women were still forced to travel to another state for abortion services. . . .

Even when women can obtain abortions within their states of residence, they may still have to travel a great distance to do so. In 1974, the year after *Roe,* the Guttmacher Institute found that between 300,000 and 400,000 women left their home communities to obtain abortions (Alan Guttmacher Institute 1976). In 1980, across the United States, more than one-quarter (27 percent) of all women who had abortions had them outside of their home counties (Henshaw and O'Reilly 1983, 5). And in 1988, fifteen years after *Roe,* an estimated 430,000 (27 percent) women who had abortions in nonhospital settings traveled more than fifty miles from their home to reach their abortion provider. This includes over 140,000 women who traveled more than 100 miles to obtain a legal abortion (Henshaw 1991, 248).[14]

The general problem that faces women who seek to exercise their constitutional right to abortion is the paucity of abortion providers. From the legalization of abortion in 1973 to the present, at least 77 percent of all U.S. counties have been without abortion providers. And the problem is not merely rural. In 1980, seven years after Court action, there were still fifty-nine metropolitan areas in which no facilities could be identified that provided abortions (Henshaw et al. 1982, 5). The most recent data suggest that the problem is worsening. In 1992, 84 percent of all U.S. counties, home to 30 percent of all women of reproductive age, had no abortion providers. Ninety-one of the country's 320 metropolitan

(28 percent) areas have no identified abortion provider, and an additional 14 (4 percent) have providers who perform fewer than fifty abortions per year. . . .

Even when abortion service is available, providers have tended to ignore the time periods set out in the Court's opinions. In 1988, fifteen years after the decisions, only 43 percent of all providers perform abortions after the first trimester. More than half (55 percent) of the hospitals that perform abortions have refused to perform second-trimester procedures, a time in pregnancy at which hospital services may be medically necessary. Only at abortion clinics have a majority of providers been willing to perform abortions after the first trimester. Indeed, in 1988 a startling 22 percent of all providers refused to perform abortions past the tenth week of pregnancy, several weeks within the first trimester, during which, according to the Court, a woman's constitutional right is virtually all-encompassing (Henshaw 1991, 251).

Finally, although abortion is "the most common surgical procedure that women undergo" (Darney et al. 1987, 161) and is reportedly the most common surgical procedure performed in the United States, an *increasing* percentage of residency programs in obstetrics and gynecology do not provide training for it. A survey taken in 1985 of all such residency programs found that 28 percent of them offered no training at all, a nearly fourfold increase since 1976. According to the results of the survey, approximately one-half of the programs made training available as an option, while only 23 percent included it routinely (Darney et al. 1987, 160). By 1992 the percentage of programs requiring abortion training had dropped nearly to half, to 12 percent (Baum 1993). In a study done in 1992 of 216 of 271 residency programs, it was found that almost half (47 percent) of graduating residents had never performed a first-trimester abortion, and only 7 percent had ever performed one in the second trimester (Cooper 1993). At least part of the reason for the increasing lack of training is harassment by antiabortion activists. "Anti-abortion groups say these numbers prove that harassment of doctors, and in turn, medical schools which train residents in abortion procedures, is an effective tactic," Cooper reported. "'You humiliate the school. . . . We hope that in 10 years, there'll be none' that train residents how to perform abortions" (Randall Terry, founder of Operation Rescue, quoted in Cooper 1993, B3). . . .

It is clear that hospital administrators, both public and private, refused to change their abortion policies in reaction to the Court decisions. In the years since the Court's decisions, abortion services have remained centered in metropolitan areas and in those states that reformed their abortion laws and regulations prior to the Court's decisions. In 1976 the Alan Guttmacher Institute (1976, 13) concluded that "[t]he response of hospitals to the legalization of abortion continues to be so limited . . . as to be tantamount to no response." Jaffe, Lindheim, and Lee (1981, 15) concluded that "the delivery pattern for abortion services that has emerged since 1973 is distorted beyond precedent." Reviewing the data in the mid-1980s, Henshaw, Forrest, and Blaine (1984, 122) summed up the situation this way: "There is abundant evidence that many women still find it difficult or impossible to obtain abortion services because of the distance of their home to the nearest provider, the cost, a lack of information on where to go, and limitations on the circumstances under which a provider will make abortions available." Most recently, Henshaw (1991, 253) concluded that "an American woman seeking abortion services will find it increasingly difficult to find a provider who will serve her in an accessible location and at an affordable cost."

Implementing Constitutional Rights: The Market

The foregoing discussion presents a seeming dilemma. There has been hostility to abortion from some politicians, most hospital administrators, many doctors, and parts of the public. On the whole, in response to the Court, hospitals did not change their policies to permit abortions. Yet, as demonstrated in Figure 1, the number of legal abortions performed in the United States continued to grow. How is it, for example, that congressional and state hostility seemed effectively to prevent progress in civil rights in the 1950s and early 1960s but did not prevent abortion in the 1970s? The answer to this question not only removes the dilemma but also illustrates why the Court's abortion decisions were effective in making legal abortion more easily available. The answer, in a word, is *clinics*.

The Court's decisions prohibited the states from interfering with a woman's right to choose an abortion, at least in the first trimester. They did not uphold hospitalization requirements, and later cases explicitly rejected hospitalization requirements for second-trimester abortions.[15] Room was left for abortion reformers, population control groups, women's groups, and individual physicians to set up clinics to perform abortions. The refusal of many hospitals, then, to perform abortions could be countered by the creation of clinics willing to do the job. And that's exactly what happened.

In the wake of the Court's decisions the number of abortion providers sharply increased. In the first year after the decisions, the number of providers grew by nearly 25 percent. Over the first three years the percentage increase was almost 58 percent. The number of providers reached a peak in 1982 and has declined more than 18 percent since then. These raw data, however, do not indicate who these providers were.

. . . [T]he number of abortion providers increased because of the increase in the number of clinics. To fill the void that hospitals had left, clinics opened in large numbers. Between 1973 and 1974, for example, the number of nonhospital abortion providers grew 61 percent. Overall, between 1973 and 1976 the number of nonhospital providers grew 152 percent, nearly five times the rate of growth of hospital providers. In metropolitan areas . . . the growth rate was 140 percent between 1973 and 1976, five times the rate for hospital providers; in nonmetropolitan areas it was a staggering 304 percent, also about five times the growth rate for nonmetropolitan hospitals.

The growth in the number of abortion clinics was matched by the increase in the number of abortions performed by them. By 1974, nonhospital clinics were performing approximately 51 percent of all abortions, and nearly an additional 3 percent were being performed in physicians' offices. Between 1973 and 1974, the number of abortions performed in hospitals rose 5 percent, while the number performed in clinics rose 39 percent. By 1976, clinics accounted for 62 percent of all reported abortions, despite the fact that they were only 17 percent of all providers (Forrest, Sullivan, and Tietze 1979). From 1973 to 1976, the years immediately following Court action, the number of abortions performed in hospitals increased by only 8 percent, whereas the number performed in clinics and physicians' offices increased by a whopping 113 percent (Forrest et al. 1979).[16] The percentages continued to rise, and by 1992, 93 percent of all abortions were performed in nonhospital settings. Clinics satisfied the need that hospitals, despite the Court's actions, refused to meet.

In permitting abortions to be performed in clinics as well as hospitals, the Court's decisions granted a way around the intransigence of hospitals. The decisions allowed individuals committed to safe and legal abortion to make use of the market and create their own structures to meet the demand. They also provided a financial incentive for services to be provided. At least some clinics were formed solely as money-making ventures. As the legal activist Janice Goodman put it, "Some doctors are going to see a very substantial amount of money to be made on this" (quoted in Goodman, Schoenbrod, and Stearns 1973, 31). Nancy Stearns, who filed a pro-choice amicus brief in *Roe,* agreed: "[In the abortion cases] the people that are necessary to effect the decision are doctors, most of whom are not opposed, probably don't give a damn, and in fact have a whole lot to gain . . . because of the amount of money they can make" (quoted in Goodman et al. 1973, 29). Even the glacial growth of hospital abortion providers in the early and mid-1970s may be due, in part, to financial considerations. In a study of thirty-six general hospitals in Harris County (Houston), Texas, the need for increased income was found to be an important determinant of whether hospitals performed abortions. Hospitals with low occupancy rates, and therefore low income, the study reported, "saw changing abortion policy as a way to fill beds and raise income" (Kemp, Carp, and Brady 1978, 27).

Although the law of the land was that the choice of an abortion was not to be denied a woman in the first trimester, and regulated only to the extent necessary to preserve a woman's health in the second trimester, American hospitals, on the whole, do not honor the law. By allowing the market to meet the need, however, the Court's decisions resulted in at least a continuation of some availability of safe and legal abortion. Although no one can be sure what might have happened if clinics had not been allowed, if the sole burden for implementing the decisions had been on hospitals, hospital practice suggests that resistance would have been strong. After all, the Court did find abortion constitutionally protected, and most hospitals simply refused to accept that decision.

The implementation of constitutional rights, then, may depend a great deal on the beliefs of those necessary to implement them. The data suggest that without clinics the Court's decisions, constitutional rights notwithstanding, would have been frustrated.

Court Decisions and Political Action

It is generally believed that winning a major Supreme Court case is an invaluable political resource. The victorious side can use the decision to dramatize the issue, encourage political mobilization, and ignite a political movement. In an older view, however, this connection is dubious. Writing at the beginning of the twentieth century, Thayer (1901) suggested that reliance on litigation weakens political organizing. Because there have been more than twenty years of litigation in regard to abortion, the issue provides a good test of these competing views.

The evidence suggests that *Roe* and *Doe* may have seriously weakened the political effectiveness of the winners—pro-choice forces—and inspired the losers. After the 1973 decisions, many pro-choice activists simply assumed they had won and stopped their activity. According to J. Hugh Anwyl, then the executive director of Planned Parenthood of Los Angeles, pro-choice activists went "on a long siesta" after the abortion decisions (quoted in Johnston 1977, 1). Alfred F. Moran, an executive vice president at Planned Parenthood of New York, put it this way: "Most of us really believed that was the end of the controversy. The Supreme Court had spoken, and while some disagreement would remain, the issue had been tried, tested and laid to rest" (Brozan 1983, A17). These views were joined by a NARAL activist, Janet Beals: "Everyone assumed that when the Supreme Court made its decision in 1973 that we'd got what we wanted and the battle was over. The movement afterwards lost steam" (quoted in Phillips 1980, 3). By 1977 a survey of pro-choice and antiabortion activity in thirteen states nationwide revealed that abortion rights advocates had failed to match the activity of their opponents (Johnston 1977).[17] The political organization and momentum that had changed laws nationwide dissipated in reaction to Court victory. This may help explain why abortion services remain so unevenly available.

Reliance on Court action seems to have harmed the pro-choice movement in a second way. The most restrictive version of the Hyde Amendment, banning federal funding of abortions even where abortion is necessary to save the life of the woman, was passed with the help of a parliamentary maneuver by pro-choice legislators. Their strategy, as reported the following day on the front pages of the *New York Times* and the *Washington Post,* was to pass such a conservative bill that the Court would have no choice but to overturn it (Russell 1977; Tolchin 1977). This reliance on the Court was totally unfounded. With hindsight, Karen Mulhauser, a former director of NARAL, suggested that "had we made more gains through the legislative and referendum processes, and taken a little longer at it, the public would have moved with us" (quoted in Williams 1979, 12). By winning a Court case "without the organization needed to cope with a powerful opposition" (Rubin 1982, 169), pro-choice forces vastly overestimated the power and influence of the Court.

By the time of *Webster* (1989), however, pro-choice forces seemed to have learned from their mistakes, while right-to-life activists miscalculated. In early August 1989, just after *Webster,* a spokesperson for the National Right to Life Committee proclaimed: "[F]or the first time since 1973, we are clearly in a position of strength" (Shribman 1989, A8). Pro-choice forces, however, went on the offensive by generating a massive political response. Commenting on *Webster,* Nancy Broff, NARAL's legislative and political director, noted, "It finally gave us the smoking gun we needed to mobilize people" (quoted in Kornhauser 1989, 11). Membership and financial support grew rapidly. "In the year after *Webster,* membership in the National Abortion Rights Action League jumped from 150,000 to 400,000; in the National Organization for Women [NOW], from 170,000 to 250,000" (Craig and O'Brien 1993, 296). Furthermore, NARAL "nearly tripled" its income in 1989, and NOW "nearly doubled" its income, as did the Planned Parenthood Federation of America (Shribman 1989, A8). In May 1989 alone, NARAL raised $1 million (Kornhauser 1989).

This newfound energy was turned toward political action. In gubernatorial elections in Virginia and New Jersey in the fall of 1989, pro-choice forces played an important role in electing the pro-choice candidates L. Douglas Wilder and James J. Florio over antiabortion opponents. Antiabortion legislation was defeated in Florida, where Gov. Bob Martinez, an opponent of abortion, called a special session of the legislature to enact it. Congress passed legislation that allowed the District of Columbia to use its own tax revenues to pay for abortions and that essentially repealed the so-called gag rule, but President Bush vetoed both bills, and the House of Representatives failed to override the vetoes. As Paige Cunningham, of the antiabortion group Americans United for Life, put it: "The pro-life movement has been organized and active for twenty years, and some of us are tired. The pro-choice movement is fresh so they're operating with a much greater energy reserve. They've really rallied in light of *Webster*" (quoted in Berke 1989, 1).

This new understanding was also seen in *Casey.* Although pro-choice forces had seen antiabortion restrictions upheld in *Webster* and *Rust,* and the sure antiabortion vote of Justice Clarence Thomas had replaced the pro-choice vote of Justice Thurgood Marshall on the Supreme Court in the interim, pro-choice forces appealed the lower-court decision to the Supreme Court. As the *New York Times* reported, this was "a calculated move to intensify the political debate on abortion before the 1992 election" (Berke 1989, 1). Further increasing the stakes, they asked the Court either to reaffirm women's fundamental right to abortion or to overturn *Roe.* Berke (1991, B8) declared that "[t]he action marked an adjustment in strategy by the abortion rights groups, who seem now to be looking to the Court as a political foil rather than a source of redress."

All this suggests that Thayer may have the stronger case. That is, Court decisions do seem to have a mobilizing potential, but for the losers! Both winners and losers appear to assume that Court decisions announcing or upholding constitutional rights will be implemented, but they behave in different ways. Winners celebrate and relax, whereas losers redouble their efforts. Note, too, that in the wake of *Webster,* public opinion moved in a pro-choice direction, counter to the tenor of the opinion. Court decisions do matter, but in complicated ways.

Conclusion

"It does no good to have the [abortion] procedure be legal if women can't get it," stated Gwenyth Mapes, the executive director of the Missoula (Montana) Blue Mountain Clinic destroyed by arson in March 1993 (quoted in Baum 1993, A1).

Courts do not exist in a vacuum. Supreme Court decisions, even those finding constitutional rights, are not implemented automatically or in any straightforward or simple way. They are merely one part of the broader political picture. At best, they can contribute to the process of change. In and of themselves, they accomplish little.

The implementation of the Court's abortion decisions, partial though it has been, owes its success to the fact that the decisions have been made in a time when the role of women in American life is changing dramatically. Out of the social turmoil of the 1960s grew a women's movement that continues to press politically, socially, and culturally for ending restrictions on women's opportunities. Access to safe and legal abortion is part of this movement. In 1973 the

Supreme Court lent its support by finding a constitutional right to abortion. And in the years since, it has maintained its support for that core constitutional right. Yet, I have argued that far more important in making safe and legal abortion available are the beliefs of politicians, relevant professionals, and the public. When these groups are supportive of abortion choice, that choice is available. Where they have opposed abortion, they have fought against the Court's decisions, successfully minimizing access to abortion. Lack of support from hospital administrators and some politicians and intense opposition from a small group of politicians and activists have limited the availability of abortion services. On the whole, in states that were supportive of abortion choice before Court action, access remains good. In the states that had the most restrictive abortion laws before *Roe,* abortion services are available but remain difficult to obtain. As Gwenyth Mapes put it, "It does no good to have the [abortion] procedure be legal if women can't get it."

This analysis suggests that in general, constitutional rights have a greater likelihood of being implemented when they reflect the preexisting beliefs of politicians, relevant professionals, and the public. When at least some of these groups are opposed, locally or nationally, implementation is less likely. The assumption that the implementation of Court decisions and constitutional rights is unproblematic both reifies and removes courts from the political, social, cultural, and economic systems in which they operate. Courts are political institutions, and their role must be understood accordingly. Examining their decisions without making the political world central to that examination may make for fine reading in constitutional-law textbooks, but it tells the reader very little about the lives people lead.

NOTES

1. Alaska, Hawaii, New York, and Washington had previously liberalized their laws. The constitutional requirements set forth in *Roe* and *Doe* were basically, although not completely, met by these state laws.

2. For a fuller examination, see Rosenberg 1991.

3. In 1971, before *Roe* and *Doe,* the Court heard an abortion case (*United States v. Vuitch*) from Washington, D.C. The decision, however, did not settle the constitutional issues involved in the abortion controversy.

4. Estimates of the number of legal abortions performed each year prior to *Roe* vary enormously, ranging from 50,000 to nearly 2 million. See Rosenberg 1991, 353–355.

5. The following discussion, except where noted, is based on Lader 1973.

6. After the 1973 decisions, NARAL kept its acronym but changed its name to the National Abortion Rights Action League.

7. Nixon's "own personal views" were that "unrestricted abortion policies, or abortion on demand" could not be squared with his "personal belief in the sanctity of human life" (quoted in Lader 1973, 176–177).

8.   Franklin and Kosaki (1989, 762) argue that in the wake of *Roe* opinions hardened. That is, those who were pro-choice before the decision became even more so after; the same held true for those opposed to abortion. Court action did not change opinions; abortion opponents did not become abortion supporters (and vice versa). See Epstein and Kobylka 1992, 203.

9.   Ford did veto the 1977 appropriations bill containing the Hyde Amendment. He stated that he did so for budgetary reasons (the bill was $4 billion over his budget request) and reasserted his support for "restrictions on the use of federal funds for abortion" (quoted in Craig and O'Brien 1993, 161).

10.   The Congressional Research Service reports that Congress enacted thirty restrictive abortion statutes during 1973–1982 (Davidson 1983).

11.   The growth in violent attacks on abortion clinics, and illegal, harassing demonstrations in front of them, may demonstrate a growing awareness of this point by the foes of abortion.

12.   Treshman is not the only antiabortion activist to express such views. Goodstein (1994, A1) writes that "there is a sizable faction among the antiabortion movement's activists . . . who have applauded Hill [the convicted killer of Dr. Britton and Mr. Barrett] as a righteous defender of babies."

13.   The East South Central states are Kentucky, Tennessee, Alabama, and Mississippi. The West South Central states are Arkansas, Louisiana, Oklahoma, and Texas. Together, these eight states contained 16 percent of the U.S. population in 1973.

14.   It is possible, of course, that some women had personal reasons for not obtaining an abortion in their home town. Still, that seems an unlikely explanation as to why 100,000 women each year would leave their home states to obtain abortions.

15.   *Akron v. Akron Center for Reproductive Health* (1983); *Planned Parenthood v. Ashcroft* (1983). The vast majority of abortions in the United States are performed in the first trimester. As early as 1976, the figure was 90 percent. See Forrest et al. 1979, 32.

16.   The percentage for clinics is not artificially high because there were only a small number of clinic abortions in the years preceding Court action. In 1973, clinics performed more than 330,000 abortions, or about 45 percent of all abortions (see Alan Guttmacher Institute 1976, 27).

17.   Others in agreement with this analysis include Tatalovich and Daynes (1981, 101, 164), participants in a symposium at the Brookings Institution (in Steiner 1983), and Jackson and Vinovskis (1983, 73), who found that after the decisions "state-level pro-choice grounds disbanded, victory seemingly achieved."

18.   This also appears to have been the case in 1954 with the Court's school desegregation decision, *Brown v. Board of Education*. After that decision, the Ku Klux Klan was reinvigorated and the White Citizen's Councils were formed, with the aim of preserving racial segregation through violence and intimidation.

REFERENCES

"Abortions Legal for Year, Performed for Thousands." 1973. *New York Times,* December 31, Sec. A.

Alan Guttmacher Institute. 1976. *Abortion 1974–1975: Need and Services in the United States, Each State and Metropolitan Area.* New York: Planned Parenthood Federation of America.

Anderson, Jack, and Michael Binstein. 1993. "Violent Shift in Abortion Battle." *Washington Post,* March 18, Sec. C.

Barringer, Felicity. 1993. "Abortion Clinics Said to Be in Peril." *New York Times,* March 6, Sec. A.

Baum, Dan. 1993. "Violence Is Driving Away Rural Abortion Clinics." *Chicago Tribune,* August 21, Sec. A.

Berke, Richard L. 1989. "The Abortion Rights Movement Has Its Day." *New York Times,* October 15, Sec. 4.

_____.1991. "Groups Backing Abortion Rights Ask Court to Act." *New York Times,* November 8, Sec. A.

Blake, Judith. 1971. "Abortion and Public Opinion: The 1960–1970 Decade." *Science,* February 12.

_____.1977a. "The Abortion Decisions: Judicial Review and Public Opinion." In *Abortion: New Directions for Policy Studies,* edited by Edward Manier, William Liu, and David Solomon. Notre Dame, Ind.: University of Notre Dame Press.

_____.1977b. "The Supreme Court's Abortion Decisions and Public Opinion in the United States." *Population and Development Review* 3:45–62.

Brody, Jane E. 1973. "States and Doctors Wary on Eased Abortion Ruling." *New York Times,* February 16, Sec. A.

Brozan, Nadine. 1983. "Abortion Ruling: 10 Years of Bitter Conflict." *New York Times,* January 15, Sec. A.

Cooper, Helene. 1993. "Medical Schools, Students Shun Abortion Study." *Wall Street Journal,* Midwest edition, March 12, Sec. B.

Craig, Barbara Hinkson, and David M. O'Brien. 1993. *Abortion and American Politics.* Chatham, N.J.: Chatham House.

Currivan, Gene. 1970. "Poll Finds Shift to Left among College Freshmen." *New York Times,* December 20, Sec. 1.

Daley, Daniel, and Rachel Benson Gold. 1994. "Public Funding for Contraceptive, Sterilization, and Abortion Services, Fiscal Year 1992." *Family Planning Perspectives* 25:244–251.

Darney, Philip D., Uta Landy, Sara MacPherson, and Richard L. Sweet. 1987. "Abortion Training in U.S. Obstetrics and Gynecology Residency Programs." *Family Planning Perspectives* 19:158–162.

Davidson, Roger H. 1983. "Procedures and Politics in Congress." In *The Abortion Dispute and the American System,* edited by Gilbert Y. Steiner. Washington, D.C.: Brookings Institution.

Ebaugh, Helen Rose Fuchs, and C. Allen Haney. 1980. "Shifts in Abortion Attitudes: 1972–1978." *Journal of Marriage and the Family* 42:491–499.

Epstein, Lee, and Joseph F. Kobylka. 1992. *The Supreme Court and Legal Change.* Chapel Hill: University of North Carolina Press.

Fiske, Edward B. 1967. "Clergymen Offer Abortion Advice." *New York Times,* May 22, Sec. A.

Forrest, Jacqueline Darroch, and Stanley K. Henshaw. 1987. "The Harassment of U.S. Abortion Providers." *Family Planning Perspectives* 19:9–13.

Forrest, Jacqueline Darroch, Ellen Sullivan, and Christopher Tietze. 1978. "Abortion in the United States, 1976–1977." *Family Planning Perspectives* 10:271–279.

_____. 1979. *Abortion 1976–1977: Need and Services in the United States, Each State and Metropolitan Area.* New York: Alan Guttmacher Institute.

Franklin, Charles H., and Liane C. Kosaki. 1989. "Republican Schoolmaster: The U.S. Supreme Court, Public Opinion, and Abortion." *American Political Science Review* 83:751–771.

Goodman, Janice, Rhonda Copelon Schoenbrod, and Nancy Stearns. 1973. "Doe and Roe." *Women's Rights Law Reporter* 1:20–38.

Goodstein, Laurie. 1994. "Life and Death Choices: Antiabortion Faction Tries to Justify Homicide." *Washington Post,* August 13, Sec. A.

Henshaw, Stanley K. 1986. "Induced Abortion: A Worldwide Perspective." *Family Planning Perspectives* 18:250–254.

_____. 1991. "The Accessibility of Abortion Services in the United States." *Family Planning Perspectives* 23:246–252, 263.

Henshaw, Stanley K., and Kevin O'Reilly. 1983. "Characteristics of Abortion Patients in the United States, 1979 and 1980." *Family Planning Perspectives* 15:5.

Henshaw, Stanley K., and Jennifer Van Vort. 1990. "Abortion Services in the United States, 1987 and 1988." *Family Planning Perspectives* 22:102–108, 142.

_____. 1994. "Abortion Services in the United States, 1991 and 1992." *Family Planning Perspectives* 26:100–106, 122.

Henshaw, Stanley K., Jacqueline Darroch Forrest, and Ellen Blaine. 1984. "Abortion Services in the United States, 1981 and 1982." *Family Planning Perspectives* 16:119–127.

Henshaw, Stanley K., Jacqueline Darroch Forrest, and Jennifer Van Vort. 1987. "Abortion Services in the United States, 1984 and 1985." *Family Planning Perspectives* 19:63–70.

Henshaw, Stanley K., Jacqueline Darroch Forrest, Ellen Sullivan, and Christopher Tietze. 1982. "Abortion Services in the United States, 1979 and 1980." *Family Planning Perspectives* 14:5–15.

Henshaw, Stanley K., Lisa M. Koonin, and Jack C. Smith. 1991. "Characteristics of U.S. Women Having Abortions, 1987." *Family Planning Perspectives* 23:75–81.

Hole, Judith, and Ellen Levine. 1971. *Rebirth of Feminism.* New York: Quadrangle.

Jackson, John E., and Maris A. Vinovskis. 1983. "Public Opinion, Elections, and the 'Single-Issue' Issue." In *The Abortion Dispute and the American System,* edited by Gilbert Y. Steiner. Washington, D.C.: Brookings Institution.

Jaffe, Frederick S., Barbara L. Lindheim, and Phillip R. Lee. 1981. *Abortion Politics.* New York: McGraw-Hill.

Johnston, Laurie. 1977. "Abortion Foes Gain Support as They Intensify Campaign." *New York Times,* October 23, Sec. 1.

Kemp, Kathleen A., Robert A. Carp, and David W. Brady. 1978. "The Supreme Court and Social Change: The Case of Abortion." *Western Political Quarterly* 31:19–31.

King, Wayne. 1973. "Despite Court Ruling, Problems Persist in Gaining Abortions." *New York Times,* May 20, Sec. 1.

Kornhauser, Anne. 1989. "Abortion Case Has Been Boon to Both Sides." *Legal Times,* July 3.

Lader, Lawrence. 1973. *Abortion II: Making the Revolution.* Boston: Beacon Press.

Lewin, Tamar. 1994. "A Cause Worth Killing For? Debate Splits Abortion Foes." *New York Times,* July 30, Sec. A.

Newport, Frank, and Leslie McAneny. 1992. "Whose Court Is It Anyhow? O'Connor, Kennedy, Souter Position Reflects Abortion Views of Most Americans." *Gallup Poll Monthly* 322 (July): 51–53.

Noonan, John T., Jr. 1973. "Raw Judicial Power." *National Review,* March 2.

Phillips, Richard. 1980. "The Shooting War over 'Choice' or 'Life' Is Beginning Again." *Chicago Tribune,* April 20, Sec. 12.

"Rhode Island Abortion Law Is Declared Unconstitutional." 1973. *New York Times,* May 17, Sec. A.

Rosen, R. A. Hudson, H.W. Werley Jr., J. W. Ager, and F.P. Shea. 1974. "Health Professionals' Attitudes toward Abortion." *Public Opinion Quarterly* 38:159–173.

Rosenberg, Gerald N. 1991. *The Hollow Hope: Can Courts Bring About Social Change?* Chicago: University of Chicago Press.

Rosenthal, Jack. 1971. "Survey Finds 50% Back Liberalization of Abortion Policy." *New York Times,* October 28, Sec. A.

Rosoff, Jeannie I. 1975. "Is Support for Abortion Political Suicide?" *Family Planning Perspectives* 7:13–22.

Rubin, Eva R. 1982. *Abortion, Politics, and the Courts.* Westport, Conn.: Greenwood Press.

Russell, Mary. 1977. "House Bars Use of U.S. Funds in Abortion Cases." *Washington Post,* June 18, Sec. A.

Shribman, David. 1989. "Abortion-Issue Foes, Preaching to the Converted in No Uncertain Terms, Step Up Funding Pleas." *Wall Street Journal,* December 26, Sec. A.

Steiner, Gilbert Y., ed. 1983. *The Abortion Dispute and the American System.* Washington, D.C.: Brookings Institution.

Sullivan, Ellen, Christopher Tietze, and Joy G. Dryfoos. 1977. "Legal Abortion in the United States, 1975–1976." *Family Planning Perspectives* 9:116.

Tatalovich, Raymond, and Byron W. Daynes. 1981. *The Politics of Abortion.* New York: Praeger.

Thayer, James Bradley. 1901. *John Marshall.* Boston: Houghton, Mifflin.

Thomas, Pierre. 1994. "U.S. Marshals Dispatched to Guard Abortion Clinics." *Washington Post,* August 2, Sec. A.

Tolchin, Martin. 1977. "House Bars Medicaid Abortions and Funds for Enforcing Quotas." *New York Times,* June 18, Sec. A.

Toner, Robin. 1993. "Clinton Orders Reversal of Abortion Restrictions Left by Reagan and Bush." *New York Times,* January 23, Sec. A.

United States. Congress. Senate. 1970a. *Congressional Record.* Daily ed. 91st Cong., 2d sess. April 23, S3746.

————. 1970b. *Congressional Record.* Daily ed. 91st Cong., 2d sess. February 24, S3501.

————. 1974. Committee on the Judiciary. *Hearings before the Subcommittee on Constitutional Amendments.* Vol. 2. 93d Cong., 2d sess.

————. 1976. Committee on the Judiciary. *Hearings before the Subcommittee on Constitutional Amendments.* Vol. 4. 94d Cong., 1st sess.

Weinstock, Edward, Christopher Tietze, Frederick S. Jaffe, and Joy G. Dryfoos. 1975. "Legal Abortions in the United States since the 1973 Supreme Court Decisions." *Family Planning Perspectives* 7:23–31.

Williams, Roger M. 1979. "The Power of Fetal Politics." *Saturday Review,* June 9.

"A Woman's Right." 1973. *Evening Star* (Washington, D.C.), January 27, Sec. A

Chapter 6

Congress

———⬥●⬥———

6–1

Congress, the Troubled Institution

Steven S. Smith

Political scientist Steven S. Smith outlines major trends in congressional politics—the polarization of Congress, the abuse of congressional procedures by the parties, the flow of power from Congress to the president, and the low public esteem of Congress. He shows how these developments are related to each other and concludes that while some reforms would improve Congress, the underlying polarization will require a more basic change in American politics.

CONGRESS IS A troubled institution. It usually is. At the moment, Congress appears handcuffed by deep partisan polarization, seems to thwart the will of the people in failing to act on important problems, looks weak in comparison with the president and other executive officials, and is held in low esteem by most Americans. Presidents of both parties complain about its slowness; the media highlights "earmarks," "pork," and other characterizations of what some consider wasteful spending; and scandals involving members of Congress surface on a seemingly regular basis. Even legislators who retire from Congress carp about the institution to which they so frequently sought reelection.

It also is true that Congress is the most powerful national legislature in the world. It is formally independent of the chief executive, its jurisdiction is very

Source: This piece is an original essay commissioned for this volume.

broad and sets its own agenda, and its members are elected independently of the executive. The executive and judicial branches cannot spend money without its approval, the president needs the approval of the Senate to appoint senior executive officials and judges and to implement treaties, and Congress has wide-ranging powers to investigate the executive branch.

Nevertheless, in everyday politics Congress is at a severe disadvantage in its relationship with the president and the courts. Congress does not speak with one voice, cannot move quickly most of the time, and is quite permeable to outside influence. Unlike the executive branch, Congress is not led by a single leader who can deliberate in private and articulate a single policy for the institution. Instead, it has two houses (each of which assign an equal vote to every member) that must negotiate their differences on legislation. Unlike any federal court, Congress is large and unwieldy, it is bicameral, its deliberations are quite visible, and its floor proceedings are televised. Citizens, including lobbyists, are free to roam the halls of Congress's office buildings and visit the offices of members. Outside groups are instrumental to legislators seeking funding for the campaigns they must mount to retain their jobs.

Congress's political weaknesses have been exposed in recent years. Partisanship, deadlock on key issues, readiness to defer to the president in a crisis, and public despair with its performance have plagued Congress. This essay outlines and evaluates those weaknesses.

A Polarized Congress

The partisan tone of legislators may be the most conspicuous feature of congressional politics over the past quarter century. There is more to it than the derisive tone of the legislators' rhetoric. Deep and wide differences exist between the parties, and it is obvious in legislators' floor voting behavior. In Figure 1, I show the distribution members of the House and Senate on a liberal-conservative scale. The scale is based on a statistical analysis of all roll-call votes. Here, I show the distribution for two Congresses, the 92nd (1971–1972) and the 110th (2009–2010).

In the early 1970s, Democrats were far more liberal than Republicans on average and Republicans were more cohesive than the Democrats, but neither house was very polarized by party. In the House, nearly half of the membership fell between the most liberal Republican and most conservative Democrat. In the Senate, it was over a third of the membership in the overlapping region. These large blocs of legislators in the middle of the policy spectrum dictated outcomes on most important issues.

The pattern has been different since the late 1980s. The middle has been vacated. No longer is there a sizable group of moderate legislators to whom party and committee leaders must appeal to build a majority coalition on most important measures. By behavior, not just rhetoric, the parties are sharply polarized.

The polarization of congressional parties was the product of multiple forces in American politics. The 1960s and early 1970s was a period of social upheaval. The civil rights movement, the women's movement, the Vietnam War, the youth culture, and other developments generated a reaction that attracted the support of conservatives of both parties, particularly in rural America and the South. *Roe v. Wade,* the 1973 Supreme Court on abortion, seemed to catalyze Christian conservatives (formerly a dormant group in American politics), who mobilized within the Republican party in most parts of the country. Republican candidates and strategists recognized an opportunity to join economic and social conservatives in a larger coalition that could upset the long-standing Democratic majorities, comprised of northern liberals and southern conservatives.

The realignment of political values and party preferences that started in the late 1960s began to alter the composition of Congress in the 1970s. In the South,

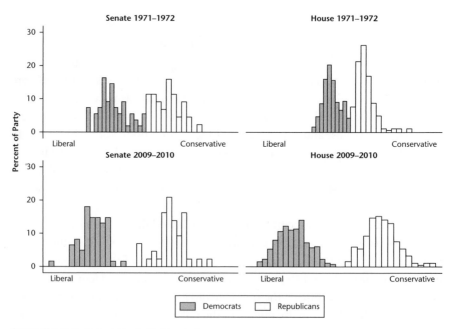

Figure 1. Liberal-Conservative Scores in Selected Congresses: Democrats in Gray, Republicans in White

Source: Common space scores (voteview.com).

many conservative Democrats were replaced by Republicans, making the congressional Democrats more uniformly liberal and reinforcing the conservative forces among congressional Republicans. In the Northeast, Midwest, and West Coast, Republicans (many of whom occupied the moderate region of the policy spectrum) lost to Democrats (most of whom were liberal), which reinforced the liberal trend among congressional Democrats and the conservative trend among Republicans. In the 1980s, the Republicans began to elect conservative leaders from the South, and the Democrats lost the mix of southern leaders who were important to the party in the mid-20th century.

As the composition of the party elites changed, the electorate began to sort itself so that political attitudes on economic and social issues were more strongly aligned with party preferences. In nearly every part of the country, the electorate supporting Democrats became more liberal and the electorate supporting Republicans became more conservative. The result was that political pressures from home became more uniform among the legislators of each party. It became more difficult for moderates to win primary elections, particularly on the Republican side, and make it to the general election ballot.

The successive elections of the 1970s, 1980s, and 1990s brought in legislators more polarized by party. This polarization was enhanced by the strategies of party leaders, first among Republicans and then Democrats. Republicans in the House, led by Georgia's Newt Gingrich, sought disciplined voting within the party in order to force Democratic leaders to draw support from conservative Democrats to win floor votes. Conservative Democrats, in turn, would have more difficulty gaining reelection in their conservative districts and states.

These developments were mutually reinforcing. As each party became more cohesive, its leadership could become more assertive and more pressure could be put on misfits within the party. As national party leaders, local party activists, and the electorate sorted themselves, primary election winners became more polarized and the electorate was more frequently given a choice between quite liberal Democrats and quite conservative Republicans. Only liberal legislators had a chance to be elected a leader among congressional Democrats; only conservative legislators had a chance to be elected a leader among congressional Republicans. The congressional parties became more polarized and their leaders were pressured to pursue more aggressive partisan strategies.

It bears noting that drawing district lines to stack House districts with the partisans of one party does not explain the polarization we have witnessed. The Senate, for which state lines are never changed, suffers from the same party polarization as the House. Instead, it has been a sorting of the electorate and legislators into parties with distinctive political attitudes that accounts for the durable pattern of the past two decades.

Legislative Pathologies in Congress

The consequences of partisan polarization in Congress are quite different in the two houses. Polarization in the House has yielded a streamlined, centralized process that can speed legislation to passage, but this is a process that often excludes the minority party in ways that intensify minority frustration and partisan passions. In contrast, polarized parties and super-majority rule in the Senate are a recipe for delay and inaction, an outcome that encourages both parties to engage in a blame game that frustrates everyone. Because both houses must approve legislation, Senate obstructionism is enough to kill many bills.

Let's begin with the House. The House majority party is able to control the floor agenda and pass legislation as long as it is reasonably cohesive. This is the product of several features of the modern House:

- The Speaker, as leader of the majority party, serves as the presiding officer and can freely recognize members to make motions on the floor, such as calling up bills for consideration.

- The Committee on Rules, which has been under the control of the Speaker since the early 1970s, can report resolutions that, if adopted by a House majority, can bring bills and conference reports to the floor and limit debate and amendments. A cohesive majority party can get these resolutions, called *special rules*, adopted.

- The Speaker appoints conference committees and can structure their membership to suit his party's needs.

Polarized parties mean that a majority party, which is cohesive when the parties are polarized, can readily gain House approval of special rules, limit minority opportunities to offer proposals, pass legislation, and control conference committee negotiations with the Senate. These features of a polarized House speed legislative action.

Unfortunately for the House minority party, partisan polarization also tends to produce a process so dominated by majority party members that minority party members get excluded from meaningful participation. Both Democratic and Republican majority parties have moved decisions on the most important policies from standing committees (where the minority is represented proportionately in most cases) to the leadership and informal work groups of the majority party (where the minority is not represented at all). Both Democratic and Republican majority parties have so restricted floor amendments on major bills that the minority party often does not have a meaningful opportunity to propose alternatives and attract some support from majority party members for them.

In contrast, the Senate has the following features:

- The majority party's leader does not preside and instead attempts to move the Senate by making motions from the floor.
- Most motions can be filibustered—that is, subject to unending debate—and so the minority can attempt to obstruct action on bills it dislikes.
- To overcome a filibuster or threatened filibuster of most bills, a three-fifths majority of all elected senators (60 when 99 or 100 seats are filled) is required to invoke cloture (close debate) and get a vote to pass a bill.
- The ability of the minority to filibuster proposals to change the rules means that the majority party cannot put in place rules similar to those that so advantage a House majority party. A two-thirds majority of senator voting (67 when 100 senators are voting) is required to invoke cloture on legislation that changes the rules.

Polarized parties mean that a sizable minority party—one that has 41 or more members—can block majority party legislation on the floor. This feature of a polarized Senate can delay or even kill legislation.

For the Senate, public expectations that the majority party can pass its legislation often fail to reflect the fact that the minority party possesses the parliamentary tools to prevent that from happening. And the minority party has been exploiting those parliamentary tools with greater frequency. Figure 2 shows the

Figure 2. The Increase in Cloture Votes, 1961–2010

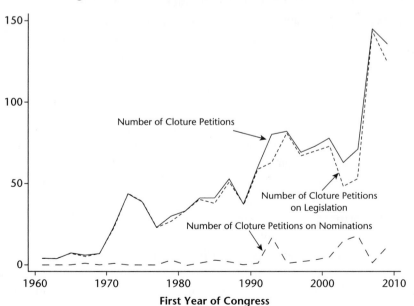

Source: http://www.senate.gov/pagelayout/reference/cloture_motions/clotureCounts.htm

number of cloture petitions filed to end or prevent filibusters in Congresses since the mid-20th century. Plainly, the record of filibustering since the late 1980s is very different than the previous decades. Minority obstructionism has become the norm on important measures and has extended from a wide variety of presidential nominations to executive and judicial positions.

Partisan polarization contributes to filibustering in powerful ways. A minority party leader finds it much easier to employ obstructionist tactics when no one from his party objects. Moreover, the obstructionism is more likely to succeed in blocking majority party legislation, forcing compromise or killing legislation, when the minority party is united and can prevent cloture. In response, the majority party leader attempts cloture more frequently, often several times on the same bill. The majority party members complain about minority obstructionism and minority party members complain that the majority is too quick to attempt to shut off debate and minority amendments.

Do filibusters matter? They do. In the polarized Congress of the last two decades, filibusters have made the Senate the primary burial ground of legislation. Political scientist Barbara Sinclair has demonstrated that in Congresses since the early 1990s, 33 of 80 major bills that died at some stage had passed the House but died in the Senate; only three died in the House after passing the Senate (others passed neither house or were vetoed). In contrast, in the 1970s and 1980s, only 12 of 42 major bills that died at some stage had passed the House but died in the Senate; eight died in the House after passing the Senate.

The problems associated with the filibuster continue to intensify. In March 2009, Senate Republicans—all 41 of them—signed a letter to President Barack Obama to encourage the president to renominate President Bush's nominees for the federal courts. They warned, "Regretfully, if we are not consulted on, and approve of, a nominee from our states, the Republican Conference will be unable to support moving forward on that nominee. And we will act to preserve this principle and the rights of our colleagues if it is not." That is, before President Obama nominated a single person to the federal courts, the Republican minority demanded that the president defer to them under threat of blocking his nominees by filibuster. In his 2012 State of the Union Address before a joint session of Congress, President Obama complained of minority party obstruction on his executive and judicial branch nominations.

In the polarized Congress, conference committees have fallen into disuse. Because conference committees approve compromise legislation with the majority support of conferees from each house, the like-minded majority party conferees do not need the support of minority party members and can largely ignore them. As a result, majority party members consult with each other without any minority legislators or staff present and appear to announce outcomes.

In recent Congresses, this went so far as to circumvent conference committees altogether by having majority party and committee leaders of the two houses negotiate compromises without appointing conference committees and then having the agreements incorporated as amendments between the houses. Even the formality of minority party participation is avoided.

These patterns have intensified and even personalized partisan conflict. Legislators who value a meaningful voice in policy making are either frustrated for being excluded (the House minority party) or for having a majority but not the super majority required to pass legislation (the Senate majority party). Tolerance of the other party has become very thin. Distrust of the other side is so widespread that opportunities for real cross-party deliberation are ignored.

Largely because of the Senate (and often with the contribution of divided party control of the House, Senate, and presidency), polarized parties create a strong bias against passing legislation. In fact, more major legislation has been killed since the parties became so polarized in the late 1980s than in the previous two decades. A polarized Senate gets hung up on filibusters, while a House, Senate, and presidency controlled by different and polarized parties cannot agree on legislation.

Aggressive Presidents and a Weakened Congress

Over the past decade, the power of Congress has been challenged on several fronts. A series of crises—terrorism, the war in Iraq, and the economic crisis—led the president to seek and receive broad powers with little detailed direction in the legislation from Congress. The president also has asserted broad powers without any participation by Congress and has acted through executive orders or other means. And President George W. Bush and his top advisers claimed a general theory of presidential power, now called *the theory of the unitary executive*, which posits that the president can control the actions of all executive branch agencies, even when the law gives authority directly to department and agency officials.

This is a large and complex subject, so I can only introduce the major ways in which Congress has yielded power to the president in recent years. Congress, under the basic constitutional framework, must delegate some power to the executive branch to implement policies it deems desirable. Unless the president has constitutional power of his own, Congress can detail how the delegated power is to be used. Failure to provide the detail, or at least to limit the delegation to a short period or carefully control spending for the purpose, grants the president power that Congress could reserve for itself.

Emergencies and National Security

Incentives to delegate broad power to the president are greatest in emergencies. A president argues that the national interest requires that he quickly be given authority to act with the flexibility required to meet unknown contingencies. Legislators can hope that their institution's control over spending and oversight activities will keep the executive in check, but, in practice, the president's advantage in public relations, control over information, and partisan considerations may limit Congress's ability to check the use of power once it is delegated to the president. In a Congress highly polarized by party, the tendency to grant unfettered power to the executive is exceptionally great when the same party controls the houses of Congress and the White House.

During 2001–2006, the six years of Republican majorities in Congress and a Republican president, the fight against terrorism and the wars in Iraq and Afghanistan led Congress to grant sweeping powers to President Bush. By historical standards, Congress held very few hearings on the broad sweep of issues during the period— prewar intelligence, the conduct of the war in Iraq, the National Security Agency's surveillance program, the treatment of detainees, and reform of the intelligence apparatus. The use of federal dollars and constitutionality of executive actions were frequently questioned by legislators and the media but seldom in congressional hearings or investigations. Once the Department of Homeland Security was created in 2003 from 22 agencies, Congress did not seriously scrutinize the functioning of the new department until one of its units, the Federal Emergency Management Agency, mismanaged the response to Hurricane Katrina. In the intensely partisan atmosphere of Washington, serious oversight of a Republican administration by a Republican Congress could only give the opposition opportunities to score points. Partisan convenience, rather than a commitment to check the use of power, seemed to drive the congressional oversight agenda.

In the meantime, President Bush took to a much greater extreme existing trends in presidential assertions of unilateral power. The administration broadened its interpretation of executive privilege to deny information to Congress. President Bush used executive orders more broadly to direct executive agencies, sometimes in contravention of statute. He used signing statements liberally when signing legislation into law to assert that he would not implement features of the law that he considered unconstitutional infringements on his power.

The Bush Theory of a Unitary Executive

More generally, President Bush and key figures in his administration subscribed to the theory of a unitary executive. The theory holds that the president has direct authority over all parts of the executive branch. Bush administration officials used the logic of the argument to justify presidential signing statements and other intrusions into statutory governance of executive agencies. To be sure, there is a compelling argument that the commander-in-chief role assigned to the president by the Constitution gives the president strong authority over the use of the armed forces. But it is reasonable to argue and seems historically accurate to say that Congress is free to direct or constrain other executive agencies by law.

Democrats, once again in the majority after the 2006 elections, objected to Bush's view of his powers but were able to do little about it before the end of Bush's second term. They did step up oversight activities, forced dozens of administration officials to testify, and attempted to impose a timetable for withdrawal from Iraq, but the president proved to have a strategic advantage in most of these confrontations with Congress. Once his policy was in place, he could rely on Senate Republicans to obstruct votes on unfriendly legislation and, if need be, veto legislation to block it. And he could delay or assert executive privilege when unfriendly congressional committees attempted to investigate executive actions—and the approaching end of his second term meant that he did not have to delay for long. President Obama, of course dealing with a friendly Congress, ordered executive agencies to ignore President Bush's signing statements unless they first consult the Department of Justice.

Emergencies and the Economy

Emergencies can motivate even an opposition Congress to grant sweeping authority to a president, as the Democrats did in 2008 in response to the economic crisis. As Wall Street investment banks were about the collapse in late 2008, the Bush administration asked for and received a $700 billion authorization for the Troubled Asset Relief Program (TARP) to "restore liquidity and stability to the financial system," primarily by purchasing soured assets (mainly mortgage-backed securities) and stabilizing the banking system. The fear, widely shared by economists and administration officials, was that the economy would suffer badly if major financial institutions failed. While some Republicans opposed the bill, most Republicans and nearly all Democrats supported the legislation. To the surprise of many members of Congress, the administration used most of the first half of the TARP funds to buy ownership stakes in banks and insurance companies to shore up their balance sheets.

Congress appeared nervous about a broad delegation of power to the Treasury and so imposed multiple mechanisms overlapping oversight and reporting responsibilities. A Congressional Oversight Panel, soon chaired by a Harvard professor, was created to review the work of Treasury and report to Congress every 30 days. The comptroller general of the General Accountability

Office, an arm of Congress, was required to monitor the program and report every 60 days. The Treasury office itself was required to file reports with Congress, a special inspector general was created, and a board comprised of executive officials was established to oversee implementation of the bill and report to Congress quarterly.

The oversight was likely to be taken seriously, but the delegation of power nevertheless represented one of the most vague delegations of power for an authorization of such a large sum of money. Moreover, the administration moved so quickly in dedicating the funds that congressional oversight would long post-date irreversible executive branch action. Later reports indicated that the executive branch had a difficult time accounting for the way the banks used federal funds.

The Continuing Battle Over Appointments

The tension between Congress and the president persists, and Congress often suffers when the president can act unilaterally on a matter on which the public appears to side with the president. During his first term, President Obama was regularly frustrated by Senate Republicans who refused to allow the Senate to vote on his nominees to executive and judicial positions. The president normally has the opportunity to make appointments on his own when Congress is in recess, appointments that last for the remainder of the next session of Congress. To block President Obama from making recess appointments, the Republican-controlled House refused to allow the Senate to recess. The House was able to do this by exploiting the constitutional provisions that "neither house . . . shall, without the consent of the other, adjourn for more than three days" (Article I, Section 5). Lacking authority to adjourn, the Senate agreed with the House to hold a *pro forma* legislative session every three days, which, in a long-accepted interpretation, meant that the Senate was not in recess and the president was not authorized to make recess appointments.

In early 2012, President Obama decided to proceed with recess appointments while the Senate was holding *pro forma* sessions once every three days. In the most noteworthy case, the confirmation of a director for the Consumer Financial Protection Bureau had been held up in the Senate since July 2011. Republicans in Congress complained bitterly about the president's move, but the new director took office. Backed by an opinion from his Justice Department, President Obama argued that the periodic *pro forma* sessions at which no legislative business was conducted were not sufficient to deny the president his constitutional power to make recess appointments. The dispute may be resolved differently in the courts, but President Obama managed to get his nominee in office in the meantime.

The Unpopular Congress

The popularity of Congress ebbs and flows with the public's confidence in government. When the president's ratings and trust in government improved after the tragic events of September 11, 2001, Congress's approval ratings improved, too (Figure 3). Nevertheless, Congress's performance ratings are almost always below those of the president and the Supreme Court—when President George W. Bush earned approval ratings in the 20s, Congress managed to fall into the teens. And in 2011, when President Obama's ratings were in the 40s, Congress dropped to all-time lows—reaching 11 percent as the year came to an end.

The legislative process is easy to dislike—it often generates political posturing and grandstanding, it necessarily involves bargaining, and it often leaves broken promises in its trail. Members of Congress often appear self-serving as they pursue their political careers and represent interests and reflect values that are controversial. And the intense partisanship that Congress has exhibited in the last two decades is quite distasteful to many Americans. The public relations efforts of the congressional parties probably make matters worse by emphasizing such

Figure 3. Percent Approving of Congress's Job Performance, Two-Year Averages, 1993–2008

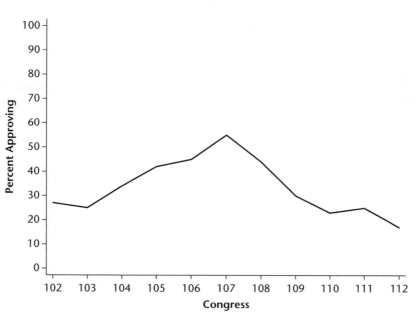

Source: Gallup Poll (http://www.gallup.com/poll/151628/Congress-Ends-2011-Record-Low-Approval.aspx).

Note: The number for the 112th Congress is for one year, 2011.

partisan and derisive messages. In contrast, the Supreme Court is cloaked in ritual and is seldom seen or heard by the general public. The president is represented by a single, large, and professional public relations machine.

A few scandals surely contribute to Congress's low standing. In fact, Congress seems to be a never-ending source of comic relief, like the joke about the legislator who kept referring to the presiding officer as "Your Honor." There is no doubt that a large majority of today's members behave ethically. No doubt the ethical standards applied by the public, the media, and Congress itself are higher today than at any other time. Yet there is no denying that the seemingly regular flow of scandals harms Congress's standing with the American people.

HIGHLIGHTS OF RECENT CONGRESSIONAL ETHICS SCANDALS

- In 1989, House Speaker James Wright (D-Texas) resigned after Republicans charged him with ethics violations for receiving extraordinarily large royalties on a book.

- In 1991, Senator David Durenberger (R-Minnesota) was condemned in a unanimously approved Senate resolution for a book deal and for seeking reimbursement for expenses for staying in a condo that he owned.

- In 1992, the disclosure that many House members had repeatedly overdrawn their accounts at the House disbursement office led people to believe that members enjoyed special privileges.

- In 1991, the Senate Ethics Committee found that three senators had substantially and improperly interfered with a federal investigation of Lincoln Savings and Loan Association. Two others were found to have exercised poor judgment in the affair. The five senators came to be known at the "Keating Five," after the name of the chair of Lincoln.

- In 1995, a long investigation of sexual harassment charges against Senator Robert Packwood (R-Oregon) led to his forced resignation from office.

- In 1995, Representative Dan Rostenkowski (D-Illinois), former chair of the House Ways and Means Committee, was found guilty of illegally receiving cash for personal use from the House post office. He later served a prison term.

- In 1995, Representative Enid Waldholtz (R-Utah) retired after her husband was charged with felonies in conjunction with raising funds for her campaign.

- In 1997, Speaker Newt Gingrich (R-Georgia) agreed to pay $300,000 in fines based on charges that he used nonprofit organizations for political purposes and misled the House Committee on Standards of Official Conduct.

- In 1998, Representative Jay Kim (R-California) pleaded guilty to charges involving over $250,000 in illegal campaign contributions.

- In 2002, Representative James A. Traficant, Jr. (D-Ohio) was convicted of receiving bribes in exchange for helping businesses get government contracts and of engaging in a pattern of racketeering since taking office in 1985.

- In 2004, House Majority Leader Tom Delay (R-Texas) was issued letters of admonition by the House ethics committee for improperly promising to endorse the son of Representative Nick Smith (R-Michigan) in exchange for Smith's vote on a bill and for attending a fundraising event with lobbyists for a company that was lobbying him on pending legislation.

- In 2005, Representative Duke Cunningham (R-California) resigned and pleaded guilty to taking more than $2.4 million in bribes and related tax evasion and fraud, the largest financial sum involving an individual member.

- In 2006, Representative Tom Delay (R-Texas) resigned after being indicted in Texas for laundering money through a national party committee in his effort to redistrict Texas congressional districts.

- In 2006, Representative William Jefferson (D-Louisiana) won reelection to the House but was denied a Ways and Means committee assignment after FBI agents videotaped him appearing to solicit a bribe and later found $90,000 of the marked cash in his freezer—making this "the cold cash scandal." Jefferson was defeated from reelection in 2008 and convicted for bribery a year later.

- In 2006, Representative Mark Foley (R-Florida) resigned after it was disclosed that he sent sexually explicit e-mail messages to underage House pages.

- In 2006, Representative Bob Ney (R-Ohio) pleaded guilty to making false statements and conspiracy in relation to receiving thousands of dollars in gifts from lobbyist Jack Abramoff. A Ney aide also pleaded guilty for receiving gifts. Separately, Abramoff pleaded guilty to charges of conspiracy, fraud, and tax evasion.

- In 2008, Senator Ted Stevens (R-Alaska) was convicted of seven counts of failing to disclose gifts related to the renovation of his Alaska home on his Senate financial disclosure forms. Stevens was defeated for reelection in November 2008.

- In 2008, Representative Tim Mahoney (D-Florida) confessed that he had had an extramarital affair with a staff member. Shortly after news reports indicated that Mahoney attempted to buy the staff member's silence, his wife filed for divorce and he was defeated for reelection.

- In 2010, Representative Charles Rangel (D-New York) was censured for violating House rules for using his office to raise money for a college building named after him, failing to disclose financial assets, and violating New York City rules by housing his campaign committees in rent-controlled apartments.

(Continued)

(Continued)

- In 2011, Senator John Ensign (R-Nevada) resigned his seat before a Senate investigation into his activities following an extramarital affair with a staff member. The activities included payments to the staff member's family and arranging for the staff member's father to be hired as a lobbyist.

- In 2011, Representative Anthony Weiner (D-New York) resigned from Congress after the public disclosure of his Twitter message to a woman with a link to a sexually suggestive photo of himself. Weiner admitted to having "exchanged messages and photos of an explicit nature with about six women."

Incumbents and candidates for Congress contribute to the generally low esteem of their colleagues in another way. Many of them, maybe most, complain about Congress—they run for Congress by running against Congress. This is an old art form in American campaigns. Candidates promise to end "business as usual" in Washington and to push through reforms to "fix" Congress—to end partisanship, reform the system of congressional perks and earmarks, to stop the influence of money and special interests, and so on. While Congress languishes with mediocre approval ratings, individual members of Congress continue to do quite well. Typically, Gallup finds that about 70 percent of the public approves of the way its own U.S. representative is handling his or her job. Most incumbents, typically more than 90 percent, successfully gain reelection when they seek it.

Congressional campaigns have become personal and often very ugly. In the polarized environment of the recent past, candidates win their parties' primaries to get on the general election ballot by demonstrating their commitment to party principles. In the general election campaign, the candidates demonize their opponents. The winning candidates emerging from these campaigns have acquired a partisan style that they carry with them into Congress, reinforcing the partisan polarization.

Directions for Reform

Partisanship, mean and ugly campaigns, congressional gridlock, and the low esteem of Congress feed on each other. They have produced a dysfunctional Congress that alienates the public, discourages qualified people from running for seats in the House and Senate, and far too often fails to act on serious problems. Presidents fill the voids created by a handcuffed Congress when they can, weakening congressional participation in important policy arenas and under-mining the representational basis for policy making.

What can be done? First, it is important to keep in mind that the partisan polarization that is behind much of Congress's problems is not readily reme-died by Congress. We have a right to expect more civil and tolerant behavior by legislators and their leaders, but we cannot expect legislators to move far from the policy positions that got them elected. Thus, in the short run, the burden is on American voters to elect more moderate candidates who, as leg-islators, will demand less partisan behavior from their leaders and insist on the compromises necessary to address the policy challenges facing the country. I am not hopeful.

Nevertheless, legislators should take steps to improve their institution. In both houses, policy making and interpersonal relations would be improved with fewer three- and four-day weeks and more five-day weeks, having less conflict between floor and committee sessions, and perhaps keeping legislators in Washington for more weekends. We cannot expect legislators to keep their partisanship in check when they spend little time with each other except to rush from place to place and cast votes. Moreover, we cannot expect Congress to engage in creative legislative activity and meaningful oversight on the part-time schedule that Congress has maintained in recent decades. Unfortunately, I would not expect legislators to happily give up time in their districts and states to make this possible.

In the House, the majority party must work much harder to protect the minority party's ability to participate in policy making in a meaningful way. The standing committees should be used whenever possible as forums for the exchange of ideas, layover rules guaranteeing the passage of time before action is taken should be observed, and amending opportunities in committee and the floor should be preserved. The majority party cannot be expected to tolerate a minority that repeatedly fails to propose serious amendments and uses nearly all of its opportunities to participate to score political points. So again, we would be asking legislators to set aside their real differences to reduce partisanship and find a way to compromise across a wide partisan divide.

In the Senate, no reform could be more important than filibuster reform. The practice is long-standing, but it is justified by neither the Constitution nor early Senate rules. It developed quite accidentally when the Senate failed to include the motion of the previous question, used in the House to limit debate, in a codification of its rules. The practice has come to be a regular means of obstruc-tionism for the minority, effectively raising the threshold for passing legislation from 51 to 60 for nearly all legislation of greater than the most modest impor-tance. I am not optimistic about the Senate minority party to endorse filibuster reform anytime soon.

The Politics of Legislative Stalemate

Sarah A. Binder

Political scientists have debated whether divided party control of the major insti-tutions of government affects policy outcomes. In this essay, political scientist Sarah Binder argues that divided party control of government, when accompa-nied by polarized parties, promotes strategic disagreement between the parties. This disagreement yields stalemate even when there is a basis for consensus on some issues and undermines Congress's ability to address important problems.

IN THE SUMMER of 2011, Democrats and Republicans on Capitol Hill battled over a looming deadline to raise the nation's debt ceiling. With the country's rating agencies on the verge of downgrading the nation's creditworthiness and top party leaders and President Barack Obama seemingly unable to cobble an agree-ment, veteran Congress observer Norman Ornstein declared that we were wit-nessing the "worst Congress ever."[1] Seeing the Congress reach new lows of congressional dysfunction, Ornstein tallied the charges against the institution:

> Look what we have now: a long-term debt disaster with viable bipartisan solutions on the table but ignored or cast aside in Congress; an impasse over the usually perfunctory matter of raising the statutory debt limit, plac-ing the United States in jeopardy of its first-ever default; sniping and guer-rilla warfare over two major policy steps enacted in the last Congress: health-care reform and financial regulation; no serious action or movement on climate change, jobs, or the continuing mortgage crisis; and major trade deals stalled yet again despite bipartisan and presidential support.

To be sure, we lack a metric to know whether these recent years have reached historic levels of dysfunction. But charges that Congress was "broken" were heard throughout the 112th Congress (2011–12) as the two parties were at log-gerheads over how to solve the nation's pressing economic and other problems. Nor did such concerns stay within the Beltway; by winter of 2012, only ten per-cent of the public was willing to admit to pollsters that they approved of Congress's on-the-job performance.

The deep stalemate of the 112th Congress stands in stark contrast to the wildly productive 111th Congress (2009–10). Under unified Democratic control,

Source: This piece is an original essay commissioned for this volume.

Congress and the White House enacted an economic stimulus bill of historic proportions, enacted landmark health care and food safety reforms into law, rewrote
the rules for Wall Street, ratified a strategic arms treaty, repealed the "don't ask,
don't tell" ban on military service by openly gay men and women, and secured
passage of a host of contentious tax measures—among other accomplishments.
Granted, the legislative process by which these accomplishments were achieved
was exceedingly partisan and contentious, at times tortuous and contorted. But
the records of the 111th and 112th Congresses compared back-to-back raise
important questions about the conditions that foster legislative stalemate. How
can Congress be remarkably productive in one year and then seemingly incapacitated the next?

In this essay, I explore the partisan, electoral, and institutional forces that seem
to underlie patterns in Congressional performance. Although scholars of American
politics have historically placed their faith in robust, cohesive political parties to
engineer a robust and productive polity, I suggest that the polarization of the
political parties has instead diminished Congress's capacity as a lawmaking
body—albeit to varying degrees in periods of unified and divided party control.
Rather than providing a mechanism of democratic accountability, today's
intensely competitive parties more often promote disagreement even when consensus is within reach. Such strategic disagreement makes legislating nearly
impossible, unless a single party is able to marshal sizable majorities on behalf of
major reforms.

Setting the Electoral Stage

Today's electoral world features an uncommon mix: a world of candidate-
centered electoral contests conducted within a system of active, nationalized
political parties. For the parties, elections have always been a proving ground,
offering them a recurring chance to make headway in gaining control of the
House, Senate, and White House. National tides of sufficient breadth and depth
to bring major partisan change—such as the 1994 wave that swept Republicans
into control of Congress for the first time in forty years or the Tea Party wave in
2010 that returned House Republicans to the majority after losing it in 2006—
may be rare, but elections nonetheless matter for the two major parties.

Elections are pivotal for the two major parties—and thus potentially for
Congress's lawmaking capacity—in four important ways. First, elections deter-
mine the numerical balance of power between the two major parties in the
House and Senate, setting the electoral context for the coming two years.
Second, elections determine the pattern of party control of government:

whether Congress and the White House will be governed by a single political party under unified government, or whether control of government will be divided between the two major parties. Third, elections determine the ideological diversity of the two political parties, shaping whether a moderate center will reign or whether the parties will occupy polar extremes—the prevailing pattern over nearly the past two decades. Finally, elections affect the bicameral nature of Congress, as they determine the array of policy views across the full House and for one-third of the Senate every two years. To understand how elections might shape Congress's policy-making performance, we need to explore these multiple ways in which elections influence the positions and capacities of the parties. Granted, how Congress performs is affected by more than the dynamics of political parties. New issues and crises—managed well or poorly—no doubt affect Congress's capacity to govern. But at the root of the legislative process lies the organization and principle of party—a mechanism for binding legislators to varying degrees through the electoral and policy interests they share with their fellow partisans.

United We Govern?

Divided party control of government predominated over the latter half of the twentieth century and again in the early years of the twenty-first, encouraging students and observers of Congress to indict split party control of Congress and the White House as the central cause of legislative stalemate. The indictment was rooted in political scientists' historic commitment to strong political parties, encapsulated in E.E. Schattschneider's *doctrine of responsible parties.* "The political parties created democracy," E.E. Schattschneider observed in his 1942 classic *Party Government,* "and . . . modern democracy is unthinkable save in terms of the parties."[2] For responsible party theorists, *American* democracy—with its separated institutions sharing constitutional powers—was unthinkable except in terms of unified party government. Political scientist V.O. Key, writing in the 1960s, offered the now-classic view: "Common partisan control of executive and legislature does not assure energetic government, but division of party control precludes it."[3]

Why might party control matter? Unified party control is said to create a natural bridge between the president and his congressional majority. That bridge is built on party members' shared electoral interest in maintaining control of government, meaning that considerations beyond policy interests will help to shape legislative coalitions. Presidents have an incentive to work toward the election and reelection of their party's congressional majority, and legislators accrue an incentive to work toward enacting the president's party agenda. Within Congress, a strong policy record for the majority party creates a good party reputation—a commodity that is said to pay off at election time.

Divided government, in contrast, is said to reinforce policy disagreements between the branches, raising obstacles to the formation of successful legislative coalitions. When two different parties control Congress and the White House, both parties have an incentive to regain control of government, rather than to work toward enacting major policy change. Moreover, given the chance that voters will reward the president for major policy achievements, the Congressional majority has a diminished interest in making the compromises necessary to force legislative success. The conventional wisdom has thus long dictated that elections affect legislative performance by determining whether party control will be divided between the two parties or concentrated within a single majority party.

In his 1991 work, *Divided We Govern,* David Mayhew was the first to provide a rigorous test of the impact of divided government on lawmaking. Mayhew asked a simple question: Does more get done in Congress during periods of unified or divided control? To answer the question, Mayhew developed a way to identify landmark laws enacted over the second half of the twentieth century and then tested whether the presence of divided government reduced the number of major laws enacted each Congress. Counter to the received wisdom, Mayhew found that unified party control of Congress and the president failed to boost legislative productivity in Washington. According to Mayhew's study, it does not matter whether a single party controls the White House and Congress: roughly the same number of important laws are enacted in periods of unified and divided control. Mayhew suggests a number of other forces that may shape Congress's performance, including shifting public moods, presidential cycles, and the rise of issues that cut across the traditional ideological spectrum.

Why might party control of government not matter? Mayhew counseled a less commanding view of parties as "policy factions," coalitions that can muster results regardless of the regime of party control. The American political system is a pluralist system, Mayhew noted, and parties adapt in such a system to the multiple crosscutting currents within the American system. Political observers and scholars alike, Mayhew suggested, demand more from parties than they can deliver in a system of separated powers. Mayhew's provocative findings have generated a growth industry in the study of divided government and lawmaking. I return to this central question below, proposing an alternative way of addressing the same question and exploring the other ways in which elections might matter in shaping congressional capacity.

The Impact of Pluralist Parties

Elections also determine the distribution of ideological views within each party. Sometimes partisans' policy views will be *polarized,* with legislators from each party situated at opposite ends of an underlying left-right ideological spectrum. From the 1980s until the present, Democrats and Republicans in both chambers have been remarkably polarized: Democrats cluster on the left of the ideological spectrum and Republicans occupy the right, with just a few legislators filling the ideological center. At other times, partisan *moderation* dominates, with a greater number of legislators standing close to the ideological center between the parties. By all accounts, the legislative parties have become more polarized over the past half-century, even as the American public remains centrist in their policy views. As shown in Figure 1, using legislators' roll call votes to identify their ideologies, partisan polarization has grown steadily since the 1970s: Very few legislators occupy the political center in either chamber. Some even claim that we now face "asymmetric" polarization: Republicans have moved farther to the right than Democrats have moved to the left.

Does it matter whether parties are polarized or centrist? There is good reason to suspect that a broad political center makes enactment of major policy change more likely. First, our political system requires broad, and usually bipartisan, coalitions to adopt major policy change—coalitions that are easier to build when legislators occupy the political center. Second, if activist constituencies polarize, parties have both electoral and policy incentives to distinguish their records and

Figure 1. Partisan Polarization, 1879–2011

Distance Between the Parties First Dimension

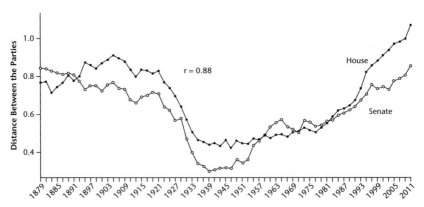

Source: "The Polarization of the Congressional Parties." Accessed February 14, 2012. http://voteview .com/political_polarization.asp

positions as well as a lesser incentive to bargain and compromise. This may help explain why President George W. Bush's push for social security reform after the 2004 elections gained little traction among Democrats: With few centrist legislators seeking bipartisan solutions, the parties preferred to stake out different grounds on reforming the program. President Obama similarly faced the consequences of a polarized Congress. As Democrats often point out, Senate Minority Leader Mitch McConnell (R-Kentucky) boasted in 2010 that the Republicans' most important goal was to make Obama a one-term president. Near or total Republican opposition to Obama proposals—from health care reform to raising income tax rates—provides ample evidence that polarization can put legislative compromise out of reach.

The conventional wisdom now suggests that today's legislative stalemate is caused in large part by the rise in polarization—a plausible hypothesis, but one that runs counter to a key assumption of the responsible party school. Party government school theorists held as a matter of faith that unified, disciplined, and coherent parties were the key to effective governance. As the parties polarized—and came to stand for different policy agendas—accountability to the electorate would increase. The parties would stand coherently for different policy prescriptions, voters would choose between stark alternatives, and the winning party would both receive a mandate to carry out that program and take responsibility for the government's action or inaction in the next election. We have, in other words, conflicting expectations about the impact of polarized parties on Congress's legislative performance. Does electoral moderation improve or harm the prospects for major policy change? I return to this question below.

Bicameral Differences

Elections might also be instrumental in shaping congressional outcomes by molding the policy views of the House and Senate. There are several reasons why House and Senate majorities might hold different views on policy questions, even when those majorities hail from the same party. First, House and Senate members face different electoral constituencies, with district-based House constituencies typically more homogenous in their views and interests than state populations represented by senators. Second, the Senate employs staggered elections, in which just one-third of the Senate is up in even-numbered years. Because Senate elections are staggered (and typically more competitive than a House race), senators are often on the ballot under different political and economic conditions—often leading to differences of opinion with their House colleagues and with each other over the most important issues and policy solutions. Third, the uneven powers afforded House and Senate party leaders and the different rules of the two chambers can often produce different legislative solutions to similar problems. In other words, unified party control of Congress does not guarantee that the two chambers will agree with each other on the big issues of the day.

Such differences in both policy and political positions between the two chambers were on full display in 2009, when House and Senate Democrats began to write President Obama's health care proposals into law. Despite unified Democratic control of the government, House and Senate Democrats failed to see eye to eye on their own Democratic president's health care reform agenda, with the two chamber caucuses opting for different approaches to broadening public access to health care. Inter-chamber disputes prolonged deliberations over a final health care bill. Indeed, the process stretched out so long that the Senate Democrats lost their filibuster-proof majority of sixty votes with the death of Senator Ted Kennedy (D-Massachusetts), vastly complicating Democrats' efforts to settle on a final bill.

In short, the House and Senate rarely exhibit identical views about public policy. As I suggest below, taking account of bicameral differences in a systematic way is essential in explaining variation in Congress's legislative performance: policy differences between the chambers are likely to increase the chances of deadlock, regardless of whether government control is unified or split between the branches. Indeed, as split party control of the House and Senate in 2011 and 2012 amply show, the legislative process can indeed grind to a halt in face of insurmountable bicameral disagreements.

When Can Congress Govern Well?

When Congress faces policy challenges—whether new or recurring problems—are legislators and the president able to muster a timely, responsive, and responsible solution? To be sure, not every one agrees on what counts as an acceptable policy solution. Still, press accounts of Congress routinely identify productive and unproductive sessions, pointing to Congress's record on addressing the major issues before it.

To assess more systematically the relevance of elections for congressional performance, I once devised a yardstick of congressional performance. As explored in detail in my book, *Stalemate,* my basic approach is to identify issues that are commonly perceived as significant national problems, and then to assess whether Congress acted to address those problems and whether seasoned observers believed that the solution was well targeted to the problem.[4] The yardstick thus tallies the share of salient issues on the nation's agenda left in limbo at the close of each Congress. I term this the *gridlock score,* and calculate each Congress's score for the period between 1947 and 2000. By comparing different Congresses' gridlock scores, I create a yardstick for measuring and assessing Congress's legislative performance over the latter half of the twentieth century.

Figure 2 shows the landscape of congressional performance between 1947 and 2000, focusing on the most salient legislative issues. The most productive Congresses in this period were the 80th (1947–1948), 88th (1963–1964), and 89th (1965–1966), the last known as the "Great Society" Congress under Lyndon Johnson. Those Congresses stalemated on less than one-third of their agendas. In contrast, the least productive Congress was the 106th (1990–2000), a Republican Congress that faced off against a Democratic Bill Clinton; stalemate occurred on over 70 percent of its agenda. The 105th (1997–1998) and 102nd (1991–1992) were close contenders for the worst performing Congresses. The highs and lows clearly comport well with the conventional wisdom about Congressional performance—from its heights in the Great Society to its lows in the period

Figure 2. Legislative Gridlock, 1947–2000

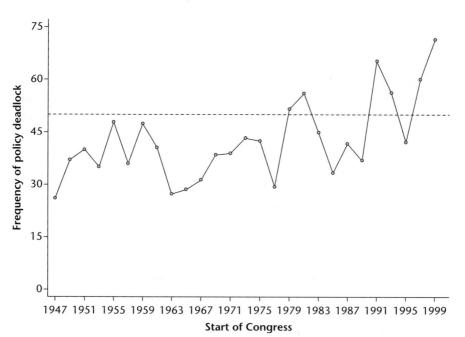

Source: Sarah A. Binder, *Stalemate: Causes and Consequences of Legislative Gridlock* (Washington, D.C.: Brookings Institution Press, 2003). The figure shows the percentage of salient issues left in stalemate at the end of each two-year Congress.

when Republicans attempted to impeach President Clinton. No doubt, if we continued to measure the Congresses after 2000, we would find that the 111th Congress (2009–2010) matches up favorably with the most productive congresses. And we can be sure that the most recent Congress (2011–2012) would give the poor performing congresses a run for their money.

What role do elections and party competition play in shaping the variation we see in Congress's legislative performance over time? We can use the gridlock scores in a statistical model that estimates how electoral, partisan, and institutional forces jointly shape the frequency of deadlock over the postwar period. The results from such a model are instructive. First, divided government accompanies more frequent bouts of stalemate: Legislative gridlock is significantly higher in periods of divided party control than in periods of unified control. Second, the array of preferences within each political party seems to matter strongly: As partisan polarization climbs, so too does gridlock. Although single party control of Congress and the White House may help to break deadlock, there are limits to the power of political parties to smooth the way for legislative agreement. Intense polarization seems counterproductive to fostering major policy change.

Third, bicameral forces seem to affect legislative outcomes: increases in the ideological gap between the two chambers make stalemate more frequent. Even controlling for the influence of party control and partisan polarization on what Congress achieves, policy differences between the House and Senate still matter. Bicameral disagreement helps to explain the several impasses Republicans encountered in the 108th Congress upon gaining control of the White House, Senate, and House. Among other issues, bankruptcy overhaul, corporate tax reform, and the annual budget resolution encountered significant delays as House and Senate Republicans could not reach common ground on each other's legislative solutions. Bicameral disagreements also plagued the divided 112th Congress, in which a Republican House and a Democratic Senate repeatedly brought the government to a standstill over funding the government and financing its debts. The combination of polarized parties and bicameral differences proved toxic to the parties' abilities to set aside differences to reach common ground.

Legislating in Polarized Times

After the Supreme Court cemented his election in 2000, George W. Bush declared that it was time to "move beyond the bitterness and partisanship of the recent past." By most accounts, however, congressional partisanship continued to rise. Democrats charged that Bush pursued a polarizing agenda of tax cuts and other measures, after his hairsplitting election arguably called for a more conciliatory approach. Republicans countered that a move toward the center would have damaged the Bush presidency, and that there was little Bush could have done given the competitive balance of two ideologically charged parties.

The terror attacks of September 11, 2001, brought a temporary respite from the intense partisanship of Congress. On measures directly related to the recovery in Washington and New York and on the war against the Taliban in Afghanistan, legislators quickly united. But on measures unrelated to September 11, and certainly in the wake of the U.S. decision to go to war in Iraq in 2003, bitter partisanship resurfaced in Congress. House Democrats derided Republican tactics that included holding open the vote on a controversial Medicare reform package for three hours in the middle of the night. Senate Democrats found themselves excluded from conference committees, and Republicans excoriated Democrats for what they deemed unconstitutional filibusters against the president's judicial nominees and relentless obstruction of Republican priorities.

The president's stance after the 2004 elections probably did not help to defuse partisan tensions. After winning with 51.4 percent of the two-party vote, the president declared: "I earned capital in the campaign, political capital, and now I intend to spend it"—an assessment that many observers questioned at the time. The second term of the Bush administration proved too late to spend down the president's capital. Although Bush enjoyed two more years of unified Republican control, by the end of 2006 Republicans had few legislative compromises to tout. The administration's flat-footed response to Hurricane Katrina in New Orleans, Americans' weariness with the wars in Iraq and Afghanistan, and the first signs of trouble in housing markets undermined public confidence in Republican rule, returning Democratic majorities to the House and Senate in the 2006 congressional elections and expanding them further with Obama's win in 2008. Since then, there has been no sign of easing in the polarization that separates the parties into warring camps. If anything, polarization continues to intensify. So today, in the run up to the 2012 elections, the parties are more polarized than they've been in more than a century.

Why has partisan polarization been so debilitating for Congress? Keep in mind that polarization reflects two trends: pronounced policy and ideological differences and intense partisan disagreement. The political parties in Washington disagree so intensely because they hold different views about the appropriate role of government in managing the economy *and* because electoral competition gives each party a strategic incentive to disagree with the other party—simply because it is the other party. Given the competitive state of the parties—and the close party margins in the House and Senate—both parties believe that control of Congress and the White House is in reach. Under such conditions, rallying the base—rather than reaching to the middle—makes the most short-term electoral sense for both parties. Rather than agree to a half-loaf compromise, both parties hold out to the next election for a full loaf. No surprise then is the increased use of lame duck December sessions in the wake of the November elections as majorities seek a final chance to lock in favored policy change before handing over the reins.

The rise in polarization also sheds some light on disputes about the impact of divided government on lawmaking. Political scientists and pundits often argue that divided party control is essential for getting things done in Washington. In some respects, the argument rings true. Facing tough choices, both parties use the cover of bipartisanship to reach agreements that are unattainable under unified party control. Standing at the edge of a cliff, the parties hold hands and jump off the ledge together—sharing credit and blame. We certainly have episodes of landmark lawmaking in periods of divided government (for instance, a grand bargain on tax reform in 1986 and historic welfare reform a decade later).

But the effectiveness of divided government in propelling solutions might be conditional on the state of the parties. Split control when polarization is low yields sustainable policy bargains; split control when polarization is high can put policy agreement out of reach. Instead of holding hands and jumping together, the parties maneuver to push the other party off the cliff and to be the last one standing. No surprise then that legislating in 2011 was a story of perpetual brinkmanship. The parties proved unable to broach compromise without the threat of a deadline to force action, typically reaching agreement with only hours to go. Facing unacceptable consequences of stalemate—shutting down the government, defaulting on the nation's debt, increasing payroll taxes in the holiday season—the two parties each time temporarily set aside their differences. Such brinkmanship takes its toll on the economy, on the public, and on Congress itself, and it leaves the nation's pressing public problems unresolved. As the events of 2011 confirm, legislating in polarized times means sometimes hardly legislating at all.

NOTES

1. Norman J. Ornstein. "Worst. Congress. Ever." *Foreign Policy*, July 19, 2011. Accessed February 9, 2012. http://www.foreignpolicy.com/articles/2011/07/19/worst_congress_ever

2. E.E. Schattschneider, *Party Government* (New York: Farrar and Reinhart, 1942), 1.

3. V. O. Key, Jr., *Politics, Parties, and Pressure Groups*, 5th ed. (New York: Crowell, 1964), 688.

4. See Sarah A. Binder, *Stalemate: Causes and Consequences of Legislative Gridlock* (Washington, D.C.: Brookings Institution Press, 2003). I use the unsigned daily editorials of the *New York Times* to identify salient issues on the agenda and then use *Congressional Quarterly* and other sources to determine whether or not Congress addressed the issue in legislation.

6-3

Congressional Committees in a Continuing Partisan Era

John H. Aldrich and David W. Rohde

*In the essay below, John Aldrich and David Rohde describe the theory of con-
ditional party government. This theory posits that a cohesive party, one in
which the party members agree on most issues, will empower its leadership to
play a central role in policymaking. With cohesive majority parties over the
last three decades, majority party leaders have directed the actions of standing committees and assumed a direct role in designing legislation.*

THE TWO PRINCIPAL organizing structures of Congress are the political parties
and the committee system. During the history of the institution, the relative
influence of the two has shifted back and forth. From 1890 to 1910, the majority party dominated the House of Representatives, with the Speaker empowered to appoint committees and their chairs and to control the legislative
agenda. After the revolt against Speaker Joe Cannon in 1910, power shifted to
committees, whose leaders were selected based on seniority. From the 1920s
through the 1970s party influence was relatively weak, and that period
became known as the era of committee government. Then, beginning with the
reform period in the 1970s, institutional changes were adopted that strengthened parties and weakened the sway of committees and their chairs. Moreover,
the extent and intensity of partisan conflict in Congress increased. Of course,
even in strong party eras Congress members did not abandon the committee
system. Speaker Cannon's powers, for example, were exercised in large part
through the committee system. This shifting balance of power therefore
reflects the degree of autonomy of the committees and their chairs from their
legislative party organizations, as well as any additional, independent powers
granted the party.

In this chapter we discuss the transformation of the party-committee balance
from the 1970s to the present, focusing mainly on the House but also considering the Senate. We begin by considering the Democratic Party reforms of the
1970s that launched the transformation and how the Democrats applied the

Source: John H. Aldrich and David W. Rohde, "The Congressional Committees in a Continuing Partisan
Era," in *Congress Reconsidered*, 9th ed., ed. Lawrence C. Dodd and Bruce I. Oppenheimer (Washington,
D.C.: CQ Press, 2009), 217–229, 232–240. Some notes appearing in the original have been deleted.

party leadership's new powers. Then we consider further developments after the Republicans won control of both houses in the 1994 elections. We also discuss additional institutional changes that the GOP made and the ways in which the Republican Party leadership interacted with the committee system to achieve its legislative goals. The return of the Democratic majority after the 2006 elections gives us a single but important session to examine the party-committee balance under new party (and committee) leadership. We will also briefly discuss Senate committees and then offer some conclusions.

The Committee System and the Era of Committee Government

The most important thing to recognize about the House and Senate committee systems is that they are designed institutions. That is, they are created by the membership to serve the interests of the chamber and its members. Committees, through division of labor, permit the chamber to stretch its capabilities by having only a subset of members consider each issue and piece of legislation in detail. Furthermore, committees encourage the development of expertise through members' specialization in the issue areas covered by their committees' jurisdictions.[1] In addition to these benefits to the chamber, committees also provide benefits to individual members. Richard Fenno has argued that members of Congress pursue one or more of three goals: reelection, power within the chamber, and good public policy.[2] The achievement of each of these goals is potentially influenced by committee membership. Members can use committee service to identify themselves with issues that are important to constituents and to secure benefits for their districts, thus enhancing their chances for reelection.[3] Committee and subcommittee chairmanships also provide members with positions of power in the chamber. And committee members are in the best position to influence public policy within their committees' jurisdictions.[4]

Congress used committees to conduct business from the beginning of the institution, although it took most of a century for the system to develop into the form we know today.[5] Standing committees (that is, permanent committees with recognized substantive jurisdictions) were widely used by the 1820s. They included members from both the majority and minority parties, and as the committees developed expertise their parent chambers began to defer to their judgments on legislative policy. Throughout the 1800s, the influence of the majority party leadership over committees grew. Speakers had the right to appoint committee members and chairs, and they chaired the Rules Committee, which set the terms of debate for bills on the House floor. The Speaker lost these powers in the revolt against Speaker Cannon in 1910. After that the Speaker could no longer appoint committees, and each party developed its own procedures for that purpose. Seniority in committee service became the almost inviolable basis for choosing committee chairs. Moreover, the Rules Committee was autonomous and the Speaker barred from serving on it.

As a result of these developments, committees became largely independent from party influence. Because committee chairs were chosen and maintained in power by seniority, they had no particular incentive to be responsive to the wishes of their party or its leaders in producing legislation. The chairs shaped their committees' agendas, appointed subcommittees (and usually chose their chairs), and decided when hearings would be held and how bills would be handled. These developments might have been less consequential if the committee leaders were ideologically representative of their party, but that was not the case. From 1930 on, the Democrats were usually in the majority, and because southern Democrats were more likely to accumulate seniority than their northern counterparts, they were disproportionately represented among committee leaders. Conservative southerners often allied with Republicans to block or alter Democratic legislation, a situation that greatly frustrated northerners. Although that pattern had begun in the 1930s, their frustration became particularly pronounced in the 1950s and 1960s.

Party Reform: Gateway to the Partisan Era

Initial attempts at reform of committee government included a successful effort in 1961 to expand the Rules Committee to reduce the influence of southern conservatives on the panel. Then in 1970 Congress passed the Legislative Reorganization Act. It contained a number of important features, such as the requirement that committees make public roll call votes, and it generally required committees to permit the public to attend their meetings. The act also made it much easier to obtain recorded votes on amendments on the House floor and set the stage for electronic voting, which markedly sped up floor voting. These changes started to shift the locus of legislative decision making from the committees to the floor. The reorganization act, however, took no action to revise the seniority system or to reduce the powers of committee chairs.[6] The conservative coalition was able to block any such actions that would have undermined their institutional position.

However, the makeup of the House (and Senate) membership was changing. The Voting Rights Act of 1965 had enfranchised black voters in the South, and their strong tilt to the Democratic Party was liberalizing the party's voter base there. Reinforcing that effect was the gradual departure from the party of conservative voters who no longer saw the Democrats as standing for their interests. As a consequence of these developments, new southern Democrats were becoming more like their northern colleagues, and the Democratic membership in Congress was becoming less divided and more homogeneous.[7] This set the stage for efforts to strengthen the majority party leadership relative to the committee system. Since the revolt against Cannon, the diverse memberships of the congressional parties had been reluctant to enhance party power because their very diversity meant that there would be great uncertainty about the ends for which that power would be used. That is, members could not be sure what policies leaders would seek, and so individual members feared that powerful leaders would seek policies far different from their own preferred outcome. If, on the other hand, the preferences of party members were to become more similar, members would not have to be as concerned that leaders with preferences different from theirs would be chosen, and it would be safer to grant leaders stronger powers.

This relationship is the essence of the theoretical perspective that we have labeled *conditional party government,* or CPG for short.[8] If the legislators in a party have very heterogeneous policy preferences, they will not be likely to grant strong powers to their leadership. As policy preferences become more homogeneous, members will be progressively more likely to empower their party leaders because they will have less reason to fear the use of those powers. This tendency will be further reinforced as the positions of the two parties become more different because the consequences to each party's members of the other party's winning the competition to control policy will become more and more negative.

By the early 1970s, liberal Democrats were a clear majority of the House Democratic caucus, but not of the entire House membership. Because they could not muster a majority on the floor for the kinds of reforms they favored, the liberals targeted the rules of the Democratic caucus instead. Only Democrats could vote on these efforts, which combined strategies dealing both with committees and with the party and its leadership. First they sought to undermine the independence and power of committee leaders, so that the remaining conservatives would be less able to impede passage of their desired legislation. This strategy followed two tracks. First, the liberals wanted to end the automatic nature of the seniority system. To this end the caucus adopted rules providing for a secret ballot vote on all committee chairs at the beginning of every Congress. If the prospective chair (usually still the most senior Democrat on the committee) was voted down, there would be a competitive election of the chair in the caucus. This change was shown to have real consequences in 1975 when three southern Democrats were removed from committee chairmanships and replaced by more loyal northerners. Chairs were put on notice that they could not buck their party's policy wishes with impunity.

The second track of the strategy involved adopting rules that restricted the powers of those chosen as chairs. The principal vehicle was a set of rules known as the Subcommittee Bill of Rights, which required that committee members bid for the chairs of subcommittees in order of seniority, ending the ability of full committee chairs simply to appoint those positions. Subcommittees had to receive specific jurisdictions, and committee legislation had to be referred to subcommittees accordingly. In addition, subcommittee chairs would control their own budgets and staffs, rather than the chair of the full committee doing so.

The other strategy of the reformers was to give more powers to the party leadership. The Speaker received the right to appoint the chair and the Democratic members of the Rules Committee. That meant that the leadership could again control the flow of legislation and strategically shape the terms of floor consideration. In addition, the power to assign Democrats to other committees was vested in a new Steering and Policy Committee, most of whose members were party leaders or appointed by the Speaker. The reformers wanted the leadership to have more influence over the allocation of prized assignments, to make members more responsive to the leaders. Finally, the Speaker was given the authority to refer bills to more than one committee and to set deadlines for reporting, further reducing the ability of committees to act as roadblocks.

Partisanship Takes Hold: 1983–1994

The reforms were adopted by the mid-1970s and some of their consequences were quickly apparent, but divisions remained in the Democratic caucus, preventing the full effects of the changes from being visible. Indeed, many observers complained that the reforms had merely made Congress less efficient by further decentralizing power to subcommittees. This viewpoint was reinforced by Ronald Reagan's success in 1981 at splitting off southern Democrats to support his budget and tax proposals. The recession of 1982, however, helped bring fifty-seven Democrats to the House, including many moderate-to-liberal southerners. Consequently the conservative coalition was no longer a majority of the House. The newcomers made up over one-fifth of the Democratic caucus, and they provided support for stronger use of the leadership's powers to advance the party agenda and to compete with the priorities of the Reagan administration.

As we noted earlier, one reform strategy sought to induce committee chairs to refrain from blocking party bills and to support the Democratic Party's legislative program. After the removal of the three southern chairs in 1975, committee chairs recognized that their continued hold on their positions depended to a degree on their party support, and their behavior changed accordingly. Research shows that members who occupied, or were close in seniority to, committee chairs dramatically increased their levels of party support between 1971 and 1982.[9] For example, in 1973–1974 the party unity score of Rep. Jamie Whitten, D-Miss., was thirty-eight points below the party average and eighteen points below the average for southern Democrats. Anticipating a liberal challenge when the chairmanship of the Appropriations Committee (where he ranked second) became vacant, Whitten began to change his behavior. By 1988, Whitten's party unity score was not only higher than the average southern Democrat's, it was two points higher than the average Democrat's.[10] Moreover, the Democratic caucus continued to use the mechanism for voting on chair candidates to pressure or remove committee leaders whose performance was deemed unsatisfactory.

The other reform strategy was to strengthen the party leadership, and it had a substantial impact on the relationship between the leadership and committees. As Barbara Sinclair has said, "Party and committee leaders must work together . . . since both are agents of and ultimately responsible to the Democratic Caucus."[11] In the changed environment, most committee leaders came to think of themselves as part of a team with the majority leadership. Committee chairs realized that they could not act independently of party priorities in drafting legislation. In turn, they expected party leaders to provide adequate staff support and assistance in moving bills to passage on the floor.[12]

One of the most important tools available to the party leadership was control of the Rules Committee. During the 1980s, the Democrats increasingly used the resolutions (called "special rules") that set the terms for floor consideration of legislation to structure the agenda to the advantage of the party.[13] For example, special rules could bar amendments completely, giving members a take-it-or-leave-it choice between the bill the leadership favored and nothing. Or the rule could permit just those amendments that the leadership wanted to consider, barring others that the Republican minority wanted but that would cause policy or electoral difficulties for some Democrats. Moreover, if the reporting committee had not adequately taken the majority party's wishes into account, special rules could be used to alter the bill as reported to bring the policy closer to the preference of the majority. This was done multiple times on defense authorization bills reported from the Armed Services Committee.

Not surprisingly, the majority party's use of its powers provoked anger and frustration among Republicans. One response from the GOP was to change its party rules to mimic those of the Democrats, so as to make its own leadership more able to compete. For example, the Republicans gave the minority leader the right to make Republican appointments to the Rules Committee and created a new committee assignment system in which the leadership had more voting power. The party leader was also empowered to designate "leadership issues," and on those bills all members of the party leadership were obliged to support the positions of the Republican Conference.

The Republicans also adopted progressively more confrontational tactics to protest their treatment and to undermine the Democratic majority. Some complaints came from GOP leaders and mainline conservatives, but most active were members of a group of populist conservatives known as the Conservative Opportunity Society (COS), led by Newt Gingrich of Georgia, then a backbencher. Gingrich and COS believed that the Republicans would be a perpetual minority unless they stopped going along with the Democrats as a means of attempting to have some influence on legislation. Instead, they argued that the GOP had to draw contrasts with the Democrats and let the public make a choice. The COS organized protests against the Democrats' management of the chamber and fought against the use of special rules to control the agenda and limit Republican influence. These efforts culminated in late 1988, when Gingrich filed a formal complaint with the House Ethics Committee against Speaker Jim Wright, D-Texas. The ensuing investigation led to Wright's resignation from the House.

Republican Rule and Its Consequences: 1994–2000

Republican confrontations with the Democratic majority continued into the 1990s, especially after President Bill Clinton was elected in 1992, restoring unified government. The GOP was able to take advantage of the political context in 1994, successfully exploiting negative public feelings about government performance, the condition of the nation, and Clinton personally.[14] The Republicans won majority control of both houses of Congress for the first time since the election of 1952. The new majority in the House chose Newt Gingrich as their Speaker, and the party set out to transform the operation of the chamber to set the stage for major changes in government policy.

Republican Procedural Changes

Gingrich's transforming efforts commenced almost immediately.[15] Little more than a week after election day he made clear his intent to depart from the seniority system in selecting committee chairs to a greater extent than the Democrats ever did, announcing that he had chosen Bob Livingston, La., as the new chair of the Appropriations Committee. Livingston ranked fifth in committee seniority but was considered more ideologically dependable and more effective than the more senior committee members. A few days later, Gingrich again bypassed seniority to select more dependable chairs for Judiciary and Commerce. Gingrich was asserting the right to name the new chairs before the newly elected majority had yet arrived in Washington, and the Republican Conference members tacitly ratified his decisions by their acquiescence.

The powers of committees and their chairs were also changed significantly. Three committees were abolished outright, and most remaining committees were limited to five subcommittees. These actions eliminated twenty-five subcommittees and 12 percent of full committee slots. As one COS member said, "Our system will prevent members from getting locked into the status quo."[16]

The Republican leadership gave its chairs the right to appoint subcommittee chairs and control over committee staff. This reflected Gingrich's view that chairs should control their committees, but he also believed that the party should control the chairs. He required committee chairs to consult with him before choosing subcommittee heads, and he pressured one chair to name two freshman representatives to head subcommittees. Gingrich also required each member of the Appropriations Committee to sign a "letter of fidelity," pledging to cut the budget as much as the Speaker wanted. To further weaken the capacities of committee leaders to build an independent power base, the Republicans adopted a six-year term limit for all committee and subcommittee chairmen.

Gingrich also announced a new Republican committee assignment process, and it was adopted by the Republican Conference in December. It gave the Speaker control over a much larger fraction of votes on the Committee on Committees. Republican House members also confirmed their leader's right to appoint the members and chair of the Rules Committee. Overall, under the new GOP majority, committees had less independent power and the party leadership had more.

It is worth noting one thing that the GOP did not do. It didn't adopt a wholesale realignment of committee jurisdictions, as some reformers had wanted. The existing pattern of jurisdictions had too many implications for the reelection, policy, and power goals of members, and most of them were unwilling to accept the risks involved in major change.[17] When the GOP took over the majority, Gingrich authorized Rep. David Dreier of California (vice chair of a joint committee on congressional reform in the previous Congress) to draft four plans of varying comprehensiveness for revamping the committee system. After it became apparent that there would be significant resistance from the chairs and members of affected committees, Gingrich opted for a version of the least-extensive plan. Thus we see that although Republican members were willing to support strengthening their leadership's influence over committees, they were not willing to sacrifice their other interests that were served by the committee system.

Party Leaders and Committees

The rules changes that the new Republican majority adopted thus set the stage for greater influence by party leaders over the activities and legislative products of committees. Because of limited space we can only present a few examples, mostly drawn from the 104th Congress (1995–1997), which we can then compare with the first session under the Democratic majority in the 110th.

Influencing Bill Creation in Committees. Majority leadership involvement in the crafting of bills in committee did not originate with the 104th Congress. As Sinclair shows,[18] such activity had become more frequent as committee autonomy decreased in the postreform era. It was, however, still infrequent in the Democrat-controlled Congresses, as most leader activity involved stages of the process after initial drafting. The 104th marked a major increase in this role for majority leadership.

The most extensive instance of leadership influence on bill creation was the drafting and revision of the legislation designed to implement the Contract with America.[19] Although there was substantial initial consultation on general matters during the crafting of the contract, the top GOP leaders determined which issues would be included and many of the particulars. For example, it was Gingrich who decided that school prayer would not be included. Committee consideration of these predrafted bills was largely pro forma, a necessary consequence of the leadership's pledge to pass them in the Congress's first hundred days.

The contract was of central importance, but the leadership's involvement in committees' initial consideration of bills was not limited to that legislation. Another example involves the major reform of agriculture subsidy policy that became known as the Freedom to Farm Act. In September 1995, the GOP leadership sent a letter to the Agriculture Committee chair, Pat Roberts of Kansas. They wrote, "We give the committee leave" to write major budget-cutting farm legislation. They indicated that they hoped the committee would support Roberts's bill, but if not "we will feel compelled" to bring the bill to the floor allowing unlimited amendments, or to replace the committee's bill with true reforms.[20] Moreover, during the consideration of the bill in committee, John Boehner of Ohio (a member, who was also GOP Conference chair) went so far as to say, "If this committee can't do it [make $13 billion in cuts called for in the budget plan], the future of this committee is seriously in doubt."[21] Rarely in congressional history has the majority leadership sought to dictate to and threaten a committee in so direct a fashion.

Bypassing Committees and Postcommittee Adjustments. In some instances, the Republican leadership simply bypassed committees altogether to achieve its policy and political goals. Gingrich had personally picked the chair of the Judiciary Committee, the independent-minded Henry Hyde of Illinois. Hyde was suitably responsive to the leadership and the Republican Conference during the speedy processing of a large number of bills from the Contract with America. However, the bill to repeal the 1994 ban on assault weapons, which Hyde opposed, went to the floor without committee consideration. When asked why Judiciary was not given the opportunity to consider the bill, the chairman said: "We have a reputation of being deliberative."[22]

Another device for bypassing committees was the use of leader-appointed party task forces.[23] Often, but not always, task forces had the assent of committees (or at least of their leaders), and they usually contained some members of the appropriate committees. A key difference, however, was that they contained only Republicans, and at times they were used to secure a different policy outcome than the committee of jurisdiction preferred. For example, in 1995 the Government Reform and Oversight Committee approved a bill to abolish the Commerce Department that was insufficiently radical to satisfy many of the GOP freshmen. The dissenters expressed their displeasure, and in response the leadership chose a different, more radical bill to accomplish the goal. The source of the bill was a GOP task force set up by Gingrich and chaired by a freshman. The bill had no hearings and no committee markup.[24]

The leadership could also use its control over the Rules Committee to make adjustments in the content of legislation after the committees had made their decisions. Barbara Sinclair's research shows that under the Republicans this kind of action was most frequent in the "revolutionary" 104th Congress, occurring on nearly half the major bills. But postcommittee adjustments continued to occur in later Congresses, for example, on more than one-third of the major bills in the 105th Congress.[25] One instance was the 1997 budget resolution, when Gingrich supervised adjustments to placate dissident Republicans and the White House. Another occurred in 1999, when moderate Republicans threatened to oppose the GOP tax bill because it was not sufficiently concerned with deficit reduction. Speaker Hastert brokered a change that made the tax rate cut dependent on a declining national debt.[26]

Special Rules and Control of the Floor. As we noted earlier, leaders of the majority can use their powers to support and defend the decisions of committees or to undermine them if the committees have not produced a result the party wanted. One way is through their general control of the floor agenda.

We saw that when they were in the minority, GOP members frequently attacked the Democrats for writing rules that barred them from offering amendments. As the majority in the 104th, however, they demonstrated that they were quite prepared to do the same thing. In one instance, on the recissions bill (legislation to make cuts in previously appropriated funds) taken up in March 1995, the Rules Committee wrote a rule that had the effect of blocking cutting defense spending to increase social spending. The rule prompted strong objections from a number of GOP moderates.[27]

In another example, a group of conservative Democrats wanted to offer a substitute amendment for the Republican Medicare reform plan, but the Rules Committee barred their amendment. Gene Taylor, D-Miss., said, "I am furious. . . . The Republicans came to power promising change, open rules." He charged, "They are no more fair than the Democrats."[28]

Not Everything Is Partisan

To this point we have focused our attention on the increased partisanship in Congress and on the strengthening of the influence of the party structure relative to committees. In this section we want to emphasize that one should not over-interpret these patterns. Specifically, it is important to recognize that much of Congress's business does not involve party conflict, as the data displayed in Table 1 demonstrate.[29] The table shows data from three Congresses on the proportion of bills over which there was some conflict, either in committee or on the floor. The standard for conflict was very minimal: Was there even one roll call on the bill on which there was a minority larger than 10 percent? Despite this low threshold, however, only about one-third of the bills saw any conflict at all.

Why was there so seldom conflict on legislation, if Congress has become ever more partisan over the period covered by these data? The reason is that the agenda that Congress deals with is multifaceted and diverse, and only a portion of it deals with the types of issues that provoke interparty disagreement. The parties care

Table 1. Conflict on Legislation in the 96th, 100th, and 104th Congresses

	96th Congress (1979–1980)	100th Congress (1987–1988)	104th Congress (1995–1996)
Prestige committees	51.3% (150)	65.7% (67)	76.3% (93)
Policy committees	40.7% (317)	28.7% (394)	34.3% (376)
Constituency committees	20.8% (438)	17.8% (499)	23.8% (315)
All committees	32.8% (905)	25.6% (960)	35.1% (784)

Note: Given above are the percentages of bills considered by those committees that exhibited some conflict, either in committee or on the floor (the number of bills in each category is in parentheses). See endnote 29.

intensely about bills that relate to divisions among their members, their activists, and their electoral coalitions—things such as tax policy, the scope of government, regulation of business, and social issues such as abortion and gay rights. Most legislation, however, does not tap into these divisive subjects. Much legislation involves renewal of, or funding for, existing programs with wide support in the country or Congress, or proposals for new policies with many perceived benefits. This type of bill provides all members the chance to (in David Mayhew's words) "claim credit" or "take positions" and thereby enhance their chances for reelection.[30] Because members do not run directly against one another, there is not a zero-sum relationship among them, and all members can potentially benefit from the adoption of legislation.

This relationship is readily apparent in Table 1 when we consider different types of committees.[31] The prestige committees—those most important to the party leadership—deal with more conflictual legislation in every Congress and also exhibit a systematic increase in conflict over time. The policy committees, which process most of Congress's substantive legislation, reveal an intermediate level of conflict and no systematic increase. Finally, the constituency committees—those most involved with providing electoral benefits to members—show the least amount of conflict on legislation.

Not only does the propensity for partisan disagreement vary across types of committees and from bill to bill, but it also varies within a single piece of legislation. Consider the Freedom to Farm Act that we mentioned earlier, which in 1996 sought to reform federal farm policy. Table 2 shows the results of two roll calls on that bill.[32] The first vote involved an effort to cut the peanut price support program, a typical "distributive" policy issue that had offered electorally important benefits to some members from agricultural districts. In this instance, within both the Democratic and Republican Parties, the members from the agriculture committees responded quite differently from other members, being much less inclined to support the abolition of peanut supports. Differences between the parties are small, and differences within them are large.

The second vote was on the Democrats' substitute proposal, which sought to keep farm policy closer to the status quo. Here the interparty differences are great. Only one Republican supported the Democrats' proposal, but 86 percent of the Democrats did. Moreover, the voting of committee members is virtually the same as that of members not on the committees. Thus some issues can provoke partisan responses while others do not, even within a single bill.

Senate Contrasts

Committees are less central to the work of the Senate than of the House because of a number of institutional differences between the two chambers. First, the

Table 2. Votes on the 1996 Freedom to Farm Act

	Phase out peanut supports	*Democratic substitute*
Republicans		
Agriculture committees	8.8% (34)	0.0% (34)
Others	61.3% (199)	0.5% (200)
All members	53.6% (233)	0.4% (234)
Democrats		
Agriculture committees	20.0% (25)	100.0% (23)
Others	48.5% (163)	84.8% (164)
All members	44.6% (188)	86.6% (187)
All members		
Agriculture committees	13.6% (59)	40.4% (57)
Others	55.5% (362)	38.5% (364)
All members	49.6% (421)	38.7% (421)

Note: Given above are the percentages of members voting "aye" on the two votes (the number of members is in parentheses). "Agriculture committees" means representatives who are on either the Committee on Agriculture or on the Appropriations Subcommittee on Agriculture and Rural Development. "Others" includes all other members.

Senate must deal with essentially the same legislative jurisdiction with less than one-fourth the number of members. Senators are therefore spread more thinly and are less specialized. For example, in 2001 senators served on an average of 3.3 standing committees and 8.9 subcommittees; the corresponding numbers for representatives were 1.9 and 3.9. On the other hand, only about half of House members are the chair or ranking minority member of a committee or subcommittee, whereas most senators are, giving them an institutional power base on which to focus.[33]

The Senate's rules and traditions also vest more power in individuals and small groups than those of the House. The most familiar manifestation of this is the ability of a minority to block passage of legislation through filibuster, but there are many other aspects of the institution that reinforce individual power to delay or block Senate action. The House is a "majoritarian" institution, in which the majority can work its will with even one more vote than the minority, but in the Senate the majority must usually pay attention to at least some minority views to achieve any results.

Another major difference is the role of the House Rules Committee that we discussed earlier. Through special rules, the majority party can decide which amendments, if any, may be considered on the floor. Moreover, regular House rules require that amendments be germane. In the Senate, neither of these conditions holds. Usually the only way to limit amendments is if senators *unanimously* consent to do so, and amendments need not be germane. Thus the Senate floor plays a much larger role in shaping the content of legislative outcomes than does the House floor, and it is much easier for senators who do not serve on the committee with jurisdiction to have an impact.

As a result of these differences, both Senate committees and Senate parties have been institutionally weaker than their House counterparts, and individual senators have been more consequential. Furthermore, because the majority party leadership usually has had to deal with some members of the minority, partisan conflict in the Senate has tended to be less frequent and less vitriolic. Nevertheless, over the last couple of decades party conflict has intensified in the Senate as well.[34] We have already considered some of the similarities and differences between the House and Senate over appropriations. As another example, in 1995 the new GOP majority adopted some rules to enhance party influence in the Senate. As in the House, six-year term limits were imposed on committee chairs. Chairs were to be chosen by successive, secret ballot votes, first among Republican committee members, then in the whole GOP Conference. Moreover, on some aspects of the Senate's business partisan conflict was as vigorous as any seen in the House. The prime example was confirmation of judicial nominations, in which only the Senate has a role. Democrats used the power of the filibuster to block nominations by President George W. Bush that they regarded as unacceptable, while frustrated Republicans railed against their actions. . . .

The House Under Speakers Hastert and Pelosi

We developed the theory of conditional party government to explain the ebb and flow of party influence in Congress over time. We have argued that as the policy preferences of party members become more homogeneous, and as the ideological centers of gravity of the two parties become more divergent, rank-and-file members will be progressively more willing to delegate strong powers to their leaders to advance the party's program and to benefit it electorally. In this chapter we described how the relationship between the party organizations in Congress and the committee systems changed, arguing that the changes were in accord with the expectations of CPG, especially after the Republican takeover in 1994. Although most observers found the arguments and evidence persuasive with respect to the Gingrich Congresses, some also raised the reasonable question of whether CPG would continue to account for congressional organization and policy making.[35] In this concluding section, we address that issue by discussing developments in Congress in the last decade, during the speakerships of Dennis Hastert and Nancy Pelosi.

CPG theory has a number of key features that we have to account for to demonstrate continued applicability: (1) Have intraparty homogeneity and interparty divergence remained high? (2) If so, has the majority party in particular continued to delegate strong powers to its leadership? and (3) Has the majority leadership continued to exercise its powers to facilitate achievement of the party's legislative and electoral goals?

With regard to the first question, the data are unequivocal. All research on the subject shows that the polarization of the parties continues.[36] The median positions of the parties on roll call measures have even been a bit farther apart during the last ten years than they were in the 104th Congress. Moreover, the proportion of Congress that takes positions in the middle of the ideological spectrum is smaller than ever. This evidence indicates that the underlying "condition" for CPG is still well satisfied. We will now consider the other two features of the argument separately for the periods of Gingrich's two successors, as each provides a separate opportunity to test the predictions of CPG against data based on new members, leaders, and circumstances.

Hastert's Speakership

The selection of Dennis Hastert, R-Ill., as Speaker provided a strong challenge for CPG theory because on taking office he promised that regular procedures would be restored. However, with regard to the willingness of members to delegate power to party leaders, none of the significant authority granted to the Republican House leadership was rescinded. To the contrary, Hastert sought and was granted additional power. For example, in late 2002 Hastert asked the GOP conference to give him and the party even more influence over the Appropriations Committee by requiring that the chairs of its subcommittees be approved by the party Steering Committee.[37] In addition the Speaker arranged to give the Steering Committee the right to approve full committee chairs. In 2001 and 2003, under Hastert's leadership, the committee bypassed a number of more senior and more moderate members to pick more junior and more conservative candidates for chairmanships. For example, Chris Shays of Connecticut, who had joined with Democrats against his party leaders in the successful fight for campaign finance reform legislation, was passed over for chair of the Government Reform Committee (where he was most senior) in favor of Tom Davis of Virginia, who had served on the committee only half as long. And in 2005, in perhaps the strongest use of leadership power against a committee chairman in a century, Chris Smith of New Jersey was removed from the top spot on Veterans Affairs because of his persistent efforts to increase spending on veterans programs. The leadership had warned Smith to be more compliant with their priorities or risk punishment.[38] When he continued, the threats were fulfilled.

Moreover, regarding the continued exercise of leadership powers, Hastert and his colleagues showed that they were more than willing to manipulate the legislative process for majority party advantage. For example, Hastert and then-Senate majority leader Bill Frist, R-Tenn., presented a compromise that they had negotiated on the Medicare bill in late 2003, and Hastert pressured Ways and Means Committee chair Bill Thomas of California to accept it against his will.[39] Around the same time, majority leader Tom DeLay of Texas gave the Armed Services Committee chair an ultimatum to pass the defense authorization bill within two days, or else the leadership would strip out a popular provision and send it to the floor alone.[40]

Thus the Republican leadership continued to pressure and influence committees' actions. They also continued to use the tools at their disposal to structure the floor agenda and actions taken after bills are passed. Despite Hastert's promise to restore the use of regular procedures, the GOP continued to use restrictive special rules to block the Democrats from offering many of their preferred amendments. David Dreier, R-Calif., noted as chair of the Rules Committee that he used to complain about Democrats' use of special rules but that he learned "pretty quickly" that the majority party needed to use that device. "'I had not known what it took to govern,' he acknowledged. Now 'our number one priority is to move our agenda.'"[41] Indeed, Don Wolfensberger, former head of the Republican staff on the Rules Committee, concluded, "By the 107th Congress (2001–2003) . . . the Republicans had far exceeded the Democrats' worst excesses in restricting floor amendments."[42]

The GOP leadership in both chambers at times restricted minority members from participation in the deliberations of conference committees. (These are temporary panels set up to resolve differences in legislation after bills have been passed by both houses.) For example, in 2003 only two moderate Democratic senators and no House Democrats were permitted to participate in the conference on the Medicare bill, and on the energy bill no Democrats at all were permitted in conference meetings. In using all of these techniques, the Republicans denied that they were being unfair to the Democrats. They contended that they were just doing what was necessary to enact their legislative agenda. As Speaker Hastert said in an interview in late 2003, "While a Speaker should strive to be fair, he is also judged by how he gets the job done. The job of the Speaker is to rule fairly, but ultimately to carry out the will of the majority."[43]

Pelosi's Speakership

The transition to Democratic rule after the elections of 2006 offered another opportunity to assess the predictions of CPG theory, especially the expectation that while polarization continued, the House Democrats could be expected to delegate strong powers to their leadership. The rules package for the 110th Congress that Speaker Nancy Pelosi, Calif., and her allies drafted and submitted confirmed the accuracy of that expectation. The package included all the main leadership powers that the Democrats exercised the last time they were the majority, plus some new ones from the era of Republican control. The most striking of these was Pelosi's decision to retain the six-year term limit for committee chairs. Moreover, she did not even inform senior Democrats of this decision until shortly before the vote on the new rules. Many of them objected (including John Dingell, the incoming chair of the Energy and Commerce Committee, who said, "I think it's dumb"), but all party members including Dingell voted for the provisions.

CPG theory would also lead us to expect the vigorous exercise of leadership powers on behalf of the party's program in the new Congress, with the support of the vast majority of Democratic representatives. This expectation is also borne out. Pelosi selected six bills—all high priorities for the party—to be considered in the first one hundred hours of legislative business. These bills bypassed committee consideration and were put together without GOP input. All were considered under closed or restrictive rules, so that Republicans were blocked from offering amendments. The Democrats successfully completed consideration of all six well before the hundred-hour deadline.

Of course the Democratic Party is not so homogeneous that it lacks any recalcitrant members. John Dingell was one, and his committee had jurisdiction over one of the Democrats' priority issues for the new Congress: the energy bill. Seeking to return processes to the regular order of the past, Dingell proceeded to construct a bill according to his own lights, and his committee's draft included two significant provisions that were at odds with leadership priorities: They were an attempt to preempt states from regulating greenhouse gases from automobiles and a provision to override a recent Supreme Court decision confirming the authority of the Environmental Protection Agency to act to combat global warming.[44]

Pelosi called Dingell and some other members of the Energy Committee to a meeting in her office with the leadership. There she demanded that Dingell remove the two provisions from the draft bill. After some negotiations, Dingell agreed to comply.[45] Rep. Henry Waxman, D-Calif., chairman of the Energy Committee's Oversight Subcommittee, who attended the meeting, later said, "I have never seen a speaker take such an active and forceful role on policy. . . . [Former Speakers] Tip O'Neill or Tom Foley would not have told John Dingell or Dan Rostenkowski [a former Ways and Means chair] not to report out a bill, or what kind of bill to report out of committee. . . . [Dingell] was shocked by her action."[46] Pelosi also succeeded in other conflicts with Dingell, including the creation of a select committee on global warming and pushing through a floor amendment to the energy bill on renewable energy standards, over the chairman's objections.[47]

Despite these conflicts, it should be clear from our earlier discussion that CPG theory does not anticipate that the general relationship between the leadership and the committee chairs would necessarily be confrontational. Just as the Speaker is the top agent of the party caucus, chairs are agents too in the current era, of both the party and the leadership. Party leaders would prefer that they be faithful agents who can be trusted to pursue shared goals on their own. Leaders must also, however, be able to monitor activity and constrain chairs if they stray. That occurred in the 2007 interactions over energy policy. As majority leader Steny Hoyer, D-Md., put it, "There is a necessity for a unity of voice and purpose in the Democratic Party . . . and the only way you're going to do that was to have a central management to create consensus, not simply individual discrete committee agendas."[48] But as Barney Frank, D-Mass., chairman of the Financial Services Committee, said, "This is not a zero-sum game. . . . It's a mutually supportive relationship."[49]

Pelosi also repeatedly demonstrated her willingness to employ control of the floor agenda through special rules to give preference to party priorities. As was the case with the six bills with which the Democrats opened the Congress, special rules that restricted or prohibited amendments were applied to the overwhelming majority of bills that came to the floor during 2007. These rules were drafted at the direction of the Democratic leadership, and partisan conflict over procedural arrangements reached unprecedented levels. In the 100th Congress, when there were substantial efforts at procedural manipulation under the direction of Speaker Wright, 90 percent of the Democrats opposed 90 percent of the Republicans on only 18 percent of the floor votes on special rules. In the 104th Congress, the first with Newt Gingrich as Speaker, that proportion increased to 58 percent. In the first session of the 110th Congress, however, fully 99 percent of the special rules votes saw this degree of party conflict![50]

Another development in this Congress regarding the Rules Committee is a remarkable and telling indicator of how much the relationship between parties and committees has changed since the prereform era. Before 1974, when the Speaker regained the right to appoint the majority members and the chair of the Rules Committee, the committee was an independent center of power, and many members desired appointment to it so that they could exercise influence within the House. Virtually all appointees to Rules had to serve a number of terms in office before they could secure a place. Moreover, the committee was deemed so important and desirable that it was designated an "exclusive" committee—a member of it could serve on no other standing committee. In 2007, however, when the Democrats had to appoint five new members because they had regained majority status, four of the five were freshmen. The exclusive designation was removed, and Rules Committee members were given additional committee assignments as well. Having lost its independent power, Rules was no longer as important or desirable a post. It was merely an extension of the majority party leadership.

Control over special rules is not the only procedural advantage the majority leadership can bring to bear on behalf of their party. For example, in April 2008 President Bush sought approval for a trade agreement that his administration had negotiated with Colombia. He expected that a vote would take place within sixty legislative days because of the stipulation in congressional rules known as "fast-track," giving such measures priority.[51] Bush knew that there was opposition to the agreement among some Democrats, but he judged that the short time frame and the oncoming election would exert pressure on Congress to comply with his wishes. Democrats, on the other hand, had been trying to persuade the administration to take some additional action to help economically distressed Americans before they addressed the trade deal. Speaker Pelosi responded to the Bush stratagem by bringing to the House floor a rules change that stripped fast-track procedures from this trade agreement. The change, which puts off a vote until the Speaker decides the time is right, secured the support of all but ten Democrats.

Moreover, the new Republican minority has sought to use its limited capabilities to encourage solidarity among its members and to compete with the majority. For example, Rep. Walter Jones, R-N.C., a generally conservative member who nonetheless had become a vigorous opponent of the war in Iraq, was passed over twice during the 110th Congress for the top minority position on a subcommittee of the Armed Services Committee because of his deviation from party orthodoxy.[52] Also, Jeff Flake, R-Ariz., another conservative who frequently disagreed with his party leaders in the previous Congress about their support for too much spending, was removed from his place on the Judiciary Committee. The minority leader, John Boehner, R-Ohio, later informed him that the action was taken because of Flake's verbal attacks on party leaders.[53]

Thus all indications are that the theoretical account offered by CPG is as applicable in 2008 as it was in 1995. Partisan policy disagreement is at least as strong and partisan conflict just as intense. Indeed, these conditions continue to be reinforced by the close division of the two chambers. In every election since 1994, members of both parties have believed that they had a good chance to win majority control. That perception makes every decision on policy and legislative strategy potentially a high-stakes choice, giving the majority party strong incentive to use its institutional powers to the maximum. Therefore, as long as the legislative parties remain ideologically homogeneous and the ideological divergence between the two parties remains great, and as long as the partisan division of the chambers is close, we expect conditional party government theory to continue to provide a good explanation for congressional organization and activity.

NOTES

1. This interest in developing and sharing expertise is the central focus in the "informational" theory of legislative organization presented by Keith Krehbiel in *Information and Legislative Organization* (Chicago: University of Chicago Press, 1991).

2. Richard F. Fenno Jr., *Congressmen in Committees* (Boston: Little Brown, 1973), chap. 1.

3. Indeed, David Mayhew contended that the institutional structure of the Congress was principally designed to foster members' reelection. See David R. Mayhew, *Congress: The Electoral Connection* (New Haven: Yale University Press, 1974). Also see E. Scott Adler, *Why Congressional Reforms Fail: Reelection and the House Committee System* (Chicago: University of Chicago Press, 2002).

4. See Richard C. Hall, *Participation in Congress* (New Haven: Yale University Press, 1996); and C. Lawrence Evans, *Leadership in Committee* (Ann Arbor: University of Michigan Press, 2001).

5. For more information on the history of the committee system, see Joseph Cooper, *The Origins of the Standing Committees and the Development of the Modern House* (Houston: Rice University Studies, 1970); and Christopher J. Deering and Steven S. Smith, *Committees in Congress,* 3rd ed. (Washington, D.C.: CQ Press, 1997).

6. For a detailed analysis of the growth of amending activity on the floors of both chambers see Steven S. Smith, *Call to Order: Floor Politics in the House and Senate* (Washington, D.C.: Brookings Institution Press, 1989).

7. For more details, see David W. Rohde, *Parties and Leaders in the Postreform House* (Chicago: University of Chicago Press, 1991), chap. 3.

8. See Rohde, *Parties and Leaders,* chap. 2; and John H. Aldrich, *Why Parties? The Origin and Transformation of Political Parties in America* (Chicago: University of Chicago Press, 1995), chaps. 6 and 7. An alternative (but compatible) theory of partisan organization of Congress is offered by Gary W. Cox and Mathew D. McCubbins, *Legislative Leviathan* (Berkeley: University of California Press, 1993).

9. Sara Brandes Crook and John R. Hibbing, "Congressional Reform and Party Discipline: The Effects of Changes in the Seniority System on Party Loyalty in the House of Representatives,"

British Journal of Political Science 15 (1985): 207–226. See also Fiona M. Wright, "The Caucus Reelection Requirement and the Transformation of Committee Chairs," *Legislative Studies Quarterly* 25 (2000): 469–480.

10. See Rohde, *Parties and Leaders*, 75–76.

11. Barbara Sinclair, *Legislators, Leaders, and Lawmaking: The U.S. House of Representatives in the Postreform Era* (Baltimore: Johns Hopkins University Press, 1995), 164.

12. For more details on this transformed relationship see Sinclair, *Legislators, Leaders, and Lawmaking,* chap. 9; and Rohde, *Parties and Leaders,* chap. 4.

13. Much has been written about the new role of the Rules Committee. See, for example, Bruce I. Oppenheimer, "The Rules Committee: New Arm of Leadership in a Decentralized House," in *Congress Reconsidered,* ed. Lawrence C. Dodd and Bruce I. Oppenheimer (New York: Praeger, 1977), 96–116; Stanley Bach and Steven S. Smith, *Managing Uncertainty in the House of Representatives* (Washington, D.C.: Brookings Institution Press, 1988); Sinclair, *Legislators, Leaders, and Lawmaking,* chap. 8; and Rohde, *Parties and Leaders,* 98–118.

14. See Gary C. Jacobson, *The Politics of Congressional Elections,* 5th ed. (New York: Longman, 2001), 178–185.

15. The discussion in this section is drawn from John H. Aldrich and David W. Rohde, "The Transition to Republican Rule in the House: Implications for Theories of Congressional Politics," *Political Science Quarterly* 112 (1997–1998): 541–567; and C. Lawrence Evans and Walter J. Oleszek, *Congress under Fire: Reform Politics and the Republican Majority* (Boston: Houghton Mifflin, 1997).

16. Quoted in Guy Gugliotta, "In New House, Barons Yield to the Boss," *Washington Post,* December 1, 1994, 1.

17. See Adler, *Why Congressional Reforms Fail.*

18. Sinclair, *Legislators, Leaders, and Lawmaking,* 163–197.

19. For more detail on the contract and Congress's actions on it, see James G. Gimpel, *Fulfilling the Contract: The First 100 Days* (Boston: Allyn and Bacon, 1996).

20. *Washington Post,* October 8, 1995, A5.

21. *Roll Call,* October 2, 1995, 20.

22. *Washington Post,* March 26, 1996, A9.

23. Task forces had been used before the GOP majority took over. See Sinclair, *Legislators, Leaders, and Lawmaking.* For more recent details on task force use, see Barbara Sinclair, *Unorthodox Lawmaking: New Legislative Processes in the U.S. Congress,* 2nd ed. (Washington, D.C.: CQ Press, 2000).

24. See *CQ Weekly,* September 23, 1995, 2886; *Roll Call,* October 12, 1995, 3. For more systematic analysis of bypassing committees, see Charles J. Finocchiaro, "Setting the Stage: Party and Procedure in the Pre-Floor Agenda Setting of the U.S. House," PhD diss., Michigan State University, 2003; and Sinclair, *Unorthodox Lawmaking.*

25. Sinclair, *Unorthodox Lawmaking,* 94.

26. Ibid., 211 and 20, respectively.

27. *Roll Call,* March 20, 1995, 18.

28. *Congressional Quarterly Weekly Report,* October 21, 1995, 3207.

29. The data are adapted from Tables 1–4 in Jamie L. Carson, Charles J. Finocchiaro, and David W. Rohde, "Consensus and Conflict in House Decision Making: A Bill-Level Examination of Committee and Floor Behavior," paper delivered at the annual meeting of the

Midwest Political Science Association, Chicago, April 2001. The data include all public bills and joint resolutions referred to a committee and either reported by the committee or debated on the floor.

30. See Mayhew, *Congress: The Electoral Connection,* 52–73.

31. The classification was developed by Deering and Smith, *Committees in Congress,* 3rd ed., chap. 3. The prestige committees are Appropriations and Ways and Means; the policy committees are Banking, Commerce, Education, Foreign Affairs, Government Operations, and Judiciary; the constituency committees are Agriculture, Armed Services, Interior, Merchant Marine, Science, Transportation, and Veterans Affairs. (Committee names change over time. These are the names for the 96th Congress.) The committees that the authors term "unrequested" are omitted, as are Rules and Budget because they consider few bills. Note that bills referred to more than one committee are counted for each committee to which they were referred.

32. These data are taken from Mark S. Hurwitz, Roger J. Moiles, and David W. Rohde, "Distributive and Partisan Issues in Agriculture Policy in the 104th House," *American Political Science Review* 95 (2001): 915.

33. The dominant role of Senate subcommittee chairs is discussed in C. Lawrence Evans, *Leadership in Committee: A Comparative Analysis of Leadership Behavior in the U.S. Senate* (Ann Arbor: University of Michigan Press, 2001).

34. For discussions of various ways in which parties can be consequential in the Senate, see *Why Not Parties? Party Effects in the United States Senate,* ed. Nathan W. Monroe, Jason M. Roberts, and David W. Rohde (Chicago: University of Chicago Press, 2008).

35. See, for example, Lawrence C. Dodd and Bruce I. Oppenheimer, "Congress and the Emerging Order: Conditional Party Government or Constructive Partisanship?" in *Congress Reconsidered,* 6th ed., ed. Lawrence C. Dodd and Bruce I. Oppenheimer (Washington, D.C.: CQ Press, 1997), 390–413.

36. See, for example, Richard Fleisher and Jon R. Bond, "The Shrinking Middle in the U.S. Congress," *British Journal of Political Science* 34 (July 2004): 429–451; and Sean Theriault, "The Case of the Vanishing Moderates: Party Polarization in the Modern Congress," manuscript, University of Texas, 2004.

37. Remember that the Steering Committee is weighted toward leadership influence. See *Roll Call,* November 18, 2002, 1.

38. *CQ Weekly,* July 26, 2003, 1910.

39. *Washington Post,* November 30, 2003, A8.

40. *CQ Weekly,* November 8, 2003, 2785.

41. Jim VandeHei, "Using the Rules Committee to Block Democrats," *Washington Post,* June 16, 2003, A21.

42. Don Wolfensberger, "The Motion to Recommit in the House: The Creation, Evisceration, and Restoration of a Minority Right," paper prepared for the Conference on the History of Congress, Stanford University, December 5–6, 2003, 31.

43. *Roll Call,* November 17, 2003, 4.

44. See Richard E. Cohen, "Power Surge," *National Journal,* July 21, 2007, 23.

45. *The Hill,* June 19, 2007, 3.

46. Quoted in Cohen, "Power Surge," 22.

47. *The Hill,* February 6, 2007, 1. Pelosi did, however, agree to Dingell's request that the select committee would not have any legislative jurisdiction.

48. Quoted in *Washington Post,* July 9, 2007, A4.

49. Quoted in *Roll Call,* November 5, 2007, 22.

50. The data on the 100th and 104th Congresses come from the PIPC House roll call database ("Roll Call Voting Data for the United States House of Representatives, 1953–2004," compiled by the Political Institutions and Public Choice Program, Michigan State University). The data are available from Michael Crespin's Web site, http://crespin.myweb.uga.edu. The data on the 110th Congress were compiled for this essay.

51. Fast-track legislation had expired in July 2007, but since the Colombia agreement was negotiated before expiration, the rules continued to apply to it.

52. See *The Hill,* October 16, 2007, 3.

53. See Robert D. Novak, "Bad Behavior?" January 13, 2007, at http://townhall.com.

Chapter 7

The Presidency

———◆◆———

7-1

from *Presidential Power*

Richard E. Neustadt

In his classic treatise Presidential Power, *Richard E. Neustadt presents a problem that confronts every occupant of the White House: His authority does not match the expectations for his performance. We expect our presidents to be leaders, Neustadt tells us, but the office guarantees no more than that they will be clerks. In the following excerpt, Neustadt explains that the key to presidential success lies in persuasion and shows how the ability to persuade depends on bargaining.*

THE LIMITS ON COMMAND suggest the structure of our government. The Constitutional Convention of 1787 is supposed to have created a government of "separated powers." It did nothing of the sort. Rather, it created a government of separated institutions *sharing* powers.[1] "I am part of the legislative process," Eisenhower often said in 1959 as a reminder of his veto.[2] Congress, the dispenser of authority and funds, is no less part of the administrative process. Federalism adds another set of separated institutions. The Bill of Rights adds others. Many public purposes can only be achieved by voluntary acts of private institutions; the press, for one, in Douglass Cater's phrase, is a "fourth branch of government."[3] And with the coming of alliances abroad, the separate institutions of a London, or a Bonn, share in the making of American public policy.

Source: Richard Neustadt, *Presidential Power and the Modern Presidents: The Politics of Leadership from Roosevelt to Reagan* (1960; New York: Simon & Schuster, 1990), 29–49.

What the Constitution separates our political parties do not combine. The parties are themselves composed of separated organizations sharing public authority. The authority consists of nominating powers. Our national parties are confederations of state and local party institutions, with a headquarters that represents the White House, more or less, if the party has a President in office. These confederacies manage presidential nominations. All other public offices depend upon electorates confined within the states.[4] All other nominations are controlled within the states. The President and congressmen who bear one party's label are divided by dependence upon different sets of voters. The differences are sharpest at the stage of nomination. The White House has too small a share in nominating congressmen, and Congress has too little weight in nominating presidents for party to erase their constitutional separation. Party links are stronger than is frequently supposed, but nominating processes assure the separation.[5]

The separateness of institutions and the sharing of authority prescribe the terms on which a President persuades. When one man shares authority with another, but does not gain or lose his job upon the other's whim, his willingness to act upon the urging of the other turns on whether he conceives the action right for him. The essence of a President's persuasive task is to convince such men that what the White House wants of them is what they ought to do for their sake and on their authority. (Sex matters not at all; for *man* read *woman*.)

Persuasive power, thus defined, amounts to more than charm or reasoned argument. These have their uses for a President, but these are not the whole of his resources. For the individuals he would induce to do what he wants done on their own responsibility will need or fear some acts by him on his responsibility. If they share his authority, he has some share in theirs. Presidential "powers" may be inconclusive when a President commands, but always remain relevant as he persuades. The status and authority inherent in his office reinforce his logic and his charm.

Status adds something to persuasiveness; authority adds still more. When Truman urged wage changes on his secretary of commerce [Charles Sawyer] while the latter was administering the [recently seized] steel mills, he and Secretary Sawyer were not just two men reasoning with one another. Had they been so, Sawyer probably would never have agreed to act. Truman's status gave him special claims to Sawyer's loyalty or at least attention. In Walter Bagehot's charming phrase, "no man can *argue* on his knees." Although there is no kneeling in this country, few men—and exceedingly few cabinet officers—are immune to the impulse to say "yes" to the President of the United States. It grows harder to say "no" when they are seated in his Oval Office at the White House, or in his study on the second floor, where almost tangibly he partakes of the aura of his physical surroundings. In Sawyer's case, moreover, the President possessed formal authority to intervene in many matters of concern to the secretary of commerce. These matters ranged from jurisdictional disputes among the defense agencies to legislation pending before Congress and, ultimately, to the tenure of the secretary, himself. There is nothing in the record to suggest that Truman voiced specific threats when they negotiated over wage increases. But given his formal powers and their relevance to Sawyer's other interests, it is safe to assume that Truman's very advocacy of wage action conveyed an implicit threat.

A President's authority and status give him great advantages in dealing with the men he would persuade. Each "power" is a vantage point for him in the degree that other men have use for his authority. From the veto to appointments, from publicity to budgeting, and so down a long list, the White House now controls the most encompassing array of vantage points in the American political system. With hardly an exception, those who share in governing this country are aware that at some time, in some degree, the doing of *their* jobs, the furthering of *their* ambitions, may depend upon the President of the United States. Their need for presidential action, or their fear of it, is bound to be recurrent if not actually continuous. Their need or fear is his advantage.

A President's advantages are greater than mere listing of his "powers" might suggest. Those with whom he deals must deal with him until the last day of his term. Because they have continuing relationships with him, his future, while it lasts, supports his present influence. Even though there is no need or fear of him today, what he could do tomorrow may supply today's advantage. Continuing relationships may convert any "power," any aspect of his status, into vantage points in almost any case. When he induces other people to do what he wants done, a President can trade on their dependence now and later.

The President's advantages are checked by the advantages of others. Continuing relationships will pull in both directions. These are relationships of mutual dependence. A President depends upon the persons whom he would persuade; he has to reckon with his need or fear of them. They too will possess status or authority, or both, else they would be of little use to him. Their vantage points confront his own; their power tempers his.

Persuasion is a two-way street. Sawyer, it will be recalled, did not respond at once to Truman's plan for wage increases at the steel mills. On the contrary, the secretary hesitated and delayed and only acquiesced when he was satisfied that publicly he would not bear the onus of decision. Sawyer had some points of vantage all his own from which to resist presidential pressure. If he had to reckon with coercive implications in the President's "situations of strength," so had Truman to be mindful of the implications underlying Sawyer's place as a department head, as steel administrator, and as a cabinet spokesman for business. Loyalty is reciprocal. Having taken on a dirty job in the steel crisis, Sawyer had strong claims to loyal support. Besides, he had authority to do some things that the White House could ill afford. . . . [H]e might have resigned in a huff (the removal power also works two ways). Or . . . he might have declined to sign necessary orders. Or he might have let it be known publicly that he deplored what he was told to do and protested its doing. By following any of these courses Sawyer almost surely would have strengthened the position of management, weakened the position of the White House, and embittered the union. But the whole purpose of a wage increase was to enhance White House persuasiveness in urging settlement upon union and companies alike. Although Sawyer's status and authority did not give him the power to prevent an increase outright, they gave him capability to undermine its purpose. If his authority over wage rates had been vested by a statute, not by revocable presidential order, his power of prevention might have been complete. So Harold Ickes [Sr.] demonstrated in the famous case of helium sales to Germany before the Second World War.[6]

The power to persuade is the power to bargain. Status and authority yield bargaining advantages. But in a government of "separated institutions sharing power," they yield them to all sides. With the array of vantage points at his disposal, a President may be far more persuasive than his logic or his charm could make him. But outcomes are not guaranteed by his advantages. There remain the counter pressures those whom he would influence can bring to bear on him from vantage points at their disposal. Command has limited utility; persuasion becomes give-and-take. It is well that the White House holds the vantage points it does. In such a business any President may need them all—and more.

THIS VIEW OF POWER as akin to bargaining is one we commonly accept in the sphere of congressional relations. Every textbook states and every legislative session demonstrates that save in times like the extraordinary Hundred Days of 1933—times virtually ruled out by definition at mid-century—a President will often be unable to obtain congressional action on his terms or even to halt action he opposes. The reverse is equally accepted: Congress often is frustrated by the President. Their formal powers are so intertwined that neither will accomplish very much, for very long, without the acquiescence of the other. By the same token, though, what one demands the other can resist. The stage is set for that great game, much like collective bargaining, in which each seeks to profit from the other's needs and fears. It is a game played catch-as-catch-can, case by case. And everybody knows the game, observers and participants alike.

The concept of real power as a give-and-take is equally familiar when applied to presidential influence outside the formal structure of the federal government. . . . When he deals with [governors, union officials, company executives and even citizens or workers] a President draws bargaining advantage from his status or authority. By virtue of their public places or their private rights they have some capability to reply in kind.

In spheres of party politics the same thing follows, necessarily, from the confederal nature of our party organizations. Even in the case of national nominations a President's advantages are checked by those of others. In 1944 it is by no means clear that Roosevelt got his first choice as his running mate. In 1948 Truman, then the President, faced serious revolts against his nomination. In 1952 his intervention from the White House helped assure the choice of Adlai Stevenson, but it is far from clear that Truman could have done as much for any other candidate acceptable to him.[7] In 1956 when Eisenhower was President, the record leaves obscure just who backed Harold Stassen's efforts to block Richard Nixon from renomination as vice president. But evidently everything did not go quite as Eisenhower wanted, whatever his intentions may have been.[8] The outcomes in these instances bear all the marks of limits on command and of power checked by power that characterize congressional relations. Both in and out of politics these checks and limits seem to be quite widely understood.

Influence becomes still more a matter of give-and-take when Presidents attempt to deal with allied governments. A classic illustration is the long unhappy wrangle over Suez policy in 1956. In dealing with the British and the French before their military intervention, Eisenhower had his share of bargaining advantages but no effective power of command. His allies had their share of counterpressures, and they finally tried the most extreme of all: action despite him. His pressure then was instrumental in reversing them. But had the British government been on safe ground at home, Eisenhower's wishes might have made as little difference after intervention as before. Behind the decorum of diplomacy—which was not very decorous in the Suez affair—relationships among allies are not unlike relationships among state delegations at a national convention. Power is persuasion, and persuasion becomes bargaining. The concept is familiar to everyone who watches foreign policy.

In only one sphere is the concept unfamiliar: the sphere of executive relations. Perhaps because of civics textbooks and teaching in our schools, Americans instinctively resist the view that power in this sphere resembles power in all others. Even Washington reporters, White House aides, and congressmen are not immune to the illusion that administrative agencies comprise a single structure, "the" executive branch, where presidential word is law, or ought to be. Yet . . . when a President seeks something from executive officials his persuasiveness is subject to the same sorts of limitations as in the case of congressmen, or governors, or national committeemen, or private citizens, or foreign governments. There are no generic differences, no differences in kind and only sometimes in degree. The incidents preceding the dismissal of [General Douglas] MacArthur and the incidents surrounding seizure of the steel mills make it plain that here as elsewhere influence derives from bargaining advantages; power is a give-and-take.

Like our governmental structure as a whole, the executive establishment consists of separated institutions sharing powers. The President heads one of these; cabinet officers, agency administrators, and military commanders head others. Below the departmental level, virtually independent bureau chiefs head many more. Under mid-century conditions, federal operations spill across dividing lines on organization charts; almost every policy entangles many agencies; almost every program calls for interagency collaboration. Everything somehow involves the President. But operating agencies owe their existence least of all to one another— and only in some part to him. Each has a separate statutory base; each has its statutes to administer; each deals with a different set of subcommittees at the Capitol. Each has its own peculiar set of clients, friends, and enemies outside the formal government. Each has a different set of specialized careerists inside its own bailiwick. Our Constitution gives the President the "take-care" clause and the appointive power. Our statutes give him central budgeting and a degree of personnel control. All agency administrators are responsible to him. But they also are responsible to Congress, to their clients, to their staffs, and to themselves. In short, they have five masters. Only after all of those do they owe any loyalty to each other.

"The members of the cabinet," Charles G. Dawes used to remark, "are a president's natural enemies." Dawes had been Harding's budget director, Coolidge's vice president, and Hoover's ambassador to London; he also had been General Pershing's chief assistant for supply in World War I. The words are highly colored, but Dawes knew whereof he spoke. The men who have to serve so many masters cannot help but be somewhat the "enemy" of any one of them. By the same token, any master wanting service is in some degree the "enemy" of such a servant. A President is likely to want loyal support but not to relish trouble on his doorstep. Yet the more his cabinet members cleave to him, the more they may need help from him in fending off the wrath of rival masters. Help, though, is synonymous with trouble. Many a cabinet officer, with loyalty ill rewarded by his lights and help withheld, has come to view the White House as innately hostile to department heads. Dawes's dictum can be turned around.

A senior presidential aide remarked to me in Eisenhower's time: "If some of these cabinet members would just take time out to stop and ask themselves, 'What would I want if I were President?' they wouldn't give him all the trouble he's been having." But even if they asked themselves the question, such officials often could not act upon the answer. Their personal attachment to the President is all too often overwhelmed by duty to their other masters.

Executive officials are not equally advantaged in their dealings with a President. Nor are the same officials equally advantaged all the time. Not every officeholder can resist like a MacArthur or Sawyer. . . . The vantage points conferred upon officials by their own authority and status vary enormously. The variance is heightened by particulars of time and circumstance. In mid-October 1950, Truman, at a press conference, remarked of the man he had considered firing in August and would fire the next April for intolerable insubordination:

> Let me tell you something that will be good for your souls. It's a pity that you . . . can't understand the ideas of two intellectually honest men when they meet. General MacArthur . . . is a member of the Government of the United States. He is loyal to that Government. He is loyal to the President. He is loyal to the President in his foreign policy. . . .There is no disagreement between General MacArthur and myself.[9]

MacArthur's status in and out of government was never higher than when Truman spoke those words. The words, once spoken, added to the general's credibility thereafter when he sought to use the press in his campaign against the President. And what had happened between August and October? Near victory had happened, together with that premature conference on postwar plans, the meeting at Wake Island.

If the bargaining advantages of a MacArthur fluctuate with changing circumstances, this is bound to be so with subordinates who have at their disposal fewer powers, lesser status, to fall back on. And when officials have no powers in their own right, or depend upon the President for status, their counterpressure may be limited indeed. White House aides, who fit both categories, are among the most responsive men of all, and for good reason. As a director of the budget once remarked to me, "Thank God I'm here and not across the street. If the President doesn't call me, I've got plenty I can do right here and plenty coming up to me, by rights, to justify my calling him. But those poor fellows over there, if the boss doesn't call them, doesn't ask them to do something, what *can* they do but sit?" Authority and status so conditional are frail reliances in resisting a President's own wants. Within the White House precincts, lifted eyebrows may suffice to set an aide in motion; command, coercion, even charm aside. But even in the White House a President does not monopolize effective power. Even there persuasion is akin to bargaining. A former Roosevelt aide once wrote of cabinet officers:

> Half of a President's suggestions, which theoretically carry the weight of orders, can be safely forgotten by a Cabinet member. And if the President asks about a suggestion a second time, he can be told that it is being investigated. If he asks a third time, a wise Cabinet officer will give him at least part of what he suggests. But only occasionally, except about the most important matters, do Presidents ever get around to asking three times.[10]

The rule applies to staff as well as to the cabinet, and certainly has been applied *by* staff in Truman's time and Eisenhower's.

Some aides will have more vantage points than a selective memory. Sherman Adams, for example, as the assistant to the President under Eisenhower, scarcely deserved the appellation "White House aide" in the meaning of the term before his time or as applied to other members of the Eisenhower entourage. Although Adams was by no means "chief of staff" in any sense so sweeping—or so simple—as press commentaries often took for granted, he apparently became no more dependent on the President than Eisenhower on him. "I need him," said the President when Adams turned out to have been remarkably imprudent in the Goldfine case, and delegated to him, at least nominally, the decision on his own departure.[11] This instance is extreme, but the tendency it illustrates is common enough. Any aide who demonstrates to others that he has the President's consistent confidence and a consistent part in presidential business will acquire so much business on his own account that he becomes in some sense independent of his chief. Nothing in the Constitution keeps a well-placed aide from converting status into power of his own, usable in some degree even against the President—an outcome not unknown in Truman's regime or, by all accounts, in Eisenhower's.

The more an officeholder's status and his powers stem from sources independent of the President, the stronger will be his potential pressure on the President. Department heads in general have more bargaining power than do most members of the White House staff; but bureau chiefs may have still more, and specialists at upper levels of established career services may have almost unlimited reserves of the enormous power which consists of sitting still. As Franklin Roosevelt once remarked:

> The Treasury is so large and far-flung and ingrained in its practices that I find it almost impossible to get the action and results I want—even with Henry [Morgenthau] there. But the Treasury is not to be compared with the State Department. You should go through the experience of trying to get any changes in the thinking, policy, and action of the career diplomats and then you'd know what a real problem was. But the Treasury and the State Department put together are nothing compared with the Na-a-vy. The admirals are really something to cope with—and I should know. To change anything in the Na-a-vy is like punching a feather bed. You punch it with your right and you punch it with your left until you are finally exhausted, and then you find the damn bed just as it was before you started punching.[12]

In the right circumstances, of course, a President can have his way with any of these people. . . . [But] as between a President and his "subordinates," no less than others on whom he depends, real power is reciprocal and varies markedly with organization, subject matter, personality and situation. The mere fact that persuasion is directed at executive officials signifies no necessary easing of his way. Any new congressman of the Administration's party, especially if narrowly elected, may turn out more amenable (though less useful) to the President than any seasoned bureau chief "downtown." *The probabilities of power do not derive from the literary theory of the Constitution.*

THERE IS a widely held belief in the United States that were it not for folly or for knavery, a reasonable President would need no power other than the logic of his argument. No less a personage than Eisenhower has subscribed to that belief in many a campaign speech and press-conference remark. But faulty reasoning and bad intentions do not cause all quarrels with Presidents. The best of reasoning and of intent cannot compose them all. For in the first place, what the President wants will rarely seem a trifle to the people he wants it from. And in the second place, they will be bound to judge it by the standard of their own responsibilities, not his. However logical his argument according to his lights, their judgment may not bring them to his view.

Those who share in governing this country frequently appear to act as though they were in business for themselves. So, in a real though not entire sense, they are and have to be. When Truman and MacArthur fell to quarreling, for example, the stakes were no less than the substance of American foreign policy, the risks of greater war or military stalemate, the prerogatives of Presidents and field commanders, the pride of a proconsul and his place in history. Intertwined, inevitably, were other stakes as well: political stakes for men and factions of both parties; power stakes for interest groups with which they were or wished to be affiliated. And every stake was raised by the apparent discontent in the American public mood. There is no reason to suppose that in such circumstances men of large but differing responsibilities will see all things through the same glasses. On the contrary, it is to be expected that their views of what ought to be done and what they then should do will vary with the differing perspectives their particular responsibilities evoke. Since their duties are not vested in a "team" or a "collegium" but in themselves, as individuals, one must expect that they will see things for themselves. Moreover, when they are responsible to many masters and when an event or policy turns loyalty against loyalty—a day-by-day occurrence in the nature of the case—one must assume that those who have the duties to perform will choose the terms of reconciliation. This is the essence of their personal responsibility. When their own duties pull in opposite directions, who else but they can choose what they will do?

When Truman dismissed MacArthur, the latter lost three posts: the American command in the Far East, the Allied command for the occupation of Japan, and the United Nations command in Korea. He also lost his status as the senior officer on active duty in the United States armed forces. So long as he held those positions and that status, though, he had a duty to his troops, to his profession, to himself (the last is hard for any man to disentangle from the rest). As a public figure and a focus for men's hopes he had a duty to constituents at home, and in Korea and Japan. He owed a duty also to those other constituents, the UN governments contributing to his field forces. As a patriot he had a duty to his country. As an accountable official and an expert guide he stood at the call of Congress. As a military officer he had, besides, a duty to the President, his constitutional commander. Some of these duties may have manifested themselves in terms more tangible or more direct than others. But it would be nonsense to argue that the last negated all the rest, however much it might be claimed to override them. And it makes no more sense to think that anybody but MacArthur was effectively empowered to decide how he himself would reconcile the competing demands his duties made upon him.

. . . Reasonable men, it is so often said, *ought* to be able to agree on the requirements of given situations. But when the outlook varies with the placement of each man, and the response required in his place is for each to decide, their reasoning may lead to disagreement quite as well—and quite as reasonably. Vanity, or vice, may weaken reason, to be sure, but it is idle to assign these as the cause of . . . MacArthur's defiance. Secretary Sawyer's hesitations, cited earlier, are in the same category. One need not denigrate such men to explain their conduct. For the responsibilities they felt, the "facts" they saw, simply were not the same as those of their superiors; yet they, not the superiors, had to decide what they would do.

Outside the executive branch the situation is the same, except that loyalty to the President may often matter *less.* There is no need to spell out the comparison with governors of Arkansas, steel company executives, trade union leaders, and the like. And when one comes to congressmen who can do nothing for themselves (or their constituents) save as they are elected, term by term, in districts and through party structures differing from those on which a President depends, the case is very clear. An able Eisenhower aide with long congressional experience remarked to me in 1958: "The people on the Hill don't do what they might *like* to do, they do what they think they *have* to do in their own interest as *they* see it." This states the case precisely.

The essence of a President's persuasive task, with congressmen and everybody else, is to induce them to believe that what he wants of them is what their own appraisal of their own responsibilities requires them to do in their interest, not his. Because men may differ in their views on public policy, because differences in outlook stem from differences in duty—duty to one's office, one's constituents, oneself—that task is bound to be more like collective bargaining than like a reasoned argument among philosopher kings. Overtly or implicitly, hard bargaining has characterized all illustrations offered up to now. This is the reason why: Persuasion deals in the coin of self-interest with men who have some freedom to reject what they find counterfeit.

A PRESIDENT DRAWS influence from bargaining advantages. But does he always need them? . . . [S]uppose most players of the governmental game see policy objectives much alike, then can he not rely on logic (or on charm) to get him what he wants? The answer is that even then most outcomes turn on bargaining. The reason for this answer is a simple one: Most who share in governing have interests of their own beyond the realm of policy objectives. The sponsorship of policy, the form it takes, the conduct of it, and the credit for it separate their interest from the President's despite agreement on the end in view. In political government the means can matter quite as much as ends; they often matter more. And there are always differences of interest in the means.

Let me introduce a case externally the opposite of my previous examples: the European Recovery Program of 1948, the so-called Marshall Plan. This is perhaps the greatest exercise in policy agreement since the Cold War began. When the then secretary of state, George Catlett Marshall, spoke at the Harvard commencement in June 1947, he launched one of the most creative, most imaginative ventures in the history of American foreign relations. What makes this policy most notable for present purposes, however, is that it became effective upon action by the Eightieth Congress, at the behest of Harry Truman, in the election year 1948.[13]

Eight months before Marshall spoke at Harvard, the Democrats had lost control of both houses of Congress for the first time in fourteen years. Truman, whom the secretary represented, had just finished his second troubled year as President-by-succession. Truman was regarded with so little warmth in his own party that in 1946 he had been urged not to participate in the congressional campaign. At the opening of Congress in January 1947, Senator Robert A. Taft, "Mr. Republican," had somewhat the attitude of a President-elect. This was a vision widely shared in Washington, with Truman relegated thereby to the role of caretaker-on-term. Moreover, within just two weeks of Marshall's commencement address, Truman was to veto two prized accomplishments of Taft's congressional majority: the Taft-Hartley Act and tax reduction.[14] Yet scarcely ten months later the Marshall Plan was under way on terms to satisfy its sponsors, its authorization completed, its first-year funds in sight, its administering agency in being: all managed by as thorough a display of executive-congressional cooperation as any we have seen since the Second World War. For any President at any time this would have been a great accomplishment. In years before mid-century it would have been enough to make the future reputation of his term. And for a Truman, at this time, enactment of the Marshall Plan appears almost miraculous.

How was the miracle accomplished? How did a President so situated bring it off? In answer, the first thing to note is that he did not do it by himself. Truman had help of a sort no less extraordinary than the outcome. Although each stands for something more complex, the names of Marshall, Vandenberg, Patterson, Bevin, Stalin tell the story of that help.

In 1947, two years after V-J Day, General Marshall was something more than secretary of state. He was a man venerated by the President as "the greatest living American," literally an embodiment of Truman's ideals. He was honored at the Pentagon as an architect of victory. He was thoroughly respected by the secretary of the Navy, James V. Forrestal, who that year became the first secretary of defense. On Capitol Hill, Marshall had an enormous fund of respect stemming from his war record as Army chief of staff, and in the country generally no officer had come out of the war with a higher reputation for judgment, intellect, and probity. Besides, as secretary of state, he had behind him the first generation of matured foreign service officers produced by the reforms of the 1920s, and mingled with them, in the departmental service, were some of the ablest of the men drawn by the war from private life to Washington. In terms both of staff talent and staff use, Marshall's years began a State Department "golden age" that lasted until the era of McCarthy. Moreover, as his undersecretary, Marshall had, successively, Dean Acheson and Robert Lovett, men who commanded the respect of the professionals and the regard of congressmen. (Acheson had been brilliantly successful at congressional relations as assistant secretary in the war and postwar years.) Finally, as a special undersecretary Marshall had Will Clayton, a man highly regarded, for good reason, at both ends of Pennsylvania Avenue.

Taken together, these are exceptional resources for a secretary of state. In the circumstances, they were quite as necessary as they obviously are relevant. The Marshall Plan was launched by a lame-duck Administration "scheduled" to leave office in eighteen months. Marshall's program faced a congressional leadership traditionally isolationist and currently intent upon economy. European aid was viewed with envy by a Pentagon distressed and virtually disarmed through budget cuts, and by domestic agencies intent on enlarged welfare programs. It was not viewed with liking by a Treasury intent on budget surpluses. The plan had need of every asset that could be extracted from the personal position of its nominal author and from the skills of his assistants.

Without the equally remarkable position of the senior senator from Michigan, Arthur H. Vandenberg, it is hard to see how Marshall's assets could have been enough. Vandenberg was chairman of the Senate Foreign Relations Committee. Actually, he was much more than that. Twenty years a senator, he was the senior member of his party in the chamber. Assiduously cultivated by FDR and Truman, he was a chief Republican proponent of bipartisanship in foreign policy and consciously conceived himself its living symbol to his party, to the country, and abroad. Moreover, by informal but entirely operative agreement with his colleague Taft, Vandenberg held the acknowledged lead among Senate Republicans in the whole field of international affairs. This acknowledgment meant more in 1947 than it might have meant at any other time. With confidence in the advent of a Republican administration two years hence, most of the gentlemen were in a mood to be responsive and responsible. The war was over, Roosevelt dead, Truman a caretaker, theirs the trust. That the senator from Michigan saw matters in this light his diaries make clear.[15] And this was not the outlook from the Senate side alone; the attitudes of House Republicans associated with the Herter Committee and its tours abroad suggest the same mood of responsibility. Vandenberg was not the only source of help on Capitol Hill. But relatively speaking his position there was as exceptional as Marshall's was downtown.

Help of another sort was furnished by a group of dedicated private citizens who organized one of the most effective instruments for public information seen since the Second World War: the Committee for the Marshall Plan, headed by the eminent Republicans whom FDR in 1940 had brought to the Department of War: Henry L. Stimson as honorary chairman and Robert P. Patterson as active spokesman. The remarkable array of bankers, lawyers, trade unionists, and editors, who had drawn together in defense of "internationalism" before Pearl Harbor and had joined their talents in the war itself, combined again to spark the work of this committee. Their efforts generated a great deal of vocal public support to buttress Marshall's arguments, and Vandenberg's, in Congress.

But before public support could be rallied, there had to be a purpose tangible enough, concrete enough, to provide a rallying ground. At Harvard, Marshall had voiced an idea in general terms. That this was turned into a hard program susceptible of presentation and support is due, in major part, to Ernest Bevin, the British foreign secretary. He well deserves the credit he has sometimes been assigned as, in effect, coauthor of the Marshall Plan. For Bevin seized on Marshall's Harvard speech and organized a European response with promptness and concreteness beyond the State Department's expectations. What had been virtually a trial balloon to test reactions on both sides of the Atlantic was hailed in London as an invitation to the Europeans to send Washington a bill of particulars. This they promptly organized to do, and the American Administration then organized in turn for its reception without further argument internally about the pros and cons of issuing the "invitation" in the first place. But for Bevin there might have been trouble from the secretary of the treasury and others besides.[16]

If Bevin's help was useful at that early stage, Stalin's was vital from first to last. In a mood of self-deprecation Truman once remarked that without Moscow's "crazy" moves "we would never have had our foreign policy . . . we never could have got a thing from Congress."[17] George Kennan, among others, had deplored the anti-Soviet overtone of the case made for the Marshall Plan in Congress and the country, but there is no doubt that this clinched the argument for many segments of American opinion. There also is no doubt that Moscow made the crucial contributions to the case.

By 1947 events, far more than governmental prescience or open action, had given a variety of publics an impression of inimical Soviet intentions (and of Europe's weakness) and a growing urge to "do something about it." Three months before Marshall spoke at Harvard, Greek-Turkish aid and promulgation of the Truman Doctrine had seemed rather to crystallize than to create a public mood and a congressional response. The Marshall planners, be it said, were poorly placed to capitalize on that mood, nor had the secretary wished to do so. Their object, indeed, was to cut across it, striking at the cause of European weakness rather than at Soviet aggressiveness, per se. A strong economy in Western Europe called, ideally, for restorative measures of continental scope. American assistance proffered in an anti-Soviet context would have been contradictory in theory and unacceptable in fact to several of the governments that Washington was anxious to assist. As Marshall, himself, saw it, the logic of his purpose forbade him to play his strongest congressional card. The Russians then proceeded to play it for him. When the Europeans met in Paris, Molotov walked out. After the Czechs had shown continued interest in American aid, a Communist coup overthrew their government while Soviet forces stood along their borders within easy reach of Prague. Molotov transformed the Marshall Plan's initial presentation; Czechoslovakia assured its final passage, which followed by a month the takeover in Prague.

Such was the help accorded Truman in obtaining action on the Marshall Plan. Considering his politically straitened circumstances he scarcely could have done with less. Conceivably some part of Moscow's contribution might have been dispensable, but not Marshall's or Vandenberg's or Bevin's or Patterson's or that of the great many other men whose work is represented by their names in my account. Their aid was not extended to the President for his own sake. He was not favored in this fashion just because they liked him personally or were spellbound by his intellect or charm. They might have been as helpful had all held him in disdain, which some of them certainly did. The Londoners who seized the ball, Vandenberg and Taft and the congressional majority, Marshall and his planners, the officials of other agencies who actively supported them or "went along," the host of influential private citizens who rallied to the cause—all these played the parts they did because they thought they had to, in their interest, given their responsibilities, not Truman's. Yet they hardly would have found it in their interest to collaborate with one another or with him had he not furnished them precisely what they needed from the White

House. Truman could not do without their help, but he could not have had it without unremitting effort on his part.

The crucial thing to note about this case is that despite compatibility of views on public policy, Truman got no help he did not pay for (except Stalin's). Bevin scarcely could have seized on Marshall's words had Marshall not been plainly backed by Truman. Marshall's interest would not have comported with the exploitation of his prestige by a president who undercut him openly or subtly or even inadvertently at any point. Vandenberg, presumably, could not have backed proposals by a White House that begrudged him deference and access gratifying to his fellow partisans (and satisfying to himself). Prominent Republicans in private life would not have found it easy to promote a cause identified with Truman's claims on 1948—and neither would the prominent New Dealers then engaged in searching for a substitute.

Truman paid the price required for their services. So far as the record shows, the White House did not falter once in firm support for Marshall and the Marshall Plan. Truman backed his secretary's gamble on an invitation to all Europe. He made the plan his own in a well-timed address to the Canadians. He lost no opportunity to widen the involvements of his own official family in the cause. Averell Harriman, the secretary of commerce; Julius Krug, the secretary of the interior; Edwin Nourse, the Economic Council chairman; James Webb, the director of the budget—all were made responsible for studies and reports contributing directly to the legislative presentation. Thus these men were committed in advance. Besides, the President continually emphasized to everyone in reach that he did not have doubts, did not desire complications and would foreclose all he could. Reportedly his emphasis was felt at the Treasury, with good effect. And Truman was at special pains to smooth the way for Vandenberg. The senator insisted on "no politics" from the Administration side; there was none. He thought a survey of American resources and capacity essential; he got it in the Krug and Harriman reports. Vandenberg expected advance consultation; he received it, step by step, in frequent meetings with the President and weekly conferences with Marshall. He asked for an effective liaison between Congress and agencies concerned; Lovett and others gave him what he wanted. When the senator decided on the need to change financing and administrative features of the legislation, Truman disregarded Budget Bureau grumbling and acquiesced with grace. When, finally, Vandenberg desired a Republican to head the new administering agency, his candidate, Paul Hoffman, was appointed despite the President's own preference for another. In all these ways Truman employed the sparse advantages his "powers" and his status then accorded him to gain the sort of help he had to have.

Truman helped himself in still another way. Traditionally and practically, no one was placed as well as he to call public attention to the task of Congress (and its

Republican leadership). Throughout the fall and winter of 1947 and on into the spring of 1948, he made repeated use of presidential "powers" to remind the country that congressional action was required. Messages, speeches, and an extra session were employed to make the point. Here, too, he drew advantage from his place. However, in his circumstances, Truman's public advocacy might have hurt, not helped, had his words seemed directed toward the forthcoming election. Truman gained advantage for his program only as his own endorsement of it stayed on the right side of that fine line between the "caretaker" in office and the would-be candidate. In public statements dealing with the Marshall Plan he seems to have risked blurring this distinction only once, when he called Congress into session in November 1947 asking both for interim aid to Europe and for peacetime price controls. The second request linked the then inflation with the current Congress (and with Taft), becoming a first step toward one of Truman's major themes in 1948. By calling for both measures at the extra session he could have been accused—and was—of mixing home-front politics with foreign aid. In the event no harm was done the European program (or his politics). But in advance a number of his own advisers feared that such a double call would jeopardize the Marshall Plan. Their fears are testimony to the narrowness of his advantage in employing his own "powers" for its benefit.[18]

It is symptomatic of Truman's situation that bipartisan accommodation by the White House then was thought to mean congressional consultation and conciliation on a scale unmatched in Eisenhower's time. Yet Eisenhower did about as well with opposition congresses as Truman did, in terms of requests granted for defense and foreign aid. It may be said that Truman asked for more extraordinary measures. But it also may be said that Eisenhower never lacked for the prestige his predecessor had to borrow. It often was remarked, in Truman's time, that he seemed a split personality, so sharply did his conduct differentiate domestic politics from national security. But personality aside, how else could he, in his first term, gain ground for an evolving foreign policy? The plain fact is that Truman had to play bipartisanship as he did or lose the game.

HAD TRUMAN LACKED the personal advantages his "powers" and his status gave him, or if he had been maladroit in using them, there probably would not have been a massive European aid program in 1948. Something of the sort, perhaps quite different in its emphasis, would almost certainly have come to pass before the end of 1949. Some American response to European weakness and to Soviet expansion was as certain as such things can be. But in 1948 temptations to await a Taft plan or a Dewey plan might well have caused at least a year's postponement of response had the outgoing Administration bungled its congressional or public or allied or executive relations. Quite aside from the specific virtues of their plan, Truman and his helpers gained that year, at least, in timing the American response.

As European time was measured then, this was a precious gain. The President's own share in this accomplishment was vital. He made his contribution by exploiting his advantages. Truman, in effect, lent Marshall and the rest the perquisites and status of his office. In return they lent him their prestige and their own influence. The transfer multiplied his influence despite his limited authority in form and lack of strength politically. Without the wherewithal to make this bargain, Truman could not have contributed to European aid.

Bargaining advantages convey no guarantees. Influence remains a two-way street. In the fortunate instance of the Marshall Plan, what Truman needed was actually in the hands of men who were prepared to "trade" with him. He personally could deliver what they wanted in return. Marshall, Vandenberg, Harriman, et al., possessed the prestige, energy, associations, staffs essential to the legislative effort. Truman himself had a sufficient hold on presidential messages and speeches, on budget policy, on high-level appointments, and on his own time and temper to carry through all aspects of his necessary part. But it takes two to make a bargain. It takes those who have prestige to lend it on whatever terms. Suppose that Marshall had declined the secretaryship of state in January 1947; Truman might not have found a substitute so well equipped to furnish what he needed in the months ahead. Or suppose that Vandenberg had fallen victim to a cancer two years before he actually did; Senator Wiley of Wisconsin would not have seemed to Taft a man with whom the world need be divided. Or suppose that the secretary of the treasury had been possessed of stature, force, and charm commensurate with that of his successor in Eisenhower's time, the redoubtable George M. Humphrey. And what if Truman then had seemed to the Republicans what he turned out to be in 1948, a formidable candidate for President? It is unlikely that a single one of these "supposes" would have changed the final outcome; two or three, however, might have altered it entirely. Truman was not guaranteed more power than his "powers" just because he had continuing relationships with cabinet secretaries and with senior senators. Here, as everywhere, the outcome was conditional on who they were and what he was and how each viewed events, and on their actual performance in response.

Granting that persuasion has no guarantee attached, how can a President reduce the risks of failing to persuade? How can he maximize his prospects for effectiveness by minimizing chances that his power will elude him? The Marshall Plan suggests an answer: He guards his power prospects in the course of making choices. Marshall himself, and Forrestal and Harriman, and others of the sort held office on the President's appointment. Vandenberg had vast symbolic value partly because FDR and Truman had done everything they could, since 1944, to build him up. The Treasury Department and the Budget Bureau—which together might have jeopardized the plans these others made—were headed by officials whose prestige depended wholly on their jobs. What Truman needed from those "givers" he received, in part, because of his past choice of men and measures. What they received in turn were actions taken or withheld by him, himself. The things they needed from him mostly involved his own conduct where his current choices ruled. The President's own actions in the past had cleared the way for current bargaining. His actions in the present were his trading stock. Behind each action lay a personal choice, and these together comprised his control over the give-and-take that gained him what he wanted. In the degree that Truman, personally, affected the advantages he drew from his relationships with other men in government, his power was protected by his choices.

By "choice" I mean no more than what is commonly referred to as "decision": a President's own act of doing or not doing. Decision is so often indecisive, and indecision is so frequently conclusive, that *choice* becomes the preferable term. "Choice" has its share of undesired connotations. In common usage it implies a black-and-white alternative. Presidential choices are rarely of that character. It also may imply that the alternatives are set before the choice maker by someone else. A President is often left to figure out his options for himself. . . .

If Presidents could count upon past choices to enhance their current influence, as Truman's choice of men had done for him, persuasion would pose fewer difficulties than it does. But Presidents can count on no such thing. Depending on the circumstances, prior choices can be as embarrassing as they were helpful in the instance of the Marshall Plan. . . . Truman's hold upon MacArthur was weakened by his deference toward him in the past.

Assuming that past choices have protected influence, not harmed it, present choices still may be inadequate. If Presidents could count on their own conduct to provide them enough bargaining advantages, as Truman's conduct did where Vandenberg and Marshall were concerned, effective bargaining might be much easier to manage than it often is. In the steel crisis, for instance, Truman's own persuasiveness with companies and union, both, was burdened by the conduct of an independent wage board and of government attorneys in the courts, to say nothing of Wilson, Arnall, Sawyer, and the like. Yet in practice, if not theory, many of *their* crucial choices never were the President's to make. Decisions that are legally in others' hands, or delegated past recall, have an unhappy way of proving just the trading stock most needed when the White House wants to trade. One reason why Truman was consistently more influential in the instance of the Marshall Plan than in the steel case or the MacArthur case is that the Marshall Plan directly involved Congress. In congressional relations there are some things that no one but the President can do. His chance to choose is higher when a message must be sent, or a nomination submitted, or a bill signed into law, than when the sphere of action is confined to the executive, where all decisive tasks may have been delegated past recall.

But adequate or not, a President's choices are the only means in his own hands of guarding his own prospects for effective influence. He can draw power from continuing relationships in the degree that he can capitalize upon the needs of others for the Presidency's status and authority. He helps himself to do so, though, by nothing save ability to recognize the preconditions and the chance advantages and to proceed accordingly in the course of the choice making that comes his way. To ask how he can guard prospective influence is thus to raise a further question: What helps him guard his power stakes in his own acts of choice?

NOTES

1. The reader will want to keep in mind the distinction between two senses in which the word *power* is employed. When I have used the word (or its plural) to refer to formal constitutional, statutory, or customary authority, it is either qualified by the adjective "formal" or placed in quotation marks as "power(s)." Where I have used it in the sense of effective influence on the conduct of others, it appears without quotation marks (and always in the singular). Where clarity and convenience permit, *authority* is substituted for "power" in the first sense and *influence* for power in the second.

2. See, for example, his press conference of July 22, 1959, as reported in the *New York Times,* July 23, 1959.

3. See Douglass Cater, *The Fourth Branch of Government* (Boston: Houghton Mifflin, 1959).

4. With the exception of the vice presidency, of course.

5. See David B. Truman's illuminating study of party relationships in the Eighty-first Congress, *The Congressional Party* (New York: Wiley, 1959), especially chaps. 4, 6, 8.

6. As secretary of the interior in 1939, Harold Ickes refused to approve the sale of helium to Germany despite the insistence of the State Department and the urging of President Roosevelt. Without the secretary's approval, such sales were forbidden by statute. See *The Secret Diaries of Harold L. Ickes* (New York: Simon & Schuster, 1954), vol. 2, especially pp. 391–93, 396–99.

In this instance the statutory authority ran to the secretary as a matter of his discretion. A President is unlikely to fire cabinet officers for the conscientious exercise of such authority. If the President did so, their successors might well be embarrassed both publicly and at the Capitol were they to reverse decisions previously taken. As for a President's authority to set aside discretionary determinations of this sort, it rests, if it exists at all, on shaky legal ground not likely to be trod save in the gravest of situations.

7. Truman's *Memoirs* indicate that having tried and failed to make Stevenson an avowed candidate in the spring of 1952, the President decided to support the candidacy of Vice President Barkley. But Barkley withdrew early in the convention for lack of key northern support. Though Truman is silent on the matter, Barkley's active candidacy nearly was revived during the balloting, but the forces then aligning to revive it were led by opponents of Truman's Fair Deal, principally Southerners. As a practical matter, the President could not

have lent his weight to their endeavors and could back no one but Stevenson to counter them. The latter's strength could not be shifted, then, to Harriman or Kefauver. Instead the other Northerners had to be withdrawn. Truman helped withdraw them. But he had no other option. See Harry S Truman, *Memoirs,* vol. 2, *Years of Trial and Hope* (Garden City, N.Y.: Doubleday, Time Inc., 1956), pp. 495–96.

8. The reference is to Stassen's public statement of July 23, 1956, calling for Nixon's replacement on the Republican ticket by Governor Herter of Massachusetts, the later secretary of state. Stassen's statement was issued after a conference with the President. Eisenhower's public statements on the vice-presidential nomination, both before and after Stassen's call, permit of alternative inferences: either that the President would have preferred another candidate, provided this could be arranged without a showing of White House dictation, or that he wanted Nixon on condition that the latter could show popular appeal. In the event, neither result was achieved. Eisenhower's own remarks lent strength to rapid party moves that smothered Stassen's effort. Nixon's nomination thus was guaranteed too quickly to appear the consequence of popular demand. For the public record on this matter see reported statements by Eisenhower, Nixon, Stassen, Herter, and Leonard Hall (the National Republican Chairman) in the *New York Times* for March 1, 8, 15, 16; April 27; July 15, 16, 25–31; August 3, 4, 17, 23, 1956. See also the account from private sources by Earl Mazo in *Richard Nixon: A Personal and Political Portrait* (New York: Harper, 1959), pp. 158–87

9. Stenographic transcript of presidential press conference, October 19, 1950, on file in the Truman Library at Independence, Missouri.

10. Jonathan Daniels, *Frontier on the Potomac* (New York: Macmillan, 1946), pp. 31–32.

11. Transcript of presidential press conference, June 18, 1958, in *Public Papers of the Presidents Dwight D. Eisenhower, 1958* (Washington, D.C.: National Archives, 1959), p. 479. In the summer of 1958, a congressional investigation into the affairs of a New England textile manufacturer, Bernard Goldfine, revealed that Sherman Adams had accepted various gifts and favors from him (the most notoriety attached to a vicuna coat). Adams also had made inquiries about the status of a Federal Communications Commission proceeding in which Goldfine was involved. In September 1958 Adams was allowed to resign. The episode was highly publicized and much discussed in that year's congressional campaigns.

12. As reported in Marriner S. Eccles (*Beckoning Frontiers,* New York: Knopf, 1951), p. 336.

13. In drawing together these observations on the Marshall Plan, I have relied on the record of personal participation by Joseph M. Jones, *The Fifteen Weeks* (New York: Viking, 1955), especially pp. 89–256; on the recent study by Harry Bayard Price, *The Marshall Plan and Its Meaning* (Ithaca: Cornell University Press, 1955), especially pp. 1–86; on the Truman *Memoirs,* vol. 2, chaps. 7–9; on Arthur H. Vandenberg Jr., ed., *The Private Papers of Senator Vandenberg* (Boston: Houghton Mifflin, 1952), especially pp. 373 ff.; and on notes of my own made at the time. This is an instance of policy development not covered, to my knowledge, by any of the university programs engaged in the production of case studies.

14. Secretary Marshall's speech, formally suggesting what became known as the Marshall Plan, was made at Harvard on June 5, 1947. On June 20 the President vetoed the Taft-Hartley Act; his veto was overridden three days later. On June 16 he vetoed the first of two tax reduction bills (HR 1) passed at the first session of the Eightieth Congress; the second of these (HR 3950), a replacement for the other, he also disapproved on July 18. In both instances his veto was narrowly sustained.

15. *Private Papers of Senator Vandenberg*, pp. 378–79, 446.

16. The initial reluctance of the Secretary of the Treasury, John Snyder, to support large-scale spending overseas became a matter of public knowledge on June 25, 1947. At a press conference on that day he interpreted Marshall's Harvard speech as a call on Europeans to help themselves, by themselves. At another press conference the same day, Marshall for his own part had indicated that the United States would consider helping programs on which Europeans agreed. The next day Truman held a press conference and was asked the inevitable question. He replied, "General Marshall and I are in complete agreement." When pressed further, Truman remarked sharply, "The secretary of the treasury and the secretary of state and the President are in complete agreement." Thus the President cut Snyder off, but had programming gathered less momentum overseas, no doubt he would have been heard from again as time passed and opportunity offered.

The foregoing quotations are from the stenographic transcript of the presidential press conference June 26, 1947, on file in the Truman Library at Independence, Missouri.

17. A remark made in December 1955, three years after he left office, but not unrepresentative of views he expressed, on occasion, while he was President.

18. This might also be taken as testimony to the political timidity of officials in the State Department and the Budget Bureau where that fear seems to have been strongest. However, conversations at the time with White House aides incline me to believe that there, too, interjection of the price issue was thought a gamble and a risk. For further comment see my "Congress and the Fair Deal: A Legislative Balance Sheet," *Public Policy,* vol. 5 (Cambridge: Harvard University Press, 1954), pp. 362–64.

7-2

The Institutional Presidency

John P. Burke

As federal obligations and services grew steadily throughout the 20th century, so too did the management responsibilities of the president. Virtually every national law delegates some responsibility to the president. The sheer growth of work was bound to cause presidents to press Congress and Congress to agree to add staff and to bring more control over departments and agencies into the White House. As a consequence, present-day presidents preside over their own bureaucracy, which poses its own control issues.

ANALYSIS OF THE workings of the White House staff, both by people who have served on it and by scholars, has a peculiar if not schizophrenic quality. For some, the staff is simply a reflection of the personality, style, and managerial skills of the incumbent president. Others emphasize characteristics of the presidency that seem to endure from administration to administration. Both of these perspectives have some merit. Presidents do seem to leave their imprint—for better or for worse—on the office. The formal and hierarchical arrangements of the Dwight Eisenhower, Richard Nixon, Ronald Reagan, George H. W. Bush, and George W. Bush presidencies and the more collegial, informal, ad hoc patterns in the John Kennedy, Lyndon Johnson, and Bill Clinton White Houses can be linked to the organizational preferences and "work ways" of each of these chief executives. Yet the White House staff, now made up of some two thousand employees in significant policy-making positions, also serves as an organizational context that can—just as in any bureaucracy—set limits on what a president can do and sometimes thwart even the best of presidential intentions. For the skillful president, the White House staff is like very hard clay that can be molded only with great effort, patience, and understanding; for the less skilled it can become a hard rock, if not a brick wall, that resists presidential management and control.

A full analysis of how presidents have succeeded or failed at this "organizational artistry" would require a detailed account of the presidential staff system that has evolved since the late 1930s and a close examination of the efforts of each of the presidents from Franklin Roosevelt through Barack Obama to organize

Source: John P. Burke, "The Institutional Presidency," in Michael Nelson, ed., *The Presidency and the Political System,* 9th ed. (Washington, DC: CQ Press, 2010), 341–366. © 2010 by CQ Press.

and manage the institutional presidency. What follows is only part of that larger project: an outline of some of the institutional characteristics of the modern presidency and the managerial challenges they present to incumbent presidents.[1]

One point that deserves mention is how odd the need for organizational leadership would have seemed to presidents in the nineteenth and early twentieth centuries. Thomas Jefferson managed his office with one secretary and a messenger. Sixty years later, in the administration of Ulysses Grant, the size of the staff had grown to three. By 1900 the staff consisted of a private secretary (formally titled "secretary to the president"), two assistant secretaries, two executive clerks, a stenographer, three lower-level clerks, and four other office personnel. Under Warren Harding the size of the staff grew to thirty-one, but most staff members were clerical. Herbert Hoover managed to persuade Congress to approve two more secretaries to the president, one of whom he assigned the job of press aide.

It was common practice for early presidents to hire immediate family and other relatives as their secretaries, an indication that their few staff members functioned as personal aides rather than as substantive policy advisers. John Quincy Adams, Andrew Jackson, John Tyler, Abraham Lincoln, and Ulysses Grant all engaged their sons as private secretaries. George Washington, James Polk, and James Buchanan employed their nephews. James Monroe employed his younger brother and two sons-in-law. Zachary Taylor hired his brother-in-law.

Early presidents also paid the salaries of their small staffs out of their own pockets. Not until 1857 did Congress appropriate money ($2,500) for a presidential clerk—one. As recently as the Coolidge presidency, the entire budget for the White House staff, including office expenses, was less than $80,000.[2] By 1963 it had climbed to $12 million. In 2009 the corresponding figure for the Executive Office of the President was estimated conservatively at $375 million. Other estimates, taking into account items that are paid for by departments and agencies, put the total at over $1 billion.[3]

As demands on the presidency mounted, more help was needed. Grappling with the Great Depression of the 1930s, President Roosevelt's solution was to "muddle through." Early in his administration he experimented with a form of cabinet government but quickly became dissatisfied with its members' parochial perspectives, infighting, and tendencies to leak information to the press— problems encountered by many of Roosevelt's successors who also took office thinking that the cabinet would play a central role in their policymaking. Roosevelt then moved to a series of coordinating bodies that included relevant cabinet officers and the heads of the new agencies that were created as part of the New Deal. Another of FDR's managerial strategies was to borrow staff from existing departments and agencies; these employees remained on their home agencies' personnel budgets while they were "detailed" to the White House. In fact, the legislative whirlwind of Roosevelt's first hundred days was the product of a loosely organized group of assistants, many of whom did not have formal positions on the White House staff.

Roosevelt's patchwork arrangement worked, but just barely. In an interview with a group of reporters shortly after his reelection in 1936, Roosevelt publicly attributed his victory to the failure of his Republican opponent, Gov. Alfred Landon of Kansas, to seize on the president's chief weakness. "What is your weakness?" one of the reporters asked. "Administration," replied the president.[4] Clearly something needed to be done.

Roosevelt had already taken steps to rectify his administrative problems by forming the Committee on Administrative Management, headed by Louis Brownlow. Roosevelt's creation of the Brownlow Committee was not the first presidential effort to seek administrative advice on how to make the presidency work more effectively. But it was the Brownlow Committee that most clearly and directly focused on the need for a larger, reorganized White House staff.[5] Concluding that "the President needs help," Brownlow and his associates proposed that "to deal with the greatly increased duties of executive management falling upon the president, the White House staff should be expanded."[6] After initially rejecting the then-controversial proposal, Congress passed the revised recommendations of the Brownlow Committee in the Reorganization Act of 1939.[7] Significant increases in the staff resources available to the president also followed passage of the Employment Act of 1946, which created the Council of Economic Advisers, and the National Security Act of 1947, which led to the development of the National Security Council and its staff, and the recommendations of the 1947 Hoover Commission on the Reorganization of the Executive Branch.[8] During Eisenhower's presidency, existing units within the White House Office (itself the core unit of the White House staff) were more clearly defined, and new offices were created. Eisenhower also designated Sherman Adams as the first White House chief of staff and assigned him significant authority to oversee and coordinate the domestic policy component of the staff system.[9]

From the handful of aides that Roosevelt and his predecessors could appoint, the numbers have increased steadily in each succeeding administration. By 1953 the size of the White House Office was about 250. Twenty years later, it had grown to almost five hundred. In 1977, criticizing the size of the staff as a symptom of the "imperial presidency," Jimmy Carter reduced it by a hundred employees, mostly by moving them to other parts of the executive bureaucracy. By 1980, Carter's last year in office, the size of the staff had inched back up to five hundred, and it has remained at about that size ever since. When other administrative units under direct presidential control (the larger Executive Office of the

President) are included—such as the Office of Management and Budget (OMB), the National Security Council, and the Council of Economic Advisers—the number of staff swells to about two thousand. Physically, the Executive Office of the President has spilled out from the East and West wings of the White House to occupy first the Old Executive Office Building next door, which was once large enough to house the Departments of State, War, and Navy, and then the New Executive Office Building on the north side of Pennsylvania Avenue, as well as other, smaller buildings in the vicinity.

A marked change in the character of the presidency has thus occurred. By recognizing that the American executive is an institution—a presidency, not merely a president—we can better understand the office, how it operates, the challenges it faces, and how it affects our politics.

The Institutional Presidency

If the presidency is best understood as an institution, then clearly it should embody some of the characteristics of an institution. But what do terms such as *institution, institutional,* and *institutionalization* mean? Our concern is the organizational character of the presidency—its growth in size, the complexity of its work ways, and the general way in which it resembles a large, well-organized bureaucracy. More specifically, an institution is complex in what it does (its functions) and how it operates (its structure); and it is well bounded—that is, differentiated from its environment.[10]

Complex Organization

Institutions are complex: they are relatively large in size; each part performs a specialized function; and some form of central authority coordinates the parts' various contributions to the work of the whole. The first aspect of complexity— the increase in size of the institutional presidency—can easily be seen by comparing the White House staff available to President Roosevelt in 1939, before the adoption of the Brownlow Committee's recommendations, with the staff at work in the Clinton, Bush, or Obama White House. The eight-person list of members of the White House staff in the 1939 *United States Government Manual* (see Table 1) is dwarfed by the long list of staff members currently serving under President Barack Obama. A comparison of the Roosevelt and Obama staffs also illustrates the second aspect of organizational complexity: increasing specialization of function. Roosevelt's aides were, by and large, generalists; they were simply called "secretary to the president" or "administrative assistant." The staff list for the Obama White House includes titles such as deputy assistant to the president for communications, deputy assistant to the president for legislative affairs, deputy assistant to the president and director of media affairs, special assistant to the president for public liaison, associate counsel to the president, and many others.

Other units of the White House staff operate within functionally defined, specialized areas, such as national security or environmental quality. In fact, one of the primary causes of the growth of the White House staff has been the addition of these units: the Bureau of the Budget (created in 1921, transferred from the Treasury Department in 1939, and reorganized as OMB in 1970), the Council of Economic Advisers (1946), the National Security Council (1947), the Office of the United States Trade Representative (1963), the Office of Policy Development (1970), the Council on Environmental Quality (1970), the Office of Science and Technology Policy (1976), the Office of Administration (1977), and the Office of National Drug Control Policy (1989). All told, the once relatively simple tasks of the president's staff—writing speeches, handling correspondence, and orchestrating the daily schedule—have evolved into substantive duties that affect the policies presidents propose and the ways they deal with the steadily increasing demands placed on the office.

The final characteristic of institutional complexity is the presence of a central authority that coordinates the contributions of the institution's functional parts. For the presidency, such authority resides nominally in the president. Since the 1950s, however, coordinating authority has gradually been taken over by the White House chief of staff—Sherman Adams under Eisenhower; H. R. Haldeman under Nixon; Hamilton Jordan and Jack Watson under Carter; James Baker, Donald Regan,

Table 1. The White House Office, 1939

Secretary to the president	Stephen Early
Secretary to the president	Brig. Gen. Edwin M. Watson
Secretary to the president	Marvin H. McIntyre
Administrative assistant	William H. McReynolds
Administrative assistant	James H. Rowe Jr.
Administrative assistant	Lauchlin Currie
Personal secretary	Marguerite A. LeHand
Executive clerk	Rudolph Forster

Source: United States Government Manual, 1939 (Washington, D.C.: U.S. Government Printing Office, 1939).

Howard Baker, and Kenneth Duberstein under Reagan; John Sununu and Samuel Skinner under George H. W. Bush; Thomas "Mack" McLarty III, Leon Panetta, Erskine Bowles, and John Podesta under Clinton; Andrew Card Jr. and Joshua Bolten under George W. Bush; and Rahm Emanuel under Obama. The chief of staff performs substantive roles in policymaking and, in most cases, wields day-to-day authority over the workings of the White House staff.

Differentiation from Environment

The complexity of the presidency and its reliance on expert advice have given the institution a unique place in the policy process, differentiating it from its political environment. One way this has occurred is through increased White House control of new policy initiatives. Presidents now routinely try to shape the nation's political agenda, and the staff resources they have at their disposal make it possible for them to do so. John Kennedy, Lyndon Johnson, and especially Richard Nixon, with his creation of the Domestic Council, emphasized White House control of policy formulation, de-emphasizing the involvement of the cabinet and the bureaucracy. Carter and Reagan began their terms of office by promising to rely more on the cabinet. They quickly found that goal unworkable in practice and turned inward to the White House staff for policy advice. Clinton, George W. Bush, and Obama followed this pattern, and their domestic and economic initiatives were largely the work of their White House staffs.

Those outside the White House—Congress, the bureaucracy, the news media, and the public—have responded to presidential direction of the national agenda by expecting more of it. Political lobbying and influence seeking, especially by those directly involved in Washington politics, focus on the president. Although American politics remains highly decentralized, incremental, and open to multiple points of access, those seeking to influence national politics try to cultivate the people who have the most to do with policy proposals: the White House staff.

A second aspect of the presidency that differentiates it from the surrounding political environment is the way parts of the staff are organized explicitly to manage external relations with the media, Congress, and various constituencies. The press secretary and staff coordinate, and in many cases control, the presidential news passed on to the media.[11] Since 1953 specific staff assistants also have been assigned to lobby Congress on the president's behalf. Today White House lobbying efforts are formally organized within the large, well-staffed Office of Legislative Affairs. The establishment of special channels of influence for important constituent groups is another way presidents manage their relations with the political environment. This practice began in the administration of Harry Truman, when David Niles became the first staff aide explicitly assigned to serve as a liaison to Jewish groups. Eisenhower hired the first black presidential assistant, E. Frederic Morrow, and added a special representative from the scientific community as well. In 1970 Nixon created the Office of Public Liaison as the organizational home within the White House staff for the aides serving as conduits to particular groups. By the time Jimmy Carter left office in 1981, special staff members were assigned to consumers, women, the elderly, Jews, Hispanics, white ethnic Catholics, Vietnam veterans, and gay men and lesbians, as well as to such traditional constituencies as African Americans, labor, and business.[12]

In George W. Bush's White House, liaison to constituency groups took on particular importance with the appointment of Karl Rove as "senior adviser" to the president. Rove not only was placed in charge of the public liaison and political affairs offices, but also was made the contact for conservative, business, and religious groups. Those contacts played an important role in Bush's successful reelection effort. The pattern continued in the Obama White House when the president appointed Valerie Jarrett, a longtime member of his inner circle, as "senior adviser" in charge of both the public liaison and intergovernmental affairs offices.

The increasing differentiation of the presidency as a discrete entity thus complements its increasing complexity and reliance on expertise as evidence of its status as an institution.

Effects of an Institutional Presidency

Even if the presidency bears the marks of an institution, do its distinctly institutional characteristics—as opposed to the individual styles, practices, and idiosyncrasies of each president—matter? Despite the tremendous growth in the size of the president's staff, perhaps it remains mainly a cluster of aides and supporting personnel, with their tasks, organization, and tenure varying greatly from administration to administration, even changing within the tenure of each president. After all, observers of the presidency, both scholarly and journalistic, have noted enormous differences between the Kennedy and Eisenhower White Houses, between Johnson and Nixon, Carter and Reagan, Reagan and George H. W. Bush, George W. Bush and Obama, and even Bush father and Bush son. It is the personality, character, and distinctive behavior of each of these presidents that have generally attracted the attention of press and public.

Some of these observations are accurate, but to the extent that the institutionalized daily workings of the presidency transcend the personal ideologies, character, and idiosyncrasies of those who work within it (especially the president), it makes sense to analyze the presidency from an institutional perspective. Not only do many of the presidency's institutional characteristics affect the office, but the effects are negative as well as positive. The institutional presidency can help determine the success or failure of a particular president.

External Centralization: Presidential Control of Policymaking

The creation of a large presidential staff has centralized much policy-making power within the presidency. This development has both positive and negative aspects. On the positive side, an institutional presidency that centralizes control of policy can protect the programs that the president wishes to foster. The Washington political climate is usually not receptive to new political initiatives, which must compete for programmatic authority and budget allocations against older programs that are generally well established in agencies and departments, have strong allies on Capitol Hill, and enjoy a supportive clientele of special interest groups.

In creating the Office of Economic Opportunity (OEO), Lyndon Johnson, a president whose legislative skills were unsurpassed, recognized precisely this problem. The OEO was designed to be a central component of Johnson's War on Poverty. As Congress was considering the legislation to create the OEO, three departments—Commerce; Labor; and Health, Education, and Welfare— lobbied to have it administratively housed within their respective bailiwicks. Johnson, recognizing that this would subordinate the OEO to whatever other goals a department might pursue, lobbied Congress to set up the OEO so that it would report directly to the president. Johnson was especially swayed by the views of Harvard economist John Kenneth Galbraith, who warned, "Do not bury the program in the departments. Put it in the Executive offices, where people will know what you are doing, where it can have a new staff and a fresh man as director."[13]

The centralization of power in presidents' staffs has not always redounded to their advantage. One of the worst effects of increasing White House control of the policy process, especially in foreign policy, has been to diminish or even exclude other sources of advice. Since the creation of the National Security Council (NSC) in 1947, presidents have tended to rely for advice on the council's staff, especially the president's assistant for national security (also known as the NSC adviser). Ironically, Congress's intent in creating the NSC was to check the foreign policy power of the president by creating a deliberative body whose members would provide an alternative source of timely advice to the president.

Except during Eisenhower's presidency, the NSC has not generally functioned as an effective deliberative body. What has developed instead is a large, White House–centered NSC staff, headed by a highly visible national security assistant, that often dominates the foreign policy-making process.[14] The reasons why the

NSC staff and the national security assistant have come to dominate are plain: proximity to the Oval Office, readily available staff resources, and a series of presidents whose views about decision-making processes differed from Eisenhower's. Beginning with McGeorge Bundy under Kennedy and continuing with Walt Rostow under Johnson, Henry Kissinger under Nixon, and Zbigniew Brzezinski under Carter, most national security assistants not only have advocated their own policy views but also have eclipsed other sources of foreign policy advice, especially the secretary of state and the State Department.

Perhaps the best testimony to the problems created by centralizing control of foreign policy in the NSC staff can be found in the memoirs of three recent secretaries of state. Cyrus Vance, who served under Carter, repeatedly battled Brzezinski. Vance's resignation as secretary of state in 1980, in fact, was precipitated by the administration's ill-fated decision—from which Vance and the State Department were effectively excluded—to try to rescue the American hostages in Iran.[15]

Alexander Haig, Reagan's first secretary of state, encountered similar problems with the NSC. In his memoirs, Haig claims he had only secondhand knowledge of many of the president's decisions. In a chapter tellingly titled, "Mr. President, I Want You to Know What's Going on around You," Haig reported,

> William Clark, in his capacity as National Security Adviser to the President, seemed to be conducting a second foreign policy, using separate channels of communications . . . bypassing the State Department altogether. Such a system was bound to produce confusion, and it soon did. There were conflicts over votes in the United Nations, differences over communications to heads of state, mixed signals to the combatants in Lebanon. Some of these, in my judgment, represented a danger to the nation.[16]

George Shultz, Haig's successor as secretary of state, also found himself cut out of a number of important decisions by the NSC staff. The most notable was the Reagan administration's secret negotiations with Iran to exchange arms for the release of American hostages in Lebanon and its covert, illegal use of the profits generated by the arms sales to fund the contra rebels in Nicaragua. The arms deal violated standing administration policy against negotiating for hostages, and the disclosure of the secret contra funds undermined congressional support for Reagan's policies in Central America. The affair not only bespoke Shultz's conflicts with the NSC but also was politically damaging to the president.

Some exceptions have been noted to the general pattern of NSC dominance in foreign policy-making: one occurred during the Ford administration, another in the elder Bush's presidency. In both cases a reasonable balance was struck in the advisory roles of the State Department and the NSC. But the two cases are revealing about the conditions under which excessive centralization can be avoided. In both presidencies the same individual, Brent Scowcroft, served as the NSC adviser, and he deliberately crafted his job to be a "neutral" or "honest" broker of the foreign policy-making process.[17] Furthermore, in both administrations the secretaries of state had extensive White House staff experience. Kissinger had served under Nixon as NSC adviser, and for part of his tenure in the Nixon and Ford administrations he was simultaneously NSC adviser and secretary of state. Bush's secretary of state, James Baker, had served as White House chief of staff and as secretary of the Treasury under Reagan.

Foreign and national security policy making in George W. Bush's presidency offers another variant. During the first term, NSC adviser Condoleezza Rice, a longtime Bush confidant, was generally considered both a policy coordinator and a policy adviser, much like her mentor Brent Scowcroft in the George H. W. Bush presidency. George W. Bush, however, had other powerful voices in his inner circle during his first term: Secretary of State Colin Powell, Secretary of Defense Donald Rumsfeld, and Vice President Dick Cheney, all of whom had served in previous administrations. Rumsfeld and Cheney were chiefs of staff under Ford, and Powell was Reagan's NSC adviser. Rumsfeld and Cheney also had served as defense secretary, and Powell had been chairman of the Joint Chiefs of Staff.

The events of September 11, 2001, radically transformed many of the internal dynamics of the Bush presidency. Although a foreign policy-making process with substantial participation by the cabinet developed after September 11, the White House staff remained a powerful force. According to one account, the "outline of the war plan often emerge[d] from the private conversations" of Bush and Rice.[18] The NSC added two new offices to deal with counterterrorism and computer security, and other White House units were created as well. Most notably, Bush signed an executive order creating the Office of Homeland Security, with a mandate to coordinate federal efforts to prevent and respond to domestic terrorism. The White House unit predated the establishment of a cabinet-level Department of Homeland Security in December 2002 (which Chief of Staff Andrew Card and members of his staff played the major role in creating). However, the White House's Office of Homeland Security remained in place after the department came into being.[19]

In domestic and economic policy, Bush generally centralized policymaking in the White House.[20] During Bush's first term, the White House staff was the dominant force in such areas as tax reform, education, the patients' bill of rights, and the faith-based initiatives proposal. In fact, in at least one of these issue areas, education policy, reports surfaced that the secretary of education was not pleased with the dominant role taken by the White House.[21] After Bush was reelected in

2004, one aide observed that the pattern would likely continue: "The Bush brand is a few priorities, run out of the White House, with no interference from the cabinet."[22] Departmental compliance with the White House's agenda, coupled with Bush's own emphasis on loyalty and discipline, was further exemplified (and bolstered) with Bush's nomination of three White House aides to cabinet positions in his second term: Rice as secretary of state, White House legal counsel Alberto Gonzales as attorney general, and Margaret Spellings (the White House domestic adviser who had largely devised the education reform proposals) as secretary of education. According to one account, "Bush and senior adviser Karl Rove are determined to 'implant their DNA throughout the government,' as one official put it."[23]

Despite his sharp policy differences with Bush, President Obama also centralized policymaking in the White House. Three longtime associates, David Axelrod, Peter Rouse, and Valerie Jarrett, were given the title of "senior adviser" to the president. New White House offices were created to coordinate energy, health care, and urban policy initiatives; a White House–based "performance evaluation" office was also added. As one account noted during the transition, although Obama built "a cabinet of prominent and strong willed players . . . he is putting together a governing structure that will concentrate more decision making over his top domestic priorities in the White House" than in the departments. These changes "shift the political center of gravity farther away from the cabinet, a trend that has accelerated under presidents of both parties in recent years."[24] The appointment of Lawrence Summers, a former secretary of the Treasury, to head the National Economic Council, also indicated a significant White House role in shaping economic policy.

Internal Centralization: Hierarchy, Gatekeeping, and Presidential Isolation

The centralization of policy-making power by the White House staff has been accompanied by a centralization of power within the staff by one or two chief aides. This internal centralization is further evidence of the institutional character of the presidency, and it too affects the way the institutional presidency operates, providing both opportunities and risks for the president.

On the positive side, centralization of authority within a well-organized staff system can ensure clear lines of responsibility, well-demarcated duties, and orderly work ways. When presidents lack a centralized, organized staff system, the policy-making process suffers.

The travails of Franklin Roosevelt's staff illustrate the problems that can arise from lack of effective organization. Roosevelt favored a relatively unorganized, competitive staff system, one in which the president acted as his own chief of staff. But rather than establishing regular patterns of duties and assignments and an orderly system of reporting and control, Roosevelt often gave several of his staff assistants the same assignment, pitting them against each other.

Some analysts have argued that redundancy—two or more staff members doing the same thing—can benefit an organization.[25] But in Roosevelt's day, staff resources were minimal. Worse, his staff arrangements generated jealousy and insecurity among his aides, neither of which is conducive to sound policy advice or effective administration. As Patrick Anderson observes, "Roosevelt used men, squeezed them dry, and ruthlessly discarded them. . . . The requirement [for success] was that they accept criticism without complaint, toil without credit, and accept unquestioningly Roosevelt's moods and machinations."[26]

In addition to making the staff more effective, a system in which one staff member serves as chief of staff or is at least *primus inter pares* (first among equals) is advantageous to a president for other reasons. It can protect the president's political standing, for example. A highly visible staff member with a significant amount of authority within the White House can act as a kind of lightning rod, handling politically tough assignments and deflecting political controversy from the president to himself or herself.

Perhaps the best example of this useful division of labor comes from the Eisenhower presidency. Part of Eisenhower's success as president derived from a leadership style in which he projected himself as a chief of state who was above the political fray, while allowing his assistants, especially Sherman Adams, the flinty former governor of New Hampshire who was Eisenhower's chief of staff, to seem like prime ministers concerned with day-to-day politics. A 1956 *Time* magazine feature on Eisenhower's staff reported that Adams's scrawled "O.K., S.A." was tantamount to presidential approval. Although it was really Eisenhower who made the decisions, Adams's reputation as the "abominable 'No!' man" helped to "preserve Eisenhower's image as a benevolent national and international leader" and protect his standing in the polls.[27]

A well-organized, centralized staff can also work against a president. Corruption and the abuse of power are among the dangers of elevating one assistant to prominence and investing that person with a large amount of power. Sherman Adams proved politically embarrassing to Eisenhower when he was accused of accepting gifts from a New England textile manufacturer. Eisenhower found it personally difficult to ask his trusted aide to resign and delegated the job to Vice President Nixon. The political and personal problems Eisenhower experienced through relying on, and then having to fire, Adams seem to be part of a pattern: Truman and Harry Vaughan, Johnson and Walter Jenkins, Nixon and Haldeman, Reagan and Donald Regan, and George H. W. Bush and John Sununu.

Another two-edged consequence of a centralized staff system is that a highly visible assistant with a large amount of authority can act as a gatekeeper, controlling and filtering the flow of information to and from the president. Both Jordan under Carter and Regan under Reagan were criticized for limiting access to the president and selectively screening the information and advice the president received. Joseph Califano Jr., Carter's secretary of health, education, and welfare, had repeated run-ins with Jordan. While lobbying Dan Rostenkowski, the Democratic representative from Illinois and influential chair of the Health Subcommittee of the House Ways and Means Committee, on a hospital cost containment bill, Califano found that Rostenkowski also resented the treatment he was receiving from Jordan. "He never returns a phone call, Joe," Rostenkowski complained. "Don't feel slighted," Califano replied. "He treats you exactly as he treats most of the Cabinet."[28] In July 1979 Carter fired Califano and promoted Jordan.

Donald Regan, who succeeded James Baker as Reagan's chief of staff in 1985, acquired tremendous power in domestic policy-making, played a major role in important presidential appointments, and was even touted in the media as Reagan's prime minister. Immediately on taking office, Regan flexed his political muscles by revamping the cabinet council system, substituting instead two streamlined bodies: the Economic Policy Council and the Domestic Policy Council. Regan retained control of the two councils' agendas. Subsequent council reports to President Reagan also flowed through Regan: "The simplified system strengthened Regan's direct control over policy, establishing him as a choke point for issues going to the President."[29]

Regan certainly was effective at centralizing power in his hands, but his attempts to exercise strong control over the policy-making process did not always serve the president's interests. In the realm of domestic policy, the tactics of Regan and his staff frequently upset House Republicans: Regan "ignored them while shaping a tax bill with [Democratic] House Ways and Means Chairman Dan Rostenkowski." President Reagan salvaged tax reform with a personal appeal to his party in Congress, "but the specter of the president traveling to Capitol Hill like a supplicant to plead for Republican House votes plainly raised doubts about the quality of White House staff work."[30]

In the realm of foreign affairs, Regan was the first chief of staff to play a major role in both making and implementing policy. His attempts to influence foreign policy precipitated the resignation of Robert McFarlane, the national security adviser, and led to the selection of Adm. John Poindexter, a Regan ally, as his replacement. The Regan-dominated, Poindexter-led NSC soon embroiled the Reagan administration in the politically embarrassing Iran-contra affair.[31]

Although George H. W. Bush was more personally involved in the policy process than Reagan, his management style fared little better. In foreign affairs he tended to operate with a close-knit group of advisers, especially his trusted longtime associate, Secretary of State James Baker. Trying simultaneously to be at the center of the decision process but avoid micromanagement of the U.S. efforts to depose Panamanian dictator Manuel Noriega and to win the Persian Gulf War, Bush appears to have been vulnerable to some of the problems Irving Janis has identified in his theory of "groupthink." These include a tendency for the leader to announce his preferences before the group has fully explored alternatives, the exclusion of dissenting opinions (for example, Colin Powell, chairman of the Joint Chiefs of Staff, was absent from several meetings soon after Iraq invaded Kuwait), and a certain degree of like-mindedness in the views of the participants.[32] Bush avoided decision fiascoes, however, because of his own foreign policy expertise and experience and his ability to reach out to other world leaders to forge effective coalitions, especially during the Gulf War.

Bush clearly preferred foreign affairs to domestic policy, largely delegating the latter to Chief of Staff John Sununu. He and OMB director Richard Darman quickly asserted control over Bush's domestic and economic policy operations, locking out cabinet secretaries and other staff members and leading to, according to Walter Williams, a "domestic policy regency."[33]

Centralized authority of the kind that Regan and Sununu practiced is preferable to organizational anarchy. But as hierarchy and centralization develop within the White House staff, presidents can find themselves isolated, relying on a small core group of advisers. If that occurs, the information the president gets will already have been selectively filtered and interpreted. Discussions and deliberations will be confined to an inner circle of like-minded advisers. Neither development is beneficial to the quality of presidential decision making or to the formulation of effective policy proposals.

George W. Bush centralized domestic policy making, but less in Chief of Staff Andrew Card than in Karl Rove, his chief political and policy adviser. Drawing on their shared experience with the elder Bush's management style, the president and Card were well aware of the dangers of investing too much power in the chief of staff position. Moreover, in planning for his new administration, Bush and Card sought to build stronger political and communications operations into the White House policy process than had existed in the first Bush White House. These operations were initially headed by Rove (politics) and Karen Hughes (communications), both of whom were longtime aides and advisers to Bush. The division of labor initially proved reasonably effective, although Rove's political contacts and advice were often subject to media scrutiny. But when Hughes resigned in April 2002, Rove's influence and visibility increased. Media accounts did not indicate any heightening of internal conflict, but questions were raised about the White House's overemphasis on loyalty and discipline, its ideological insularity, and the need for Bush to have other channels of information and advice.[34]

President Bush's response to the events of September 11 and his decisions to wage war in Afghanistan and Iraq were not the products of a deliberative process driven by the White House staff, although NSC adviser Rice's private counsel remained important to Bush. Considering the presence of such powerful and experienced players as Cheney, Powell, and Rumsfeld, a staff-driven process was unlikely to develop. Moreover, most accounts of Bush's decision making after September 11 stressed his deep personal involvement in the details of policy and his frequent meetings with the war cabinet.[35] What was problematic was whether intelligence had been properly shared, analyzed, and vetted before September 11 about a potential terrorist attack. With Iraq, the intelligence issue arose again, first with respect to the falsely reported presence of weapons of mass destruction and then with respect to the difficulties postwar reconstruction would encounter. Perhaps Rice would have served the president better by acting more assertively as an honest broker of the decision process: testing assumptions, challenging evidence for its reliability, questioning deeper ideological commitments, making sure a full range of policy options was on the table, coordinating information, and fostering bureaucratic cooperation. Greater White House involvement of this sort might have contributed to a more thorough decision-making process.

Barack Obama's selection of Rahm Emanuel as chief of staff brought on board someone with impressive credentials who was likely to hew to the strong chief of staff model. Emanuel had been Clinton's chief White House political adviser (akin to Rove), he had strong political credentials as the fourth-ranking Democrat in the House of Representatives, and he had a reputation as a tough and demanding manager and fierce partisan infighter. If all works out well, he may serve as a policy adviser and a tough but effective manager along the lines of Leon Panetta and James Baker. If not, the difficulties experienced under John Sununu or Don Regan are likely to emerge. The situation is complicated by the appointment of three longtime Obama advisers—Axelrod, Jarrett, and Rouse—as "senior advisers" to the president with authority over various units of the staff. How well Emanuel and these senior advisers work together will have major consequences for the Obama presidency.

Bureaucratization

As the top levels of the White House staff have gained authority and political visibility, the rest of the staff has taken on the character of a bureaucratic organization. Among its bureaucratic characteristics are complex work routines, which often stifle originality and reduce differences on policy to their lowest common denominator. Drawing on his experience in the Carter White House, Greg Schneiders complained that if one feeds "advice through the system . . . what may have begun as a bold initiative comes out the other end as unrecognizable mush. The system frustrates and alienates the staff and cheats the President and the country."[36] Schneiders also noted that the frustrations of staffers do not end with the paper flow:

> There are also the meetings. The incredible, interminable, boring, ever-multiplying meetings. There are staff meetings and task force meetings, trip meetings and general schedule meetings, meetings to make decisions and unmake them and to plan future meetings, where even more decisions will be made.[37]

"All of this might be more tolerable," Schneiders suggested, "if the staff could derive satisfaction vicariously from personal association with the President." But few aides have any direct contact with the president: "Even many of those at the highest levels—assistants, deputy assistants, special assistants—don't see the President once a week or speak to him in any substantive way once a month."[38] Similarly, Karen Hult observes that "So much of it is symbolic." In her view, staff members "want to get close to the president because it signals . . . the person really has the president's ear. Now, of course, the more people you have like that, the less likely they really are to have the president's ear."[39]

What develops as a substitute for work satisfaction or personal proximity to the president are typical patterns of organizational behavior: "bureaucratic" and "court" politics. With regard to court politics, for example, White House staff members often compete for assignments and authority that serve as a measure of their standing and prestige on the staff and ultimately with the president. Sometimes these turf battles are physical in character, with staff members competing for larger office space and closer proximity to central figures in the administration, especially to the president and the Oval Office in the West Wing. At the beginning of each presidential term, journalists take an intense interest in the size of staff offices and their location in relation to the president; these are taken as signs of relative power and influence by the Washington political community.

Not only are staff members concerned about their standing within the White House, but they also care about how they are perceived by outsiders. Patterns of behavior—bureaucratic politics—can develop that relate to a staff member's place in the organization: "Where one stands depends on where one sits." Staff members often develop allies on the outside—members of the press, members of Congress, lobbyists, and other political influentials—who can aid the programs and political causes of particular parts of the institutional presidency or the personal careers of staffers. Conversely, they can also create hostility and enmity among those outside the staff who compete with them for the president's attention. One classic example of this is the "us versus them" attitude that develops between White House staff members (inside) and the regular departments (outside) in domestic and economic policy and between the NSC staff (inside) and the State Department (outside) in foreign policy. In part, such attitudes may stem from different views and perspectives of a personal nature. But these attitudes may also inhere in the endemic bureaucratic competition and politics that any complex, bureaucratic institution generates.

Politicization

As a response to the bureaucratization of the White House staff, presidents are increasingly politicizing the institutional presidency. That is, they are attempting to make sure that staff members heed their policy directives and serve the president's political needs, rather than their own.

In most cases, the president's reasons for politicizing the staff are understandable. The Constitution's system of shared powers deals presidents a weak hand in Washington. To advance their goals, presidents need broad agreement among their aides and assistants with their political programs and policy goals. President Nixon, for example, created the Domestic Council as a discrete unit within the White House staff to serve as his principal source of policy advice on domestic affairs because he feared that the agencies and departments were staffed with unsympathetic liberal Democrats.

The difficulty for presidents comes in determining to what extent they should politicize their staffs. Excessive politicization can limit the range of opinions among (and thus the quality of advice from) the staff. Taken to extremes, politicization may result in a phalanx of like-minded sycophants.

Excessive politicization can also weaken the objectivity of the policy analysis at the president's disposal, especially if the newly politicized staff unit has a tradition of neutral competence and professionalism. As Terry Moe summarized the argument, "Politicization is deplored for its destructive effects on institutional memory, expertise, professionalism, objectivity, communications, continuity, and other bases of organizational competence."[40]

The part of the president's staff in which politicization has been most noticeable—and the debate over politicization most charged—is OMB. When Nixon created the Domestic Council he also reorganized the old Bureau of the Budget into the present OMB. Although the Bureau of the Budget was an arm of the presidential staff and certainly not wholly above politics, it was regarded as a place where neutral competence was paramount—that is, "a place where you were both a representative for the President's particular view and the top objective resource for the continuous institution of the Presidency."[41]

Nixon increased the number of political appointees in OMB. Moreover, some functions once assigned to professionals were given to political appointees; for example, presidentially appointed program associate directors were placed in OMB's examining divisions.[42] The effects of these changes have been noticeable: greater staff loyalty to political appointees, less cooperation with other parts of the White House staff and with Congress, and reduced impartiality and competence in favor of ideology and partisanship. The role of OMB in the policy process has also changed: it now gives substantive policy advice—not just objective budget estimates—and takes an active and visible role in lobbying Congress.

The experience of the Reagan administration is particularly revealing of the risks of excessive politicization in budget making, an area where expertise and objective analysis must complement the policy goals expressed in the president's budget proposal. Reagan relied heavily on OMB, especially during the directorship of David Stockman, both in formulating an economic policy and in trying to get its legislative provisions passed by Congress. Stockman himself concluded—and announced that conclusion in the title of his memoirs—that the so-called Reagan revolution failed.[43] Part of Stockman's thesis was that Reagan was done in by normal Washington politics, which is particularly averse to a budget-conscious president. But Stockman's own words reveal a politicized, deprofessionalized OMB, which may not have been able to give the president the kind of objective advice that he needed, at times, to win over his critics and political opponents:

> The thing was put together so fast that it probably should have been put together differently. . . . We were doing the whole budget-cutting exercise so frenetically . . . juggling details, pushing people, and going from one session to another. . . . The defense program was just a bunch of numbers written on a piece of paper. And it didn't mesh.[44]

The politicization of OMB cannot explain all of Stockman's difficulties. But as Stockman's account attests, Reagan and his advisers needed hard questioning, objective analysis, and criticism of the sort that the old Bureau of the Budget, but not the new OMB, could provide a president.

Putting the President Back In

Since its inception under Franklin Roosevelt, the institutional presidency has undoubtedly offered presidents some of the important resources they need to meet the complex policy tasks and expectations of the office. But as we have seen, the by-products of an institutional presidency—centralization of policymaking in the president's staff, hierarchy, bureaucratization, and politicization—have detracted from as well as served presidents' policy goals.

Presidents are not, however, simply at the mercy of the institution. Having emphasized the institutional character of the presidency, we should not neglect the presidential character of the institution. Although the presidency is an institution, it is an intensely personal one, which can take on a different character from administration to administration, from one set of staff advisers to another. Presidents and their staffs are by no means hostages to the institution. They have often been able to benefit from the positive resources it provides while deflecting or overcoming the institutional forces that detract from their goals.

The most obvious management task a president faces is to recognize on first being elected that organizing and staffing the White House are matters of highest priority. All of Washington and the media wait in eager anticipation for the president-elect to announce the names of the new cabinet. But it is how presidents-elect organize the White House staff and select the people who work for them that will make or break their presidencies.[45]

Clinton's difficulties during his first years as president can be attributed in great measure to his failure, during the transition period before he took office, to understand what it takes to create an effective staff system. According to one report, "Though it had studied the operations of every other major government agency, [Clinton's transition team] assigned no one to study the workings of the White House."[46] This failure was "an insane decision," according to one senior Clinton aide. "We knew more about FEMA [Federal Emergency Management Agency] and the Tuna Commission than we did about the White House. We arrived not knowing what was there, had never worked together, had never worked in these positions."[47]

Clinton's early appointments of top aides exhibit another pattern of which presidents need to be wary: the tendency to offer staff positions to longtime political loyalists and campaign workers. As one Clinton aide noted, "Unable to shift from a campaign mode, it [Clinton's transition team] made staffing decisions with an eye to rewarding loyal campaign workers instead of considering the broader task of governing."[48] Presidents surely need assistants who are personally loyal to them and share their deeply held political views. But presidents also need aides who are adept in Washington politics or have expertise in a particular policy area. Too many friends from Little Rock, Sacramento, or rural Georgia can doom a presidency very quickly.

In contrast, George W. Bush had a more successful transition to office, despite the unusual circumstances of determining who won the 2000 election. Much preliminary planning had been undertaken before the election, including the selection of a chief of staff. Furthermore, even as the uncertainty over how

Florida voted dragged on (not to be settled until December 12), transition planning was well under way in the Bush camp. Bush made a particularly wise choice in placing Cheney in charge of the transition. Cheney was not only a veteran of past administrations but also a participant in the outgoing Ford and senior Bush transitions. Bush's early selection of Card as chief of staff enabled White House planning and organization to proceed on course. By the end of the first week of January, Bush was only a week behind where Clinton had been in picking his cabinet, and he was well ahead in announcing White House appointments.[49]

Like Bush, Barack Obama used his transition period wisely in preparing to take office. During summer 2008, John Podesta, a former Clinton chief of staff, was assigned to head Obama's preelection transition. Podesta ambitiously began by developing lists of potential nominees, formulating a legislative agenda, reviewing President Bush's executive orders, planning for Obama's first 100 days in office, and organizing the postelection transition. On November 6, two days after the election, Obama tapped Rahm Emanuel as chief of staff, and in the ensuing weeks key White House staff appointments were announced. Cabinet appointments also were swiftly made public, often in teams that stressed Obama's agenda and priorities.

Obama was somewhat less surefooted in his choice of department heads. On the one hand, by December 19 his roster of cabinet nominees was complete. No transition since Nixon's in 1968 had made swifter progress. But this progress came at a price. Two of Obama's appointees—Bill Richardson as secretary of commerce and Tom Daschle as secretary of health and human services—withdrew when serious ethical questions emerged after their nominations were announced. His next choice as commerce secretary, New Hampshire Republican senator Judd Gregg, first accepted and then declined a nomination, citing "irresolvable conflicts" with the president on public policy. Not until spring 2009 were the two seats filled. The Senate confirmed former Washington governor Gary Locke as secretary of commerce on March 24, 2009. One month later, on April 28, Kansas governor Kathleen Sebelius was confirmed to head the Department of Health and Human Services.

Beyond striking a good balance between loyalty, on the one hand, and Washington experience and policy expertise on the other, presidents must also be aware of the strengths, and especially the weaknesses, of the various ways of organizing the staff members they have selected. For example, to reduce some of the negative effects of relying on a large White House staff, Eisenhower complemented his use of the formal machinery of the NSC and Adams's office with informal channels of advice. In foreign affairs, he turned not just to his trusted secretary of state, John Foster Dulles, but also to a network of friends and associates with political knowledge and substantive experience, such as his brother

Milton Eisenhower and Gen. Alfred Gruenther, the supreme allied commander in Europe. Eisenhower also held regular meetings with his cabinet and with congressional leaders to inform them of his actions, to garner their support, and to hear their views and opinions.[50]

When dealing with his staff, Eisenhower encouraged his aides to air their disagreements and doubts in a candid and straightforward manner. He especially emphasized the need to avoid expressing views that simply reflected departmental or other bureaucratic interests. Herbert Brownell, his attorney general from 1953 until 1957, recalls that "time after time" Eisenhower would tell his cabinet members, "You are not supposed to represent your department, your home state, or anything else. You are my advisers. I want you to speak freely and, more than that, I would like to have you reflect and comment on what other members of the cabinet say."[51] Minutes of Eisenhower's NSC meetings reveal a president who was exposed to the policy divisions within his staff and who engaged in lively discussions with Dulles, Nixon, Harold Stassen, Henry Cabot Lodge, and others. But Eisenhower was also careful to reserve for himself the ultimate power of decision. Although they had a voice in the process, neither the NSC nor Adams decided for the president.

Kennedy dismantled most of the national security staff that had existed under Eisenhower, preferring instead to use smaller, more informal and collegial decision-making forums. Kennedy's abandonment of more formal procedures may have been unwise, but his experience with the "Ex-Com" (his executive committee of top foreign policy advisers) offers lessons about how presidents can make good use of informal patterns of seeking and giving advice. In April 1961 Kennedy's advisers performed poorly, steering him into an ill-conceived, poorly planned, hastily decided, and badly executed invasion of Cuba—the Bay of Pigs disaster. In the aftermath of that fiasco, Kennedy commissioned a study to find out what had gone wrong. On the basis of its findings, he reorganized his decision-making procedures—including major changes in the Central Intelligence Agency—and explored the faults in his own leadership style. By the time of the Cuban missile crisis, in October 1962, Kennedy and his advisers had become an effective decision-making group. Information was readily at hand, the assumptions and implications of policy options were probed, pressures that could lead to a false group consensus were avoided, and Kennedy deliberately concealed his own policy preferences—sometimes absenting himself from meetings—to facilitate candid discussions and to head off a premature decision.

In addition to developing a suitable leadership style, presidents can also take steps to deal with the bureaucratic tendencies that crop up in their staffs. Kennedy's New Frontier agenda, for example, included a number of programs, such as the Peace Corps, that did not resemble traditional bureaucracies; and his personal style generated loyalty and trust. Eisenhower lacked the youthful vigor of his successor, but his broad organizational experience made him a good judge of character with a sure instinct for what and how much he could delegate to subordinates and how best to organize and use their various talents. As with members of his cabinet, Eisenhower emphasized to his staff aides that they worked for him, not for the NSC, Adams, or anyone else.

Finally, although the tendencies toward centralization of policymaking within the White House and politicization of the advisory process have been powerful, all presidents have the capacity to choose how they will act and react within a complex political context populated by other powerful political institutions, processes, and participants. Too much politicization weakens any special claims of expertise, experience, and institutional primacy that the president might make in a particular policy area. Too much centralization eclipses the role of other political actors in a system that is geared to share, rather than exclude, domains of power; it may also set in motion a powerful reaction against the president.

Presidents would be well-advised not to neglect the observation about presidential success that Richard Neustadt made nearly fifty years ago: "Presidential power is the power to persuade."[52] But what presidents also need to know is that the character and intended audience of that persuasion must be tailored not just to the requirements of legislative bargaining and enhancing popular support but to the institutional character of the presidency itself.

NOTES

1. For a fuller account, see John P. Burke, *The Institutional Presidency: Organizing and Managing the White House from FDR to Clinton* (Baltimore: Johns Hopkins University Press, 2000).

2. Stephen J. Wayne, *The Legislative Presidency* (New York: Harper and Row, 1978), 30.

3. Bradley H. Patterson, *To Serve the President: Continuity and Innovation in the White House Staff* (Washington, D.C.: Brookings Institution, 2008), 31–32.

4. Quoted in Louis Brownlow, *A Passion for Anonymity: The Autobiography of Louis Brownlow*, vol. 2 (Chicago: University of Chicago Press, 1958), 392.

5. I use the term *larger* to refer to the Brownlow Committee's recognition that the president needed greater staff resources and its recommendations that the Bureau of the Budget be brought over from the Treasury Department and that the Executive Office of the President be created. In its advice on increasing the size of the president's immediate staff, the committee's recommendations were rather modest: the addition of six administrative aides who would avoid the political spotlight and have a "passion for anonymity." These new positions added a more formal structure to the Roosevelt White House and set out new responsibilities for the once–ad hoc staffing arrangement. It is also interesting to note that Roosevelt rejected Brownlow's recommendations that the position of a chief of staff be created and that a more hierarchical, formally organized White House be established; their implementation would

await FDR's successors. For further analysis of FDR and the institutional presidency, see Matthew J. Dickinson, *Bitter Harvest: FDR, Presidential Power, and the Growth of the Presidential Branch* (Cambridge: Cambridge University Press, 1997). For fuller discussion of earlier reorganization efforts, see Peri Arnold, *Making the Managerial Presidency: Comprehensive Reorganization Planning, 1905–1980* (Princeton: Princeton University Press, 1986).

6. President's Committee on Administrative Management, *Administrative Management in the Government of the United States* (Washington, D.C.: U.S. Government Printing Office, 1937), 4.

7. The initial Brownlow Committee recommendation for reorganizing the executive branch also included proposals to redefine the jurisdiction of cabinet departments, regroup autonomous and independent agencies and bureaus, and give the president virtually unchecked authority to determine and carry out the reorganization and any needed in the future. The more controversial proposals were either dropped or made more palatable in the reorganization act passed by Congress in 1939.

8. For further discussion of the Brownlow and Hoover Commissions, as well as other efforts at reorganizing the presidency, see Arnold, *Making the Managerial Presidency.*

9. On the growth of the White House staff during the Eisenhower presidency, see John Hart, "Eisenhower and the Swelling of the Presidency," *Polity* 24 (1992): 673–691.

10. The characteristics of institutionalization are adapted, in part, from Nelson Polsby, "The Institutionalization of the U.S. House of Representatives," *American Political Science Review* 52 (1968): 144–168. On the notion of the presidency as an institution, also see Lester Seligman, "Presidential Leadership: The Inner Circle and Institutionalization," *Journal of Politics* 18 (1956): 410–426; *The Institutionalized Presidency*, ed. Norman Thomas and Hans Baade (Dobbs Ferry, N.Y.: Oceana Press, 1972); Robert S. Gilmour, "The Institutionalized Presidency: A Conceptual Clarification," in *The Presidency in Contemporary Context*, ed. Norman Thomas (New York: Dodd, Mead, 1975), 147–159; John Kessel, *The Domestic Presidency: Decision-Making in the White House* (North Scituate, Mass.: Duxbury Press, 1975); Lester Seligman, "The Presidency and Political Change," *Annals* 466 (1983): 179–192; John Kessel, "The Structures of the Carter White House," *American Journal of Political Science* 27 (1983): 431–463; John Kessel, "The Structures of the Reagan White House," *American Journal of Political Science* 28 (1984): 231–258; Colin Campbell, *Managing the Presidency* (Pittsburgh: University of Pittsburgh Press, 1986); and Peri Arnold, "The Institutionalized Presidency and the American Regime," in *The Presidency Reconsidered*, ed. Richard Waterman (Itasca, Ill.: F. E. Peacock, 1993), 215–245.

11. On White House relations with the media, see Martha J. Kumar, *Managing the President's Message: The White House Communications Operation* (Baltimore: Johns Hopkins University Press, 2007).

12. For further discussion, see Joseph Pika, "Interest Groups and the Executive: Federal Intervention," in *Interest Group Politics*, ed. Allan J. Cigler and Burdett A. Loomis (Washington, D.C.: CQ Press, 1983), 298–323.

13. Galbraith quoted in Lyndon Johnson, *Vantage Point: Perspectives of the Presidency, 1963–69* (New York: Holt, Rinehart and Winston, 1971), 76. For a more extensive analysis of White House centralization, see Andrew Rudalevige, *Managing the President's Program: Presidential Leadership and Legislative Policy Formulation*, Princeton: Princeton University Press, 2002).

14. On the development of the role of NSC adviser, see John P. Burke, *Honest Broker? The National Security Advisor and Presidential Decision Making* (College Station: Texas A&M University Press, 2009).

15. Cyrus Vance, *Hard Choices: Critical Years in America's Foreign Policy* (New York: Simon and Schuster, 1983), 409–410.

16. Alexander Haig, *Caveat: Realism, Reagan, and Foreign Policy* (New York: Macmillan, 1984), 306–307.

17. On Scowcroft's role as honest broker, see Burke, *Honest Broker?*, 151–197.

18. Jane Perlez, David Sanger, and Thom Shanker, "From Many Voices, One Battle Strategy," *New York Times*, September 23, 2001.

19. For further discussion on centralization post–September 11, see John P. Burke, *Becoming President: The Bush Transition, 2000–2003* (Boulder: Lynne Rienner, 2004), 175–180, 186–188.

20. There were, however, some exceptions. Early in the new administration Vice President Cheney was asked to develop a comprehensive energy program. Bush also chose a special task force to flesh out his campaign proposals for Social Security reform.

21. See, for example, Noam Scheiber, "Rod Paige Learns the Hard Way," *New Republic*, July 2, 2001; and Diana Schemo, "Education Chief Seeks More Visible Role," *New York Times*, August 5, 2001.

22. Quoted in Jim VandeHei and Glenn Kessler, "President to Consider Changes for New Term," *Washington Post*, November 5, 2004.

23. Mike Allen, "Bush to Change Economic Team," *Washington Post*, November 29, 2004.

24. Peter Baker, "Reshaping White House with a Domestic Focus," *New York Times*, December 20, 2008.

25. Martin Landau, "Redundancy, Rationality, and the Problem of Duplication and Overlap," *Public Administration Review* 29 (1969): 346–358.

26. Patrick Anderson, *The President's Men* (Garden City: Anchor Books, 1969), 10.

27. Fred I. Greenstein, *The Hidden-Hand Presidency* (New York: Basic Books, 1982), 147. Adams's counterpart in foreign affairs was Secretary of State John Foster Dulles.

28. Joseph A. Califano Jr., *Governing America: An Insider's Report from the White House and the Cabinet* (New York: Simon and Schuster, 1981), 148.

29. Ronald Brownstein and Dick Kirschsten, "Cabinet Power," *National Journal*, June 28, 1986, 1589.

30. Bernard Weinraub, "How Donald Regan Runs the White House," *New York Times Magazine*, January 5, 1986, 14.

31. On the involvement of the chief of staff in foreign policy, see David A. Cohen, Chris J. Dolan, and Jerel A. Rosati, "A Place at the Table: The Emerging Foreign Policy Roles of the White House Chief of Staff," *Congress and the Presidency* 29 (2002): 119–149.

32. Irving Janis, *Groupthink: Psychological Studies of Policy Decisions and Fiascoes*, 2nd ed. (Boston: Houghton Mifflin, 1982). On possible problems with Bush's small-group decision making in the Gulf War, see Bob Woodward, *The Commanders* (New York: Simon and Schuster, 1991); Daniel P. Franklin and Robert Shepard, "Analyzing the Bush Foreign Policy" (paper presented at the annual meeting of the American Political Science Association, Washington, D.C., August 29–September 1, 1991); and Cecil V. Crabb Jr. and Kevin V. Mulcahy, "The Elitist Presidency: George Bush and the Management of Operation Desert Storm," in *Presidency Reconsidered*, 275–300. On problems in the Panama invasion of 1989, see John Broder and Melissa Healy, "Panama Operation Hurt by Critical Intelligence Gaps," *Los Angeles Times*, December 24, 1989, 1.

33. Walter Williams, "George Bush and White House Policy Competence" (paper presented at the annual meeting of the American Political Science Association, Chicago, September 3–6, 1992), 12–13.

34. See, for example, Ron Suskind, *The Price of Loyalty: George W. Bush, the White House, and the Education of Paul O'Neill* (New York: Simon and Schuster, 2004).

35. On the response to September 11 and the war in Afghanistan, see, for example, Bob Woodward, *Bush at War* (New York: Simon and Schuster, 2002); on the war in Iraq, see Bob Woodward, *Plan of Attack* (New York: Simon and Schuster, 2004).

36. Greg Schneiders, "My Turn: Goodbye to All That," *Newsweek*, September 24, 1979, 23.

37. Ibid.

38. Ibid.

39. Quoted in Baker, "Reshaping White House with a Domestic Focus."

40. Terry M. Moe, "The Politicized Presidency," in *The New Direction in American Politics*, ed. John Chubb and Paul Peterson (Washington, D.C.: Brookings Institution Press, 1985), 235.

41. Hugh Heclo, "OMB and the Presidency: The Problem of 'Neutral Competence,'" *Public Interest* 38 (1975): 81.

42. Ibid., 85.

43. David A. Stockman, *The Triumph of Politics: Why the Reagan Revolution Failed* (New York: Harper and Row, 1986).

44. Quoted in William Greider, *The Education of David Stockman and Other Americans* (New York: Dutton, 1982), 33, 37.

45. For an analysis of the Carter through Clinton transitions, see John P. Burke, *Presidential Transitions: From Politics to Practice* (Boulder: Lynne Rienner, 2000). For an early analysis of the Obama transition, see John P. Burke, "The Obama Presidential Transition: An Early Assessment," *Presidential Studies Quarterly* 39, no. 3 (September 2009): 572–602

46. Jack Nelson and Robert Donovan, "The Education of a President," *Los Angeles Times Sunday Magazine*, August 1, 1993, 14.

47. Quoted in ibid.

48. Ibid.

49. For further analysis of the George W. Bush transition, see Burke, *Becoming President*.

50. On Eisenhower's "binocular" use of informal and formal patterns of advice, see Greenstein, *Hidden-Hand Presidency*, 100–151. On his decision-making processes, see John P. Burke and Fred I. Greenstein, with Larry Berman and Richard Immerman, *How Presidents Test Reality: Decisions on Vietnam, 1954 and 1965* (New York: Russell Sage, 1989).

51. Herbert Brownell with John P. Burke, *Advising Ike: The Memoirs of Attorney General Herbert Brownell* (Lawrence: University Press of Kansas, 1993), 294.

52. Richard E. Neustadt, *Presidential Power: The Politics of Leadership* (New York: Wiley, 1960).

7-3

from *Going Public*

Samuel Kernell

Richard Neustadt, writing in 1960, judged that the president's ability to lead depended on skill at the bargaining table in cutting deals with other politicians. In the following essay Samuel Kernell examines how the leadership strategy of modern presidents has evolved. He finds that, rather than limiting their leadership to quiet diplomacy with fellow Washingtonians, modern presidents often "go public," a set of activities borrowed from presidential election campaigns and directed toward persuading other politicians to adopt their policy preferences. Some examples of going public are a televised press conference, a special prime-time address to the nation, traveling outside Washington to deliver a speech to a business or professional convention, and a visit to a day care center with network cameras trailing behind.

Introduction: Going Public in Theory and Practice

WHEN PRESIDENT GEORGE H. W. BUSH delivered his State of the Union address to the joint assembly of the mostly Democratic Congress on January 28, 1992, he assumed what was becoming a familiar stance:

> I pride myself that I am a prudent man, and I believe that patience is a virtue. But I understand that politics is for some a game. . . . I submit my plan tomorrow. And I am asking you to pass it by March 20. And I ask the American people to let you know they want this action by March 20. From the day after that, if it must be: The battle is joined. And you know when principle is at stake, I relish a good fair fight.

Once upon a time, these might have been fighting words, but by the 1990s presidents had so routinely come to appeal for public support in their dealings with Congress that Bush's rhetoric scarcely caused a stir among his Washington audience. Presidential appeals for public support had, in fact, become commonplace.

Source: Samuel Kernell, *Going Public: New Strategies of Presidential Leadership,* 3d ed. (Washington, D.C.: CQ Press, 1997), 1–12, 17–26, 34–38, 57–64; and Samuel Kernell, *Going Public: New Strategies of Presidential Leadership,* 4th ed. (Washington, D.C.: CQ Press, 2006), 40–57. Some notes appearing in the original have been deleted.

Two years later Bill Clinton would use the same forum to launch a six-month public relations campaign to persuade Congress to expand coverage of federal health care beyond Medicare to include everyone not covered by employer insurance. What raised eyebrows was not the announcement or even the scope of the plan. Rather it was the bravado—some would say hubris—with which Clinton warned the assembled legislators that if they failed to give him a fully comprehensive program "I will take this pen and veto it." Two days after his 2004 reelection George W. Bush held a press conference in which he outlined an ambitious policy agenda headed by overhaul of the Social Security system. He matter-of-factly told reporters, "I earned capital in the campaign, political capital, and now I intend to spend it. It is my style."[1] Six weeks later he unveiled in his State of the Union address his partial privatization scheme for Social Security and announced a "sixty cities in sixty days" campaign to push it through Congress.

I call the approach to presidential leadership that has come into vogue at the White House "going public." It is a strategy whereby a president promotes himself and his policies in Washington by appealing directly to the American public for support. Forcing compliance from fellow Washingtonians by going over their heads to enlist constituents' pressure is a tactic that was known but seldom attempted during the first half of the century. Theodore Roosevelt probably first enunciated the strategic principle of going public when he described the presidency as the "bully pulpit." Moreover, he occasionally put theory into practice with public appeals for his Progressive Party reforms. During the next thirty years, other presidents also periodically summoned public support to help them in their dealings with Congress. Perhaps the most famous such instance is Woodrow Wilson's ill-fated whistle-stop tour of the country on behalf of his League of Nations treaty. Equally noteworthy, historically, is Franklin D. Roosevelt's series of radio "fireside chats," which were designed less to subdue congressional opposition than to remind politicians of his continuing national mandate for the New Deal.

These historical instances are significant in large part because they are rare. Unlike Richard Nixon, who thought it important "to spread the White House around" by traveling and speaking extensively,[2] these earlier presidents were largely confined to Washington and obliged to address the country through the nation's newspapers. The concept and legitimizing precedents of going public may have been established during these years, but the emergence of presidents who *routinely* did so to promote their policies outside Washington awaited the development of modern systems of transportation and mass communications. Going public should be appreciated as a strategic adaptation to the information age.

The regularity with which recent presidents have sought public backing for their Washington dealings has altered the way politicians both inside and outside the White House regard the office. The following chapters present numerous instances of presidents preoccupied with public relations, as if these activities chiefly determined their success. Cases are recounted of other Washington politicians intently monitoring the president's popularity ratings and his addresses on television, as if his performance in these realms governed their own behavior. We shall also examine various testimonials of central institutional figures, including several Speakers of the House of Representatives, citing the president's prestige and rhetoric as they explain Congress's actions. If the public ruminations of politicians are to be believed, the president's effectiveness in rallying public support has become a primary consideration for those who do business with him.

Presidential Theory

Going public has become routine. This was not always the case. After World War I Congress refused to support President Wilson's League of Nations, a peace treaty the president himself had helped negotiate. In this instance Congress determined to amend the treaty and a president equally determined to finalize the agreement the other countries had ratified left him with little choice but to go public to try to marshal public opinion to force the Senate's agreement. Today our information-age presidents opt to go public regardless of the political climate in Washington.

There is another reason to systematically study this leadership strategy. Compared with many other aspects of the modern presidency, scholarship has only recently directed its attention toward this feature of the president's repertoire. Although going public had not become a keystone of presidential leadership in the 1950s and 1960s, when much of the influential scholarship on the subject was written, sufficient precedents were available for scholars to consider its potential for presidential leadership in the future.

Probably the main reason traditional presidential scholarship shortchanged going public is its fundamental incompatibility with bargaining. Presidential power is the "power to bargain," Richard E. Neustadt taught a generation of students of the presidency.[3] When Neustadt published his definitive study of presidential leadership in 1960, the "bargaining president" had already become a centerpiece of pluralist theories of American politics. Nearly a decade earlier, Robert A. Dahl and Charles E. Lindblom had described the politician in America generically as "the human embodiment of a bargaining society." They made a special point to include the president in writing that despite his possessing "more hierarchical controls than any other single figure in the government . . . like everyone else . . . the President must bargain constantly."[4] Since Neustadt's landmark treatise, other major works on the presidency have reinforced and elaborated this theme.[5]

Going public violates bargaining in several ways. First, it rarely includes the kinds of exchanges necessary, in pluralist theory, for the American political system to function properly. At times, going public will be merely superfluous—fluff compared with the substance of traditional political exchange. Practiced in a dedicated way, however, it may displace bargaining.

Second, going public fails to extend benefits for compliance, but freely imposes costs for noncompliance. In appealing to the public to "tell your senators and representatives by phone, wire, and Mailgram that the future hangs in balance," the president seeks the aid of a third party—the public—to force other politicians to accept his preferences.[6] If targeted representatives are lucky, the president's success may cost them no more than an opportunity at the bargaining table to shape policy or to extract compensation. If unlucky, they may find themselves both capitulating to the president's wishes and suffering the reproach of constituents for having resisted him in the first place. By imposing costs and failing to offer benefits, going public is more akin to force than to bargaining. Nelson W. Polsby makes this point when he says that members of Congress may "find themselves ill disposed toward a president who prefers to deal indirectly with them [by going public] through what they may interpret as coercion rather than face-to-face in the spirit of mutual accommodation."[7] This senator may echo the sentiments, if not the actions, of those on Capitol Hill who find themselves repeatedly pressured by the president's public appeals: "A lot of Democrats, even if they like the President's proposal, will vote against him because of his radio address on Saturday."[8]

Third, going public entails public posturing. To the extent that it fixes the president's bargaining position, posturing makes subsequent compromise with other politicians more difficult. Because negotiators must be prepared to yield some of their clients' preferences to make a deal, bargaining proverbially proceeds best behind closed doors. Consider the difficulty Ronald Reagan's widely publicized challenge "My tax proposal is a line drawn in dirt" posed for subsequent budget negotiations in Washington.[9] Similarly, during his nationally televised State of the Union address in 1994, President Bill Clinton sought to repair his reputation as someone too willing to compromise away his principles by declaring to the assembled joint session of Congress, "If you send me [health care] legislation that does not guarantee every American private health insurance that can never be taken away, you will force me to take this pen, veto the legislation, and we'll come right back here and start all over again."[10] Not only did these declarations threaten to cut away any middle ground on which a compromise might be constructed, they probably stiffened the resolve of the president's adversaries, some of whom would later be needed to pass the administration's legislative program.

Finally, and possibly most injurious to bargaining, going public undermines the legitimacy of other politicians. It usurps their prerogatives of office, denies their role as representatives, and questions their claim to reflect the interests of their constituents. For a traditional bargaining stance with the president to be restored, these politicians would first have to reestablish parity, probably at a cost of conflict with the White House.[11]

Given these fundamental incompatibilities, one may further speculate that by spoiling the bargaining environment, going public renders the president's future influence ever more dependent upon his ability to generate popular support for himself and his policies. The degree to which a president draws upon public opinion determines the kind of leader he will be.

Presidential Practice

Bargaining and going public have never been particularly compatible styles of leadership. In the early twentieth century, when technology limited presidents' capacity to engage in public relations, they did so sparingly. On rare occasions, presidents might enlist public support as their contribution to bargains with politicians for whom their position was potentially risky. But generally, these two leadership strategies coexisted in a quiet tension. In modern times, though, going public is likely to take the form of an election campaign. George W. Bush's "sixty cities in sixty days" Social Security reform tour in 2005 is a recent example to which we shall later return. When presidents adopt intensive public relations as their leadership strategy they render bargaining increasingly difficult. The decision to go public at one juncture may preclude and undermine the opportunity to bargain at another, and vice versa. All this means that the decision to bargain or to go public must be carefully weighed.

The two case studies below reveal that modern presidents and their advisers carefully attend to this strategic issue. We compare instances of presidential success and failure in order to understand the potential gains and losses embedded in presidents' choices.

Ronald Reagan Enlists Public Opinion as a Lever

No president has enlisted public strategies to better advantage than did Ronald Reagan. Throughout his tenure, he exhibited a full appreciation of bargaining and going public as the modern office's principal strategic alternatives. The following examples from a six-month survey of White House news coverage show how entrenched this bifurcated view of presidential strategy has become. The survey begins in late November 1984, when some members of the administration were pondering how the president might exploit his landslide victory and others were preparing a new round of budget cuts and a tax reform bill for the next Congress.

November 29, 1984. Washington Post columnist Lou Cannon reported the following prediction from a White House official: "We're going to have confrontation on spending and consultation on tax reform." The aide explained, "We have somebody to negotiate with us on tax reform, but may not on budget cuts."[12] By "confrontation" he was referring to the president's success in appealing to the public on national television, that is, in going public. By "consultation" he meant bargaining.

January 25, 1985. The above prediction proved accurate two months later, when another staffer offered as pristine an evocation of going public as one is likely to find: "We have to look at it, in many ways, like a campaign. He [Reagan] wants to take his case to the people. You have a constituency of 535 legislators as opposed to 100 million voters. But the goal is the same—to get the majority of voters to support your position."[13]

February 10, 1985. In a nationally broadcast radio address, President Reagan extended an olive branch, inviting members of Congress to "work with us in the spirit of cooperation and compromise" on the budget. This public statement probably did little to allay the frequently voiced suspicion of House Democratic leaders that such overtures were mainly intended for public consumption. One Reagan aide insisted, however, that the president simply sought to reassure legislators that "he would not 'go over their heads' and campaign across the country for his budget without trying first to reach a compromise."[14] In this statement the aide implicitly concedes the harm public pressure can create for bargaining but seeks to incorporate it advantageously into the strategic thinking of the politicians with whom the administration must deal by not forswearing its use.

March 9, 1985. After some public sparring, the administration eventually settled down to intensive budget negotiations with the Republican-led Senate Finance Committee. Failing to do as well as he would like, however, Reagan sent a message to his party's senators through repeated unattributed statements to the press that, if necessary, he would "go to the people to carry our message forward." * Again, public appeals, though held in reserve, were threatened.

March 11, 1985. In an interview with a *New York Times* correspondent, a senior Reagan aide sized up his president: "He's liberated, he wants to get into a fight,

*Jonathan Fuerbringer, "Reagan Critical of Budget View of Senate Panel," *New York Times*, March 9, 1985. Senate Majority Leader Bob Dole told reporters that if the president liked the Senate's final budget package he would campaign for it "very vigorously . . . going to television, whatever he needs to reduce federal spending." Karen Tumulty, "Reagan May Get Draft of Budget Accord Today," *Los Angeles Times*, April 4, 1985, 1.

he feels strongly and wants to push his program through himself. . . . Reagan never quite believed his popularity before the election, never believed the polls. Now he has it, and he's going to push . . . ahead with our agenda."[15]

May 16, 1985. To avoid entangling tax reform with budget deliberations in Congress, Reagan, at the request of Republican leaders, delayed unveiling his tax reform proposal until late May. A couple of weeks before Reagan's national television address on the subject, White House aides began priming the press with leaks on the proposal's content and promises that the president would follow it with a public relations blitz. In the words of one White House official, the plan was to force Congress to make a "binary choice between tax reform or no tax reform."[16] The administration rejected bargaining, as predicted nearly six months earlier by a White House aide, apparently for two strategic reasons. First, Reagan feared that in a quietly negotiated process, the tax reform package would unravel under the concerted pressure of the special interests. Second, by taking the high-profile approach of "standing up for the people against the special interests," in the words of one adviser, tax reform might do for Republicans what Social Security did for Democrats—make them the majority party.[17]

During these six months, when bargaining held out promise—as it had during negotiations with the Senate Finance Committee—public appeals were held in reserve. The White House occasionally, however, threatened an appeal in trying to gain more favorable consideration. On other occasions, when opponents of the president's policies appeared capable of extracting major concessions—House Democrats on the budget and interest groups on tax reform, for example—the White House disengaged from negotiations and tried through public relations to force Congress to accept the president's policies. Although by 1985 news items such as the preceding excerpts seemed unexceptional as daily news, they are a recent phenomenon. One does not routinely find such stories in White House reporting twenty years earlier when, for example, John Kennedy's legislative agenda was stalled in Congress.

President Clinton Snares Himself by Bargaining

Shortly after assuming office, Bill Clinton received some bad news. The Bush administration had underestimated the size of the next year's deficit by $50 billion. The president's campaign promises of new domestic programs and a middle-class tax cut would have to be put on hold in favor of fulfilling his third, now urgent pledge to trim $500 billion from the deficit over the next five years. On February 17, 1993, President Clinton appeared before a joint session of Congress and a national television audience to unveil his deficit reduction package. The president's deficit-cutting options were constrained by two considerations: he wanted to include minimal stimulus spending to honor his campaign promise, and he faced a Congress controlled by fellow Democrats who were committed to many of the programs under the budget ax. Even with proposed cuts in defense spending, the only way the budget could accommodate these constraints was through a tax increase. The package raised taxes on the highest-income groups and introduced a broad energy consumption tax. During the following weeks, the president and his congressional liaison team quietly lobbied Congress. He would not again issue a public appeal until the eve of the final vote in August.

The president soon learned that Republicans in both chambers had united in opposition to the administration proposal. Led by Newt Gingrich in the House of Representatives and Bob Dole in the Senate, Republicans retreated to the sidelines and assumed the role of Greek chorus, ominously chanting "tax and spend liberals." This meant that the administration needed virtually every Democratic vote to win. Democratic members appreciated this, and many began exploiting the rising value of their votes to extract concessions that would make the legislation more favorable to their constituents.

By June the president's bargaining efforts had won him a watered-down bill that even he had difficulty being enthusiastic about. Meanwhile, the Republicans' public relations campaign had met with success: the American public had come to regard President Clinton as a "tax and spend liberal." Whereas shortly after the February speech, the *Los Angeles Times* had found half of its polling respondents willing to describe the president's initiative as "bold and innovative" and only 35 percent of them willing to describe it as "tax and spend," by June these numbers had reversed. Now, 53 percent labeled it "tax and spend" and only 28 percent still regarded it as "bold and innovative."[18] Given this turnaround in the public's assessment of the initiative, it was not surprising that the public also downgraded its evaluation of the initiative's sponsor. During the previous five months, President Clinton's approval rating had plunged from 58 to 41 percent.

This was the situation when several of Clinton's senior campaign consultants sounded the alarm in a memo: in only six months the president had virtually exhausted his capacity for leadership. If he did not turn back the current tide of public opinion, he would be weakened beyond repair. In response, the president assembled his senior advisers to evaluate current strategy. This set the stage for a confrontation between those advisers who represented the president in bargaining with other Washingtonians and those staffers who manned the White House public relations machinery. The argument that erupted between these advisers should disabuse anyone of the notion that bargaining and cultivating public support are separate, self-contained spheres of action that do not encroach on one another.[19]

The president's chief pollster, Stanley Greenberg, opened the discussion by stating his and his fellow consultants' position: "We do not exaggerate when we say that our current course, advanced by our economic team and Congressional leaders, threatens to sink your popularity further and weaken your presidency. . . . The immediate problem," he explained, "is that thanks to the Republican effort no one views your economic package as anything other than a tax scheme. You must exercise a 'bold zero option,' which is consultant talk for 'rid your policy of any taxes that affect the middle class.'" (In fact, the only tax still in the bill was a 4.3-cent-per-gallon gasoline tax that would raise a modest $20 billion.) Greenberg then unveiled polling data that found broad public support for such a move. He closed by warning everyone in the room, "We have a very short period of time. And if we don't communicate something serious and focused in the period, we're going to be left with what our detractors used to characterize our plan. . . . Don't assume we can fix it in August." This concluded the case for going public. And in order to use this strategy, Clinton had to change course on taxes.

According to those present, the economic and congressional advisers had listened to this argument "with a slow burn." Finally, the president's chief lobbyist, Howard Paster, blurted out, "This isn't an election! The Senate breaks its ass to get a 4.3-cent-a-gallon tax passed, and we can't just abandon it." Besides, they needed the $20 billion provided by the tax to offset other concessions that would be necessary to get the bill passed. "I need all the chips that are available," Paster pleaded. "Don't bargain them away here. Let me have maximum latitude."

From here, the discussion deteriorated into name calling and blame assigning that stopped only when Clinton started screaming at everyone—"a purple fit" is how one participant described it. In the end the president decided that he had to stay the course but that he would begin traveling around the country to explain to the public that his economic package was the "best" that could be enacted. In mid-August, after a concerted public relations campaign that concluded with a nationally televised address, the legislation barely passed. (In the Senate, Vice President Al Gore cast the tie-breaking vote.) The new administration's first legislative initiative had drained its resources both in Congress and across the nation. From here, the Clinton administration limped toward even more difficult initiatives represented by the North American Free Trade Agreement (NAFTA) and health care reform.

Clearly, as both case studies show, going public appears to foster political relations that are quite at odds with those traditionally cultivated through bargaining. One may begin to examine this phenomenon by asking, what is it about modern politics that would inspire presidents to go public in the first place?

How Washington and Presidents Have Changed

The incompatibility of bargaining and going public presents some pressing theoretical questions. Why should presidents come to favor a strategy of leadership that appears so incompatible with the principles of pluralist theory? Why, if other Washington elites legitimately and correctly represent the interests of their clients and constituents, would anything be gained by going over their heads? The answers to these questions are complex, reflecting changes in the capital and in presidents. In this chapter we consider the changes within Washington, the locale of presidential activity. . . .

Some would account for the rise of going public by resorting to the imperative of technology. Certainly, advances in transportation and communications have been indispensable to this process, but they have not been sufficient in themselves to alter political relations in such a contradictory way. . . .

There are more fundamental reasons for the discrepancy between theory and current practice. Politics in Washington may no longer be as tractable to bargaining as it once was. Presidents prefer to go public because the strategy offers a better prospect of success than it did in the past. Perhaps the most consequential development in the modern era is the regularity of divided party control of government. Every president since Jimmy Carter has at some time had to deal with a Congress in which the opposition party controlled one or both chambers. On such occasions, each side frequently finds political advantage in frustrating the other and playing a blame game. Posturing in preparation for the next election takes precedence over bargaining and passing new policy.

Moreover, beginning in the 1970s close observers of American politics detected a pervasive decoupling of traditional allegiances. The most prominent of these trends saw voters abandoning their political party affiliations. From the 1960s to the 1980s the proportion of survey respondents who classified themselves as Independent (or some other noncommittal category) grew from 24 to 41 percent; twenty-five years later, despite a resurgent partisanship among both voters and politicians on a number of dimensions, this basic, defining fact has not changed. Entering the 2006 midterm election period, most surveys show Independent to be the single most popular choice when respondents are asked their party identification.[20] And voters continue to split their ballots, if not quite at the record rates of the 1980s, still to a degree unknown in the 1950s and 1960s.*
Consequently, political relations among politicians in Washington remain loose

---

*During the 1990s, the American National Election Surveys found 30 percent of respondent voters reporting that they had split their ballot between the presidential and House candidates. This compares to 18 percent in 2004 and the 1960s and 14 percent during the 1950s. The author wishes to thank Martin B. Wattenberg for supplying these figures in a personal communication, March 10, 2006.

and individualistic. In part ballot splitting reflects the dramatic growth of incumbency advantage, especially in House elections, during the 1980s. From 1976 until 1992 at least 90 percent of these incumbents who sought reelection won both their primary and general elections. Some years the figure reached a 98 percent success rate. If this success better insulated these politicians from party and institutional leaders, it served paradoxically to make many of them more sensitive to public opinion from their constituencies. After all, they were winning, in their view, by dint of heroic effort to respond to their constituents.[21]

As politicians in Washington became more sensitive (and perhaps responsive) to public pressure, presidents learned that mobilizing these pressures worked. For exposition I classify the earlier era up to the 1970s as "institutionalized pluralism" and the latter era as "individualized pluralism." Since the 1994 midterm congressional elections, when an ideologically infused resurgent Republican Party surprisingly took over control of the House of Representatives and the Senate for the first time in a generation, politics in Washington has in one important respect shifted away from those relations described by individualized pluralism. Specifically, a series of vigorous Republican Party leaders in Congress have restored a level of discipline and policy coherence unseen since the 1960s. Nonetheless, given the recentness and limited scope of this development and continuing, unabated expectations of presidential leadership via public relations, I have retained this bifurcated classification of the modern evolution of Washington politics from predominantly private elite transactions to the mobilization of interested publics. We will consider how recently strengthened partisanship in Congress may temper presidents' incentives to go public. . . .

The President's Place in Institutionalized Pluralism

Constructing coalitions across the broad institutional landscape of Congress, the bureaucracy, interest groups, courts, and state governments requires a politician who possesses a panoramic view and commands the resources necessary to engage the disparate, parochial interests of Washington's political elites. Only the president enjoys such vantage and resources. Traditional presidential scholarship leaves little doubt as to how they should be employed. Nowhere has Dahl and Lindblom's framework of the bargaining society been more forcefully employed than in Richard E. Neustadt's classic *Presidential Power*, published in 1960. Neustadt observes:

> Status and authority yield bargaining advantages. But in a government of "separated institutions sharing powers," they yield them to all sides. With the array of vantage points at his disposal, a President may be far more persuasive than his logic or his charm could make him. But outcomes are not guaranteed by his advantages. There remain the counter pressures

those whom he would influence can bring to bear on him from vantage points at their disposal. Command has limited utility; persuasion becomes give-and-take. . . .

The President's advantages are checked by the advantages of others. Continuing relationships will pull in both directions. These are relationships of mutual dependence. A President depends upon the men he would persuade; he has to reckon with his need or fear of them. They too will possess status, or authority, or both, else they would be of little use to him. Their vantage points confront his own; their power tempers his.*

Bargaining is thus the essence of presidential leadership, and pluralist theory explicitly rejects unilateral forms of influence as usually insufficient and ultimately costly. The ideal president is one who seizes the center of the Washington bazaar and actively barters with fellow politicians to build winning coalitions. He must do so, according to this theory, or he will forfeit any claim to leadership. . . .

The Calculus of Those Who Deal with the President

Those Washingtonians who conduct business with the president observe his behavior carefully. Their judgment about his leadership guides them in their dealings with him. Traditionally, the professional president watchers have asked themselves the following questions: What are his priorities? How much does he care whether he wins or loses on a particular issue? How will he weigh his options? Is he capable of winning?

Each person will answer these questions about the president's will and skill somewhat differently, of course, depending upon his or her institutional vantage. The chief lobbyist for the United Auto Workers, a network White House correspondent, and the mayor of New York City may size up the president differently depending upon what they need from him. Nonetheless, they arrive at their judgments about the president in similar ways. Each observes the same behavior, inspects the same personal qualities, evaluates the views of the same recognized opinion leaders—columnists and commentators, among others—and tests his or her own tentative opinions with those of fellow community members. Local opinion leaders promote a general agreement among Washingtonians in their assessments of the president. Their agreement is his reputation.[22]

---

* Richard E. Neustadt, *Presidential Power*, 28–29. Copyright 1980. Reprinted by permission of John Wiley and Sons, Inc. Compare with Dahl and Lindblom's earlier observation: "The President possesses more hierarchical controls than any other single figure in the government; indeed, he is often described somewhat romantically and certainly ambiguously as the most powerful democratic executive in the world. Yet like everyone else in the American policy process, the President must bargain constantly—with Congressional leaders, individual Congressmen, his department heads, bureau chiefs, and leaders of nongovernmental organizations" (Dahl and Lindblom, *Politics, Economics, and Welfare*, 333).

A president with a strong reputation does better in his dealings largely because others expect fewer concessions from him. Accordingly, he finds them more compliant; an orderly marketplace prevails. Saddled with a weak reputation, conversely, a president must work harder. Because others expect him to be less effective, they press him harder in expectation of greater gain. Comity at the bargaining table may give way to contention as other politicians form unreasonable expectations of gain. Through such expectations, the president's reputation regulates community relations in ways that either facilitate or impede his success. In a world of institutionalized pluralism, bargaining presidents seldom actively traded upon their prestige, leaving it to influence Washington political elites only through their anticipation of the electorate's behavior. As a consequence, prestige remained largely irrelevant to other politicians' assessments of the president.* Once presidents began going public and interjecting prestige directly into their relations with fellow politicians, and once these politicians found their resistance to this pressure diminished because of their own altered circumstances, the president's ability to marshal public opinion soon became an important ingredient of his reputation. New questions were added to traditional ones: Does the president feel strongly enough about an issue to go public? Will he follow through on his threats to do so? Does his standing in the country run so deep that it will likely be converted into mail to members of Congress, or is it so shallow that it will expire as he attempts to use it?

In today's Washington, the answers to these questions contribute to the president's reputation. Consequently, his prestige and reputation have lost much of their separateness. The community's estimates of Carter and Reagan rose and fell with the polls. Through reputation, prestige has begun to play a larger role in regulating the president's day-to-day transactions with other community members. Grappling with the unclear causes of Carter's failure in Washington, Neustadt arrived at the same conclusion:

> A President's capacity to draw and stir a television audience seems every bit as interesting to current Washingtonians as his ability to wield his formal powers. This interest is his opportunity. While national party organizations fall away, while congressional party discipline relaxes, while interest groups proliferate and issue networks rise, a President who wishes to compete for leadership in framing policy and shaping coalitions has to make the most he can out of his popular connection. Anticipating home reactions, Washingtonians . . . are vulnerable to any breeze from home

* Neustadt observed that President Truman's television appeal for tighter price controls in 1951 had little visible effect on how Washington politicians viewed the issue. This is the only mention of a president going public in the original eight chapters of the book. Neustadt, *Presidential Power*, 45.

that presidential words and sights can stir. If he is deemed effective on the tube they will anticipate. That is the essence of professional reputation.[23]

The record supports Neustadt's speculation. In late 1978 and early 1979, with his monthly approval rating dropping to less than 50 percent, President Carter complained that it was difficult to gain Congress's attention for his legislative proposals. As one congressional liaison official stated, "When you go up to the Hill and the latest polls show Carter isn't doing well, then there isn't much reason for a member to go along with him."[24] A member of Congress concurred: "The relationship between the President and Congress is partly the result of how well the President is doing politically. Congress is better behaved when he does well. . . . Right now, it's almost as if Congress is paying no attention to him."[25]

The President's Calculus

The limited goods and services available for barter to the bargaining president would be quickly exhausted in a leaderless setting where every coalition partner must be dealt with individually. When politicians are more subject to environmental forces, however, other avenues of presidential influence open up. No politician within Washington is better positioned than the president to go outside the community and draw popular support. With members more sensitive to influences beyond Washington, the president's hand in mobilizing public opinion has been strengthened. For the new Congress—indeed, for the new Washington generally—going public may at times be the most effective course available.

Under these circumstances, the president's prestige becomes his political capital. It is something to be spent when the coffers are full, to be conserved when they are low, and to be replenished when they are empty. Early in 1997, when asked by campaign-weary news reporters why President Clinton maintained such a heavy travel schedule after his election victory, press secretary Michael D. McCurry lectured them on modern political science: "Campaigns are about framing a choice for the American people. . . .When you are responsible for governing you have to use the same tools of public persuasion to advance your program, to build public support for the direction you are attempting to lead."[26]

If public relations are to be productive the message must be tailored to a correctly targeted audience. For this, presidents require accurate, precisely measured readings of public opinion. Modern presidents must be attentive to the polls, but they need not crave the affection of the public. Their relationship with it may be purely instrumental. However gratifying public approval may be, popular support is a resource the expenditure of which must be coolly calculated. As another Clinton aide explained, "Clinton has come to believe that if he keeps his approval ratings up and sells his message as he did during the campaign, there will be greater acceptability for his program. . . . The idea is that you have to sell it as if in a campaign."[27]

Bargaining presidents require the sage advice of politicians familiar with the bargaining game; presidents who go public need pollsters. Compare the relish with which President Nixon reportedly approached the polls with the disdain Truman expressed. "Nixon had all kinds of polls all the time," recalled one of his consultants. "He sometimes had a couple of pollsters doing the same kind of survey at the same time. He really studied them. He wanted to find the thing that would give him an advantage."[28] The confidant went on to observe that the president wanted poll data "on just about anything and everything" throughout his administration.

Indicative of current fashion, presidents from Carter through Bush have all had in-house pollsters taking continuous—weekly, even daily—readings of public opinion.[29] When George H. W. Bush reportedly spent $216,000 of Republican National Committee (RNC) money on in-house polling in one year, many Washington politicians probably viewed it as an excessive indulgence, reflecting the RNC's largesse more than any practical need for data. But this figure soon looked modest after Clinton spent nearly ten times that amount in 1993, when he averaged three or four polls and an equal number of focus groups each month.[30]

Pollsters vigilantly monitor the pulse of opinion to warn of slippage and to identify opportunities for gain. Before recommending a policy course, they assess its costs in public support. Sometimes, as was the case with Clinton's pollsters, they go so far as to ask the public whether the president should bargain with congressional leaders or challenge them by mobilizing public opinion. These advisers' regular and frequently unsolicited denials that they affected policy belie their self-effacement.

To see how the strategic prescriptions of going public differ from those of bargaining, consider the hypothetical case of a president requiring additional votes if he is to prevail in Congress. If a large number of votes is needed, the most obvious and direct course is to go on prime-time television to solicit the public's active support. Employed at the right moment by a popular president, the effect may be dramatic. This tactic, however, has considerable costs and risks. A real debit of lost public support may occur when a president takes a forthright position. There is also the possibility that the public will not respond, which damages the president's future credibility. Given this, a president understandably finds the *threat* to go public frequently more attractive than the *act*. To the degree that such a threat is credible, the anticipated responses of some representatives and senators may suffice to achieve victory.

A more focused application of influence via public relations becomes available as an election nears. Fence-sitting representatives and senators may be plied with promises of reelection support. This may be done privately and selectively, or it may be tendered openly to all who may vote on the president's program. Presidential support can be much more substantial than endorsement. Presidents at least as far back as 1938, when Franklin Roosevelt failed to purge anti–New Deal Democrats in the midterm elections, have at times actively sought to improve their own fortunes in the next Congress by influencing the current election. During the 1970 midterm congressional election campaigns, President Nixon raced around the country "in a white heat," trying desperately to secure a Republican Congress that would not convene for another generation.[31] In the 1999–2000 election cycle outgoing President Clinton pushed the modern president's efforts to serve his party's candidates to what would seem to be an individual's physical limits. By one count he participated in 295 congressional fund-raising events garnering more than $160 million for his party's candidates. Were it not for the tragic events of 9/11 and the subsequent invasion of Afghanistan, President Bush might have matched his predecessor. After getting off to a slow start in the next election cycle, the president made up ground rapidly. By the 2002 election he had attended seventy-four fund-raisers, an impressive number except when compared to Clinton, but he garnered significantly more money for Republican congressional candidates than had his Democratic counterpart. . . .

The variety of methods for generating publicity notwithstanding, going public offers fewer and simpler stratagems than does its pluralist alternative. At the heart of the latter lies bargaining, which must involve choice: choice among alternative coalitions, choice of specific partners, and choice of the goods and services to be bartered. Above all, it requires empathy, the ability of one politician to discern what his or her counterpart minimally needs in return for cooperation. The number, variety, and subtlety of choices place great demands upon strategic calculation, so much so that pluralist leadership must be understood as an art. In Neustadt's schema, the president's success ultimately reduces to intuition an ability to sense "right choices."[32]

Going public also requires choice, and it leaves ample room for the play of talent. If anyone doubts it, consider the obviously staged town meetings that President Bush's advance team assembled during his [2005] "sixty cities in sixty days" promotion of Social Security reform. Public relations is a less obscure matter than bargaining with fellow politicians, every one of them a professional bent on extracting as much from the president while surrendering as little as possible. Going public promises a more straightforward presidency than its pluralist counterpart—its options fewer, its strategy simpler, and consequently, its practitioner's actions both more predictable and easily observed.

NOTES

1. Dan Froomkin, "Bush Agenda: Bold but Blurry," *Washington Post*, November 5, 2004.

2. Robert B. Semple Jr., "Nixon Eludes Newsmen on Coast Trip," *New York Times*, August 3, 1970, 16.

3. Richard E. Neustadt, *Presidential Power* (New York: John Wiley and Sons, 1980).

4. Robert A. Dahl and Charles E. Lindblom, *Politics, Economics, and Welfare* (New York: Harper and Row, 1953), 333.

5. Among them are Aaron Wildavsky, *The Politics of the Budgetary Process* (Boston: Little, Brown, 1964); Graham T. Allison, *The Essence of Decision: Explaining the Cuban Missile Crisis* (New York: HarperCollins, 1987); Hugh Heclo, *The Government of Strangers* (Washington, D.C.: Brookings Institution, 1977); and Nelson W. Polsby, *Consequences of Party Reform* (New York: Oxford University Press, 1983).

6. From Ronald Reagan's address to the nation on his 1986 budget. Jack Nelson, "Reagan Calls for Public Support of Deficit Cuts," *Los Angeles Times*, April 25, 1985, 1.

7. Nelson W. Polsby, "Interest Groups and the Presidency: Trends in Political Intermediation in America," in *American Politics and Public Policy*, ed. Walter Dean Burnham and Martha Wagner Weinbey (Cambridge: MIT Press, 1978), 52.

8. Hedrick Smith, "Bitterness on Capitol Hill," *New York Times*, April 24, 1985, 14.

9. Ed Magnuson, "A Line Drawn in Dirt," *Time*, February 22, 1982, 12–13.

10. William J. Clinton, *Public Papers of the Presidents of the United States: William J. Clinton, 1994*, vol. 1 (Washington, D.C.: Government Printing Office, 1995), 126–135.

11. See David S. Broder, "Diary of a Mad Majority Leader," *Washington Post*, December 13, 1981, C1, C5; David S. Broder, "Rostenkowski Knows It's His Turn," *Washington Post National Weekly Edition*, June 10, 1985, 13.

12. Lou Cannon, "Big Spending-Cut Bill Studied," *Washington Post*, November 29, 1984, A8.

13. Bernard Weinraub, "Reagan Sets Tour of Nation to Seek Economic Victory," *New York Times*, January 25, 1985, 43.

14. Bernard Weinraub, "Reagan Calls for 'Spirit of Cooperation' on Budget and Taxes," *New York Times*, February 10, 1985, 32. On Democratic suspicions of Reagan's motives see Hedrick Smith, "O'Neill Reflects Democratic Strategy on Budget Cuts and Tax Revisions," *New York Times*, December 6, 1984, B20; and Margaret Shapiro, "O'Neill's New Honeymoon with Reagan," *Washington Post National Weekly Edition*, February 11, 1985, 12.

15. Bernard Weinraub, "In His 2nd Term, He Is Reagan the Liberated," *New York Times*, March 11, 1985, 10.

16. David E. Rosenbaum, "Reagan Approves Primary Elements of Tax Overhaul," *New York Times*, May 16, 1985, 1.

17. Robert W. Merry and David Shribman, "G.O.P. Hopes Tax Bill Will Help It Become Majority Party Again," *Wall Street Journal*, May 23, 1985. See also Rosenbaum, "Reagan Approves Primary Elements of Tax Overhaul," 14. Instances such as those reported here continued into summer. See, for example, Jonathan Fuerbringer, "Key Issues Impede Compromise on Cutting Deficit," *New York Times*, June 23, 1985, 22.

18. These figures are reported in Richard E. Cohen, *Changing Course in Washington* (New York: Macmillan, 1994), 180.

19. The account of this meeting comes from Bob Woodward, *The Agenda* (New York: Simon and Schuster, 1994).

20. An excellent source for monitoring these trends is www.pollingreport.com.

21. Gary C. Jacobson, *The Politics of Congressional Elections*, 5th ed. (New York: Longman, 2001), 21–34.

22. This discussion of reputation follows closely that of Neustadt in *Presidential Power*, chap. 4.

23. Neustadt, *Presidential Power*, 238.

24. Cited in Gary C. Jacobson, *The Politics of Congressional Elections*, 4th ed. (New York: Longman, 1997), 193–194.

25. Statement by Rep. Richard B. Cheney cited in Charles O. Jones, "Congress and the Presidency," in *The New Congress*, eds. Thomas E. Mann and Norman J. Ornstein (Washington, D.C.: American Enterprise Institute, 1981), 241.

26. Alison Mitchell, "Clinton Seems to Keep Running Though the Race Is Run and Won," *New York Times*, February 12, 1997, A1, A12.

27. Ibid., A12.

28. Cited in George C. Edwards III, *The Public Presidency* (New York: St. Martin's Press, 1983), 14.

29. B. Drummond Ayres Jr., "G.O.P. Keeps Tabs on Nation's Mood," *New York Times*, November 16, 1981, 20.

30. These figures are cited in George C. Edwards III, "Frustration and Folly: Bill Clinton and the Public Presidency," in *The Clinton Presidency: First Appraisals*, eds. Colin Campbell and Bert A. Rockman (Chatham, N.J.: Chatham House, 1996), 234.

31. Rowland Evans and Robert Novak, *Nixon in the White House: The Frustration of Power*, (New York: Random House, 1971).

32. Neustadt, *Presidential Power*, especially chap. 8.

Chapter 8

The Bureaucracy

8-1

The Politics of Bureaucratic Structure

Terry M. Moe

Legislators, presidents, and other political players care about the content and implementation of policy. They also care about the way executive agencies are structured: Where in the executive branch are new agencies placed? What kind of bureaucrat will be motivated to aggressively pursue, or to resist the pursuit of, certain policy goals? Who should report to whom? What rules should govern bureaucrats' behavior? In the following essay, Terry M. Moe observes that these questions are anticipated and answered by politicians as they set policy. They are the subjects of "structural" politics. The federal bureaucracy is not structured on the basis of a theory of public administration, Moe argues, but should instead be viewed as the product of politics.

AMERICAN PUBLIC BUREAUCRACY is not designed to be effective. The bureaucracy arises out of politics, and its design reflects the interests, strategies, and compromises of those who exercise political power.

This politicized notion of bureaucracy has never appealed to most academics or reformers. They accept it—indeed, they adamantly argue its truth—and the social science of public bureaucracy is a decidedly political body of work as a result. Yet, for the most part, those who study and practice public administration have a thinly

Source: John E. Chubb and Paul E. Peterson, eds., *Can the Government Govern?* (Washington, D.C.: Brookings Institution Press, 1989), 267–285. Some notes appearing in the original have been deleted.

veiled disdain for politics, and they want it kept out of bureaucracy as much as possible. They want presidents to stop politicizing the departments and bureaus. They want Congress to stop its incessant meddling in bureaucratic affairs. They want all politicians to respect bureaucratic autonomy, expertise, and professionalism.[1]

The bureaucracy's defenders are not apologists. Problems of capture, inertia, parochialism, fragmentation, and imperialism are familiar grounds for criticism. And there is lots of criticism. But once the subversive influence of politics is mentally factored out, these bureaucratic problems are understood to have bureaucratic solutions—new mandates, new rules and procedures, new personnel systems, better training and management, better people. These are the quintessential reforms that politicians are urged to adopt to bring about effective bureaucracy. The goal at all times is the greater good: "In designing any political structure, whether it be the Congress, the executive branch, or the judiciary, it is important to build arrangements that weigh the scale in favor of those advocating the national interest."[2]

The hitch is that those in positions of power are not necessarily motivated by the national interest. They have their own interests to pursue in politics—the interests of southwest Pennsylvania or cotton farmers or the maritime industry—and they exercise their power in ways conducive to those interests. Moreover, choices about bureaucratic structure are not matters that can be separated off from all this, to be guided by technical criteria of efficiency and effectiveness. Structural choices have important consequences for the content and direction of policy, and political actors know it. When they make choices about structure, they are implicitly making choices about policy. And precisely because this is so, issues of structure are inevitably caught up in the larger political struggle. Any notion that political actors might confine their attention to policymaking and turn organizational design over to neutral criteria or efficiency experts denies the realities of politics.

This essay is an effort to understand bureaucracy by understanding its foundation in political choice and self-interest. The central question boils down to this: what sorts of structures do the various political actors—interest groups, presidents, members of Congress, bureaucrats—find conducive to their own interests, and what kind of bureaucracy is therefore likely to emerge from their efforts to exercise political power? In other words, why do they build the bureaucracy they do? . . .

A Perspective on Structural Politics

Most citizens do not get terribly excited about the arcane details of public administration. When they choose among candidates in elections, they pay attention to such things as party or image or stands on policy. If pressed, the candidates would probably have views or even voting records on structural issues—for example, whether the Occupational Safety and Health Administration should be required to carry out cost-benefit analysis before proposing a formal rule or whether the Consumer Product Safety Commission should be moved into the Commerce Department—but this is hardly the stuff that political campaigns are made of. People just do not know or care much about these sorts of things.

Organized interest groups are another matter. They are active, informed participants in their specialized issue areas, and they know that their policy goals are crucially dependent on precisely those fine details of administrative structure that cause voters' eyes to glaze over. Structure is valuable to them, and they have every incentive to mobilize their political resources to get what they want. As a result, they are normally the only source of political pressure when structural issues are at stake. Structural politics is interest group politics.

Interest Groups: The Technical Problem of Structural Choice

Most accounts of structural politics pay attention to interest groups, but their analytical focus is on the politicians who exercise public authority and make the final choices. This tends to be misleading. It is well known that politicians, even legislators from safe districts, are extraordinarily concerned about their electoral popularity and, for that reason, are highly responsive to their constituencies. To the extent this holds true, their positions on issues are not really their own, but are induced by the positions of others. If one seeks to understand why structural choices turn out as they do, then, it does not make much sense to start with politicians. The more fundamental questions have to do with how interest groups decide what kinds of structures they want politicians to provide. This is the place to start.

In approaching these questions about interest groups, it is useful to begin with an extreme case. Suppose that, in a given issue area, there is a single dominant group (or coalition) with a reasonably complex problem—pollution, poverty, job safety, health—it seeks to address through governmental action, and that the group is so powerful that politicians will enact virtually any proposal the group offers, subject to reasonable budget constraints. In effect, the group is able to exercise public authority on its own by writing legislation that is binding on everyone and enforceable in the courts.

The dominant group is an instructive case because, as it makes choices about structure, it faces no political problems. It need not worry about losing its grip on public authority or about the influence of its political opponents—considerations which would otherwise weigh heavily in its calculations. Without the usual uncertainties and constraints of politics, the group has the luxury of concerning itself entirely with the technical requirements of effective organization. Its job is to identify those structural arrangements that best realize its policy goals.

It is perhaps natural to think that, since a dominant group can have anything it wants, it would proceed by figuring out what types of behaviors are called for by what types of people under what types of conditions and by writing legislation spelling all this out in the minutest detail. If an administrative agency were necessary to perform services, process applications, or inspect business operations, the jobs of bureaucrats could be specified with such precision that they would have little choice but to do the group's bidding.

For simple policy goals—requiring, say, little more than transfer payments—these strategies would be attractive. But they are quite unsuited to policy problems of any complexity. The reason is that, although the group has the political power to impose its will on everyone, it almost surely lacks the knowledge to do it well. It does not know what to tell people to do.

In part, this is an expertise problem. Society as a whole simply has not developed sufficient knowledge to determine the causes of or solutions for most social problems; and the group typically knows much less than society does, even when it hires experts of its own. These knowledge problems are compounded by uncertainty about the future. The world is subject to unpredictable changes over time, and some will call on specific policy adjustments if the group's interests are to be pursued effectively. The group could attempt to specify all future contingencies in the current legislation and, through continuous monitoring and intervention, update it over time. But the knowledge requirements of a halfway decent job would prove enormously costly, cumbersome, and time-consuming.

A group with the political power to tell everyone what to do, then, will typically not find it worthwhile to try. A more attractive option is to write legislation in general terms, put experts on the public payroll, and grant them the authority to "fill in the details" and make whatever adjustments are necessary over time. This compensates nicely for the group's formidable knowledge problems, allowing it to pursue its own interests without knowing exactly how to implement its policies and without having to grapple with future contingencies. The experts do what the group is unable to do for itself. And because they are public officials on the public payroll, the arrangement economizes greatly on the group's resources and time.

It does, however, raise a new worry: there is no guarantee the experts will always act in the group's best interests. Experts have their own interests—in career, in autonomy—that may conflict with those of the group. And, due largely to experts' specialized knowledge and the often intangible nature of their outputs, the group cannot know exactly what its expert agents are doing or why. These are problems of conflict of interest and asymmetric information, and they are unavoidable. Because of them, control will be imperfect.

When the group's political power is assured, as we assume it is here, these control problems are at the heart of structural choice. The most direct approach is for the group to impose a set of rules to constrain bureaucratic behavior. Among other things, these rules might specify the criteria and procedures bureaucrats are to use in making decisions; shape incentives by specifying how bureaucrats are to be evaluated, rewarded, and sanctioned; require them to collect and report certain kinds of information on their internal operations, and set up oversight procedures by which their activities can be monitored. These are basic components of bureaucratic structure.

But some slippage will remain. The group's knowledge problems, combined with the experts' will and capacity to resist (at least at the margins), make perfect control impossible. Fortunately, though, the group can do more than impose a set of rules on its agents. It also has the power to choose who its agents will be— and wise use of this power could make the extensive use of rules unnecessary.

The key here is reputation. Most individuals in the expert market come with reputations that speak to their job-relevant traits: expertise, intelligence, honesty, loyalty, policy preferences, ideology. "Good" reputations provide reliable information. The reason is that individuals value good reputations, they invest in them—by behaving honestly, for instance, even when they could realize short-term gains through cheating—and, having built up reputations, they have strong incentives to maintain them through consistent behavior. To the group, therefore, reputation is of enormous value because it allows predictability in an uncertain world. And predictability facilitates control.

To see more concretely how this works, consider an important reputational syndrome: professionalism. If individuals are known to be accountants or securities lawyers or highway engineers, the group will immediately know a great deal about their "type." They will be experts in certain issues. They will have specialized educations and occupational experiences. They will analyze issues, collect data, and propose solutions in characteristic ways. They will hew to the norms of their professional communities. Particularly when professionalism is combined with reputational information of a more personal nature, the behavior of these experts will be highly predictable.

The link between predictability and control would seem especially troublesome in this case, since professionals are widely known to demand autonomy in their work. And, as far as restrictive rules and hierarchical directives are concerned, their demand for autonomy does indeed pose problems. But the group is forced to grant experts discretion anyway, owing to its knowledge problems. What professionalism does—via reputation—is allow the group to anticipate how expert discretion will be exercised under various conditions; it can then plan accordingly as it designs a structure that takes best advantage of their expertise. In the extreme, one might think of professionals as automatons, programmed to behave in specific ways. Knowing how they are programmed, the group can select those with the desired programs, place them in a structure designed to accommodate them, and turn them loose to exercise free choice. The professionals would see themselves as independent decision makers. The group would see them as under control. And both would be right.

The purpose of this illustration is not to emphasize professionalism per se, but to clarify a general point about the technical requirements of organizational design. A politically powerful group, acting under uncertainty and concerned with solving a complex policy problem, is normally best off if it resists using its power to tell bureaucrats exactly what to do. It can use its power more productively by selecting the right types of bureaucrats and designing a structure that affords them reasonable autonomy. Through the judicious allocation of bureaucratic roles and responsibilities, incentive systems, and structural checks on bureaucratic choice, a select set of bureaucrats can be unleashed to follow their expert judgment, free from detailed formal instructions.

Interest Groups: The Political Problem of Structural Choice

Political dominance is an extreme case for purposes of illustration. In the real world of democratic politics, interest groups cannot lay claim to unchallenged legal authority. Because this is so, they face two fundamental problems that a dominant group does not. The first I will call political uncertainty, the second political compromise. Both have enormous consequences for the strategic design of public bureaucracy—consequences that entail substantial departures from effective organization.

Political uncertainty is inherent in democratic government. No one has a perpetual hold on public authority nor, therefore, a perpetual right to control public agencies. An interest group may be powerful enough to exercise public authority today, but tomorrow its power may ebb, and its right to exercise public authority may then be usurped by its political opponents. Should this occur, they would become the new "owners" of whatever the group had created, and they could use their authority to destroy—quite legitimately—everything the group had worked so hard to achieve.

A group that is currently advantaged, then, must anticipate all this. Precisely because its own authority is not guaranteed, it cannot afford to focus entirely on technical issues of effective organization. It must also design its creations so that they have the capacity to pursue its policy goals in a world in which its enemies may achieve the right to govern. The group's task in the current period, then, is to build agencies that are difficult for its opponents to gain control over later. Given the way authority is allocated and exercised in a democracy, this will often mean building agencies that are insulated from public authority in general—and thus insulated from formal control by the group itself.

There are various structural means by which the group can try to protect and nurture its bureaucratic agents. They include the following:

- It can write detailed legislation that imposes rigid constraints on the agency's mandate and decision procedures. While these constraints will tend to be flawed, cumbersome, and costly, they serve to remove important types of decisions from future political control. The reason they are so attractive is rooted in the American separation-of-powers system, which sets up obstacles that make formal legislation extremely difficult to achieve—and, if achieved, extremely difficult to overturn. Should the group's opponents gain in political power, there is a good chance they would still not be able to pass corrective legislation of their own.

- It can place even greater emphasis on professionalism than is technically justified, since professionals will generally act to protect their own autonomy and resist political interference. For similar reasons, the group can be a strong supporter of the career civil service and other personnel systems that insulate bureaucratic jobs, promotion, and pay from political intervention. And it can try to minimize the power and number of political appointees, since these too are routes by which opponents may exercise influence.

- It can oppose formal provisions that enhance political oversight and involvement. The legislative veto, for example, is bad because it gives opponents a direct mechanism for reversing agency decisions. Sunset provisions, which require reauthorization of the agency after some period of time, are also dangerous because they give opponents opportunities to overturn the group's legislative achievements.

- It can see that the agency is given a safe location in the scheme of government. Most obviously, it might try to place the agency in a friendly executive department, where it can be sheltered by the group's allies. Or it may favor formal independence, which provides special protection from presidential removal and managerial powers.

- It can favor judicialization of agency decision making as a way of insulating policy choices from outside interference. It can also favor making various types of agency actions—or inactions—appealable to the courts. It must take care to design these procedures and checks, however, so that they disproportionately favor the group over its opponents.

The driving force of political uncertainty, then, causes the winning group to favor structural designs it would never favor on technical grounds alone: designs that place detailed formal restrictions on bureaucratic discretion, impose complex procedures for agency decision making, minimize opportunities for oversight, and otherwise insulate the agency from politics. The group has to protect itself and its agency from the dangers of democracy, and it does so by imposing structures that appear strange and incongruous indeed when judged by almost any reasonable standards of what an effective organization ought to look like.

But this is only part of the story. The departure from technical rationality is still greater because of a second basic feature of American democratic politics: legislative victory of any consequence almost always requires compromise. This means that opposing groups will have a direct say in how the agency and its mandate are constructed. One form that this can take, of course, is the classic compromise over policy that is written about endlessly in textbooks and newspapers. But there is no real disjunction between policy and structure, and many of the opponents' interests will also be pursued through demands for structural concessions. What sorts of arrangements should they tend to favor?

- Opponents want structures that work against effective performance. They fear strong, coherent, centralized organization. They like fragmented authority, decentralization, federalism, checks and balances, and other structural means of promoting weakness, confusion, and delay.

- They want structures that allow politicians to get at the agency. They do not want to see the agency placed within a friendly department, nor do they favor formal independence. They are enthusiastic supporters of legislative veto and reauthorization provisions. They favor onerous requirements for the collection and reporting of information, the monitoring of agency operations, and the review of agency decisions—thus laying the basis for active, interventionist oversight by politicians.

- They want appointment and personnel arrangements that allow for political direction of the agency. They also want more active and influential roles for political appointees and less extensive reliance on professionalism and the civil service.

- They favor agency decision making procedures that allow them to participate, to present evidence and arguments, to appeal adverse agency decisions, to delay, and, in general, to protect their own interests and inhibit effective agency action through formal, legally sanctioned rules. This means that they will tend to push for cumbersome, heavily judicialized decision processes, and that they will favor an active, easily triggered role for the courts in reviewing agency decisions.

- They want agency decisions to be accompanied by, and partially justified in terms of, "objective" assessments of their consequences: environmental impact statements, inflation impact statements, cost-benefit analysis. These are costly, time-consuming, and disruptive. Even better, their methods and conclusions can be challenged in the courts, providing new opportunities for delaying or quashing agency decisions.

Political compromise ushers the fox into the chicken coop. Opposing groups are dedicated to crippling the bureaucracy and gaining control over its decisions, and they will pressure for fragmented authority, labyrinthine procedures, mechanisms of political intervention, and other structures that subvert the bureaucracy's performance and open it up to attack. In the politics of structural choice, the inevitability of compromise means that agencies will be burdened with structures fully intended to cause their failure.

In short, democratic government gives rise to two major forces that cause the structure of public bureaucracy to depart from technical rationality. First, those currently in a position to exercise public authority will often face uncertainty about their own grip on political power in the years ahead, and this will prompt them to favor structures that insulate their achievements from politics. Second, opponents will also tend to have a say in structural design, and, to the degree they do, they will impose structures that subvert effective performance and politicize agency decisions.

Legislators and Structural Choice

If politicians were nothing more than conduits for political pressures, structural choice could be understood without paying much attention to them. But politicians, especially presidents, do sometimes have preferences about the structure of government that are not simple reflections of what the groups want. And when this is so, they can use their control of public authority to make their preferences felt in structural outcomes.

The conduit notion is not so wide of the mark for legislators, owing to their almost paranoid concern for reelection. In structural politics, well informed interest groups make demands, observe legislators' responses, and accurately assign credit and blame as decisions are made and consequences realized. Legislators therefore have strong incentives to do what groups want—and, even in the absence of explicit demands, to take entrepreneurial action in actively representing group interests. They cannot satisfy groups with empty position taking. Nor can they costlessly "shift the responsibility" by delegating tough decisions to the bureaucracy. Interest groups, unlike voters, are not easily fooled.

This does not mean that legislators always do what groups demand of them. Autonomous behavior can arise even among legislators who are motivated by nothing other than reelection. This happens because politicians, like groups, recognize that their current choices are not just means of responding to current pressures, but are also means of imposing structure on their political lives. This will sometimes lead them to make unpopular choices today in order to reap political rewards later on.

It is not quite right, moreover, to suggest that legislators have no interest of their own in controlling the bureaucracy. The more control legislators are able to exercise, the more groups will depend on them to get what they want; and this, in itself, makes control electorally attractive. But the attractiveness of control is diluted by other factors. First, the winning group—the more powerful side—will pressure to have its victories removed from political influence. Second, the capacity for control can be a curse for legislators in later conflict, since both sides will descend on them repeatedly. Third, oversight for purposes of serious policy control is time-consuming, costly, and difficult to do well; legislators typically have much more productive ways to spend their scarce resources.

The result is that legislators tend not to invest in general policy control. Instead, they value "particularized" control: they want to be able to intervene quickly, inexpensively, and in ad hoc ways to protect or advance the interests of particular clients in particular matters. This sort of control can be managed by an individual legislator without collective action; it has direct payoffs; it will generally be carried out behind the scenes; and it does not involve or provoke conflict. It generates political benefits without political costs. Moreover, it fits in quite nicely with a bureaucratic structure designed for conflict avoidance: an agency that is highly autonomous in the realm of policy yet highly constrained by complex procedural requirements will offer all sorts of opportunities for particularistic interventions.

The more general point is that legislators, by and large, can be expected either to respond to group demands in structural politics or to take entrepreneurial action in trying to please them. They will not be given to flights of autonomous action or statesmanship.

Presidents and Structural Choice

Presidents are motivated differently. Governance is the driving force behind the modern presidency. All presidents, regardless of party, are expected to govern effectively and are held responsible for taking action on virtually the full range of problems facing society. To be judged successful in the eyes of history—arguably the single most important motivator for presidents—they must appear to be strong leaders. They need to achieve their policy initiatives, their initiatives must be regarded as socially valuable, and the structures for attaining them must appear to work.

This raises two basic problems for interest groups. The first is that presidents are not very susceptible to the appeals of special interests. They want to make groups happy, to be sure, and sometimes responding to group demands will contribute nicely to governance. But this is often not so. In general, presidents have incentives to think in grander terms about what is best for society as a whole, or at least broad chunks of it, and they have their own agendas that may depart substantially from what even their more prominent group supporters might want. Even when they are simply responding to group pressures—which is more likely, of course, during their first term—the size and heterogeneity of their support coalitions tend to promote moderation, compromise, opposition to capture, and concern for social efficiency.

The second problem is that presidents want to control the bureaucracy. While legislators eagerly delegate their powers to administrative agencies, presidents are driven to take charge. They do not care about all agencies equally, of course. Some agencies are especially important because their programs are priority items on the presidential agenda. Others are important because they deal with sensitive issues that can become political bombshells if something goes wrong. But most all agencies impinge in one way or another on larger presidential responsibilities—for the budget, for the economy, for national defense—and presidents must have the capacity to direct and constrain agency behavior in basic respects if these larger responsibilities are to be handled successfully. They may often choose not to use their capacity for administrative control; they may even let favored groups use it when it suits their purposes. But the capacity must be there when they need it.

Presidents therefore have a unique role to play in the politics of structural choice. They are the only participants who are directly concerned with how the bureaucracy as a whole should be organized. And they are the only ones who actually want to run it through hands-on management and control. Their ideal is a rational, coherent, centrally directed bureaucracy that strongly resembles popular textbook notions of what an effective bureaucracy, public or private, ought to look like.

In general, presidents favor placing agencies within executive departments and subordinating them to hierarchical authority. They want to see important oversight, budget, and policy coordination functions given to department superiors—and, above them, to the Office of Management and Budget and other presidential management agencies—so that the bureaucracy can be brought under unified direction. While they value professionalism and civil service for their contributions to expertise, continuity, and impartiality, they want authority in the hands of their own political appointees—and they want to choose appointees whose types appear most conducive to presidential leadership.

This is just what the winning group and its legislative allies do not want. They want to protect their agencies and policy achievements by insulating them from politics, and presidents threaten to ruin everything by trying to control these agencies from above. The opposing groups are delighted with this, but they cannot always take comfort in the presidential approach to bureaucracy either. For presidents will tend to resist complex procedural protections, excessive judicial review, legislative veto provisions, and many other means by which the losers try to protect themselves and cripple bureaucratic performance. Presidents want agencies to have discretion, flexibility, and the capacity to take direction. They do not want agencies to be hamstrung by rules and regulations—unless, of course, they are presidential rules and regulations designed to enhance presidential control.

Legislators, Presidents, and Interest Groups

Obviously, presidents and legislators have very different orientations to the politics of structural choice. Interest groups can be expected to anticipate these differences from the outset and devise their own strategies accordingly.

Generally speaking, groups on both sides will find Congress a comfortable place in which to do business. Legislators are not bound by any overarching notion of what the bureaucracy as a whole ought to look like. They are not intrinsically motivated by effectiveness or efficiency or coordination or management or any other design criteria that might limit the kind of bureaucracy they are willing to create. They do not even want to retain political control for themselves.

The key thing about Congress is that it is open and responsive to what the groups want. It willingly builds, piece by piece—however grotesque the pieces, however inconsistent with one another—the kind of bureaucracy interest groups incrementally demand in their structural battles over time. This "congressional bureaucracy" is not supposed to function as a coherent whole, nor even to constitute one. Only the pieces are important. That is the way groups want it.

Presidents, of course, do not want it that way. Interest groups may find them attractive allies on occasion, especially when their interests and the presidential agenda coincide. But, in general, presidents are a fearsome presence on the political scene. Their broad support coalitions, their grand perspective on public policy, and their fundamental concern for a coherent, centrally controlled bureaucracy combine to make them maverick players in the game of structural politics. They want a "presidential bureaucracy" that is fundamentally at odds with the congressional bureaucracy everyone else is busily trying to create.

To the winning group, presidents are a major source of political uncertainty over and above the risks associated with the future power of the group's opponents. This gives it even greater incentives to pressure for structures that are insulated from politics—and, when possible, disproportionately insulated from presidential politics. Because of the seriousness of the presidency's threat, the winning group will place special emphasis on limiting the powers and numbers of political appointees, locating effective authority in the agency and its career personnel, and opposing new hierarchical powers—of review, coordination, veto—for units in the Executive Office or even the departments.

The losing side is much more pragmatic. Presidents offer important opportunities for expanding the scope of conflict, imposing new procedural constraints on agency action, and appealing unfavorable decisions. Especially if presidents are not entirely sympathetic to the agency and its mission, the losing side may actively support all the trappings of presidential bureaucracy—but only, of course, for the particular case at hand. Thus, while presidents may oppose group efforts to cripple the agency through congressional bureaucracy, groups may be able to achieve much the same end through presidential bureaucracy. The risk, however, is that the next president could turn out to be an avid supporter of the agency, in which case presidential bureaucracy might be targeted to quite different ends indeed. If there is a choice, sinking formal restrictions into legislative concrete offers a much more secure and permanent fix.

Bureaucracy

Bureaucratic structure emerges as a jerry-built fusion of congressional and presidential forms, their relative roles and particular features determined by the powers, priorities, and strategies of the various designers. The result is that each agency cannot help but begin life as a unique structural reflection of its own politics.

Once an agency is created, the political world becomes a different place. Agency bureaucrats are now political actors in their own right. They have career and institutional interests that may not be entirely congruent with their formal missions, and they have powerful resources—expertise and delegated authority—that might be employed toward these selfish ends. They are new players whose interests and resources alter the political game.

It is useful to think in terms of two basic types of bureaucratic players: political appointees and careerists. Careerists are the pure bureaucrats. As they carry out their jobs, they will be concerned with the technical requirements of effective organization, but they will also face the same problem that all other political actors face: political uncertainty. Changes in group power, committee composition, and presidential administration represent serious threats to things that bureaucrats hold dear. Their mandates could be restricted, their budgets cut, their discretion curtailed, their reputations blemished. Like groups and politicians, bureaucrats cannot afford to concern themselves solely with technical matters. They must take action to reduce their political uncertainty.

One attractive strategy is to nurture mutually beneficial relationships with groups and politicians whose political support the agency needs. If these are to provide real security, they must be more than isolated quid pro quos; they must be part of an ongoing stream of exchanges that give all participants expectations of future gain and thus incentives to resist short-term opportunities to profit at one another's expense. This is most easily done with the agency's initial supporters.

Over time, however, the agency will be driven to broaden its support base, and it may move away from some of its creators—as regulatory agencies sometimes have, for example, in currying favor with the business interests they are supposed to be regulating. All agencies will have a tendency to move away from presidents, who, as temporary players, are inherently unsuited to participation in stable, long-term relationships.

Political appointees are also unattractive allies. They are not long-term participants, and no one will treat them as though they are. They have no concrete basis for participating in the exchange relationships of benefit to careerists. Indeed, they may not want to, for they have incentives to pay special attention to White House policy, and they will try to forge alliances that further those ends. Their focus is on short-term presidential victories, and relationships that stabilize politics for the agency may get in the way and have to be challenged.

As this begins to suggest, the strategy of building supportive relationships is inherently limited. In the end, much of the environment remains out of control. This prompts careerists to rely on a second, complementary strategy of uncertainty avoidance: insulation. If they cannot control the environment, they can try to shut themselves off from it in various ways. They can promote further professionalization and more extensive reliance on civil service. They can formalize and judicialize their decision procedures. They can base decisions on technical expertise, operational experience, and precedent, thus making them "objective" and agency-centered. They can try to monopolize the information necessary for effective political oversight. These insulating strategies are designed, moreover, not simply to shield the agency from its political environment, but also to shield it from the very appointees who are formally in charge.

All of this raises an obvious question: why can't groups and politicians anticipate the agency's alliance and insulationist strategies and design a structure ex ante that adjusts for them? The answer, of course, is that they can. Presidents may push for stronger hierarchical controls and greater formal power for appointees than they otherwise would. Group opponents may place even greater emphasis on opening the agency up to political oversight. And so on. The agency's design, therefore, should from the beginning incorporate everyone's anticipations about its incentives to form alliances and promote its own autonomy.

Thus, however active the agency is in forming alliances, insulating itself from politics, and otherwise shaping political outcomes, it would be a mistake to regard the agency as a truly independent force. It is literally manufactured by the other players as a vehicle for advancing and protecting their own interests, and their structural designs are premised on anticipations about the roles the agency and its bureaucrats will play in future politics. The whole point of structural choice is to anticipate, program, and engineer bureaucratic behavior. Although groups and politicians cannot do this perfectly, the agency is fundamentally a product of their designs, and so is the way it plays the political game. That is why, in our attempt to understand the structure and politics of bureaucracy, we turn to bureaucrats last rather than first.

Structural Choice as a Perpetual Process

The game of structural politics never ends. An agency is created and given a mandate, but, in principle at least, all of the choices that have been made in the formative round of decision making can be reversed or modified later.

As the politics of structural choice unfolds over time, three basic forces supply its dynamics. First, group opponents will constantly be on the lookout for opportunities to impose structures of their own that will inhibit the agency's performance and open it up to external control. Second, the winning group must constantly be ready to defend its agency from attack—but it may also have attacks of its own to launch. The prime reason is poor performance: because the agency is burdened from the beginning with a structure unsuited to the lofty goals it is supposed to achieve, the supporting group is likely to be dissatisfied and to push for more productive structural arrangements. Third, the president will try to ensure that agency behavior is consistent with broader presidential priorities, and he will take action to impose his own structures on top of those already put in place by Congress. He may also act to impose structures on purely political grounds in response to the interests of either the winning or opposing group.

All of this is going on all the time, generating pressures for structural change that find expression in both the legislative and executive processes. These are potentially of great importance for bureaucracy and policy, and all the relevant participants are intensely aware of it. However, the choices about structure that are made in the first period, when the agency is designed and empowered with a mandate, are normally far more enduring and consequential than those that will be made later. They constitute an institutional base that is protected by all the impediments to new legislation inherent in separation of powers, as well as by the political clout of the agency's supporters. Most of the pushing and hauling in subsequent years is likely to produce only incremental change. This, obviously, is very much on everyone's minds in the first period.

NOTES

1. Harold Seidman and Robert Gilmour, *Politics, Position, and Power: From the Positive to the Regulatory State,* 4th ed. (Oxford University Press, 1986); and Frederick C. Mosher, *Democracy and the Public Service,* 2d ed. (Oxford University Press, 1982).

2. Seidman and Gilmour, *Politics, Position, and Power,* p. 330.

Bush and the Bureaucracy: A Crusade for Control

Paul Singer

*Every president seeks to influence policy by controlling the decisions of execu-
tive agencies and their personnel. Presidents accomplish this by means such as
increasing the authority of presidential appointees and establishing procedures that govern the regulatory activities of agencies. In this essay, reporter
Paul Singer reports on the efforts of the George W. Bush administration
(2001–2009) and considers the views of its critics.*

TWO WEEKS BEFORE George W. Bush's 2001 inauguration, the Heritage
Foundation issued a paper offering the new president advice on "taking charge
of federal personnel."

The authors—two former officials at the Office of Personnel Management
and a former congressional staffer who is now at OPM—laid out an ambitious
agenda to overhaul civil service rules and "reassert managerial control of government." The paper emphasized the importance of appointing strong leaders to
key government positions and holding bureaucrats "personally accountable for
achievement of the president's election-endorsed and value-defined program."

Reminded of this paper recently, co-author Robert Moffit, who has moved on
to other issues at Heritage, dusted off a copy and called a reporter back with a hint
of rejoicing in his voice. "They apparently are really doing this stuff," he said.

To Moffit and other proponents of strong management, the Bush White
House has indeed initiated a dramatic transformation of the federal bureaucracy,
trying to create a leaner, more results-oriented government that can better
account for taxpayer dollars. Reshaping the agenda of government to match the
president's priorities is the purpose of democratic elections, Moffit said.

But critics charge that the White House is embarking on a crusade to replace
expert judgment in federal agencies with political calculation, to marginalize or
eliminate longtime civil servants, to change laws without going through
Congress, to silence dissenting views within the government, and to centralize
decision-making in the White House.

"A president cannot wave a wand and wipe prior policy, as implemented by
duly enacted statutes, off the books," said Rena Steinzor, a founder and board

Source: Paul Singer, "Bush and the Bureaucracy: A Crusade for Control," *National Journal*, March 25, 2005.

member of the Center for Progressive Regulation, a think tank of liberal academics. "We have made a judgment as a nation, for decades, that an independent bureaucracy is very important." The Bush administration, she said, is "politicizing and terrorizing the bureaucracy, and turning it 180 degrees."

Critics point to a long list of manifestations of greater White House control. Among them:

> Reorganizations in various federal agencies, such as major staff cuts anticipated at NASA, that eliminate career civil service staff, or replace managers with political appointees;
>
> New management systems to grade federal agencies on the results they achieve, with the White House in charge of defining "success";
>
> Increased White House oversight of regulations issued by the Environmental Protection Agency, the Department of Labor, and other departments and agencies;
>
> The president's proposal to replace the civil service employment system with new, government-wide "pay-for-performance" rules that make it easier for managers to promote, reward, or fire employees;
>
> "Competitive sourcing" requirements that force thousands of federal workers to compete against private contractors to keep their jobs;
>
> A series of steps that may weaken traditional watchdogs and the office that protects whistle-blowers;
>
> New restrictions on the public release of government information, including a huge jump in the number of documents labeled "classified";
>
> A growing cadre of government employees who are going public with charges that their recommendations were ignored, their reports edited, or their conclusions reversed by their political-appointee managers, at the behest of the White House.

Many presidents have tried to reshape the federal bureaucracy to their liking. President Nixon had his "Management by Objective" program that attempted to rein in anti-poverty programs; President Clinton had his "Reinventing Government" initiative that aimed to improve government services and streamline rules. But under Bush, White House control of the federal agencies is "more coordinated and centralized than it has ever been," said New York University professor of public service Paul Light, who is also a senior fellow at the Brookings Institution. "It is a sea change from what it was under the Clinton administration."

Clay Johnson, who as deputy director for management at the Office of Management and Budget is the point man for Bush's "management agenda," denied any "Republican conspiracy" to control the bureaucracy or silence civil servants. "It's about things working better; it's not about controlling," Johnson said. "The thing that we can impose more of than anything else is clarity—clarity of purpose. We want to have a real clear definition of what success is," he said.

"The overall goal of all that we are doing," Johnson added, "is, we want to get to the point in three or four years where we can say to the American taxpayer that every program is getting better every year."

The federal bureaucracy is a notoriously unwieldy beast. It includes about 1.9 million civilian employees, many of whom have agendas that differ from the president's. Each administration, Republican or Democratic, struggles with its relationship with an army of workers who were on the job before the new political team arrived, and who expect to be there after the team leaves.

"You have this bizarre cycle, where the leader comes into the room and says, 'We are going to march north,' and the bureaucracy all applaud," said former House Speaker Newt Gingrich, R-Ga. "Then the leader leaves the room, and the bureaucracy says, 'Yeah, well, this "march north" thing is terrific, but this year, to be practical, we have to keep marching south. But what we'll do is, we'll hire a consultant to study marching north, so that next year we can begin to think about whether or not we can do it.'"

The White House is proud of its management initiatives and Bush's reputation as "the M.B.A. president." The administration regularly issues press releases to announce progress on the President's Management Agenda—a list of priorities that includes competitive sourcing and development of "e-government." And Bush's fiscal 2006 budget includes cuts based on performance assessments for hundreds of individual federal programs. But critics fear that the management agenda, combined with an array of other administration initiatives, has established a framework that makes it easier for political appointees to overrule, marginalize, or even fire career employees who question the president's agenda.

For example, the Environmental Protection Agency issued a rule earlier this month to regulate emissions of mercury from power plants. In unveiling the rule, the EPA asserted that it represents the most stringent controls on mercury ever issued. According to the agency, the requirements are cost-effective, will achieve significant health benefits, and will create an economic incentive for companies to continually improve their environmental performance.

But the rule is driven by the Bush administration's novel—some say, illegal—interpretation of the Clean Air Act that allows the EPA to avoid imposing mandatory emissions controls on each facility. Environmentalists, and some EPA staff, contend that the mercury rule is far weaker than one the Clinton administration proposed, and that political appointees at the agency ignored the scientific and legal judgment of career staff to push the rule through the regulatory process.

The battle over the mercury rule has been bitter and public. Many other efforts to tighten central control are buried deep within the bowels of the bureaucracy.

Structures

The Natural Resources Conservation Service is not generally a political hotbed. A division of the Agriculture Department, the NRCS—working through "conservationist" offices in each state—is responsible for helping farmers implement soil and water conservation measures, such as restoring wetlands, building dams, and designing systems to prevent animal waste from running off into waterways.

In a major reorganization over the past two years, NRCS chief Bruce Knight eliminated the service's six regional offices, which were headed by career managers and oversaw the state offices. He replaced the six regional managers with three political appointees in Washington and shuffled 200 career staffers from the regional offices into other offices throughout the agency.

Knight said the reorganization is "really just a strong business case." It created a "flatter, leaner structure" that relies much more heavily on the expertise of the state conservationists and makes better use of employees, he said. "I had about 200 highly valuable [employees] scattered around the country, and I needed to put them at the mission of the agency."

But in so doing, Knight has also raised concerns about the independence of the technical staffers who oversee conservation measures across the country.

Under the new structure, career NRCS scientists might worry that their technical decisions about where to spend money and how to implement programs will be overruled for political purposes, said Rich Duesterhaus, a former NRCS staffer and now director of government affairs for the National Association of Conservation Districts.

"They clearly now have a direct line from the politically appointed chief, through these three politically appointed regional assistant chiefs, to the line officers who supervise and carry out these programs," Duesterhaus said. And why should political control over a soil and water conservation agency matter? Because the 2002 farm bill doubled the NRCS's budget for assistance to farmers, from about $1.5 billion in 2001 to $2.8 billion in 2006, with a total increase of $18 billion slated through 2012.

"In the old days, the money wasn't big enough to matter," Duesterhaus said, but the influx of cash in 2002 has made the NRCS "a contender in terms of spoils, and where those spoils go becomes an issue." With direct political oversight of the state conservationists, Duesterhaus said, "it becomes a little easier to say, 'Well, we need Ohio, so make sure we put a little extra money in Ohio.'"

Earlier this month, Charles Adams, one of the six career regional conservationists who were unseated in the reorganization, filed a discrimination complaint against Knight and other agency officials, arguing that the reorganization
derailed his 37-year career in favor of three political appointees with far less
expertise. "I allege that . . . a calculated, arbitrary, and capricious decision was
made to preclude me from the line and leadership of this agency," Adams wrote
in his complaint to the Agriculture Department's Office of Civil Rights.

Knight rejects any suggestion that he has politicized the work of a technical
agency. "The real power is in the state conservationist, the career individual in
the state who manages the budget and the people," he said. "Most people will
agree that we are more scientifically and technologically based now" than before
the reorganization. The agency has about 12,500 staff members and only a dozen
political appointees, Knight said.

But employees in other federal agencies have also asserted that reorganization
plans have bumped career managers from senior positions, or diluted their
authority.

The Centers for Disease Control and Prevention is instituting a major overhaul that will create a new layer of "coordinating centers"—including a strategic
center responsible for developing long-term goals for the agency—between
CDC Director Julie Gerberding and the health and science centers that formerly
reported directly to her. Gerberding said, "I don't think our goal is to have control over the organization—our goal is to have an impact on health."

But some career staffers say they are being pushed aside and losing the ability
to manage their programs. *The Washington Post* earlier this month reported a
memo from a top CDC official warning that CDC employees are suffering a
"crisis of confidence" and that they feel "cowed into silence." CDC aides—who
are unwilling to have their names published for fear of reprisals—say they are
losing the ability to make independent professional judgments on topics ranging
from sexual abstinence, to drug use, to influenza. Gerberding replied, "I think
that is a very inaccurate assessment of what is going on at CDC."

Nevertheless, throughout the federal government, complaints can be heard
from disgruntled civil servants who feel they are being elbowed aside by the political leadership—though it is hard to assess whether the invariably anonymous
sources have been targeted for elimination or are simply frightened of the change.

Some of the administration's efforts have attracted congressional scrutiny. On
March 16, the House Science panel's Space and Aeronautics Subcommittee held
a hearing on the administration's plan to slash funding for aeronautics research
at NASA and to eliminate 2,000 jobs in order to focus the agency on the president's "Vision for Space Exploration," which includes the goal of manned missions to Mars.

But the administration is not backing down. In fact, it wants more authority to carry out these reorganizations. The White House has said it is drafting legislative proposals to create a "sunset" process requiring federal programs to rejustify their existence every 10 years and to set up "reform" commissions giving the president authority to initiate major restructuring of programs. House Government Reform Committee Chairman Tom Davis, R-Va., said in an interview this month that he believes that Congress should restore the president's unilateral authority to reorganize executive branch agencies—authority that presidents held from the late 1930s until 1984, and that Nixon used when he created the Environmental Protection Agency in 1970.

Procedures

Beyond its tinkering with organizational structures, the White House is pursuing a sweeping overhaul of personnel rules that is aimed at giving managers across the federal government more flexibility to promote, punish, or fire hundreds of thousands of civil servants. While a proposed transformation of the pay systems at the Defense and Homeland Security departments has spurred vigorous debate—fueled by the administration's announcement in January that it wants to extend these systems to the rest of the federal government—less fanfare attended last year's rollout of a new pay-for-performance plan for the roughly 6,000 veteran federal government managers who constitute the Senior Executive Service.

Together, the two new approaches give political appointees in federal agencies greater authority to reward or discipline senior career managers, and give managers the same authority over the civil servants below them. The White House calls this a "modern" personnel system, where everyone is judged on results. Critics call it a process for weeding out recalcitrant civil servants or political opponents.

The new pay-for-performance plan for the Senior Executive Service eliminates annual raises for top career managers and replaces them with a system of merit ratings. Some career executives fear that the system will allow the White House to simply push aside managers who are unenthusiastic about the president's agenda.

"We all know that performance is in the eyes of the beholder, no matter what you say about wanting to have many numerical indicators and so forth," said Carol Bonosaro, president of the Senior Executives Association, which represents members of the SES. "The concern is that if you know that your boss has the total authority to not give you a pay raise, are you going to be more inclined to skirt an ethics requirement for them? Are you going to be more inclined to do what is perhaps not really right?"

And the layers of performance ratings based on the president's goals serve to reinforce the agenda throughout the bureaucracy, Bonosaro said. "You kick the general, and the general comes back and kicks the soldiers, and it goes down the line."

In another move, which could affect thousands of civil servants, Bush has made "competitive sourcing" one of his primary management goals for federal agencies, requiring government workers to compete for their jobs against private contractors.

In January, OMB reported that government employees had won about 90 percent of the 30,000 jobs awarded in 2003 and 2004, with decisions still to be made on about 15,000 jobs offered for competition in those years. But in February, the Federal Aviation Administration announced that Lockheed Martin had won the government's largest-ever job competition, covering about 2,300 flight-service jobs. FAA workers slated to be displaced under the contract filed an appeal this month, complaining that the agency's bidding process was flawed.

"Everything they do is sending the signal [to employees] that they can be replaced easily by contractors, if the work they do isn't done by whatever standards the president is going to put out in his new measurement system," said Colleen Kelley, president of the National Treasury Employees Union.

"It's all about putting more power in the hands of the appointees and making it easier to downgrade, get rid of, use the rules as a weapon against employees who are not in lockstep with you," said Mark Roth, general counsel of the American Federation of Government Employees.

OMB's Johnson denies any intent to enforce political orthodoxy on the civil service. "Rewarding people for their political views is against the law. It's like incest: verboten. Not allowed. Doesn't happen," Johnson said.

"You are being encouraged, and evaluated, and mentored, and managed, and held accountable for doing things that the administration considers to be important," he said. "That does not mean vote Republican versus Democrat; that doesn't mean be pro-life or pro-choice, or be for strict-constructionist judges, or be against strict-constructionist judges," Johnson contended.

"We are controlling what the definition of success is, but shame on us if that's a bad idea. I think it's a really good idea," Johnson said. "It is a mind-set and an approach, and it is a focus on results that [the president] is imposing. It's not 'I want everyone to be like me and have the same political beliefs as me.'"

Checks and Balances

But what if "incest" does happen? Where would a civil servant go to report "verboten" behavior?

Critics of the administration charge that the White House is tampering with the independent structures that protect against waste, fraud, abuse, and political retribution—the federal inspectors general and the Office of General Counsel. The White House vehemently denies the charge.

Rep. Henry Waxman, D-Calif., the top Democrat on the House Government Reform Committee, issued a report last October—and updated it in January— declaring that the Bush administration was appointing inspectors general with political connections to the White House much more frequently than the Clinton administration did. Working with a very small sample—11 IGs appointed by Bush, 32 appointed by Clinton—Waxman's report concludes that 64 percent of the Bush appointees had political experience on their resumes, and only 18 percent had audit experience. For the Clinton appointees, the ratios were reversed: 22 percent had political backgrounds, 66 percent had audit experience.

Gaston Gianni, who until his retirement in December was the Clinton-appointed inspector general at the Federal Deposit Insurance Corporation and vice chairman of the President's Council on Integrity and Efficiency—an IG professional group—said, "I've read the Waxman report. Factually, it's correct. The conclusions, I don't think flow from the facts."

Gianni said it is true that the Bush administration is favoring political background rather than investigative experience in appointing IGs, but he said there is no evidence that the people Bush has appointed have any less independence or zeal for their work.

Nevertheless, Gianni said, the practice worries him. "The environment is such, as we go forward, that the perception will be that, rather than 'small-p' political appointees, they are going to become 'capital-P' Political appointees. Even though nothing else has changed, that is what the perception will be."

Steinzor and NYU's Light agree that the White House has generally sent the message to inspectors that an excess of independence may be bad for their careers.

Last July, Johnson and Gianni signed a memo to inspectors general and agency heads, spelling out the "working relationship principles" for both positions and emphasizing the need for mutual respect, objectivity, and communication between an IG and his or her agency head. Johnson serves as the chairman of the president's council on integrity, and the memo was his idea. Some critics read it as a warning to IGs not to be too aggressive, but Johnson denies any such message.

"The IGs should not be, by definition, adversarial agents," Johnson said. "They are there to prevent waste, fraud, and abuse. The heads of agency are there to prevent waste, fraud, and abuse. The IGs, by definition, are for positive change. . . . Where you get into disagreements is when somebody tries to constantly play 'gotcha,' or where the IG gets a little too enamored of their independent status and tries to do things in a negative fashion, tries to uproot things, or identify things that will hurt the agency," he said. "The IG is there to help the agency."

Johnson said that he had recommended the "relationship principles" to the professional group, but that IGs and agency officials drafted the principles.

Light said there is nothing untoward about principles extolling the virtues of communication and common decency, but he argued that the memo—together with the pattern noted in the Waxman report and some high-profile firings of IGs early in the Bush administration—sets a tone that may have a chilling effect on inspectors.

Johnson dismisses this concern. "I don't think there is any information that suggests that the IGs are less critical than they have been. I don't think there is anything that says they are finding less waste, fraud, and abuse, that they are being less effective IGs as a result of this 'Republican conspiracy.'"

The Office of Special Counsel is a bigger concern for administration critics. Established as an independent agency charged with protecting whistle-blowers and civil servants who are mistreated for political or other reasons unconnected with their performance, the office is in a bitter feud with several of its employees who argue that they are being punished for resisting attempts by Bush's appointee to dismantle the operation.

Among other things, current and former employees charge that Special Counsel Scott Bloch has summarily dismissed hundreds of whistle-blower complaints, instigated a reorganization of the office that will significantly increase political control of investigations, and forced senior staff members critical of his work to choose between relocating to regional offices or being fired. Several anonymous employees, joined by four public-interest groups, filed formal charges against Bloch on March 3, and at least half a dozen staff members have resigned or been fired for refusing to relocate.

Bloch characterizes the complaints against his office as the work of a few disgruntled employees, reinforced by groups that are on a mission to embarrass the White House. Together, these critics are "going out and making reckless allegations that have no truth. They don't like the success Bush officials are having in dealing with the bureaucracy," Bloch said. "They don't want a Bush appointee like myself to get credit" for reducing a large backlog of old cases that were languishing when Bloch took office in 2004. "We have doubled our enforcement over prior years in all areas," Bloch said. His critics "hurl accusations at the office and basically say insulting things about their fellow employees, and they are false."

Levers of Government

An Interior Department official who has worked in the federal government for 30 years denied that the White House is trying to marginalize the civil service, arguing that what people are seeing is simply better executive management from the White House.

"This administration runs a more effective management of the government than did the previous administration, which was a lot more loosey-goosey," this person said, requesting anonymity to speak freely about his bosses. "They bring more of a business mind-set, but I don't think that's a particularly bad thing. They are more organized, and they are smart about it."

The sharper management focus extends into the minutiae of government, giving the White House oversight and control of the executive branch at several levels. In some cases, the Bush administration is creating new approaches, but in most cases, officials are simply using authorities created under prior administrations and applying them more aggressively.

For example, Clinton issued a regulatory-review executive order in 1993, charging OMB's Office of Information and Regulatory Affairs with ensuring that regulations "are consistent with applicable law [and] the president's priorities." The order emphasized use of the best available science and the most cost-effective approach to regulations.

The Bush administration has built on this executive order, setting new requirements for reviewing the costs and benefits of regulatory proposals, establishing a higher threshold for reaching scientific certainty in regulatory decisions, and creating new opportunities for outside experts to challenge the government's conclusions about the dangers that a rule is designed to mitigate.

A regulatory agency career official who demanded anonymity said that OIRA, under the Bush administration, is "much more active" in the regulatory process. "They get involved much earlier in the process on large rules," the official said. "They are reviewing drafts of preambles as they are being written for some rules, or sections of rules."

The executive order gives OMB 90 days to review agency rules, but OIRA Administrator John Graham said in an e-mail response to a reporter's query: "During an important rule-making, OIRA may work informally with agencies at the early stages of the rule-making. This early OIRA participation is designed to make sure that our benefit-cost perspective receives a fair hearing, before key decisions are made and final documents are drafted."

Graham added, "A key benefit of early OIRA involvement is that the pace of rule-making is accelerated by building consensus early in the process and avoiding contentious delays beyond the 90-day review period." He said that the majority of OMB staffers are career civil servants with significant expertise in their issue areas and that, contrary to the assumptions of many critics, OMB involvement does not always result in an outcome that is more favorable to industry. For example, he said, OMB initiated a Food and Drug Administration rule-making to require that producers add the trans-fat content of foods to nutritional labels.

Sally Katzen, who held both John Graham's job and Clay Johnson's job during her years in the Clinton administration, said, "There is nothing wrong with more-centralized review, guidance, and oversight. It is, after all, a president—singular—who is the head of the executive branch." But, she cautioned, "the problems we face are often highly technical or otherwise highly complicated, and those who serve in the White House or OMB do not have all the answers. And they certainly don't have the manpower, the expertise, or the intimate familiarity with the underlying detail. They cannot—and, in my mind, should not—replace the agency expertise, the agency knowledge, and the agency experience."

While OIRA serves as the central regulatory-review office for the White House, OMB has also positioned itself as the central performance-accountability office, with the establishment of the "President's Management Agenda" and the Program Assessment Rating Tool, or PART, under which the White House grades every agency and program on the basis of its management activities and real-world results. After several years of conducting the assessments without imposing any real consequences for failure, the administration, in the first budget proposal of Bush's second term, used the results assessments to justify eliminating or significantly reducing funding for about 150 federal programs.

John Kamensky, who was deputy director of the National Performance Review (the "reinventing government" initiative) in the Clinton administration, said that Bush's White House is, in many ways, simply expanding on efforts begun in the previous administration.

"We had proposed, in the Clinton administration, tying performance to budget, but there wasn't enough performance information to do that. The Bush administration has that information, finally, so it's sort of a natural progression," Kamensky said.

But critics worry that the review process gives the administration the opportunity to establish its own measures of success for programs, without taking into account the requirements established by Congress.

For example, OMB's review declared the Housing and Urban Development Department's Community Development Block Grant program "ineffective," charging that its mission is unclear, it has few measures of success, and it "does not effectively target funds to the most-needy communities."

But a study by a National Academy of Public Administration panel in February disputed OMB's assessment. The program's "statutory mission or purpose seems clear," the panel said. As a block grant, CDBG is able to fund a broad range of community-development functions, and "if the CDBG program lacks clarity, it is likely because the statute intended it so," according to the report. The breadth of the program's activities makes it difficult to provide specific measures of success, the panel concluded, and the White House suggestion that funding be geographically targeted "seems to contradict the statute's intent."

Donald Plusquellic, mayor of Akron, Ohio, and president of the U.S. Conference of Mayors, defends the CDBG program. "I can evaluate anything as a failure if I get to set up the standards," he said.

Johnson acknowledges that CDBG fails the test in part because the administration is applying a new definition of success. "We believe the goal of housing programs is not just to build houses, but the economic development that comes with them. So those are the results we want to focus on," Johnson said. "You can say we are imposing our political views on people, or our favored views of the housing world or the CDBG world on people. Well, guilty as charged. It's important to focus on outcomes, not outputs."

The president has proposed to eliminate the $4 billion block-grant program and shift its functions into a new community and economic development initiative in the Commerce Department. The Senate voted 66–32 last week for a budget amendment designed to block the administration plan.

NYU's Light says the administration has instituted a host of other procedures that centralize power in the White House, ranging from a vetting process for political appointees that allows little independent decision-making for Cabinet officials, to regular conference calls between the White House and the agency chiefs of staff that help to "focus [the staffers'] attention up Pennsylvania Avenue to the White House, and away from down in your department."

But is that a bad thing? The Heritage Foundation's Moffit doesn't think so. "Why would that be anything other than 100 percent American?" Moffit asks. "I elected a president, and I expect the president to run the executive branch of the government. And there is an issue about whether he is? That's absurd."

The role of the civil service is "to make the car run," Moffit said. "And if they have been driving the car east for the past 25 years of their professional life, but the president says, 'Fine, I know you've been going east, but now we're going to go west; you're going to do a 180-degree turn and go in exactly the opposite direction,' their job is to make sure the car goes exactly in the opposite direction. Nobody elected them to do anything else."

Roth of the American Federation of Government Employees disagrees. "You do not entirely change your entire focus every time a president is elected, because it is not the job of the president to pass the laws. It is the job of the president to execute the laws," Roth said. "These laws are on the books, these programs are in regulations." An administration "can't just say, 'We don't like it, so don't do it.'"

8-3

from *The Politics of Presidential Appointments*

David E. Lewis

In this essay, political scientist David Lewis outlines the remarkable history of presidential efforts to control the federal bureaucracy through personnel appointments. Presidents have replaced merit-based positions with presidential appointments, created new layers of political appointees over civil servants, added staff aides to top offices, laid off civil servants, and reorganized departments to accommodate more presidential appointees. As a result, the merit-based civil service today comprises a smaller portion of the federal workforce than it did in the mid-twentieth century.

FEW PEOPLE have heard of Schedule C appointments to the federal service. If queried most would connect a discussion of "Schedule C" to Internal Revenue Service tax forms, but in 1953 the creation of the Schedule C by President Eisenhower was a watershed event in the history of federal personnel management. Eisenhower created this new category of appointments after his inauguration not only in response to pressure from Republican partisans to create more jobs for party members, but also to help rein in the sprawling New Deal bureaucracy created and staffed by presidents Roosevelt and Truman for the previous twenty years. The creation of this new category of federal personnel gave the administration the authority to add over one thousand new appointees to the executive branch and immediately gain substantial influence in important public-policy areas like conservation and the environment.

Prior to Eisenhower's order, important bureaucratic jobs—like director and assistant director of the U.S. Fish and Wildlife Service, director of the National Park Service, and chief and deputy chief of the Soil Conservation Service—had to be filled by career employees who had worked their way up through the agency according to nonpolitical criteria. After Eisenhower's order, these jobs could and were filled by political appointees reviewed by the Republican National Committee and named by the White House. Future presidential administrations expanded the number of jobs included in Schedule C, both managerial positions and other confidential positions like staff, counsel, and special assistant positions.

Source: David E. Lewis, *The Politics of Presidential Appointments: Political Control and Bureaucratic Performance,* by David E. Lewis (Princeton, N.J.: Princeton University Press, 2008), 11–25, 27–37, 39–43, 49–50. Notes appearing in the original have been deleted.

It is hard to understand the details or importance of President Eisenhower's order without an understanding of the history and details of the civil service system in the United States. Very important and practical choices about the number and location of appointees occur in the context of a unique history and sometimes complex set of civil service laws and rules.

This chapter . . . begins with a brief history of the federal personnel system. It then describes the contours of the modern personnel system, including an explanation of the different types of appointed positions and how they get created. The chapter then describes the presidential personnel operation and how it responds to pressures to fill existing positions and satisfy demands for patronage. The next section describes the most common politicization techniques and the tools Congress has used to rein them in. The chapter concludes with a case study of the reorganization of the Civil Service Commission to illustrate the different politicization techniques and demonstrate how politicization is used to change public policy.

A Brief History of the Federal Personnel System

One of the unique features of the Constitution is that it makes virtually no mention of the bureaucracy; its few limited references to departments or officers give virtually no detail apart from the fact that principal officers are to be nominated by the president and confirmed by the Senate. Congress is empowered to determine the means of appointing inferior officers, and the president is granted the ability to request information from principal officers in writing. Apart from these few details the Constitution is silent about the design, function, and administration of the bureaucratic state.

The Constitution's silence leaves responsibility for the creation, nurturing, and maintenance of the continuing government to elected officials, who are divided by different constituencies, institutional responsibilities, and political temperaments. It is the decisions of these persons in the context of a shifting electoral, partisan, and historical landscape that shapes the nature and history of the modern personnel system.

The Personnel System before Merit

The personnel system that presided from 1789 to 1829 was selected and populated by and with persons from the same social class, who were defined by enfranchisement, property, common upbringing, and shared values. They were drawn from what Leonard White calls "a broad class of gentlemen." The selection of federal personnel was dictated in large part by "fitness for public office," but fitness for office was itself defined by standing, wealth, or public reputation rather than relevant experience, expertise, or demonstrated competence.

Long tenure and expectations of continued service were the norm, reinforced by the long dominance of one party in power from 1800 to 1829, the absence of a national party system, and, apparently, the personal conviction of early presidents that persons should not be removed from office because of their political beliefs. Presidents did fill vacancies and newly created offices in the expanding federal government with their partisans, but outright removals of Federalists by Republicans were rare. Regular rotation only occurred at the level of department heads.

The increasingly permanent and class-based federal service did have its detractors. There was a growing sentiment, particularly with expanded franchise, that more positive action needed to be taken to democratize the public service itself. Of particular concern to many were instances where sons inherited the jobs of their fathers, accentuating fears that federal jobs were becoming a type of property or privilege. In 1820 Congress enacted the Tenure of Office Act, requiring the explicit reappointment of all federal officials every four years as a way of contravening the establishment of a professional class.

The old system was not overturned fully until the presidency of Andrew Jackson. Upon assuming office in 1829 Jackson said, "The duties of all public officers are, or at least admit of being made, so plain and simple that men of intelligence may readily qualify themselves for their performance; I can not but believe that more is lost by the long continuance of men in office than is generally to be gained by their experience." Jackson believed that public office was not reserved for a particular class or incumbents in government. Rather, it should be opened to the broader public. The political benefits of such an action were not lost on Jackson.

While his actions to democratize the federal service only led to the turnover of 10 percent of the federal workforce, his actions set in motion a full-fledged patronage system in the United States. Undergirded by the development of national parties hungry for federal office as a way of securing funds and votes, the regular rotation of a large percentage of federal offices became the norm. The national parties, loose confederations of state and local parties, gave out offices and expected activity for the party and political assessments in return. Office holders would return 1 to 6 percent of their salaries to the party. . . .

The vast majority of federal jobs were located outside of Washington, D.C. They were an important political resource and were viewed proprietarily by congressmen who sought to distribute patronage to local and state machines that brought them to power. Presidents were expected to consult with the senators and, to a lesser extent, representatives in the states where appointments were made. The power of this norm was reinforced by the practice of senatorial courtesy whereby the Senate would refuse to confirm a nomination if an objection was raised by the senator from the state where the appointment was being made. While some strong presidents, such as Jackson or Polk, resisted this norm in principle, all usually followed it in practice.

The deleterious consequences of the spoils system for bureaucratic performance were somewhat mitigated by several factors. First, Andrew Jackson was partly right that many federal jobs did not require a tremendous amount of expertise or special training. . . . Most of the work in the civil service was still clerical and very little authority or discretion was delegated to subcabinet officials. In addition, many of the persons turned out of office with electoral turnover would return once their party returned to power.

Second, jobs requiring more expertise were sometimes filled by persons who did not turn over with each administration. Certain auditors, comptrollers, clerks, and personnel in the scientific offices stayed from administration to administration to conduct the business of government. . . . Indeed, some employees of long tenure moved up to key positions because of their expertise. Their competence and expertise in public work outweighed party patronage considerations in their selection.

This dual personnel system persisted during a period when the size and activities of government were limited. As the federal government grew in size and complexity, however, the weaknesses of the spoils system became increasingly apparent. The quality of the federal service suffered. Rotation in office did lead to the dismissal of many qualified federal officials, such as those who kept the accounts and records, made it difficult to sustain reforms, and prevented the development of consistent, purposeful management practices. Rotation-induced instability prevented functional specialization and the development of managerial and policy-specific expertise. These factors, coupled with low pay, decreased the prestige of federal jobs and their reliability as long-term careers. Day-to-day performance was also hindered by the low quality of patronage appointees who were only competent in their jobs by happy accident or the limited requirements of their occupations. Many appointees spent a portion of their time in other jobs, in work for the party, or in leisure.

. . . The challenges of the Civil War, economic and territorial expansion, periodic monetary crises, massive immigration, and technological change meant the federal government would need to take on new responsibilities and expand to fit its new roles; and public pressure for greater federal government involvement meant the administration of government would have to change. It would have to specialize, organize, and stabilize in order to provide the expertise and services demanded by agricultural interests, businesses, pensioners, consumers, and voters

of all types through their elected officials. Congress and the president faced increasing pressure to build a professional bureaucracy by enacting civil service reforms.

The Creation and Extension of Merit

A number of different groups were involved in the nascent push for civil service
reform. Included among these groups were urban merchants, bankers, and brokers, often motivated by their own frustrating experience with corrupt and inefficient postal offices and customs houses. A larger class of professionals including
lawyers, academics, journalists, and clergy were also supportive of reform, partly
as a moral crusade against the corruptions of the spoils system but also as a
means of confronting a political system not responsive enough to their interests.
Agency officials were also supportive of reform as a means of improving the
performance of offices they were supposed to manage.

Efforts to alter the system usually engendered hostility from the parties and
their sympathizers in Congress. As public pressure to change the personnel system mounted, however, the national parties acquiesced reluctantly, fearful of
giving up the patronage they held or hoped to gain in the next election. They
became more supportive when they needed to cultivate reform-oriented voters.
They were also more supportive when they were out of power or expected to
lose power since civil service would limit the opposition party's control over
spoils. . . .

The first serious government-wide attempt at reform came in the 1870s during the Grant Administration. The reform was motivated more by a desire to
heal divisions in the Republican Party than that for substantive reform.
Republicans had experienced significant losses in the 1870 elections and a split
emerged among reformers within the party and Grant-aligned machine elements, particularly in the Senate. To appease reformers, Grant requested a law
authorizing the president to issue regulations governing the admission of persons to the civil service, to hire employees to assess the fitness of persons for the
civil service, and to establish regulations governing the conduct of civil servants
appointed under the new regulations. In response, the Republican majority delegated to the president sweeping authority to create a civil service system with
the hope of bridging the rift before the 1872 elections.

When the commission recommended its first set of rules in 1872, Republicans
in Congress said little. After the 1872 elections, however, their tone changed.
When the first civil service examinations came on-line in the Treasury
Department in 1873, members of Congress were openly hostile. They responded
by refusing appropriations for the commission in 1874. Since Grant's primary
interest in the commission was to hold together the different factions in the

party, he did little to defend it. When Congress refused to appropriate funds again in 1875, Grant revoked the commission's rules and closed its offices.

Rutherford B. Hayes pledged to support civil service reform during his candidacy in 1876. When he assumed office in 1877 he requested appropriations from Congress to reactivate the Grant Civil Service Commission. Congress turned down his request, but Hayes took a number of other actions to further the cause of civil service. He appointed noted civil service reformer Carl Schurz as Secretary of the Interior, where Schurz installed a vigorous merit system. Hayes also instituted competitive examinations in the New York City customhouse and post office after a public investigation of the customhouse and a bitter feud with Senator Conkling from New York over patronage.

Hayes's actions coincided with the formation of a number of civil service reform associations. These organizations appeared earliest in the northeast where Hayes's controversy over appointments to the New York customhouse drew the most attention. By 1881 the number of groups had grown substantially and societies existed from San Francisco to New York.

The assassination of Hayes's successor, James Garfield, by a disappointed office seeker in the summer of 1881 galvanized popular support for a more concrete and permanent merit system. One month after Garfield's assassination, the local civil service reform associations that started during the Hayes administration coalesced into the National Civil Service Reform League. In December 1881, Democratic Senator George Pendleton introduced reform legislation drafted by the league. The bill was reported from committee in May 1882 but had little support in the Republican Congress. The league, however, pressured for the legislation with a poster campaign and the publication of lists of opponents to civil service reform. With Garfield's assassination reformers had their crystallizing event and leading journals and newspapers aided their efforts.

Enthusiasm for reform increased after the elections in the fall of 1882. Republicans fared poorly and reform was clearly an issue. President Chester Arthur expressed his support for the legislation, and debate on the Pendleton bill began as soon as Congress convened on December 12, 1882. Debate lasted through December 27 and on January 16, 1883, President Arthur signed the Pendleton Act into law. The law created—for the first time in the United States—a merit-based federal civil service.

The law provided for the creation of a three-person bipartisan Civil Service Commission (CSC) that would administer exams and promulgate rules under the act. Under the provisions of the Pendleton Act only 10.5 percent of all federal workers were included in the merit system, and these were primarily employees in large post offices or customs houses. Some employees from the departmental service in Washington, D.C.[,] were also included. At this time being under the merit system meant only that persons had to do well on competitive examinations to be appointed. There were no effective protections against adverse job actions or firing after appointment. Job tenure was only protected by the requirement that new persons appointed to the job had to have done well on the same competitive examination. Formal job tenure and protection from partisan dismissal were not established until the late 1890s. Rigorous prohibition on political activity by civil servants was not enacted until Congress passed the Hatch Act in 1939.

The Pendleton Act delegated to the president authority to add the remaining unclassified federal jobs into the merit system with the exception of positions requiring Senate confirmation and common laborers. Presidents added significantly to the civil service through presidential action; 65 percent of the growth in civil service coverage between 1884 and 1903 was through executive order. Once positions were added, it was difficult for Congress to remove them since they would presumably have to do so over the president's veto. They were unlikely to override a president's veto given that one party was sure to prefer to have these positions under civil service at any given time. . . .

Presidents, with a few exceptions, resisted pressures to remove positions once they had been included in the merit system. Presidents were bolstered by the interests that had pushed for the enactment of civil service reform in the first place. Notably, civil service reform leagues continued to push for the preservation and expansion of the federal merit system while also pressuring states and localities to adopt reforms of their own. Efforts to roll back merit system gains were met with howls of protest . . . .

Nascent government unions also pushed for the expansion of the merit system. The passage of the Pendleton Act provided an environment in which federal employees could organize more easily since the act weakened the ties of federal employees to political patrons. Workers in several occupations, such as mail carriers and postal clerks, organized in the late 1880s and early 1890s. Postal unions were particularly effective at lobbying for pay increases and tenure protections. . . .

These unions were instrumental in the passage of the Lloyd-Lafollette Act in 1912 that formally allowed the unionization of government workers (provided they joined unions that would not strike). The act also prohibited dismissal for reasons other than efficiency, and gave employees the right to be notified of possible firing in writing and respond.

The Lloyd-Lafollette [A]ct spurred a period of more aggressive unionization and the National Federation of Federal Employees organized in 1917 under the auspices of the American Federation of Labor (AFL). This was followed by the American Federation of Government Employees (AFGE) in 1932 and the United Federal Workers of America (under the Congress of Industrial Organizations [CIO]) in 1937. These unions, along with the occupation-specific unions like the postal unions, were instrumental in securing higher salaries and benefits for federal workers. They helped secure the enactment of the Civil Service Retirement Act of 1920 and the Classification Acts of 1923 and 1949. The former provided retirement and survivor benefits as well as improved tenure protections for civil service workers. The latter two acts created a job classification and pay system on the principle of equal pay for equal work and outlined detailed grievance procedures that strengthened worker protections against adverse personnel actions. . . .

The merit system continued to expand as all nineteenth-century and most twentieth-century presidents through Franklin Delano Roosevelt used executive orders to include new classes of employees in the merit system. Presidents frequently blanketed positions into the civil service just prior to leaving office. It was not unusual for Congress to allow new agencies to be created outside the merit system originally, only to add them into the system later. For example, many agencies created to mobilize for war or to combat the Great Depression were originally created outside the merit system. In some cases, the creation of new agencies and new programs provided patronage opportunities that excited either the president or Congress. In fact, in the 1930s Congress on occasion specifically prohibited the president from placing agencies in the merit system. Once these agencies were populated according to the dictates of the politicians in power, they moved to blanket them into the civil service system. This protected their partisans from removal and ensured a degree of long-term loyalty to the programmatic mission of the agencies or to the patrons themselves.

The percentage of federal jobs in the traditional merit system has varied substantially over time (Figure 1). By 1897, the advent of the McKinley presidency, close to 50 percent of the federal civilian workforce was under the merit system, and by 1932 close to 80 percent of federal workers held merit positions, a proportion that dipped during the New Deal but reached its peak of almost 88 percent in 1951. This figure underestimates the actual extension of the merit system because many employees not covered by the traditional merit system were employed under other agency-specific personnel systems, like the Tennessee Valley Authority (TVA) or the Foreign Service, which included merit-like provisions. In addition, many of the excluded employees were employed overseas and were unlikely to be consequential for patronage.

While the percentage of jobs included in the merit system peaked at midcentury, it is now decreasing as the federal government shifts its strategy away from a one-size-fits-all personnel system to an agency-specific model. This trend has accelerated at the start of the twenty-first century, since Congress enacted legislation providing both the Department of Homeland Security and the Department of Defense with authority to create their own personnel systems. If these new systems are implemented effectively, the number of federal employees under

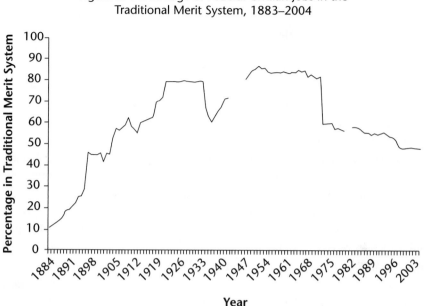

Figure 1. Percentage of Federal Civilian Jobs in the
Traditional Merit System, 1883–2004

the traditional merit system will dip below 30 percent of the federal civilian workforce.

The Modern Personnel System

Today the federal government employs 2.5 million civilians in full-time positions (and 1.4 million uniformed military personnel). Each civilian job is defined by a pay category and an appointment authority. To ensure equal pay for equal work, an elaborate pay system, including three primary classification schemes for blue-collar, white-collar, and top-level management positions, has been developed. The Federal Wage System (FWS) covers trade, craft, skilled, and unskilled laborers. The General Schedule (GS) defines the pay rates for administrative, technical, and professional jobs, while the Senior Level and Scientific and Professional (SL/ST) system does the same for high-level, but nonmanagerial, positions. Top-level management and professional jobs are covered under the Senior Executive Service (SES) pay schedule or the Executive Schedule (EX). The EX, with a few exceptions, is reserved for positions requiring presidential nomination and Senate confirmation. In each pay system there is a series of numerical pay categories that in the GS system are called *grades*. There are currently fifteen grades in the GS system. These pay categories define a pay range for jobs with equivalent levels of responsibility, qualifications, or experience. Each pay category allows for some flexibility in differentiating between employees who hold similar positions but have different levels of experience or backgrounds. In the GS system these are called *steps*. . . .

Of the 2.5 million full-time civilian employees, about 1.32 million are included in the traditional merit system. At the heart of the civil service system is a series of rules and regulations governing how people can obtain federal jobs and what their rights are with regard to promotion, removal, and other personnel actions. Merit system principles demand that persons be hired, promoted, and fired only on the basis of merit rather than on other factors, such as party membership, gender, or race. Persons initially establish their merit through competitive examination or, in some cases, appropriate background qualifications. Once a person's qualifications have been established, a determination is made about his or her eligibility for both position and pay grade. Persons employed under the merit system have a series of rights formerly defined in the *Federal Personnel Manual*, most notably rights to notification and appeal in cases of adverse personnel actions such as demotion or removal. These rights are now defined in the *Code of Federal Regulations* and various Office of Personnel Management (OPM) handbooks.

Excepted Positions

As suggested above, more than half of all federal jobs are now "excepted" from the traditional merit system described above (Figure 1). The excepted service is a residual category, catching all jobs that are not subject to the appointment provisions of Title 5 of the United States Code. There are four categories of excepted jobs: positions requiring presidential nomination and Senate confirmation (PAS); jobs filled by persons in the SES; positions in what are known as Schedules A, B, and C; and positions in agency-specific personnel systems.

The most visible positions outside the traditional merit system are those that require presidential nomination and Senate confirmation. These positions are at the top of the federal personnel hierarchy. The United States Constitution (Article II, sec. 2, cl. 2) requires that all "ambassadors, other public ministers and consuls, judges of the Supreme Court, and all other officers of the United States" be appointed in this manner. The manner of appointing "inferior" officers is up to Congress (and the president) as the result of legislative determinations. Where one draws the line between "principal" and "inferior" officers, however, is unclear. In 2004 there were 1,137 PAS positions in the executive branch, about 945 of which were policymaking positions. The remainder is comprised of appointments to minor advisory or committee-supervisory roles often requiring only part-time employment, paid on a per diem basis. Of the 945 positions, about 186 were U.S. attorneys or U.S. marshals and 154 were ambassadors, leaving

Figure 2. Federal Civilian Personnel System Appointment Authorities

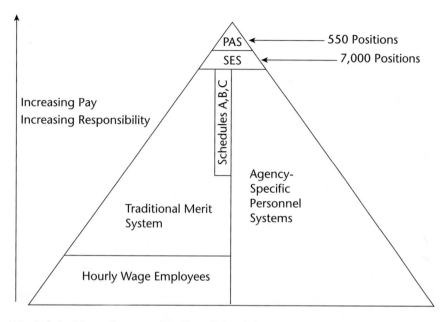

Note: Excludes job-specific excepted positions. PAS excludes part-time, advisory, U.S. Attorneys, U.S. Marshals, and ambassadorial positions. The "excepted service" includes PAS, SES, Schedules A, B, C, and personnel in agency-specific personnel systems.

550–600 key executive PAS positions in the cabinet departments and major independent agencies. The average cabinet department dealing with domestic affairs has fifteen to thirty PAS positions, including a secretary, a deputy secretary, a handful of under- and assistant secretaries, an inspector general, and a chief financial officer.

Between PAS positions and the competitive civil service in the federal hierarchy is a space filled by a mixture of career employees from the Senior Executive Service (SES) and political appointees who will be designated noncareer members of this service. The SES was created by the Civil Service Reform Act of 1978 and is comprised of a cadre of approximately 7,000 senior management officials. The OPM, based on its own assessment and the requests of agencies, allocates a certain number of SES positions to each department or agency, and the administration chooses which of the jobs in the agency will be SES jobs. Presidents or their subordinates can choose either an existing member of the SES (a career civil servant who applied to be a part of the SES) or a political appointee from outside who will fill an SES job. By law political appointees cannot exceed 10 percent of the entire SES or 25 percent of the allocated SES positions in a specific agency. In 2004 there were 6,811 persons in the SES, 674 of whom were appointees. Some examples of appointed SES positions include Chief of Staff at the U.S Agency for

International Development, Director of Intergovernmental Affairs for the Department of Defense, Deputy Assistant Secretary for Special Education and Rehabilitative Services, and Deputy General Counsel in the Department of Health and Human Services.

A key motivation in creating the SES was to give presidents more flexibility in controlling policy and programmatic positions pivotal for implementing the administration's program. One way in which it did this was to provide more appointees at this level; another was to increase the ease with which presidents could reassign career senior management officials. Under the law the president can reassign a career SES executive to any other position, provided the president and the new agency head have been in office for at least 120 days and the executive has been given 15 days notice (60 if the reassignment includes a geographical change).

Since the creation of the merit system it has been clear that there are some positions for which it is not feasible to hold exams, even in agencies where the merit system is otherwise entirely appropriate. There are three classes of such positions, designated as Schedules A, B, and C. There are no examinations at all for Schedule A positions, which historically have included lawyers, military chaplains, or positions in isolated localities. Schedule B positions have examinations attached to them but they establish a threshold level of acceptability and do not utilize comparisons among applicants. This schedule has included positions in new agencies or programs for which there are no established directions or guidelines, federal work-study positions, and positions set aside for those with certain types of disabilities.

The third schedule, Schedule C, is reserved for positions of a confidential or policy-determining nature. As the start of the chapter suggested, the schedule was created by President Eisenhower in 1953. Schedule C originally included both management positions below the PAS level and the assorted staff assigned to appointees (confidential assistants, drivers, and so forth). As such, the pay range for Schedule C appointees varied dramatically according to position. Top-level management positions in Schedule C were eventually converted to NEA [National Education Association] positions in 1966 and SES positions in 1978. Lower-paying Schedule C positions remain (GS 15 and below). In 2004 there were 1,596 persons appointed to Schedule C positions in the federal government.

These constitute an important subtype of political appointment and, while technically selected by agency officials, presidents since Reagan have exercised substantial control over them. . . . Typical Schedule C posts include special or confidential assistants to PAS appointees, directors of communications, press, or outreach offices, and officials in legislative liaison offices. Some current examples include the White House liaison in the Department of Interior, the confidential assistant to the Assistant Secretary of Education for Vocational and Adult Education, and the Director of Media Affairs in the Department of Labor.

The last, and by far the largest, set of positions are excepted because they are located in agencies that have authority to govern their own personnel systems (Table 1). They can be low- or high-paying jobs of varying levels of responsibility and character. Calling them "excepted" is something of a misnomer, however, since the rights of employees in these personnel systems are usually very similar to those in the Title 5 civil service system. There has been a dramatic increase in the number of "excepted" jobs because recent congressional decisions give certain agencies authority to create their own personnel systems outside the merit system defined by Title 5. The most significant actions in this regard have been the reorganization in 1970 of the postal service into a government corporation, with its own personnel system (800,000 employees); the creation of the Department of Homeland Security in 2002, with authority to create its own personnel system (170,000 civilian employees); and Congress's decision in 2003 to grant the Department of Defense authority to create its own personnel system (660,000 civilian employees). Agencies, bolstered by outside critiques of the federal personnel system, have long clamored for more control over their own personnel systems, claiming that they need more flexibility in hiring, promoting, and firing in order to improve performance. Flexible personnel systems allow them to respond more quickly to changes in the job market, agency personnel

Table 1. Examples of Agencies with Broad Exceptions from
the Traditional Merit Personnel System

Department of Defense
Department of Homeland Security
Federal Aviation Agency
United States Postal Service
Postal Rates Commission
Central Intelligence Agency
National Security Agency
Tennessee Valley Authority
Federal Bureau of Investigation
General Accounting Office
Panama Canal Commission
Board of Governors, Federal Reserve System
Peace Corps
Railroad Retirement Board
Overseas Private Investment Corporation
Nuclear Regulatory Commission
Federal Election Commission

Source. U.S. General Accounting Office 1997a; U.S. Senate 2000.

needs, and new programmatic responsibilities. Increased flexibility, however, can also lead to fewer protections against abuses in hiring, firing, and promotion, as well as inequities in pay, benefits, and treatment for comparable work.

In sum, politicization, when it does occur, is, at the top levels, defined both by pay and by appointment authority. It involves an increase in the number of PAS, SES, Schedule C, and similarly excepted agency-specific appointees.

The Modern Presidential Personnel Process

Given these different types of appointments, it is worth reviewing how presidents and their staffs go about filling PAS positions and determining where to place SES and Schedule C appointees. Both policy and patronage concerns shape modern personnel politics. On the policy side, presidents are confronted with a need to fill hundreds of executive-level PAS positions across the government requiring specific skills, experience, and expertise. These jobs range from the Secretary of Defense to the Assistant Secretary of Labor for Occupational Safety and Health to the Under Secretary of Commerce for Intellectual Property. The success of the administration in controlling the bureaucracy depends upon their success in filling these slots. . . .

There is almost uniform concern articulated voluntarily by persons involved in presidential personnel about how important it is to find loyal people with the right skills and background to fill these jobs. . . . Personnel is policy and White House officials recognize that in order to get control of policy, you need people who are loyal to the president and qualified for the job to which they have been appointed. In practice, evaluations of competence can be colored by ideology and the immediate need to fill literally thousands of jobs. Reagan aide Lyn Nofziger, for example, stated, "As far as I'm concerned, anyone who supported Reagan is competent." That said, and importantly, most senior personnel officials define their job as finding the most competent people for senior administration posts.

Starting with President Nixon, many presidents have employed professional recruiters to help identify qualified persons for top executive posts. The most important personnel task at the start of each administration is that of identifying candidates to fill these positions. Each administration has produced lists of positions to be filled first. These include positions important for public safety but also usually positions that need to be filled early to advance the president's policy agenda. Transition advice to President Kennedy focused on the "pressure points" in government. In the Reagan administration the transition focused first on the "Key 87" positions, which included executive posts necessary for implementation of Reagan's economic program. These priority positions naturally receive the most attention throughout the president's term whenever vacancies occur. In some cases, the existing number of positions is sufficient to gain control and advance the president's agenda; in others, it is not.

On the patronage side, presidents and their personnel operations are besieged by office seekers who have a connection to the campaign, to the party, interest groups, or patrons in Congress important to the administration. Recent administrations have received tens of thousands of resumes, and even more recommendations and communications dealing with specific candidates or jobs. . . . Overall, the Clinton administration received over 100,000 resumes. . . .

Dealing with requests for jobs involves evaluating the skills and backgrounds of priority job seekers and locating appropriate or defensible jobs in levels of pay and responsibility. In many cases, priority placements are young, inexperienced, or primarily qualified through political work. This makes them unqualified for top executive posts. The less background experience, the harder it is to find them jobs. Such applicants are usually given staff, liaison, advance, and public affairs jobs for which they are best qualified given their campaign experience. In other cases, people connected to the candidates either through personal relationships or contributions are too senior to take such jobs but are either not qualified for or not interested in top executive posts. Personnel officials often recommend these persons for ambassadorships, positions on commissions, or advisory posts. . . .

In practice, presidents and their subordinates in presidential personnel (PPO) determine the number and location of political appointees by starting with where their predecessor had appointees and then making incremental adjustments. Each administration learns what jobs were filled by appointees in the last administration through a variety of sources, including transition reports produced by teams sent to the different agencies in the executive branch prior to the inauguration, contacts with the previous administration, and government publications. Subsequent adjustments to the number and location of appointees are made based upon concerns about policy and the need to satisfy concerns for patronage.

The distinction drawn between policy and patronage activities in presidential personnel is not to suggest that policy-driven personnel practices have no patronage component or that efforts to reward campaign supporters cannot influence policy. On the contrary, patronage concerns invariably influence appointments, and appointees of all types can influence policy outputs. Rather, the point is that one process revolves primarily around filling *positions* and the other process revolves primarily around placing *persons*. These two fundamentally different goals are managed differently and have different effects on the number and penetration of political appointments in the bureaucracy.

Common Politicization Techniques

One factor that can influence the number and penetration of appointees in specific cases is the extent to which presidents and their appointees confront career personnel in management positions that do not share their ideology or priorities. Conflict between the president and agencies can emerge for a number of reasons. Sometimes the disagreement stems from what agencies do. Some agencies are designed with a specific policy goal in mind. For example, the Office of Economic Opportunity was the hallmark of Lyndon Johnson's Great Society. It was anathema to Richard Nixon, and he set about politicizing (and dismantling) it in the early 1970s.

In other cases the political biases of a particular agency have less to do with the mission of the agency embedded in law or executive decree than with issues of personnel. Career managers can be unresponsive because they are known to be partisans from the other party. For example, surveys of top executives from the Nixon and Ford administrations showed that many top managers, particularly executives in social service agencies, were unsympathetic to the policy goals of the Nixon administration. More recent surveys confirm that top careerists in defense agencies are more likely to be Republican and conservative, whereas top careerists in social welfare agencies are likely to be Democrats and liberal.

Career managers also often feel bound by legal, moral, or professional norms to certain courses of action and these courses of action may be at variance with the president's agenda. Agencies act to implement policy directives spelled out in statutes, executive decrees, or informal directions from Congress. They are legally bound to implement the laws enacted, and the amount of discretion administrators possess to alter policy is not always clear. Differences of opinion arise about both managers' power and their responsibilities given this power. This is starkly illustrated in cases where career employees are asked to implement administrative policies they believe to be of questionable legality. For instance, career employees make administrative changes in the level and type of civil rights enforcement that might or might not include affirmative action as a remedy. Directions from political appointees can also bump up against professional norms. The ranger in the Forest Service, the statistician in the Bureau of Labor Statistics, and the lawyer in the Justice Department has a point beyond which they cannot go and still maintain their professional integrity. . . .

A number of different techniques for politicizing agencies address the perceived lack of responsiveness from career officials. These techniques are often used concurrently with other strategies for gaining control of the bureaucracy, such as budgeting, public statements, and administrative actions. To help visualize what this problem looks like, consider Figure 3, an organizational chart from a hypothetical department in which the top three levels are filled by presidential

Figure 3. Hypothetical Agency Problem

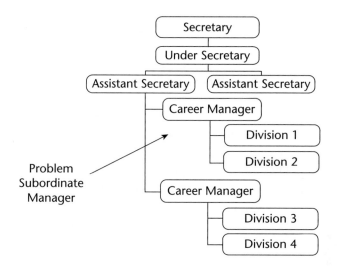

appointments with Senate confirmation. Below this is a level of career managers who direct the operating programs and bureaus. Assume that one of these career managers is unresponsive or problematic to the administration in power for one of the reasons listed above.

Replacement

The first and most obvious solution to this dilemma is to remove the resistant career manager and replace this person with an appointee or more acceptable career person. If the position is a general SES position the president can replace the career SES manager with an appointee after a period of time, provided doing so will not put the agency over the statutory limit for the number of appointees in the SES or agency.

The president can also try to change the appointment authority of the position in question (Figure 4). For example, a presidential administration could change a GS 15 career management position to a Schedule C position or a general SES position. Changes in appointment authority can sometimes be performed internally, as in the case of deciding which jobs are SES jobs. In other cases changes are performed with a request to the Office of Personnel Management (or earlier, the CSC). Most experienced personnel officers know how to use the appropriate terms of art to ensure their applications are approved. The OPM director and many of her subordinates serve at the pleasure of the president, easing the way for the White House to get its way. . . .

Figure 4. Replacement

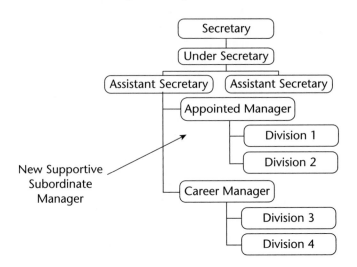

There are . . . three techniques well known in bureaucratic lore for getting unwanted employees to leave their current jobs. The first and most obvious strategy for convincing a careerist to leave is the *frontal assault*. Political appointees meet privately with the career manager in question and tell the manager that her services are no longer needed. Career managers are offered help finding another job, a going-away party, and even a departmental award. The career manager is informed that if she refuses to leave, her employment record and references will suffer.

The career manager can also be *transferred* within the agency to a position she is unlikely to accept. The transfer offer is usually accompanied by a raise and perhaps a promotion to a newly created position. In such cases, appointees know ahead of time the types of jobs the career employee is likely or unlikely to accept. For example, the career manager known to have strong ties to the East Coast may be offered a job in Dallas or St. Louis. Appointees inform the career employee that if she does not want the new job, she can resign without prejudice from the agency and stay on in their current position for a limited amount of time until she finds another position.

With a change in administration, careerists identified with the past administration's policies worry about being transferred to "turkey farms"—jobs with few responsibilities, limited staff, and no access to policymaking. . . . As noted above, by law SES careerists cannot be removed without consent for 120 days by the new administration, but many waive these rights if the new administration requests it. If career employees do not waive this right, the new administration can transfer them after 120 days, provided they have been given appropriate written notice.

A related strategy is the *new-activity* technique. Political appointees hatch plans for a new agency initiative, and the career employee in question is selected for the job ostensibly on the basis of his past performance and unique qualifications. The career manager is even promoted and given an increase in pay. The new initiative appears to be meaningful, but the real purpose behind it is to move the career manager out of his current position. . . .

Layering

Political appointees' difficulty in getting what they want through attempting to remove career employees and reclassifying their jobs often leads them to adopt other strategies. One of the most prominent is *layering,* the practice of adding politically appointed managers on top of career managers as a means of enhancing political control. . . . These new appointees can more carefully monitor the career managers and assume some of their policy-determining responsibilities through their influence in budget preparation, personnel decisions, and other administrative responsibilities. . . .

Add Appointed Ministerial Staff

A similar strategy is to *add appointed ministerial staff.* For instance, the Senate-confirmed assistant secretary adds two special assistants. Titled positions like assistant secretaries often acquire title-riding appointees like chiefs of staff, special assistants, counsels, and public affairs personnel to help them perform their job. The strategy of adding ministerial staff is different from layering in that the appointees added have little formal authority. While they have little formal authority, such appointees can acquire substantial informal authority as experts, gatekeepers, and public spokespeople.

Ministerial staff of this type usually comprises Schedule C appointees. Schedule C positions are created specifically for persons attached to the incoming appointees. Schedule C appointees gain power from being the primary advisors to higher-level appointees and from speaking with the implied authority of the appointee. In other contexts ministerial staff is given special projects, review budgets and legal documents, and help in personnel and administrative decisions. Schedule C positions can be training grounds for other appointed positions. Persons working for higher-level appointees often gain valuable experience and exposure and move from these positions into managerial positions with more formal responsibility.

Reorganization

A fourth common politicization technique is *reorganization*. Reorganization has been used strategically by managers to diminish the influence of problematic career managers and enhance political control. . . . The nominal purpose of the reorganization can be to align organizational structure to better meet the bureau's stated goals or to increase efficiency but have the real or dual purpose of getting better control of the bureau. In large, modern agencies with complicated organizational structures, reorganizations can be subtle and effective means of getting political appointees in charge of important administrative responsibilities. In reorganizations, positions are created and disbanded, upgraded and downgraded, and these decisions are informed by the political needs of administration officials.

For example, in the 1980s enforcement activities within the Environmental Protection Agency (EPA) were reorganized at least three times. In 1981 the Office of Enforcement was disbanded and the legal staff was parsed out to various other offices within the agency. EPA director Anne Burford assembled a new Office of Legal and Enforcement Counsel not long after, but key positions remained vacant into 1982. In 1983 a distinct Office of Enforcement Counsel was created under an assistant administrator. The effect of Burford's reorganizations, however, was to diminish the influence of inherited personnel partly through a decline in morale and high turnover among attorneys who had served in the old Office of Enforcement.

Reorganization can also be used to create parallel bureaucratic structures or processes to circumvent existing structures. This form of politicization takes two common forms. In the first, a new manager who is sympathetic to the goals of the administration is added to the management structure with staff and resources. . . . In this case, however, it is not the problematic career manager who is given this post; rather, it is the trusted, sympathetic manager with closer ties to the administration. This manager duplicates or explicitly assumes tasks performed by the division headed by the less-responsive career manager. The administration then cuts the disfavored manager out of decision making and downgrades the manager's division. . . .

Reductions-in-Force (RIF)

The final prominent technique for politicizing is the *reduction-in-force (RIF)*. While RIFs are a normal part of organizational life in both the private and public sectors, they can also be used strategically to transform an unresponsive agency. Through RIFs federal officials cut employment as a way of getting control of the bureau.

According to a general rule of "save grade, save pay," those career employees with the least experience lose their jobs first during RIFs, but those who stay with more seniority are bumped down in position and often assume tasks that are new or are different from what they were doing before. They often have to do more work for the same amount of pay, and the new tasks they assume are frequently jobs not performed by people in their pay scale. These ripple effects increase attrition beyond that caused by the initial RIF. For example, reducing the employment of Division 1 and Division 2 will lead to attrition in both divisions. The career manager in charge of these divisions and her subordinates will have to do more work with fewer employees and manage through declining morale for an administration with whom they likely disagree ideologically.

The Reagan administration's treatment of the Council on Environmental Quality (CEQ) is a good example of this approach. In 1982 the CEQ's staff had been reduced from forty-nine, under President Carter, to fifteen. The administration fired all of the immediate council staff, some of whom had served since the Nixon and Ford administrations. Appointees from the campaign staff replaced those removed.

Informal Aids to Politicization

There are also a number of ways to augment politicization efforts informally. One common technique for politicizing administration is to leave career positions vacant for significant periods of time and have appointees take over these responsibilities in an acting role. For example, during the second George W. Bush administration, when Sandra Bates, a career manager within the General Services Administration (GSA), decided to leave her position as Commissioner of the Federal Technology Service (FTS), Barbara Shelton was selected to fill that job in an acting role until a replacement was found. Although career managers generally assume acting roles when appointees leave, Shelton was an appointee. She was the politically appointed regional administrator of the GSA's Mid-Atlantic region. No immediate plans were announced to select a permanent replacement in the agency. GSA was pursuing an internal reorganization wherein the FTS would be merged with the Federal Supply Service.

With lax oversight and informal norms, different presidential administrations have also been successful in influencing personnel choices inside the *civil service* without changing the appointment authority of the jobs themselves. Technically, personnel chosen for positions under the merit system are to be chosen outside the influence of politics. In reality, both Congress and the president can strongly influence the hiring of careerists at higher levels in the permanent federal service. The most formal and blatant attempt to do this was the Eisenhower administration's

"Willis Directive." Charles Willis, an assistant to Eisenhower chief-of-staff Sherman Adams, wrote and circulated an elaborate personnel plan for the new administration. The plan invited officials from the Republican National Committee (RNC), Republican congressmen, or other prominent state Republicans to recommend personnel for jobs both *inside* and outside the civil service. All jobs at GS 14 and above were called "controlled" positions. Federal agencies were to announce vacancies on forms supplied by the RNC and make regular reports to the RNC on how vacancies were filled. Both the spirit and contents of the plan violated Civil Service Rule 4, which state[s] that career positions are to be filled "without regard to political or religious affiliation." . . .

In total, the numbers and percentages of appointees vary from administration to administration because of replacement, layering, reorganization, and RIFs. These politicization techniques can be augmented by less formal techniques, such as strategic vacancies, political influence in the hiring of careerists, and bending of the rules in administrative determinations and rulings.

Congressional Responses

Of course, politicization choices happen with an eye toward Congress since the legislative branch has both the means of learning about politicization and a variety of ways to respond. . . . Civil servants in the affected agencies complain to the press or friendly members of Congress. As one personnel official explained to me, "the *Washington Post* is their inspector general." Others confirmed that the possibility that their actions might appear on the front page of the *Washington Post* constrained personnel actions. Personnel officials also suggested that members of Congress were attentive to appointee head-counts, and the existence of congressional reports including such counts confirms their claim.

Personnel officials recognize that their missteps can lead to problems for the president and adjust their behavior accordingly. At minimum, an influential member of Congress can informally communicate his displeasure with the agency or the White House. Members can also publicize the president's action, creating an embarrassing situation for the White House. For example, in 1987 several Democratic members of Congress accused the Reagan administration of "packing" the top ranks of government with appointees to the detriment of the federal service. Backed by a GAO report tracking appointments, these members denounced an increase in appointees to the SES, particularly in the agencies that manage the government such as the OPM (personnel), the GSA (facilities), and the OMB (finances). During the Clinton administration, Republicans publicly complained about the politicization of the Commerce Department, and they requested that the GAO investigate the burrowing of Democratic appointees and staff into civil service positions. In the second George W. Bush administration, the

Democratic minority used charges of cronyism coupled with data on appointee increases to score political points.

More concretely, Congress can refuse presidential requests to create new Senate-confirmed positions or use their appropriations power to limit these and other types of appointed positions. For example, efforts to elevate the EPA to a cabinet department in the George H. W. Bush administration were derailed partly due to Congress's refusal to accede to the president's requests for additional appointees. Congress has also enacted limits on the number of positions that could be paid at appointee-level salaries as a means of limiting the number of appointees. They occasionally include specific language in appropriations bills mandating that none of the appropriations be used to pay the salaries of more than a set number of appointees. For example, the Department of Transportation and Related Agencies Appropriations Act, enacted in the late 1980s, includes the following language, "None of the funds in this Act shall be available for salaries and expenses of more than [insert number] political and Presidential appointees in the Department of Transportation." The number of appointees allowed has varied in other bills from a low of 88 to a high of 138.

These instances are rare but this should not be taken as evidence that presidents can act with a free hand. On the contrary, White House officials anticipate the likely response of Congress and adjust their behavior accordingly. They are less likely to politicize if they expect Congress to overturn their action or impose serious political costs on the president. . . .

Conclusion

To understand politicization decisions from administration to administration one has to understand the context of both the history of the merit system and the details defining the different strategies and techniques employed. The professional merit-based civil service system was a late arrival in the United States. The United States federal government operated for almost one hundred years without a formal professional civil service, yet the importance of ensuring both loyalty and competence in the federal service was already evident. During the height of the spoils system, a dual personnel system existed with a continuing body of professionals working side by side with patronage appointees. The dual system presaged numerous attempts to institute merit systems in the period leading up to the formal creation of the merit system.

The 1883 reforms embodied in the Pendleton Act were focused on the task of eliminating spoils. Reformers sought to end assessments, political activity by public employees, and patronage hiring and firing through the expansion of merit protection and the merit system. The U.S. personnel system's narrow focus on spoils had a lasting effect on public personnel management. The United States was slow to focus on positive human resource management activities like recruitment, training, morale, and benefits. Instead, the personnel system was defined by rules designed to protect workers from the evil of spoils. Part of Congress's recent motivation for allowing individual agencies to develop personnel systems outside the traditional merit-based civil service system is to allow them to escape the cumbersome and antiquated federal personnel system. Isolated exceptions to Title 5 have now become a landslide, with less than one-half of all federal personnel under the traditional merit system. The Merit Systems Protection Board, the appellate body that hears employee complaints, is cutting its budget and closing regional offices.

While the federal personnel system continues to change dramatically, the politicization calculus remains much the same. Political actors are making decisions about the numbers of Senate-confirmed, noncareer SES, and Schedule C appointees in an effort to make the bureaucracy responsive to them and satisfy demands for patronage. In the same way they feared turning over competent, long-tenured professionals in the Jacksonian era, so, too, they fear politicizing too much now. . . . .

8-4

Administrative Procedures as Instruments of Political Control

Mathew D. McCubbins, Roger G. Noll, and Barry R. Weingast

Specifying the procedures by which executive agencies make decisions is one way for Congress and the president to limit the exercise of power delegated to those agencies. In this paper, social scientists McCubbins, Noll, and Weingast outline two forms of delegation as well as the kinds of administrative procedures that Congress and the president establish to influence agency decisions.

A CENTRAL PROBLEM of representative democracy is how to ensure that policy decisions are responsive to the interests or preferences of citizens. The U.S. Constitution deals with the electoral side of this problem by constructing institutional safeguards and incentive structures designed to make elected representatives responsive to citizens. But making policy involves more than decisions by elected legislators and the president. Inevitably, elected officials delegate considerable policymaking authority to unelected bureaucrats. Because elected officials have limited resources for monitoring agency performance, the possibility arises that bureaucrats will not comply with their policy preferences. This gives rise to the question how—or, indeed, whether—elected political officials can reasonably effectively assure that their policy intentions will be carried out.

This paper explores the principles of the political control of bureaucratic decisions. In so doing, we seek to develop a unifying conceptual framework for two general types of controls: "oversight"—monitoring, rewarding, and punishing bureaucratic behavior—and administrative procedures.

We begin with the premise that the political control of agencies is a principal-agent problem. In general, principal-agent problems do not have first-best solutions that guarantee perfect compliance. Moreover, the best available solution typically consists of a method for altering the incentives of the agent (here, the agency). Usually this involves some mechanism for (costly) monitoring of the agent, combined with a system of rewards and punishments. Standard political

Source: Mathew D. McCubbins, Roger G. Noll, and Barry R. Weingast, "Administrative Procedures as Instruments of Political Control," *Journal of Law, Economics, and Organization* 3(2), Fall 1987, 243–277. Notes and some bibliographic references appearing in the original have been deleted.

oversight—hearings, investigations, budget reviews, legislative sanctions—corresponds nicely with this form of solution to a principal-agent problem.

Administrative procedures are another mechanism for inducing compliance. Procedural requirements affect the institutional environment in which agencies make decisions and thereby limit an agency's range of feasible policy actions. In recognition of this, elected officials can design procedures to solve two prototypical problems of political control. First, procedures can be used to mitigate informational disadvantages faced by politicians in dealing with agencies. Second, procedures can be used to enfranchise important constituents in agency decisionmaking processes, thereby assuring that agencies are responsive to their interests.

The most subtle and . . . most interesting aspect of procedural controls is that they enable political leaders to assure compliance without specifying, or even necessarily knowing, what substantive outcome is most in their interest. By controlling processes, political leaders assign relative degrees of importance to the constituents whose interests are at stake in an administrative proceeding and thereby channel an agency's decisions toward the substantive outcomes that are most favored by those who are intended to be benefited by the policy. Thus, political leaders can be responsive to their constituencies without knowing, or needing to know, the details of the policy outcomes that these constituents want. . . .

The traditional view of administrative law provides a partial solution to the puzzle in political theory. Judicial review of agency decisions includes an examination of the conformity of an agency's decision to its mandate (which is derived not only from the actual legislation, but from committee reports, floor debates, veto messages, and other detritti of the legislative process). It also considers the conformity of the legislation and agency decision processes with individual rights and democratic values. In reviewing agency decisions, then, an impartial court can veto agency choices which do not conform with legislative intent and democratic procedural values.

Nevertheless, the mechanism of judicial review is insufficient for assuring political control. First, legislative mandates are often vague and broad, thereby placing only loose boundaries on agency decisions. Second, even when legislation is relatively specific, it is unlikely to foresee completely all contingent circumstances that might confront an agency, which inevitably leaves some degree of discretion to administrative officials. Hence, judicial review can only hold administrative discretion within reasonable bounds. Third, to the extent that administrative law does more than simply protect democratic values, the nature of political forces that give rise to administrative law becomes a puzzle in the problem of political control of agencies. Fourth, as argued by Shapiro (1986), traditional views of judicial review rest on an analytically weak foundation, for they assume that the objectives of the judiciary (unlike those of elected officials and bureaucrats) are purely to pursue principles of fairness and legitimacy. To the extent the courts pursue policy objectives that do not conform to the wishes of elected officials, administrative law (through legislation or executive order) may be in part a means for controlling the judiciary as well as for assuring adherence to democratic values.

This paper examines the role of administrative law in assisting political actors in controlling the bureaucracy. . . . [M]uch of administrative law—indeed, most administrative law that is not derived from judicial interpretation of the Constitution and common law principles of administrative fairness—is written for the purpose of helping elected politicians retain control of policymaking. Our hypothesis primarily concerns Congress, but it also applies to the Executive, which often helps develop and always approves legislative changes in administrative law and which directly alters administrative procedures through the issuance of executive orders. . . .

Solutions to the Problem of Bureaucratic Compliance

Creating an agency with discretionary authority to make policy decisions causes a potentially important problem: the agency may make decisions that depart from the policies (including distributive benefits and costs) that Congress and the president would otherwise have chosen. The mechanics of how and why agency decisions would depart from the policies preferred by members of Congress and the president are the subject of a vast literature, and we review it only briefly here. The fundamental premise of this literature is that bureaucrats have personal preferences which conflict with members of Congress and the president. The policy choices of the latter are disciplined by the requirement that periodically they seek ratification of their performance in office by their constituents. The choices of agency officials are not subjected to electoral discipline. Consequently, in the absence of effective oversight, they are likely to reflect personal preferences, derived from some combination of private political values, personal career objectives, and, all else equal, an aversion to effort, especially effort that does not serve personal interests.

The crime of runaway bureaucracy requires opportunity as well as motive, and this is supplied by asymmetric information. A consequence of delegating authority to bureaucrats is that they may become more expert about their policy responsibilities than the elected representatives who created their bureau. Information about cause-effect relations, the details of existing policies and regulations, the pending decision agenda, and the distribution of benefits and costs of agency actions is costly and time-consuming to acquire. As in all agency relationships, it may be possible for the agency to take advantage of its private information.

Several consequences can emerge from this situation. One is simple shirking: an agency becomes a Club Med for government officials who undersupply policy decisions. Another is corruption: agency officials allow the bureau to be "captured" by selling out to an external group. Still another is oligarchy: the peculiar political preferences of the agency override democratic preferences. The challenge for political overseers is to prevent these outcomes.

Because monitoring and enforcement are not costless, no method of influencing administrative decisions will be perfect. Rather, elected representatives face a tradeoff between the extent of compliance they can command and the effort that is expended to assure it, effort which has an opportunity cost because it can also be used for other politically relevant purposes. Moreover, political actors can be expected to engage in delegation even if they find perfect compliance to be excessively costly. Delegation confers a benefit by expanding the scope of politically relevant activity available to them. Imperfect compliance, then, is simply a cost of delegation to be balanced against this benefit.

The problem of bureaucratic compliance has long been recognized as a principal-agent problem. Specifically, members of Congress and the president are principals in an agency relationship with an executive bureau. As in all agency relationships, the principals will seek methods to ensure that delegation is more beneficial than costly. . . .

Politicians have several means available to reward or punish agencies. Under extreme circumstances, civil servants can be removed from office, and even prosecuted, if their actions stray too far from the grey areas surrounding the mandate and power of their agency. The top officials in an agency are usually political appointees and can be impeached by Congress or, with a few exceptions, fired by the president. Appropriations and reauthorizations bills also provide a means for either general or programmatically targeted rewards and punishments. Public hearings and investigations, while part of the monitoring function, also can serve to subject recalcitrant bureaucrats to public humiliation that devastates their careers. Finally, legislation or executive order can reorganize agencies and shuffle policy responsibilities among them, thereby reallocating policymaking authority.

Although these actions are reactive in that they take place after a suspected impropriety has occurred, their availability affects the incentives facing bureaucratic decisionmakers. The value of a political punishment, multiplied by the likelihood that improper behavior will be detected and punished, enters as a cost in the calculation of net benefits by a bureaucrat who contemplates straying from the preferences of political overseers. If detection and punishment are sufficiently likely, and the magnitude of the punishment sufficiently great, a non-complying action can be deterred. Thus, the presence of sanctions, by forcing administrators to anticipate political reactions to their policy decisions, provides some measure of protection from noncompliance. . . .

. . . By themselves, rewards and punishments do not deal directly with the problem of asymmetric information. If agencies have better information, they have a range of discretion that is undetectable to political overseers, and so, in the absence of monitoring, some noncomplying decisions will not be subject to retribution. Thus, if noncompliance is a serious problem, one would expect political actors to invest substantial resources in monitoring; indeed, this appears to be the case (Aberbach).

Policy monitoring in Congress takes two forms. The more apparent, but probably less important, is ongoing oversight and evaluation by congressional sub-committees and agencies that are arms of Congress, such as the Congressional Budget Office (CBO) and the General Accounting Office (GAO). Less apparent, but probably more important (judging from how members of Congress allocate their time and staff), is "fire-alarm" monitoring. This form of monitoring consists of disappointed constituents pulling a member's fire alarm whenever an agency harms them. Oversight is then a form of constituency service for members. Constituency service has become an increasingly important activity of members of Congress in the postwar era, to the point where it now accounts for more than half of the staff effort in Congress and is a critical factor in assuring the reelection success of members.

Policy monitoring in the executive branch is concentrated in the evaluation process. The Executive Office of the President is comprised of numerous organizations, most notably the Office of Management and Budget (OMB), that scrutinize budgets, programs, and operations of agencies. Furthermore, cabinet officials—the people most politically responsive to the president—also have their own independent evaluation staffs.

To facilitate the monitoring process, political actors impose information collection and reporting requirements on agencies. Both Congress and the OMB receive oceans of data and reports from offices within agencies about ongoing programs. And, through GAO and the General Services Administration (GSA), political actors impose rigid accounting and record-keeping requirements on agencies that can be used subsequently as the basis for sanctions.

Though monitoring is probably far more pervasive and effective than was once thought, it imposes costs on political actors. First, resources devoted to monitoring have an opportunity cost, for they presumably could be devoted to delivering more government services to constituents or shrinking the burden of the public sector. Second, the time used by political principals in acquiring information, assessing the degree of noncompliance, and deciding what punishment strategy, if any, to undertake also has an opportunity cost. Easy and quick compliance is preferred, for it enables political actors to provide more service to constituents in a given amount of time. . . .

. . . [B]y themselves, monitoring and sanctions do not comprise a perfect solution to the problem of bureaucratic compliance because they are costly, inexact, and subject to fundamental limitations. Thus, one would expect politicians to welcome other measures that may be available for altering the incentive structure of agencies, especially if these alternatives have relatively low cost. An optimal mix of the measures, where each measure complements the strengths of the other and substitutes for the other's weaknesses, will establish less costly and more effective control of the bureaucracy by political principals. Hence, the stage is set for analyzing administrative law as such a mechanism.

Procedural Solutions to Compliance Problems

Administrative procedures can be solutions to problems of noncompliance by agencies only if procedures actually affect the outcomes of decisionmaking processes. Such is not necessarily the case, for elaborate procedures can serve at least two other ends. First, . . . procedures may be ends in their own right. Regardless of the outcome, people may derive greater value from processes that treat them respectfully and give the appearance of rationality than from processes that are perceived to be cruel, unfair, and arbitrary. Second, procedures may be a ruse aimed at the electorate in that they have no effect on outcomes but transfer apparent responsibility for decisions from elected political officials to agencies or courts. Whereas as usually stated this implies irrationality or gullibility on the part of the electorate, this is not necessarily the case. Administrative procedures in some form may be necessary to protect other values (such as constitutional rights and procedural characteristics referred to above) and so bound (but not determine) outcomes while simultaneously increasing the complexity of decisionmaking processes and the informational requirements to comprehend them. If so, administrative procedures can simultaneously provide a net benefit to citizens and attenuate the ability of citizens to allocate political responsibility for policy outcomes.

While both lines of argument point to plausible features of administrative processes, we argue that this is not all there is to procedures. Specifically, we assume that the details of administrative law as applied to any given decision problem will affect the outcome. The basis for this assumption is the presumption that decisions depend on the information that underpins them and on the means for relating that information to decisions that are permissible according to the strictures of administrative law. If decisionmakers must take account of all of the relevant information that is available to them, and if participants in an administrative process can be relied upon to provide information that is, on balance, favorable to their interests, then rules of standing and evidence and the allocation of burdens of proof will affect the range of decisions available to an agency. . . .

If procedures do affect outcomes, political officials have available to them another tool for inducing bureaucratic compliance. Specifically, alterations in procedures will change the expected policy outcomes of administrative agencies by affecting the relative influence of people who are affected by the policy. Moreover, because policy is controlled by participants in administrative processes, political officials can use procedures to control policy without bearing costs themselves, or even having to know what policy is likely to emerge. . . .

. . . [W]e wish to advance the hypothesis that administrative procedures enhance the ability of political principals in general to solve their agency control problems.

There are two general forms of control problems. First, *political principals in both branches of government suffer an informational disadvantage with respect to the bureaucracy.* Because of this ubiquitous problem, the political principals will seek a ubiquitous solution. We argue that many of the provisions of the Administrative Procedures Act solve this asymmetric information problem. Second, *the coalition that forms to create an agency—the committee that drafted the legislation, the chamber majorities that approved it, and the president who signed it into law—will seek to ensure that the bargain struck among the members of the coalition does not unravel once the coalition disbands.* Specifically, the coalition will seek to combine sanctions with an institutional structure to create pressures on agencies that replicate the political pressures applied when the relevant legislation was enacted. Here, the point of administrative procedures is *not* to preselect specific policy outcomes, but to create a decisionmaking environment that mirrors the political circumstances that gave rise to the establishment of the policy. Whereas political officials may not know what specific policy outcome they will want in the future, they will know which interests ought to influence a decision and what distributive outcomes will be consistent with the original coalitional arrangement. In other words, the coalition "stacks the deck" in the agency's decisionmaking to enhance the durability of the bargain struck among members of the coalition. . . .

If these uses of administrative process are effective, *the agency, without any need for input, guidance, or attention from political principals, is directed toward the decisions its principals would make on their own, even if the principals are unaware, ex ante, of what that outcome would be.* [italics added for emphasis] By structuring the rules of the game for the agency, administrative procedures sequence agency activity, regulate its information collection and dissemination, limit its available choices, and define its strategic advantage. Moreover, an important feature of this system is that constituents, agencies, and the courts bear much of the costs of ensuring compliance. Indeed, courts are the key, for without them political actors could not rely on decentralized enforcement.

Political Consequences of the Administrative Procedures Act

The Administrative Procedures Act [APA] of 1946 codified over a half-century of court decisions affecting administrative proceedings. The court's rationale for establishing the procedural requirements embodied in the act was to ensure that procedural justice applies in agency decisionmaking. But the APA did more than this. Indeed, it took Congress and the president a decade to work out the details of an act to which they could both agree. Thus the APA is in part a political document, written to enhance political control. The twin goals of procedural justice and agency control were noted in the Report of the House Judiciary Committee accompanying the proposed act: the act "is designed to provide . . . fairness in administrative operation" and "to assure . . . the effectuation of the declared policies of Congress" (U.S. Congress, 1947: 252). . . .

Incentives to the Gain Relevant Political Information

Politicians delegate authority to an agency for a variety of reasons. One is that the policy is inherently controversial and so politicians may seek to distance themselves from the ultimate policy choice by "shifting responsibility" to an agency designed to take blame (Fiorina, 1985). In this case, the principle design criterion for an administrative process is likely to be procedural fairness, as perceived by the warring interests, and a propensity to find compromise, so that in the end the participants will have a blunted incentive to take further political action to alter the policy outcome.

Another motive for broad delegation of authority occurs when political leaders are uncertain about what politically is the most desirable policy. It can then be in their interest to set in motion processes that will resolve these uncertainties and that will use the newly acquired information to carry out the policy preferences they would have if fully informed. To accomplish this, political principals must first provide bureaucrats with the means to collect information about the consequences of various policy options. Second, political leaders must impose procedures that cause the information to be used to make decisions that serve their interests. . . .

The constraints of due process imposed by the APA and the courts are primarily procedural. Courts ensure that agency actions are neither "arbitrary" nor "capricious." The requirements are as follows:

1. The agency cannot announce a new policy without warning, but must instead give "notice" that it will consider an issue, and do so without prejudice or bias in favor or any particular action.

2. Agencies must solicit "comments" and allow all interested parties to communicate their views.

3. Agencies must allow "participation" in the decisionmaking process, with the extent often mandated by the organic statute creating the agency as well as by the courts. If hearings are held, then parties may be allowed to bring forth testimony and evidence and often to cross-examine other witnesses.

4. Agencies must deal explicitly with the evidence presented to them and provide a rationalizable link between the evidence and their decisions.

These requirements play an important role in governing information collection and dissemination by agencies. Their paramount political implications are fivefold.

First, they ensure that agencies cannot secretly conspire against elected officials by presenting them with a fait accompli, that is, a new policy with already mobilized supporters. Rather, the agency must announce its intentions to consider an issue well in advance of any decision.

Second, agencies must solicit valuable political information. The notice and comment provisions assure that the agency learns what are the relevant political interests to the decision and something about the political costs and benefits associated with various actions. That participation is not universal (and may even be stacked) does not entail political costs. Diffuse groups who do not participate, even when their interests are at stake, are much less likely to become an electoral force in comparison with those that do participate.

Third, the entire proceeding is public and the rules against ex parte contact protect against secret deals between the agency and some constituency it might seek to mobilize against Congress or the president.

Fourth, the entire sequence of decisionmaking—notice, comment, deliberation, collection of evidence, and construction of a record in favor of a chosen action—afford numerous opportunities for political principals to respond when an agency seeks to move in a direction that officials do not like. These procedures also ensure that relevant political information is available to form the basis of such action. Neither Congress nor the president need first undertake costly collection of this information, nor need they contend with an agency which has substantial private information. An important consequence is that this allows political reaction prior to agency choice, and prior to the agency's ability to mobilize a constituency. The strategic advantage of agencies is therefore limited.

Fifth, administrative participation also works as a gauge of political interest and controversiality. In administrative processes with broad rights of standing and relatively harsh evidentiary standards pertaining to the agency's basis for its decisions, interested parties have an incentive to burden the record with voluminous evidence supporting a decision favorable to their interests. But marshalling this evidence and its supporting legal argument is expensive, so that parties will face a tradeoff between the likely effect of more evidence on the agency's decision and the costs of submitting it. In noncontentious proceedings, a party need not participate intensely to affect outcomes favorably; however, in highly controversial policy decisions, intense participation is an absolute necessity to prevent a catastrophic outcome (assuming that an interest's position is in some measure defensible). Hence, demanding procedural requirements (including a "hard-look" judicial review) have the political side benefit of selectively causing the most politically contentious issues—and the ones in which political overseers would be most concerned about the distributive aspects of the decision—to generate the most complete information, as well as to provide substantial advance warning about the likely decision that, in the absence of political intervention, the agency is most likely to make. . . .

Deck-Stacking

. . . [P]olitical actors control the extent of representation of various interests in administrative processes. Through these decisions, political actors assure that the influence accorded to different constituents is not random; indeed, by controlling the details of procedures and participation, *political actors stack the deck in favor of constituents who are the intended beneficiaries of the bargain struck by the coalition which created the agency.* Because administrative processes, once established, endure far into the future and may deal with issues in which there is considerable uncertainty over key economic and technical phenomena, elected representatives can be expected to be unsure about the substantive details of their most desired policy, even though they are certain about who should benefit and how the costs should be shared. In such a circumstance, political leaders could undertake to become [so] sufficiently expert that they could fashion legislation that was rich in substantive policy content, as is often the case in tax legislation. Alternatively, the organic statute can be vague in policy objectives, seemingly giving an agency great policy discretion, but the administrative process can be designed to assure that the outcomes will be responsive to the constituents that the policy is intended to favor.

. . . [T]he resources available for representation in administrative processes vary systematically and predictably among interests for reasons other than their stakes in the issue. Some constituents are likely to be well represented regardless of the cost and complexity of the processes that affect them, and still others not at all. Moreover, among the less well-represented constituents there may also be considerable differences in the extent to which they are politically relevant in Congress or the White House, owing to their participation in elections or because some are better represented on relevant congressional committees.

. . . All else equal, elaborate procedures with stiff evidentiary burdens for decisions and numerous opportunities for seeking judicial review before the final policy decision is reached will benefit constituents that have considerable resources for representation. Coupled with no budget for subsidizing other representation, or for independent staff analysis in the agency or in other agencies that might participate in its proceedings, cumbersome procedures exemplify deck-stacking in favor of well-organized, well-financed interests. . . .

Decentralized Enforcement and the Courts

Procedures will only have their desired effect if their requirements are enforced. If the constraints they impose are binding, they will establish an automatic control mechanism for Congress that keeps the agency from choosing undesirable outcomes. Moreover, they will do so with minimal effort required on the part of politicians. Administrative procedures have the advantage that their enforcement is left to constituents, who file suit for violations of prescribed procedure, and to the courts.

The courts thus play a key role in assuring political control. If the agency violates its procedures, judicial remedy must be highly likely. If so, the courts, and constituents who bring suit, guarantee compliance with procedural constraints, which in turn guarantees that the agency choice will mirror political preferences without any need for political oversight. Put another way, enforcement of procedures is *decentralized* in that enforcement does not depend on the action of political principals. This lowers enforcement costs and preserves the influence of politicians without direct participation or explicit knowledge on their part. . . .

Congress, the President, and the Courts

The legislative department derives a superiority in our government from other circumstances. Its constitutional powers being at once more extensive, and less susceptible of precise limits, it can with greater facility, mask, under complicated and indirect measures, the encroachments which it makes on the co-ordinate departments. . . . On the other side, the executive power being more simple in its nature, and the judiciary being described by landmarks still less uncertain, immediately betray and defeat themselves. Nor is this all: As the legislative department has access to the pockets of the people, and has in some constitutions full discretion, and in all a prevailing influence, over the pecuniary rewards of those who fill the other departments, a dependence is thus created in the latter, which gives still greater facility to encroachments of the former.

—Madison, *The Federalist*, no. 48.

The extent to which the courts can and should "encroach" upon legislative and executive responsibilities has been a point of debate in legal scholarship. That they do encroach is unquestioned. Our thesis concerning the political ramifications of the administrative system provides a new perspective on this debate.

Administrative procedures can be viewed as an "indirect" means by which politicians, in anticipation of judicial encroachment, use the courts to maintain political control. The courts, of course, use procedures as an "indirect" means of encroaching upon the prerogatives of other branches. The evolution of procedural standards has often occurred for policy-based reasons. For example, throughout the late 1960s and early 1970s, courts increased the procedural rights of nonregulated interests. By enabling increased participation by environmental and consumer groups, and by enfranchising these groups to challenge agencies in court, agencies were made to accommodate new interests. . . .

. . . [O]ne of the great advantages of procedural—as opposed to substantive—constraints is that they allow considerable flexibility with regard to the ultimate policy chosen. This is most important in circumstances in which the substantive content of the politically most desirable choice is uncertain. In this circumstance, substantive constraints would prove limiting. Defining safety in the workplace rather than delegating the task to OSHA [Occupational Safety and Health Administration] may rule out policies that turn out to be politically desirable, while promoting others that prove to be undesirable. . . .

Conclusions

Assuring bureaucratic compliance with the preferences of political overseers is an especially rich example of the principal-agent problem. Noncompliance can be manifested in several ways: shirking by undersupplying policy outcomes; pursuing policy objectives that are inconsistent with the preferences of elected political officials; or creating new, organized political interests that are a political threat to political overseers. To cope with these problems, political actors engage in the kinds of activities that are emphasized in the principal-agent literature. They set up mechanisms to monitor agency activities, either directly or through constituent complaints, and they offer rewards and punishments to alter the incentives faced by agencies.

As can be expected, monitoring and sanctions are unlikely to provide a perfect solution to the noncompliance problem. Both are costly to use, and economic incentives have a limited range. Consequently, in the best of circumstances noncompliance is likely to be present in combination with extensive monitoring activity and at least some instances of punishment.

Administrative procedures constitute an additional mechanism for achieving greater compliance. First, because they ameliorate the problem of asymmetric information, administrative procedures are a useful, cost-reducing supplement to methods for monitoring and punishing agencies. They reduce the informational costs of following agency activities and especially facilitate "fire-alarm" monitoring through constituencies affected by an agency's policies. They also sharpen decisions to punish by facilitating the assessment of the extent and importance of noncompliance. Thus, by lowering the costs of monitoring and sharpening sanctions, administrative procedures produce an equilibrium in which compliance is greater than it otherwise would be.

A second role of administrative procedures is that they can be used by agencies to avoid inadvertent noncompliance of such a magnitude that it would lead to sanctions. In politics, sanctions are costly to both the principal and the agent, that is, they are *not* simply wealth transfers from the latter to the former but involve legislation, executive order, or litigation to punish an agency and change its policies.

Hence, sanctions impose a net loss that all sides have a common interest to avoid. Administrative procedures aid an agency in avoiding sanctions in three ways. By stacking the deck to benefit favored political interests, they channel decisions in directions preferred by political overseers. By mirroring the political environment faced by the agency's overseers, an agency's processes give it information about which constituencies, if any, might threaten the agency politically should they be dissatisfied with its policies. And by facilitating early dissemination of information about further feasible policy decisions, administrative procedures increase the chance that the "fire alarm" will be sounded by an offended constituency before an agency is fully committed to a policy. Thus, administrative procedures reduce the likelihood that sanctions will actually have to be used.

Together, the legal constraints imposed by procedures and the incentives created by threat of sanction establish a decisionmaking environment that channels agency policy choices in favor of constituencies important to political overseers. Thus, the administrative system is automatic. The infrequency of visible oversight activities (and especially sanctions) does not mean that there is an absence of political control.

Of course, not every group will be included in an agency's environment. Influence will be accorded to those represented in the coalition that gave rise to the agency's organic statute. Well-organized special interests and the parochial interests of congressional districts will be well represented. Interests of a national constituency that is not well organized will not achieve representation unless it is built into the agency's process. And this will occur only if these broader interests are influential with elected politicians, usually because they are electorally significant. Thus, in the end, the politics of the bureaucracy will mirror the politics surrounding Congress and the president.

REFERENCES

Fiorina, Morris. 1985. "Group Concentration and the Delegation of Legislative Authority," in R. G. Noll, ed., *Regulatory Policy and the Social Sciences*. Berkeley: University of California Press.

Noll, Roger, and Bruce Owen. 1983. *Political Economy of Deregulation*. Washington, D. C.: American Enterprise Institute.

Olson, Mancur. 1965. *The Logic of Collective Action*. Cambridge: Harvard University Press.

Spitzer, Matthew. 1986. "Rational Choice Political Economy and Administrative Law: One View of the Synagogue," Working Paper, University of Southern California Law Center.

Stewart, Richard B. 1975. "The Reformation of Administrative Law," 88 *Harvard Law Review* 1669–1813.

Taylor, Serge. 1984. *Making Bureaucracies Think: The Environmental Impact Statement Strategy of Administrative Reform*. Palo Alto: Stanford University Press.

U.S. Senate. 1947. *The Administrative Procedure Act: Legislative History*. 79th Congress. Document no. 248. Washington, D.C.: Government Printing Office.

————. Committee on Government Operations. 1977. *Study on Federal Regulation: Congressional Oversight of Regulatory Agencies*, vol. 2. Washington, D.C.: Government Printing Office.

Wallis, John. 1986. "Political-economy of the New Deal: Federal Emergency Relief Administration." Paper delivered at the American Economic Association Meetings, New Orleans.

Wehr, Elizabeth. 1977. "House, Senate Committees Propose Changes in FTC," *Congressional Quarterly* (June 11): 1156-57.

Weingast, Barry R. 1984. "The Congressional-Bureaucratic System: A Principal-Agent Perspective," 44 *Public Choice* 147–92.

————, and Mark Moran. 1983. "Bureaucratic Discretion or Congressional Control: Regulatory Policymaking by the Federal Trade Commission," 91 *Journal of Political Economy* 765–800.

Wildavsky, Aaron. 1979. *The Politics of the Budgetary Process*. 3rd ed. Boston: Little, Brown.

Wines, Michael. 1981. "Miller's Directive to the FTC: Quit Acting Like a 'Consumer Cop.'" *National Journal* (December 5): 2149–53.

Chapter 9

The Judiciary

9-1

from *A Matter of Interpretation: Federal Courts and the Law*

Antonin Scalia

Supreme Court judges and indeed—as we learn in the essay by Carp, Manning, and Stidham, later in this section—judges at every level of the federal judiciary decide cases in close accord with the political views of those who appointed them. Years of Democratic control of the White House and Congress created the activist federal judiciary of the 1960s and 1970s that advanced federal protections of civil rights and civil liberties. With the resurgence of the Republican Party in national politics, the federal judiciary has gradually, with turnover in members, become more conservative. Some observers note these trends and conclude that judges are little more than partisan politicians disguised in robes. Unsurprisingly, judges do not view themselves this way. Instead, they account for their sometimes sharply differing opinions on criteria that do not fit neatly on the familiar partisan or ideological dimensions that are used to classify elected officeholders. In the next two essays, two current Supreme Court justices—one conservative and appointed by a Republican president, the other a moderate, appointed by a Democrat— explain how they approach decisions, decisions on which they frequently

Source: Antonin Scalia, "Common-Law Courts in a Civil-Law System: The Role of United States Federal Courts in Interpreting the Constitution and Laws," from *A Matter of Interpretation: Federal Courts and the Law* (Princeton University Press: 1997), 3–47. Some notes appearing in the original have been deleted.

disagree. As you read and weigh these alternative views, note that both judges begin with the same assumption—that as the unelected branch the judiciary should, when possible, defer to the decisions of democratically elected officeholders.

In the following essay, excerpted from his highly regarded series of lectures to Princeton law students, Justice Antonin Scalia explains how he approaches decisions. Some call this style "literalist" or "originalist," in that Scalia weighs decisions against a close reading of the texts of laws and the Constitution. He reminds us that in a constitutional democracy judges are not charged with deciding what fair and just policy should be. This responsibility belongs with elected officials, who better reflect their citizenry's views on such matters. Nor should judges try to read the minds of those who make the law. A judge's role begins and ends with applying the law (including the Constitution) to the particular circumstances of a legal disagreement. Scalia's critics have complained that the application of law is frequently not so simple. Laws conflict or fail to consider the many contingencies that reach the Supreme Court.

THE FOLLOWING ESSAY attempts to explain the current neglected state of the science of construing legal texts, and offers a few suggestions for improvement. It is addressed not just to lawyers but to all thoughtful Americans who share our national obsession with the law.

The Common Law

The first year of law school makes an enormous impact upon the mind. Many students remark upon the phenomenon. They experience a sort of intellectual rebirth, the acquisition of a whole new mode of perceiving and thinking. Thereafter, even if they do not yet know much law, they do—as the expression goes—"think like a lawyer."

The overwhelming majority of the courses taught in that first year, and surely the ones that have the most profound effect, teach the substance, and the methodology, of the common law—torts, for example; contracts; property; criminal law. American lawyers cut their teeth upon the common law. To understand what an effect that must have, you must appreciate that the common law is not really common law, except insofar as judges can be regarded as common. That is to say, it is not "customary law," or a reflection of the people's practices, but is rather law developed by the judges. Perhaps in the very infancy of Anglo-Saxon law it could have been thought that the courts were mere expositors of generally accepted social practices; and certainly, even in the full maturity of the common law, a well-established commercial or social practice could form the basis for a court's decision. But from an early time—as early as the Year Books, which record English judicial decisions from the end of the thirteenth century to the beginning of the sixteenth—any equivalence between custom and common law had ceased to exist, except in the sense that the doctrine of *stare decisis* rendered prior judicial decisions "custom." The issues coming before the courts involved, more and more, refined questions to which customary practice provided no answer.

Oliver Wendell Holmes's influential book *The Common Law*[1]—which is still suggested reading for entering law students—talks a little bit about Germanic and early English custom. . . . This is the image of the law—the common law— to which an aspiring American lawyer is first exposed, even if he has not read Holmes over the previous summer as he was supposed to. He learns the law, not by reading statutes that promulgate it or treatises that summarize it, but rather by studying the judicial opinions that invented it. This is the famous case-law method, pioneered by Harvard Law School in the last century, and brought to movies and TV by the redoubtable Professor Kingsfield of *Love Story* and *The Paper Chase*. The student is directed to read a series of cases, set forth in a text called a "casebook," designed to show how the law developed. . . . Famous old cases are famous, you see, not because they came out right, but because the rule of law they announced was the intelligent one. Common-law courts performed two functions: One was to apply the law to the facts. All adjudicators—French judges, arbitrators, even baseball umpires and football referees—do that. But the second function, and the more important one, was to *make* the law.

If you were sitting in on Professor Kingsfield's class when *Hadley* v. *Baxendale* was the assigned reading, you would find that the class discussion would not end with the mere description and dissection of the opinion. [This case, a familiar example of 19th century English common law, involves liability in failing to perform a contracted obligation.-Ed.] Various "hypotheticals" would be proposed by the crusty (yet, under it all, good-hearted) old professor, testing the validity and the sufficiency of the "foreseeability" rule. What if, for example, you are a blacksmith, and a young knight rides up on a horse that has thrown a shoe. He tells you he is returning to his ancestral estate, Blackacre, which he must reach that very evening to claim his inheritance, or else it will go to his wicked, no-good cousin, the sheriff of Nottingham. You contract to put on a new shoe, for the going rate of three farthings. The shoe is defective, or is badly shod, the horse goes lame, and the knight reaches Blackacre too late. Are you really liable for the full amount of his inheritance? Is it reasonable to impose that degree of liability for three farthings? Would not the parties have set a different price if liability of that amount had been contemplated? Ought there not to be, in other words, some limiting principle to damages beyond mere foreseeability? Indeed, might not that principle—call it presumed assumption of risk—explain why *Hadley* v. *Baxendale* reached the right result after all, though not for the precise reason it assigned?

What intellectual fun all of this is! It explains why first-year law school is so exhilarating: because it consists of playing common-law judge, which in turn consists of playing king—devising, out of the brilliance of one's own mind, those laws that ought to govern mankind. How exciting! And no wonder so many law students, having drunk at this intoxicating well, aspire for the rest of their lives to be judges!

Besides the ability to think about, and devise, the "best" legal rule, there is another skill imparted in the first year of law school that is essential to the making of a good common-law judge. It is the technique of what is called "distinguishing" cases. That is a necessary skill, because an absolute prerequisite to common-law lawmaking is the doctrine of *stare decisis*—that is, the principle that a decision made in one case will be followed in the next. Quite obviously, without such a principle common-law courts would not be making any "law"; they would just be resolving the particular dispute before them. It is the requirement that future courts adhere to the principle underlying a judicial decision which causes that decision to be a legal rule. (There is no such requirement in the civil-law system, where it is the text of the law rather than any prior judicial interpretation of that text which is authoritative. Prior judicial opinions are consulted for their persuasive effect, much as academic commentary would be; but they are not *binding*.)

Within such a precedent-bound common-law system, it is critical for the lawyer, or the judge, to establish whether the case at hand falls within a principle that has already been decided. Hence the technique—or the art, or the game—of "distinguishing" earlier cases. It is an art or a game, rather than a science, because what constitutes the "holding" of an earlier case is not well defined and can be adjusted to suit the occasion. . . .

It should be apparent that by reason of the doctrine of *stare decisis*, as limited by the principle I have just described, the common law grew in a peculiar fashion—rather like a Scrabble board. No rule of decision previously announced could be *erased*, but qualifications could be *added* to it. The first case lays on the board: "No liability for breach of contractual duty without privity"; the next player adds "unless injured party is member of household." And the game continues.

As I have described, this system of making law by judicial opinion, and making law by distinguishing earlier cases, is what every American law student, every newborn American lawyer, first sees when he opens his eyes. And the impression remains for life. His image of the great judge—the Holmes, the Cardozo—is the man (or woman) who has the intelligence to discern the best rule of law for the case at hand and then the skill to perform the broken-field running through earlier cases that leaves him free to impose that rule: distinguishing one prior case on the left, straight-arming another one on the right, high-stepping away from another precedent about to tackle him from the rear, until (bravo!) he reaches the goal—good law. That image of the great judge remains with the former law student when he himself becomes a judge, and thus the common-law tradition is passed on.

Democratic Legislation

All of this would be an unqualified good, were it not for a trend in government that has developed in recent centuries, called democracy. In most countries, judges are no longer agents of the king, for there are no kings. . . . [O]nce we have taken this realistic view of what common-law courts do, the uncomfortable relationship of common-law lawmaking to democracy (if not to the technical doctrine of the separation of powers) becomes apparent. Indeed, that was evident to many even before legal realism carried the day. It was one of the principal motivations behind the law-codification movement of the nineteenth century. . . .

The nineteenth-century codification movement . . . was generally opposed by the bar, and hence did not achieve substantial success, except in one field: civil procedure, the law governing the trial of civil cases.[2] (I have always found it curious, by the way, that the only field in which lawyers and judges were willing to abandon judicial lawmaking was a field important to nobody except litigants, lawyers, and judges. Civil procedure used to be the *only* statutory course taught in first-year law school.) Today, generally speaking, the old private-law fields—contracts, torts, property, trusts and estates, family law—remain firmly within the control of state common-law courts.[3] Indeed, it is probably true that in these fields judicial lawmaking can be more freewheeling than ever, since the doctrine of *stare decisis* has appreciably eroded. Prior decisions that even the cleverest mind cannot distinguish can nowadays simply be overruled.

My point in all of this is not that the common law should be scraped away as a barnacle on the hull of democracy. I am content to leave the common law, and the process of developing the common law, where it is. It has proven to be a good method of developing the law in many fields—and perhaps the very best method. An argument can be made that development of the bulk of private law by judges (a natural aristocracy, as Madison accurately portrayed them)[4] is a desirable limitation upon popular democracy. . . .

But though I have no quarrel with the common law and its process, I do question whether the *attitude* of the common-law judge—the mind-set that asks, "What is the most desirable resolution of this case, and how can any impediments to the achievement of that result be evaded?"—is appropriate for most of the work that I do, and much of the work that state judges do. We live in an age of legislation, and most new law is statutory law. . . . Every issue of law resolved by a federal judge involves interpretation of text—the text of a regulation, or of a statute, or of the Constitution. Let me put the Constitution to one side for the time being, since many believe that that document is in effect a charter for judges to develop an evolving common law of freedom of speech, of privacy rights, and the like. I think that is wrong—indeed, as I shall discuss below, I think it frustrates the whole purpose of a written constitution. But we need not pause to debate that point now, since a very small proportion of judges' work is constitutional interpretation in any event. (Even in the Supreme Court, I would estimate that well less than a fifth of the issues we confront are constitutional issues—and probably less than a twentieth if you exclude criminal-law cases.) By far the greatest part of what I and all federal judges do is to interpret the meaning of federal statutes and federal agency regulations. Thus the subject of statutory interpretation deserves study and attention in its own right, as the principal business of judges and (hence) lawyers. It will not do to treat the enterprise as simply an inconvenient modern add-on to the judge's primary role of common-law lawmaker. Indeed, attacking the enterprise with the Mr. Fix-it mentality of the common-law judge is a sure recipe for incompetence and usurpation.

The Science of Statutory Interpretation

The state of the science of statutory interpretation in American law is accurately described by a prominent treatise on the legal process as follows:

> Do not expect anybody's theory of statutory interpretation, whether it is your own or somebody else's, to be an accurate statement of what courts actually do with statutes. The hard truth of the matter is that American courts have no intelligible, generally accepted, and consistently applied theory of statutory interpretation.[5]

Surely this is a sad commentary: We American judges have no intelligible theory of what we do most.

Even sadder, however, is the fact that the American bar and American legal education, by and large, are unconcerned with the fact that we have no intelligible theory. Whereas legal scholarship has been at pains to rationalize the common law—to devise the *best* rules governing contracts, torts, and so forth—it has been seemingly agnostic as to whether there is even any such thing as good or bad rules of statutory interpretation. There are few law-school courses on the subject, and certainly no required ones; the science of interpretation (if it is a science) is left to be picked up piecemeal, through the reading of cases (good and bad) in substantive fields of law that happen to involve statutes, such as securities law, natural resources law, and employment law. . . .

"Intent of the Legislature"

Statutory interpretation is such a broad subject that the substance of it cannot be discussed comprehensively here. It is worth examining a few aspects, however, if only to demonstrate the great degree of confusion that prevails. We can begin at the most fundamental possible level. So utterly unformed is the American law of statutory interpretation that not only is its methodology unclear, but even its very *objective* is. Consider the basic question: What are we looking for when we construe a statute?

You will find it frequently said in judicial opinions of my court and others that the judge's objective in interpreting a statute is to give effect to "the intent of the legislature." This principle, in one form or another, goes back at least as far as Blackstone.[6] Unfortunately, it does not square with some of the (few) generally accepted concrete rules of statutory construction. One is the rule that when the text of a statute is clear, that is the end of the matter. Why should that be so, if what the legislature *intended*, rather than what it *said*, is the object of our inquiry? In selecting the words of the statute, the legislature might have misspoken. Why not permit that to be demonstrated from the floor debates? Or indeed, why not accept, as proper material for the court to consider, later explanations by the legislators—a sworn affidavit signed by the majority of each house, for example, as to what they *really* meant?

Another accepted rule of construction is that ambiguities in a newly enacted statute are to be resolved in such fashion as to make the statute, not only internally consistent, but also compatible with previously enacted laws. We simply assume, for purposes of our search for "intent," that the enacting legislature was aware of all those other laws. Well of course that is a fiction, and if we were really looking for the subjective intent of the enacting legislature we would more likely find it by paying attention to the text (and legislative history) of the new statute in isolation.

The evidence suggests that, despite frequent statements to the contrary, we do not really look for subjective legislative intent. We look for a sort of "objectified" intent—the intent that a reasonable person would gather from the text of the law, placed alongside the remainder of the *corpus juris*. As Bishop's old treatise nicely put it, elaborating upon the usual formulation: "[T]he primary object of all rules for interpreting statutes is to ascertain the legislative intent; *or, exactly,*

the meaning which the subject is authorized to understand the legislature intended." [7]
And the reason we adopt this objectified version is, I think, that it is simply incompatible with democratic government, or indeed, even with fair government, to have the meaning of a law determined by what the lawgiver meant, rather than by what the lawgiver promulgated. That seems to me one step worse than the trick the emperor Nero was said to engage in: posting edicts high up on the pillars, so that they could not easily be read. Government by unexpressed intent is similarly tyrannical. It is the *law* that governs, not the intent of the lawgiver. That seems to me the essence of the famous American ideal set forth in the Massachusetts constitution: A government of laws, not of men. Men may intend what they will; but it is only the laws that they enact which bind us.

In reality, however, if one accepts the principle that the object of judicial interpretation is to determine the intent of the legislature, being bound by genuine but unexpressed legislative intent rather than the law is only the *theoretical* threat. The *practical* threat is that, under the guise or even the self-delusion of pursuing unexpressed legislative intents, common-law judges will in fact pursue their own objectives and desires, extending their lawmaking proclivities from the common law to the statutory field. When you are told to decide, not on the basis of what the legislature said, but on the basis of what it *meant*, and are assured that there is no necessary connection between the two, your best shot at figuring out what the legislature meant is to ask yourself what a wise and intelligent person *should* have meant; and that will surely bring you to the conclusion that the law means what you think it *ought* to mean—which is precisely how judges decide things under the common law. As Dean Landis of Harvard Law School (a believer in the search for legislative intent) put it in a 1930 article:

> [T]he gravest sins are perpetrated in the name of the intent of the legislature. Judges are rarely willing to admit their role as actual lawgivers, and such admissions as are wrung from their unwilling lips lie in the field of common and not statute law. To condone in these instances the practice of talking in terms of the intent of the legislature, as if the legislature had attributed a particular meaning to certain words, when it is apparent that the intent is that of the judge, is to condone atavistic practices too reminiscent of the medicine man.[8] . . .

The text is the law, and it is the text that must be observed. I agree with Justice Holmes's remark, quoted approvingly by Justice Frankfurter in his article on the construction of statutes: "Only a day or two ago—when counsel talked of the intention of a legislature, I was indiscreet enough to say I don't care what their intention was. I only want to know what the words mean." [9] And I agree with Holmes's other remark, quoted approvingly by Justice Jackson: "We do not inquire what the legislature meant; we ask only what the statute means." [10]

Textualism

The philosophy of interpretation I have described above is known as textualism. In some sophisticated circles, it is considered simpleminded—"wooden," "unimaginative," "pedestrian." It is none of that. To be a textualist in good standing, one need not be too dull to perceive the broader social purposes that a statute is designed, or could be designed, to serve; or too hidebound to realize that new times require new laws. One need only hold the belief that judges have no authority to pursue those broader purposes or write those new laws.

Textualism should not be confused with so-called strict constructionism, a degraded form of textualism that brings the whole philosophy into disrepute. I am not a strict constructionist, and no one ought to be—though better that, I suppose, than a nontextualist. A text should not be construed strictly, and it should not be construed leniently; it should be construed reasonably, to contain all that it fairly means. The difference between textualism and strict constructionism can be seen in a case my Court decided four terms ago.[11] The statute at issue provided for an increased jail term if, "during and in relation to . . . [a] drug trafficking crime," the defendant "uses . . . a firearm." The defendant in this case had sought to purchase a quantity of cocaine; and what he had offered to give in exchange for the cocaine was an unloaded firearm, which he showed to the drug-seller. The Court held, I regret to say, that the defendant was subject to the increased penalty, because he had "used a firearm during and in relation to a drug trafficking crime." The vote was not even close (6–3). I dissented. Now I cannot say whether my colleagues in the majority voted the way they did because they are strict-construction textualists, or because they are not textualists at all. But a proper textualist, which is to say my kind of textualist, would surely have voted to acquit. The phrase "uses a gun" fairly connoted use of a gun for what guns are normally used for, that is, as a weapon. As I put the point in my dissent, when you ask someone, "Do you use a cane?" you are not inquiring whether he has hung his grandfather's antique cane as a decoration in the hallway.

But while the good textualist is not a literalist, neither is he a nihilist. Words do have a limited range of meaning, and no interpretation that goes beyond that range is permissible. My favorite example of a departure from text—and certainly the departure that has enabled judges to do more freewheeling law-making than any other—pertains to the Due Process Clause found in the Fifth and Fourteenth Amendments of the United States Constitution, which says that no person shall "be deprived of life, liberty, or property without due process of law." It has been interpreted to prevent the government from taking away certain liberties *beyond* those, such as freedom of speech and of religion, that are specifically named in the Constitution. (The first Supreme Court case to use the Due Process Clause in this fashion was, by the way, *Dred Scott*[12]—not a desirable parentage.) Well, it may or may not be a good thing to guarantee additional liberties, but the Due Process Clause quite obviously does not bear that interpretation. By its inescapable terms, it guarantees only process. Property can be taken by the state; liberty can be taken; even life can be taken; but not without the *process* that our traditions require—notably, a validly enacted law and a fair trial. To say otherwise is to abandon textualism, and to render democratically adopted texts mere springboards for judicial lawmaking.

Of all the criticisms leveled against textualism, the most mindless is that it is "formalistic." The answer to that is, *of course it's formalistic!* The rule of law is *about* form. If, for example, a citizen performs an act—let us say the sale of certain technology to a foreign country—which is prohibited by a widely publicized bill proposed by the administration and passed by both houses of Congress, *but not yet signed by the President*, that sale is lawful. It is of no consequence that everyone knows both houses of Congress and the President wish to prevent that sale. Before the wish becomes a binding law, it must be embodied in a bill that passes both houses and is signed by the President. Is that not formalism? A murderer has been caught with blood on his hands, bending over the body of his victim; a neighbor with a video camera has filmed the crime; and the murderer has confessed in writing and on videotape. We nonetheless insist that before the state can punish this miscreant, it must conduct a full-dress criminal trial that results in a verdict of guilty. Is that not formalism? Long live formalism. It is what makes a government a government of laws and not of men. . . .

Legislative History

Let me turn now . . . to an interpretive device whose widespread use is relatively new: legislative history, by which I mean the statements made in the floor debates, committee reports, and even committee testimony, leading up to the enactment of the legislation. My view that the objective indication of the words, rather than the intent of the legislature, is what constitutes the law leads me, of course, to the conclusion that legislative history should not be used as an authoritative indication of a statute's meaning. This was the traditional English, and the traditional American, practice. Chief Justice Taney wrote:

> In expounding this law, the judgment of the court cannot, in any degree, be influenced by the construction placed upon it by individual members of Congress in the debate which took place on its passage, nor by the motives or reasons assigned by them for supporting or opposing amendments that were offered. The law as it passed is the will of the majority of both houses, *and the only mode in which that will is spoken is in the act itself;* and we must

gather their intention from the language there used, comparing it, when any ambiguity exists, with the laws upon the same subject, and looking, if necessary, to the public history of the times in which it was passed.[13]

That uncompromising view generally prevailed in this country until the present century. The movement to change it gained momentum in the late 1920s and 1930s, driven, believe it or not, by frustration with common-law judges' use of "legislative intent" and phonied-up canons to impose their own views—in those days views opposed to progressive social legislation. I quoted earlier an article by Dean Landis inveighing against such judicial usurpation. The solution he proposed was not the banishment of legislative intent as an interpretive criterion, but rather the use of legislative history to place that intent beyond manipulation.[14]

Extensive use of legislative history in this country dates only from about the 1940s. . . . In the past few decades, however, we have developed a legal culture in which lawyers routinely—and I do mean routinely—make no distinction between words in the text of a statute and words in its legislative history. My Court is frequently told, in briefs and in oral argument, that "Congress said thus-and-so"—when in fact what is being quoted is not the law promulgated by Congress, nor even any text endorsed by a single house of Congress, but rather the statement of a single committee of a single house, set forth in a committee report. Resort to legislative history has become so common that lawyerly wags have popularized a humorous quip inverting the oft-recited (and oft-ignored) rule as to when its use is appropriate: "One should consult the text of the statute," the joke goes, "only when the legislative history is ambiguous." Alas, that is no longer funny. Reality has overtaken parody. A few terms ago, I read a brief that *began* the legal argument with a discussion of legislative history and then continued (I am quoting it verbatim): "Unfortunately, the legislative debates are not helpful. Thus, we turn to the other guidepost in this difficult area, statutory language." [15]

As I have said, I object to the use of legislative history on principle, since I reject intent of the legislature as the proper criterion of the law. What is most exasperating about the use of legislative history, however, is that it does not even make sense for those who *accept* legislative intent as the criterion. It is much more likely to produce a false or contrived legislative intent than a genuine one. . . .

Ironically, but quite understandably, the more courts have relied upon legislative history, the less worthy of reliance it has become. In earlier days, it was at least genuine and not contrived—a real part of the legislation's *history*, in the sense that it was part of the *development* of the bill, part of the attempt to inform and persuade those who voted. Nowadays, however, when it is universally known and expected that judges will resort to floor debates and (especially) committee reports as authoritative expressions of "legislative intent," affecting the courts rather than informing the Congress has become the primary purpose of the exercise. It is less that the courts refer to legislative history because it exists than that legislative history exists because the courts refer to it. One of the routine tasks of the Washington lawyer-lobbyist is to draft language that sympathetic legislators can recite in a prewritten "floor debate"—or, even better, insert into a committee report. . . .

I think that Dean Landis, and those who joined him in the prescription of legislative history as a cure for what he called "willful judges," would be aghast at the results a half century later. On balance, it has facilitated rather than deterred decisions that are based upon the courts' policy preferences, rather than neutral principles of law. Since there are no rules as to how much weight an element of legislative history is entitled to, it can usually be either relied upon or dismissed with equal plausibility. If the willful judge does not like the committee report, he will not follow it; he will call the statute not ambiguous enough, the committee report too ambiguous, or the legislative history (this is a favorite phrase) "as a whole, inconclusive." . . .

Interpreting Constitutional Texts

Without pretending to have exhausted the vast topic of textual interpretation, I wish to address a final subject: the distinctive problem of constitutional interpretation. The problem is distinctive, not because special principles of interpretation apply, but because the usual principles are being applied to an unusual text. Chief Justice Marshall put the point as well as it can be put in *McCulloch* v. *Maryland*:

> A constitution, to contain an accurate detail of all the subdivisions of which its great powers will admit, and of all the means by which they may be carried into execution, would partake of the prolixity of a legal code, and could scarcely be embraced by the human mind. It would probably never be understood by the public. Its nature, therefore, requires, that only its great outlines should be marked, its important objects designated, and the minor ingredients which compose those objects be deduced from the nature of the objects themselves.[16]

In textual interpretation, context is everything, and the context of the Constitution tells us not to expect nit-picking detail, and to give words and phrases an expansive rather than narrow interpretation—though not an interpretation that the language will not bear.

Take, for example, the provision of the First Amendment that forbids abridgment of "the freedom of speech, or of the press." That phrase does not list the full range of communicative expression. Handwritten letters, for example, are neither speech nor press. Yet surely there is no doubt they cannot be censored. In this constitutional context, speech and press, the two most common forms of communication, stand as a sort of synecdoche for the whole. That is not strict construction, but it is reasonable construction.

It is curious that most of those who insist that the drafter's intent gives meaning to a statute reject the drafter's intent as the criterion for interpretation of the Constitution. I reject it for both. . . . [T]he Great Divide with regard to constitutional interpretation is not that between Framers' intent and objective meaning, but rather that between *original* meaning (whether derived from Framers' intent or not) and *current* meaning. The ascendant school of constitutional interpretation affirms the existence of what is called The Living Constitution, a body of law that (unlike normal statutes) grows and changes from age to age, in order to meet the needs of a changing society. And it is the judges who determine those needs and "find" that changing law. Seems familiar, doesn't it? Yes, it is the common law returned, but infinitely more powerful than what the old common law ever pretended to be, for now it trumps even the statutes of democratic legislatures. . . .

If you go into a constitutional law class, or study a constitutional law casebook, or read a brief filed in a constitutional law case, you will rarely find the discussion addressed to the text of the constitutional provision that is at issue, or to the question of what was the originally understood or even the originally intended meaning of that text. The starting point of the analysis will be Supreme Court cases, and the new issue will presumptively be decided according to the logic that those cases expressed, with no regard for how far that logic, thus extended, has distanced us from the original text and understanding. Worse still, however, it is known and understood that if that logic fails to produce what in the view of the current Supreme Court is the *desirable* result for the case at hand, then, like good common-law judges, the Court will distinguish its precedents, or narrow them, or if all else fails overrule them, in order that the Constitution might mean what it *ought* to mean. Should there be—to take one of the less controversial examples—a constitutional right to die? If so, there is.[17] Should there be a constitutional right to reclaim a biological child put out for adoption by the other parent? Again, if so, there is.[18] If it is good, it is so. Never mind the text that we are supposedly construing; we will smuggle these new rights in, if all else fails, under the Due Process Clause (which, as I have described, is textually incapable of containing them). Moreover, what the Constitution meant yesterday it does not necessarily mean today. As our opinions say in the context of our Eighth Amendment jurisprudence (the Cruel and Unusual Punishments Clause), its meaning changes to reflect "the evolving standards of decency that mark the progress of a maturing society."[19]

This is preeminently a common-law way of making law, and not the way of construing a democratically adopted text. . . . Proposals for "dynamic statutory construction," such as those of Judge Calabresi . . . are concededly avant-garde. The Constitution, however, even though a democratically adopted text, we formally treat like the common law. What, it is fair to ask, is the justification for doing so?

One would suppose that the rule that a text does not change would apply *a fortiori* to a constitution. If courts felt too much bound by the democratic process to tinker with statutes, when their tinkering could be adjusted by the legislature, how much more should they feel bound not to tinker with a constitution, when their tinkering is virtually irreparable. It certainly cannot be said that a constitution naturally suggests changeability; to the contrary, its whole purpose is to prevent change—to embed certain rights in such a manner that future generations cannot readily take them away. A society that adopts a bill of rights is skeptical that "evolving standards of decency" always "mark progress," and that societies always "mature," as opposed to rot. Neither the text of such a document nor the intent of its framers (whichever you choose) can possibly lead to the conclusion that its only effect is to take the power of changing rights away from the legislature and give it to the courts.

Flexibility and Liberality of the Living Constitution

The argument most frequently made in favor of the Living Constitution is a pragmatic one: Such an evolutionary approach is necessary in order to provide the "flexibility" that a changing society requires; the Constitution would have snapped if it had not been permitted to bend and grow. This might be a persuasive argument if most of the "growing" that the proponents of this approach have brought upon us in the past, and are determined to bring upon us in the future, were the *elimination* of restrictions upon democratic government. But just the opposite is true. Historically, and particularly in the past thirty-five years, the "evolving" Constitution has imposed a vast array of new constraints—new inflexibilities—upon administrative, judicial, and legislative action. To mention only a few things that formerly could be done or not done, as the society desired, but now cannot be done:

- admitting in a state criminal trial evidence of guilt that was obtained by an unlawful search;[20]

- permitting invocation of God at public-school graduations;[21]

- electing one of the two houses of a state legislature the way the United States Senate is elected, i.e., on a basis that does not give all voters numerically equal representation;[22]

- terminating welfare payments as soon as evidence of fraud is received, subject to restoration after hearing if the evidence is satisfactorily refuted;[23]

- imposing property requirements as a condition of voting;[24]

- prohibiting anonymous campaign literature;[25]

- prohibiting pornography.[26]

And the future agenda of constitutional evolutionists is mostly more of the same—the creation of *new* restrictions upon democratic government, rather than the elimination of old ones. *Less* flexibility in government, not *more*. As things now stand, the state and federal governments may either apply capital punishment or abolish it, permit suicide or forbid it—all as the changing times and the changing sentiments of society may demand. But when capital punishment is held to violate the Eighth Amendment, and suicide is held to be protected by the Fourteenth Amendment, all flexibility with regard to those matters will be gone. No, the reality of the matter is that, generally speaking, devotees of The Living Constitution do not seek to facilitate social change but to prevent it.

There are, I must admit, a few exceptions to that—a few instances in which, historically, greater flexibility has been the result of the process. But those exceptions serve only to refute another argument of the proponents of an evolving Constitution, that evolution will always be in the direction of greater personal liberty. (They consider that a great advantage, for reasons that I do not entirely understand. All government represents a balance between individual freedom and social order, and it is not true that *every* alteration of that balance in the direction of greater individual freedom is necessarily good.) But in any case, the record of history refutes the proposition that the evolving Constitution will invariably enlarge individual rights. The most obvious refutation is the modern Court's limitation of the constitutional protections afforded to property. The provision prohibiting impairment of the obligation of contracts, for example, has been gutted.[27] I am sure that We the People agree with that development; we value property rights less than the Founders did. So also, we value the right to bear arms less than did the Founders (who thought the right of self-defense to be absolutely fundamental), and there will be few tears shed if and when the Second Amendment is held to guarantee nothing more than the state National Guard. But this just shows that the Founders were right when they feared that some (in their view misguided) future generation might wish to abandon liberties that they considered essential, and so sought to protect those liberties in a Bill of Rights. We may *like* the abridgment of property rights and *like* the elimination of the right to bear arms; but let us not pretend that these are not *reductions of rights*.

Or if property rights are too cold to arouse enthusiasm, and the right to bear arms too dangerous, let me give another example: Several terms ago a case came before the Supreme Court involving a prosecution for sexual abuse of a young child. The trial court found that the child would be too frightened to testify in the presence of the (presumed) abuser, and so, pursuant to state law, she was permitted to testify with only the prosecutor and defense counsel present, with the defendant, the judge, and the jury watching over closed-circuit television. A reasonable enough procedure, and it was held to be constitutional by my Court.[28] I dissented, because the Sixth Amendment provides that "[i]n *all* criminal prosecutions the accused shall enjoy the right . . . to be confronted with the witnesses against him" (emphasis added). There is no doubt what confrontation meant— or indeed means today. It means face-to-face, not watching from another room. And there is no doubt what one of the major purposes of that provision was: to induce *precisely* that pressure upon the witness which the little girl found it difficult to endure. It is difficult to accuse someone to his face, particularly when you are lying. Now no extrinsic factors have changed since that provision was adopted in 1791. Sexual abuse existed then, as it does now; little children were more easily upset than adults, then as now; a means of placing the defendant out of sight of the witness existed then as now (a screen could easily have been erected that would enable the defendant to see the witness, but not the witness the defendant). But the Sixth Amendment nonetheless gave *all* criminal defendants the right to *confront* the witnesses against them, because that was thought to be an important protection. The only significant things that *have* changed, I think, are the society's sensitivity to so-called psychic trauma (which is what we are told the child witness in such a situation suffers) and the society's assessment of where the proper balance ought to be struck between the two extremes of a procedure that assures convicting 100 percent of all child abusers, and a procedure that assures acquitting 100 percent of those falsely accused of child abuse. I have no doubt that the society is, as a whole, happy and pleased with what my Court decided. But we should not pretend that the decision did not *eliminate* a liberty that previously existed. . . .

It seems to me that that is where we are heading, or perhaps even where we have arrived. Seventy-five years ago, we believed firmly enough in a rock-solid, unchanging Constitution that we felt it necessary to adopt the Nineteenth Amendment to give women the vote. The battle was not fought in the courts, and few thought that it could be, despite the constitutional guarantee of Equal Protection of the Laws; that provision did not, when it was adopted, and hence did not in 1920, guarantee equal access to the ballot but permitted distinctions on the basis not only of age but of property and of sex. Who can doubt that if the issue had been deferred until today, the Constitution would be (formally) unamended, and the courts would be the chosen instrumentality of change? The American people have been converted to belief in The Living Constitution, a "morphing" document that means, from age to age, what it ought to mean. And with that conversion has inevitably come the new phenomenon of selecting and confirming federal judges, at all levels, on the basis of their views regarding a whole series of proposals for constitutional evolution. If the courts are free to write the Constitution anew, they will, by God, write it the way the majority wants; the appointment and confirmation process will see to that. This, of course, is the end of the Bill of Rights, whose meaning will be committed to the very body it was meant to protect against: the majority. By trying to make the Constitution do everything that needs doing from age to age, we shall have caused it to do nothing at all.

NOTES

I am grateful for technical and research assistance by Matthew P. Previn, and for substantive suggestions by Eugene Scalia.

1. Oliver Wendell Holmes, Jr., *The Common Law* (1881).

2. The country's first major code of civil procedure, known as the Field Code (after David Dudley Field, who played a major role in its enactment), was passed in New York in 1848. By the end of the nineteenth century, similar codes had been adopted in many states. *See* Lawrence M. Friedman, *A History of American Law* 340–47 (1973).

3. The principal exception to this statement consists of so-called Uniform Laws, statutes enacted in virtually identical form by all or a large majority of state legislatures, in an effort to achieve nationwide uniformity with respect to certain aspects of some common-law fields. *See, e.g.*, Uniform Commercial Code, 1 U.L.A. 5 (1989); Uniform Marriage and Divorce Act 9A U.L.A. 156 (1987); Uniform Consumer Credit Code, 7A U.L.A. 17 (1985).

4. "The [members of the judiciary department], by the mode of their appointment, as well as by the nature and permanency of it, are too far removed from the people to share much in their prepossessions." *The Federalist* No. 49, at 341 (Jacob E. Cooke ed., 1961).

5. Henry M. Hart, Jr. & Albert M. Sacks, *The Legal Process* 1169 (William N. Eskridge, Jr. & Philip P. Frickey eds., 1994).

6. *See* 1 William Blackstone, *Commentaries on the Laws of England* 59–62, 91 (photo reprint 1979) (1765).

7. Joel Prentiss Bishop, *Commentaries on the Written Laws and Their Interpretation* 57–58 (Boston: Little, Brown, & Co. 1882) (emphasis added) (citation omitted).

8. James M. Landis, *A Note on "Statutory Interpretation,"* 43 Harv. L. Rev. 886, 891 (1930).

9. Felix Frankfurter, *Some Reflections on the Reading of Statutes*, 47 Colum. L. Rev. 527, 538 (1947).

10. Oliver Wendell Holmes, *Collected Legal Papers* 207 (1920), *quoted in* Schwegmann Bros. v. Calvert Distillers Corp., 341 U.S. 384, 397 (1951) (Jackson, J., concurring).

11. Smith v. United States, 508 U.S. 223 (1993).

12. Dred Scott v. Sandford, 60 U.S. (19 How.) 393, 450 (1857).

13. Aldridge v. Williams, 44 U.S. (3 How.) 9, 24 (1845) (emphasis added).

14. *See* Landis, *supra* note 17, at 891–92.

15. Brief for Petitioner at 21, Jett v. Dallas Indep. Sch. Dist., 491 U.S. 701 (1989), *quoted in* Green v. Bock Laundry Machine Co., 490 U.S. 504, 530 (1989) (Scalia, J., concurring).

16. McCulloch v. Maryland, 17 U.S. (4 Wheat.) 316, 407 (1819).

17. *See* Cruzan v. Director, Mo. Dep't of Health, 497 U.S. 261, 279 (1990).

18. *See In re* Kirchner, 649 N.E.2d 324, 333 (Ill.), *cert. denied*, 115 S. Ct. 2599 (1995).

19. Rhodes v. Chapman, 452 U.S. 337, 346 (1981), quoting from Trop v. Dulles, 356 U.S. 86, 101 (1958) (plurality opinion).

20. *See* Mapp v. Ohio, 367 U.S. 643 (1961).

21. *See* Lee v. Weisman, 505 U.S. 577 (1992).

22. *See* Reynolds v. Sims, 377 U.S. 533 (1964).

23. *See* Goldberg v. Kelly, 397 U.S. 254 (1970).

24. *See* Kramer v. Union Free Sch. Dist., 395 U.S. 621 (1969).

25. *See* McIntyre v. Ohio Elections Comm'n, 115 S. Ct. 1511 (1995).

26. Under current doctrine, pornography may be banned only if it is "obscene," *see* Miller v. California, 413 U.S. 15 (1973), a judicially crafted term of art that does not embrace material that excites "normal, healthy sexual desires," Brocket v. Spokane Arcades, Inc., 472 U.S. 491, 498 (1985).

27. *See* Home Building & Loan Ass'n v. Blaisdell, 290 U.S. 398 (1934).

28. *See* Maryland v. Craig, 497 U.S. 836 (1990).

9-2

from *Active Liberty*

Stephen Breyer

Justice Stephen Breyer's book Active Liberty, *from which this essay is excerpted, has been widely viewed as an activist judge's response to Justice Scalia's paean to judicial restraint. Yet Breyer does not envision a broadly activist role for judges in shaping social policy. For one thing, he agrees fundamentally with Scalia that unelected, life-tenured judges should subordinate their personal views on policy to those who are elected to make these decisions. Reflecting this, Breyer's decisions show his reluctance to overrule acts of Congress and executive decisions. For Breyer, the primacy of democracy requires that judges play a special role as guardians of citizens' rights and opportunities to influence government. On a variety of issues, this hierarchy of values leads Breyer to decide cases in ways that Scalia believes overstep judges' mandate. Breyer accepts broad regulation of campaign finance as advancing the performance of democracy, whereas Scalia argues that such laws affront First Amendment protections of free speech.*

THE THEME AS I here consider it falls within an interpretive tradition. . . . That tradition sees texts as driven by *purposes*. The judge should try to find and "honestly . . . say what was the underlying purpose expressed" in a statute. The judge should read constitutional language "as the revelation of the great purposes which were intended to be achieved by the Constitution" itself, a "framework for" and a "continuing instrument of government." The judge should recognize that the Constitution will apply to "new subject matter . . . with which the framers were not familiar." Thus, the judge, whether applying statute or Constitution, should "reconstruct the past solution imaginatively in its setting and project the purposes which inspired it upon the concrete occasions which arise for their decision." Since law is connected to life, judges, in applying a text in light of its purpose, should look to *consequences*, including "contemporary conditions, social, industrial, and political, of the community to be affected." And since "the purpose of construction is the ascertainment of meaning, nothing that is logically relevant should be excluded."[1]

Source: Stephen Breyer, from *Active Liberty: Interpreting Our Democratic Constitution* (Alfred A. Knopf: 2005), 17–34, 85–101. Some notes appearing in the original have been deleted.

That tradition does not expect highly general instructions themselves to determine the outcome of difficult concrete cases where language is open-ended and precisely defined purpose is difficult to ascertain. Certain constitutional language, for example, reflects "fundamental aspirations and . . . 'moods,' embodied in provisions like the due process and equal protection clauses, which were designed not to be precise and positive directions for rules of action." A judge, when interpreting such open-ended provisions, must avoid being "willful, in the sense of enforcing individual views." A judge cannot "enforce whatever he thinks best." "In the exercise of" the "high power" of judicial review, says Justice Louis Brandeis, "we must be ever on our guard, lest we erect our prejudices into legal principles." At the same time, a judge must avoid being "wooden, in uncritically resting on formulas, in assuming the familiar to be the necessary, in not realizing that any problem can be solved if only one principle is involved but that unfortunately all controversies of importance involve if not a conflict at least an interplay of principles."[2]

How, then, is the judge to act between the bounds of the "willful" and the "wooden"? The tradition answers with an *attitude*, an attitude that hesitates to rely upon any single theory or grand view of law, of interpretation, or of the Constitution. It champions the need to search for purposes; it calls for restraint, asking judges to "speak . . . humbly as the voice of the law." And it finds in the democratic nature of our system more than simply a justification for judicial restraint. Holmes reminds the judge as a general matter to allow "[c]onsiderable latitude . . . for differences of view." . . .

[O]ne can reasonably view the Constitution as focusing upon active liberty, both as important in itself and as a partial means to help secure individual (modern) freedom. The Framers included elements designed to "control and mitigate" the ill effects of more direct forms of democratic government, but in doing so, the Framers "did not see themselves as repudiating either the Revolution or popular government." Rather, they were "saving both from their excesses." The act of ratifying the Constitution, by means of special state elections with broad voter eligibility rules, signaled the democratic character of the document itself.[3]

As history has made clear, the original Constitution was insufficient. It did not include a majority of the nation within its "democratic community." It took a civil war and eighty years of racial segregation before the slaves and their descendants could begin to think of the Constitution as theirs. Nor did women receive the right to vote until 1920. The "people" had to amend the Constitution, not only to extend its democratic base but also to expand and more fully to secure basic individual (negative) liberty.

But the original document sowed the democratic seed. Madison described something fundamental about American government, then and now, when he said the Constitution is a "charter . . . of power . . . granted by liberty," not (as in Europe) a "charter of liberty . . . granted by power."[4]. . .

In sum, our constitutional history has been a quest for workable government, workable democratic government, workable democratic government protective of individual personal liberty. Our central commitment has been to "government of the people, by the people, for the people." And the applications following illustrate how this constitutional understanding helps interpret the Constitution—in a way that helps to resolve problems related to *modern* government. . . .

Statutory Interpretation

The [first] example concerns statutory interpretation. It contrasts a literal text-based approach with an approach that places more emphasis on statutory purpose and congressional intent. It illustrates why judges should pay primary attention to a statute's purpose in difficult cases of interpretation in which language is not clear. It shows how overemphasis on text can lead courts astray, divorcing law from life—indeed, creating law that harms those whom Congress meant to help. And it explains why a purposive approach is more consistent with the framework for a "delegated democracy" that the Constitution creates.[5]

The interpretive problem arises when statutory language does not clearly answer the question of what the statute means or how it applies. Why does a statute contain such language? Perhaps Congress used inappropriate language. Perhaps it failed to use its own drafting expertise or failed to have committee hearings, writing legislation on the floor instead. Perhaps it chose politically symbolic language or ambiguous language over more precise language—possibilities that modern, highly partisan, interest-group-based politics (responding to overly simplified media accounts) make realistic. Perhaps no one in Congress thought about how the statute would apply in certain circumstances. Perhaps it is impossible to use language that foresees how a statute should apply in all relevant circumstances.

The founding generation of Americans understood these or similar possibilities. They realized that judges, though mere "fallible men," would have to exercise judgment and discretion in applying newly codified law. But they expected that judges, when doing so, would remain faithful to the legislators' will. The problem of statutory interpretation is how to meet that expectation.

Most judges start in the same way. They look first to the statute's language, its structure, and its history in an effort to determine the statute's purpose. They then use that purpose (along with the language, structure, and history) to determine the proper interpretation. Thus far, there is agreement. But when the problem is truly difficult, these factors without more may simply limit the universe of possible answers without clearly identifying a final choice. What then?

At this point judges tend to divide in their approach. Some look primarily to text, i.e., to language and text-related circumstances, for further enlightenment. They may try to tease further meaning from the language and structure of the statute itself. They may look to language-based canons of interpretation in the search for an "objective" key to the statute's proper interpretation, say a canon like *noscitur a sociis*, which tells a judge to interpret a word so that it has the same kind of meaning as its neighbors. Textualism, it has been argued, searches for "meaning . . . in structure." It means "preferring the language and structure of the law whenever possible over its legislative history and imputed values." It asks judges to avoid invocation of vague or broad statutory purposes and instead to consider such purposes at "lower levels of generality." It hopes thereby to reduce the risk that judges will interpret statutes subjectively, substituting their own ideas of what is good for those of Congress.[6]

Other judges look primarily to the statute's purposes for enlightenment. They avoid the use of interpretive canons. They allow context to determine the level of generality at which they will describe a statute's purpose—in the way that context tells us not to answer the lost driver's request for directions, "Where am I?" with the words "In a car." They speak in terms of congressional "intent," while understanding that legal conventions govern the use of that term to describe, not the intent of any, or every, individual legislator, but the intent of the group—in the way that linguistic conventions allow us to speak of the intentions of an army or a team, even when they differ from those of any, or every, soldier or member. And they examine legislative history, often closely, in the hope that the history will help them better understand the context, the enacting legislators' objectives, and ultimately the statute's purposes. At the heart of a purpose-based approach stands the "reasonable member of Congress"—a legal fiction that applies, for example, even when Congress did not in fact consider a particular problem. The judge will ask how this person (real or fictional), aware of the statute's language, structure, and general objectives (actually or hypothetically), *would have wanted* a court to interpret the statute in light of present circumstances in the particular case.

[A] recent case illustrate[s] the difference between the two approaches. In [it] the majority followed a more textual approach; the dissent, a more purposive approach. . . . The federal habeas corpus statute is ambiguous in respect to the time limits that apply when a state prisoner seeks access to federal habeas corpus. It says that a state prisoner (ordinarily) must file a federal petition within one year after his state court conviction becomes final. But the statute tolls that one-year period during the time that "a properly filed application for State post-conviction *or other collateral review*" is pending. Do the words "other collateral review" include an earlier application for a federal habeas corpus petition? Should the one-year period be tolled, for example, when a state prisoner mistakenly files a habeas petition in federal court before he exhausts all his state collateral remedies?

It is unlikely that anyone in Congress thought about this question, for it is highly technical. Yet it is important. More than half of all federal habeas corpus petitions fall into the relevant category—i.e., state prisoners file them prematurely before the prisoner has tried to take advantage of available state remedies. In those cases, the federal court often dismisses the petition and the state prisoner must return to state court to exhaust available state remedies before he can once again file his federal habeas petition in federal court. If the one-year statute of limitations is not tolled while the first federal habeas petition was pending, that state prisoner will likely find that the one year has run—and his federal petition is time-barred—before he can return to federal court.[7]

A literal reading of the statute suggests that this is just what Congress had in mind. It suggests that the one-year time limit is tolled only during the time that *state* collateral review (or similar) proceedings are in process. And that reading is supported by various linguistic canons of construction.[8]

Nonetheless, the language does not foreclose an alternative interpretation— an interpretation under which such petitions would fall within the scope of the phrase "other collateral review." The word "State" could be read to modify the phrase "post-conviction . . . review," permitting "*other* collateral review" to refer to federal proceedings. The phrase "properly filed" could be interpreted to refer to purely formal filing requirements rather than calling into play more important remedial questions such as the presence or absence of "exhaustion." A purposive approach favors this latter linguistic interpretation.[9]

Why? [Consider] our hypothetical legislator, the reasonable member of Congress. Which interpretation would that member favor (if he had thought of the problem, which he likely had not)? Consider the consequences of the more literal interpretation. That interpretation would close the doors of federal habeas courts to many or most state prisoners who mistakenly filed a federal habeas petition too soon, but not to all such prisoners. Whether the one-year window was still open would depend in large part on how long the federal court considering the premature federal petition took to dismiss it. In cases in which the court ruled quickly, the short time the federal petition was (wrongly) present in the federal court might not matter. But if a premature federal petition languishes on the federal court's docket while the one year runs, the petitioner would likely lose his one meaningful chance to seek federal habeas relief. By way of contrast, state court delay in considering a prisoner petition in state court would not matter. Whenever *state* proceedings are at issue, the statute tolls the one-year limitations period.

Now ask *why* our reasonable legislator would want to bring about these consequences. He might believe that state prisoners have too often abused the federal writ by filing too many petitions. But the distinction that a literal interpretation would make between those allowed to file and those not allowed to file—a distinction that in essence rests upon federal court processing delay—is a *random* distinction, bearing no logical relation to any abuse-related purpose. Would our reasonable legislator, even if concerned about abuse of the writ, choose to deny access to the Great Writ on a *random* basis? Given our traditions, including those the Constitution grants through its habeas corpus guarantees, the answer to this question is likely no. Would those using a more literal text-based approach answer this question differently? I do not think so. But my real objection to the text-based approach is that it would prevent them from posing the question at all.[10]

[This] example suggest[s] the danger that lurks where judges rely too heavily upon just text and textual aids when interpreting a statute. . . . [W]hen difficult statutory questions are at issue, courts do better to focus foremost upon statutory purpose, ruling out neither legislative history nor any other form of help in order to locate the role that Congress intended the statutory words in question to play.

For one thing, near-exclusive reliance upon canons and other linguistic interpretive aids in close cases can undermine the Constitution's democratic objective. Legislation in a delegated democracy is meant to embody the people's will, either directly (insofar as legislators see themselves as translating how their constituents feel about each proposed law) or indirectly (insofar as legislators see themselves as exercising delegated authority to vote in accordance with what they see as the public interest). Either way, an interpretation of a statute that tends to implement the legislator's will helps to implement the public's will and is therefore consistent with the Constitution's democratic purpose. For similar reasons an interpretation that undercuts the statute's objectives tends to undercut that constitutional objective. . . .

Use of a "reasonable legislator" fiction also facilitates legislative accountability. Ordinary citizens think in terms of general purposes. They readily understand their elected legislators' thinking similarly. It is not impossible to ask an ordinary citizen to determine whether a particular law is consistent with a general purpose the ordinary citizen might support. It is not impossible to ask an ordinary citizen to determine what general purpose a legislator sought to achieve in enacting a particular statute. And it is not impossible for the ordinary citizen to judge the legislator accordingly. But it *is* impossible to ask an ordinary citizen (or an ordinary legislator) to understand the operation of linguistic canons of interpretation. And it *is* impossible to ask an ordinary citizen to draw any relevant electoral conclusion from consequences that might flow when courts reach a purpose-thwarting interpretation of the statute based upon their near-exclusive use of interpretive canons. Were a segment of the public unhappy about application of the Arbitration Act to ordinary employment contracts, whom should it blame?

For another thing, that approach means that laws will work better for the people they are presently meant to affect. Law is tied to life, and a failure to understand how a statute is so tied can undermine the very human activity that the law seeks to benefit. The more literal text-based, canon-based interpretation of the Foreign Sovereign Immunities jurisdictional statute, for example, means that foreign nations, those using tiered corporate ownership, will find their access to federal courts cut off, undermining the statute's basic jurisdictional objectives. The textual approach to the habeas corpus statute randomly closes courthouse doors in a way that runs contrary to our commitment to basic individual liberty. And it does so because it tends to stop judges from asking a relevant purpose-based question: Why would Congress have wanted a statute that produces those consequences?[11]

In sum, a "reasonable legislator" approach is a workable method of implementing the Constitution's democratic objective. It permits ready translation of the general desire of the public for certain ends, through the legislator's efforts to embody those ends in legislation, into a set of statutory words that will carry out those general objectives. I have argued that the Framers created the Constitution's complex governmental mechanism in order better to translate public will, determined through collective deliberation, into sound public policy. The courts constitute part of that mechanism. And judicial use of the "will of the reasonable legislator"—even if at times it is a fiction—helps statutes match their means to their overall public policy objectives, a match that helps translate the popular will into sound policy. An overly literal reading of a text can too often stand in the way.

Constitutional Interpretation: Speech

The [next] example focuses on the First Amendment and how it . . . show[s] the importance of reading the First Amendment not in isolation but as seeking to maintain a system of free expression designed to further a basic constitutional purpose: creating and maintaining democratic decision-making institutions.

The example begins where courts normally begin in First Amendment cases. They try to classify the speech at issue, distinguishing among different speech-related activities for the purpose of applying a strict, moderately strict, or totally relaxed presumption of unconstitutionality. Is the speech "political speech," calling for a strong pro-speech presumption, "commercial speech," calling for a mid-range presumption, or simply a form of economic regulation presumed constitutional?

Should courts begin in this way? Some argue that making these kinds of categorical distinctions is a misplaced enterprise. The Constitution's language makes no such distinction. It simply protects "the freedom of speech" from government restriction. "Speech is speech and that is the end of the matter." But to limit distinctions to the point at which First Amendment law embodies the slogan "speech is speech" cannot work. And the fact that the First Amendment seeks to protect active liberty as well as modern liberty helps to explain why.[12]

The democratic government that the Constitution creates now regulates a host of activities that inevitably take place through the medium of speech. Today's workers manipulate information, not wood or metal. And the modern information-based workplace, no less than its more materially based predecessors, requires the application of community standards seeking to assure, for example, the absence of anti-competitive restraints; the accuracy of information; the absence of discrimination; the protection of health, safety, the environment, the consumer; and so forth.

Laws that embody these standards obviously affect speech. Warranty laws require private firms to include on labels statements of a specified content. Securities laws and consumer protection laws insist upon the disclosure of information that businesses might prefer to keep private. Health laws forbid tobacco advertising, say, to children. Anti-discrimination laws insist that employers prevent employees from making certain kinds of statements. Communications laws require cable broadcasters to provide network access. Campaign finance laws restrict citizen contributions to candidates.

To treat all these instances alike, to scrutinize them all as if they all represented a similar kind of legislative effort to restrain a citizen's "modern liberty" to speak, would lump together too many different kinds of activities under the aegis of a single standard, thereby creating a dilemma. On the one hand, if strong First Amendment standards were to apply across the board, they would prevent a democratically elected government from creating necessary regulation. The strong free speech guarantees needed to protect the structural democratic governing process, if applied without distinction to all governmental efforts to control speech, would unreasonably limit the public's substantive economic (or social) regulatory choices. The limits on substantive choice would likely exceed what any liberty-protecting framework for democratic government could require, depriving the people of the democratically necessary room to make decisions, including the leeway to make regulatory mistakes. . . . Most scholars, including "speech is speech" advocates, consequently see a need for distinctions. The question is, Which ones? Applied where?

At this point, reference to the Constitution's more general objectives helps. First, active liberty is particularly at risk when law restricts speech directly related to the shaping of public opinion, for example, speech that takes place in areas related to politics and policy-making by elected officials. That special risk justifies especially strong pro-speech judicial presumptions. It also justifies careful review whenever the speech in question seeks to shape public opinion, particularly if that opinion in turn will affect the political process and the kind of society in which we live.

Second, whenever ordinary commercial or economic regulation is at issue, this special risk normally is absent. Moreover, strong pro-speech presumptions risk imposing what is, from the perspective of active liberty, too severe a restriction upon the legislature—a restriction that would dramatically limit the size of the legislative arena that the Constitution opens for public deliberation and action. The presence of this second risk warns against use of special, strong pro-speech judicial presumptions or special regulation-skeptical judicial review.

The upshot is that reference to constitutional purposes in general and active liberty in particular helps to justify the category of review that the Court applies to a given type of law. But those same considerations argue, among other things, against category boundaries that are too rigid or fixed and against too mechanical an application of those categories. Rather, reference to active liberty will help courts define and apply the categories case by case.

Consider campaign finance reform. The campaign finance problem arises out of the explosion of campaign costs, particularly those related to television advertising, together with the vast disparity in ability to make a campaign contribution. In the year 2000, for example, election expenditures amounted to $1.4 billion, and the two presidential candidates spent about $310 million. In 2002, an off-year without a presidential contest, campaign expenditures still amounted to more than $1 billion. A typical House election cost $900,000, with an open seat costing $1.2 million; a typical Senate seat cost about $4.8 million, with an open contested seat costing about $7.1 million.[13] . . .

A small number of individuals and groups underwrite a very large share of these costs. In 2000, about half the money the parties spent, roughly $500 million, was soft money, i.e., money not subject to regulation under the then current campaign finance laws. Two-thirds of that money—almost $300 million—came from just 800 donors, each contributing a minimum of $120,000. Of these donors, 435 were corporations or unions (whose *direct* contributions the law forbids). The rest, 365, were individual citizens. At the same time, 99 percent of the 200 million or so citizens eligible to vote gave less than $200. Ninety-six percent gave nothing at all.[14]

The upshot is a concern, reflected in campaign finance laws, that the few who give in large amounts may have special access to, and therefore influence over, their elected representatives or, at least, create the appearance of undue influence. (One study found, for example, that 55 percent of Americans believe that large contributions have a "great deal" of impact on how decisions are made in Washington; fewer than 1 percent believed they had no impact.) These contributions (particularly if applied to television) may eliminate the need for, and in that sense crowd out, smaller individual contributions. In either case, the public may lose confidence in the political system and become less willing to participate in the political process. That, in important part, is why legislatures have tried to regulate the size of campaign contributions.[15]

Our Court in 1976 considered the constitutionality of the congressional legislation that initially regulated campaign contributions, and in 2003 we considered more recent legislation that tried to close what Congress considered a loophole— the ability to make contributions in the form of unregulated soft money. The basic constitutional question does not concern the desirability or wisdom of the legislation but whether, how, and the extent to which the First Amendment permits the legislature to impose limits on the amounts that individuals or organizations or parties can contribute to a campaign. Here it is possible to sketch an approach to decision-making that draws upon the Constitution's democratic objective.[16]

It is difficult to find an easy answer to this basic constitutional question in language, in history, or in tradition. The First Amendment's language says that Congress shall not abridge "the freedom of speech." But it does not define "the freedom of speech" in any detail. The nation's Founders did not speak directly about campaign contributions. . .

Neither can we find the answer through the use of purely conceptual arguments. Some claim, for example, that "money is speech." Others say, "money is not speech." But neither contention helps. Money is not speech, it is money. But the expenditure of money enables speech, and that expenditure is often necessary to communicate a message, particularly in a political context. A law that forbade the expenditure of money to communicate could effectively suppress the message.

Nor does it resolve the problem simply to point out that campaign contribution limits inhibit the political "speech opportunities" of those who wish to contribute more. Indeed, that is so. But the question is whether, in context, such a limitation is prohibited as an abridgment of "the freedom of speech." To announce that the harm imposed by a contribution limit is under no circumstances justified is simply to state an ultimate constitutional conclusion; it is not to explain the underlying reasons.[17]

Once we remove our blinders, however, paying increased attention to the Constitution's general democratic objective, it becomes easier to reach a solution. To understand the First Amendment as seeking in significant part to protect active liberty, "participatory self-government," is to understand it as protecting more than the individual's modern freedom. It is to understand the amendment as seeking to facilitate a conversation among ordinary citizens that will encourage their informed participation in the electoral process. It is to suggest a constitutional purpose that goes beyond protecting the individual from government restriction of information about matters that the Constitution commits to individual, not collective, decision-making. It is to understand the First Amendment as seeking primarily to encourage the exchange of information and ideas necessary for citizens themselves to shape that "public opinion which is the final source of government in a democratic state." In these ways the Amendment helps to maintain a form of government open to participation (in Constant's words) by "all the citizens, without exception." [18]

To focus upon the First Amendment's relation to the Constitution's democratic objective is helpful because the campaign laws seek to further a similar objective. They seek to democratize the influence that money can bring to bear upon the electoral process, thereby building public confidence in that process, broadening the base of a candidate's meaningful financial support, and encouraging greater public participation. Ultimately, they seek thereby to maintain the integrity of the political process—a process that itself translates political speech into governmental action. Insofar as they achieve these objectives, those laws, despite the limits they impose, will help to further the kind of open public political discussion that the First Amendment seeks to sustain, both as an end and as a means of achieving a workable democracy.

To emphasize the First Amendment's protection of active liberty is not to find the campaign finance laws automatically constitutional. Rather, it is to recognize that basic democratic objectives, including some of a kind that the First Amendment seeks to further, lie on both sides of the constitutional equation. Seen in terms of modern liberty, they include protection of the citizen's speech from government interference; seen in terms of active liberty, they include promotion of a democratic conversation. That, I believe, is why our Court has refused to apply a strong First Amendment presumption that would almost automatically find the laws unconstitutional. Rather the Court has consistently rejected "strict scrutiny" as the proper test, instead examining a campaign finance law "close[ly]" while applying what it calls "heightened scrutiny." In doing so, the Court has emphasized the power of large campaign contributions to "erod[e] public confidence in the electoral process." It has noted that contribution limits are "aimed at protecting the integrity of the process"; pointed out that in doing so they "tangibly benefit public participation in political debate"; and concluded that that is why "there is no place for the strong presumption against constitutionality, of the sort often thought to accompany the words 'strict scrutiny.'" In this statement it recognizes the possibility that, just as a restraint of trade is sometimes lawful because it furthers, rather than restricts, competition, so a restriction on speech, even when political speech is at issue, will sometimes prove reasonable, hence lawful. Consequently the Court has tried to look realistically both at a campaign finance law's *negative* impact upon those primarily wealthier citizens who wish to engage in more electoral communication and its *positive* impact upon the public's confidence in, and ability to communicate through, the electoral process. And it has applied a constitutional test that I would describe as one of proportionality. Does the statute strike a reasonable balance between electoral speech-restricting and speech-enhancing consequences? Or does it instead impose restrictions on speech that are disproportionate when measured against their electoral and speech-related benefits, taking into account the kind, the importance, and the extent of those benefits, as well as the need for the restriction in order to secure them?[19]

In trying to answer these questions, courts need not totally abandon what I have referred to as judicial modesty. Courts can defer to the legislature's own judgment insofar as that judgment concerns matters (particularly empirical matters) about which the legislature is comparatively expert, such as the extent of the campaign finance problem, a matter that directly concerns the realities of political life. But courts should not defer when they evaluate the risk that reform legislation will defeat the participatory self-government objective itself. That risk is present, for example, when laws set contribution limits so low that they elevate the reputation-related or media-related advantages of incumbency to the point of insulating incumbent officeholders from effective challenge.[20]

A focus upon the Constitution's democratic objective does not offer easy answers to the difficult questions that campaign finance laws pose. But it does clarify the First Amendment's role in promoting active liberty and suggests an approach for addressing those and other vexing questions. In turn, such a focus can help the Court arrive at answers faithful to the Constitution, its language, and its parts, read together as a consistent whole. Modesty suggests when, and how, courts should defer to the legislature in doing so. . . .

My argument is that, in applying First Amendment presumptions, we must distinguish among areas, contexts, and forms of speech. Reference . . . back to at least one general purpose, active liberty, helps both to generate proper distinctions and also properly to apply the distinctions generated. The active liberty reference helps us to preserve speech that is essential to our democratic form of government, while simultaneously permitting the law to deal effectively with such modern regulatory problems as campaign finance. . . .

NOTES

1. Hand, *supra* note I, at 109; *United States v. Classic,* 313 U.S. 299, 316 (1941) (Stone, J.); Hand, *id.*, at 157; Aharon Barak, *A Judge on Judging: The Role of a Supreme Court in a Democracy,* 116 Harv. L. Rev. 16, 28 (2002) ("The law regulates relationships between people. It prescribes patterns of behavior. It reflects the values of society. The role of the judge is to understand the purpose of law in society and to help the law achieve its purpose."); Goldman, *supra* note I, at 115; Felix Frankfurter, *Some Reflections on the Reading of Statutes,* 47 Colum. L. Rev. 527, 541 (1947).

2. Felix Frankfurter, *The Supreme Court in the Mirror of Justices,* in *Of Law and Life & Other Things That Matter* 94 (Philip B. Kurland ed., 1965); *id.* at 95; Hand, *supra* note I, at 109; *New State Ice Co. v. Liebmann,* 285 U.S. 262, 311 (1932) (Brandeis, J., dissenting); Frankfurter, *supra* note 3, at 95.

3. *Id.* at 517.

4. Bailyn, *supra* note I, at 55 (quoting James Madison).

5. Aharon Barak, *A Judge on Judging: The Role of a Supreme Court in a Democracy,* 116 Harv. L. Rev. 28–29 (2002).

6. See, e.g., Antonin Scalia, *Common-Law Courts in a Civil-Law System: The Role of United States Federal Courts in Interpreting the Constitution and Laws,* in *A Matter of Interpretation: Federal Courts and the Law* 26–27 (Amy Gutmann ed., 1997); see William N. Eskridge Jr., Philip P. Frickey, & Elizabeth Garrett, *Cases and Materials on Legislation-Statutes and the Creation of Public Policy* 822 (3d ed. 2001); Frank H. Easterbrook, *Text, History, and Structure in Statutory Interpretation,* 17 Harv. J. L. & Pub. Pol'y 61, 64 (1994).

7. *Duncan,* 533 U.S. 167 at 185 (Breyer, J. dissenting) (citing U.S. Dept. of Justice, Office of Justice Programs, Bureau of Justice Statistics, *Federal Habeas Corpus Review: Challenging State Court Criminal Convictions* 17 [1995]).

8. See *id.* at 172–75.

9. *Id.* at 190–93 (Breyer, J., dissenting).

10. *Id.* at 190 (Breyer, J., dissenting).

11. Barak, *supra* note I, at 28–29.

12. See, e.g., Alex Kozinski & Stuart Banner, *Who's Afraid of Commercial Speech?* 76 Va. L. Rev. 627, 631 (1990); Martin H. Redish, *The First Amendment in the Marketplace: Commercial Speech and the Values of Free Expression,* 39 Geo. Wash. L. Rev. 429, 452–48 (1971); cf. 44 *Liquormart, Inc. v. Rhode Island,* 517 U.S. 484, 522 (1996) (Thomas, J., concurring in part and concurring in the judgment); U.S. Const. art. I.

13. Ctr. for Responsive Politics, *Election Overview, 2000 Cycle: Stats at a Glance,* at http://www.opensecrets.org/overview/index.asp?Cycle=2000 accessed Mar. 8, 2002 (aggregating totals using Federal Election Commission data); Ctr. for Responsive Politics, *Election Overview,* at http://www.opensecrets.org/overview/stats.asp accessed Nov. 21, 2003 (based on FEC data).

14. Taken from the record developed in *McConnell v. Federal Election Comm'n,* No. 02-1674 et al., Joint Appendix 1558. In the 2002 midterm election, less than one-tenth of one percent of the population gave 83 percent of all (hard and soft) itemized campaign contributions. Ctr. for Responsive Politics, see *supra* note 2.

15. Taken from the record developed in *McConnell,* No. 02-1674 et al., Joint Appendix 1564.

16. *Buckley v. Valeo,* 424 U.S. I (1976); *McConnell v. FEC,* 540 U.S. 93 (2003).

17. U.S. Const. amend. I.

18. *Masses Publishing Co. v. Patten,* 244 F.535, 540 (S.D.N.Y. 1917 [(Hand, J.)]; Benjamin Constant, *The Liberty of the Ancients Compared with That of the Moderns* (1819), in *Political Writings,* at 327 (Biancamaria Fontana trans. & ed., 1988).

19. *McConnell,* 540 U.S. at 136, 231; see also *Nixon v. Shrink Mo. Gov't PAC,* 528 U.S. 377, 399–402 (2000) (Breyer, J., concurring); *id.* at 136 (internal quotation marks omitted); *id.* at 137 (internal quotation marks omitted); see *Board of Trade of Chicago v. United States,* 246 U.S. 231 (1918); see *McConnell,* 540 U.S. at 134–42.

20. *McConnell,* 540 U.S. at 137.

9-3

Federalist No. 78

Alexander Hamilton
May 28, 1788

Of the several branches laid out in the Constitution, the judiciary is the least democratic—that is, the least responsive to the expressed preferences of the citizenry. Indeed, it is hard to imagine an institution designed to be less responsive to the public than the Supreme Court, whose unelected judges enjoy lifetime appointments. During the Constitution's ratification, this fact exposed the judiciary to all sorts of wild speculation from opponents about the dire consequences the judiciary would have for the new republic. In one of the most famous passages of The Federalist, *Alexander Hamilton seeks to calm fears by declaring the judiciary to be "the least dangerous branch." Unlike the president, the Court does not control a military force, and unlike Congress, it cannot confiscate citizens' property through taxation. At the same time, Hamilton does not shrink from assigning the judiciary a critical role in safeguarding the Constitution against congressional and presidential encroachments he sees as bound to occur from time to time. By assigning it this role, he assumed that the Supreme Court has the authority of "judicial review" even though there was no provision for it in the Constitution.*

WE PROCEED now to an examination of the judiciary department of the proposed government. In unfolding the defects of the existing Confederation, the utility and necessity of a federal judicature have been clearly pointed out. It is the less necessary to recapitulate the considerations there urged, as the propriety of the institution in the abstract is not disputed; the only questions which have been raised being relative to the manner of constituting it, and to its extent. To these points, therefore, our observations shall be confined.

The manner of constituting it seems to embrace these several objects: 1st. The mode of appointing the judges. 2d. The tenure by which they are to hold their places. 3d. The partition of the judiciary authority between different courts, and their relations to each other.

First.

As to the mode of appointing the judges; this is the same with that of appointing the officers of the Union in general, and has been so fully discussed . . . that nothing can be said here which would not be useless repetition.

Second.

As to the tenure by which the judges are to hold their places; this chiefly concerns their duration in office; the provisions for their support; the precautions for their responsibility.

According to the plan of the convention, all judges who may be appointed by the United States are to hold their offices during good behavior. . . . The standard of good behavior for the continuance in office of the judicial magistracy, is certainly one of the most valuable of the modern improvements in the practice of government. In a monarchy it is an excellent barrier to the despotism of the prince; in a republic it is a no less excellent barrier to the encroachments and oppressions of the representative body. And it is the best expedient which can be devised in any government, to secure a steady, upright, and impartial administration of the laws.

Whoever attentively considers the different departments of power must perceive, that, in a government in which they are separated from each other, the judiciary, from the nature of its functions, will always be the least dangerous to the political rights of the Constitution; because it will be least in a capacity to annoy or injure them. The Executive not only dispenses the honors, but holds the sword of the community. The legislature not only commands the purse, but prescribes the rules by which the duties and rights of every citizen are to be regulated. The judiciary, on the contrary, has no influence over either the sword or the purse; no direction either of the strength or of the wealth of the society; and can take no active resolution whatever. It may truly be said to have neither FORCE nor WILL, but merely judgment; and must ultimately depend upon the aid of the executive arm even for the efficacy of its judgments.

This simple view of the matter suggests several important consequences. It proves incontestably, that the judiciary is beyond comparison the weakest of the three departments of power[1]; that it can never attack with success either of the other two; and that all possible care is requisite to enable it to defend itself against their attacks. It equally proves, that though individual oppression may now and then proceed from the courts of justice, the general liberty of the people can never be endangered from that quarter; I mean so long as the judiciary remains truly distinct from both the legislature and the Executive. For I agree, that "there is no liberty, if the power of judging be not separated from the legislative and executive powers."[2] And it proves, in the last place, that as liberty can have nothing to fear from the judiciary alone, but would have every thing to fear from its union with either of the other departments; that as all the effects of such a union must ensue from a dependence of the former on the latter, notwithstanding a nominal and apparent separation; that as, from the natural feebleness of the judiciary, it is in continual jeopardy of being overpowered, awed, or influenced by its co-ordinate branches; and that as nothing can contribute so much to its firmness and independence as permanency in office, this quality may therefore be justly regarded as an indispensable ingredient in its constitution, and, in a great measure, as the citadel of the public justice and the public security.

The complete independence of the courts of justice is peculiarly essential in a limited Constitution. By a limited Constitution, I understand one which contains certain specified exceptions to the legislative authority; such, for instance, as that it shall pass no bills of attainder, no ex post facto laws, and the like. Limitations of this kind can be preserved in practice no other way than through the medium of courts of justice, whose duty it must be to declare all acts contrary to the manifest tenor of the Constitution void. Without this, all the reservations of particular rights or privileges would amount to nothing.

Some perplexity respecting the rights of the courts to pronounce legislative acts void, because contrary to the Constitution, has arisen from an imagination that the doctrine would imply a superiority of the judiciary to the legislative power. It is urged that the authority which can declare the acts of another void, must necessarily be superior to the one whose acts may be declared void. As this doctrine is of great importance in all the American constitutions, a brief discussion of the ground on which it rests cannot be unacceptable.

There is no position which depends on clearer principles, than that every act of a delegated authority, contrary to the tenor of the commission under which it is exercised, is void. No legislative act, therefore, contrary to the Constitution, can be valid. To deny this, would be to affirm, that the deputy is greater than his principal; that the servant is above his master; that the representatives of the people are superior to the people themselves; that men acting by virtue of powers, may do not only what their powers do not authorize, but what they forbid.

If it be said that the legislative body are themselves the constitutional judges of their own powers, and that the construction they put upon them is conclusive upon the other departments, it may be answered, that this cannot be the natural presumption, where it is not to be collected from any particular provisions in the Constitution. It is not otherwise to be supposed, that the Constitution could intend to enable the representatives of the people to substitute their will to that of their constituents. It is far more rational to suppose, that the courts were designed to be an intermediate body between the people and the legislature, in order, among other things, to keep the latter within the limits assigned to their authority. The interpretation of the laws is the proper and peculiar province of the courts. A constitution is, in fact, and must be regarded by the judges, as a fundamental law. It therefore belongs to them to ascertain its meaning, as well as the meaning of any particular act proceeding from the legislative body. If there should happen to be an irreconcilable variance between the two, that which has the superior obligation and validity ought, of course, to be preferred; or, in other words, the Constitution ought to be preferred to the statute, the intention of the people to the intention of their agents.

Nor does this conclusion by any means suppose a superiority of the judicial to the legislative power. It only supposes that the power of the people is superior to both; and that where the will of the legislature, declared in its statutes, stands in opposition to that of the people, declared in the Constitution, the judges ought to be governed by the latter rather than the former. They ought to regulate their decisions by the fundamental laws, rather than by those which are not fundamental.

This exercise of judicial discretion, in determining between two contradictory laws, is exemplified in a familiar instance. It not uncommonly happens, that there are two statutes existing at one time, clashing in whole or in part with each other, and neither of them containing any repealing clause or expression. In such a case, it is the province of the courts to liquidate and fix their meaning and operation. So far as they can, by any fair construction, be reconciled to each other, reason and law conspire to dictate that this should be done; where this is impracticable, it becomes a matter of necessity to give effect to one, in exclusion of the other. The rule which has obtained in the courts for determining their relative validity is, that the last in order of time shall be preferred to the first. But this is a mere rule of construction, not derived from any positive law, but from the nature and reason of the thing. It is a rule not enjoined upon the courts by legislative provision, but adopted by themselves, as consonant to truth and propriety, for the direction of their conduct as interpreters of the law. They thought it reasonable, that between the interfering acts of an EQUAL authority, that which was the last indication of its will should have the preference.

But in regard to the interfering acts of a superior and subordinate authority, of an original and derivative power, the nature and reason of the thing indicate the converse of that rule as proper to be followed. They teach us that the prior act of a superior ought to be preferred to the subsequent act of an inferior and subordinate authority; and that accordingly, whenever a particular statute contravenes the Constitution, it will be the duty of the judicial tribunals to adhere to the latter and disregard the former.

It can be of no weight to say that the courts, on the pretense of a repugnancy, may substitute their own pleasure to the constitutional intentions of the legislature. This might as well happen in the case of two contradictory statutes; or it might as well happen in every adjudication upon any single statute. The courts must declare the sense of the law; and if they should be disposed to exercise WILL instead of JUDGMENT, the consequence would equally be the substitution of their pleasure to that of the legislative body. The observation, if it prove any thing, would prove that there ought to be no judges distinct from that body.

If, then, the courts of justice are to be considered as the bulwarks of a limited Constitution against legislative encroachments, this consideration will afford a strong argument for the permanent tenure of judicial offices, since nothing will contribute so much as this to that independent spirit in the judges which must be essential to the faithful performance of so arduous a duty.

This independence of the judges is equally requisite to guard the Constitution and the rights of individuals from the effects of those ill humors, which the arts of designing men, or the influence of particular conjunctures, sometimes disseminate among the people themselves, and which, though they speedily give place to better information, and more deliberate reflection, have a tendency, in the meantime, to occasion dangerous innovations in the government, and serious oppressions of the minor party in the community. . . . Until the people have, by some solemn and authoritative act, annulled or changed the established form, it is binding upon themselves collectively, as well as individually; and no presumption, or even knowledge, of their sentiments, can warrant their representatives in a departure from it, prior to such an act. But it is easy to see, that it would require an uncommon portion of fortitude in the judges to do their duty as faithful guardians of the Constitution, where legislative invasions of it had been instigated by the major voice of the community.

But it is not with a view to infractions of the Constitution only, that the independence of the judges may be an essential safeguard against the effects of occasional ill humors in the society. These sometimes extend no farther than to the injury of the private rights of particular classes of citizens, by unjust and partial laws. Here also the firmness of the judicial magistracy is of vast importance in mitigating the severity and confining the operation of such laws. It not only serves to moderate the immediate mischiefs of those which may have been passed, but it operates as a check upon the legislative body in passing them; who, perceiving that obstacles to the success of iniquitous intention are to be expected from the scruples of the courts, are in a manner compelled, by the very motives of the injustice they meditate, to qualify their attempts. . . .

That inflexible and uniform adherence to the rights of the Constitution, and of individuals, which we perceive to be indispensable in the courts of justice, can certainly not be expected from judges who hold their offices by a temporary commission. Periodical appointments, however regulated, or by whomsoever made, would, in some way or other, be fatal to their necessary independence. If the power of making them was committed either to the Executive or legislature, there would be danger of an improper complaisance to the branch which possessed it; if to both, there would be an unwillingness to hazard the displeasure of either; if to the people, or to persons chosen by them for the special purpose, there would be too great a disposition to consult popularity, to justify a reliance that nothing would be consulted but the Constitution and the laws.

There is yet a further and a weightier reason for the permanency of the judicial offices, which is deducible from the nature of the qualifications they require. It has been frequently remarked, with great propriety, that a voluminous code of laws is one of the inconveniences necessarily connected with the advantages of a free government. To avoid an arbitrary discretion in the courts, it is indispensable that they should be bound down by strict rules and precedents, which serve to define and point out their duty in every particular case that comes before them; and it will readily be conceived from the variety of controversies which grow out of the folly and wickedness of mankind, that the records of those precedents must unavoidably swell to a very considerable bulk, and must demand long and laborious study to acquire a competent knowledge of them. Hence it is, that there can be but few men in the society who will have sufficient skill in the laws to qualify them for the stations of judges. And making the proper deductions for the ordinary depravity of human nature, the number must be still smaller of those who unite the requisite integrity with the requisite knowledge. . . .

NOTES

1. The celebrated Montesquieu, speaking of them, says: "Of the three powers above mentioned, the judiciary is next to nothing." "Spirit of Laws." vol. i., page 186. [See Charles de Secondat, Baron de Montesquieu, *The Spirit of Laws*, trans. Thomas Nugent, rev. J. V. Pritchard (London: G. Bell & Sons Ltd., 1914).]

2. Idem, page 181.

The Voting Behavior of Barack Obama's Judges: As Far Left as Some Opponents Say or Just Mainstream Liberals?

Robert A. Carp, Kenneth L. Manning, and Ronald Stidham

In recent years, politics in Washington have become as intensely partisan and polarized ideologically as at any time in the past half-century. Partisanship periodically flares up in its most virulent form during divided government, when the Senate deliberates confirmation of the president's judicial nominees. Democratic President Clinton complained continually that the Republican Senate was not giving his nominees a fair shake. Similarly, President Bush blasted Democratic obstructionism. President Obama has issued similar complaints, but unlike his predecessors, he appears to have been less attentive to judicial appointments and confirmation politics. The early assessment of Obama's federal district judges finds them following the long-established pattern of rendering more liberal decisions than their Republican-appointed counterparts.

WHAT IS THE ideological direction of the judges whom President Barack Obama has appointed during his first three and a half years in office? Until now, virtually all of the information about this question has been anecdotal in nature. Critics of the president, who are typically Republican, have suggested that Obama's judicial appointees are ultraliberals who are hostile to the interests of private property and to those who wish to be free of most forms of governmental restraint and that the jurists are slavishly following the wishes of those who comprise the Democratic electorate—that is, racial minorities, gays, labor union members, and so on. For example, in his run for the Republican nomination, Texas Governor Rick Perry promised that, if elected, he would appoint only U.S. Supreme Court and federal judges who will "reject the idea [that] our Founding Fathers inserted a right to gay marriage into our Constitution."[1] And former House speaker Newt Gingrich said in December of 2011 that as president, he would abolish whole courts in order to be rid of judges whose decisions he feels are out of step with the country. Gingrich furthermore suggested that "the president could send federal law enforcement authorities to arrest judges who make

Source: This piece is an original essay commissioned for this volume.

controversial rulings in order to compel them to justify their decisions before congressional hearings."[2] While no one would contend that the views of these two Republican candidates are characteristic of all members of the GOP, still it is probably fair to say that most Republicans regard Obama's jurists as too liberal and as far out-of-center from America's political mainstream. Democrats, on the other hand, seem satisfied with the Obama appointees to the bench, while some actually believe that he has been too reserved in not pushing a more liberal agenda. For example, one law professor and former Obama colleague from the University of Chicago, Geoffrey Stone, said of the Obama administration, "They have been playing it a little too carefully. This administration has been very cautious in terms of nominating people who are in any way subject to attack from the right. We want to make sure that he's willing to take some risks."[3]

So which side is correct—conservatives who contend that Obama's appointees are leading the charge down the proverbial "slippery slopes of socialism" or their Democratic counterparts who are either satisfied with the status quo or who would like to see Obama move the federal judiciary to the left? Empirical data is always useful in addressing such queries, and such data will be the primary contribution of this research endeavor. For in this chapter, we seek to shed some light on whether or not President Obama is making ideologically based appointments and whether his judicial cohort is deciding cases in the manner anticipated by most court observers. We have organized the chapter around two basic questions: What might we expect of the Obama administration's potential to have an ideological impact on the federal courts? And what do the empirical data tell us so far about the way that the Obama cohort has been deciding cases during the three and a half years of his presidency?

Presidential Support for Ideologically Based Appointments

One key aspect of the success of chief executives in appointing a federal judiciary that mirrors their own political beliefs is the depth of the commitment to doing so. Some presidents may be content merely to fill the federal bench with party loyalists and pay little attention to their nominees' specific ideologies. Some may consider ideological factors when appointing Supreme Court justices but may not regard them as important for trial and appellate judges. Other presidents may discount ideologically based appointments because they themselves tend to be nonideological. Still others may place factors such as past political loyalty ahead of ideology in selecting judges.

For example, Harry Truman had strong political views, but when selecting judges, he placed loyalty to himself ahead of the candidate's overall political orientation. On the other hand, Ronald Reagan, Lyndon Johnson, and George W. Bush are examples of presidents who had strong ideological beliefs on many issues and took great pains to select judges who shared those beliefs. What do we know about whether Barack Obama is committed to making ideologically based judicial appointments?

On the campaign trail four year ago, candidate Obama placed a lot of emphasis on the word *change*, although he was rather short on the specifics of that vague term. *Change* might suggest that the new president would seek to chart a very different course than his predecessor and that Obama would wish to appoint an unabashedly liberal judiciary to counterbalance George W. Bush's staunchly conservative approach. However, President Obama's nominees have so far not generated unanimous antipathy from all persons of right-wing persuasion. Indeed, in September 2009, Republican senator John Thune of South Dakota called two of Obama's nominees to federal judgeships in his state "good picks."[4] And as recently as July 2011, two of President Obama's federal district court nominees in Texas, Assistant U.S. Attorney Gregg Costa of Houston and U.S. Magistrate David Guaderrama in El Paso, were recommended by both of Texas's conservative Republican Senators, John Cornyn and Kay Bailey Hutchison.[5] It was also reported that the State's leading Democrats and the White House were equally pleased with the judicial nominations. While not all lower court appointments have been this convivial, they have generally not reflected the hard-hitting rhetoric of the current 2012 presidential campaign.

Somewhat similar dynamics have occurred with regard to Obama's Supreme Court nominations. In May 2009, the president selected Sonia Sotomayor as his first Supreme Court nominee to fill the vacancy that occurred when Justice David Souter announced he would retire from the bench. Sotomayor, who was initially selected for a federal judgeship by President George H.W. Bush, was the first Hispanic nominated to the Supreme Court and would become only the third woman to serve there. Obama's pick received plaudits for her rise from humble family roots, her distinguished educational background, and her years of experience as a federal district court and courts of appeals jurist. Although Sotomayor was widely recognized as a Democrat, a review of her judicial and legal record turned up no real instances of liberal ideological extremism. Nevertheless, many Republicans criticized Sotomayor for comments she had made in some past speeches about a "wise Latina" being better able to reach a conclusion "than a white male who hadn't lived that life."[6] These attacks yielded little political fruit for the GOP, however. Given Sotomayor's solid qualifications and her ethically unimpeachable background, Republicans were unable to mount a serious challenge to her nomination. She was confirmed easily by a vote of 68–31.[7]

About nine months later, President Obama was presented with a second Supreme Court opening with the retirement of Justice John Paul Stevens. And again the President chose to downplay ideology and nominate a more mainstream, middle-of-the road candidate for this High Court office—Elena Kagan. Or, as one seasoned commentator quipped, President Obama's announcement of Elena Kagan "was perfectly boring—and that's what makes her such a bold choice."[8] This commentator then added, "Nominating Kagan . . . required some courage. Obama defied those populists who said he should reach beyond the Eastern elite for somebody with more 'real world' experience. He defied liberal interest groups—his own base—that favored a more ideological liberal . . . . Instead, he chose brain over bio, sending to the Senate neither a compelling American story nor a liberal warrior but a superbly skilled, nonideological builder of bridges."[9] On August 5, 2010, the Senate confirmed Kagan's appointment by a vote of 63–37.

We now return to our original question: Does the evidence suggest that President Obama is trying to move the courts' center of gravity to the far ideological left of center? In reality, there is virtually no evidence for that proposition. The indication is that the Obama administration is generally trying to avoid acrimonious political battles by appointing mainstream Democrats and eschewing nominees with especially controversial pasts. Furthermore, the elevation of Sotomayor to become the first Latin American to serve on the Supreme Court and the nomination of Kagan to increase the number of women on the Court suggests that the Obama administration may be following in the footsteps of George W. Bush and Bill Clinton in seeking to increase the diversity of the judiciary. And ethnic and gender diversity may not be the only goals that the Obama While House has in mind. One administration official noted that "the unifying quality that we are looking for is excellence, but also diversity, and diversity in the broadest sense of the word. We are looking for experiential diversity, not just race and gender. We want people who are not the usual suspects, not just judges and prosecutors but public defenders and lawyers in private practice."[10]

Not only does the evidence indicate that Obama has not been extremely ideological in his judicial nominations, some expert observers have even questioned how important judicial selection is to the Obama administration. One group of observers noted, "The surest key to understanding the politics, processes, and outcomes of the Obama judicial selection record in the 111th Congress is the recognition that judges were not seen as a priority by those closest to the President. Judicial selection was not a major focal point in the administration's legislatively driven domestic policy agenda nor was it seen as a 'legacy' issue. There was a failure to understand that the judiciary would inevitably become particularly central to the very legislative agenda (health care reform) that was the President's greatest priority."[11]

In sum, when we consider the bipartisan support that Obama's nominees have received in some instances, the relatively few cases of outright rejection of Obama's judicial picks, the paucity of discussion by the White House about pushing the courts in a directly leftward direction, and the occasional grumbling by some about the lack of enthusiasm exhibited by the administration toward judicial nominations, it is difficult to conclude that Obama has made ideology a paramount priority in selecting judicial nominees. To be sure, Obama has largely appointed reliable fellow party members to positions on the bench. But this makes him no different than most prior presidents, and the evidence so far suggests that Obama is approaching his responsibility of filling court vacancies in a rather familiar fashion.

The Number of Vacancies to Be Filled

A second element affecting the capacity of chief executives to establish a policy link between themselves and the judiciary is the number of appointments available to them. The more judges a president can select, the greater his potential to put his stamp on the judicial branch. For example, George Washington's influence on the Supreme Court was significant, because he was able to nominate ten individuals to the High Court. Jimmy Carter's was nil because no vacancies occurred during his term as president.

The number of appointment opportunities depends on several factors: how many judicial vacancies are inherited from the previous administration (Clinton, for example, was left with a whopping one hundred lower court vacancies—14 percent of the total—by his predecessor George H.W. Bush), how many judges and justices die or resign during the president's term, how long the president serves, and whether Congress passes legislation that significantly increases the number of judgeships.

Historically, the last factor seems to have been the most important in influencing the number of judgeships available, and politics in its most basic form permeates that process. A study of proposals in thirteen Congresses to create new judgeships tested the following two hypotheses: (1) "Proposals to add new federal judges are more likely to pass if the same party controls the Presidency and Congress than if different parties are in power," and (2) "Proposals to add new federal judges are more likely to pass during the first two years of the president's term than during the second two years." The study author concluded that his "data support both hypotheses—proposals to add new judges are about five times more likely to pass if the same party controls the presidency and the Congress than if different parties control [each] and about four times more likely to pass during the first two years of the president's term than during the second two years." He then noted that these findings serve "to remind us that not only is judicial selection a political process, but so is the creation of judicial posts."[12]

When Barack Obama assumed the presidency in 2009, he inherited 59 judicial vacancies—44 at the district court level and 15 in the courts of appeals. Democrats who controlled the Senate in the final years of the George W. Bush administration were in no mood to approve the judicial nominees of the then-unpopular, lame duck president. President Obama thus came into office with a sizable number of vacancies to fill. However, the number was not as high as that which greeted George W. Bush when he took the reins of power in early 2001. At that time, Bush was presented with 29 courts of appeals and 62 district court vacancies. Still, with 59 judicial positions open, Obama had the opportunity to make a good start in filling the bench with judges who share his philosophy.

Despite this initial opening opportunity for the president, the record indicates that he has been slow to fill many of these judicial vacancies and he has been subjected to much criticism for this lack of enthusiasm and activity. As of December 1, 2011, there were some 82 unfilled judicial vacancies, 15 at the appellate court level and 67 in the district courts. Indeed, the Obama administration has been continually criticized by court observers as being too slow in the judicial appointment process. Two court watchers at the *Washington Post* noted, "Federal judges have been retiring at a rate of one per week this year, driving up vacancies that have nearly doubled since President Obama took office. The departures are increasing workloads dramatically and delaying trials in some of the nation's courts." And later they observed, "Since Obama took office, federal judicial vacancies have risen steadily as dozens of judges have left without being replaced by presidential nominees. Experts blame Republican delaying tactics, slow White House nominations, and a dysfunctional Senate confirmation system."[13]

Despite the ponderous way in which the Obama administration has made judicial appointments so far, as well as the hurdles of the Republican Senate confirmation process, the Obama mark is slowly being made in the judiciary. As of mid-January 2012, there were 787 active trial and appellate court judges and an additional 522 senior status jurists, making a total of 1,309. Of these 787 active judges, President Obama had appointed 124 (none of whom had left their positions), which represented almost 16 percent of the total at the time. This is in keeping with the percentage of recent presidents. For example, former President George W. Bush appointed about 20 percent of the active judiciary during each of his terms, and President Obama should be able to meet or come close to that mark in the months remaining in his term.

What about the possibility of Congress passing a new omnibus judges bill that would give the president the opportunity to pack the judiciary with men and women who share his values? Such an enactment greatly enhanced President Kennedy's and President Carter's ideological impacts on the judiciary. Unfortunately for President Obama, he has had no such luck. Measures have been introduced in Congress to create a few new emergency judicial positions, but between the budget-cutting mentality that pervades the current Congress and the sharp political divisions that characterize this body, it is not likely that Congress will offer the president the bonanza of an omnibus judges bill that would serve to increase his impact on the federal judiciary.

So what is one to conclude about this second predictor of whether President Obama will potentially have a substantial impact on the ideological direction of the federal judiciary—the number of vacancies he can fill? The data suggest that in terms of pure numbers, the president is having about an average set of opportunities to make an ideological impact on the federal bench. That means that after his first term, about one in five federal judges will likely bear the Obama stamp—a factor of some consequence.

The President's Political Clout

Presidential skill in overcoming political obstacles is also a factor in leaving a mark upon the judiciary. The U.S. Senate can be a stumbling block. If the Senate is controlled by the president's party, the White House will find it much easier to secure confirmations. Sometimes when the opposition is in power in the Senate, presidents are forced into political horse-trading to get their nominees approved. For example, in the summer of 1999, President Clinton was obliged to make a deal with the conservative chair of the Senate Judiciary Committee, Orrin Hatch. To obtain smooth sailing for at least ten of Clinton's judicial nominations that were blocked in the Senate, the president agreed to nominate a Utah Republican, Ted Stewart, who was vigorously opposed by liberals and environmental groups.

The Senate Judiciary Committee can be another roadblock. Some presidents have been more adept than others at easing their candidates through the jagged rocks of the Judiciary Committee rapids. Both Presidents Kennedy and Johnson, for example, had to deal with the formidable Senator James Eastland of Mississippi, then committee chair, but only Johnson seemed to have had the political adroitness to get most of his liberal nominees approved; Kennedy lacked that skill. Even Clinton, despite his considerable political acumen, was never able to parlay those skills into much clout with the conservative and often hostile Senate Judiciary Committee.

The president's personal popularity is another element in the political power formula. Chief executives who are very well liked by the public and who command respect among opinion makers in the news media, the rank-and-file of their political party, and the leaders of the nation's major interest groups are much more likely to prevail over forces that seek to thwart their judicial nominations.

How would we assess President Obama's capacity to make an ideological impact on the federal judiciary in light of this "political clout" variable? On this dimension, the data are clearly of a mixed nature. Although the president was elected by a decisive majority of the electorate and he carried both houses of Congress, his glory days were short-lived. The high unemployment rate and the economic recession, which had dogged his predecessor George W. Bush, have not abated as fast as many Americans had hoped. The high approval numbers given to the president during his early days in office have fallen to only 48 percent as the nation enters this presidential election year. And while these approval ratings are certainly not at record-low levels, they still detract from the president's overall political clout. It is true that President Obama was able to get a number of major pieces of legislation passed during his first two years in office, but this arguably was due just as much to skillfulness by the Democratic leadership in Congress over their large majorities and a clear willingness by Obama to compromise at key points as it was sheer political clout. Furthermore, the Obama legislative agenda ground to a virtual halt after the 2010 elections, when Republicans made big gains and regained control of the House of Representatives.

There have been some notable successes in the international and foreign policy realm, notably the killing of Osama bin Laden and other key Al Qaida operatives and also the withdrawal of American troops from Iraq. President Obama also was successful in getting the New START (Strategic Arms Reduction Treaty) nuclear arms treaty passed. But domestic economic issues seem to be on the minds of most Americans, and on this variable, the president's support level has been decidedly mixed.

In terms of Obama's success vis-à-vis the Senate Judiciary confirmation process, the president has had some modest success. As Sheldon Goldman and his team of researchers have noted, "It is a fair generalization to note that the Senate Judiciary Committee facets of the processes . . . offered, at least on the surface, a picture of relative calm. The Committee did its job, with the greatest obstruction and delay of Obama nominees occurring at the floor stages of confirmation. Behind such a generalization are layers of nuance that shaped both committee and floor activity and, at times, the lack thereof."[14] These observers further noted that this "surface cooperation" was somewhat deceptive. They commented that "it would be a vast overstatement to suggest that the minority members on the committee simply 'went along' with the administration's picks. To the contrary, there was a pattern of regularized and systematic opposition that had an impact on the processing of virtually all Obama nominees, but that impact could be seen, in most instances, in processing delay, not definitive and resolute obstruction save for a handful of . . . nominees."[15]

What about the president's success in obtaining Senate confirmation for his judicial nominees? Here there was moderate success—but at the price of continual delays. Republicans used a variety of tactics to delay floor action in the Senate. For example, there were constant refusals of unanimous consent to floor votes on nominations, the extensive use of holds on nominees by individual senators, and, "when played out to the end game of opposition, utilization of the threat of filibusters and the necessity for cloture votes to bring a nominee to the floor."[16] What's more, Obama suffered a high-profile failed nomination when Republicans used a filibuster to block his nomination of Goodwin Liu to a position on the Ninth Circuit Court of Appeals.[17] Still, the bottom-line confirmation numbers for the president were not disastrous. Looking at the figures for his first two years in office, 44 of his 78 nominees to the district courts (56.4 percent) and 15 of his 22 nominees to the courts of appeals (68.2 percent) were confirmed by the Senate. Nevertheless, these confirmation numbers are at the low end of the spectrum and bespeak the increasing levels of partisanship, which have interjected themselves into the confirmation process of lower court judges in recent years. As the Goldman research team observed, "for the district courts, the proportion of confirmed Obama appointees was the lowest since the first half of [George] W. Bush's second term (the 109th Congress), which in turn was the lowest proportion in over 75 years and likely historically."[18]

So what is one to conclude about the impact of the president's political clout in terms of his success in shaping the judiciary with his court appointments? Despite the president's diminished political effectiveness that quickly followed his election victory and despite the delaying tactics of Republican opponents on the Judiciary Committee and in the Senate, a decided majority of his nominees were confirmed. One might speculate that had his nominees been more left-of-center, his success scores would have been lower than they were. But, still, the mainstream Democrats that were approved by the Judiciary Committee and by the Senate were surely more liberal than those who would have been appointed by a modern-day Republican president.

The Judicial Climate the New Judges Enter

A final matter affects the capacity of chief executives to secure a federal judiciary that reflects their own political values: the philosophical orientations of the current sitting district and appellate court judges with whom the new appointees would interact. Because federal judges serve lifetime appointments during good behavior, presidents must accept the composition and value structure of the judiciary as it exists when they take office. If the existing judiciary already reflects the president's political and legal orientations, the impact of the new judicial appointees will be immediate and substantial. However, if the new chief executive faces a trial and appellate judiciary whose values are radically different from his own, the impact of that president's subsequent judicial appointments will be weaker and slower to materialize. New judges must respect the controlling legal precedents and the constitutional interpretations that prevail in the judiciary at the time they enter it or they risk being overruled by a higher court. That reality may limit the capacity of a new set of judges to go their own way—at least in the short run.

Consider, for example, President Reagan's impact on the judicial branch, which continued to be substantial for a long time. By the end of his second term, he had appointed an unprecedented 368 federal judges, 50 percent of those on the bench. When he entered the White House, the Supreme Court was already teetering to the right because of Richard Nixon's and Gerald R. Ford's conservative appointments. Although Jimmy Carter's liberal appointees were still serving on trial and appellate benches, Reagan found a good many conservative judges from Nixon and Ford on the bench when he took office. Thus he had a major role in shaping the entire federal judiciary in his own conservative image for some time to come. George H.W. Bush's judges had a much easier time making their impact felt, because they entered a judicial realm wherein well over half of the judges already professed conservative Republican values.

On the other hand, President Clinton's impact on the judiciary was slower to manifest itself, because his judicial nominees entered an arena in which more than 75 percent of the trial and appellate court judgeships were held by the appointees of GOP presidents with very conservative orientations. When George W. Bush entered the White House, 51 percent of the federal judges had been appointed by Democratic presidents. At the end of his eight years in office, roughly 60 percent of lower federal judges bore the Republican label. Thus, when Obama assumed office, the judiciary was clearly dominated by those who did not share his mainstream Democratic values.

What is the scorecard like in January of 2012, as President Obama is about to complete his first term on office? As of January 2012, 45.3 percent of "active" federal judges have been appointed by Democratic presidents, while 54.7 percent have been selected by Republican chief executives. When one factors in judges with "senior judge" status, the numbers are fairly similar: for all federal jurists on the bench today, 43.3 percent are Democratic appointees while 56.7 are those chosen by GOP presidents.[19] With Obama expected to add about 5 percent of additional Democratic judges to the bench during the remainder of his term (a large number of whom will likely be replacing conservative Republican retirees), it seems fair to predict that by the end of 2012, the federal bench should be split almost evenly between Democrats and Republicans. The real question, then, is whether or not the president will be reelected. If so, by the end of a second Obama term, the judiciary will very likely be distinctly more Democratic—perhaps by some 20 percentage points—by the end of his second term in 2016. If Obama loses his reelection bid to a Republican, the federal bench will almost certainly once again be dominated by the GOP and by a similar percentage. This makes the presidential election of 2012 a particularly critical one in terms of the future ideological direction of the federal judiciary.

Sources and Definitions

Let us now turn to a quantitative analysis of the decision making by Obama judges. Before we examine the data we have collected, we need to say a word about the data's source, and offer working definitions of the terms *conservative* and *liberal*. The data on trial courts were taken from a database consisting of more than 102,000 opinions by more than 2,200 judges published in the *Federal Supplement* from 1933 through early 2011. Included in this overall data set were 91 decisions handed down by judges appointed by President Barack Obama.[20] Only cases that fit easily into one of thirty case types and that contained a clear, underlying liberal-conservative dimension were used. This included cases such as state and federal habeas corpus pleas, labor-management disputes, questions involving the right to privacy, and environmental protection cases. Excluded were cases involving matters that do not exhibit a clear ideological dimension such as patent cases, admiralty disputes, and land condemnation hearings. The number of cases not selected was about the same as the number included.

In the realm of civil rights and civil liberties, *liberal* judges would generally take a broadening position; that is, they would seek in their rulings to extend those freedoms. *Conservative* judges, by contrast, would prefer to limit such rights. For example, in a case in which a government agency wanted to prevent a controversial person from speaking in a public park or at a state university, a liberal judge would be more inclined than a conservative to uphold the right of the would-be speech giver. Or, in a case concerning affirmative action in public higher education, a liberal judge would be more likely to take the side favoring special admissions for minority petitioners.

In the area of government regulation of the economy, liberal judges would probably uphold legislation that benefited working people or the economic underdog. Thus, if the secretary of labor sought an injunction against an employer for paying less than the minimum wage, a liberal judge would be more disposed to endorse the labor secretary's arguments, whereas a conservative judge would tend to side with business, especially big business.

Another broad category of cases often studied by judicial scholars is criminal justice. Liberal judges are, in general, more sympathetic to the motions made by criminal defendants. For instance, in a case in which the accused claimed to have been coerced by the government to make an illegal confession, liberal judges would be more likely than their conservative counterparts to agree that the government had acted improperly.

What the Data Reveal

In Figure 1, we compare the total "liberalism" scores of the judicial cohorts appointed by nine of the most recent chief executives, four Democrats and five Republicans.[21] The data indicate that 51.1 percent of the decisions of Barack

Figure 1. Decisions Scored as Liberal by Judges Appointed
by the Ten Most Recent Presidents

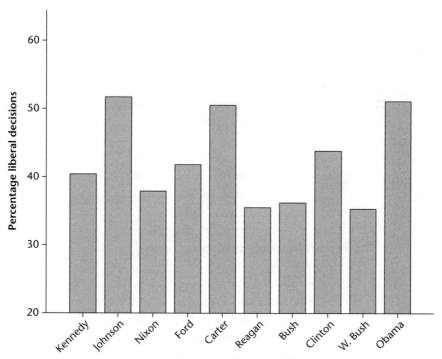

Obama's jurists have decided in a liberal direction. This puts him around seven points ahead of the Clinton cohort and very similar to the judges appointed by Lyndon Johnson and Jimmy Carter, whose liberalism scores were respectively 51.7 and 50.5. The Obama jurists are clearly more liberal than those of his immediate predecessor, George W. Bush, whose liberalism score was the lowest for all presidents in our data set (going back to the time of Woodrow Wilson)—35.3 percent. The Obama judges are also more liberal than the judges of other Republican presidents, whose ideology scores are as follows: Nixon, 37.9 percent; Ford, 41.8 percent; Reagan, 35.5 percent; and George H.W. Bush, 36.2 percent.[22]

We previously noted that President Obama has not directly called for moving the judiciary's center of gravity to the ideological left, and we have observed that he has been accorded no more than an average number of judicial openings to fill. Likewise we concluded that his political clout vis-à-vis the American public and the Senate has been only at moderate levels but that he has had the opportunity to move the lower federal judiciary closer to a partisan equilibrium by increasing the number of Democratic jurists on the bench by about 10 percentage points for every two years in office. So far, President Obama has been able to fill most of his judicial vacancies with mainstream Democrats, and such Democrats are on the whole more liberal than typical members of the GOP. It therefore seems fair to conclude that the president has moved the center of gravity of the federal judiciary somewhat toward the left. Despite this, it is worth noting that at this point, the ideological middle position of the lower federal judiciary still remains conservative, given the substantial partisan advantage Republicans had when Obama took office (around 62 percent of sitting judges at that time had been appointed by Republican presidents). The early evidence indicates that Obama's judges are mainstream liberals entering a bench that has been dominated by conservatives and, as such, his judicial nominees are moving the overall direction of the federal judiciary toward the political center.

Traditional versus Nontraditional Judges

One final subject of interest is the decision-making patterns of Obama traditional appointees (that is, white males) compared with those of his nontraditional appointees (women and minorities). Such comparisons are increasingly meaningful, because recent presidents have been appointing an increasing number of women and minorities to the federal bench. For example, President Clinton appointed the largest number of women and minorities of any previous

Democratic president—51 percent—and President George W. Bush chose the largest percentage of such individuals of any prior Republican chief executive—34 percent. President Obama has appointed around 62 percent of his lower court jurists from among the ranks of women and/or racial minorities, and this has included a number of judges who are openly gay.[23] Conventional wisdom often suggests that women and minorities might be somewhat more liberal in their voting patterns than their white male counterparts, but the actual scholarly evidence on this tends to be conflicting and inconclusive.[24] Regardless, at this point it is clear that a large majority of President Obama's judicial nominees have been from groups that have been historically underrepresented on the bench. What's more, if the current trajectory continues, President Obama is on track to have a greater percentage of women and/or racial minorities as his appointees to the federal judiciary than any other president in U.S. history.

Conclusion

We have explored the ideological impact that President Barack Obama has had so far on the decision-making patterns of the trial court judiciary. To perform this task, we sought to determine the degree to which Obama and his appointment team have possessed a strong commitment to make ideologically based appointments, the number of vacancies to be filled, the extent of the president's political clout, and the ideological climate that his judicial cohort is entering.

Our estimation is that President Obama is having a notable impact on the ideological orientation of the federal judiciary. Although cautious and pragmatic in his approach to judicial appointments, and downplaying ideological factors, it is nonetheless clear that Obama is appointing mainstream liberal-Democrats to the federal bench. And with today's sharp partisan cleavages, such individuals are decidedly more left-of-center than members of the GOP. (The "liberal Republicans" and the "conservative Democrats" of the past have become rare breeds in the highly charged politics of 21st-century America.) By the end of his first term, Obama will likely have appointed about 20 percent of the federal judiciary. Given the distinctly conservative tilt of the federal bench when he began office, in this way, he will almost certainly be effective in shifting the ideological balance of the courts to the political center. If President Obama is defeated for a second term, he will still have made his mark on the judiciary, albeit a modest one. On the other hand, if the president is reelected, then his judges, coupled with the Clinton cohort still on the bench, should give moderately liberal Democrats a firm control of the federal judiciary.

NOTES

1. Will Weissert, "Perry Signs Pledge on Anti-Gay Marriage Amendment," *Associated Press,* available online at http://news.yahoo.com/perry-signs-pledge-anti-gay-marriage-amendment-161046437.html

2. Amy Gardner and Matt Delong, "Newt Gingrich's Assault on 'Activist Judges' Draws Criticism, Even from Right," *Washington Post,* December 18, 2011, available online at http://www.washingtonpost.com/politics/newt-gingrichs-assault-on-activist-judges-draws-criticism-even-from-right/2011/12/17/gIQAoYa800_story.html

3. Michael D. Shear, "Obama Nominates Berkeley Professor Goodwin Liu to Federal Appeals Court," *Washington Post,* February 25, 2010, A 21.

4. Associated Press, "Thune: Federal Judge Nominees Are 'Good Picks,'" *Rapid City Journal,* September 9, 2009, available at www.rapidcityjournal.com/articles/2009/09/09/news/doc4aa7f74c398bf352231062.txt

5. Gary Martin, "State's Senators Recommended Two for Federal Bench," *Houston Chronicle,* July 20, 2011, B2.

6. Carolina A. Miranda, "Just What Is a 'Wise Latina," Anyway?" *Time,* July 14, 2009, available at http://www.time.com/time/politics/article/0,8599,1910403,00.html

7. Fox News, "Senate Confirms Sotomayor to U.S. Supreme Court," August 6, 2009, available at http://www.foxnews.com/politics/2009/08/06/senate-confirms-sonia-sotomayor-supreme-court/

8. Dana Milbank, "In Kagan, Obama Picks a Nominee, Not a Fight," *Washington Post,* May 11, 2010, A2.

9. *Ibid.* Also, for an excellent discussion of President Obama's quest for diversity on the federal bench, see Sheldon Goldman, Elliot Slotnick, and Sara Schiavoni, "Obama's Judiciary at Midterm: The Confirmation Drama, *Judicature* 94(2011): 262–304.

10. Jeffrey Toobin, "Are Obama Judges Really Liberals?" *The New Yorker,* September 21, 2009, available at http://www.newyorker.com/reporting/2009/09/21/090921fa_fact_toobin?currentPage=all

11. Goldman et al., "Obama's Judiciary at Midterm," 272.

12. Jon R. Bond, "The Politics of Court Structure: The Addition of New Federal Judges," *Law and Policy Quarterly* 2 (1980): 182, 183, and 187.

13. Jerry Markon and Shailagh Murry, "Federal Judicial Vacancies Reaching Crisis Point," *Washington Post,* February 8, 2011, available online at http://www.washingtonpost.com/national/vacancies-on-federal-bench-hit-crisis-point/2011/02/07/ABzpkZF_story.html

14. Goldman et al., 280.

15. *Ibid.*

16. *Ibid,* 287.

17. Paul Kane, "Senate Republicans Block Judicial Nominee Goodwin Liu," *Washington Post,* May 19, 2011, available online at http://www.washingtonpost.com/politics/judicial-nominee-goodwin-liu-faces-filibuster-showdown/2011/05/18/AF6ak76G_story.html

18. *Ibid,* 293.

19. It should be emphasized that when one is discussing a president's potential to make an ideological impact on the judiciary, it is not sufficient to count only the number of appointments he can make. One also has to factor in which cohorts of judges are retiring from the

bench. Thus if Obama appoints a mainstream Democrat to replace a retiring Clinton judge who is also a mainstream Democrat, there is no ideological gain for the administration. However, if Obama appoints a moderate Democrat to replace a retiring conservative Reagan jurist, there is a two-fold gain. And at the present time, the oldest cohorts of any size still on the federal bench are those appointed by Ronald Reagan and by George H.W. Bush. This enhances Obama's potential to nudge the judiciary to the left, because he is more likely to replace a conservative Republican with a Democrat who is likely to be more liberal. To be more precise, since Obama took office some 75 active and senior judges appointed by Republicans have departed the bench due to death or retirement, while only 60 jurists selected by Democrats have done so.

20. These rulings were handed down in three key issue areas: civil liberties and rights; criminal justice; and labor and economic regulation. Though we coded only district court rulings, prior research suggests that the behavior of jurists at this level is comparable to that of judges appointed by the same presidents to the courts of appeals. See Ronald Stidham, Robert A. Carp, and Donald R. Songer, "The Voting Behavior of President Clinton's Judicial Appointees," *Judicature* 80 (1996): 16–20; and Robert A. Carp, Donald Songer, C.K. Rowland, and Lisa Richey-Tracy, "The Voting Behavior of Judges Appointed by President Bush," *Judicature* 76 (1993): 298–302.

21. The reader will note that we have made few references to President Gerald Ford in our generalizations about the voting behavior of recent Republican presidential cohorts. The reason is that President Ford was something of an outlier and an exception to the rule that the judges appointed by GOP chief executives are generally more conservative than those selected by Democratic presidents. Ford's overall liberalism score of 44 percent makes him the most liberal of recent Republican presidents, although still more conservative than recent Democratic chief executives. There are at least two reasons for this. First, Ford was much less of a political ideologue than his predecessor in the White House, Richard Nixon, or his Republican successors, Reagan, George H. W. Bush, and George W. Bush. Also, because Ford's circuitous route to the presidency did not enhance his political effectiveness with the Senate, he would not have the clout to force highly conservative Republican nominees through a liberal, Democratic Senate, even if he had wished to.

22. In previous studies of judicial decision-making, we have broken down the liberalism numbers for each presidential cohort into our three subcategories of civil rights and civil liberties, labor and economic regulation, and criminal justice. However, because our total "n" for the Obama cohort is still relatively small, it would be methodologically unsound to publish results produced by such diminutive samples. Indeed we acknowledge that even our total "n" for the Obama cohort—91 decisions—is quite modest. We consequently we put forth our observations and conclusions here in a very tentative fashion and caution that our results could change with the addition of more cases to our sample.

23. For a superb discussion of President Obama's appointments of women and minorities to the federal bench, see Goldman et. al., "Obama's Judiciary at Midterm," 262–304.

24. See Robert A. Carp, Kenneth L. Manning, and Ronald Stidham, "President Clinton's District Judges: 'Extreme Liberals' or Just Plain Moderates," *Judicature* 84 (2001):284–288; and Robert A. Carp et al., *Judicial Process in America,* 8th ed., chap. 5 (Washington, DC: CQ Press, 2011).

Chapter 10

Public Opinion

———•:•———

10-1

Analyzing and Interpreting Polls

Herbert Asher

Public opinion polls have gained a prominent place in modern American poli-
tics. Polls themselves often are newsworthy, particularly during campaigns
and times of political crisis. Unfortunately, as Herbert Asher shows in the
following essay, polls are open to misinterpretation and misuse. The wording
of questions, the construction of a sample, the choice of items to analyze and
report, the use of surveys to measure trends, and the examination of subsets
of respondents all pose problems of interpretation. Every consumer of polling
information must understand these issues to properly use the information
polls provide.

INTERPRETING A POLL is more an art than a science, even though statistical analysis of poll data is central to the enterprise. An investigator examining poll results
has tremendous leeway in deciding which items to analyze, which sample subsets or breakdowns to present, and how to interpret the statistical results. Take
as an example a poll with three items that measure attitudes toward arms control
negotiations. The investigator may construct an index from these three
items. . . . Or the investigator may emphasize the results from one question, perhaps because of space and time constraints and the desire to keep matters simple,

Source: Herbert Asher, *Polling and the Public: What Every Citizen Should Know,* 4th ed. (Washington, D.C.: CQ Press, 1998), 141–169.

or because those particular results best support the analyst's own policy preferences. The investigator may examine results from the entire sample and ignore subgroups whose responses deviate from the overall pattern. Again time and space limitations or the investigator's own preferences may influence these choices. Finally, two investigators may interpret identical poll results in sharply different ways depending on the perspectives and values they bring to their data analysis; the glass may indeed be half full or half empty.

As the preceding example suggests, the analysis and interpretation of data entail a high degree of subjectivity and judgment. Subjectivity in this context does not mean deliberate bias or distortion, but simply professional judgments about the importance and relevance of information. Certainly, news organizations' interpretations of their polls are generally done in the least subjective and unbiased fashion. But biases can slip in—sometimes unintentionally, sometimes deliberately—when, for example, an organization has sponsored a poll to promote a particular position. Because this final phase of polling is likely to have the most direct influence on public opinion, this chapter includes several case studies to illustrate the judgmental aspects of analyzing and interpreting poll results.

Choosing Items to Analyze

Many public opinion surveys deal with multifaceted, complex issues. For example, a researcher querying Americans about their attitudes toward tax reform might find initially that they overwhelmingly favor a fairer tax system. But if respondents are asked about specific aspects of tax reform, their answers may reflect high levels of confusion, indifference, or opposition. And depending upon which items the researcher chooses to emphasize, the report might convey support, indifference, or opposition toward tax reform. American foreign policy in the Middle East is another highly complex subject that can elicit divergent reactions from Americans depending on which aspects of the policy they are questioned about.

Some surveys go into great depth on a topic through multiple items constructed to measure its various facets. The problem for an investigator in this case becomes one of deciding which results to report. Moreover, even though an extensive analysis is conducted, the media might publicize only an abbreviated version of it. In such a case the consumer of the poll results is at the mercy of the media to portray accurately the overall study. Groups or organizations that sponsor polls to demonstrate support for a particular position or policy option often disseminate results in a selective fashion which enables them to put the organization and its policies in a favorable light.

In contrast with in-depth surveys on a topic, *omnibus surveys* are superficial in their treatment of particular topics because of the need to cover many subjects in the same survey. Here the problem for an investigator becomes one of ensuring that the few questions employed to study a specific topic really do justice to the substance and complexity of that topic. It is left to the consumer of both kinds of polls to judge whether they receive the central information on a topic or whether other items might legitimately yield different substantive results.

The issue of prayer in public schools is a good example of how public opinion polling on a topic can be incomplete and potentially misleading. Typically, pollsters ask Americans whether they support a constitutional amendment that would permit voluntary prayer in public schools, and more than three-fourths of Americans respond that they would favor such an amendment. This question misses the mark. Voluntary prayer by individuals is in no way prohibited; the real issue is whether there will be *organized* voluntary prayer. But many pollsters do not include items that tap this aspect of the voluntary prayer issue. Will there be a common prayer? If so, who will compose it? Will someone lead the class in prayer? If so, who? Under what circumstances and when will the prayer be uttered? What about students who do not wish to participate or who prefer a different prayer?

The difficulty with both the in-depth poll and the omnibus survey is that the full set of items used to study a particular topic is usually not reported and thus the consumer cannot make informed judgments about whether the conclusions of the survey are valid. Recognizing this, individuals should take a skeptical view of claims by a corporate executive or an elected officeholder or even a friend that the polls demonstrate public support for or opposition to a particular position. The first question to ask is: What is the evidence cited to support the claim? From there one might examine the question wording, the response alternatives, the screening for nonattitudes, and the treatment of "don't know" responses. Then one might attempt the more difficult task of assessing whether the questions used to study the topic at hand were really optimal. Might other questions have been used? What aspects of the topic were not addressed? Finally, one might ponder whether different interpretations could be imposed on the data and whether alternative explanations could account for the reported patterns.

In evaluating poll results, there is always the temptation to seize upon those that support one's position and ignore those that do not. The problem is that one or two items cannot capture the full complexity of most issues. For example, a *Newsweek* poll conducted by the Gallup Organization in July 1986 asked a number of questions about sex laws and lifestyles. The poll included the following three items (Alpern 1986, 38):

> Do you approve or disapprove of the Supreme Court decision upholding a
> state law against certain sexual practices engaged in privately by consenting

adult homosexuals? [This question was asked of the 73 percent who knew about the Supreme Court decision.]

Disapprove	47%
Approve	41%

In general, do you think that states should have the right to prohibit particular sexual practices conducted in private between consenting adult homosexuals?

No	57%
Yes	34%

Do you think homosexuality has become an accepted alternative lifestyle or not?

Yes	32%
No	61%
Don't know	7%

Note that the first two items tap citizens' attitudes toward the legal treatment of homosexuals, while the third addresses citizens' views of homosexuality as a lifestyle. Although differently focused, all three questions deal with aspects of gay life. It would not be surprising to see gay rights advocates cite the results of the first two questions as indicating support for their position. Opponents of gay rights would emphasize the results of the third question.

An Eyewitness News/*Daily News* poll of New York City residents conducted in February 1986 further illustrates how the selective use and analysis of survey questions can generate very different impressions of popular opinion on an issue. This poll asked a number of gay rights questions:

On another matter, would you say that New York City needs a gay rights law or not?

Yes, need gay rights law	39%
No, do not need gay rights law	54%
Don't know/no opinion	8%

On another matter, do you think it should be against the law for landlords or private employers to deny housing or a job to someone because that person is homosexual or do you think landlords and employers should be allowed to do that if they want to?

Yes, should be against law	49%
No, should not be against law	47%

Volunteered responses

Should be law only for landlord	1%
Should be law only for employers	8%
Don't know/no opinion	3%

Although a definite majority of the respondents oppose a gay rights law in response to the first question, a plurality also believe that it should be illegal for landlords and employers to deny housing and jobs to persons because they are homosexual. Here the two questions both address the legal status of homosexuals, and it is clear which question gay rights activists and gay rights opponents would cite in support of their respective policy positions. It is not clear, however, which question is the better measure of public opinion. The first question is unsatisfactory because one does not know how respondents interpreted the scope of a gay rights law. Did they think it referred only to housing and job discrimination, or did they think it would go substantially beyond that? The second question is inadequate if it is viewed as equivalent to a gay rights law. Lumping housing and jobs together constitutes another flaw since citizens might have divergent views on these two aspects of gay rights.

Additional examples of the importance of item selection are based on polls of Americans' attitudes about the Iraqi invasion of Kuwait in 1990. Early in the Persian Gulf crisis, various survey organizations asked Americans, using different questions, how they felt about taking military action against Iraq. Not surprisingly, the organizations obtained different results.

Do you favor or oppose direct U.S. military action against Iraq at this time? (Gallup, August 3–4, 1990)

Favor	23%
Oppose	68%
Don't know/refused	9%

Do you agree or disagree that the U.S. should take all actions necessary, including the use of military force, to make sure that Iraq withdraws its forces from Kuwait? (ABC News/ *Washington Post,* August 8, 1990)

Agree	66%
Disagree	33%
Don't know	1%

Would you approve or disapprove of using U.S. troops to force the Iraqis to leave Kuwait? (Gallup, August 9–12, 1990, taken from *Public Perspective,* September/October 1990, 13)

Approve	64%
Disapprove	36%

(I'm going to mention some things that may or may not happen in the Middle East and for each one, please tell me whether the U.S. should or should not take military action in connection with it). . . . If Iraq refuses to withdraw from Kuwait? (NBC News/*Wall Street Journal,* August 18–19, 1990, taken from *Public Perspective,* September/October 1990, 13)

No military action	51%
Military action	49%

Note that the responses to these questions indicate varying levels of support for military action even though most of the questions were asked within two weeks of each other. The first question shows the most opposition to military action. This is easily explained: the question concerns military action *at this time,* an alternative that many Americans may have seen as premature until other means had been tried. The other three questions all indicate majority support for military action, although that support ranges from a bare majority to about two-thirds of all Americans. It is clear which question proponents and opponents of military action would cite to support their arguments.

Throughout the Persian Gulf crisis, public opinion was highly supportive of President Bush's policies; only in the period between October and December 1990 did support for the president's handling of the situation drop below 60 percent. For example, a November 1990 CBS News/*New York Times* poll showed the following patterns of response:

Do you approve or disapprove of the way George Bush is handling Iraq's invasion of Kuwait?

Approve	50%
Disapprove	41%
Don't know/NA	8%

Likewise, an ABC News/*Washington Post* poll in mid-November reported:

Do you approve or disapprove of the way George Bush is handling the situation caused by Iraq's invasion of Kuwait?

Approve	59%
Disapprove	36%
Don't know/NA	5%

Some opponents of the military buildup tried to use these and similar polls to demonstrate that support for the president's policies was decreasing, since earlier polls had indicated support levels in the 60–70 percent range. Fortunately, the *Washington Post* poll cited above asked respondents who disapproved of Bush's policy whether the president was moving too slowly or too quickly. It turned out that 44 percent of the disapprovers said "too slowly" and 37 percent "too quickly." Thus, a plurality of the disapprovers preferred more rapid action against Iraq—a result that provided little support for those critics of the president's policies who were arguing against a military solution.

Shortly before the outbreak of the war, the *Washington Post* conducted a survey of American attitudes about going to war with Iraq. To assess the effects of question wording, the *Post* split its sample in half and used two different versions of the same question followed by the identical follow-up question to each item.

Version 1

As you may know, the U.N. Security Council has authorized the use of force against Iraq if it doesn't withdraw from Kuwait by January 15. If Iraq does not withdraw from Kuwait, should the United States go to war against Iraq to force it out of Kuwait at some point after January 15 or not?

Go to war sometime after January 15	62%
No, do not go to war	32%

How long after January 15 should the United States wait for Iraq to withdraw from Kuwait before going to war to force it out?

Do not favor war at any point	32%
Immediately	18%
Less than one month	28%
1–3 months	8%
4 months or longer	2%

Version 2

The United Nations has passed a resolution authorizing the use of military force against Iraq if they do not withdraw their troops from Kuwait by January 15. If Iraq does not withdraw from Kuwait by then, do you think the United States should start military actions against Iraq, or should the United States wait longer to see if the trade embargo and economic sanctions work?

U.S. should start military actions	49%
U.S. should wait longer to see if sanctions work	47%

How long after January 15 should the United States wait for Iraq to withdraw from Kuwait before going to war to force it out?

U.S. should start military actions	49%

For those who would wait:

Less than a month	15%
1–3 months	17%
4 months or longer	9%

Morin (1991) points out how very different portraits of the American public can be painted by examining the two versions with and without the follow-up question. For example, version 1 shows 62 percent of Americans supporting war against Iraq, while version 2 shows only 49 percent. These different results stem from inclusion of the embargo and sanctions option in the second version. Thus it appears that version 2 gives a less militaristic depiction of the American public. Responses to the follow-up question, however, provide a different picture of the public. For example, the first version shows that 54 percent of Americans (18 + 28 + 8) favor going to war within three months. But the second version shows that 81 percent of Americans (49 + 15 + 17) favor war within three months. The point, of course, is that the availability of different items on a survey can generate differing descriptions of the public's preferences.

The importance of item selection is illustrated in a final example on the Gulf War from an April 3, 1991, ABC News/*Washington Post* poll conducted just after the conflict. It included the following three questions:

Do you approve or disapprove of the way that George Bush is handling the situation involving Iraqi rebels who are trying to overthrow Saddam Hussein?

Approve	69%
Disapprove	24%
Don't know	7%

Please tell me if you agree or disagree with this statement: The United States should not have ended the war with Iraqi President Saddam Hussein still in power.

Agree	55%
Disagree	40%
Don't know	5%

Do you think the United States should try to help rebels overthrow Hussein or not?

Yes	45%
No	51%
Don't know	4%

Note that the responses to the first item indicate overwhelming approval for the president. But if one analyzed the second question in isolation, one might conclude that a majority of Americans did not support the president and indeed wanted to restart the war against Saddam Hussein. But the third item shows that a majority of Americans oppose helping the rebels. The lesson of this and the previous examples is clear. Constructing an interpretation around any single survey item can generate a very inaccurate description of public opinion. Unfortunately, advocates of particular positions have many opportunities to use survey results selectively and misleadingly to advance their cause.

The health care debate in 1993 and 1994 also provides examples of how the selection of items for analysis can influence one's view of American public opinion. *Washington Post* polls asked Americans whether they thought the Clinton health plan was better or worse than the present system (Morin 1994). In one version of the question, the sample was given the response options "better" or "worse," while in the other version respondents could choose among "better," "worse," or "don't know enough about the plan to say." The following responses were obtained:

Version 1		Version 2	
better	52%	better	21%
worse	34%	worse	27%
don't know (volunteered)	14%	don't know enough	52%

Clearly, very different portrayals of American public opinion are presented by the two versions of the question. The first version suggests that a majority of Americans believed that the Clinton plan was better than the status quo, while the second version suggests that a plurality of citizens with opinions on the issue felt that the Clinton plan was worse. It is obvious which version of the question supporters and opponents of the Clinton health plan would be more likely to cite.

Another example from the health care reform area deals with Americans' feelings about the seriousness of the health care problem. Certainly, the more seriously the problem was viewed, the greater the impetus for changing the health care system. Different polling organizations asked a variety of questions designed to tap the importance of the health care issue (questions taken from the September/October 1994 issue of *Public Perspective,* 23, 26):

> Louis Harris and Associates (April 1994): Which of the following statements comes closest to expressing your overall view of the health care system in this country? . . . There are some good things in our health care system, but fundamental changes are needed to make it better. . . . Our health care system has so much wrong with it that we need to completely rebuild it. . . . On the whole, the health care system works pretty well and only minor changes are necessary to make it work.

Fundamental changes needed	54%
Completely rebuild it	31%
Only minor changes needed	14%

> NBC/*Wall Street Journal* (March 1994): Which of the following comes closest to your belief about the American health care system—the system is in crisis; the system has major problems, but is not in crisis; the system has problems, but they are not major; or the system has no problems?

Crisis	22%
Major problems	50%
Minor problems	26%

> Gallup (June 1994): Which of these statements do you agree with more: The country has health care problems, but no health care crisis, or, the country has a health care crisis?

Crisis	55%
Problems but no crisis	41%
Don't know	4%

> Gallup (June 1994): Which of these statements do you agree with more: The country has a health care crisis, or the country has health care problems, but no health care crisis?

Crisis	35%
Problems but no crisis	61%
Don't know	4%

Certainly if one were trying to make the case that health care reform was an absolute priority, one would cite the first version of the Gallup question in which 55 percent of the respondents labeled health care a crisis. But if one wanted to move more slowly and incrementally on the health care issue, one would likely cite the NBC News/ *Wall Street Journal* poll in which only 22 percent of Americans said there was a crisis. Health care reform is the kind of controversial public policy issue that invites political leaders to seize upon those poll results to advance their positions. In such situations, citizens should be sensitive to how politicians are selectively using the polls.

Schneider (1996) has provided an excellent example of how examination of a single trial heat question may give a misleading impression of the electoral strength of presidential candidates. A better sense of the candidates' true electoral strength is achieved by adding to the analysis information about the incumbent's job approval rating. For example, in a trial heat question in May 1980 incumbent president Jimmy Carter led challenger Ronald Reagan by 40 to 32 percent, yet at the time Carter's job rating was quite negative: 38 percent approval and 51 percent disapproval. Thus Carter's lead in the trial heat item was much more fragile than it appeared; indeed, Reagan went on to win the election. Four years later, in May of 1984, President Reagan led challenger Walter Mondale by 10 percentage points in the trial heat question. But Reagan's job rating was very positive: 54 percent approval compared with 38 percent disapproval. Thus Reagan's 10-point lead looked quite solid in view of his strong job ratings, and he won overwhelmingly in November. Finally, in April 1992, incumbent president George Bush led challenger Bill Clinton by 50 to 34 percent in the trial heat question, a huge margin. But Bush's overall job rating was negative—42 percent approval versus 48 percent disapproval. Bush's lead over Clinton, then, was not as strong as it appeared, and Clinton ultimately won the election.

By collecting information on multiple aspects of a topic, pollsters are better able to understand citizens' attitudes (Morin and Berry 1996). One of the anomalies of 1996 was the substantial number of Americans who were worried about the health of the economy at a time when by most objective indicators the economy was performing very well. Part of the answer to this puzzle was Americans' ignorance and misinformation about the country's economic health. For example, even though unemployment was substantially lower in 1996 than in 1991, 33 percent of Americans said it was higher in 1996 and 28 percent said the same. The average estimate of the unemployment rate was 20.6 percent when in reality it was just over 5 percent. Americans' perceptions of inflation and the deficit were similar; in both cases Americans thought that the reality was much worse than it actually was. It is no wonder that many Americans expressed economic insecurity during good economic times; they were not aware of how strongly the economy was performing.

The final example in this section focuses on how the media selects what we learn about a poll even when the complete poll and analyses are available to the citizenry. The example concerns a book entitled *Sex in America: A Definitive*

Survey by Robert T. Michael et al., published in 1994, along with a more specialized and comprehensive volume, *The Social Organization of Sexuality: Sexual Practices in the United States* by Edward O. Laumann et al. Both books are based on an extensive questionnaire administered by the National Opinion Research Center to 3,432 scientifically selected respondents. . . .

Because of the importance of the subject matter and because sex sells, media coverage of the survey was widespread. How various media reported the story indicates how much leeway the media have and how influential they are in determining what citizens learn about a given topic. For example, the *New York Times* ran a front-page story on October 7, 1994, entitled "Sex in America: Faithfulness in Marriage Thrives After All." Less prominent stories appeared in subsequent issues, including one on October 18, 1994, inaccurately entitled "Gay Survey Raises a New Question."

Two of the three major news magazines featured the sex survey on the covers of their October 17, 1994, issues. The *Time* cover simply read "Sex in America: Surprising News from the Most Important Survey since the Kinsey Report." The *U.S. News & World Report* cover was more risqué, showing a partially clad man and woman in bed; it read "Sex in America: A Massive New Survey, the Most Authoritative Ever, Reveals What We Do Behind the Bedroom Door." In contrast, *Newsweek* simply ran a two-page story with the lead "Not Frenzied, But Fulfilled. Sex: Relax. If you do it—with your mate—around twice a week, according to a major new study, you basically wrote the book of love."

Other magazines and newspapers also reported on the survey in ways geared to their readership. The November issue of *Glamour* featured the survey on its cover with the teaser "Who's doing it? And how? MAJOR U.S. SEX SURVEY." The story that followed was written by the authors of the book. While the cover of the November 15, 1994, *Advocate* read "What That Sex Survey Really Means," the story focused largely on what the survey had to say about the number of gays and lesbians in the population. The lead stated "10%: Reality or Myth? There's little authoritative information about gays and lesbians in the landmark study *Sex in America*—but what there is will cause big trouble." Finally, the *Chronicle of Higher Education,* a weekly newspaper geared to college and university personnel, in its October 17, 1994, issue headlined its story "The Sex Lives of Americans. Survey that had been target of conservative attacks produces few startling results."

Both books about the survey contain a vast amount of information and a large number of results and findings. But most of the media reported on such topics as marital fidelity, how often Americans have sex, how many sex partners people have, how often people experience orgasm, what percentages of the population are gay and lesbian, how long sex takes, and the time elapsed between a couple's first meeting and their first sexual involvement. Many of the reports also presented results for married vs. singles, men vs. women, and other analytical groupings. While most of the media coverage cited above was accurate in reporting the actual survey results, it also was selective in focusing on the more titillating parts of the survey, an unsurprising outcome given the need to satisfy their readerships.

Examining Trends with Polling Data

Researchers often use polling data to describe and analyze trends. To isolate trend data, a researcher must ensure that items relating to the topic under investigation are included in multiple surveys conducted at different points in time. Ideally, the items should be identically worded. But even when they are, serious problems of comparability can make trend analysis difficult. Identically worded items may not mean the same thing or provide the same stimulus to respondents over time because social and political changes in society have altered the meaning of the questions. For example, consider this question:

> Some say that the civil rights people have been trying to push [have been pushed] too fast. Others feel they haven't pushed fast enough. How about you? Do you think that civil rights leaders are trying to push too fast, are going too slowly, or are they moving at about the right speed?

The responses to this item can be greatly influenced by the goals and agenda of the civil rights leadership at the time of the survey. A finding that more Americans think that the civil rights leaders are moving too fast or too slowly may reflect not a change in attitude from past views about civil rights activism but a change in the civil rights agenda itself. In this case, follow-up questions designed to measure specific components of the civil rights agenda are needed to help define the trend.

There are other difficulties in achieving comparability over time. For example, even if the wording of an item were to remain the same, its placement within the questionnaire could change, which in turn could alter the meaning of a question. Likewise, the definition of the sampling frame and the procedures used to achieve completed interviews could change. In short, comparability entails much more than simply wording questions identically. Unfortunately, consumers of poll results seldom receive the information that enables them to judge whether items are truly comparable over time.

Two studies demonstrate the advantages and disadvantages of using identical items over time. Abramson, Silver, and Anderson (1990) complained that the biennial National Election Studies (NES) conducted by the Survey Research Center at the University of Michigan, Ann Arbor, were losing their longitudinal comparability as new questions were added to the surveys and old ones removed. Baumgartner and Walker (1988), in contrast, complained that the use of the same standard question over time to assess the level of group membership in the United States had systematically underestimated the extent of such activity. They argued that new measures of group membership should be employed, which, of course, would make comparisons between past and present surveys more problematic. Although both the old and the new measures can be included in a survey, this becomes very costly if the survey must cover many other topics.

Two other studies show how variations in question wording can make the assessment of attitude change over time difficult. Borrelli and colleagues (1987) found that polls measuring Americans' political party loyalties in 1980 and in 1984 varied widely in their results. They attributed the different results in these polls to three factors: whether the poll sampled voters only; whether the poll emphasized "today" or the present in inquiring about citizens' partisanship; and whether the poll was conducted close to election day, which would tend to give the advantage to the party ahead in the presidential contest. The implications of this research for assessing change in party identification over time are evident— that is, to conclude that genuine partisan change occurred in either of the two polls, other possible sources of observed differences, such as modifications in the wording of questions, must be ruled out. In a study of support for aid to the Nicaraguan contras between 1983 and 1986, Lockerbie and Borrelli (1990) argue that much of the observed change in American public opinion was not genuine. Instead, it was attributable to changes in the wording of the questions used to measure support for the contras. Again, the point is that one must be able to eliminate other potential explanations for observed change before one can conclude that observed change is genuine change.

Smith's (1993) critique of three major national studies of anti-Semitism conducted in 1964, 1981, and 1992 is an informative case study of how longitudinal comparisons may be undermined by methodological differences across surveys. The 1981 and 1992 studies were ostensibly designed to build upon the 1964 effort, thereby facilitating an analysis of trends in anti-Semitism. But, as Smith notes, longitudinal comparisons among the three studies were problematic because of differences in sample definition and interview mode, changes in question order and question wording, and insufficient information to evaluate the quality of the sample and the design execution. In examining an eleven-item anti-Semitism scale, he did find six items highly comparable over time that indicated a decline in anti-Semitic attitudes.

Despite the problems of sorting out true opinion change from change attributable to methodological factors, there are times when public opinion changes markedly and suddenly in response to a dramatic occurrence and the observed change is indeed genuine. Two examples from CBS News/*New York Times* polls in 1991 about the Persian Gulf war illustrate dramatic and extensive attitude change. The first example concerns military action against Iraq. Just before the January 15 deadline imposed by the UN for the withdrawal of Iraq from Kuwait, a poll found that 47 percent of Americans favored beginning military action against Iraq if it did not withdraw; 46 percent were opposed. Two days after the deadline and after the beginning of the allied air campaign against Iraq, a poll found 79 percent of Americans saying the United States had done the right thing in beginning military action against Iraq. The second example focuses on people's attitudes toward a ground war in the Middle East. Before the allied ground offensive began, only 11 percent of Americans said the United States should begin fighting the ground war soon; 79 percent said bombing from the air should continue. But after the ground war began, the numbers shifted dramatically: 75 percent of Americans said the United States was right to begin the ground war, and only 19 percent said the nation should have waited longer. Clearly, the Persian Gulf crisis was a case in which American public opinion moved dramatically in the direction of supporting the president at each new stage.

Examining Subsets of Respondents

Although it is natural to want to know the results from an entire sample, often the most interesting information in a poll comes from examining the response patterns of subsets of respondents defined according to certain theoretically or substantively relevant characteristics. For example, a January 1986 CBS News/*New York Times* poll showed President Reagan enjoying unprecedented popularity for a six-year incumbent: 65 percent approved of the president's performance, and only 24 percent disapproved. But these overall figures mask some analytically interesting variations. For example, among blacks only 37 percent approved of the president's performance; 49 percent disapproved. The sexes also differed in their views of the president, with men expressing a 72 percent approval rate compared with 58 percent for women. (As expected among categories of party loyalists, 89 percent of the Republicans, 66 percent of the independents, and only 47 percent of the Democrats approved of the president's performance.) Why did blacks and whites—and men and women—differ in their views of the president?

There is no necessary reason for public opinion on an issue to be uniform across subgroups. Indeed, on many issues there are reasons to expect just the opposite. That is why a fuller understanding of American public opinion is gained by taking a closer look at the views of relevant subgroups of the sample. In doing so, however, one should note that dividing the sample into subsets increases the sampling error and lowers the reliability of the sample estimates. For example, a sample of 1,600 Americans might be queried about their attitudes on abortion. After the overall pattern is observed, the researcher might wish to break down the sample by religion—yielding 1,150 Protestant, 400 Catholic, and 50 Jewish respondents—to determine whether religious affiliation is associated with specific attitudes toward abortion. The analyst might observe that Catholics on the whole are the most opposed to abortion. To find out which Catholics are most likely to oppose abortion, she might further divide the 400 Catholics into young and old Catholics or regular church attenders and nonregular attenders, or into four categories of young Catholic churchgoers, old Catholic churchgoers, young Catholic nonattenders, and old Catholic nonattenders. The more breakdowns done at the same time, the quicker the sample size in any particular category plummets, perhaps leaving insufficient cases in some categories to make solid conclusions.

Innumerable examples can be cited to demonstrate the advantages of delving more deeply into poll data on subsets of respondents. An ABC News/*Washington Post* poll conducted in February 1986 showed major differences in the attitudes of men and women toward pornography; an examination of only the total sample would have missed these important divergences. For example, in response to the question "Do you think laws against pornography in this country are too strict, not strict enough, or just about right?" 10 percent of the men said the laws were too strict, 41 percent said not strict enough, and 47 percent said about right. Among women, only 2 percent said the laws were too strict, a sizable 72 percent said they were not strict enough, and 23 percent thought they were about right (Sussman 1986b, 37).

A CBS News/*New York Times* poll of Americans conducted in April 1986 found widespread approval of the American bombing of Libya; 77 percent of the sample approved of the action, and only 14 percent disapproved. Despite the overall approval, differences among various subgroups are noteworthy. For example, 83 percent of the men approved of the bombing compared with 71 percent of the women. Of the white respondents, 80 percent approved in contrast to only 53 percent of the blacks (Clymer 1986). Even though all of these demographically defined groups gave at least majority support to the bombing, the differences in levels of support are both statistically and substantively significant.

Polls showed dramatic differences by race in the O. J. Simpson case, with blacks more convinced of Simpson's innocence and more likely to believe that he could not get a fair trial. For example, a field poll of Californians (*U.S. News & World Report,* August 1, 1994) showed that only 35 percent of blacks believed that Simpson could get a fair trial compared with 55 percent of whites. Also, 62 percent of whites thought Simpson was "very likely or somewhat likely" to be guilty of murder compared with only 38 percent for blacks. Comparable results were found in a national *Time*/CNN poll (*Time*, August 1, 1994): 66 percent of whites thought Simpson got a fair preliminary hearing compared with only 31 percent of black respondents, while 77 percent of the white respondents thought the case against Simpson was "very strong" or "fairly strong" compared with 45 percent for blacks. A *Newsweek* poll (August 1, 1994) revealed that 60 percent of blacks believed that Simpson was set up (20 percent attributing the setup to the police); only 23 percent of whites believed in a setup conspiracy. When asked whether Simpson had been treated better or worse than the average white murder suspect, whites said better by an overwhelming 52 to 5 percent margin, while blacks said worse by a 30 to 19 percent margin. These reactions to the Simpson case startled many Americans who could not understand how their compatriots of another race could see the situation so differently.

School busing to achieve racial integration has consistently been opposed by substantial majorities in national public opinion polls. A Harris poll commissioned by *Newsweek* in 1978 found that 85 percent of whites opposed busing (Williams 1979, 48). An ABC News/*Washington Post* poll conducted in February 1986 showed 60 percent of whites against busing (Sussman 1986a). The difference between the two polls might reflect genuine attitude change about busing in that eight-year period, or it might be a function of different question wording or different placement within the questionnaire. Whatever the reason, additional analysis of both these polls shows that whites are not monolithic in their opposition to busing. For example, the 1978 poll showed that 56 percent of white parents whose children had been bused viewed the experience as "very satisfactory." The 1986 poll revealed sharp differences in busing attitudes among younger and older whites. Among whites age thirty and under, 47 percent supported busing and 50 percent opposed it, while among whites over age thirty, 32 percent supported busing and 65 percent opposed it. Moreover, among younger whites whose families had experienced busing firsthand, 54 percent approved of busing and 46 percent opposed it. (Of course, staunch opponents of busing may have moved to escape busing, thereby guaranteeing that the remaining population would be relatively more supportive of busing.)

Another example of the usefulness of examining poll results within age categories is provided by an ABC News/*Washington Post* poll conducted in May 1985 on citizens' views of how the federal budget deficit might be cut. One item read, "Do you think the government should give people a smaller Social Security cost-of-living increase than they are now scheduled to get as a way of reducing the budget deficit, or not?" Among the overall sample, 19 percent favored granting a smaller cost-of-living increase and 78 percent opposed. To test the widespread view that young workers lack confidence in the Social Security system and doubt they will ever get out of the system what they paid in, Sussman (1985c) investigated how different age groups responded to the preceding question. Basically, he found that all age groups strongly opposed a reduction in cost-of-living increases. Unlike the busing issue, this question showed no difference among age groups—an important substantive finding, particularly in light of the expectation that there would be divergent views among the old and young. Too often people mistakenly dismiss null (no difference) results as uninteresting and unexciting; a finding of no difference can be just as substantively significant as a finding of a major difference.

An example where age does make a difference in people's opinions is the topic of physician-assisted suicide. A *Washington Post* poll conducted in 1996 asked a national sample of Americans, "Should it be legal or illegal for a doctor to help a terminally ill patient commit suicide?" (Rosenbaum 1997). The attitudes of older citizens and younger citizens were markedly different on this question—the older the age group, the greater the opposition to doctor-assisted suicide. For example, 52 percent of respondents between ages eighteen and twenty-nine thought doctor-assisted suicide should be legal; 41 percent said it should be illegal. But for citizens over age seventy, the comparable figures were 35 and 58 percent. Even more striking were some of the racial and income differences on this question. Whites thought physician involvement in suicide should be legal by a 55 to 35 percent margin; blacks opposed it 70 to 20 percent. At the lowest income levels, doctor-assisted suicide was opposed by a 54 to 37 percent margin; at the highest income level it was supported by a 58 to 30 percent margin.

In many instances the categories used for creating subgroups are already established or self-evident. For example, if one is interested in gender or racial differences, the categories of male and female or white and black are straightforward candidates for investigation. Other breakdowns require more thought. For example, what divisions might one use to examine the effects of age? Should they be young, middle-aged, and old? If so, what actual ages correspond to these categories? Is middle age thirty-five to sixty-five, forty to sixty, or what? Or should more than three categories of age be defined? In samples selected to study the effects of religion, the typical breakdown is Protestant, Catholic, and Jewish. But this simple threefold division might overlook some interesting variations; that is, some Protestants are evangelical, some are fundamentalist, and others are considered mainline denominations. Moreover, since most blacks are Protestants, comparisons of Catholics and Protestants that do not also control for race may be misleading.

Establishing categories is much more subjective and judgmental in other situations. For example, religious categories can be defined relatively easily by denominational affiliation, as mentioned earlier, but classifying respondents as evangelicals or fundamentalists is more complicated. Those who actually belong to denominations normally characterized as evangelical or fundamentalist could be so categorized. Or an investigator might identify some evangelical or fundamentalist beliefs, construct some polling questions around them, and then classify respondents according to their responses to the questions. Obviously, this would require some common core of agreement about the definition of an evangelical or fundamentalist. Wilcox (1984, 6) argues:

> Fundamentalists and evangelicals have a very similar set of religious beliefs, including the literal interpretation of the Bible, the need for a religious conversion known as being "born-again," and the need to convert sinners to the faith. The evangelicals, however, are less anti-intellectual and more involved in the secular world, while the fundamentalists criticize the evangelicals for failing to keep themselves "pure from the world."

Creating subsets by ideology is another common approach to analyzing public opinion. The most-often-used categories of ideology are liberal, moderate, and conservative, and the typical way of obtaining this information is to ask respondents a question in the following form: "Generally speaking, do you think of yourself as a liberal, moderate, or conservative?" However, one can raise many objections to this procedure, including whether people really assign common meanings to these terms. Indeed, the levels of ideological sophistication and awareness have been an ongoing topic of research in political science.

Journalist Kevin Phillips (1981) has cited the work of political scientists Stuart A. Lilie and William S. Maddox, who argue that the traditional liberal-moderate-conservative breakdown is inadequate for analytical purposes. Instead, they propose a fourfold classification of liberal, conservative, populist, and libertarian, based on two underlying dimensions: whether one supports or opposes governmental intervention in the economy and whether one supports or opposes expansion of individual behavioral liberties and sexual equality. They define liberals as those who support both governmental intervention in the economy and expansion of personal liberties, conservatives as those who oppose both, libertarians as citizens who favor expanding personal liberties but oppose governmental intervention in the economy, and populists as persons who favor governmental economic intervention but oppose the expansion of personal liberties. According to one poll, populists made up 24 percent of the electorate, conservatives 18 percent, liberals 16 percent, and libertarians 13 percent, with the rest of the electorate not readily classifiable or unfamiliar with ideological terminology.

This more elaborate breakdown of ideology may help us to better understand public opinion, but the traditional categories still dominate political discourse. Thus, when one encounters citizens who oppose government programs that affect the marketplace but support pro-choice court decisions on abortion, proposed gay rights statutes, and the Equal Rights Amendment, one feels uncomfortable calling them liberals or conservatives since they appear to be conservative on economic issues and liberal on lifestyle issues. One might feel more confident in classifying them as libertarians.

Additional examples of how an examination of subsets of respondents can provide useful insights into the public's attitudes are provided by two CBS News/*New York Times* surveys conducted in 1991, one dealing with the Persian Gulf crisis and the other with attitudes toward police. Although the rapid and successful conclusion of the ground war against Iraq resulted in widespread approval of the enterprise, before the land assault began there were differences of opinion among Americans about a ground war. For example, in the February 12–13 CBS News/*New York Times* poll, Americans were asked: "Suppose several thousand American troops would lose their lives in a ground war against Iraq. Do you think a ground war against Iraq would be worth the cost or not?" By examining the percentage saying it would be worth the cost, one finds the following results for different groups of Americans:

All respondents	45%	Independents	46%
Men	56%	Republicans	54%
Women	35%	Eighteen to twenty-nine year-olds	50%
Whites	47%	Thirty to forty-four year-olds	44%
Blacks	30%	Forty-five to sixty-four year-olds	51%
Democrats	36%	Sixty-five years and older	26%

Note that the youngest age group, the one most likely to suffer the casualties, is among the most supportive of a ground war. Note also the sizable differences between men and women, whites and blacks, and Democrats and Republicans.

Substantial racial differences in opinion also were expressed in an April 1–3, 1991, CBS News/*New York Times* poll on attitudes toward local police. Overall, 55 percent of the sample said they had substantial confidence in the local police, and 44 percent said little confidence. But among whites the comparable percentages were 59 percent and 39 percent, while for blacks only 30 percent had substantial confidence and fully 70 percent expressed little confidence in the police. Even on issues in which the direction of white and black opinion was the same, there were still substantial racial differences in the responses. For example, 69 percent of whites said that the police in their own community treat blacks and whites the same, and only 16 percent said the police were tougher on blacks than on whites. Although a plurality—45 percent—of blacks agreed that the police treat blacks and whites equally, fully 42 percent of black respondents felt that the police were tougher on blacks. Certainly if one were conducting a study to ascertain citizens' attitudes about police performance, it would be foolish not to examine the opinions of relevant subgroups.

Another example of the importance of examining subsets of respondents is provided by a January 1985 ABC News/*Washington Post* poll that queried Americans about their attitudes on a variety of issues and presented results not only for the entire sample but also for subsets of respondents defined by their attentiveness to public affairs (Sussman 1985b). Attentiveness to public affairs was measured by whether the respondents were aware of four news events: the subway shooting in New York City of four alleged assailants by their intended victim; the switch in jobs by two key Reagan administration officials, Donald Regan and James Baker; the Treasury Department's proposal to simplify the tax system; and protests against South African apartheid held in the United States. Respondents then were divided into four levels of awareness, with 27 percent in the highest category, 26 percent in the next highest, 25 percent in the next category, and 22 percent falling in the lowest. The next step in the analysis was to compare the policy preferences of the highest and lowest awareness subsets.

There were some marked differences between these two groups. For example, on the issue of support for the president's military buildup, 59 percent of the lowest awareness respondents opposed any major cuts in military spending to lessen the budget deficit. In contrast, 57 percent of the highest awareness group said that military spending should be limited to help with the budget deficit. On the issue of tax rates, a majority of both groups agreed with the president that taxes were too high, but there was a difference in the size of the majority. Among the lowest awareness respondents, 72 percent said taxes were too high and 24 percent said they were not, while among the highest awareness respondents, 52 percent said taxes were too high and 45 percent said they were not (Sussman 1985b).

Opinions about the future of Social Security and Medicare also are affected by citizens' knowledge about the two programs (Pianin and Brossard 1997). In one poll, the more people knew about Social Security and Medicare, the more likely they were to believe that these programs were in crisis and that major governmental action was needed. For example, among highly knowledgeable respondents, 88 percent believed that Social Security either was in crisis or had major problems; only 70 percent of respondents with little knowledge agreed. Likewise, 89 percent of the highly knowledgeable respondents believed Social Security would go bankrupt if Congress did nothing compared to only 61 percent for the less-informed respondents.

All these findings raise some interesting normative issues about public opinion polls. . . . [T]he methodology of public opinion polls is very democratic. All citizens have a nearly equal chance to be selected in a sample and have their views counted; all respondents are weighted equally (or nearly so) in the typical data analysis. Yet except at the polls all citizens do not have equal influence in shaping public policy. The distribution of political resources, whether financial or informational, is not uniform across the population. Polls themselves become a means to influence public policy, as various decision makers cite poll results to legitimize their policies. But should the views of all poll respondents be counted equally? An elitist critic would argue that the most informed segments of the population should be given the greatest weight. Therefore, in the preceding example of defense spending, more attention should be given to the views of the highest awareness subset (assuming the validity of the levels of awareness), which was more supportive of reducing military spending. An egalitarian argument would assert that all respondents should be counted equally. . . .

Interpreting Poll Results

An August 1986 Gallup poll on education showed that 67 percent of Americans would allow their children to attend class with a child suffering from AIDS, while 24 percent would not. What reaction might there be to this finding? Some people might be shocked and depressed to discover that almost one-fourth of Americans could be so mean-spirited toward AIDS victims when the scientific evidence shows that AIDS is not a disease transmitted by casual contact. Others might be reassured and relieved that two-thirds of Americans are sufficiently enlightened or tolerant to allow their children to attend school with children who have AIDS. Some people might feel dismay: How could 67 percent of Americans foolishly allow their children to go to school with a child who has AIDS when there is no absolute guarantee that AIDS cannot be transmitted casually?

Consider this example from a 1983 poll by the National Opinion Research Center (NORC): "If your party nominated a black [man] for President, would you vote for him if he were qualified for the job?" Eighty-five percent of the white respondents said yes. How might this response be interpreted? One might feel positive about how much racial attitudes have changed in the United States. A different perspective would decry the fact that in this supposedly tolerant and enlightened era, 15 percent of white survey respondents could not bring themselves to say they would vote for a qualified black candidate.

In neither example can we assign a single correct meaning to the data. Instead, the interpretation one chooses will be a function of individual values and beliefs, and purposes in analyzing the survey. This is demonstrated in an analysis of two national surveys on gun control, one sponsored by the National Rifle Association (NRA) and conducted by Decision/Making/Information, Inc., and the other sponsored by the Center for the Study and Prevention of Handgun Violence and conducted by Cambridge Reports, Inc. (pollster Patrick Caddell's firm). Although the statistical results from both surveys were comparable, the two reports arrived at substantially different conclusions. The NRA's analysis concluded:

> Majorities of American voters believe that we do *not* need more laws governing the possession and use of firearms and that more firearms laws would *not* result in a decrease in the crime rate. (Wright 1981, 25)

In contrast, the center's report stated:

> It is clear that the vast majority of the public (both those who live with handguns and those who do not) want handgun licensing and registration. . . . The American public wants some form of handgun control legislation. (Wright 1981, 25)

Wright carefully analyzed the evidence cited in support of each conclusion and found that

> the major difference between the two reports is not in the findings, but in what is said about or concluded about the findings: what aspects of the evidence are emphasized or de-emphasized, what interpretation is given to a finding, and what implications are drawn from the findings about the need, or lack thereof, for stricter weapons controls. (Wright 1981, 38)

In essence, it was the interpretation of the data that generated the difference in the recommendations.

Two polls on tax reform provide another example of how poll data can be selectively interpreted and reported (Sussman 1985a). The first poll, sponsored by the insurance industry, was conducted by pollster Burns Roper. Its main conclusion, reported in a press conference announcing the poll results, was that 77 percent of the American public "said that workers should not be taxed on employee benefits" and that only 15 percent supported such a tax, a conclusion very reassuring to the insurance industry. However, Roper included other items in the poll that the insurance industry chose not to emphasize. As Sussman points out, the 77 percent opposed to the taxing of fringe benefits were then asked, "Would you still oppose counting the value of employee benefits as taxable income for employees if the additional tax revenues went directly to the reduction of federal budget deficits and not into new spending?" Twenty-six percent were no longer opposed to taxing fringe benefits under this condition, bringing the overall opposition down to 51 percent of the sample.

A second follow-up question asked, "Would you still oppose counting the value of employee benefits as taxable income for employees if the additional tax revenues permitted an overall reduction of tax rates for individuals?" (a feature that was part of the Treasury Department's initial tax proposals). Now only 33 percent of the sample was opposed to taxing fringes, 50 percent supported it, and 17 percent were undecided. Thus, depending upon which results one used, one could show a majority of citizens supportive of or opposed to taxing fringe benefits.

The other poll that Sussman analyzed also tapped people's reactions to the Treasury Department's tax proposal. A number of questions in the survey demonstrated public hostility to the Treasury proposal. One item read:

> The Treasury Department has proposed changing the tax system. Three tax brackets would be created, but most current deductions from income would be eliminated. Non-federal income taxes and property taxes would not be deductible, and many deductions would be limited. Do you favor or oppose this proposal? (Sussman 1985a)

Not surprisingly, 57 percent opposed the Treasury plan, and only 27 percent supported it. But as Sussman points out, the question is highly selective and leading since it focuses on changes in the tax system that hurt the taxpayer. For example, nowhere does it inform the respondent that a key part of the Treasury plan was to reduce existing tax rates so that 80 percent of Americans would be paying either the same amount or less in taxes than they were paying before. Clearly, this survey was designed to obtain a set of results compatible with the sponsor's policy objectives.

Morin (1995) describes a situation in which polling data were misinterpreted and misreported in the *Washington Post* because of faulty communication between a *Post* reporter and a local polling firm that was conducting an omnibus survey in the Washington, D.C., area. Interested in how worried federal employees were about their jobs given the budgetary battles between the Clinton White House and the Republican Congress in 1995, the reporter commissioned the polling firm to include the following questions in its survey: "Do you think your agency or company will probably be affected by federal budget cutbacks? Do you think your own job will be affected?" The poll discovered that 40 percent of the federal workers interviewed believed their own jobs might be affected. Unfortunately, when the polling outfit prepared a report for its client, the reporter, the report concluded that these federal workers felt their jobs were jeopardized. And then the reporter's story stated, "Four out of every 10 federal employees fear losing their jobs because of budget reductions." As Morin points out, this conclusion does not follow from the polling questions asked. The belief that one's job will likely be affected is not equivalent to the fear of losing one's job. Instead, the effects might be lower salary increases, decreased job mobility, increased job responsibilities, and the like. A correction quickly appeared in the

Post clarifying what the polling data actually had said. One lesson of this example is the responsibility that pollsters have to clients to communicate carefully and accurately what poll results mean. Another lesson is that one should not try to read too much into the responses to any single survey item. In this case, if the reporter wanted to know exactly how federal workers thought their jobs would be affected, a specific question eliciting this information should have been included in the survey.

Weighting the Sample

Samples are selected to be representative of the population from which they are drawn. Sometimes adjustments must be made to a sample before analyzing and reporting results. These adjustments may be made for substantive reasons or because of biases in the characteristics of the selected sample. An example of adjustments made for substantive reasons is pollsters' attempts to determine who the likely voters will be and to base their election predictions not on the entire sample but on a subset of likely voters.

To correct for biases, weights can be used so that the sample's demographic characteristics more accurately reflect the population's overall properties. Because sampling and interviewing involve statistics and probability theory as well as logistical problems of contacting respondents, the sample may contain too few blacks, or too few men, or too few people in the youngest age category. Assuming that one knows the true population proportions for sex, race, and age, one can adjust the sample by the use of weights to bring its numbers into line with the overall population values. For example, if females constitute 60 percent of the sample but 50 percent of the overall population, one might weight each female respondent by five-sixths, thereby reducing the percentage of females in the sample to 50 percent (five-sixths times 60 percent).

A 1986 *Columbus Dispatch* preelection poll on the gubernatorial preferences of Ohioans illustrates the consequences of weighting. In August 1986 the *Dispatch* sent a mail questionnaire to a sample of Ohioans selected from the statewide list of registered voters. The poll showed that incumbent Democratic governor Richard Celeste was leading former GOP governor James Rhodes, 48 percent to 43 percent, with Independent candidate and former Democratic mayor of Cleveland Dennis Kucinich receiving 9 percent; an undecided alternative was not provided to respondents (Curtin 1986a). Fortunately, the *Dispatch* report of its poll included the sample size for each category (unlike the practice of the national media). One table presented to the reader showed the following relationship between political party affiliation and gubernatorial vote preference (Curtin 1986b):

Gubernatorial preference	Democrat	Republican	Independent
Celeste	82%	14%	33%
Rhodes	9	81	50
Kucinich	9	5	17
Total %	100	100	100
(N)	(253)	(245)	(138)

Given the thrust of the news story that Celeste was ahead, 48 to 43 percent, the numbers in the table were surprising because Rhodes was running almost as well among Republicans as Celeste was among Democrats, and Rhodes had a substantial lead among Independents. Because the N's were provided, one could calculate the actual number of Celeste, Rhodes, and Kucinich votes in the sample as follows:

Celeste votes $= .82(253) + .14(245) + .33(138) = 287$

Rhodes votes $= .09(253) + .81(245) + .50(138) = 291$

Kucinich votes $= .09(253) + .05(245) + .17(138) = 58$

The percentages calculated from these totals show Rhodes slightly *ahead*, 46 to 45 percent, rather than trailing. At first I thought there was a mistake in the poll or in the party affiliation and gubernatorial vote preference. In rereading the news story, however, I learned that the sample had been weighted. The reporter wrote, "Results were adjusted, or weighted, slightly to compensate for demographic differences between poll respondents and the Ohio electorate as a whole" (Curtin 1986b). The reporter did inform the reader that the data were weighted, but nowhere did he say that the adjustment affected who was ahead in the poll.

The adjustment probably was statistically valid since the poll respondents did not seem to include sufficient numbers of women and blacks, two groups that were more supportive of the Democratic gubernatorial candidate. However, nowhere in the news story was any specific information provided on how the weighting was done. This example illustrates that weighting can be consequential, and it is probably typical in terms of the scant information provided to citizens about weighting procedures.

When Polls Conflict: A Concluding Example

A variety of factors can influence poll results and their subsequent interpretation. Useful vehicles for a review of these factors are the polls that led up to the 1980, 1984, 1988, 1992, and 1996 presidential elections—polls that were often highly inconsistent. For example, in the 1984 election, polls conducted at comparable times yielded highly dissimilar results. A Harris poll had Reagan leading Mondale by 9 percentage points, an ABC News/*Washington Post* poll had Reagan ahead by 12 points, a CBS News/*New York Times* survey had Reagan leading by 13 points, a *Los Angeles Times* poll gave Reagan a 17-point lead, and an NBC News poll had the president ahead by 25 points (Oreskes 1984). In September 1988 seven different polls on presidential preference were released within a three-day period with results ranging from Bush ahead by 8 points to a Dukakis lead of 6 points (Morin 1988). In 1992 ten national polls conducted in the latter part of August showed Clinton with leads over Bush ranging from 5 to 19 percentage points (Elving 1992). And in 1996, the final preelection polls showed Clinton leading Dole by margins ranging from 7 to 18 percentage points. How can polls on an ostensibly straightforward topic such as presidential vote preference differ so widely? Many reasons can be cited, some obvious and others more subtle in their effects.

Among the more subtle reasons are the method of interviewing and the number of callbacks that a pollster uses to contact respondents who initially were unavailable. According to Lewis and Schneider (1982, 43), Patrick Caddell and George Gallup in their 1980 polls found that President Reagan received less support from respondents interviewed personally than from those queried over the telephone. Their speculation about this finding was that weak Democrats who were going to desert Carter found it easier to admit this in a telephone interview than in a face-to-face situation.

With respect to callbacks, Dolnick (1984) reports that one reason a Harris poll was closer than others in predicting Reagan's sizable victory in 1980 was that it made repeated callbacks, which at each stage "turned up increasing numbers of well-paid, well-educated Republican-leaning voters." A similar situation occurred in 1984. Traugott (1987) found that persistence in callbacks resulted in a more Republican sample, speculating that Republicans were less likely to have been at home or available initially.

Some of the more obvious factors that help account for differences among compared polls are question wording and question placement. Some survey items mention the presidential and vice-presidential candidates, while others mention only the presidential challengers. Some pollsters ask follow-up questions of undecided voters to ascertain whether they lean toward one candidate or another; others do not. Question order can influence responses. Normally, incumbents and better known candidates do better when the question on vote intention is asked at the beginning of the survey rather than later. If vote intention is measured after a series of issue and problem questions have been asked, respondents may have been reminded of shortcomings in the incumbent's record and may therefore be less willing to express support for the incumbent.

Comparable polls also can differ in how the sample is selected and how it is treated for analytical purposes. Some polls sample registered voters; others query adult Americans. There are differences as well in the methods used to identify likely voters. As Lipset (1980) points out, the greater the number of respondents who are screened out of the sample because they do not seem to be likely voters, the more probable it is that the remaining respondents will be relatively more Republican in their vote preferences. Some samples are weighted to guarantee demographic representativeness; others are not.

It is also possible that discrepancies among polls are not due to any of the above factors, but may simply reflect statistical fluctuations. For example, if one poll with a 4 percent sampling error shows Clinton ahead of Dole, 52 to 43 percent, this result is statistically congruent with other polls that might have a very narrow Clinton lead of 48 to 47 percent or other polls that show a landslide Clinton lead of 56 to 39 percent.

Voss et al. (1995) summarized and compared many of the methodological differences among polls conducted by eight polling organizations for the 1988 and 1992 presidential elections. Even though all eight organizations were studying the same phenomenon, there were enough differences in their approaches that polls conducted at the same time using identical questions might still get somewhat different results for reasons beyond sampling error. One feature Voss et al. examined was the sampling method—how each organization generated a list of telephone numbers from which to sample. Once the sample was selected, polling organizations conducting telephone interviews still had to make choices about how to handle "busy signals, refusals, and calls answered by electronic devices, how to decide which household members are eligible to be interviewed, and how to select the respondent from among those eligible" (Voss et al. 1995). The investigators also examined the various weighting schemes used by each survey operation to ensure a representative sample. Much of this methodological information is not readily available to the consumer of public opinion polls, and if it were many consumers would be overwhelmed by the volume of methodological detail. Yet these factors can make a difference. For example, the eight polling organizations analyzed by Voss et al. treated refusals quite differently. Some of the outfits did not call back after receiving a refusal from a potential respondent; other organizations did make callbacks. One organization generally tried to call back but with a different interviewer, but then gave up if a second refusal was obtained.

Just as different methodological features can affect election polls, they also can influence other surveys. One prominent example dealt with the widely divergent estimates of rape obtained from two different national surveys. Much of this discrepancy stemmed from the methodological differences between the two surveys (Lynch 1996). Because the poll consumer is unaware of many of the design features of a survey, he or she must assume the survey design was appropriate for the topic at hand. Then the consumer can ask whether the information collected by the survey was analyzed and interpreted correctly.

REFERENCES

Abramson, Paul R., Brian Silver, and Barbara Anderson. 1990. "The Decline of Overtime Comparability in the National Election Studies." *Public Opinion Quarterly* 54 (summer): 177–190.

Alpern, David M. 1986. "A *Newsweek* Poll: Sex Laws." *Newsweek,* 14 July, 38.

Baumgartner, Frank R., and Jack L. Walker. 1988. "Survey Research and Membership in Voluntary Associations." *American Journal of Political Science* 32 (November): 908–928.

Borrelli, Stephen, Brad Lockerbie, and Richard G. Niemi. 1987. "Why the Democrat-Republican Partisan Gap Varies from Poll to Poll." *Public Opinion Quarterly* 51 (spring): 115–119.

Clymer, Adam. 1986. "A Poll Finds 77% in U.S. Approve Raid on Libya." *New York Times,* 17 April, A-23.

Curtin, Michael. 1986a. "Celeste Leading Rhodes 48% to 43%, with Kucinich Trailing." *Columbus Dispatch,* 10 August, 1-A.

_____. 1986b. "Here Is How Poll Was Taken." *Columbus Dispatch,* 10 August, 8-E.

Dolnick, Edward. 1984. "Pollsters Are Asking: What's Wrong." *Columbus Dispatch,* 19 August, C-1.

Elving, Ronald D. 1992. "Polls Confound and Confuse in This Topsy-Turvy Year." *Congressional Quarterly Weekly Report,* 12 September, 2725–2727.

Laumann, Edward O., et al. 1994. *The Social Organization of Sexuality.* Chicago: University of Chicago Press.

Lewis, I. A., and William Schneider. 1982. "Is the Public Lying to the Pollsters?" *Public Opinion* 5 (April/May): 42–47.

Lipset, Seymour Martin. 1980. "Different Polls, Different Results in 1980 Politics." *Public Opinion* 3 (August/September): 19–20, 60.

Lockerbie, Brad, and Stephen A. Borrelli. 1990. "Question Wording and Public Support for Contra Aid, 1983–1986." *Public Opinion Quarterly* 54 (summer): 195–208.

Lynch, James P. 1996. "Clarifying Divergent Estimates of Rape from Two National Surveys." *Public Opinion Quarterly* 60 (winter): 558–619.

Michael, Robert T., John H. Gagnon, Edward O. Laumann, and Gina Kolata. 1994. *Sex in America: A Definitive Survey.* Boston: Little, Brown.

Morin, Richard. 1988. "Behind the Numbers: Confessions of a Pollster." *Washington Post,* 16 October, C-1, C-4.

_____. 1991. "2 Ways of Reading the Public's Lips on Gulf Policy." *Washington Post,* 14 January, A-9.

_____. 1994. "Don't Know Much About Health Care Reform." *Washington Post* National Weekly Edition, 14–20 March, 37.

_____. 1995. "Reading between the Numbers." *Washington Post* National Weekly Edition, 4–10 September, 30.

Morin, Richard, and John M. Berry. 1996. "Economic Anxieties." *Washington Post* National Weekly Edition, 4–10 November, 6–7.

Oreskes, Michael. 1984. "Pollsters Offer Reasons for Disparity in Results." *New York Times,* 20 October, A-8.

Phillips, Kevin P. 1981. "Polls Are Too Broad in Analysis Divisions." *Columbus Dispatch,* 8 September, B-3.

Pianin, Eric, and Mario Brossard. 1997. "Hands Off Social Security and Medicare." *Washington Post* National Weekly Edition, 7 April, 35.

Rosenbaum, David E. 1997. "Americans Want a Right to Die. Or So They Think." *New York Times,* 8 June, E3.

Schneider, William. 1996. "How to Read a Trial Heat Poll." Transcript, CNN "Inside Politics Extra," 12 May (see AllPolitics Web site).

Smith, Tom W. 1993. "Actual Trends or Measurement Artifacts? A Review of Three Studies of Anti-Semitism." *Public Opinion Quarterly* 57 (fall): 380–393.

Sussman, Barry. 1985a. "To Understand These Polls, You Have to Read the Fine Print." *Washington Post* National Weekly Edition, 4 March, 37.

_____. 1985b. "Reagan's Support on Issues Relies Heavily on the Uninformed." *Washington Post* National Weekly Edition, 1 April, 37.

_____. 1985c. "Social Security and the Young." *Washington Post* National Weekly Edition, 27 May, 37.

_____. 1986a. "It's Wrong to Assume that School Busing Is Wildly Unpopular." *Washington Post* National Weekly Edition, 10 March, 37.

_____. 1986b. "With Pornography, It All Depends on Who's Doing the Looking." *Washington Post* National Weekly Edition, 24 March, 37.

Traugott, Michael W. 1987. "The Importance of Persistence in Respondent Selection for Preelection Surveys." *Public Opinion Quarterly* 51 (spring): 48–57.

Voss, D. Stephen, Andrew Gelman, and Gary King. 1995. "Preelection Survey Methodology: Details from Eight Polling Organizations, 1988 and 1992." *Public Opinion Quarterly* 59 (spring): 98–132.

Wilcox, William Clyde. 1984. "The New Christian Right and the White Fundamentalists: An Analysis of a Potential Political Movement." Ph.D. diss., Ohio State University.

Williams, Dennis A. 1979. "A New Racial Poll." *Newsweek,* 26 February, 48, 53.

Wright, James D. 1981. "Public Opinion and Gun Control: A Comparison of Results from Two Recent National Surveys." *Annals of the American Academy of Political and Social Science* 455 (May): 24–39.

10-2

Dynamic Representation

James A. Stimson, Michael B. MacKuen, and Robert S. Erikson

The relationship between public opinion and government action is complex. In the United States, with single-member congressional districts, we often consider relationship at the "micro" level—that is, whether individual elected officials are following the wishes of their home constituencies. But the overall relationship between public preferences and government behavior, the "macro" level, is more difficult to assess. In the following essay, James Stimson, Michael MacKuen, and Robert Erikson provide a look at this relationship with the help of a creative invention. These scholars use a statistical technique to build an aggregate measure of public opinion from dozens of polls. The technique allows them to measure change in the liberalism of views expressed in the polls over several decades. Then, using similarly aggregated measures of the behavior of Congress, the president, and the Supreme Court, they evaluate the relationship between the liberalism of public opinion and the behavior of the institutions. Government as a whole proves responsive to public opinion, and Congress and the presidency prove more responsive to public opinion than the Supreme Court.

WHAT DOES IT mean that a government represents public feelings? Responsiveness must be a central part of any satisfactory answer. Representative governments respond to—meaning act as a consequence of—changes in public sentiment. To "act as a consequence of" changes in public sentiment implies a sequence, inherently structured in time. We may say that if, by knowing about earlier changes in public sentiment, we can improve the prediction of public policy over what we could have done from knowing only the history of public policy itself, then opinion causes policy, and this is dynamic representation. . . .

The *dynamic* character of representation has a second aspect. Most political decisions are about change or the prevention of change. Governments decide to change health care systems, to reduce environmental regulations, to develop new weapons systems, or to increase subsidies for long staple cotton growers. Or not. Thus, political decisions have a directional force to them, and their incremental

Source: James A. Stimson, Michael B. MacKuen, and Robert S. Erikson, "Dynamic Representation," *American Political Science Review* 89 (September 1995): 543–564. Notes appearing in the original have been deleted.

character is inherently dynamic. Further, most public opinion judgments concern change as well. The public expresses preferences for "more" or "less" governmental action across different spheres: "faster school integration," "cuts in welfare spending," "getting tougher on crime," and so on. The main difference is that public sentiment is generally more vague, diffuse, than the more concrete government action.

This understanding suggests something akin to the familiar "thermostat" analogy. The public makes judgments about current public policy—most easily that government's actions need to be enhanced or trimmed back. These judgments will change as policy changes, as real-world conditions change, or as "politically colored" perceptions of policy and conditions change. And as the simple model indicates, politicians and government officials sense these changes in public judgment and act accordingly. Thus, when public policy drifts away from the public's demands for policy, the representation system acts as a control mechanism to keep policy on course.

The question now is how. If public opinion governs, how does it find its way into the aggregation of acts that come to be called public policy.

The Mechanisms of Dynamic Representation

Start with a politician facing a policy choice. With both preferences over policy options and a continuing need to protect the electoral career from unwanted termination, the elected official will typically need to balance personal preference against electoral expediency. We presume that politicians have personal preferences for and against particular policies and also that they value reelection. Then for each choice, we can define (1) a personal ideal point in the space of policy options and (2) an *expediency point* (that position most likely to optimize future reelection changes). The expediency point might be the median voter of the relevant constituency or some similar construct. We are not concerned here about particular rules. All that matters is that the politician have a *perception* of the most expedient position.

. . . Politicians create an appropriate margin of safety: those who highly value policy formulation or who feel safe at home choose policy over security; those who face competitive challenge in the next election lean toward "expediency" and security. . . .

. . . [E]lectoral turnover stems from events that overwhelm the margin of safety that the politicians select. Campaign finance, personal scandals, challenger tactics, the framing of electoral choice—all affect outcomes. The victims come both from those who take electoral risk by pursuing policy and also from those who ignore personal preference and concentrate solely on reelection: what matters is the force of electoral events relative to the politician's expectations. . . .

To breathe life into this system, let us put it into motion to see its aggregate and dynamic implications. Assume that public opinion—global attitudes toward the role of government in society—moves over time. Immediately we can expect greater turnover as the force of public opinion augments the normal electoral shocks to upset incumbent politicians' standard calculus. Now, the changes in personnel will prove systematic: rightward shifts in public opinion will replace Democrats with Republicans, and leftward shifts Republicans with Democrats. . . .

Rational Anticipation, Turnover, and Policy Consequence

Turnover from elections works most transparently with politicians who are neither well informed (until hit on the head by the club of election results) nor strategic. But that does not look at all like the politicians we observe. The oft-painted picture of members of Congress, for example, as people who read five or six daily newspapers, work 18-hour days, and leave no stone unturned in anticipating the electoral problems that might arise from policy choices does not suggest either limited information or naïveté.

We explicitly postulate the reverse of the dumb and naïve politician: (1) elected politicians are rational actors; (2) they are well informed about movements in public opinion; and (3) they agree with one another about the nature of those movements. This was well said by John Kingdon: "People in and around government sense a national mood. They are comfortable discussing its content, and believe they know when the mood shifts. The idea goes by different names. . . . But common to all . . . is the notion that a rather large number of people out in the country are thinking along certain common lines, that this national mood changes from one time to another in discernible ways, and that these changes in mood or climate have important impacts on policy agendas and policy outcomes" (1984, 153). . . .

Elected politicians, we believe, sense the mood of the moment, assess its trend, and anticipate its consequence for future elections. Changes in opinion, correctly perceived, will lead politicians to revise their beliefs about future election opportunities and hazards. Revised beliefs imply also revised expedient positions. Such strategic adjustment will have two effects: (1) it will dampen turnover, the conventional path of electoral influence; and (2) it will drive policy through rational anticipation.

When politicians perceive public opinion change, they adapt their behavior to please their constituency and, accordingly, enhance their chances of reelection.

Public opinion will still work through elections, however. When they are surprised by the suddenness or the magnitude of opinion change or when they are unable credibly to alter their policies, politicians, despite their best efforts, will occasionally face defeat at the polls. Rather more fitfully than was the case with dumb politicians, public preferences will operate on electoral institutions by changing the personnel and thus the aggregated preferences of elected officials.

But that is not the only public opinion effect. Changing policy from shifting perceptions of what is electorally expedient we will refer to as *rational anticipation*. In a world of savvy politicians, rational anticipation produces dynamic representation without need for actual electoral defeats.

Politicians modify their behavior at the margin. Liberals and conservatives do not change their stripes, but they do engage in strategic behavior either to minimize risk from movements adverse to their positions or to maximize electoral payoff from movements supportive of their positions. For example, in a conservative era, such as the early 1980s, conservative Democrats found it easier to break with their party and did it more often, while liberal Republicans found it more difficult and dangerous and did it less often. The result of such conditions can be substantial shifts in winning and losing coalitions without any change of personnel.

Moreover, such direct anticipation of the electoral future does not exhaust the possibilities. For other actors also anticipate the effects of future elections on the current behavior of elected officials. Those who advance policy proposals—bureaucrats, lobbyists, judges, and citizens—are concerned with what can be done successfully, be it administrative act, judicial decision, or legislative proposal. And other politicians—those who pursue a leadership role or advocate particular policies—may choose to push ahead of the curve, to multiply the effects of even marginal shifts in opinion by anticipating others' anticipated reactions.

The impact of rational anticipation is thus a net shift in policy outputs from the aggregation of all these smallish strategic decisions, which (responding to the same signal) tend to move all in the same direction. It should be observable as the direct response of policy to opinion change, when election turnover effects are controlled.

A Design for Assessing Representation

This two-part setup permits three possible empirical outcomes: (1) two-stage representation may occur through the mechanism of electoral turnover, where candidate success depends upon the public opinion of the moment, which is then reflected in policy behavior; (2) movements in policy acts may reflect opinion without changes in elite personnel, the rational anticipation scheme; and (3) no representation might occur if both schemes fail. The alternatives are laid out in Figure 1. There we can see three testable linkages. The first, A, is the first stage of the electoral sequence. The question to be answered is, Does public opinion affect election outcomes? The second stage, B, is not much in doubt. Its question is no cliff-hanger: Is there a difference in policy behavior between liberals and conservatives? The third linkage, C, is rational anticipation. Its question is, Does public policy move with public opinion independently of the effects of (past) elections? . . .

. . . The scheme of Figure 1 takes account of reality by positing other sets of causes of all phenomena as disturbances. The first, u_o, is the exogenous factors that account for changes in opinion. Not a focus of attention here (but see Durr 1993), they are such plausible forces as national optimism or pessimism arising from economic performance and reactions to past policies as experienced in daily life.

Elections are influenced by factors such as incumbent party performance, incumbency, macropartisanship, and so forth. Those factors appear as u_e on Figure 1. And finally, u_p captures sets of causes of public policy other than representation—such things as the events and problems to which policy is response or

Figure 1. The Pathways to Dynamic Representation

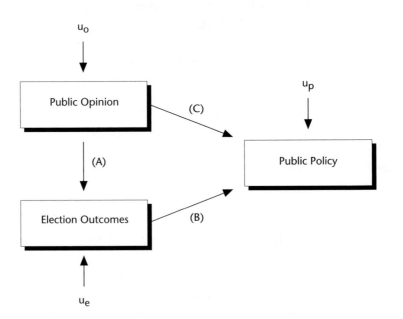

solution. Some of these "disturbances" are amenable to modeling, and will be. Some are irreducible, and must remain unobserved. . . .

Measurement

The raw materials of dynamic representation are familiar stuff: public opinion, elections, and public policy together form the focus of a major proportion of our scholarly activity. But familiar as these concepts are, longitudinal measures of them are (excepting elections) ad hoc at best and more often nonexistent. It is easy to think of movements of public opinion over time and public policy over time. It is not easy to quantify them. The situation—familiar concepts but novel measures—requires more than the usual cursory attention to measurement concerns. We begin with public opinion.

The Measures: Public Opinion and Elections

To tap public opinion over time we have [to] measure domestic policy mood (Stimson 1991). Mood is the major dimension underlying expressed preferences over policy alternatives in the survey research record. It is properly interpreted as left versus right—more specifically, as global preferences for a larger, more active federal government as opposed to a smaller, more passive one across the sphere of all domestic policy controversies. Thus our public opinion measure represents the public's sense of whether the political "temperature" is too hot or too cold, whether government is too active or not active enough. The policy status quo is the baseline, either explicit or implicit, in most survey questions. What the questions (and the mood measure) tap then is relative preference—the preferred direction of policy change.

Displayed in Figure 2, the *policy mood* series portrays an American public opinion that moves slowly back and forth from left (up on the scale) to right (down) over time and is roughly in accord with popular depictions of the eras of modern American politics. It reaches a liberal high point in the early 1960s, meanders mainly in the liberal end of its range through the middle 1970s, moves quite dramatically toward conservatism approaching 1980, and then begins a gradual return to liberalism over the 1980s. Note as well that the neutral point (50% liberal, 50% conservative) means something: points above 50 mean that the public wants more conservative policy. Thus, while the public's conservatism peaked in 1980, the public continued to demand more conservative policy (though by smaller margins) until 1984. (Thus we may think of our mood

Figure 2. Public Opinion over Time: Domestic Policy Mood, 1956–1993

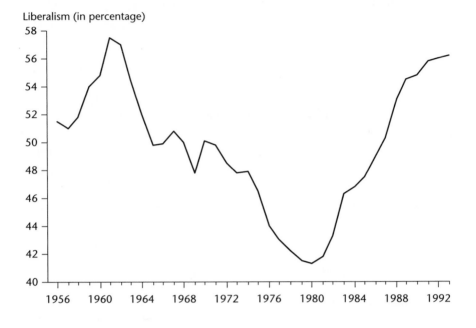

measure as a signal to politicians about the intensity and the direction of political pressure. It represents a demand for change.) . . .

The Measures: Policy Change

What is policy liberalism, and how can we measure it? What we observe is decisions such as congressional votes—not quite "policy." Our view is that each involves policy *change* at the margin. The issue as it is typically confronted is, Should we move current government policy in more liberal (expansive) directions or in more conservative ones? What we observe is who votes how. We see, for example, a particular vote in which the liberal forces triumph over conservative opponents. We take such a vote to mean that in fact the (unobserved) content of the vote moves policy in a liberal direction—or resists movement in the conservative direction.

This is a direct analogy to public opinion as we measure it. We ask the public whether government should "do more" or "spend more" toward some particular purpose. We take the response, "do more," "do less," "do about the same" to indicate the preferred direction of policy *change*. In both cases direction of change from the status quo is the issue.

Measuring this net liberalism or conservatism of global policy output seems easy enough in concept. We talk about some Congresses being more or less liberal than others as if we knew what that meant. But if we ask how we know, where those intuitions come from, the answer is likely to be nonspecific. The intuitions probably arise from fuzzy processing of multiple indicators of, for example, congressional action. And if none of them by itself is probably "the" defensible measure, our intuitions are probably correct in netting out the sum of many of them, all moving in the same direction. That, at least, is our strategy here. We will exploit several indicators of annual congressional policy output, each by itself dubious. But when they run in tandem with one another, the set will seem much more secure than its members.

Congressional Rating Scales. Rating scales are a starting point. Intended to tap the policy behaviors of individual House members and Senators, scales produced by groups such as Americans for Democratic Action (ADA) and Americans for Constitutional Action (ACA), later American Conservative Union (ACU), are now available for most of the period in question. Neither of these is intended to be a longitudinal measure of congressional action; and from a priori consideration of the properties such a measure would want, this is not how we would derive one. But if scales move similarly across chambers and scales from different organizations move in common over time, then we begin to believe that whatever it is they are measuring is probably global liberalism or conservatism of roll-call voting. Thus, as a measure of *net group rating,* we take the yearly average of the House's (or Senate's) ADA score and (100 minus) the ACA/ACU score.

Congressional Roll-Call Outcomes. The strength of the rating scales is their cross-sectional validity: they discriminate liberals from moderates from conservatives in any given year. Their weakness is longitudinal validity: we are less confident that they discriminate liberal from moderate from conservative Congresses. For greater face validity, we turn to the roll calls themselves as measures of policymaking. A quite direct measure is the answer to the questions, On ideological votes, who wins? and By how much do they win? Provided that we can isolate a set of roll calls that polarize votes along the left-versus-right main dimension of American domestic politics, measuring the degree of, say, liberalism is as easy as counting the votes. If we know which position on the vote is liberal and which conservative, then all that remains is to observe who won and by how much (and then aggregate that roll-call information to the session).

We exploit the cross-sectional strength of the rating scales (specifically, ADA) to classify roll calls. For each of the 25,492 roll-call votes in both houses for 1956–90, we classify the vote as left-right polarized or not (and then in which direction). The criterion for the classification as polarized is that the vote must show a greater association with member ADA scores than a hypothetical party-line vote for the particular members of each Congress. The intuition of this criterion is that we know we are observing a left-right cleavage when defection from party lines is itself along left-right lines—conservative Democrats voting with Republicans, liberal Republicans voting with Democrats. Although the party vote itself might be ideological, we cannot know that it is. One measure of the net liberalism of the session (for each house separately) is then simply the median size of the liberal coalition (on votes where the liberal and conservative sides are defined). A second approach to the same raw data is to focus on winning and losing, rather than coalition size. In this set of measures we simply count the percentage of liberal wins. We are observing quite directly then who wins, who loses, and by how much.

The Dramatic Acts of Congress: Key Votes. Scales of roll-call votes tell us about the overall tenor of public policy. Probably an excellent basis for inference about the net direction of policy movement, they do not distinguish between minor matters and those of enormous public consequence and visibility. Getting a good measure of "importance" presents a formidable challenge, requiring great numbers of subtle judgments about content and context. It is nonetheless desirable to have some indication of whether legislative activity produces something of import. A particular subset of legislation, the *Congressional Quarterly* "key votes" for each session of Congress, does attempt to distinguish the crucial from the trivial. The virtues of this set of votes are that it reflects the wisdom of expert observers of Congress at the time about what was important, and the measures are readily coded into liberal or conservative actions (and some that are neither).

We quantify the key votes as a combination of who wins and by how much. Accordingly, we average (1) the percentage of liberal wins and (2) the size of the liberal winning coalition. Crude, the measures nonetheless tap the issue in question, the direction of highly visible outcomes. The resulting time series are noisy (as would be expected from the small numbers of votes for each year), evincing a good deal of year-to-year fluctuation that seems meaningless. But they also show a picture of episodes of major policy change occurring exactly when expected for the Great Society (liberalism, peaking in 1965) and the Reagan Revolution (conservatism, peaking in 1981) periods respectively.

To get a sense of how legislative policy has moved over the years, look at Figure 3. [Figure 3a] presents our four measures for the House of Representatives. (To keep the eye on systematic movement, we have smoothed the graphs by taking a centered three-year moving average for each series. Note that we smooth only in this graph: we use the measured data for the statistical analysis.) It is clear that each indicator (wins, coalition size, ADA–ACA ratings, and key votes) contains both a common component and an idiosyncratic component. The lines move together, with a bit of zig and zag around the main flow. The panel for the Senate (Figure 3b) carries a similar message. Peaks of liberalism came during the early 1960s and the late 1980s,

Figure 3. Indicators of Public Policy Change in Four Parts of American Government (Three-Year Moving Averages)

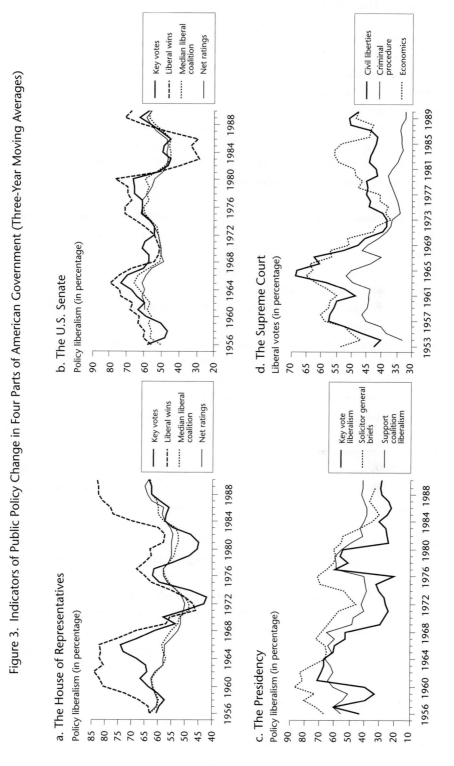

a. The House of Representatives
Policy liberalism (in percentage)

Key votes
Liberal wins
Median liberal coalition
Net ratings

1956 1960 1964 1968 1972 1976 1980 1984 1988

b. The U.S. Senate
Policy liberalism (in percentage)

Key votes
Liberal wins
Median liberal coalition
Net ratings

1956 1960 1964 1968 1972 1976 1980 1984 1988

c. The Presidency
Policy liberalism (in percentage)

Key vote liberalism
Solicitor general briefs
Support coalition liberalism

1956 1960 1964 1968 1972 1976 1980 1984 1988

d. The Supreme Court
Liberal votes (in percentage)

Civil liberties
Criminal procedure
Economics

1953 1957 1961 1965 1969 1973 1977 1981 1985 1989

475

with conservatism at its height around 1980. While thus similar in outline, the patterns are not quite identical.

Presidential Policy Liberalism. The beginning point of dealing with the presidency is noting the near impossibility of direct measures of presidential liberalism from what presidents say and do. While we have an intuition about various acts and speeches, any attempt to quantify that intuition, to extract acts from the context of actions, quickly becomes hopelessly subjective. The alternative is to look instead at presidents through their quantifiable records of interacting with the legislature and judiciary.

We know how often particular members of Congress support and oppose the president. And we can measure the liberalism of individual members in several ways. The most convenient of these is ADA scores, which are present for the entire period, as other comparable indicators are not. And we know that ADA ratings are very highly correlated with other ratings when available—positively or negatively—so that they can serve as a useful instrument of the underlying concept.

How then to combine these different pieces of information? A first approach is to ask the question, How liberal are the regular supporters of the president each year?, and then adopt that standard as a reflection of what the president wanted from Congress. That, however, is confounded by shared partisanship between president and member. We expect members of the president's party to be more likely to be regular supporters—independent of ideological agreement with the president's program. To deal with shared party ties as a confounding factor in presidential support, we opt instead to focus on presidential support within party. The strategy is first to divide each party into support and opposition groups based upon whether member presidential support is above or below the average for the party. The mean ADA rating of each party's "support" group is then an estimate of the president's ideological position. The opposition groups similarly measure the reverse. The measurement question then may be reduced to how such separate estimates are to be combined. For a summary measure of presidential position we perform a principal components analysis of the eight indicators (*support* vs. *oppose,* by party, by house). That analysis shows decisively that each of the eight taps a single underlying dimension. Such a dimension is estimated with a factor score and rescaled . . . to approximate the ADA scales from which it was derived.

For a second legislative presidential position measure we simply take the recorded presidential position for the key votes and compute the percentage of presidential stands each year that are liberal, where again the votes are classified by polarization with individual ADA ratings.

Presidential Interaction with the Court. With less regularity and on a quite different set of issues, presidents make their policy views known to the U.S. Supreme Court. The mechanism for doing so formally is the amicus curiae brief filed by the presidency's designated agent to the courts, the solicitor general. On over 700 occasions in the 1953–89 terms, the solicitor general went on record with the

Court, arguing that the holdings of particular judicial decisions ought to be affirmed or reversed. About 90% of these briefs take positions on cases that are themselves classifiably liberal or conservative.

We employ the solicitor general briefs data as leverage to measure presumed presidential position on judicial issues. Using the direction coding from the Spaeth Supreme Court data base for the case and our knowledge of whether the solicitor general argued to affirm or reverse, we code each of the briefs as to direction— liberal, conservative, or nonideological. It is then an easy matter to produce aggregated annual scales as percentage liberal of the ideological positions taken.

A quick comparison of the presidential series with the legislative series (in Figure 3) suggests less coherence in the presidential measures. Much of the discord comes from the *Solicitor General* series (which we retain, nevertheless, for its substantive value). Note also that the presidential series is typically more conservative than the two congressional series, as we might reasonably expect from the historical party control of the two institutions.

Supreme Court Liberalism. For data we have the Supreme Court data base for the period 1953–90. From that, we can content-classify the majority position in individual cases as liberal, conservative, or neither; and from that, the lifetime liberalism or conservatism of individual justices is readily derived. Then we return to the individual cases and scale the majority and dissenting votes by the justices who cast them. This allows a content-free second classification of the majority position as liberal, conservative, or not ideological. From this we build annual measures of the major-case content categories. We have chosen four such categories—*civil rights and liberties, criminal procedure, economics,* and *other*— the number a compromise between separating matters which might in principle produce different alignments and grouping broadly enough to have sufficient cases in each for reliable annual measures.

For each measure we construct a time series consisting of the percentage of all votes cast by the justices on the liberal side of the issue, whichever that is, for the year. This focus on justice decisions, rather than aggregate outcomes of the Court, appears to produce a more moderate measure over time than the alternative. . . .

We examine the first three domains in Figure 3. There we see that the issue domains move pretty much in tandem. All domains show the famous liberalism of the Warren Court in the mid-1960s and the conservative reaction of the Burger Court. Most show a modest rebound of liberalism in the early 1980s, which then reverses from the influence of new Reagan justices.

The pattern of more substantive notice is that the *"criminal procedure"* cases produce no liberal rebound in the 1980s. This is an interesting exception, for public attitudes toward crime and criminals are themselves an exception to the growing liberalism of the 1980s (Stimson 1991). This is a case where the conservative message ("The solution is more punitive law enforcement") is still dominant. . . .

A Summary Analysis of Governmental Responsiveness

For a summation of dynamic representation we slice across the institutional structure of American politics, returning to the familiar questions, Does public opinion influence public policy? and By what process? Our combining the policy output of the four institutions is, of course, a fiction: a single national public policy is not the average of independent branches. We "average" across different branches to provide a rough answer to a rough question. Here we select two indicators from each of the four prior analyses (president, House, Senate, and Supreme Court) and then estimate representation as it works on the American national government as a whole. . . .

We get a better sense of the historical dynamic by examining Figure 4. Plotted here are measures of public opinion, public policy and predicted policy. The first (in the light, solid line) is public opinion, with its liberal peaks during the early 1960s and late 1980s and its conservative peak around 1980. The dark, solid line represents policy, a simple average of our eight policy indicators. Without much work, it is clear that the two series are basically similar: policy reflects the timing and range of public opinion change.

Yet the two paths are not identical. Policy turned much more conservative during the late 1960s and early 1970s than the public demanded. Then, contrary to

Figure 4. Global Public Opinion and Global Public Policy:
Predicted and Actual Policy

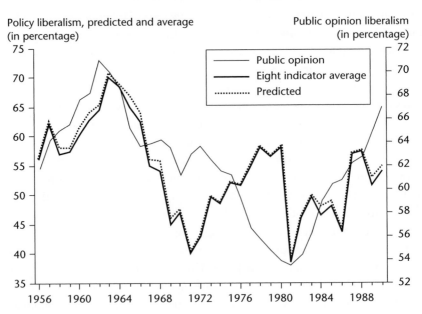

Policy liberalism, predicted and average
(in percentage)

Public opinion liberalism
(in percentage)

the continuing turn to the right, policy temporarily shifted leftward under Carter's leadership. Now look at the small dots that show predicted policy. . . . The exceptionally good fit is apparent. More important, the model is now able to account for the otherwise surprising conservatism just before 1972 and the liberalism of the late 1970s by including the Vietnam War and the composition variables. Thus, while the main part of policy moves in accord with public preferences, significant deviations can and do occur. Those deviations seem explicable but not by public preferences. Public opinion is powerful but not all-powerful.

Figure 4 takes us back to where we started, public policy preferences, and forward to the end of the story, the policy liberalism of American government, 1956–90. The point is that the two are a lot alike. . . .

Some Reflections on American Politics

The past four decades of United States history show that politicians translate changes in public opinion into policy change. Further, the evidence suggests that this translation varies by institution, both in the mechanisms that produce the link and in the nature of the dynamics.

Most important, dynamic representation finds strong support. Our work indicates that when the public asks for a more activist or a more conservative government, politicians oblige. The early peak of public opinion liberalism during the early 1960s produced liberal policy; the turn away from activism and the steady move toward conservatism was similarly reflected in national policy; and the recent 1980s upsurge of public demand for action was also effective (with the exception of the Court). To be sure, other things matter too. We have modeled a late 1960s shift rightward in policy (beyond that driven by public opinion) as a function of the Vietnam War's dominance over domestic political agendas. In addition, we modeled the shift leftward during the years of the Carter presidency (a shift contrary to the prevailing movement in public opinion) as a coincidence of compositional factors.

While we are confident that the basic result holds, we know that we do not yet fully understand movement in public policy. Nevertheless, the main story is that large-scale shifts in public opinion yield corresponding large-scale shifts in government action.

The link between opinion and policy is undoubtedly more complicated. While concentrating on policy response to opinion, we have seen little evidence of opinion reaction to policy. Elementary analyses generate contradictory inferences: the matter is subtle, the timing probably complex. We do know enough to assert that opinion reaction cannot explain the structural associations we uncover. We do not know enough to characterize the fuller relationship. This, of course, is a compelling subject for hard work.

Beyond the basic result, we can say that American national institutions vary in the mechanisms that produce responsiveness. It is the Senate, not the House of Representatives, that most clearly mimics the eighteenth-century clockwork meant to produce electoral accountability. When comparing the effectiveness of turnover and rational anticipation, we find that for the Senate (and also for the presidency), the most important channel for governmental representation is electoral replacement. Equally responsive, however, is the House of Representatives. Its members employ rational anticipation to produce a similarly effective public policy response, without the overt evidence of personnel change. The Supreme Court appears to reflect public opinion far more than constitutionally expected; but, in comparison, it is the institution that responds least.

Finally, the dynamics prove interesting. Each of the electoral institutions translates immediately public opinion into public policy. That is to say, when electoral politicians sense a shift in public preferences, they act directly and effectively to shift the direction of public policy. We find no evidence of delay or hesitation. The Court, not surprisingly, moves at a more deliberate speed. But equally important, rational anticipation is based not only on the long-term trends in public opinion but also on year-to-year shifts. That is to say, politicians constantly and immediately process public opinion changes in order to stay ahead of the political curve. Understanding politics well, the constitutional framers were correct in expecting short-term politics to be a fundamental part of dynamic representation.

The United States government, as it has evolved over the years, produces a complex response to public demands. The original constitutional design mixed different political calculations into different institutions so that no personal ambition, no political faction, no single political interest, or no transient passion could dominate. We now see the founders' expectations about complexity manifest in contemporary policymaking. Constitutional mechanisms harness politicians' strategies to the public's demands. In the end, the government combines both short- and long-term considerations through both rational anticipation and compositional change to produce a strong and resilient link between public and policy. . . .

REFERENCES

Durr, Robert H. 1993. "What Moves Policy Sentiment?" *American Political Science Review* 87:158–70.

Kingdon, John W. 1984. *Agendas, Alternatives, and Public Policies.* Boston: Little, Brown.

Stimson, James A. 1991. *Public Opinion in America: Moods, Cycles, and Swings.* Boulder: Westview.

10-3

from *Culture War? The Myth of a Polarized America*

Morris P. Fiorina

Many observers of politics have asserted that Americans are increasingly polarized, particularly over cultural or social issues. That polarization, it is claimed, has intensified partisanship in the electorate and in Washington. In the following essay, Morris Fiorina challenges the assumption that Americans have become more deeply divided on cultural issues. He argues, rather, that political elites, particularly candidates for office, have become more polarized along party and ideological lines, thus changing the choices available to the voters. That, in turn, has produced a sorting of the electorate and the deceptive appearance of polarization in the mass public.

[MANY OBSERVERS OF American politics in recent years refer] to "the 50:50 nation." During the late 1990s and early 2000s this phrase began to appear in popular discussions of American politics, as did a similar phrase, "the 49 percent nation." Such phraseology referred to the closely divided national elections of the late 1990s, when the winning party's popular vote share repeatedly came in right around 49 percent of the total vote:

- 1996 Clinton Vote   49.2%
- 1996 Republican House Vote   48.9
- 1998 Republican House Vote   48.9
- 2000 Gore Vote   48.4
- 2000 Republican House Vote   48.3
- 2002 Republican House Vote   50.9

If we consider only the two-party vote, the parties are almost exactly evenly matched nationally—50:50—or at least they were until the 2002 House elections, when the Republicans broke through that ceiling and got to 52.9 percent. Clearly, recent national elections have been exceedingly close. No presidential candidate has won a majority of the popular vote since 1988, the past three elections

Source: Morris P. Fiorina, *Culture War? The Myth of a Polarized America* (Upper Saddle River, N.J.: Pearson Education, Inc., 2005), 11–26.

constituting the longest such streak since the so-called "era of indecision," when no presidential candidate won a majority of the popular vote in the four elections from 1880 to 1892.

The question is what to make of these recent close elections? For most commentators, the answer is obvious: the American electorate is polarized. In the previously quoted words of the *Economist*, the close recent U.S. elections " . . . *reflect deep demographic divisions. . . . The 50-50 nation appears to be made up of two big, separate voting blocks, with only a small number of swing voters in the middle.*" The top panel of Figure 1 depicts this claim graphically. The electorate is highly polarized: a large number of "progressives" on the left support the Democrats, a large number of "orthodox" on the right support the Republicans, and very few people occupy the middle ground. With a polarized electorate like this, elections will be very close, half the voters will cheer, and half the voters will seethe, as *USA Today* asserts.

But the U-shaped distribution in the top panel of the figure is not the only electoral configuration that will produce close elections. Most obviously, consider the bell-shaped distribution in the bottom panel of Figure 1, which is the inverse of the U-shaped distribution in the top. In the lower figure most people hold moderate or centrist positions and relatively few are extreme partisans. But if the Democratic and Republican parties position themselves equidistant from

Figure 1. Two Very Different Close Election Scenarios

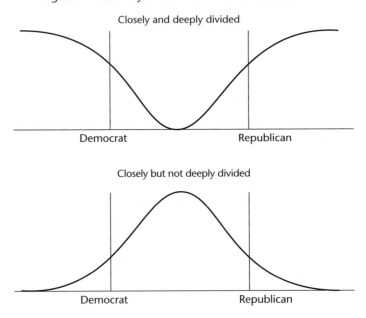

Closely and deeply divided

Democrat   Republican

Closely but not deeply divided

Democrat   Republican

the center on opposite sides, then the bottom configuration too produces close elections. In both examples the electorate is *closely* divided, but only in the top panel of the figure would we say that the voters are *deeply* divided. In the top panel it would be accurate to say that voters are polarized, but in the bottom panel we would more accurately call most voters ambivalent or indifferent.

When an election results in a near 50:50 outcome, the standard interpretation seems to be that the electorate is polarized as in the top panel of Figure 1. Why should that be the default interpretation? When an individual voter reports that he or she is on the fence (50:50) about whom to vote for, everyone understands that there are a number of plausible interpretations; the individual likes both candidates equally, dislikes both candidates equally, or really doesn't give a damn. No one suggests that the individual is polarized. But the aggregate and individual situations are analogous. In each case a continuous variable (percent of the vote/probability of voting for a given candidate) is compressed into a dichotomous variable (Republican or Democratic victory/Republican or Democratic vote), with enormous loss of information.

In sum, close elections may reflect equal numbers of voters who hate one candidate and love the other, voters who like both, voters who do not care much at all about either candidate, or various combinations of these conditions. Without taking a detailed look at voter attitudes, we cannot determine whether close elections reflect a polarized electorate that is deeply divided, or an ambivalent electorate that is closely divided between the choices it is offered. So, let us take a closer look at the public opinion that underlies the knife-edge elections of the past few years. Is it as divided as election outcomes seem to suggest?

Is the Country Polarized?

You've got 80% to 90% of the country that look at each other like they are on separate planets. (Bush reelection strategist, Matthew Dowd).

Is America polarized? Strictly speaking the question should be "has America become *more* polarized?" for that is the claim. But if the country is not polarized to begin with, the question of whether it has become more polarized is moot. Barely two months before the supposed "values chasm separating the blue states from the red ones" emerged in the 2000 election, the Pew Research Center for the People & the Press conducted an extensive national survey that included a wide sampling of issues, a number of those which figure prominently in discussions of the culture war. We have divided the Pew survey respondents into those who resided in states that two months later were to be categorized as blue states and states that two months later were to be categorized as red states. The question is whether there is any indication in these data that the election results would leave one half the country "seething" and one half "cheering," as *USA Today* reports.

Table 1 indicates that the residents of blue and red states certainly intended to vote differently: the percentage expressing an intention to vote for George Bush was ten points higher in the red states. Reminiscent of our discussion of dichotomous choices, however, the partisan and ideological predispositions underlying these voting differences were less distinct. The difference between the proportions of red and blue state respondents who consider themselves Democrats is not statistically significant, and the difference in the proportions who consider themselves Republicans is barely so—in both red and blue states self-identified independents are the largest group. Similarly, about a fifth of the respondents in both red and blue states consider themselves liberals (the four point difference is not statistically significant), and while there are more conservatives in the red states, there are more conservatives than liberals even in the blue states. In both the red and blue states the largest group of people classified themselves as moderates. In sum, while the aggregate voting patterns of red and blue states would turn out to be quite distinct in November, the underlying patterns of political identification were much less so.

Table 2 reports similar results for the group evaluations reported by residents of red and blue states. Unsurprisingly, red state residents regard the Republican Party more favorably than the Democrats, but 55 percent of them regard the Democratic Party favorably. Conversely, blue state residents regard the Democratic Party more favorably than the Republicans, but 50 percent report favorable evaluations of the Republican Party. Evangelical Christians are evaluated equally positively by solid majorities in both red and blue states, as are Jews and Catholics. Muslims fare less well overall and red state residents regard them lower still, but one wonders how much experience many people have with actual Muslims—especially in many of the red states—as opposed to the abstract

Table 1. Red Versus Blue States: Political Inclinations

	Blue	Red
Vote intention: Bush	34%	44%
Democratic self-ID	36	32
Republican self-ID	25	31
Liberal self-ID	22	18
Conservative self-ID	33	41
Moderate self-ID	45	41

Table 2. Red Versus Blue States: Group Evaluations
(Percent very/mostly favorable toward . . .)

	Blue	Red
Republican Party	50%	58%
Democratic Party	64	55
Evangelical Christians	60	63
Jews	79	77
Catholics	77	79
Muslims	56	47
Atheists	37	27

concept of a Muslim. Finally, in a standard finding, neither red nor blue state residents like atheists: Americans do not care very much what or how people believe, but they are generally negative toward people who don't believe in anything.

Across a range of other matters, blue and red state residents differ little, if at all. Figures in Table 3 indicate that similar proportions regard the government as *almost always* wasteful and inefficient—relative to the red states, the blue states clearly are not wellsprings of support for big government. Only small minorities in either category regard discrimination as the main reason that African

Table 3. Red Versus Blue States: Beliefs and Perceptions:
(Percent strongly supporting statement)

Gov't almost always wasteful and inefficient	39%	44%
Discrimination main reason blacks cannot get ahead	25	21
Immigrants strengthen our country	44	32
Fight for country right or wrong	35	43
Too much power concentrated in large companies	64	62
Corporations make too much profit	44	43
Al Gore is more liberal than he lets on	55	59
George Bush is more conservative than he lets on	59	57
Wish Clinton could run again (strongly disagree)	51	61

Americans can't get ahead—the blue states are not hotbeds of racial liberalism. Immigrants receive a warmer reception among blue state residents, but multiculturalism remains a minority position even in the blue states. Blue state residents are less likely to endorse unqualified patriotism.

On the other hand, red state residents are just as likely as blue state residents to believe that large companies have too much power and to think that corporations make too much profit—the red states are not the running dogs of corporate America. Amusingly, majorities in both red and blue states agree that Al Gore is more of a liberal than he lets on, and that George Bush is more of a conservative than he lets on—they were not fooled by all the talk about "progressives" and "compassionate conservatives." And finally—and counter to suggestions of numerous Democrats after the election—majorities in both red and blue states *strongly* disagree with the proposition that they wish Bill Clinton could run again. Clinton was more favorably regarded in the blue states, but Clinton fatigue by no means was limited to the red states.

When it comes to issue sentiments, Table 4 shows that in many cases the small differences we have seen so far become even smaller. Contrary to Republican dogma, red state citizens are equally as unenthusiastic about using the surplus (har!) to cut taxes as blue state citizens. Nearly equal numbers of blue and red state residents think the surplus should be used to pay off the national

Table 4. Red Versus Blue States: Issue Sentiments

	Blue	Red
Should use the surplus to cut taxes	14%	14%
. . . pay off the national debt	21	23
. . . increase domestic spending	28	24
. . . bolster SS and Medicare	35	38
Favor abolition of inheritance tax	70	72
. . . gov't grants to religious organizations	67	66
. . . school vouchers for low and middle income parents	54	50
. . . partial privatization of SS	69	71
. . . Medicare coverage of prescription drugs	91	92
. . . increasing defense spending	30	37
Do whatever it takes to protect the environment	70	64

debt, increase domestic spending, and bolster Social Security and Medicare. Contrary to Democratic dogma, blue state citizens are equally as enthusiastic as red state citizens about abolishing the inheritance tax, giving government grants to religious organizations, adopting school vouchers, and partially privatizing Social Security. Overwhelming majorities in both red and blue states favor providing prescription drugs through Medicare, and solid majorities endorse protecting the environment, whatever it takes. Neither red nor blue state residents attach high priority to increasing defense spending. Looking at this series of issue items, one wonders why anyone would bother separating respondents into red and blue categories—the differences are insignificant.

But, we have not considered the specific issues that define the culture war. Table 5 brings us to the heart of the matter—questions of religion, morality, and sexuality. The proportion of Protestants is significantly higher in the red states, of course, as is the proportion of respondents who report having a "born again" experience. There is a real difference here between the heartland and the coasts. But the significance of this difference fades when we dig deeper. Only a minority of red state respondents reports being very involved in church activities—only marginally more than those blue state respondents who report heavy involvement. A higher proportion of red state respondents report that religion is very important in their lives, but a healthy 62 percent majority of blue state respondents feel similarly. Very similar proportions think churches should stay out of politics, and the minority of red state residents who approve of the clergy talking

Table 5. Red Versus Blue States: Religion and Morals

	Blue	Red
Protestant	50%	69%
"Born again" or Evangelical Christian	28	45
Very involved in church activities	21	29
Religion is very important in my life	62	74
Churches should keep out of politics	46	43
Ever right for clergy to discuss candidates or issues from the pulpit? (yes)	35	33
Ban dangerous books from school libraries (yes)	37	42
Homosexuality should be accepted by society		
Agree strongly	41	31
Agree not strongly	16	14

politics from the pulpit is slightly smaller than the minority in the blue states. Book-burners are only slightly more common in the red states. Finally, there is a clear difference in one of the major issues of the culture war, homosexuality, but probably less of a difference than many would have expected. The level of support for societal acceptance of homosexuality is ten percentage points higher in the blue states (twelve points if we add those who waffle to those who fully accept homosexuality). The difference is statistically significant, but it hardly conjures up an image of two coalitions of deeply opposed states engaged in a culture war. Opinion is almost as divided within the red and the blue states as it is between them. Significantly, this ten- to twelve-point difference on the issue of homosexual acceptance is about as large a difference as we found between red and blue state respondents in the survey. Readers can judge for themselves whether differences of this magnitude justify the military metaphors usually used to describe them.

A legitimate objection to the preceding comparisons is that they include all citizens rather than just voters. Only about half of the age-eligible electorate goes to the polls in contemporary presidential elections, and far fewer vote in lower-level elections. It is well known that partisanship and ideology are strong correlates of who votes: more intense partisans and more extreme ideologues are more likely to vote. Thus, it is possible that the *voters* in red states differ more from the *voters* in blue states than the residents do. To consider this possibility we turn to the 2000 National Election Study which—after the election—asks individuals whether and how they voted. In 2000, the NES reported a vote distribution reasonably close to the actual national division: 50.6 percent of the respondents reported voting for Gore, 45.5 percent for Bush, and the remainder for minor candidates.

Tables 6 and 7 report differences among reported voters in the NES that are only marginally larger than those reported among all respondents in the Pew Survey. Again, the largest difference is for the vote itself. To reiterate, even if an individual feels 55:45 between the two candidates, she has to vote one way or the other. The reported vote for Bush is 54 percent in the red states versus 37 percent in the blue states—a seventeen-point gap, which is larger than the ten-point gap in vote *intention* in the earlier Pew Survey. Self-identified Democrats were significantly more common among blue state voters and self-identified Republicans significantly more common among red state voters, but in neither case does the difference reach double digits; independents and minor party affiliates were a third of the actual electorate in both categories. Self-identified liberals are more common in the blue states, but self-identified conservatives were at least as numerous as liberals in blue states. Again, moderates or centrists were the majority in both categories. An overwhelming majority of blue state voters approved

Table 6. Red Versus Blue States: Political Inclinations

	Blue	Red
Bush vote	37%	54%
Democratic self-ID*	40	32
Republican self-ID	25	34
Liberal self-ID	20	11
Conservative self-ID	24	31
Clinton job approval**	71	57
Clinton foreign policy job approval	70	63
Clinton economic job approval	81	74
Democrats better able to handle economy	35	27
Republicans better able to handle economy	24	29
Prefer unified control	24	24

*Party identifiers include strong and weak identifiers, not independent leaners.
Liberal identifiers are scale postions 1–2, conservative identifiers 6–7.
**Unless otherwise noted approval figures in the table combine "strongly approve" and "approve."

of Bill Clinton's general job performance as well as his foreign policy job performance and his economic job performance, but so did a heavy, if smaller, majority of red state voters. Only minorities of both blue state and red state voters thought that one party could better handle the economy. Finally, rather than blue state residents favoring Democratic control of the Presidency and Congress and red state residents favoring Republican control, nearly identical majorities of both prefer divided control.

Table 7 indicates that issue preferences in the two categories of states are surprisingly similar in many instances. Four in ten voters in both red and blue states agree that immigration should decrease, and seven in ten believe that English should be the official language of the United States (the proportion is actually slightly higher in the blue states). Four in ten voters in both categories put environmental considerations above employment considerations, a surprising similarity in light of the image of red states as hotbeds of clear-cutters and blue states as strongholds of tree-huggers. Narrow majorities of voters in both categories support school vouchers, and large majorities support the death penalty. In neither blue nor red states are people wildly in favor of government intervention to

Table 7. Red Versus Blue States: Issue Preferences

	Blue	Red
Immigration should decrease*	41%	43%
Make English official language	70	66
Environment over jobs	43	42
Favor school vouchers	51	54
Favor death penalty	70	77
Government should ensure fair treatment of blacks in employment	57	51
Blacks should get preferences in hiring	13	14
Stricter gun control	64	52
Equal women's role**	83	82
Attend church regularly	50	65
Moral climate: much worse	26	30
somewhat worse	25	25
Tolerate others' moral views	62	62
Abortion—always legal	48	37
Allow homosexual adoption	52	40
No gay job discrimination	73	62
Favor gays in military (strongly)	60	44

*Unless otherwise noted, the figures in the table combine "strongly" or "completely agree" responses with "mostly" or "somewhat agree" responses.
**Scale positions 1–2

ensure fair treatment of African Americans in employment, and virtually identical (small) proportions support racial preferences in hiring.

Again, when we turn to the specific issues that define the culture war, larger differences emerge, but there also are numerous surprises. A solid majority of blue state voters support stricter gun control laws, but so does a narrow majority of red state voters. Support for women's equality is overwhelming and identical among voters in both categories of states. Although regular church attenders are significantly more common in the red states, similar proportions in both red and blue states believe the moral climate of the country has deteriorated since 1992, and identical proportions believe that others' moral views should be tolerated. Support for unrestricted abortion is eleven points higher among blue state voters, but such unqualified support falls short of a majority, and more than a third of red state voters offer similarly unqualified support. The 2000 NES is particularly rich in items tapping people's views about matters related to sexual orientation. Here we find differences between blue and red state voters that are statistically significant, though smaller in magnitude than regular consumers of the news might have expected. A narrow majority of blue state voters would allow homosexuals to adopt children, but so would four in ten red state voters. Solid majorities of voters in both categories support laws that would ban employment discrimination against gays. Sixty percent of blue state voters fully support gays in the military, contrasted with 44 percent of red state voters. This 16 percent difference is the single largest disparity we found between the issue preferences of red and blue state voters. Perhaps Bill Clinton picked the one issue in the realm of sexual orientation that was most likely to create controversy. But the evidence supports the alternative hypothesis that Clinton's executive order polarized the electorate: according to Gallup data, popular support for gays in the military rose through the 1980s and had reached 60 percent in 1989 before plummeting in the wake of Clinton's executive order.

All in all, the comparison of blue and red state residents who claim to have voted in 2000 seems consistent with the picture reflecting comparisons of all residents of blue and red states. There are numerous similarities between red and blue state voters, some differences, and a few notable differences, but little that calls to mind the portrait of a culture war between the states.

10-4

How Divided Are We?

James Q. Wilson

In response to Fiorina, political scientist James Q. Wilson argues that American politics has become more polarized. Wilson traces this polarization to changes in congressional elections, media, interest groups, and education. Moreover, Wilson argues that the polarization matters. It has reduced America's ability to address serious policy problems, contributed to public alienation from politics, and threatens the role of the United States in the world.

THE 2004 ELECTION left our country deeply divided over whether our country is deeply divided. For some, America is indeed a polarized nation, perhaps more so today than at any time in living memory. In this view, yesterday's split over Bill Clinton has given way to today's even more acrimonious split between Americans who detest George Bush and Americans who detest John Kerry, and similar divisions will persist as long as angry liberals and angry conservatives continue to confront each other across the political abyss. Others, however, believe that most Americans are moderate centrists, who, although disagreeing over partisan issues in 2004, harbor no deep ideological hostility. I take the former view.

By polarization I do not have in mind partisan disagreements alone. These have always been with us. Since popular voting began in the 19th century, scarcely any winning candidate has received more than 60 percent of the vote, and very few losers have received less than 40 percent. Inevitably, Americans will differ over who should be in the White House. But this does not necessarily mean they are polarized.

By polarization I mean something else: an intense commitment to a candidate, a culture, or an ideology that sets people in one group definitively apart from people in another, rival group. Such a condition is revealed when a candidate for public office is regarded by a competitor and his supporters not simply as wrong but as corrupt or wicked; when one way of thinking about the world is assumed to be morally superior to any other way; when one set of political beliefs is considered to be entirely correct and a rival set wholly wrong. In extreme form, as defined by Richard Hofstadter in *The Paranoid Style in American Politics* (1965),

Source: James Q. Wilson, "How Divided Are We?", *Commentary*, February 2006. http://www.commentarymagazine.com/article/how-divided-are-we/. Notes appearing in the original have been deleted.

polarization can entail the belief that the other side is in thrall to a secret conspiracy that is using devious means to obtain control over society. Today's versions might go like this: "Liberals employ their dominance of the media, the universities, and Hollywood to enforce a radically secular agenda"; or, "conservatives, working through the religious Right and the big corporations, conspired with their hired neocon advisers to invade Iraq for the sake of oil."

Polarization is not new to this country. It is hard to imagine a society more divided than ours was in 1800, when pro-British, pro-commerce New Englanders supported John Adams for the presidency while pro-French, pro-agriculture Southerners backed Thomas Jefferson. One sign of this hostility was the passage of the Alien and Sedition Acts in 1798; another was that in 1800, just as in 2000, an extremely close election was settled by a struggle in one state (New York in 1800, Florida in 2000).

The fierce contest between Abraham Lincoln and George McClellan in 1864 signaled another national division, this one over the conduct of the Civil War. But thereafter, until recently, the nation ceased to be polarized in that sense. Even in the half-century from 1948 to (roughly) 1996, marked as it was by sometimes strong expressions of feeling over whether the presidency should go to Harry Truman or Thomas Dewey, to Dwight Eisenhower or Adlai Stevenson, to John F. Kennedy or Richard Nixon, to Nixon or Hubert Humphrey, and so forth, opinion surveys do not indicate widespread detestation of one candidate or the other, or of the people who supported him.

Now they do. Today, many Americans and much of the press regularly speak of the President as a dimwit, a charlatan, or a knave. A former Democratic presidential candidate has asserted that Bush "betrayed" America by launching a war designed to benefit his friends and corporate backers. A senior Democratic Senator has characterized administration policy as a series of "lies, lies, and more lies" and has accused Bush of plotting a "mindless, needless, senseless, and reckless" war. From the other direction, similar expressions of popular disdain have been directed at Senator John Kerry (and before him at President Bill Clinton); if you have not heard them, that may be because (unlike many of my relatives) you do not live in Arkansas or Texas or other locales where the *New York Times* is not read. In these places, Kerry is widely spoken of as a scoundrel.

In the 2004 presidential election, over two-thirds of Kerry voters said they were motivated explicitly by the desire to defeat Bush. By early 2005, President Bush's approval rating, which stood at 94 percent among Republicans, was only 18 percent among Democrats—the largest such gap in the history of the Gallup poll. These data, moreover, were said to reflect a mutual revulsion between whole geographical sections of the country, the so-called Red (Republican) states versus the so-called Blue (Democratic) states. As summed up by the distinguished social scientist who writes humor columns under the name of Dave Barry, residents of Red states are "ignorant racist fascist knuckle-dragging NASCAR-obsessed cousin-marrying road-kill-eating tobacco-juice-dribbling gun-fondling religious fanatic rednecks," while Blue-state residents are "godless unpatriotic pierced-nose Volvo-driving France-loving leftwing Communist latte-sucking tofu-chomping holistic-wacko neurotic vegan weenie perverts."

To be sure, other scholars differ with Dr. Barry. To them, polarization, although a real enough phenomenon, is almost entirely confined to a small number of political elites and members of Congress. In *Culture War?* (2004), which bears the subtitle "The Myth of a Polarized America," Morris Fiorina of Stanford argues that policy differences between voters in Red and Blue states are really quite small, and that most are in general agreement even on issues like abortion and homosexuality.

But the extent of polarization cannot properly be measured by the voting results in Red and Blue states. Many of these states are in fact deeply divided internally between liberal and conservative areas, and gave the nod to one candidate or the other by only a narrow margin. Inferring the views of individual citizens from the gross results of presidential balloting is a questionable procedure.

Nor does Fiorina's analysis capture the very real and very deep division over an issue like abortion. Between 1973, when *Roe* v. *Wade* was decided, and now, he writes, there has been no change in the degree to which people will or will not accept any one of six reasons to justify an abortion: (1) the woman's health is endangered; (2) she became pregnant because of a rape; (3) there is a strong chance of a fetal defect; (4) the family has a low income; (5) the woman is not married; (6) and the woman simply wants no more children. Fiorina may be right about that. Nevertheless, only about 40 percent of all Americans will support abortion for any of the last three reasons in his series, while over 80 percent will support it for one or another of the first three.

In other words, almost all Americans are for abortion in the case of maternal emergency, but fewer than half if it is simply a matter of the mother's preference. That split—a profoundly important one—has remained in place for over three decades, *and* it affects how people vote. In 2000 and again in 2004, 70 percent of those who thought abortion should always be legal voted for Al Gore or John Kerry, while over 70 percent of those who thought it should always be illegal voted for George Bush.

Division is just as great over other high-profile issues. Polarization over the war in Iraq, for example, is more pronounced than any war-related controversy in at least a half-century. In the fall of 2005, according to Gallup, 81 percent of Democrats but only 20 percent of Republicans thought the war in Iraq was a mistake. During the Vietnam war, by contrast, itself a famously contentious cause, there was more unanimity across party lines, whether for or against: in late 1968 and early 1969, about equal numbers of Democrats and Republicans thought the intervention there was a mistake. Pretty much the same was true of Korea: in early 1951, 44 percent of Democrats and 61 percent of Republicans thought the war was a mistake—a partisan split, but nowhere near as large as the one over our present campaign in Iraq.

Polarization, then, is real. But what explains its growth? And has it spread beyond the political elites to influence the opinions and attitudes of ordinary Americans?

The answer to the first question, I suspect, can be found in the changing politics of Congress, the new competitiveness of the mass media, and the rise of new interest groups.

That Congress is polarized seems beyond question. When, in 1998, the House deliberated whether to impeach President Clinton, all but four Republican members voted for at least one of the impeachment articles, while only five Democrats voted for even one. In the Senate, 91 percent of Republicans voted to convict on at least one article; every single Democrat voted for acquittal.

The impeachment issue was not an isolated case. In 1993, President Clinton's budget passed both the House and the Senate without a single Republican vote in favor. The same deep partisan split occurred over taxes and supplemental appropriations. Nor was this a blip: since 1950, there has been a steady increase in the percentage of votes in Congress pitting most Democrats against most Republicans.

In the midst of the struggle to pacify Iraq, Howard Dean, the chairman of the Democratic National Committee, said the war could not be won and Nancy Pelosi, the leader of the House Democrats, endorsed the view that American forces should be brought home as soon as possible. By contrast, although there was congressional grumbling (mostly by Republicans) about Korea and complaints (mostly by Democrats) about Vietnam, and although Senator George Aiken of Vermont famously proposed that we declare victory and withdraw, I cannot remember party leaders calling for unconditional surrender.

The reasons for the widening fissures in Congress are not far to seek. Each of the political parties was once a coalition of dissimilar forces: liberal Northern Democrats and conservative Southern Democrats, liberal coastal Republicans and conservative Midwestern Republicans. No longer; the realignments of the

South (now overwhelmingly Republican) and of New England (now strongly Democratic) have all but eliminated legislators who deviate from the party's leadership. Conservative Democrats and liberal Republicans are endangered species now approaching extinction. At the same time, the ideological gap between the parties is growing: if there was once a large overlap between Democrats and Republicans—remember "Tweedledum and Tweedledee"?—today that congruence has almost disappeared. By the late 1990's, virtually every Democrat was more liberal than virtually every Republican.

The result has been not only intense partisanship but a sharp rise in congressional incivility. In 1995, a Republican-controlled Senate passed a budget that President Clinton proceeded to veto; in the loggerhead that followed, many federal agencies shut down (in a move that backfired on the Republicans). Congressional debates have seen an increase not only in heated exchanges but in the number of times a representative's words are either ruled out of order or "taken down" (that is, written by the clerk and then read aloud, with the offending member being asked if he or she wishes to withdraw them).

It has been suggested that congressional polarization is exacerbated by new districting arrangements that make each House seat safe for either a Democratic or a Republican incumbent. If only these seats were truly competitive, it is said, more centrist legislators would be elected. That seems plausible, but David C. King of Harvard has shown that it is wrong: in the House, the more competitive the district, the more extreme the views of the winner. This odd finding is apparently the consequence of a nomination process dominated by party activists. In primary races, where turnout is low (and seems to be getting lower), the ideologically motivated tend to exercise a preponderance of influence.

All this suggests a situation very unlike the half-century before the 1990's, if perhaps closer to certain periods in the 18th and 19th centuries. Then, too, incivility was common in Congress, with members not only passing the most scandalous remarks about each other but on occasion striking their rivals with canes or fists. Such partisan feeling ran highest when Congress was deeply divided over slavery before the Civil War and over Reconstruction after it. Today the issues are different, but the emotions are not dissimilar.

Next, the mass media. Not only are they themselves increasingly polarized, but consumers are well aware of it and act on that awareness. Fewer people now subscribe to newspapers or watch the network evening news. Although some of this decline may be explained by a preference for entertainment over news, some undoubtedly reflects the growing conviction that the mainstream press generally does not tell the truth, or at least not the whole truth.

In part, media bias feeds into, and off, an increase in business competition. In the 1950's, television news amounted to a brief 30-minute interlude in the day's programming, and not a very profitable one at that; for the rest of the time, the three networks supplied us with westerns and situation comedies. Today, television news is a vast, growing, and very profitable venture by the many broadcast and cable outlets that supply news twenty-four hours a day, seven days a week.

The news we get is not only more omnipresent, it is also more competitive and hence often more adversarial. When there were only three television networks, and radio stations were forbidden by the fairness doctrine from broadcasting controversial views, the media gravitated toward the middle of the ideological spectrum, where the large markets could be found. But now that technology has created cable news and the Internet, and now that the fairness doctrine has by and large been repealed, many media outlets find their markets at the ideological extremes.

Here is where the sharper antagonism among political leaders and their advisers and associates comes in. As one journalist has remarked about the change in his profession, "We don't deal in facts [any longer], but in attributed opinions." Or, these days, in unattributed opinions. And those opinions are more intensely rivalrous than was once the case.

The result is that, through commercial as well as ideological self-interest, the media contribute heavily to polarization. Broadcasters are eager for stories to fill their round-the-clock schedules, and at the same time reluctant to trust the government as a source for those stories. Many media outlets are clearly liberal in their orientation; with the arrival of Fox News and the growth of talk radio, many are now just as clearly conservative.

The evidence of liberal bias in the mainstream media is very strong. The Center for Media and Public Affairs (CMPA) has been systematically studying television broadcasts for a quarter-century. In the 2004 presidential campaign, John Kerry received more favorable mentions than any presidential candidate in CMPA's history, especially during the month before election day. This is not new: since 1980 (and setting aside the recent advent of Fox News), the Democratic candidate has received more favorable mentions than the Republican candidate in every race except the 1988 contest between Michael Dukakis and George H. W. Bush. A similarly clear orientation characterizes weekly newsmagazines like *Time* and *Newsweek*.

For its part, talk radio is listened to by about one-sixth of the adult public, and that one-sixth is made up mostly of conservatives. National Public Radio has an audience of about the same size; it is disproportionately liberal. The same breakdown affects cable-television news, where the rivalry is between CNN (and MSNBC) and Fox News. Those who watch CNN are more likely to be Democrats than Republicans; the reverse is emphatically true of Fox. As for news and opinion on the Internet, which has become an important source for college graduates in particular, it, too, is largely polarized along political and ideological lines, emphasized even more by the culture that has grown up around news blogs.

At one time, our culture was only weakly affected by the media because news organizations had only a few points of access to us and were largely moderate and audience-maximizing enterprises. Today the media have many lines of access, and reflect both the maximization of controversy and the cultivation of niche markets. Once the media talked to us; now they shout at us.

And then there are the interest groups. In the past, the major ones—the National Association of Manufacturers, the Chamber of Commerce, and labor organizations like the AFL-CIO—were concerned with their own material interests. They are still active, but the loudest messages today come from very different sources and have a very different cast to them. They are issued by groups concerned with social and cultural matters like civil rights, managing the environment, alternatives to the public schools, the role of women, access to firearms, and so forth, and they directly influence the way people view politics.

Interest groups preoccupied with material concerns can readily find ways to arrive at compromise solutions to their differences; interest groups divided by issues of rights or morality find compromise very difficult. The positions taken by many of these groups and their supporters, often operating within the two political parties, profoundly affect the selection of candidates for office. In brief, it is hard to imagine someone opposed to abortion receiving the Democratic nomination for President, or someone in favor of it receiving the Republican nomination.

Outside the realm of party politics, interest groups also file briefs in important court cases and can benefit from decisions that in turn help shape the political debate. Abortion became a hot controversy in the 1970's not because the American people were already polarized on the matter but because their (mainly centrist) views were not consulted; instead, national policy was determined by the Supreme Court in a decision, *Roe* v. *Wade,* that itself reflected a definition of "rights" vigorously promoted by certain well-defined interest groups.

Polarization not only is real and has increased, but it has also spread to rank-and-file voters through elite influence.

In *The Nature and Origins of Mass Opinion* (1992), John R. Zaller of UCLA listed a number of contemporary issues—homosexuality, a nuclear freeze, the war in Vietnam, busing for school integration, the 1990–91 war to expel Iraq from Kuwait—and measured the views held about them by politically aware citizens. (By "politically aware," Zaller meant people who did well answering neutral factual questions about politics.) His findings were illuminating.

Take the Persian Gulf war. Iraq had invaded Kuwait in August 1990. From that point through the congressional elections in November 1990, scarcely any elite voices were raised to warn against anything the United States might contemplate doing in response. Two days after the mid-term elections, however, President George H. W. Bush announced that he was sending many more troops to the Persian Gulf. This provoked strong criticism from some members of Congress, especially Democrats.

As it happens, a major public-opinion survey was under way just as these events were unfolding. Before criticism began to be voiced in Congress, both registered Democrats and registered Republicans had supported Bush's vaguely announced intention of coming to the aid of Kuwait; the more politically aware they were, the greater their support. *After* the onset of elite criticism, the support of Republican voters went up, but Democratic support flattened out. As Bush became more vigorous in enunciating his aims, politically aware voters began to differ sharply, with Democratic support declining and Republican support increasing further.

Much the same pattern can be seen in popular attitudes toward the other issues studied by Zaller. As political awareness increases, attitudes split apart, with, for example, highly aware liberals favoring busing and job guarantees and opposing the war in Vietnam, and highly aware conservatives opposing busing and job guarantees and supporting the war in Vietnam.

But why should this be surprising? To imagine that extremist politics has been confined to the chattering classes is to believe that Congress, the media, and American interest groups operate in an ideological vacuum. I find that assumption implausible.

———————

As for the extent to which these extremist views have spread, that is probably best assessed by looking not at specific issues but at enduring political values and party preferences. In 2004, only 12 percent of Democrats approved of George Bush; at earlier periods, by contrast, three to four times as many Democrats approved of Ronald Reagan, Gerald Ford, Richard Nixon, and Dwight D. Eisenhower. Over the course of about two decades, in other words, party affiliation had come to exercise a critical influence over what people thought about a sitting President.

The same change can be seen in the public's view of military power. Since the late 1980's, Republicans have been more willing than Democrats to say that "the best way to ensure peace is through military strength." By the late 1990's and on into 2003, well over two-thirds of all Republicans agreed with this view, but far fewer than half of all Democrats did. In 2005, three-fourths of all Democrats but fewer than a third of all Republicans told pollsters that good diplomacy was the best way to ensure peace. In the same survey, two-thirds of all Republicans but only one fourth of all Democrats said they would fight for this country "whether it is right or wrong."

Unlike in earlier years, the parties are no longer seen as Tweedledum and Tweedledee. To the contrary, as they sharpen their ideological differences, attentive voters have sharpened *their* ideological differences. They now like either the Democrats or the Republicans more than they once did, and are less apt to feel neutral toward either one.

How deep does this polarization reach? As measured by opinion polls, the gap between Democrats and Republicans was twice as great in 2004 as in 1972. In fact, rank-and-file Americans disagree more strongly today than did politically active Americans in 1972.

To be sure, this mass polarization involves only a minority of all voters, but the minority is sizable, and a significant part of it is made up of the college-educated. As Marc Hetherington of Vanderbilt puts it: "people with the greatest ability to assimilate new information, those with more formal education, are most affected by elite polarization." And that cohort has undeniably grown.

In 1900, only 10 percent of all young Americans went to high school. My father, in common with many men his age in the early 20th century, dropped out of school after the eighth grade. Even when I graduated from college, the first in my family to do so, fewer than one-tenth of all Americans over the age of twenty-five had gone that far. Today, 84 percent of adult Americans have graduated from high school and nearly 27 percent have graduated from college. This extraordinary growth in schooling has produced an ever larger audience for political agitation.

Ideologically, an even greater dividing line than undergraduate education is postgraduate education. People who have proceeded beyond college seem to be very different from those who stop with a high-school or college diploma. Thus, about a sixth of all voters describe themselves as liberals, but the figure for those with a postgraduate degree is well over a quarter. In mid-2004, about half of all voters trusted George Bush; less than a third of those with a postgraduate education did. In November of the same year, when over half of all college graduates voted for Bush, well over half of the smaller cohort who had done postgraduate work voted for Kerry. According to the Pew Center for Research on the People and the Press, more than half of all Democrats with a postgraduate education supported the antiwar candidacy of Howard Dean.

The effect of postgraduate education is reinforced by being in a profession. Between 1900 and 1960, write John B. Judis and Ruy Teixeira in *The Emerging Democratic Majority* (2002), professionals voted pretty much the same way as business managers; by 1988, the former began supporting Democrats while the latter supported Republicans. On the other hand, the effect of postgraduate education seems to outweigh the effect of affluence. For most voters, including college graduates, having higher incomes means becoming more conservative; not so for those with a postgraduate education, whose liberal predilections are immune to the wealth effect.

The results of this linkage between ideology, on the one hand, and congressional polarization, media influence, interest-group demands, and education on the other are easily read in the commentary surrounding the 2004 election. In their zeal to denigrate the President, liberals, pronounced one conservative pundit, had "gone quite around the twist." According to liberal spokesmen, conservatives with their "religious intolerance" and their determination to rewrite the Constitution had so befuddled their fellow Americans that a "great nation was felled by a poisonous nut."

If such wholesale slurs are not signs of polarization, then the word has no meaning. To a degree that we cannot precisely measure, and over issues that we cannot exactly list, polarization has seeped down into the public, where it has assumed the form of a culture war. The sociologist James Davison Hunter, who has written about this phenomenon in a mainly religious context, defines culture war as "political and social hostility rooted in different systems of moral understanding." Such conflicts, he writes, which can involve "fundamental ideas about who we are as Americans," are waged both across the religious/secular divide and within religions themselves, where those with an "orthodox" view of moral authority square off against those with a "progressive" view.

To some degree, this terminology is appropriate to today's political situation as well. We are indeed in a culture war in Hunter's sense, though I believe this war is itself but another component, or another symptom, of the larger ideological polarization that has us in its grip. Conservative thinking on political issues has religious roots, but it also has roots that are fully as secular as anything on the Left. By the same token, the liberal attack on conservatives derives in part from an explicitly "progressive" religious orientation—liberal Protestantism or

Catholicism, or Reform Judaism—but in part from the same secular sources shared by many conservatives.

But what, one might ask, is wrong with having well-defined parties arguing vigorously about the issues that matter? Is it possible that polarized politics is a good thing, encouraging sharp debate and clear positions? Perhaps that is true on those issues where reasonable compromises can be devised. But there are two limits to such an arrangement.

First, many Americans believe that unbridgeable political differences have prevented leaders from addressing the problems they were elected to address. As a result, distrust of government mounts, leading to an alienation from politics altogether. The steep decline in popular approval of our national officials has many causes, but surely one of them is that ordinary voters agree among themselves more than political elites agree with each other—and the elites are far more numerous than they once were.

In the 1950's, a committee of the American Political Science Association (APSA) argued the case for a "responsible" two-party system. The model the APSA had in mind was the more ideological and therefore more "coherent" party system of Great Britain. At the time, scarcely anyone thought our parties could be transformed in such a supposedly salutary direction. Instead, as Governor George Wallace of Alabama put it in his failed third-party bid for the presidency, there was not a "dime's worth of difference" between Democrats and Republicans.

What Wallace forgot was that, however alike the parties were, the public liked them that way. A half-century ago, Tweedledum and Tweedledee enjoyed the support of the American people; the more different they have become, the greater has been the drop in popular confidence in both them and the federal government.

A final drawback of polarization is more profound. Sharpened debate is arguably helpful with respect to domestic issues, but not for the management of important foreign and military matters. The United States, an unrivaled superpower with unparalleled responsibilities for protecting the peace and defeating terrorists, is now forced to discharge those duties with its own political house in disarray.

We fought World War II as a united nation, even against two enemies (Germany and Italy) that had not attacked us. We began the wars in Korea and Vietnam with some degree of unity, too, although it was eventually whittled away. By the early 1990's, when we expelled Iraq from Kuwait, we had to do so over the objections of congressional critics; the first President Bush avoided putting the issue to Congress altogether. In 2003 we toppled Saddam Hussein in the face of catcalls from many domestic leaders and opinion-makers. Now, in stabilizing Iraq and helping that country create a new free government, we have proceeded despite intense and mounting criticism, much of it voiced by politicians who before the war agreed that Saddam Hussein was an evil menace in possession of weapons of mass destruction and that we had to remove him.

Denmark or Luxembourg can afford to exhibit domestic anguish and uncertainty over military policy; the United States cannot. A divided America encourages our enemies, disheartens our allies, and saps our resolve—potentially to fatal effect. What General Giap of North Vietnam once said of us is even truer today: America cannot be defeated on the battlefield, but it can be defeated at home. Polarization is a force that can defeat us.

10-5

Religion in American Politics

Robert D. Putnam and David E. Campbell

Religiosity—that is, the extent to which people observe religious practices—
has become a more open feature of American politics in recent decades. In this
chapter from their book, American Grace, *political scientists Robert Putnam*
and David Campbell trace the relationship between religious and political
attitudes in the American public over recent decades. They observe a "God
gap"—politically important differences between the religious and nonreli-
gious, between generations, and between Democrats and Republicans in their
religious and political views.

PERHAPS THE MOST visible change in American religion over the last generation is
the role it has come to play in the nation's politics. Religiosity has partisan over-
tones now that it did not have in the past. While there are notable exceptions,
the most highly religious Americans are likely to be Republicans; Democrats
predominate among those who are least religious. Among the punditry, this connection between religiosity and the vote has been given the unfortunate but
alliterative label of the God gap—the gap in question referring to the political
differences between people at varying levels of religiosity. It is thus like the so-
called gender gap, the difference in the partisan tendencies of men and women.
And, like the gender gap, the coupling between religiosity and partisanship has
become one of those unquestioned generalizations of American political life—an
election day fault line endlessly discussed by political pundits and shrewdly
exploited by political operatives. . . .

We will first show that the glue which holds religiosity and partisanship
together is the political salience of two issues in particular: abortion and same-sex
marriage. Attitudes on both are tightly connected to religiosity—which is not a
new development. The new part is that they have become politically salient, as
the Democratic and Republican parties have taken opposing positions on both
abortion and homosexual rights. As the parties have moved apart on these issues,
religious and nonreligious voters have moved apart also. But, we suggest, should
attitudes on these issues change, the religious divide in politics would likely also

Source: Robert D. Putnam and David E. Campbell, *American Grace: How Religion Divides and Unites Us* (New
York: Simon & Schuster, 2010), 369–418. Notes from the original have been deleted.

change. For while attitudes on same-sex marriage are moving sharply in a liberal direction, those on abortion are becoming somewhat more conservative—with both shifts most pronounced among young people. . . .

Religiosity and Party Preference

We begin by confirming the conventional wisdom: Religious and nonreligious voters differ dramatically in their partisan preferences. While the extent and endurance of the religious divide between the parties easily can be exaggerated, as a broad generalization it is accurate to say that religiosity and support for the Republican Party are bound together. While there are many ways to make this point, it is instructive to focus on the frequency of saying grace as a good tracer of religiosity. The more often you say grace, the more likely you are to find a home in the Republican Party, and the less likely you are to identify with the Democrats. Being a political independent, though, is unrelated to grace saying. Indeed, few things about a person correspond as tightly to partisanship as grace saying. We stress that the connection between grace and the GOP is not a fluky result owing to the fact that grace saying is somehow an idiosyncratic measure of religiosity. No matter the yardstick of religious devotion or practice, the story comes out the same. See Figure 1. When using our more complete index of religiosity (which does not actually include saying grace as one of its components), the picture looks virtually identical: The highly religious are far more likely to be Republicans than Democrats, those who are low on our religiosity scale largely favor Democrats over the GOP, and religiosity has no bearing on partisan independence. Even when we account statistically for other things that often go along with religiosity—such as marital status, age, region of the country—the connection between religiosity and partisanship remains.

A focus on the broad contours of the religious divide between the parties can obscure as well as reveal. While it is generally the case that a higher level of religious devotion predicts greater support for the Republicans, the connection between religiosity and partisan preference varies in important ways—both across religious traditions and over time. Consider, first, the fact that highly religious members of different traditions vary widely in their Republicanness. Roughly 70 percent of highly religious evangelical Protestants and Mormons identify as Republicans, with highly religious mainline Protestants right behind at 62 percent. However, only half as many highly religious Catholics describe themselves as Republican (35 percent). And, as we saw in Chapter 9, Black Protestants are arguably the most highly religious group in America—including the most frequent grace sayers—and yet are also the least likely to identify as

Figure 1. The "Grace Gap": Frequency of Saying
Grace Predicts Party Identification
(with standard demographic characteristics held constant)

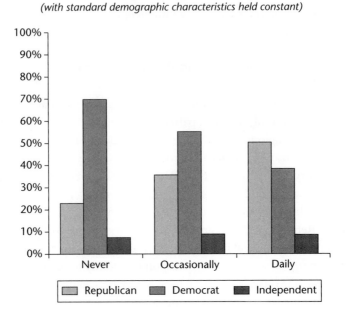

The "God Gap": Strength of Religiosity Predicts Party Identification
(with standard demographic characteristics held constant)

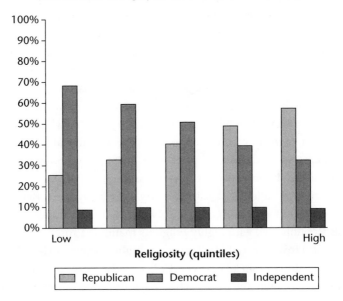

Source: Faith Matters survey, 2006.

Republicans (merely 14 percent of highly religious Black Protestants do so). In Figure 1, the percentage of Republicans among the most frequent grace sayers and/or highly religious would be considerably higher if we were to exclude African Americans. It is highly religious evangelicals, mainline Protestants, and Mormons who are the most likely to be Republicans. . . .

The Religious Divide Overtime

The religious divide between the parties has become well entrenched. However, its emergence was not predestined. For while the political differences between the religious and nonreligious run deep, they are not necessarily permanent. Nor are they a constant, as the religiosity-partisanship connection has varied over time. The General Social Survey is the most convincing source of data to examine the connection between religiosity and partisanship. Figure 2, therefore, displays the relationship between the frequency with which someone attends religious services and their party identification, while also accounting for a bundle of other demographic characteristics that might plausibly explain any connection between them. A positive number means that more church attendance predicts a higher likelihood of identifying as a Republican—the higher the number, the greater the relationship. As we see in the figure, the Republicans had a modest advantage among churchgoers in the early 1970s, which likely was fallout from the George McGovern campaign of 1972. McGovern's campaign . . . helped trigger the first aftershock. McGovern was famously labeled the candidate of "abortion, amnesty [for draft evaders], and acid." He was also supported by an unusually secular group of activist supporters, which only added to the wariness of religious voters. In the mid-1970s, though, the modest "religiosity advantage" that Republicans had over Democrats disappeared with Jimmy Carter's successful presidential campaign. Carter cultivated an image of being morally upright and was outwardly religious, being the first presidential candidate to describe himself as born again. Then, beginning in the 1980s, the Republicans gained an advantage among highly religious voters, which has continued to grow since. We can take a slightly longer historical view with the National Election Studies, which date back to 1952. Again, we see that there was little to no religious divide in partisanship in the 1950s and 1960s, with a pattern similar to the GSS from the 1970s to the present. The presidential vote affirms the trends in partisanship. In 1952 in the midst of the post-war religious boom, Republican Dwight Eisenhower received exactly the same percentage of support (59 percent) among Americans who attended religious services frequently and among those who never

Figure 2. The Link Between Religious Attendance and Party Identification Has
Varied Over Time (General Social Survey)
(whites only, with standard demographic characteristics held constant)

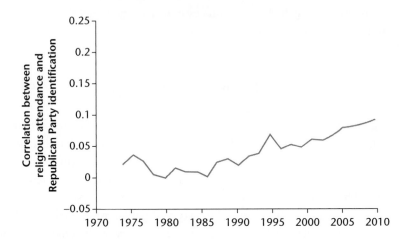

The Link Between Religious Attendance and Party Identification Has Varied
Over Time (National Election Studies)
(whites only, with standard demographic characteristics held constant)

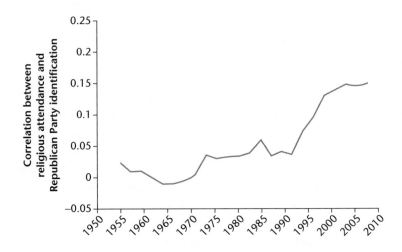

Source: General Social Survey and National Election Studies.

attended. Compare that to 2008, when there was a 22 percentage point difference in support for John McCain between those who attended religious services
at least weekly (61 percent) and those who never attended (39 percent).

In other words, the connection between religiosity and partisanship has varied
over time, and has grown considerably since the mid-1980s. Indeed, American

history teaches us that religion is neither exclusively left nor right, progressive nor conservative. Instead, religion of different sorts has been associated with political causes of different sorts. On some issues, notably those related to race, religion has been invoked to justify both sides of the debate. In the nineteenth century, religion animated advocates of both abolition and slavery. No one put the point better than Abraham Lincoln, who, in his second inaugural address, referred to the two sides of the Civil War by noting that "both read the same Bible and pray to the same God, and each invokes His aid against the other." Lincoln's words, however, obscure an important point about the way religion relates to politics, since they imply a symmetry between the religious justifications of pro- and antislavery advocates. Actually, white Southerners would have been pro-slavery without religion; while white Northerners likely would have been antislavery only because of religion. Likewise during the civil rights era, while the civil rights movement relied substantially on black churches as sources of both organization and inspiration and also found allies in many Northern mainline Protestant churches, some segregationists also found a religious rationale for their beliefs.

Beyond race, throughout America's history other issues have had an explicitly religious impulse, whether it was the drive in the early 1800s to stop the delivery of mail on Sunday, or the campaign for Prohibition, or the broader Progressive movement. Given the close association of religion and American patriotism, opinions motivated by nationalism are often given a religious inflection. The American Revolution had religious impulses. So did anticommunism in the Cold War era, and so does support for the Iraq and Afghan wars today. Religion, however, has also inspired the political left—from pacifists to anti-apartheid advocates to the movement to provide sanctuary for undocumented workers.

What is unusual about the current period, then, is not that religion matters in American politics. In a highly religious nation like the United States, we should not be surprised that religion and politics would intertwine. Nor is it unusual that religion has come to matter in the specific domain of presidential politics. For example, John F. Kennedy in 1960—and before him, Al Smith in 1928—faced a stained glass ceiling, as many Protestant voters were wary of a Catholic president. What makes the current period unusual is that church-attending evangelicals and Catholics (and other religious groups too) have found common political cause. We call this the "coalition of the religious." Given that not all religious traditions are equally likely to identify with the Republicans—and Black Protestants barely do at all—it is more accurately labeled the coalition of most of the religious. At the same time, the growing ranks of (most) nonreligious voters are also allied, but on the opposite end of the political spectrum.

The Political Generation Gap

The creation of a new coalition of the religious represents a major change in the foundation of the American political system. But will this be an enduring feature of American politics? The answer lies partly in the process by which the coalition emerged. There are two different but potentially complementary ways in which a partisan shift of this magnitude can occur. The first is change among individual voters, such as when a frequent churchgoer switches from identifying as a Democrat to a Republican. To the extent this occurred, it would suggest that the current divide could disappear rather rapidly as those individuals switch again. Or the shift could occur because of generational replacement, which is much more gradual but also more enduring. That is, as an older generation whose partisan allegiances reflect the coalitions of a previous political era die off, they are replaced by political newcomers who came of age in a period of new political alliances. As the younger generation replaces the older, the new alliances supplant the existing political coalitions.

The evidence suggests both a large generational shift in the connection between religiosity and partisanship and a more modest change among individual voters. The generational differences can be seen in our analysis of the Faith Matters surveys, as the God gap is widest among people under the age of thirty-five, growing progressively weaker among voters in ever older generational cohorts, with the weakest relationship of all observed for those sixty-five and older. Such a pattern is consistent with generational replacement, as the differences could reflect the different eras in which each generation entered the electorate. Older voters formed their political loyalties at a time when there was little or no relationship between religiosity and partisanship, and so their initial partisan orientation was not associated with their level of religious involvement. Younger voters, however, have known only a political system in which religiosity and partisanship are closely aligned.

While suggestive, data from one period of time cannot determine definitively whether the differences we see are owing to generational replacement or simply to maturation as people move through the life cycle. More convincing evidence is found when we track the connection between religiosity and partisanship by interviewing the same people, and their children, over time. By doing so, we can follow changes within the same individuals over time, as well as across generations.

Studies that follow intergenerational trends over time are rare, but fortunately one has been conducted since the mid-1960s, precisely the period of time in which we are interested. In the Youth-Parent Socialization Study, a nationally representative sample of high school seniors and their parents was interviewed in 1965. Researchers reinterviewed both generations in 1973 and again in 1982.

In 1997, they returned again to the second generation and then also interviewed the children of the second generation (post-boomers). The resulting data provide an unrivaled opportunity to trace intergenerational trends, including the connections between religiosity and partisanship.

As seen in Figure 3, in 1965 we find a modest connection between frequency of worship attendance and voters' party identification. Frequent attenders were slightly more likely to be Republicans. Not surprisingly, the parents and their adolescent children (generations 1 and 2) show almost exactly the same correlation. We can see the generational differences emerge when comparing generations 1 and 2 over time, as by 1973 the baby boomers display a very different relationship between religiosity and partisanship than their parents. In 1973, when those of generation 2 were in their mid-twenties and just reaching political maturity, they show no connection between church attendance and party identification. Among their parents, however, the modest connection observed in 1965 held steady. By 1982, the story changes. The modest relationship between religiosity and partisanship observed in 1965 and 1973 had disappeared among the older generation, but had reappeared among their children, the boomers.

Figure 3. The Religious Divide Has Grown Among Baby Boomers, but Is Widest Among Their Children

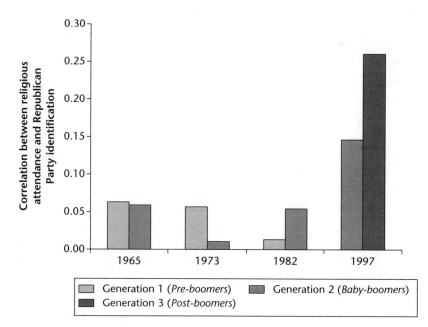

The changes from the mid-1960s to the early 1980s were small. The real change occurred between 1982 and 1997. In that period, the link between religiosity and partisanship grew substantially among baby boomers; the strength of the connection between religious attendance and party affiliation among the second generation was almost three times as strong as in 1982. Since these are interviews with the same people at different points in time, we can be confident that the emergence of the religiosity divide has entailed some individual-level change, as churchgoing and partisanship have come into alignment. . . .

While individual change is part of the story, the comparison between generations 2 and 3—the baby boomers and their post-boomer children—suggests that generational replacement has played an even more significant role in the appearance of the connection between religiosity and partisanship. The post-boomers have nearly twice the correlation between attendance at religious services and party affiliation as their parents. The strength of the tie between religiosity and party affiliation among this generation is all the more striking when we consider that, in 1997, the post-boomers were roughly the same average age as their parents were in 1973—when their parents' generation evinced no connection between religiosity and partisanship.

In sum, data from this long-running panel study suggest that the current religious divide has cracked open because of both generational replacement and, to a lesser degree, individual change. The strong generational component of the God gap's emergence suggests that it will likely endure—while the smaller individual-level calibration between church and party reminds us that changes in political alignments can, and do, happen. . . . [T]his calibration process can even be observed over a single year. And while political allegiances are sometimes calibrated to be in tune with one's religion, in our current political environment we also see evidence that people calibrate their religious involvement to align with their politics. In any given year, these are small changes but, cumulatively, they add up.

This process of generational replacement is typical of change in the partisan landscape. In spite of the usual election year hype about this or that voting bloc swinging dramatically from one party to another, changes generally occur through a process more akin to plate tectonics than earthquakes—steadily over a period of time, not suddenly. Once parties' brand labels take hold among the electorate they do not disappear overnight. Individuals' own partisanship is often a form of self-identity, and is long-standing. This is why we can speak of people being Republicans or Democrats, almost as though party label is a demographic category. Fundamental change in the partisan configuration of the electorate requires large blocs of voters to move from one party to another, and this is far more likely to happen among voters coming of political age than those who have had a long-term partisan affiliation.

Today's religious divide opened up in a gradual process; should it close, that too is likely to be a gradual process.

Country Club vs. Sunday School Republicans

In discussing changes in the partisan landscape, it is important that we take a moment to correct a widely held misconception about the Republicans' coalition of the religious. Many pundits speak as though today's Republican Party is split between two opposing factions, defined by what those Republicans do on Sunday mornings. There are those Republicans who spend Sunday mornings on the links—the affluent country club wing of the party. Then, allegedly, there is the downscale Sunday school wing of the party, who spend their Sunday mornings in the pews. Since religion, it is often said, is a salve for the poor, these two wings are thought to inhabit different worlds. If true, this would significantly dampen the electoral significance of the God gap, since it would mean that the two wings of the Republican coalition could easily rupture.

Really, though, the two wings are largely one and the same. Many of those country clubbers are the Sunday schoolers. In our 2006 Faith Matters survey, we divided people into four mutually exclusive categories defined by their level of education and frequency of church attendance. People are either frequent or infrequent church attenders, and have either high or low education (as a reliable marker of socioeconomic status), thus creating four mutually exclusive categories:

1. More than a high school education / Attend church monthly or more

2. A high school education or less / Attend church monthly or more

3. More than a high school education / Attend church less than monthly

4. A high school education or less / Attend church less than monthly

Of these four groups, the highest percentage of Republicans is found among people who attend church frequently *and* have high education. Furthermore, as shown in Figure 4, since the 1970s, Republicans have seen gains among college-educated churchgoers—voters with one foot in the country club wing and another in the Sunday School wing of the party.

These Republican gains among college-educated churchgoers go hand in hand with the fact that class and religion have become mutually reinforcing. . . . [R]eligion is not only for the poor. Recall that Americans with high socioeconomic status are no less likely to attend religious services as those with low socioeconomic status. In fact, over roughly the last thirty years, it is the working class

Figure 4. College-Educated Churchgoers Are Most Likely
to Be Republicans (Whites Only)

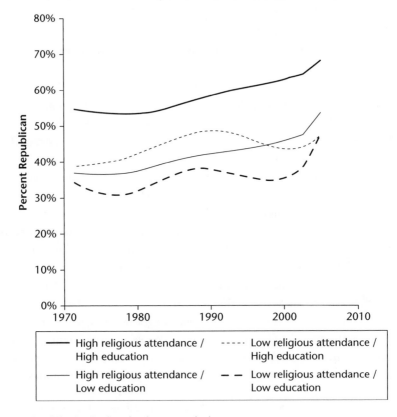

Legend:

— High religious attendance / High education
— High religious attendance / Low education
----- Low religious attendance / High education
– – Low religious attendance / Low education

Source: National Election Studies; data loess-smoothed.

who have become less likely to attend church relative to the upper class. An increasing skew in the socioeconomic status of churchgoers has accompanied the increasing Republicanness of high-socioeconomic-status churchgoers. So, relative to the working class, college grads are more likely to be church attenders, and those church-attending college grads are increasingly likely to be Republicans. Importantly, these changes are not driven solely by the political transformation of the South, which was once monolithically Democratic but is now a far more Republican region (in presidential elections, overwhelmingly so). When we examine the same trends in education, church attendance, and party identification but leave Southerners out of the picture, the results are nearly identical.

The political implications of the country club-Sunday school fusion are profound, as it explains how the GOP succeeds by simultaneously advocating both social and economic conservatism. If a high level of religiosity were coupled with economic desperation, the Republicans would have to say very different things to the two wings of the party. As long as those college grads are in the pews, the Republicans can preach a single sermon that blends social conservatism with economic policies favored by the educated class. As a matter of fact, political scientist Larry Bartels shows that cultural issues like abortion and same-sex marriage have the greatest impact on the votes cast by upper-class voters.

Abortion and Homosexuality: The Glue that Holds the Coalition Together

We have determined that the God gap is neither new, nor fleeting, nor necessarily permanent. Nor does it conflict with the class division between America's parties, another foundational element in the nation's political chemistry What, though, explains why, beginning in the mid-1980s and continuing to the present, religiosity and partisanship have become so intertwined? Any explanation must be able to account not only for why we see a connection between religiosity and partisanship now, but also why that connection appeared when it did.

The answer, we suggest, lies in the issues that have brought the coalition of the religious together. Politics is always a matter of building coalitions. Coalitions, in turn, come together in reaction to the political issues that are salient. Successful politicians, parties, and movements frame issues in such a way that otherwise disparate groups see themselves as allies in a cause. Coalitions come together around issues, but those issues have to come from somewhere. Because the United States has an extremely porous political system, there are many points of entry for issue entrepreneurs. Political scientist John Kingdon evokes a fitting metaphor when he describes the "policy primeval soup" found in Washington. It is survival of the fittest, and the issues that win—those that rise from the soup to become the big issues voters care about—are often the issues that can bring new groups together, or even create a shared identity among people who previously had little in common.

Given the strength of the religiosity-partisanship connection, one could be forgiven for thinking that religiosity, like one's party preference, shapes opinions on a wide range of issues. This is not so. Instead, religiosity has a tight connection to attitudes regarding abortion and gay marriage, and a more modest correlation—or none at all—to issues that do not pertain to sex and the family. The coalition of the religious has come together around a small bundle of issues.

We base that conclusion on a statistical analysis which accounts for the impact of other personal characteristics that might plausibly be related to the positions people take on the issues of the day (using our standard bundle of demographic controls). By controlling for these other factors, we can be sure that religiosity is not standing in for another factor (like gender or living in the South) that is itself related to religiosity. Religion is only one of myriad factors that affect where people stand on public issues, although the specific factors vary depending on the issue. For some, race matters. For others, gender matters. For still others, economic background matters. And so we account for these many other influences on people's political opinions.

While we cannot claim to have examined every issue imaginable, the 2006 Faith Matters survey did include a wide array, including:

Death penalty

Foreign aid

Immigration

U.S. intervention in world affairs

Protecting civil liberties vs. safety from terrorism

Government efforts to close income gaps between rich and poor

Same-sex marriage

Abortion

As shown in Figure 5, the issues fall into three categories: those for which religiosity matters a lot, for which it matters less, and for which it does not matter at all. Of all the issues included in the 2006 Faith Matters survey, only two unequivocally fall into the category where religiosity matters a lot: abortion and same-sex marriage.

Holding everything else steady, when we move from the bottom of the religiosity index to the top, the percentage of Americans who oppose abortion in all but cases of rape, incest, and endangerment of the mothers life rises from about 18 percent to 78 percent—an enormous 60 percentage point gain. We observe a similar, if slightly less substantial, connection between religiosity and attitudes toward same-sex marriage: From the bottom to the top of the religiosity index, the percentage opposing same-sex unions rises 44 percentage points (16 percent to 60 percent). . . .

Religiosity's influence on public opinion thus has a narrow scope. It does not matter at all for some issues, matters only a little for most, and matters a lot for only two. Abortion and same-sex marriage are the glue holding the coalition of the religious together.

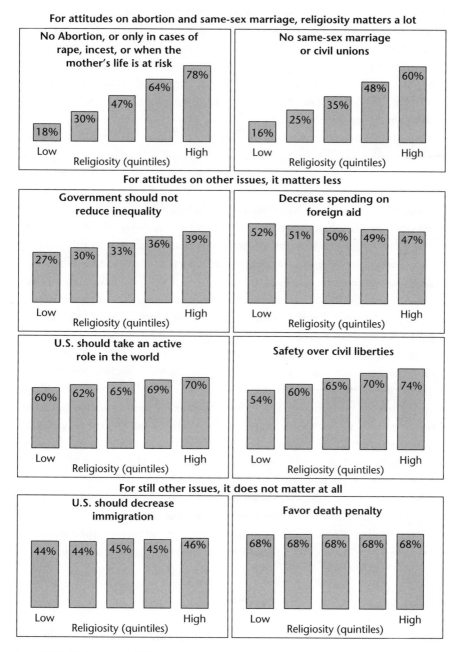

Figure 5. Religiosity and Political Attitudes
(with standard demographic controls held constant)

Source: Faith Matters survey, 2006.

The connection between religiosity and these sex and family issues is necessary to explain the religious divide between the parties, but it is not sufficient. For while the tie between religiosity and partisanship has varied, the link between religiosity and attitudes on both abortion and same-sex marriage has been constant. Since at least 1972, the first year of the General Social Survey, and almost certainly much longer, frequency of religious attendance has consistently been a strong predictor of opposition to abortion and disapproval of homosexuality. . . .

So what did change? The answer is that, beginning in the 1980s, sex and family issues—which had long been aligned with religiosity—also become aligned with positions taken by America's two major political parties. As a result, religiosity and partisanship came into alignment.

This alignment occurred because of a change in the political choices offered to voters. If the political choices placed before Americans are uncorrelated with religion, then any political decisions that might be affected by religion are moot. Consequently, for religion to affect the choices voters make, the candidates on the ballot must have contrasting positions on the issues shaped by religion.

To see why the two criteria work in tandem, pretend that you have taken a side in the cola wars and are a partisan of Pepsi rather than Coke. Accordingly, when given a choice of restaurants that are otherwise equal you would prefer one that serves Pepsi. Imagine that we conducted a study in which we tried to predict the restaurants that you frequent. You would expect us to find a correlation between your preference for Pepsi and your preferred restaurants—you are more likely to eat in Pepsi-serving restaurants. From that study, we would conclude that there is a relationship between the brand of soda you like and where you eat. Now, suppose that we ran the same study, but this time all the restaurants in the city serve only Coke. We would no longer find a correlation between soda preference and restaurant choice, as it would appear that whether you like Coke or Pepsi has no bearing on your decision of where to eat. However, the absence of a correlation only reflects the absence of choices. Politics works the same way. Unless candidates in an election differ on an issue—that is, offer voters a choice—that issue cannot be a factor affecting how people vote. It seems obvious, but the changing choices offered to voters are too rarely acknowledged as the explanation for the emergence of the strong relationship between religiosity and the vote.

Choices

We have seen that prior to the 1970s whether one went to church had little to do with party preference. Subjects like abortion and homosexuality were not to be uttered in polite company, let alone included in a political platform. Then, American society, and thus politics, underwent a dramatic change. The new divisions within American politics are succinctly captured in the slogan popular-ized by the women's movement: The personal is the political. Owing to the social tumult of the Sixties, politics came to be defined by a new set of issues that were very personal indeed, including abortion. . . . [T]he long Sixties were a shock to American society, the effects of which are still being felt. Then came the first aftershock, which reverberated through American religion, as theo-logically conservative—largely evangelical—religion was revitalized. This first aftershock also rippled through American politics, causing new cleavages and alliances within the electorate. The coalition of the religious began to come together, and the political movement known as the Religious Right was born.

The many activists who comprise the Religious Right movement, particularly the evangelicals who stand at the center of the movement, are animated by an array of issues: school prayer, pornography, creationism, public displays of reli-gious symbols and monuments, and even a concern for global human rights. However, the specialized issues that motivate small numbers of activists do not necessarily trigger a tectonic shift in the foundations of the parties' coalitions. As political scientist Geoffrey Layman puts it, "Only those issues that capture the sustained attention of the mass public and change its perceptions of and feelings about the parties are capable of creating long-term partisan change." Most of the issues that mobilize activists, who almost by definition have opinions and inter-ests outside the mainstream, do not matter much to "regular" people, the vast majority of whom do not make politics a priority. Few issues spur deep-seated change in the partisan makeup of the general population. Those that do often touch an emotional chord. Civil rights is one example, given the visceral reaction many Americans have to race. Abortion is another.

Why does abortion have such political potency? At the risk of profound under-statement, we note that abortion symbolizes more than merely an obstetrical procedure. For people on both sides of the issue, abortion is a highly symbolic issue that touches a raw nerve. In describing the reaction to the Supreme Court's landmark abortion decision, *Roe* v. *Wade,* political scientist David Leege and his colleagues write that "Religious traditionalists reacted so strongly against the decision because it seemed to threaten and devalue the unique quality that set women, as bearers of children, apart from men." Based on her comprehensive study of abortion activists on both sides of the issue, sociologist Kristin Luker goes even further and describes how, to them, abortion is a referendum on the totality of one's moral worldview:

> The pro-life world view, notwithstanding the occasional atheist or agnostic attached to it, is at the core one that centers around God. . . . [T]he pro-choice world view is not centered around a Divine Being, but rather around a belief in the highest abilities of human beings. For them, reason—the

human capacity to use intelligence, rather than faith, to understand and alter the environment—is at the core of their world.

To be pro-life typically, then, indicates more than one's position on abortion. Abortion stands in for a bundle of beliefs that, grouped together, can be called moral traditionalism. Luker was studying activists, that rare breed who have a passion for politics and whose opinions are the most strident. Within the general public, the link between attitudes on abortion and a moral worldview is admittedly weaker, but still easily detected. People with pro-life attitudes are not only more religious when compared to those on the pro-choice side, they are far more likely to disapprove of premarital sex, to believe that it is best if women do not work outside the home, and to say that children should be taught obedience over self-reliance. No matter the measure, pro-life advocates come out as more morally traditional. While we are not suggesting that abortion sits as the prime mover of all sex and family attitudes—among such a cluster of closely related opinions, trying to single out one is undoubtedly a fool's errand—we simply note that abortion is inextricably bound up with moral traditionalism across the board, and has become a potent symbol for a morally traditionalist worldview.

Remember, though, that a political issue can only divide the electorate when voters are presented with a choice on that particular issue. In the case of abortion, the Democratic and Republican parties did not diverge sharply on the issue until the 1980s. In 1976, the Republican platform was more or less neutral on abortion. By 1980 it unequivocally endorsed a constitutional amendment to ban abortion, language that has been preserved ever since. . . . Beginning in the 1980s, voters had a choice on abortion. The battle lines had been drawn.

Let us be clear about why we draw attention to the parties' national platforms. While few voters read or pay any attention whatsoever to them, they nonetheless reflect the priorities of the activists, donors, and candidates of the party—those who establish the party's brand label in the minds of rank and file voters. Increasingly, abortion was becoming a line of demarcation between Republicans and Democrats. Candidates, especially presidential candidates, learned that they had to toe their party's line on abortion in order to win over the ardent activists. The process is self-reinforcing. Activists and partisans come to learn that "good Republicans" are pro-life (and, likewise, "good Democrats" are pro-choice). As a result, a strong position on abortion feeds on itself—pro-lifers are attracted to the Republican Party, while Republican partisans come to be pro-life. . . . The changes occurring in the parties were accompanied by an increasing emphasis on abortion in the nation's churches. However, just as the parties did not react immediately to *Roe* v. *Wade,* so too was there a delayed reaction to the decision in at least some religious circles. When the Supreme Court decided *Roe* v. *Wade,* opinion about abortion was in flux. While Catholic leaders were decidedly against it, opinion within evangelical circles was unsettled. In 1971, just two years prior to *Roe*, the Southern Baptist Convention even approved a resolution that called for the legalization of abortion in some circumstances. Following *Roe*, it took a few years for evangelical leaders to embrace the pro-life cause as fully as their Catholic counterparts. By the late 1970s, though, evangelical opposition to abortion hardened, setting the stage for the coalition of the religious to come together. The old interreligious tensions manifested in Kennedy's 1960 presidential race were forgotten. These former antagonists found that what united them was greater than what divided them.

As the effects of the parties' divergence on abortion rippled through the electorate, attitudes on abortion came to be highly correlated with partisanship. Figure 6 shows this clearly, again using data from the General Social Survey (which has used the same measure of abortion attitudes since 1972). As before, even when accounting for the same array of demographic controls, we see that abortion became strongly associated with party identification in the mid- to late 1980s, precisely the time at which the God gap—the link between church attendance and partisanship—also appeared. Since the mid-1980s, the growing linkage between opinion on abortion and partisanship parallels the increasing connection between church attendance and party identification. Today religiosity, abortion,

Figure 6. Attitudes Against Abortion and Homosexuality Have Become More Strongly Connected to Republican Party Identification
(whites only, with standard demographic characteristics held constant)

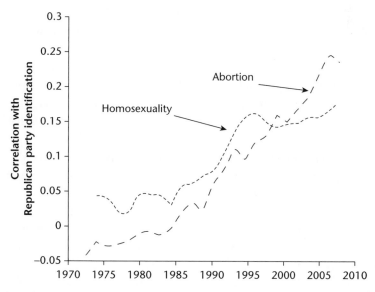

Source: General Social Survey

and partisanship form an interlocking triumvirate, but this has not always been the case. When abortion was emerging as a major issue during the 1970s, Democrats were somewhat more likely to oppose abortion than Republicans, because, in that period, Catholics were overwhelmingly Democratic and pro-life. It was not until the Democratic and Republican parties took distinctive stands on abortion in the 1980s that the issue became a predictor of party sympathies.

The rise of abortion as a dominant dividing line between the parties can easily leave the wrong impression about the nature of public opinion on abortion. Abortion's link to partisanship does not mean that Americans are grouped in either an ardently pro-choice or pro-life camp, with few holding a moderate position. To the contrary, most Americans are in the moderate middle on abortion as they are on most issues. . . . Most people's views on abortion lies in between the two poles of the issue—few Americans endorse a hard-line position banning all abortion and few believe in unfettered abortion on demand. Still, Americans do disagree on just where to draw the line on regulating abortion, and even those moderate differences are enough to divide Republicans from Democrats. Even if few people occupy the extremes of the spectrum of opinion on abortion, it is still the case that those who are more willing to limit abortion (even if they do not want to ban it outright) are more likely to identify as Republicans, while those who are more willing to permit abortion (even if they do not endorse abortion under all circumstances) are more likely to be Democrats. If anything, the relatively modest differences on abortion in the aggregate make its salience as a political issue all the more remarkable. It also suggests that even seemingly small shifts in abortion attitudes can have significant political implications—and, we will show, such a shift appears to be underway.

Recall, though, that abortion is not the only sex and family issue with a strong connection to religiosity. Attitudes toward homosexual rights and same-sex marriage specifically are tightly connected, too. Figure 6 also shows the connection between religiosity and attitudes toward homosexuality, which, like opinion on abortion, began to be more strongly associated with Republican Party affiliation in the mid-1980s (although, unlike abortion, its relationship to partisanship has leveled off over the last decade or so).

Given that religiosity and attitudes on sex and family issues are tightly linked, it is not surprising that a majority of Americans who say that religion is very important when they make political decisions also see abortion and same-sex marriage as very important issues to them personally. In contrast, people who say that they do not draw on religion when making political decisions are far less likely to ascribe as much significance to either abortion or same-sex marriage. Those at the poles of these issues place more importance on them than do people with opinions in the middle, and abortion and same-sex marriage opponents place far more importance on these issues than do supporters (see Figures 7 and 8).

Figure 7. Those Who Oppose Abortion Place More Importance on the Issue than Those Who Favor It

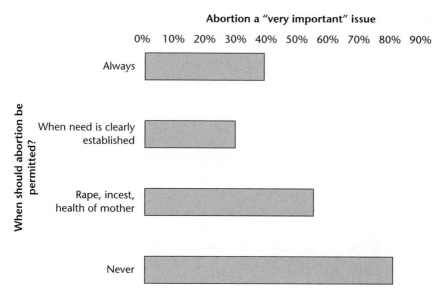

Source: Faith Matters survey, 2007.

Figure 8. Those Who Oppose Same-Sex Marriage Place More Importance on the Issue than Those Who Favor It

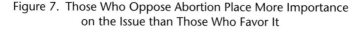

Source: Faith Matters survey, 2007.

Eighty-one percent of people who say that abortion should never be permitted say that it is a very important matter, compared to 39 percent of those who say abortion should always be available as an option; 49 percent of those who oppose same-sex marriage say it is very important, compared to 28 percent of those who favor it. In other words, opponents of abortion and same-sex marriage place a higher priority on sex and family issues than do Americans who favor abortion rights and legal recognition for same-sex relationships. . . .

Are the Times A-Changin'?

We have seen how the sex and family issues of abortion and gay marriage are the glue that holds the coalition of the religious together. By implication, then, if abortion and gay marriage were not on the political agenda, religious and secular Americans would be much closer to finding common political ground. Indeed, this was the situation in American politics before these sex and family issues came to the fore. We make this point because these two sex and family issues may be on their way to losing their political potency. There are no guarantees in any prognostication, especially about politics, but there is evidence suggesting that change may be coming.

Homosexuality: Increasing Acceptance

We turn first to the changing opinions on homosexuality, and gay marriage specifically. Just as there has been a liberalization of attitudes regarding the propriety of women working outside the home, so is there a similar trend on the acceptance of homosexuality, and the idea of legal recognition for homosexual unions. In 1988, before gay marriage had erupted as an issue of national prominence, the General Social Survey asked a representative sample of Americans whether "homosexual couples should have the right to marry one another." At that time, only 12 percent of Americans agreed that homosexuals should be permitted to marry. By 2006, after the issue had simmered for years, that figure had risen to 35 percent. In 2008, it rose again to 39 percent. In our 2006 Faith Matters survey we find 34 percent in support of gay marriage. However, we also find another 30 percent who support a middle way, civil unions for homosexual couples.

Given generational differences in views toward gay marriage, acceptance of homosexual nuptials will likely keep growing. Young people are increasingly likely to approve of gay marriage, as the generation gap is getting wider. As seen in Figure 9, back in 1988, there were only small generational differences in approval of same-sex marriage; overall support for the idea was very low. Fifteen percent of young Americans (born after 1965) favored marriage for same-sex couples, compared to 13 percent among the baby boomers (born between 1945 and 1965), and 9 percent among Americans born before 1945. By 2008, half of young Americans expressed support for same-sex marriage—this is 17 percentage points higher than the baby boomers, and 28 points higher than Americans born before 1945. We even see a rise in support for gay marriage after 2004, the year in which same-sex marriage came to the fore. From 2004 to 2008, overall support for gay marriage rose by roughly 8 percentage points. It would be tempting to extrapolate from the shift between 2004 and 2008 and predict that support for gay marriage will grow by 2 percentage points per year. If that were true, gay marriage would soon become highly popular. As with mutual funds, however, in public opinion past performance is no guarantee of future returns. Opinion change on gay marriage likely accelerated in the wake of 2004, as this was a time in which gay marriage was very much in the news, which would be expected to maximize the flux in public opinion. Whether the trend will continue with the same trajectory remains to be seen. Nonetheless, it seems highly likely that liberalization on attitudes toward same-sex marriage will continue, as younger Americans have a generally more accepting attitude toward homosexuality. For example, in 2008 while two thirds of the over-sixty-fives believe that homosexual

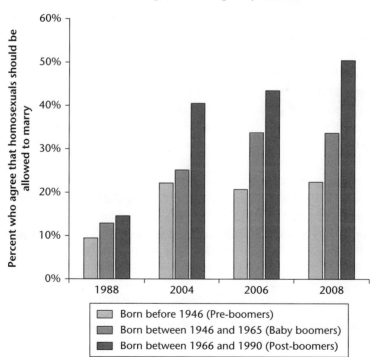

Figure 9. Americans of All Ages Have Become More Accepting of Same-Sex Marriage, but Young People Most of All

Source: General Social Survey.

acts are "always wrong," that opinion is shared by only 46 percent of 18–34-year-olds (with 35–49- and 50–64-year-olds falling in between).

Over the last generation, attitudes to homosexuality (discussed here) and attitudes to gender roles . . . have traced parallel paths. Both working mothers and gay marriage have won increasing acceptance among both religious and secular Americans, though the level of acceptance of both remains lower among the religious. Indeed, the impact of religiosity on support for gay marriage is actually starker now than two decades ago—a function of the fact that twenty years ago, virtually everyone opposed gay marriage. Today, the generations differ from each other in their level of support such that the most religious post-boomer is as likely to support gay marriage (32 percent) as the least religious pre-boomer (32 percent).

When put together, all of this evidence points to one unmistakable trend: Homosexuality is increasingly acceptable, especially among young people. Among young people, religiosity still drives up opposition to gay marriage, but does so starting at a much lower level of opposition. Undoubtedly, part of the explanation for young people's acceptance of same-sex marriage is that they have become politically and socially aware during a period in which homosexuality has been increasingly featured positively in the popular media. Gay characters are common in TV programs and movies and many prominent gay celebrities project an image of respectability.

Pop culture, though, is not the whole story, as there is another overriding explanation for young people's acceptance of homosexuality and same-sex marriage. Young people are also the least religious age group. Since religiosity is such a strong predictor of attitudes toward same-sex marriage, and homosexuality more generally, it comes as no surprise that the most secular cohort of the population is the most accepting of gay marriage.

Based on the inexorable process of generational replacement, we would thus also expect gay marriage to become increasingly acceptable as time passes. As young people become a larger portion of the population, overall approval of homosexuality, including but not limited to gay marriage, will rise. If and when that happens, homosexuality will become less attractive as a wedge issue in politics and will likely cease to be a potent issue at all. . . .

Abortion: Increasing Ambivalence

We also see evidence that abortion's political potency may weaken, but for the opposite reason that gay marriage will likely diminish in significance. As with gay marriage, the opinions of young people differ from those of their elders. Instead of being more liberal, however, they are somewhat more conservative. It would not be accurate to describe the post-baby boomer generation as ardently pro-life, as few endorse a total ban on abortion, but they are more willing than their parents to place restrictions on abortion. In fact, their attitudes on abortion more closely resemble the opinions of their grandparents. Since this increase in opposition to, or at least unease with, abortion appears in multiple sources of data, we are confident that it is not an idiosyncratic quirk in one survey.

The best source of data over time on attitudes toward abortion is the General Social Survey. Beginning in 1972, the General Social Survey has asked an extremely detailed question about whether respondents would approve of abortion in a wide-ranging series of situations:

If there is a strong chance of serious defect in the baby.

If the woman is married and does not want any more children.

If the woman's own health is seriously endangered by the pregnancy.

If the family has a very low income and cannot afford any more children.

If the woman became pregnant as a result of rape.

If the woman is not married and does not want to marry the man.

We can thus combine the responses into an index, charted in Figure 10, that ranges from 0 to 6—from approval of abortion under no circumstances to approval in all of them, with plenty of options in between. Since this same set of questions has been asked in the General Social Survey since 1972, we can trace opinion on abortion over nearly four decades. When viewed in the aggregate, opinion on abortion has remained largely stable. However, there have been some slight peaks and valleys. The most compelling explanation for the ups and downs in support for abortion is that they correspond to the way abortion was framed by opinion leaders in each time period. When, in the 1970s, support for abortion was framed as upholding women's autonomy, attitudes toward abortion warmed. In the mid-1980s, opponents of abortion advocated popular ideas such as parental consent laws, and abortion support dropped slightly. Support for abortion then rose again when, in the late 1980s through early 1990s, there was a real possibility that the Supreme Court would overturn *Roe v. Wade*, which would enable states to ban abortion altogether. The last decade or so, however, has seen support for abortion drop— modestly—again.

Our interest is less in the ebbs and flows of overall abortion opinion, and more in the differences across generations. Before we turn to what we find, recall what we saw regarding attitudes on gay marriage. Young people support gay marriage far more than their elders, which is entirely consistent with their low average level of religiosity. Accordingly, we should expect to find that young people are

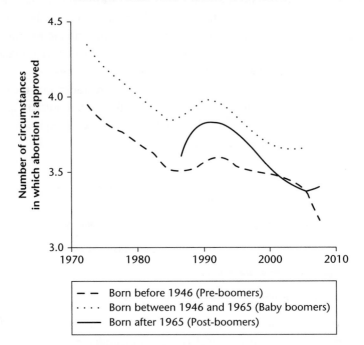

Figure 10. Young People Are More Ambivalent about
Abortion than Their Parents' Generation

Source: General Social Survey; data loess-smoothed.

also the most likely to support abortion. In fact, however, people born after 1965 are less pro-choice than their baby boomer parents. . . .

We stress that it is not accurate to describe post-boomers as ardently pro-life. On average, they are willing to support abortion in at least three circumstances, which is a far cry from opposing all abortions. Nor is there a gaping chasm in the abortion attitudes of young people and their parents; the difference is modest— but statistically significant. Furthermore, there has been a slight uptick in approval of abortion among young people in the last few years, suggesting that they might be on a pro-choice trajectory and in years to come may converge with their parents' generation.

Nonetheless, the discrepancy between where we would expect young people's opinion on abortion to be—based on their relatively high levels of secularism— and where it is cries out for an explanation. We can better comprehend the abortion attitudes of the young by parsing the circumstances under which they would permit it. Recall that the General Social Survey asks people whether they approve of abortion in six different situations. Three of them are related to either the physical or mental health of the mother: a serious defect in the baby, the woman's own health is endangered, or a pregnancy resulting from rape. The other three can be described as social or economic reasons: a woman is married and does not want more children, the family cannot afford more children, or an unmarried woman does not want to marry the father.

Whether a hypothetical abortion is for health or social/economic reasons, we see a similar drop-off in support, especially among the post-boomers. When we look just at approval of abortion for health reasons, the post-boomers converge with their grandparents, and even great-grandparents. That is, the baby boomers are a little more likely to support abortion for health-related reasons than either their parents' or their children's generations. The baby boom generation diverges even further from the others on abortion for social/economic reasons. And while recent years have seen a slight uptick in support for this justification for abortion among the post-boomers, they still remain below their parents' generation.

While the cultural barometric pressure is pushing support for gay marriage upward, it appears to have been pressing downward on approval of abortion. Why? There are many plausible explanations. As is often the case when explaining social change, multiple factors are likely working in concert. Recall our earlier mention of how abortion opinion appears to shift, slightly, as the terms of the public debate over abortion shift. Such a perspective can help us make sense of the growing reluctance to endorse elective abortion. In the aftermath of *Roe v. Wade* (decided in 1973), antiabortion advocates pushed for a repeal of the decision and a total ban on abortion, while supporters of abortion rights stressed the dangers of the back-alley abortions that were in living memory In such a climate, there was little room for nuance. As *Roe* endured and became entrenched, the debate changed. Opponents of abortion increasingly adopted an incremental approach by not focusing on achieving a full-fledged ban on all abortions. Instead, they have centered their attention on advocating abortion restrictions like requiring parental notification for minors, ending intact dilation and extraction (aka partial birth) abortions, requiring pre-abortion counseling, and ending federal funding for groups that provide abortions. . . .

It is important to draw a distinction between the old debate over the legality of abortion and the new one over which restrictions should be placed on abortion. A debate over restrictions, without the serious threat that abortion would be banned outright, is a far cry from a debate over whether abortion should ever be permitted. In the current environment, political space has opened up for ambivalence toward abortion, particularly abortion for economic and social reasons, without advocating an absolute ban. Likewise, in this environment one can be pro-choice without defending abortion in all circumstances. Just as post-boomers have only known a world where women commonly work outside the home and where homosexuality is increasingly accepted, so also have they only known a world with the new debate over abortion. Today's young people have also grown up in an era with widespread acceptance and availability of birth control. If contraception is easy to obtain, unplanned pregnancies can appear less like a tragic mistake and more like the consequence of sexual irresponsibility. Pregnancy, in such a view, is the consequence of not taking responsibility for being sexually active and, therefore, abortion means avoiding consequences. The mantra of taking responsibility and owning up to consequences is a powerful political idea, as it applies to issues such as welfare reform, standardized testing, and strictness on crime. While there can always be debate over individual cases, the meaning of "unplanned" changes when birth control is readily available. No one would say that a rape victim should "take responsibility" for not having used birth control, and contraception is irrelevant to cases where delivery puts the mother s life at risk. In both hypothetical situations, young people are as likely as their elders to agree that abortion should be permitted.

We propose still another hypothesis for young people s unease with abortion that, we concede, remains a plausible hunch rather than a tested proposition—the prevalence of in utero ultrasound images. It has become a rite of passage during pregnancy for a woman to have ultrasound photos taken of her developing fetus; often, the expectant mother can even bring home a video of her ultrasound. While we admittedly do not have hard data to test this hypothesis, we strongly suspect that the antiabortion movement has benefited from the improvement in ultrasound quality. When pro-life advocates show films of aborted bloody fetuses, many react with queasiness rather than sympathy. However, ultrasound photos pasted into scrapbooks and passed along by e-mail are a different story. Both of us have had many friends and relatives display ultrasound photos, and never once has an expectant mother used the impersonal word "fetus" to describe what we are seeing. Ultrasounds are pictures of their baby-to-be. Similarly, other improvements in medical technology have likely weakened support for abortion. Operations are performed in utero, while premature babies are increasingly able to survive outside the womb. Like the social ritual of passing around the ultrasound photos, these developments subtly reinforce the strongest argument made by pro-life advocates—the fetus is a not-yet-born baby. . .

To bring us back to the data, we offer some important caveats. . . . First, the subtleties in the abortion attitudes of young people do not mean that they are ripe for political mobilization for strict restrictions on abortion, or for the pro-life cause in general. Recent ballot initiatives in California and South Dakota, both of which would have made abortions more difficult to obtain, found little support among young voters. In both cases, voters under thirty were the most likely to vote against the initiatives and thus against restricting access to abortion. This is a voting bloc that may be uncomfortable with abortion, at least for some reasons, but has not embraced the pro-life political movement.

The nuance in the attitudes of young people toward abortion is also revealed when we compare how they respond to different ways of asking about abortion. The detailed questions asked in the General Social Survey are sufficiently subtle to detect young people's ambivalence about abortion. When given coarser options, young people don't always display such generational differences. However, even when the abortion opinions of young people look just like the opinions of older generations, this is surprising because we would have many reasons—particularly their low religiosity—to expect them to show a high degree of support for abortion.

Conclusion

We began by affirming that the oft-discussed God gap in American politics is real. The Republicans have forged a coalition of the religious—although with exceptions, notably Black Protestants. Over roughly the last three decades, sex and family issues like abortion and same-sex marriage have brought this religious-political coalition together. The coalition will likely hold when sex and family issues are at stake in an election, and as long as the Republicans maintain their religion-friendly image. However, should sex and family issues recede in political significance, religion—or religiosity—will gradually cease to be such a salient political division. The data suggest that abortion and gay marriage may recede as political issues.

There has been a liberalizing trend on same-sex marriage, with younger Americans far more accepting of homosexuality generally, and same-sex unions specifically, than their elders. On abortion, though, we see evidence of a conservative tilt among young people, even though they are also the most secular age group in the population.

Each of these trends has a different implication for the future of American politics. The trend on homosexual rights is likely to follow the same pattern as attitudes toward women's rights. Religiosity will remain a predictor of more conservative attitudes, but the floor for those attitudes will keep moving higher and higher. Recall that, in 2008, the most religious young person is just as likely to support gay marriage as the most secular member of his or her grandparents' generation. As the floor rises, opposition to homosexuality, like opposition to women's rights, will cease to be politically viable.

The trend on attitudes toward abortion among young people likely has a different, but no less portentous, implication. First, acceptance of abortion and same-sex marriage differ in that they are moving in opposite directions. For that reason, it would seem less likely that these issues would continue to share the same political platform. And since today's young people will constitute an ever greater share of the future electorate, continuation of this trend would lead aggregate opinion on abortion to shift modestly in a pro-life direction.

Secondly, and more subtly, abortion attitudes appear to have a weakening connection to religiosity among the rising generation. Since it was the tie between abortion and religiosity that brought the coalition of the religious together, any loosening of the abortion-religiosity connection has the potential to pull it apart. This would not necessarily mean that abortion ceases to be contentious, only that the debate over abortion is less likely to be waged along religious lines.

If we are reading the tea leaves right, these trends would not mean the immediate breakup of the coalition of the religious. Nor would they mean the immediate demise of the Religious Right as a political movement, as we are reminded that past rumors of the death of the Religious Right have been greatly exaggerated. Instead, we expect the Republicans' image as the religion-friendly party to endure, as images outlast issues. But party images can change. Adding to the potential for change, more and more Democratic candidates have begun using religious rhetoric and symbolism in an effort to neutralize the Republican advantage among churchgoers. In the short term, these efforts have had little effect, especially with the most religious voters, but over time they might lead to a change in whether the Republicans continue to be identified as the most religion-friendly party. . . .

Given the dynamism of American religion, we should not be surprised that over time the ways in which it intersects with politics change. Going all the way back to the election of 1800, Thomas Jefferson's opponents accused him of being an atheist intent on confiscating the Bibles of New England housewives. Later in the 1800s, there were sharp divisions between the liturgical (Episcopalians, Lutherans, Catholics) and pietistic (Baptists, Methodists) religions. As Catholic immigration swelled, tensions between Catholics and Protestants rose, fanned by Al Smith's candidacy in 1928 but then largely extinguished by Kennedy in 1960. The demise of Catholic-Protestant conflict brought us a new source of religious division between the religious and the secular. Sex and family issues have now united a historically unique coalition of (most of) the religious but, we suggest, should the salience of those issues diminish, the coalition would likely unravel slowly. If so, we would not expect religion to cease to be a significant factor in American politics.

The particular constellation of religion and politics in contemporary America is the product of a particular set of historical contingencies—the shock and aftershocks that realigned the world of morality and religion and the strategic decisions of party leaders about how to respond to that new cleavage. History teaches us that if the current God gap were to fade, we should expect religion and politics to align in new ways, as political entrepreneurs work to construct new coalitions. The change will be in *how* religion affects our politics, not *whether* it does.

Chapter 11

Voting, Campaigns, and Elections

11-1

from *The Reasoning Voter*

Samuel L. Popkin

*Voters confront difficult choices with incomplete and usually biased informa-
tion. Many voters are not strongly motivated to learn more. Even if they want
to learn more, the information they need is often not available in a convenient
form. In the following essay, Samuel L. Popkin argues that this predicament
does not necessarily lead voters to make irrational decisions. Voters instead
rely on low-cost shortcuts to obtain information and make decisions. Popkin's
analysis can help us to better understand the role of campaigns in voters'
decision-making processes as well as other features of American politics.*

IN RECENT DECADES, journalists and reformers have complained with increasing
force about the lack of content in voting and the consequent opportunities for
manipulating the electorate. And yet over the same period academic studies of
voting have begun to expose more and more about the substance of voting decisions and the limits to manipulation of voters. The more we learn about what
voters know, the more we see how campaigns matter in a democracy. And the
more we see, the clearer it becomes that we must change both our critiques of
campaigns and our suggestions for reforming them.

Source: Samuel L. Popkin, *The Reasoning Voter: Communication and Persuasion in Presidential Campaigns,* 2d ed.
(Chicago: University of Chicago Press, 1994), 212–219. Notes appearing in the original have been deleted.

In this [essay] I summarize my findings about how voters reason and show how some modest changes which follow from my theory could ameliorate some defects of the campaign process.

I have argued . . . that the term *low-information rationality,* or "gut" rationality, best describes the kind of practical reasoning about government and politics in which people actually engage. . . . [L]ow-information reasoning is by no means devoid of substantive content, and is instead a process that economically incorporates learning and information from past experiences, daily life, the media, and political campaigns. . . .

Gut rationality draws on the information shortcuts and rules of thumb that voters use to obtain and evaluate information and to choose among candidates. These information shortcuts and rules of thumb must be considered when evaluating an electorate and considering changes in the electoral system.

How Voters Reason

It is easy to demonstrate that Americans have limited knowledge of basic textbook facts about their government and the political debates of the day. But evaluating citizens only in terms of such factual knowledge is a misleading way to assess their competence as voters.

Because voters use shortcuts to obtain and evaluate information, they are able to store far more data about politics than measurements of their textbook knowledge would suggest. Shortcuts for obtaining information at low cost are numerous. People learn about specific government programs as a by-product of ordinary activities, such as planning for retirement, managing a business, or choosing a college. They obtain economic information from their activities as consumers, from their workplace, and from their friends. They also obtain all sorts of information from the media. Thus they do not need to know which party controls Congress, or the names of their senators, in order to know something about the state of the economy or proposed cuts in Social Security or the controversies over abortion. And they do not need to know where Nicaragua is, or how to describe the Politburo, in order to get information about changes in international tensions which they can relate to proposals for cutting the defense budget.

When direct information is hard to obtain, people will find a proxy for it. They will use a candidate's past political positions to estimate his or her future positions. When they are uncertain about those past positions, they will accept as a proxy information about the candidate's personal demographic characteristics and the groups with which he or she has associated. And since voters find it difficult to gather information about the past competence of politicians who have performed outside their district or state, they will accept campaign competence as a proxy for competence in elected office—as an indication of the political skills needed to handle the issues and problems confronting the government.

Voters use evaluations of personal character as a substitute for information about past demonstrations of political character. They are concerned about personal character and integrity because they generally cannot infer the candidate's true commitments from his past votes, most of which are based on a hard-to-decipher mixture of compromises between ideal positions and practical realities. Evaluating any sort of information for its relevance to politics is a reasoning process, not a reflex projection directly from pocketbook or personal problems to votes. But in making such evaluations, voters use the shortcut of relying on the opinions of others whom they trust and with whom they discuss the news. These opinions can serve as fire alarms that alert them to news deserving more than their minimal attention. As media communities have developed, voters have the additional shortcut of validating their opinions by comparing them with the opinions of political leaders whose positions and reputations people grow to know over time.

People will use simplifying assumptions to evaluate complex information. A common simplifying assumption is that a politician had significant control over an observable result, such as a loss of jobs in the auto industry. This saves people the trouble of finding out which specific actions really caused the result. Another example of a simplifying assumption is the notion that "My enemy's enemy is my friend."

People use party identification as running tallies of past information and shortcuts to storing and encoding their past experiences with political parties. They are able to encode information about social groups prominent in the party, the priorities of the party, and the performance of the party and its president in various policy areas. This generalized information about parties provides "default values" from which voters can assess candidates about whom they have no other information. In keeping generalized tallies by issue area, they avoid the need to know the specifics of every legislative bill.

As a shortcut in assessing a candidate's future performance, without collecting more data, people assemble what data they have about the candidate into a causal narrative or story. Because a story needs a main character, they can create one from their knowledge of people who have traits or characteristics like those of the candidate. This allows them to go beyond the incomplete information they have about a candidate, and to hold together and remember more information than they otherwise could. Because these stories are causal narratives, they allow voters to think about government in causal terms and to evaluate what it will do. Narratives thus help people incorporate their reasoning about government into their projections about candidates; their assumptions "confer political significance on some facts and withhold it from others." They offer people a way to connect personal and political information, to project that information into the future, and to make a complete picture from limited information.

Finally, people use shortcuts when choosing between candidates. When faced with an array of candidates in which some are known well and some are known poorly, and all are known in different and incomparable ways, voters will seek a clear and accessible criterion for comparing them. This usually means looking for the sharpest differences between the candidates which can be related to government performance. Incorporating these differences into narratives allows them to compare the candidates without spending the calculation time and the energy needed to make independent evaluations of each candidate.

Working Attitudes

People do not and cannot use all the information they have at one time. What they use will depend in part on the point of view or frame with which they view the world; attitudes and information are brought to bear if they fit the frame. Of the attitudes and bits of information available, people tend to use those they consider important or those they have used recently. As the changes in voter attitudes entailed by the emergence of new candidates in primaries suggest, attitudes and information will also be brought to the foreground when they fit with what is *expected* in a situation. Our realizations, the thoughts that come clearly to mind, depend in part on what others say about their own thoughts and perceptions.

Thus, as options change, expectations change. If a Democrat were asked in early 1984 what he or she thought of Walter Mondale as a presidential candidate, and the reply was "He'll be all right," that response could be interpreted as coming from a nonthinking voter who was passively following a media report about the thinking of others. But the same response could also be interpreted as an indication of a complex ability to come to grips with the available choices, with issue concerns that cannot be satisfied simultaneously, and with the compromises considered necessary to reach consensus with other people. Similarly, if the same voter were asked a few weeks later what he or she thought about Gary Hart and the reply was "He's just what we need," the response could be interpreted to mean that this voter was simply following the media-reported bandwagon. On the other hand, it could be interpreted to mean that reported changes in public expectations had brought other attitudes and concerns forward in the voter's mind. As this example suggests, the information voters use depends on the reasoning they do, and the reasoning they do depends in part on their expectations. It also indicates that the way in which the content of a voter's response is interpreted depends on a theory about how voters use information and make choices. And I am convinced that any such theory must account for the "working attitudes" of voters—the combinations of feeling, thought, and information they bring to bear when they make their choices at the polls.

Why Campaigns Matter

Changes in government, in society, and in the role of the mass media in politics have made campaigns more important today than they were fifty years ago, when modern studies of them began. Campaign communications make connections between politics and benefits that are of concern to the voter; they offer cognitive focal points, symbolic "smoking guns," and thus make voters more aware of the costs of misperception. Campaigns attempt to achieve a common focus, to make one question and one cleavage paramount in voters' minds. They try to develop a message for a general audience, a call that will reach beyond the "disinterested interest" of the highly attentive, on one hand, and the narrow interests of issue publics, on the other. Each campaign attempts to organize the many cleavages within the electorate by setting the political agenda in the way most favorable to its own candidates. . . .

The spread of education has both broadened and segmented the electorate. Educated voters pay more attention to national and international issues and they are now connected in many more electronic communities—groups of people who have important identifications maintained through media rather than direct, personal contact. There are also today more government programs—Medicare, Social Security, welfare, and farm supports are obvious examples—that have a direct impact on certain groups, which become issue publics. Other issue publics include coalitions organized around policies toward specific countries, such as Israel or Cuba; various conservation and environmental groups; and groups concerned with social issues, such as abortion and gun control. Furthermore, there are now a great many more communications channels with which these people can keep in touch with those outside their immediate neighborhoods or communities. Such extended groups are not new, and modern communications technology is not necessary to mobilize them, as the abolitionist and temperance movements remind us; but the channels to mobilize such groups are more available today, and I believe that the groups they have nurtured are more numerous. When the national political conventions were first telecast in 1952, all three networks showed the same picture at the same time because there was only one national microwave relay; today, with the proliferation of cable systems and satellite relays, television can now show . . . hundred[s of] channels. Furthermore, as channels and options have proliferated, and as commuting time has increased and two-career families become more common, the proportion of people watching mainstream networks and network news is also dropping.

Over the past fifty years, as surveys have become increasingly available to study public opinion, there have been many gains in knowledge about voting and elections. There have also been losses, as national surveys have replaced the detailed community orientation of the original Columbia studies. We know much more about individuals and much less about extended networks, and we have not adequately examined the implications for society and campaigning of the transitions from face-to-face to electronic communities.

Both primaries and the growth of media communication have increased the amount of exposure people get to individual candidates, particularly the quantity of personal information they get about the candidates. This increases the importance of campaigns because it gives voters more opportunities to abandon views based on party default values in favor of views based on candidate information, and also more opportunities to shift from views based on a candidate's record to views based on his or her campaign image. Moreover, as primaries have expanded, parties have had to deal with the additional task of closing ranks after the campaign has pitted factions within the party against each other. Primaries have also changed the meaning of political party conventions. Conventions no longer deliberate and choose candidates; instead, they present the electorate with important cues about the social composition of the candidate's coalition and about the candidate's political history and relations with the rest of the party. The more primaries divide parties, the more cues are needed to reunite parties and remind supporters of losing candidates about their differences with the other party.

The Implications of Shortcuts

Recognizing the role of low-information rationality in voting behavior has important implications for how we measure and study attitudes, how we evaluate the effects of education, and how we evaluate electoral reforms. To begin with, we must acknowledge that the ambivalence, inconsistency, and changes in preference that can be observed among voters are not the result of limited information. They exist because as human beings we can never use all of what we know at any one time. We can be as ambivalent when we have a lot of information and concern as when we have little information and limited concern. Nor do inconsistency, ambivalence, and change result from a lack of education (especially civic education) or a lack of political interest. Ambivalence is simply an immutable fact of life. Economists and psychologists have had to deal with the inconsistencies people demonstrate in cognitive experiments on framing and choice: prefer-ence reversals and attitude changes can no longer be attributed to a lack of information, a lack of concern, a lack of attention, low stakes, or the existence of "non-attitudes."

The use of information shortcuts is likewise an inescapable fact of life, and will occur no matter how educated we are, how much information we have, and how much thinking we do. Professionals weighing résumés and past accomplishments against personal interviews, or choosing from an array of diverse objects, have the same problems and use the same shortcuts as voters choosing presidents. What we have called Gresham's law of information—that new and personal information, being easier to use, tends to drive old and impersonal political information out of circulation—applies not only to the inattentive and the uneducated but to all of us. We must therefore stop considering shortcuts pejoratively, as the last refuge of citizens who are uneducated, lacking in the political experience and expertise of their "betters," or cynically content to be freeloaders in our democracy.

Drunkard's Searches and information shortcuts provide an invaluable part of our knowledge and must therefore be considered along with textbook knowl-edge in evaluating any decision-making process. As Abraham Kaplan has noted, the Drunkard's Search—metaphorically, looking for the lost keys under the nearest streetlight—seems bothersome because of the assumption that we should begin any search rationally, in the most likely places rather than in those that are the best lit and nearest to hand. He adds, "But the joke may be on us. It may be sensible to look first in an unlikely place just *because* 'it's lighter there.' . . . The optimal pattern of search does not simply mirror the pattern of probability density of what we seek. We accept the hypothesis that a thing sought is in a certain place because we remember having seen it there, or because it is usually in places of that kind, or for like reasons. But . . . we look in a certain place for additional reasons: we happen to be in the place already, others are looking else-where." At least when people look under the streetlight, they will almost cer-tainly find their keys if they are there; if they look by the car, in the dark, they are far less likely to find them even if they are there.

. . . [W]e should keep in mind the main features about how voters obtain information and reason about their political choices. The Drunkard's Search is an aid to calculation as well as an information shortcut. By telling us where to look, it also tells us how to choose, how to use easily obtained information in making comparisons and choices. As long as this is how we search and choose, people will neither have nor desire all the information about their government that theorists and reformers want them to have.

The faith that increased education would lead to higher levels of textbook knowledge about government, and that this knowledge in turn would enable the electorate to measure up to its role in democratic theory, was misplaced. Education doesn't change *how* we think. Education broadens the voter, because educated voters pay attention to more problems and are more sensitive to connections between their lives and national and international events. However, educated voters still *sample* the news, and they still rely on shortcuts and calculation aids in assessing information, assembling scenarios, and making their choices. Further, an educated, broadened electorate is a more diffuse electorate, an electorate segmented by the very abundance of its concerns. Such an electorate will be harder to form into coalitions. The more divided an electorate, the more time and communication it takes to assemble people around a single cleavage.

Since all citizens sample the news and use shortcuts, they must be judged in part by the quality of the "fire alarms" to which they respond. They must be judged in part by *who* they know and respond to, not simply by *what* they know. Furthermore, this use of fire alarms has an important implication. Since people can only respond to the fire alarms they hear, it matters how the fire alarms to which they are exposed are chosen. If it matters whether the responses to a policy or crisis are mediated electronically by Jesse Jackson and Jesse Helms, or by Bill Bradley and Robert Dole, then attention must be given to how the mediators are chosen by the networks.

11-2

No Compromise: The Electoral Origins of Legislative Gridlock

Gary C. Jacobson

Political scientist Gary Jacobson argues that the polarization of the parties in Congress, and the gridlock it has produced, is a product of elections—that is, of who gets elected and by whom. In recent decades, party realignment in the South and intensified party loyalty throughout the nation have made the coalitions of voters supporting Democrats and Republicans more different. Serving those coalitions has reinforced the polarization of parties in Congress and generated gridlock when party control of the House, Senate, and presidency becomes divided.

DURING THE SUMMER of 2011, congressional Republicans played chicken with the Barack Obama administration over the United States' fiscal future. The Republican strategy, a brainchild of the party's radically conservative Tea Party faction, was to force Obama's Democrats to accept massive cuts in federal spending by refusing to raise the legal debt ceiling if they did not comply. Without a higher debt limit, the government would be unable to borrow enough money to pay all of its bills, threatening national and global economic turmoil. The administration was agreeable to some cuts but insisted on raising revenues—mainly by rescinding tax breaks enjoyed by wealthy individuals and corporations—as part of any deficit reduction package. Republicans adamantly refused to consider any revenue increases.

In the end, both sides blinked. The final agreement raised the debt ceiling enough to assure the government's borrowing capacity until 2013, made much more modest spending cuts than Republicans had initially demanded, and raised no new revenues. It did nothing to address the long-term fiscal challenge posed by the major entitlement programs, Social Security, Medicare, and Medicaid. That chore was handed off to a new bipartisan, bicameral committee of twelve that was supposed to come up with a comprehensive deficit reduction plan and submit it to Congress by November 23; its failure would trigger $1.2 trillion in spending cuts starting January 2013 and extending over the next decade, half from defense, half from domestic programs (excluding the major entitlements).

Source: This piece is an original essay commissioned for this volume.

The committee also failed to break the fiscal gridlock, as Republicans rejected any tax increases and Democrats refused to attack the deficit through cuts alone. With the axe not scheduled to fall until 2013, it was left to the 2012 electorate to resolve the stalemate—although, from the evidence examined in this essay, voters far are more likely to perpetuate than to break it.

Although rarely as dramatic as in the 112th Congress, legislative gridlock is nothing new. The governing institutions set up by the United States Constitution are inherently prone to stalemate and, according to James Madison's famous account in *Federalist* no. 51, designedly so. The bicameral legislature, presidential veto, and the distinct electoral bases and calendars of representatives, senators, and presidents were meant to thwart simple majority rule, and they always have. In abstract terms, the framers imposed high transaction costs (the time, effort, and resources needed to build cross-institutional coalitions to enact laws) in return for low conformity costs (living under new laws passed over one's objection).[1] The Senate's requirement of a supermajority of (at present) 60 votes to overcome filibusters on most types of legislation added yet another barrier to action. As one astute analyst of the American political process has observed, "It is perhaps more surprising that we get policy innovation at all . . . instead of unremitting stalemate."[2]

Both formal and informal studies of legislative gridlock agree on its institutional foundations, but they also find that its actual prevalence depends on the distribution of preferences within and across institutions: the wider the ideological distance between chambers, between partisans within each chamber, or between the president and the median representative or the 41st most distant opposition senator (the so-called "veto pivot"), the smaller the set of mutually agreeable changes in the status quo and thus the higher the likelihood of gridlock. In abstract terms, the greater the distance between participants capable of blocking action on any policy dimension, the wider the range of alternatives to the status quo that fall between their ideal positions and thus cannot pass, because any change within this range represents a move away from one side's ideal point, which it will therefore block.[3]

Ideological distances in turn reflect the preferences of the disparate electoral coalitions responsible for electing the president and each chamber's Democratic and Republican delegations. Institutionally, the potential for gridlock is a constant (barring a rare change in institutional rules); the extent to which that potential is fulfilled depends ultimately on electoral politics. In this essay, I first document the increasing partisan divergence—and thus propensity toward legislative gridlock—in national politics since the 1970s. I then examine and confirm the sturdy electoral underpinnings of this trend. Finally, I focus on politics and policy during the first three years of the Barack Obama administration to illustrate how electoral and congressional politics interact in an era when the conditions for legislative gridlock are at their maximum.

Partisan Polarization in Congress

The propensity for legislative gridlock varies with the ideological distance between the congressional parties; and by every measure, the congressional parties have become increasingly distant from one another since the mid-1970s. One widely used measure of polarization is the distance between the House and Senate parties' median first-dimension DW-Nominate scores (Figure 1).[4] DW-Nominate scores are calculated from all nonunanimous roll-call votes cast during each Congress and locate each member for each Congress on a liberal-conservative scale that ranges from -1.0 to 1.0; the higher the score, the more conservative the member.[5] Since the 1970s, the Republican medians have moved sharply to the right on this scale, Democratic medians rather less sharply to the left, leaving the parties in the 111th Congress (2009–2010) more distant from one another, ideologically, than at any previous time in American history.

Figure 1. Median DW-Nominate Scores of the Congressional Parties 93rd–111th Congresses

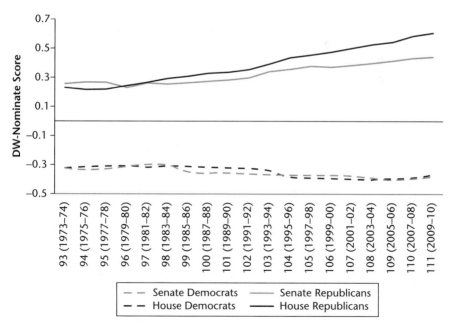

Source: Keith T. Poole at http://voteview.com/pmediant.htm

The potential for more frequent gridlock inherent in these trends is evident from Figures 2a through 2d. Figures 2a and 2b show the distribution of DW-Nominate scores for each House party's members for the two congresses bracketing this period, the 93rd (1973–74) and the 111th (2009–10); figures 2c and 2d display the comparable Senate data. In the 1970s, the distribution of ideological locations of the congressional parties, while clearly distinct, overlapped in the middle. By the first Congress of the Obama administration, every Republican was to the right of every Democrat in both chambers, and the parties' modal positions were much further apart than they had been earlier.[6] As the parties drew apart, the proportion of moderates in each party and chamber—defined here as members near the ideological center with DW-Nominate scores between -0.2 and 0.2—also declined sharply (Figure 3). The change was particularly notable in the House, in which, by this standard, not a single Republican moderate remained after the 2008 election. The proportion of moderate House Democrats increased somewhat after the 2006 and 2008 elections, when the party took several dozen seats in Republican-leaning districts, where any hope of electoral survival required moderation, but 29 of the 41 Democrats with DW-Nominate scores greater than -0.2 were replaced by Republicans in 2010. When the final data are in, the 112th Congress (2011–2012) will almost certainly contain fewer moderates than any Congress in at least the past century.

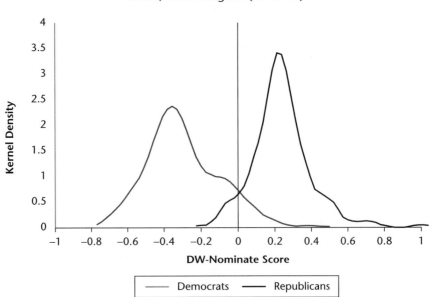

Figure 2a. Ideological Positions on Roll-Call Votes, House, 93rd Congress (1973–74)

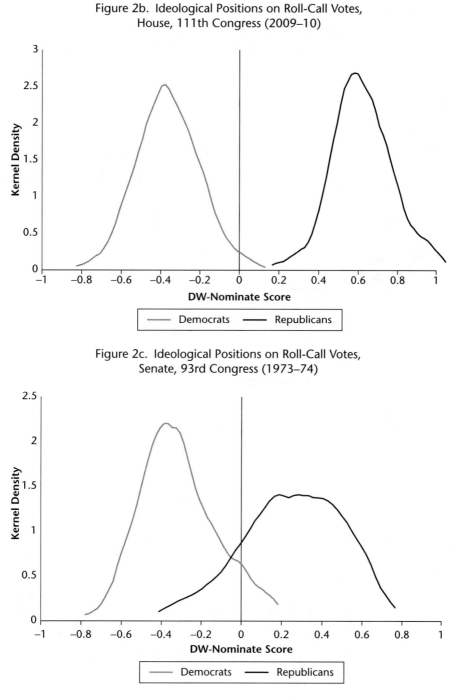

Figure 2b. Ideological Positions on Roll-Call Votes,
House, 111th Congress (2009–10)

Figure 2c. Ideological Positions on Roll-Call Votes,
Senate, 93rd Congress (1973–74)

(Continued)

(Continued)

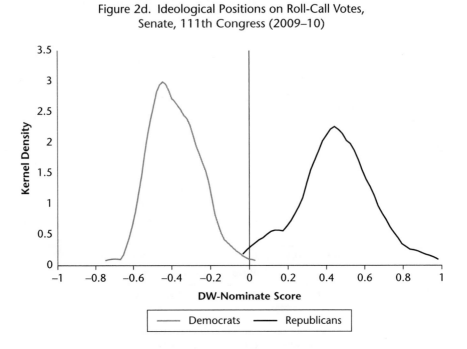

Figure 2d. Ideological Positions on Roll-Call Votes, Senate, 111th Congress (2009–10)

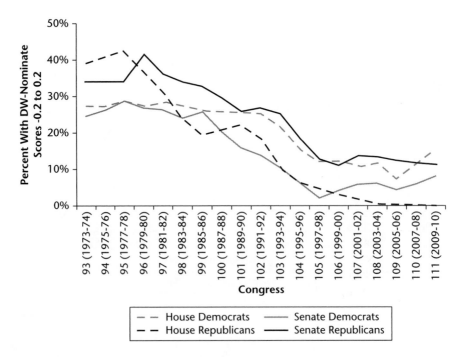

Figure 3. The Disappearance of the Moderates

Another common measure of roll-call voting in Congress—the frequency with which partisans have supported the president's initiatives—reiterates the polarizing trend observed in the DW-Nominate data (Figure 4). Since the 1970s, the president's partisans have become much more consistently supportive of his policies and the other party's partisans much less so, with the partisan gap growing from about 30 to more than 70 percentage points. Party unity in the House and Senate on divisive votes has also risen steadily, reaching its highest point in at least five decades during 111th Congress.[7]

All of these trends point to a heightened propensity for partisan disagreement and a diminished range of politically attainable changes in the direction of national policy when neither party has the votes to impose its will unilaterally—which is almost always the case. Congressional polarization also encourages the unrestrained use of procedural devices to obstruct or to circumvent obstruction that make legislative politics so frustrating and embittering to participants and so ugly to the public.[8]

The Electoral Origins of Congressional Polarization

The congressional parties have been driven apart by a diverse array of interacting internal and external forces. A full account of this complex story is beyond the

Figure 4. Presidential Support in Congress, 93rd–111th Congresses

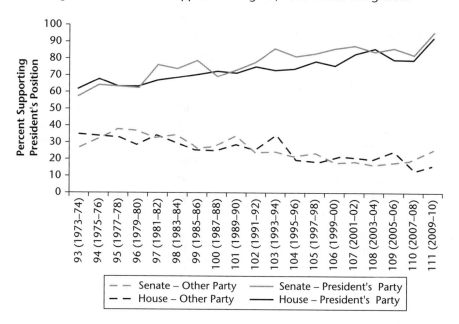

Source: Compiled by George C. Edwards III and posted at http://presdata.tamu.edu, annual scores averaged for each two-year Congress.

scope of this essay,[9] but one essential component has clearly been the corresponding polarization of the congressional parties' respective electoral constituencies. Two major trends have given the congressional parties increasingly divergent electoral coalitions. First, the partisan, ideological, and policy views of voters have grown more internally consistent, more distinctive between parties, and more predictive of voting in national elections.[10] Second, electoral units into which voters are sorted have become more homogeneously partisan.[11] That is, over the last several decades, changes in the preferences, behavior, and distribution of congressional voters have given the congressional parties more internally homogenous, divergent, and polarized electoral bases.

A principal source of this electoral transformation was the historic partisan realignment of the South.[12] The civil rights revolution, and particularly the Voting Rights Act of 1965, brought southern blacks into the electorate as Democrats, while moving conservative whites to abandon their ancestral allegiance to the Democratic party in favor of the ideologically and racially more compatible Republicans. In-migration also contributed to an increasingly Republican electorate, which gradually replaced conservative Democrats with conservative Republicans in southern House and Senate seats. Conservatives whites outside the South also moved toward the Republican Party, while liberals become overwhelmingly Democratic. The level of consistency between party identification and ideology thus grew across the board; in 1972, self-identified liberals and conservatives identified with the "appropriate" party 71 percent of the time; in 2008, they did so 88 percent of the time.[13]

Party loyalty among congressional voters also increased over this period,[14] so the relationship between ideology and voting became much stronger. Figure 5 displays the growing proportion of self-identified liberals and diminishing proportion of self-identified conservatives voting for Democratic candidates for House and Senate in elections since 1972. The shift among conservatives is particularly notable, as is the pivotal role of the 1994 election in solidifying support for Republican candidates among conservatives. In 2010, according to the exit polls, nearly 90 percent of self-identified liberals voted for Democrats in the House elections, while nearly 90 percent of conservatives voted for Republicans.

As a consequence of these trends, the ideological leanings of the parties' respective electoral constituencies—defined as those voters who reported voting for the winning Republican and Democratic House and Senate candidates— have become increasingly divergent (Figure 6). In the 1970s, average ideological differences between the parties' electoral constituencies were modest, about 0.5 points on the National Election Studies' 7-point liberal-conservative scale.[15] By 2008, the ideological gap had more than tripled in both chambers.[16]

The divergence of electoral constituencies is equally striking in aggregate voting data. The presidential vote in a state or district offers a serviceable measure

Figure 5. Ideology and Voting in Congressional Elections, 1972–2010

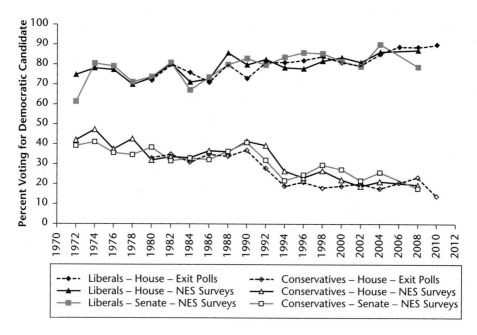

Source: National Election Studies, 1972–2008; "Portrait of the Electorate," *New York Times* (November 13,1994): A15, and National Exit Polls, 1996–2010.

Figure 6. Ideological Divergence of Electoral Constituencies of House and Senate Parties, 1972–2008

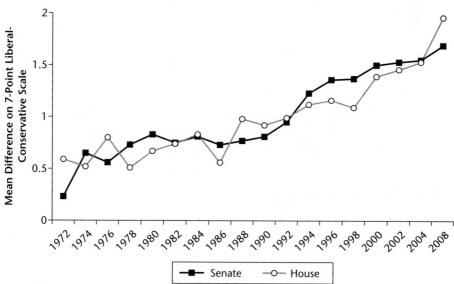

Source: Compiled by author from National Election Studies data.

of its relative political leanings.[17] Figure 7 displays the average difference in the share of the major party presidential votes between districts won by House Democrats and Republicans in elections since 1972 (the midterm data are from the presidential election two years prior). Back in the early 1970s, House districts won by Democrats and Republicans differed in their average presidential vote by only about 7 percentage points, which was a low point for the postwar period. Since then, the gap has tripled, with most of the increase occurring since 1992. In 2010, Obama's (2008) share of the vote in districts won by Democrats was on average 23 percentage points higher than in districts won by Republicans (67 percent compared to 44 percent). A similar though less-pronounced trend appears in comparable Senate data (Figure 8); the divergence is smaller because states tend to be more heterogeneous, politically and otherwise, than House districts. But in both chambers, the congressional party coalitions now represent constituencies that are far more dissimilar, politically, than they did in the 1970s.

Figures 9a and 9b offer an additional perspective on this development that echoes the patterns depicted in Figures 2a and 2b. Figure 9a displays the distribution of the 1972 presidential vote (normalized as a deviation from the major-party vote for the Democrat) in the House districts won by Democrats and

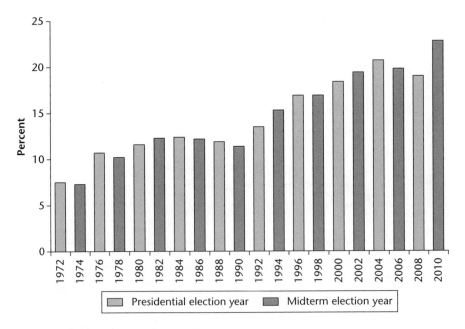

Figure 7. Difference in the Democratic Presidential Vote between Districts Won by Democratic and Republican Representatives, 1972–2010

Source: Compiled by author.

Figure 8. Difference in the Democratic Presidential Vote between States
Won by Democratic and Republican Senators, 1972–2010

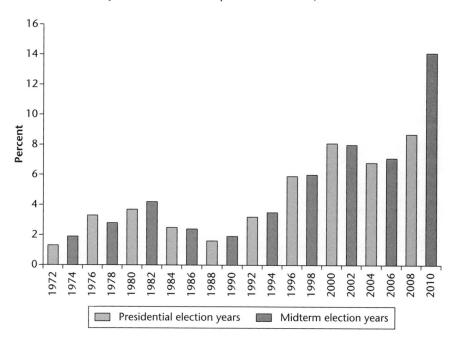

Source: Compiled by author.

Republicans in the 1974 election. Figure 9b does the same (using 2008 presidential data) for the districts won by each party's candidates in 2010. After 1974, each party's delegation represented a set of districts that were largely similar in their political leanings, although some Democrats did represent lopsidedly Democratic (largely urban and minority) districts. The Republicans and Democrats elected in 2010 represent much more politically dissimilar sets of districts. After 1974, 38 percent of House members represented districts where their party's presidential candidate's vote was below its national average; after 2010, only 9 percent did so. Comparable data from the Senate elections of 1974 and 2010 (not shown) reveal the same pattern of change toward more polarized electorates.

Viewed together, these figures suggest a close relationship between the increasing divergence of partisans in Congress and the electorate, and the correlation coefficients listed in Table 1 provide strong support for this interpretation. The correlations over the last four decades between the two measures of House and Senate divergence (differences in average DW-Nominate and presidential support scores calculated from the data in Figures 1 and 4) and the two measures of constituency divergence (the ideological differences in Figure 6 and the district and

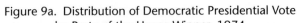

Figure 9a. Distribution of Democratic Presidential Vote
by Party of the House Winner, 1974

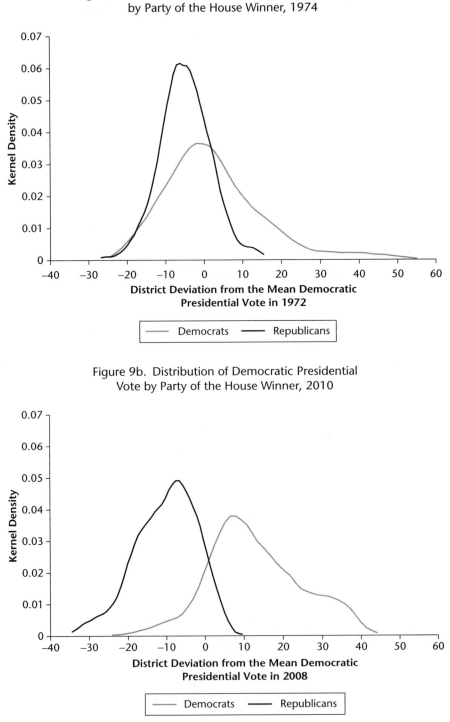

Figure 9b. Distribution of Democratic Presidential
Vote by Party of the House Winner, 2010

Table 1. Electoral and Congressional Polarization, 1972–2010

Correlations Between Congressional Party Differences in:	House	Senate
DW-Nominate scores and local presidential vote	.96	.77
Presidential support scores and local presidential vote	.89	.89
DW-Nominate scores and electoral constituents' ideology	.93	.94
Presidential support scores and electoral constituents' ideology	.88	.90

state presidential vote gaps in Figures 7 and 8) are all very high, averaging 0.90. These measures are silent about the direction of causation, but both logic and evidence point to an interactive process: voters have sorted themselves into political camps by responding to the more sharply differentiated alternatives presented by the national parties and their candidates, while changes in roll-call voting have reflected the parties' increasingly divergent electoral coalitions.[18] Through this inherently interactive process, electoral and congressional politics have coevolved in a way that has made gridlock and stalemate increasingly likely, with consequences fully on display during the first three years of the Obama administration.

Action and Gridlock during the Obama Administration

The Obama administration illustrates both gridlocked politics and the conditions under which gridlock can be broken, even when partisan polarization is at a peak. During the 111th Congress, Obama pushed through a $787 billion economic stimulus package targeting the deep recession he had inherited, initiated comprehensive reforms of the nation's health care system, and signed a major redesign of financial regulation aimed at preventing a repeat of the financial meltdown that had made the recession so severe.[19] Not every major initiative was successful—an ambitious clean energy bill died in the Senate—but these legislative achievements made the 111th Congress among the most productive in many years. What happened to gridlock?

The government managed to avoid gridlock despite the extreme partisan divisions in the House and Senate because Democratic victories in the 2006 and 2008 elections had left them with a 257–178 House margin and between July 2009 and January 2010, a 60–40 majority in the Senate[20] and because a handful of moderate Republicans remained in the Senate. The Democratic House majority was large enough to pass the stimulus, health care reform, and financial regulation bills over nearly unanimous Republican opposition (no Republican voted for the first two bills, only three for the third) despite some Democratic defections (of 7, 34, and 19 members, respectively, on the three bills).

In the Senate, the stimulus bill needed three Republican votes to overcome a filibuster, because two Democratic senators were unavailable.[21] The three votes came from Arlen Specter (who left the Republican Party in April to become an independent, voting organizationally with the Democrats) and the Senate's two most moderate Republicans, both from Maine: Olympia Snowe (DW-Nominate, .040) and Susan Collins (DW-Nominate, .059). The filibuster-breaking vote on health care reform in December 2009, in contrast, was a strictly party line vote, with all 60 Democrats in favor and all 40 Republicans opposed. Democrats lost their 60th Senate vote when Republican Scott Brown won the special election for the late Ted Kennedy's Massachusetts seat in January 2010. Final enactment of health care reform in March 2010 depended on the use of a special budget reconciliation procedure that disallows filibusters.[22] Again, no Republican voted for the bill; with three Democratic defectors, the final vote was 56–43. Finally, financial reform, like the stimulus bill, needed three Republican votes to reach the 60 needed for cloture (Snowe and Collins again, plus Brown).

The Democratic president and congressional majorities were able to act, then, not because they were able to bridge the partisan divide, but because they had, for a time, sufficient votes to proceed in the face of intense Republican opposition (with a little help from the few remaining moderate Senate Republicans). And the Republican opposition was extraordinarily intense. The Obama administration made a concerted effort to win Republican votes on all of these bills, especially the health care legislation, but with the few exceptions noted, completely failed. Failure was assured by the strategy of all-out opposition to Obama that Republican congressional leaders had adopted as their ticket back to majority status. The appeal of that strategy, and its success, is a direct result of electoral realities. Republicans went with the conservatives who dominate their electoral constituencies and whose disdain for Obama preceded his presidency.[23] Any hesitation they may have had about pursuing a deliberate gridlock strategy ended with the emergence of the raucous Tea Party movement, largely an expression of the Republican Party's extreme right wing,[24] whose anger and energy convinced Republican leaders that they had nothing to gain by compromise and potentially much to gain from unbending opposition.

The electoral logic and effect of this strategy can be discerned in survey data from the 2008 and 2010 Cooperative Congressional Election Studies (CCES), which provide large enough national samples to permit analyses at the House district level.[25] Regarding health care reform, the 2008 CCES asked, "Do you favor or oppose the U. S. government guaranteeing health insurance for all citizens, even if it means raising taxes?" About 62 percent of respondents said they supported the idea, 38 percent opposed it, and so it was generally popular at the time. Partisan divisions were substantial, however, with 88 percent of Democrats, 61 percent of independents, but only 23 percent of Republicans supporting such a plan. More important, the distribution of opinion across House voters and districts provided little reason for congressional Republicans to support such a policy. Figure 10 displays the distribution of district-level opinion on the health care question among four sets of respondents: The dotted lines show the distribution of opinion among all constituents across the set of districts won in 2008 by Republicans (black) or Democrats (gray). The solid lines show the distributions for those respondents who said they voted for Republican or Democratic winner—that is, the voters who formed the electoral constituencies of each party's House delegation. Taken as a whole, the two parties' constituencies differed only modestly on this question: In the median Democratic district, 65 percent of respondents supported this kind of health care reform; in the median Republican district, it was 58 percent. The parties' electoral constituencies, in contrast, were thoroughly polarized on the issue: A large majority of House Democrats' electoral constituencies strongly favored the idea, while few of the Republicans' electoral constituencies gave it more than minimal support. Partisan divisions that emerged in Congress on the health care issue were thus firmly rooted in the opinions of those constituents whose opinions matter most to reelection-oriented representatives.

The fierce partisan debate over the health care bill in the months leading up to final passage in 2010 left the public thoroughly divided on its virtues. Ordinary

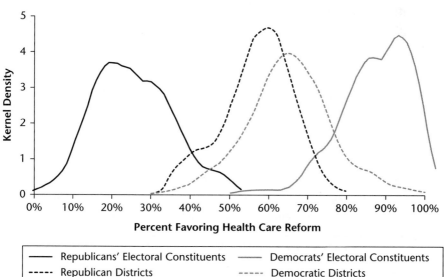

Figure 10. Distribution of Opinions on Health Care Reform
Across U.S. House Districts, 2008

| Republicans' Electoral Constituents | Democrats' Electoral Constituents |
| Republican Districts | Democratic Districts |

Source: 2008 Cooperative Congressional Election Study.

Republicans remained as opposed to the idea as they had been in 2008, while its support dropped a few points among Democrats and quite substantially among independents, which proved costly to Democrats on election day.[26] "Obamacare" was a prime target of the Republicans' 2010 campaigns, which won a 242–193 Republican House majority and reduced the Democrats' Senate majority by six, to 53–47, for the 112th Congress. The election left the House parties' bases even further apart on health care than they had been in 2008 (Figure 11). The average difference between Republican and Democratic districts grew from 8 points to 14 points, the difference between electoral constituencies, from 62 to 75 points. It is thus no surprise that the first bill the House Republican leadership introduced in the 112th Congress was a repeal of the legislation enacted in 2010, nor that it failed. The bill passed the House with the votes of all 242 Republicans and all but three Democrats opposed. It went no further, because every Senate Democrat voted against it and Obama would have vetoed it had it passed. Gridlock prevailed, preserving the new status quo, at least for the time being.

Health care reform generated the widest differences of opinion among the congressional parties' constituencies, but they were also sharply divided on most other items on Obama's legislative agenda. Table 2 lists the distribution of responses to 2010 CCES questions concerning support for seven of his major

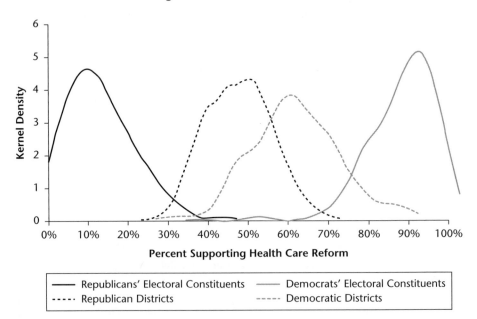

Figure 11. Distribution of Support for Obama's Health Care Reform Legislation Across House Districts, 2010

Source: 2010 Cooperative Congressional Election Study.

initiatives that were subject to roll-call votes in the House.[27] The table distinguishes not only electoral constituents from all constituents but also, within electoral constituencies, the respective parties' primary constituencies, defined as those who voted for the winning candidate and who had also participated in the winner's party's primary in 2010. The threat of primary challenges to members who stray too far from party orthodoxy is thought to be one source of partisan intransigence in Congress, because primaries are low-turnout affairs that attract a disproportionate share of strong partisans and ideologues.[28] This view is supported by the CCES data, particularly for Republicans. On average, across these agenda items, the House parties' full constituencies are only 9 points apart, while their electoral constituencies are 56 points apart and their primary constituencies are 67 points apart.

The message in these data is that insofar as members of Congress faithfully represent the views of the people who put and keep them in office, sharp partisan divisions on roll-call votes will be the norm. The intransigence that produces gridlock is evidence of individual responsiveness and collective responsibility—to the people and parties who actually elect members, if not to their broader constituencies or to the nation as a whole. It is thus no surprise that the 2010 elections, which resulted in House and Senate majorities with unusually disparate electoral bases

Table 2. Constituents' Support for Obama's Agenda (in Percentages)

	House Democrats' Constituents			House Republicans' Constituents		
	Primary	Electoral	All	All	Electoral	Primary
Health Care Reform	91	88	61	48	13	7
Economic Stimulus	87	85	60	48	14	8
Clean Energy	89	86	66	56	25	17
Repeal Don't Ask—Don't Tell	86	84	67	59	35	28
Financial Reform	96	95	75	68	44	36
Stem Cell Research	90	87	69	48	43	35
Children's Health Insurance	95	94	77	71	47	40
Average	91	88	68	57	32	24
Average number supported:	6.4	6.2	4.7	4.1	2.2	1.7

Source: 2010 Cooperative Congressional Election Study; weighted N's range from 3,972 to 20,593.

and thus locations on the ideological spectrum, ushered in a year of spectacular gridlock on budgets, deficits, and other issues regarding the scope of government, for these are issues that fundamentally divide the parties' electoral coalitions.

The 2010 election reinstituted divided government, putting the House in Republican hands and leaving the Democratic Senate majority well short of the 60 votes needed to overcome a filibuster. The resulting sharp increase in the prospects for legislative gridlock is illustrated by the data in Table 3 and Figure 12. The table lists the DW-Nominate scores for holders of the key locations in the legislative process in the 111th and 112th congresses: President Obama,[29] the median members of the House and Senate, the Senate Republican filibuster pivot (the one 41st from the most conservative end of the spectrum), and the chambers' veto pivots (the Democrats ranked 34th and 190th from the liberal end of the spectrum in, respectively, the Senate and House, who would presumably vote to sustain a veto of any legislation to their ideological right). The list also includes the median member of the majority party in the House, another key participant according to the *party cartel* theory, which posits that the House majority uses agenda control to keep any bill off the floor if it is not supported by a majority of the majority members.[30] For the House, the entries for the 112th Congress are estimates derived by recalculating the medians for the 111th Congress under the conservative assumption that the distribution of locations for the new Republican House majority would match that of Republicans in the 111th Congress.[31] For the Senate, the new median was estimated at six positions to the right on the scale for the previous Senate. Figure 12 displays the differences in the ideological locations of the key participants in each of the two congresses.

Table 3. Ideological Location of the Parties in the 111th and 112th Congresses

DW-Nominate Score	111th Congress	112th Congress
Barack Obama	−.431	−.431
House median	−.198	.394
House majority party median	−.370	.604
House veto pivot	−.347	−.225
Senate median	−.263	−.180
Senate Republican filibuster pivot	−.021	.337
Senate Democratic filibuster pivot	−.309	−.309
Senate veto pivot	−.380	−.309

The election brought a huge increase in the ideological distance between the House and Senate medians; the gap is even larger under the *party cartel* scenario, where the House majority party median is supposed to be decisive. The distances between the House floor and majority party medians and the opposite-party Senate filibuster pivot also grew dramatically, as did the distance between the two Senate filibuster pivots. Clearly, the range of changes in the status quo that would be blocked by one chamber or the other and within the Senate greatly increased after the election. The same is true for Obama and the House, particularly under the *party cartel* scenario. The ideological distance between the president and the median Senator grew only modestly, but the gap between the president and the Republican filibuster pivot became much wider. The ideological location at which the president's veto would be overridden moved a bit rightward but remained well to the left of center; even if Republicans had taken the Senate as well as the House in 2010, they would have found it impossible to repeal the health care or financial regulation bills over Obama's objection. The gaps between the House and Senate medians, the Senate parties' filibuster pivots, and the president and the House floor and party medians were all the widest since at least the 93rd Congress.

These dramatically enlarged gridlock intervals severely reduced the range of possible agreements on departures from the status quo. Only where the failure to agree would result, not in continuation of the status quo, but in an outcome completely unacceptable to large majorities on both sides—for example, no budget and hence no money to keep the government running or no increase in the debt ceiling

Figure 12. Ideological Distances between Key Participants
111th and 112th Congresses

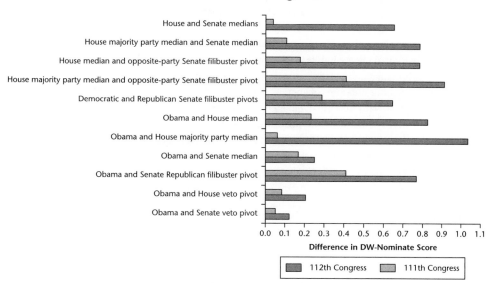

and hence a default on government bonds and chaos in the financial markets—could important legislation pass during the first year of 112th Congress. And even in these cases, the process was unusually ugly. Hence, the partisan disputes over taxes, spending, and deficits that brought the U.S. government to the brink of paper insolvency in the summer of 2011, for example, unified the public on at least one thing: disdain for Congress. Public comments on the process were scathing, with "ridiculous," "disgusting," and "stupid" topping the list of one-word descriptions reported in the July 28–31 Pew Survey.[32] In surveys taken through the rest of the year, disapproval of Congress's performance averaged 83 percent and approval averaged 12 percent; as minority leader Nancy Pelosi remarked on the *Daily Show*, "You wonder who are these people who approve of Congress?"[33] Disapproval of Congress in 2011 was thoroughly bipartisan.[34] It was also predictable; Americans invariably say they detest the kind of partisan bickering and stalemate epitomized by the showdowns and stop-gap measures arising from unresolved fights over the nation's finances in 2011.[35] The irony is that the divisive politics and partisan gridlock they condemn is largely the product of their own electoral decisions and of the winners' fidelity to the people who put them in Congress.

NOTES

1. Samuel Kernell, Gary C. Jacobson, and Thad Kousser, *The Logic of American Politics*, 5th ed. (Washington, DC: CQ Press, 2012), 22–26.

2. Charles Stewart III, *Analyzing Congress* (New York: Norton), 80.

3. Ibid.; Keith Krehbiel, *Pivotal Politics: A Theory of U.S. Lawmaking* (Chicago: University of Chicago Press, 1998); Sarah H. Binder, *Stalemate: Causes and Consequences of Legislative Gridlock* (Washington, DC: The Brookings Institution, 2003); David W. Brady and Craig Volden, *Revolving Gridlock: Politics and Policy from Jimmy Carter to George W. Bush,* 2nd ed. (Boulder CO: Westview Press, 2006).

4. The means and medians are virtually identical in these data and can be used interchangeably for making the points in this section.

5. For an explanation of the methodology for computing these scores and justification for their interpretations measures of liberal–conservative ideology, see Nolan M. McCarty, Keith T. Poole, and Howard Rosenthal, *Income Redistribution and the Realignment of American Politics* (Washington, DC: American Enterprise Institute Press, 1997); and Keith T. Poole and Howard Rosenthal, *Congress: A Political History of Roll Call Voting* (New York: Oxford University Press, 1997), Chapters 3 and 11. The data used here are from Keith T. Poole, at http://voteview.uh.edu/dwnomin.htm, accessed July 12, 2011.

6. The apparent overlap in Figure 2d is an artifact of the kernel density estimator; the most conservative Senate Democrat had a DW-Nominate score of -.021, the most liberal Republican, .040.

7. Gary C. Jacobson, *The Politics of Congressional Elections*, 8th ed. (New York: Pearson, 2012), pp. 261–262.

8. Barbara Sinclair, *Unorthodox Lawmaking: New Legislative Processes in the U.S. Congress*, 4th ed. (Washington, DC: CQ Press, 2012), pp. 141–165.

9. See Barbara Sinclair, *Party Wars: Polarization and the Politics of National Policy Making* (Norman, OK: University of Oklahoma Press, 2006) for a lucid and thorough account.

10. Gary C. Jacobson, "The Electoral Basis of Partisan Polarization in Congress," presented at the Annual Meeting of the American Political Science Association, Washington, DC, August 31–September 3, 2000; Larry M. Bartels, "Partisanship and Voting Behavior, 1952–1996," *American Journal of Political Science* 44 (January 2000):35–50.

11. Jeffrey M., Stonecash, Mark D. Brewer, and Mach D. Mariani, *Diverging Parties: Social Change, Realignment, and Party Polarization* (Boulder, Colorado: Westview Press, 2003); Gary C. Jacobson, *The Politics of Congressional Elections*, 6th ed. (New York: Longman, 2004), pp. 236–243; Matthew Levendusky, *The Partisan Sort: How Liberals Became Democrats and Conservatives Became Republicans* (Chicago: University of Chicago Press, 2009), pp. 38–77; Alan I. Abramowitz, *The Disappearing Center: Engaged Citizens, Polarization, and American Democracy* (New Haven CT: Yale University Press, 2010), pp. 34–61.

12. Earle Black and Merle Black, *Politics and Society in the South* (Cambridge, MA: Harvard University Press, 1987); Paul Frymer, "The 1994 Aftershock: Dealignment or Realignment in the South," in Philip A. Klinkner, ed., *Midterm: The Elections of 1994 in Context* (Boulder, Colorado: Westview Press, 1995), pp. 99–113; Richard Nadeau and Harold W. Stanley, "Class Polarization Among Native Southern Whites, 1952-90," *American Journal of Political Science* 37 (August 1993):900–919; M. V. Hood, III, Quentin Kidd, and Irwin L. Morris, "Of Byrd[s] and Bumpers: Using Democratic Senators to Analyze Political Change in the South, 1960–1995," *American Journal of Political Science* 43 (April 1999):465–487; Martin P. Wattenberg, "The Building of a Republican Regional Base in the South: The Elephant Crosses the Mason-Dixon Line," *Public Opinion Quarterly* 55 (1991):424–31; Charles S. Bullock III, Donna R. Hoffman, and Ronald Kieth Gaddie, "The Consolidation of the White Southern Congressional Vote," *Political Research Quarterly* 58 (June 2005):231–243.

13. Based on analysis of data in the American National Election Study Cumulative Data File; see Gary C. Jacobson, "Partisanship, Money, and Competition: Elections and the Transformation of Congress since the 1970s," in Lawrence C. Dodd and Bruce I. Oppenheimer, eds. *Congress Reconsidered*, 10th ed. (Washington, DC: CQ Press, forthcoming).

14. Jacobson, *Politics of Congressional Elections*, pp. 19–120.

15. The scale points are: extremely liberal, liberal, slightly liberal, middle-of-the-road, slightly conservative, conservative, and extremely conservative.

16. Realignment in the South explains only part of this change, since the gap between Republican and Democratic constituencies outside the South also grew (from 0.7 to 1.6 points in the House and from 0.6 to 1.4 points in the Senate).

17. *Relative* because the differences in district-level votes between election years produced by the ups and downs of party fortunes in presidential elections have to be factored out of the measurement.

18. Gary C. Jacobson, "Polarization in National Politics: The Electoral Connection," in Jon R. Bond and Richard Fleisher, eds., *Polarized Politics: Congress and the President in a Partisan Era* (Washington, DC: CQ Press, 2000), pp. 25–28. Statistical analysis also indicates reciprocal causation; Granger causation tests find significant effects in both directions for three of the four House pairings; in the four Senate pairings, one or the other causal directions is significant (at p<.10 or better) but the direction varies.

19. The specific bills were the American Recovery and Reinvestment Act of 2009, signed into law on February 17, 2009; the Patient Protection and Affordable Care Act, signed on

March 22, 2010; and the Dodd–Frank Wall Street Reform and Consumer Protection Act, signed on July 21, 2010. 20.   The Democratic total includes two independents who vote to organize with the Democrats.

21. Ted Kennedy of Massachusetts because of illness, Al Franken of Minnesota because his disputed election kept him from taking his seat until July 7.

22. Sinclair, *Unorthodox Lawmaking*, pp. 210–230.

23. Gary C. Jacobson, "Obama and the Polarized Public," in James A. Thurber, ed., *Obama in Office: The First Two Years* (Boulder, CO: Paradigm Publishers, 2011), pp. 19–40.

24. Gary C. Jacobson, "The President, the Tea Party, and the Voting Behavior in 2010: Insights From the Cooperative Congressional Election Study," presented at the Annual Meeting of the American Political Science Association, Seattle, Washington, September 1–4, 2011.

25. The 2008 CCES included 32,800 respondents; the 2010 CCES, 55,399 respondents. For details on these surveys, see Stephen Ansolabehere, "Guide to the 2008 Cooperative Congressional Elections Survey," Harvard University, 2009, draft of February 9, 2009; Stephen Ansolabehere, *Cooperative Congressional Election Study, 2010: Common Content*. [Computer File] Release 1: May 17, 2011, Cambridge, MA: Harvard University [producer] http://projects.iq.harvard.edu/cces

26. Jacobson, "Obama and the Polarized Public," p. 31.

27. Except for the stem cell bill, which was never brought to a vote.

28. Levendusky, *Partisan Sort*, 135–136.

29. The president's DW-Nominate score is calculated from his stated positions, if any, on bills before Congress.

30. Gary W. Cox and Mathew D. McCubbins, *Setting the Agenda: Responsible Party Government in the U.S. House of Representatives* (New York: Cambridge University Press, 2005), pp. 37–49; and "Agenda Power in the House of Representatives, 1877–1986," in David W. Brady and Mathew D. McCubbins, eds., *Party, Process, and Political Change in Congress: New Perspectives on the History of Congress* (Stanford CA: Stanford University Press, 2002), pp. 113–118.

31. With its influx of Tea Party favorites, the Republican House median is probably more conservative than this estimate; the actual data will become available after the end of the 112th Congress.

32. Results reported at http://people-press.org/files/legacy-questionnaires/08-1-11%20Topline%20For%20Release.pdf, accessed November 11, 2011.

33. *The Daily Show with Jon Stewart*, broadcast November 9, 2011; at http://www.thedailyshow.com/watch/wed-november-9-2011/nancy-pelosi, accessed December 20, 2011.

34. The question was asked in 21 surveys between August and December; see "Congress—Job Rating," at http://www.pollingreport.com/CongJob.htm, accessed December 20, 2011; Frank Newport, "Congress' Job Approval Entrenched at Record Low of 13%," at http://www.gallup.com/poll/150728/Congress-Job-Approval-Entrenched-Record-Low.aspx, accessed November 14, 2011.

35. John R. Hibbing and Elizabeth Theiss-Morse, *Congress as Public Enemy: Public Attitudes Toward American Political Institutions* (New York: Cambridge University Press, 1995), pp. 16–20.

11-3

from *Air Wars*

Darrell M. West

*Complaints about negative advertising, voter manipulation, and ever-mount-
ing costs are voiced in all national, and most statewide, election campaigns.
Many voters describe campaign advertising as misleading and as not providing adequate information about the candidates. In this essay, Darrell West
reviews the criticisms of modern campaigns and describes the strategies and
mechanics of television advertising in political campaigns.*

IT WAS A HISTORIC ELECTION. After defeating Sen. Hillary Clinton for the
Democratic nomination and triumphing over Republican nominee John McCain,
Sen. Barack Obama made history by becoming America's first African American
president. Noting that the country was mired in a financial meltdown and
engulfed in controversial wars in Iraq and Afghanistan, Obama broadcast advertisements explaining that he represented "Change We Can Believe In." His commercials linked McCain to unpopular GOP President George W. Bush with the
slogan "More of the Same." Employing McCain's own words from the nominating process, Obama put forth that the Arizona senator supported Bush 90 percent
of the time on legislative votes.

For his part, McCain ran a scorched earth strategy that characterized Obama
as a vacuous celebrity similar to Paris Hilton and Britney Spears, then as someone who palled around with domestic terrorists, and finally as a tax-and-spend
liberal whose philosophy bordered on socialism. One ad hammered Obama with
the attack of "Higher Taxes. More Spending. Not Ready." In the end, though,
people's fears about the national economy led Obama to a 52 percent to 46 percent margin win over his Republican rival.

As illustrated throughout the campaign, advertisements are a major component of political races. In recent presidential campaigns, campaign spots accounted
for the largest item in total fall expenditures.[1] Commercials are used to shape
citizens' impressions and affect news coverage.[2] As such, they represent a major
strategic tool for campaigners. However, not all spots produce the same results.
Some ads work; others do not. To determine which spots are effective, analysts

Source: Darrell M. West, "Overview of Ads," from *Air Wars: Television Advertising in Election Campaigns,
1952–2008*, 5th ed. (Washington, D.C.: CQ Press: 2010), 1–24.

must look at production techniques, ad buys (the frequency and location of ad broadcasting), opposition responses, news coverage, and citizens' predispositions. Through detailed studies of ad campaigns since the 1950s, this book shows how to assess ad messages, media coverage of ads, and ad impact on voters.

The History of Ads

From the earliest days of the Republic, communications devices have been essential to political campaigns. In 1828, handbills distributed by Andrew Jackson's supporters portrayed John Quincy Adams as "driving off with a horse-whip a crippled old soldier who dared to speak to him, to ask an alms." A circular distributed by Adams's forces, meanwhile, attacked Jackson for "ordering other executions, massacring Indians, stabbing a Samuel Jackson in the back, murdering one soldier who disobeyed his commands, and hanging three Indians."[3]

The method, though perhaps not the tone, of communicating with the electorate has changed dramatically since 1828. Handbills have virtually disappeared. Radio became the most popular vehicle in the 1920s and 1930s. After World War II, television emerged as the advertising medium of choice for political candidates. And now, in the twenty-first century, the media marketplace has fragmented into a bewildering variety of communication channels from cable television and talk radio to late-night entertainment shows and the World Wide Web. A new Internet-based lexicon has appeared that distinguishes banner ads (large boxes that span the top of a Web site), interstitial ads (spots that flash while a Web site is being loaded), pop-up ads (spots that appear after a Web site is loaded), transactional ads (spots that allow viewers to make a purchase or request information), and rich media ads (spots that have audio, video, or motion embedded within them).[4] Somehow, in this multifaceted situation, candidates must figure out how to reach voters who will decide key election contests.

The 1952 presidential campaign was the first one to feature television ads. In that year, each party ran television and print ads evoking World War II memories. Republicans, in an effort to support Gen. Dwight Eisenhower and break two decades of Democratic control, reminded voters in a *New York Times* ad that "one party rule made slaves out of the German people until Hitler was conquered by Ike." Not to be outdone, Democratic ads informed voters that "General Hindenburg, the professional soldier and national hero, [was] also ignorant of domestic and political affairs. . . . The net result was his appointment of Adolf Hitler as Chancellor."[5]

In the 1960s, television spots highlighted differences in candidates' personal traits. The 1964 presidential campaign with Lyndon Johnson and Barry Goldwater was one of the most negative races since the advent of television. Johnson's campaign characterized Goldwater as an extremist not to be trusted with America's future. One five-minute ad, "Confession of a Republican," proclaimed, "This man scares me. . . . So many men with strange ideas are working for Goldwater."[6] Johnson's "Daisy" ad made a similar point in a more graphic manner. Along with speeches and news coverage, the visual image of a mushroom cloud rising behind a little girl picking daisies in a meadow helped raise doubts about Goldwater's fitness for office in the nuclear age, even though a firestorm of protest forced the ad off the air after only one showing.

Ads in the 1970s and 1980s took advantage of public fear about the economy. When the United States started to experience the twin ills of inflation and unemployment, a phenomenon that led experts to coin a new word, *stagflation,* campaign commercials emphasized economic themes. In 1980, Republican challenger Ronald Reagan effectively used ads to criticize economic performance under President Jimmy Carter. When the economy came roaring back in 1984, Reagan's serene "Morning in America" ad communicated the simple message that prosperity abounded and the United States was at peace.

The 1988 presidential contest was the zenith of attack politics in the post–World War II period. This campaign illustrated the powerful ability of ads to alter impressions of a candidate who was not well known nationally. Early in the summer of 1988, Massachusetts governor Michael Dukakis held a 17-percentage-point lead over his Republican rival, then vice president George H.W. Bush. Women preferred Dukakis over Bush by a large margin, and the governor was doing well among blacks, elderly citizens, and Democrats who previously had supported Reagan.

Meanwhile, Republicans were test marketing new advertising material. Over Memorial Day weekend in Paramus, New Jersey, Bush aides Jim Baker, Lee Atwater, Roger Ailes, Robert Teeter, and Nicholas Brady stood behind a one-way mirror observing a small group of so-called Reagan Democrats. Information concerning Willie Horton, a convicted black man who—while on furlough from a Massachusetts prison—brutally raped a white woman, was being presented, and the audience was quite disturbed. Atwater later boasted to party operatives, "By the time this election is over, Willie Horton will be a household name."[7] Bush went on to beat Dukakis 53 percent to 46 percent.

The 1992 campaign represented the dangers of becoming overly reliant on attack ads and the power of thirty-minute "infomercials" by Reform Party candidate Ross Perot. Throughout the race, Bush used ads to attack Democratic nominee Bill Clinton's character and his record as governor of Arkansas. But unlike in his 1988 race, Bush did not prevail. The poor economy, the backlash that developed against Bush's advertising attacks, and Clinton's quick responses to criticisms led to Clinton beating Bush 43 percent to 38 percent. Perot finished in third place with 19 percent, the best showing for a third-party candidate since Theodore Roosevelt in 1912.

In 1996, President Clinton coasted to reelection through the help of ads broadcast more than a year before the election. With the advice of political strategist Dick Morris, Clinton defied the conventional wisdom arguing against early advertising. He ran ads both on television and over the Internet that positioned him as the bulwark against GOP extremism. Linking Republican nominee Bob Dole to unpopular House Speaker Newt Gingrich, Clinton portrayed the Republican Party as insensitive to women, children, and minorities and not to be trusted with important issues such as Social Security, Medicare, and education.

In 2000, Al Gore and George W. Bush ran in the closest presidential election in decades. Featuring cautious advertising that played to undecided voters, each candidate, along with outside groups, ran commercials that challenged the integrity and experience of the other. Bush emphasized education reform, whereas Gore focused on health care and Social Security. One Bush ad, popularly known as "RATS," featured the first use of a subliminal message in presidential campaign history when the word *RATS* was superimposed over a few frames criticizing Gore's prescription drug plan.[8] The election even saw a remake of the infamous 1964 "Daisy" ad ("Daisy II"), when a group of Texans paid for an ad with an image of a girl plucking petals off a daisy while an announcer complained that because of Clinton–Gore deals with "communist Red China" in return for campaign contributions, Democrats had compromised the country's security and made the nation vulnerable to Chinese missile attacks.

In 2004, Bush used images of firefighters carrying victims away from the World Trade Center to explain how he was a "tested" individual who could provide steady leadership in turbulent times. At the same time, he characterized his opponent, Democrat John Kerry, as an unprincipled and untrustworthy "flip-flopper." The campaign produced a commercial showing Senator Kerry wind-surfing while a narrator intoned, "In which direction would John Kerry lead? Kerry voted for the Iraq War, opposed it, supported it, and now opposes it again. . . . John Kerry: Whichever way the wind blows."[9] Kerry, meanwhile, attacked Bush's economic record and complained about Bush's foreign policy. One advertisement said "only Herbert Hoover had a worse record on jobs." Another spot showed a picture of Saudi Crown Prince Abdullah and suggested that "the Saudi royal family gets special favors, while our gas prices skyrocket."[10]

The 2008 presidential campaign represented one of the most wide-open races in decades. There was no incumbent or heir-apparent on the ballot of either major party. The result was that eight Democrats and nine Republicans sought their party's nomination. This included a woman (Hillary Clinton), an African American (Barack Obama), a Hispanic (Bill Richardson), a Mormon (Mitt Romney), and a former prisoner of war (John McCain). Between the primaries and the general election, the airwaves were saturated with political commercials. In the fall, McCain attacked Obama in terms of policy vision, lack of foreign policy experience, and personal associations. Obama, meanwhile, said McCain represented "Bush's Third Term" and that his GOP rival was not the party maverick he claimed to be.

Throughout these elections, commercials were a valuable lens on the inner workings of each campaign. Candidates revealed crucial aspects of their vision, leadership style, and substantive positions. As stated by Elizabeth Kolbert, then a news reporter for the *New York Times,* "Every advertising dollar spent represents a clue to a campaign's deepest hopes and a potential revelation about its priorities."[11]

Principles of Advertising

Strategists use the principles of stereotyping, association, demonization, and code words to influence the electorate. A *stereotype* refers to a common portrait or an oversimplified judgment that people hold toward groups or sets of individuals. For example, Republicans are often portrayed as strong on defense, but not very compassionate toward poor people. Democrats are viewed as caring and compassionate toward the downtrodden, but overly eager to raise taxes. Because television ads are brief, generally no more than thirty seconds, campaigners evoke stereotypes knowing they appeal to voters' prejudices and commonly held views.

However, ads cannot create perceptions that do not already exist in people's minds. There must be a kernel of truth in the stereotype for these types of appeals to be effective. If people do not already think that college professors are absentminded, nurses are caring, or car salespeople are sleazy, it is hard for election ads to play to these kinds of sentiments.

Association is based on linking a candidate or cause to some other idea or person. Politicians love to connect themselves to widely esteemed popular objects while tying their opponents to things that are unpopular, controversial, or divisive. Flags, patriotism, and prominent celebrities are examples of objects with which candidates surround themselves. In contrast, opponents are pictured with unpopular causes or organizations or cast in a light that bonds them to unfavorable objects such as higher taxes, funding cuts for social programs, and ties to fringe groups or corporate "big money."[12]

During the Cold War, it was popular to portray leftist-leaning candidates as communist sympathizers having allegiance to foreign powers. When Kerry received the Democratic nomination, opponents sought to tie him to controversial Vietnam War protester, actress Jane Fonda. The Swift Boat Veterans for Truth ran an ad entitled "Friends" that asserted, "even before Jane Fonda went to Hanoi to meet with the enemy and mock America, John Kerry secretly met with enemy leaders in Paris. . . . Jane Fonda apologized for her activities, but John Kerry refuses to."[13]

In the campaign for the 2008 Democratic presidential nomination, Hillary Clinton used association techniques to tie Obama to controversial African American minister Jeremiah Wright, Obama's hometown minister at Trinity United Church of Christ in Chicago. Using videos of Wright complaining that America was "the No. 1 killer in the world" and that the U.S. government had "started the AIDS virus," she suggested that Obama was outside the political meanstream because he associated with such a controversial speaker.[14]

The 2008 general election saw a similar tactic on the part of McCain. The GOP nominee attempted to link Obama to former 1960s radical William Ayers. Noting that Ayers had admitted to participating in a police station bombing in 1970 and that Obama had held a benefit coffee at Ayers's home in 1995 during his first run for public office, McCain said that this personal link between the men proved that Obama was too extreme for America and not to be trusted.

However, after endorsements by Warren Buffett and Colin Powell, Obama ran spots touting support by these prominent Americans and used these associations to make the point that he represented a safe choice for America. Combined with his own calm demeanor and steady voice, Obama defused what could have come to be seen as negative associations with controversial figures.

To gain credibility, politicians like to associate themselves with such popular people as public figures, sports heroes, astronauts, or Hollywood celebrities. These individuals come from outside the political world and often have a great deal of mainstream influence and respect. By associating with them and winning their endorsements, politicians attempt to piggyback onto the high credibility these individuals have among voters in general.[15]

Demonization is the process of turning an opponent into an evil being or satanic figure. Wartime enemies are condemned as murderers, terrorists, or barbarians. Political opponents are portrayed as extremists out of touch with the mainstream or guilty of immoral behavior. Adversaries are identified with policy actions that are widely condemned or seen as socially destructive.

For example, an entry in an anti-Bush ad contest sponsored by the MoveOn .org Voter Fund intermingled pictures of Adolf Hitler and George W. Bush making speeches. In a clear effort to demonize the sitting president, the spot concluded with the tagline, "What were war crimes in 1945 is foreign policy in 2003."[16]

Meanwhile, commercials sponsored by the Progress for America Voter Fund, a conservative political action committee, attacked Kerry by showing pictures of Osama bin Laden and September 11 hijacker Mohamed Atta. The unmistakable message in these spots was that Kerry was not to be trusted with defending America's security.[17]

As with the other principles, demonizing the opposition is a tactic that must be used carefully. There must be some believability in the specific appeal for an ad to have credibility. One cannot simply make charges that are unsubstantiated or so far out of bounds as to exceed voters' ability to internalize them. Demonization must bear some resemblance to the facts for this tactic to influence citizens.

Code words are shorthand communication devices that play on common stereotypes and connotations associated with particular kinds of language. Even in the limited space of thirty seconds, campaigns can use short messages to communicate broader messages to the public. Many people feel that thirty seconds is too brief a period to convey much in the way of substantive themes, but during election campaigns, single words or expressions can take on enormous importance.

For example, in the 1960s and 1970s, Republicans used the phrase "law and order" to play to voter conceptions that Democrats were permissive on crime, race, and morality, whereas Republicans could be counted on to protect the social order. Democrats were paired with images and voice-overs of urban riots and social protests to convey complex political messages.

Democrats, meanwhile, have used a similar tactic in regard to the code word of *right wing*. Following the surprise GOP takeover of the House and Senate in 1994 and Newt Gingrich's ascension to the Speakership, Democrats played to voter stereotypes about Republicans being uncaring and insensitive. Using examples of extreme rhetoric and policy proposals that sought to slow the rate of increase in spending on various federal programs, Democrats associated GOP candidates with unsympathetic and extremist images. Throughout the country in 2000, House Democrats used the phrase *right-wing extremists* to refer to their Republican counterparts.[18]

Code words are powerful communication devices because they allow voters to associate a particular message with a specific code word. One of the most frequently used code words has been *liberal* by Republicans. In 1988, George Bush Sr. called Democratic candidate Dukakis a liberal thirty-one times in his speeches. The message got through to voters. Whereas 31 percent in May 1988 believed Dukakis was liberal, the figure rose to 46 percent by September 1988.

In 1992, Bush's use of the term *liberal* rose to sixty-two times. Similar to 1988, the word took on a number of negative meanings, such as being fiscally irresponsible, soft on crime, and dangerously out of touch with the American public. This approach allowed Bush to condemn Clinton with the single word liberal without having to voice more detailed descriptions of his opponent's position.[19]

By 1996, the country's airwaves were filled with ads using the *L*-word. Dole ran ads condemning Clinton as a tax-and-spend liberal and as someone whose failed policies were liberal. In one speech in September 1996, Dole used the word fourteen times. Republican congressional candidates used the same appeal all across the country. Ads financed by the Republican National Committee criticized Democratic House and Senate candidates as "liberals," "ultra-liberals," "super-liberals," "unbelievably liberal," "embarrassingly liberal," "foolishly liberal," and "taxingly liberal." Because of the country's changed political climate after the abortive Republican Revolution to downsize government, though, the use of the word liberal as an epithet did not resonate with voters. As one voter in a focus group put it, the term liberal meant helping people. Others felt that "liberal is having an open mind."

This view was supported in a 1996 CBS News/*New York Times* survey asking people what they thought of when they heard someone described as liberal or conservative, respectively. The most common responses for liberal were open minded (14 percent), free spending (8 percent), high degree of government involvement (7 percent), helps people (5 percent), and pro-handouts (5 percent). The most common responses for conservative were fiscally responsible (17 percent), closed minded (10 percent), careful (8 percent), against change (7 percent), and low degree of government involvement (6 percent).[20]

In the 2004 campaign, however, use of the *liberal* epithet returned to the campaign trail. President George W. Bush criticized Kerry for advocating a return to "massive new government agencies" with power over health care. Through an ad showing a map of a complex federal bureaucracy, Bush charged that Kerry's health care program would cause "rationing" and that "Washington bureaucrats, not your doctor, [would] make final decisions on your health."[21] In addition, the Republican National Committee sent a mass mailing to voters in Arkansas and West Virginia accusing "liberals" of seeking to ban the Bible in order to promote policies on gay marriage.[22]

With conservative disgust over the decision of the French government not to support the war in Iraq, the 2004 election introduced the code word *French* to political discourse. Not only did some lawmakers seek to rename French fries "freedom fries," Bush's Commerce secretary, Don Evans, accused Kerry of looking "French" because he spoke the language, was cosmopolitan, and had French relatives.[23] The National Rifle Association also associated Kerry with France by using a mailing with a French poodle wearing a Kerry campaign sweater and having a bow in its hair to condemn the Democrat's record.[24]

As explained by Françoise Meltzer, a humanities professor at the University of Chicago, in the 2004 electoral context, "French really means un-American." It was a striking contrast to earlier periods, when France was viewed favorably in the United States because it had aided the thirteen colonies during the American Revolution and given America the gift of the Statue of Liberty.[25]

The 2008 presidential election was a code word bonanza. Democrats argued that McCain was an "out of touch" politician who didn't even use a computer or e-mail. Meanwhile, Republicans complained that Obama was a liberal or even a socialist, and that he associated with domestic terrorists. Obama sought to disarm these attacks by joking at the end of the campaign that some people thought he was a secret communist because he'd "shared [his] toys in kindergarten."[26]

How Ads Are Put Together

Production techniques for commercials have improved dramatically since the 1950s. Early ads were rudimentary by contemporary standards. Political spots often took the form of footage from press conferences or testimonials from prominent citizens. Many were of the "talking head" variety in which the candidate (or his or her supporter) looked straight into the camera and spoke for thirty or sixty seconds without any editing.

Contemporary ads, in contrast, are visually enticing. Technological advances in television and on the Internet allow ad producers to use colorful images and sophisticated editing techniques to make spots more compelling. Images can be spliced together, and animated images visually transpose one person into another in a split second using a technique called "morphing." As we see in the next sections, catchy visuals, music, and color capture viewer attention and convey particular political messages in a variety of ways.

Visual Images

The visual aspect of advertising is the most important part of commercials. According to the old adage, a picture is worth a thousand words. Contemporary ads use graphic imagery to grab the public's attention and convey messages. Whereas traditional research focused on the spoken content of ads to determine ways of conveying messages, modern analysts study both audio and visual aspects of advertising.

Candidates often attempt to undermine political opponents by associating them with unfavorable visuals. A 1990 campaign ad by Sen. Bennett Johnston, D-La., against his opponent, state representative David Duke, showed pictures of Duke addressing a Ku Klux Klan rally in the presence of a burning cross to make his point that Duke was an extremist who should not be elected to a seat in the U.S. Senate.

A similar phenomenon happened in 1996. Taking advantage of House Speaker Newt Gingrich's unpopularity, Democrats across the United States broadcast ads showing pictures of Gingrich side by side with Bob Dole and House and Senate Republican candidates. The message was clear: A vote for the Republican Dole was a vote for Gingrich.

In 2000, George W. Bush positioned himself as a "compassionate conservative" and frequently appeared at election rallies with retired general Colin Powell, a popular African American leader who later became Bush's secretary of state. Bush surrounded himself in photo opportunities and ads with women, minorities, and children to convey the idea he was a different kind of Republican than Gingrich. For his part, Gore relied on pictures of himself with his wife, Mary Elizabeth (Tipper) Gore, to communicate the idea that he was a candidate with firm values and a strong marriage. It was a way to distinguish himself from the personal scandals of the Clinton era.

In 2004, terrorism was mentioned in 13 percent of all the ads run after Labor Day.[27] Some advertisements mentioned Osama bin Laden by name or showed pictures of him. One Republican Senate candidate in Wisconsin even invoked the visual image of a burning World Trade Center on September 11, 2001, to charge that "Russ Feingold voted against the Patriot Act and the Department of Homeland Security."[28]

However, by 2008, public fear over domestic terrorism had faded. In his campaign for the Republican presidential nomination, former New York City mayor Rudy Giuliani attempted to play to citizen concerns by broadcasting ads reminding people of 9/11. But unlike 2004, when these fears helped Bush win reelection, visual images of past terrorist attacks did not resonate with voters; the electorate was much more worried about the economy.

Indeed, the powerful imagery in the fall general election centered on the economy. With the startling meltdown of major financial institutions in the weeks leading up to the November election, voters saw major companies failing or merging and an extraordinary amount of taxpayer dollars infused into banks and insurance companies. Images of unemployed workers, people losing health benefits, and senior citizens forced to scrimp on needed prescription drugs were commonplace. Through these and other devices, Obama effectively tied McCain to Bush and negative perceptions about the Republican Party's economic policies.

The visual aspect of campaign advertising is important because it is the one that has the most impact on viewers. The reason is simple—people remember visuals longer than they do spoken words. Images also have the advantage of creating an emotional response much more powerful than that which results from hearing the spoken word.

CBS news reporter Lesley Stahl tells the story of a hard-hitting evening news piece broadcast on Reagan's presidency in 1984. The story claimed that Reagan had done certain things, such as cut the budget for the elderly, that were contrary to what he said he had done. Accompanying the story was a series of pleasant visual images of Reagan "basking in a sea of flag-waving supporters, beaming beneath red-white-and-blue balloons floating skyward, sharing concerns with farmers in a field." After the story aired, Stahl was surprised by a favorable telephone call from a top Reagan assistant. Asked why he liked the story, given her harsh words, the Reagan adviser explained she had given the White House four and a half minutes of positive pictures of President Reagan: "They don't hear what you are saying if the pictures are saying something different."[29]

Visual Text

Visual text is a print message appearing onscreen, generally in big, bold letters. Printed messages grab viewers' attention and tell them to pay attention to an ad. As an example, Ross Perot's 1992 ads used visual text scrolling up the screen to persuade the American public to vote for him. Spots for Clinton in 1996 used big, splashy text onscreen to make the political point that Republicans wanted to "CUT MEDICARE." Dole sought to characterize Clinton as "LIBERAL" and "UNTRUSTWORTHY." In 2000, Democratic ads often noted that Texas ranked "50TH" in family health care, and Republican ads complained that Gore was guilty of "EXAGGERATIONS." Republican ads against Obama in 2008 superimposed text such as "INEXPERIENCED" or "NOT READY" to argue that the Democrat lacked the necessary credentials for the chief executive position. Obama countered by saying that McCain was "More of the Same." Advertisers have found that memory of a message is greatly enhanced by combining visual text with spoken words and descriptive images.

Music and Sounds

Music sets the tone for an ad. Just as party hosts use upbeat music to accompany festivities or an educational institution plays "Pomp and Circumstance" to set the scene for a graduation ceremony, campaign ads use music to convey the mood of a particular commercial.

Uplifting ads use cheery music to make people feel good about a candidate. For example, the 1984 campaign featured an independently produced ad called "I'm Proud To Be an American" that used music from country singer Lee Greenwood's song by that same name. The music played over scenes of Reagan, the American flag, and cheerful scenes of happy Americans. It conveyed the message that things were good in America and people should vote for Reagan.

Conversely, somber or ominous music in an ad seeks subliminally to undermine support for the opponent. In George H.W. Bush's "Revolving Door" ad in 1988, dark and threatening music accompanied scenes of prisoners walking through a revolving door while an announcer attacked Dukakis's record on crime. The sounds of drums, the footsteps of guards on metal stairs, and threatening voices were integral to the ad's message that voters should reject Dukakis in the November election because he was soft on crime.

Color

Color communicates vivid messages in ads. Media consultants use bright colors to associate their candidates with a positive image and grayish or black and white to associate opponents with a negative image. In 2000, for example, the NAACP-sponsored spot about the dragging death of James Byrd was broadcast in black and white to make the point that something dramatically different and calamitous had taken place and viewers should pay close attention.

The 1992 Bush campaign developed an ad called "Arkansas Record" that featured a vulture looking out over a dark and barren landscape to make its point that Clinton had poorly governed Arkansas. That year, Bush also used a low-quality, grayish photographic negative of Clinton from an April 20, 1992, *Time* magazine cover to exhort voters to defeat the Arkansas governor in November. The cover with the photographic negative of Clinton was entitled, "Why Voters Don't Trust Clinton." Bush's ad juxtaposed a nice color image of himself to reinforce the message that voters should not vote for Clinton.

A 1996 Dole commercial took a color videotape clip in which Clinton said if he had it to do over again, he would inhale marijuana, and rebroadcast the image in black and white to make Clinton look sinister. The opposite technique (going from black and white to color) was used by Gore in his 2000 ad called "Veteran." It opened with a black and white photo of a youthful Gore in Vietnam, then shifted to color frames of Gore with Tipper.

Editing

Editing determines the sequencing and pacing of an ad. The *sequencing* of ad images refers to how images in one scene are related to following scenes. For example, the

1984 Reagan ad "Morning in America" showed images of Reagan interspersed with scenes of Americans at work and a country at peace. The sequencing linked the president with the popular themes of peace and prosperity. These images were accompanied by music that enhanced the emotional impact of the ad.

An Obama attack ad in 2008 showed a shifty-eyed McCain grimacing, raising his eyebrows, and smiling awkwardly to suggest he was not the right man for the presidency. At a time of domestic crisis, according to the spot, the United States needed someone better equipped to handle economic and foreign policy issues.

The *pacing* of an ad refers to whether the images flow smoothly or abruptly from scene to scene. Abrupt cuts from image to image create a jarring effect that tells viewers something bad is appearing before them. Such cuts are commonly used to convey negative feelings in attack ads.

Voice-Overs

Through an off-screen announcer, a voice-over provides a road map that knits together visual scenes. A campaign ad is composed of different pictures that convey particular points. The announcer guides viewers through these scenes to clearly communicate the message of the ad.

Typically, attack ads use male announcers to deliver blistering criticisms, but Dole made history in 1996 by using a female announcer to condemn Clinton's "failed liberal drug policies." The use of a woman for the voice-over was designed to soften any potential backlash from going on the attack and to appeal to women concerned about drug use and moral permissiveness in American society.

However, in 2000, both George W. Bush and Gore reverted to the historical pattern and relied more frequently on male announcers for the audio components of their ads. One exception was a Bush ad called "Compare," which used a female announcer to criticize Gore's prescription drug plan. Female narrators are used for health care ads because market research reveals that women make the preponderance of health care decisions in U.S. households. Another exception took place in 2004 during a Bush ad known as "Wolves." This spot used the image of a pack of wolves to argue that the United States was surrounded by dangerous enemies. It used a female announcer to take the edge off what was a hard-hitting attack on the opposition.

How Ads Are Financed

The financing of campaign ads has changed dramatically in recent decades. In the post-Watergate reforms of the 1970s, candidates generally paid for the bulk of their advertisements out of so-called hard money contributions. These were gifts given directly to candidate organizations for voter persuasion. Campaigners would use these funds to produce and broadcast ads that were put out on the airwaves under a candidate's direct sponsorship. Both the Republican and Democrat nominees broadcast ads designed to frame the contest and set the agenda of political dialogue.

Over time, though, a series of loopholes appeared that transformed campaign ad financing. Interest groups and party organizations began to exploit a loophole that allowed unlimited amounts of money (so-called soft money gifts) to be spent on voter education and get-out-the-vote efforts. Originally created by the 1976 *Buckley v. Valeo* Supreme Court case on the post-Watergate reforms, this loophole was designed to strengthen political parties and outside groups and allow them to mobilize and educate supporters. Donors could give whatever money they desired without being limited to the $1,000 per individual and $5,000 per organization rules for hard money contributions.

This loophole reached its zenith in the 1990s when President Bill Clinton used large amounts of soft money contributions to the Democratic National Committee (DNC) to run ads extolling his virtues and lambasting those of the Republican opposition. Rather than using the money for get-out-the-vote or party-building activities, the DNC ran commercials that were virtually indistinguishable from hard money–financed candidate spots. Republicans did the same thing through the Republican National Committee to criticize Clinton and campaign against Democratic House and Senate candidates.[30]

The ensuing controversy over these funding practices (and a post-election investigation into Clinton's campaign spending) eventually led to enactment of the 2002 Bipartisan Campaign Reform Act (BCRA) sponsored by John McCain and Democrat Russell Feingold. Among its key principles were the outlawing of soft money gifts at the national party level (although state party organizations still could accept these contributions), an increase in individual contributions to $2,000 per candidate per election cycle, and a requirement that candidates personally appear in ads saying they paid for their commercials and took responsibility for their contents.

Groups still could run issue ads that talked about specific policies. For example, they could say that Republicans were harming poor people or that Democrats loved to raise taxes. But ads broadcast by these organizations in the sixty days before a general election could not engage in electoral advocacy. Groups could not criticize the policy stances of a specific federal candidate without registering as a political action committee and being subject to disclosure requirements.

The result of this legislation is a hodgepodge of rules concerning ad financing. Candidates can use hard money gifts to run advertisements, as can national party organizations. State party groups can rely on soft money contributions for political advertisements. Interest groups can spend unlimited amounts of money on issue ads without any disclosure of spending or contributors, except in the last sixty days before a general election. At that point in the campaign, they can run ads criticizing federal candidates, but they have to disclose who paid for the spots.

Unaffected by the 2002 reform legislation are radio ads, direct mail, phone calls, and Internet advertisements. Officials had focused on television ads because they form the bulk of political communications and are the technology that critics most worry about in terms of misleading voters. By restraining the most worrisome television maladies, the hope is that this reform will improve the content and tone of civic discourse. However, as discussed later in this volume, there is little evidence from 2004 or 2008 that the new rules made candidate appeals any more civil.

The 2004 and 2008 elections saw the rise of ad financing through Internet contributions. Howard Dean in 2004 and Obama in 2008 democratized fund-raising by using Web sites to raise large amounts of money from many small donors. With the Democratic base upset at President George W. Bush and alarmed at the Iraq War, these anti-war candidates raised huge amounts of money. Obama's total contributions exceeded $600 million, an all-time record for an American presidential candidate. This allowed him to fund a wide variety of television commercials, radio spots, Internet advertisements, a thirty-minute infomercial the week before the election, and get-out-the-vote efforts on Election Day.

The Impact of Ads on Voters

Ads are fascinating not only because of the manner in which they are put together but also because of their ability to influence voters. People are not equally susceptible to the media, and political observers have long tried to find out how media power actually operates.[31]

Consultants judge the effectiveness of ads by the ultimate results—who wins. This type of test, however, is never possible to complete until after the election. It leads invariably to the immutable law of advertising: Winners have great ads and losers do not.

As an alternative, journalists evaluate ads by asking voters to indicate whether commercials influenced them. When asked directly whether television commercials helped them decide how to vote, most voters say they did not. For example, the results of a Media Studies Center survey placed ads at the bottom of the heap in terms of possible information sources. Whereas 45 percent of voters felt they learned a lot from debates, 32 percent cited newspaper stories, and 30 percent pointed to television news stories, just 5 percent believed they learned a lot from political ads. When asked directly about ads in a CBS News/*New York Times* survey, only 11 percent reported that any presidential candidate's ads had helped them decide how to vote.[32]

But this is not a meaningful way of looking at advertising. Such responses undoubtedly reflect an unwillingness to admit that external agents have any effect on individual voting behavior. Many people firmly believe that they make up their minds independently of the campaign. Much in the same way teenagers do not like to concede parental influence, few voters are willing to admit they are influenced by television.

In studying campaign ads, one needs to emphasize the overall context in which people make decisions. The same ad can have very different consequences depending on the manner in which an opponent responds, the way a journalist reports the ad, the number of times the spot is broadcast, or the predispositions of the viewer.

A vivid example is found in Kathleen Hall Jamieson's study of the 1988 presidential campaign.[33] The effectiveness of Bush's "Revolving Door" ad on Dukakis's crime record was enhanced by the majority culture's fears about black men raping white women and by earlier news stories that had sensationalized Horton's crime spree. Bush did not have to mention Horton in his ad for viewers to make the connection between Dukakis and heinous crimes.

This idea is central to understanding campaign advertisements. Commercials cannot be explored in isolation from candidate behavior and the general flow of media information. An analysis of thirty-second spots requires a keen awareness of the structure of electoral competition, strategic candidate behavior, media coverage, and public opinion. A variety of long- and short-term factors go into voter decision-making. In terms of long-term forces, things such as party loyalties, ideological predispositions, the rules of the game, and socioeconomic status linked to education, income, sex, race, and region affect how people interpret ads and judge candidates. Meanwhile, there are a variety of short-term factors during a campaign that affect people. These include how the media cover ads, what reporters say about the candidates, candidate strategies, and debate performance.

Generally, the better known candidates are, the less ads are able to sway voter impressions. In a situation in which voters have firm feelings about campaigners based on long-term forces such as party and ideology, it is difficult for any of the short-term forces to make a difference. However, if the candidate is not well known or there is volatility in the political climate, news, ads, and debates can make a substantial difference in the election outcome.

The Structure of Electoral Competition

The structure of the electoral process defines the general opportunities available to candidates. The most important development at the presidential level has been the dramatic change in how convention delegates are selected. Once controlled by party leaders in small-scale caucus settings thought to be immune from media influence, nominations have become open and lengthy affairs significantly shaped by the mass media. The percentage of delegates to national nominating conventions selected through primaries increased significantly after 1968. From the 1920s to the 1960s, about 40 percent of delegates were selected in primaries, with the remainder chosen in caucus settings dominated by party leaders. However, after rule changes set in motion by the Democratic Party's McGovern-Fraser Commission following the 1968 election, about 70 percent of convention delegates in each party now are chosen directly by voters in presidential primaries.

Nominating reforms have required candidates to appeal directly to voters for support and in the eyes of many observers have altered the character of the electoral system.[34] No longer are candidates dependent on negotiations with a handful of party leaders. Instead, they must demonstrate public appeal and run campaigns that win media attention. Campaigns have become longer and have come to depend increasingly on television as a means of attracting public support.[35]

Some campaigns get far more attention than others. Citizens are more interested in and knowledgeable about presidential general election campaigns than nominating contests. Although variation exists among individual contests depending on the candidates involved, nomination races typically generate less citizen interest and less media coverage. Of course, the 2008 Democratic nominating contest sparked unusual interest because of the clash of superstar candidates Obama and Clinton.

These differences in the visibility of the candidates and the extent of media coverage are important for the study of television advertisements. Because less visible races feature candidates who are not well known, ad effects on citizens' opinions of the candidates often are significant. Past research has demonstrated that television's impact is strongest when viewers have weakly formulated views.[36] It is easier to run ads against a candidate who is not well known because there is no preexisting attitudinal profile to shield that individual against critical claims.

In addition, candidate behavior is conditioned by the rules of the game. Presidential elections in the United States are determined by the state-based Electoral College. Candidates seek to assemble a majority of Electoral College votes by winning targeted states. This electoral structure has enormous implications for advertising strategies. Most candidates do not run a fifty-state campaign. Instead, because many states tend to vote consistently over time, they focus on the fifteen to twenty states that swing back and forth between the two major parties.

Daron Shaw has undertaken an innovative study of Electoral College strategies and found that candidates apportion their time and advertising dollars in systematic ways. According to his study, strategies center on five categories: base Republican, marginal Republican, battleground state, marginal Democratic, and base Democratic.[37] Factors such as electoral history, size of the state's electoral vote, and current competitiveness dictate how campaigners allocate their resources. These decisions tend to be stable across presidential elections. This demonstrates the way in which electoral rules affect candidate strategies.

Advertising and Strategic Politicians

Early research downplayed the power of ads to mold the public images of candidates. The pioneering study in this area was Thomas Patterson and Robert McClure's innovative effort, The Unseeing Eye.[38] Looking at both content and effects, they sought to dispel the concerns of the public and journalists regarding political commercials. Using a model of psychological reasoning based on voters' knowledge about candidates, these researchers examined whether television ads enabled voters to learn more about the policy views or about the personal qualities of campaigners. They found that voters learned more about the issues from ads than from the news, because the ads addressed issues whereas the news was dominated by coverage of the "horse race"—who is ahead at a given time. Popular concerns about the strategic dangers of ads affecting how viewers thought of candidates were minimized as uninformed hand-wringing.

The study's results fit with the general view among election experts of the 1960s and 1970s that political strategies were not very decisive in determining election results. Researchers in the era following the 1960 publication of Campbell et al.'s classic work on voting behavior, The American Voter, proclaimed such long-term forces as party identification as the most important. Few scholars disputed this interpretation, even as many argued that short-term factors related to media coverage, candidates' advertisements, and campaign spending simply were not crucial to vote choice. For example, Harold Mendelsohn and Irving Crespi claimed in 1970 that the "injection of high doses of political information during the frenetic periods of national campaigns does very little to alter the deeply rooted, tightly held political attitudes of most voters."[39] Even the later emergence of models based on pocketbook considerations did little to change this interpretation. Paid ads were thought to have limited capacity to shape citizens' impressions of economic performance.

Recent decades, though, have begun to see changes in previous viewpoints. Candidates have started to use commercials more aggressively, reporters have devoted more attention to paid advertising, and ad techniques have grown more sophisticated. It now is thought that voters' assessments can change based on short-term information and that candidates have the power to sway undecided voters who wait until the closing weeks of the campaign to make up their minds. Evidence from elections across the United States suggests that ads are successful in helping candidates develop impressions of themselves.[40]

This is particularly true when campaigners are unknown or in multicandidate nominating contests. The more strategic options that are available with the larger number of candidates involved, the more potential there is for the campaign to affect citizen judgments. One study of the New Hampshire primary by Lynn Vavreck, Constantine Spiliotes, and Linda Fowler, for example, found that a variety of campaign activities affected voters' recognition of and favorability toward specific candidates.[41]

Furthermore, candidates no longer hold a monopoly on advertising. Political parties, interest groups, and even private individuals run commercials around election time. In fact, there are discernible differences in the percentage of attack ads run by different sources. The most negative messages involve issue ads run by interest groups. Fifty-six percent of those ads were attack oriented in recent elections, compared with 20 percent of candidate-sponsored advertisements.[42]

Because paid ads are so important in contemporary campaigns, candidates take the development of advertising strategies quite seriously. Commercials often are pretested through focus groups or public opinion surveys.[43] Themes as well as styles of presentation are tried out before likely voters. What messages are most appealing? When and how often should particular ads be aired? Who should be targeted? How should ads best convey information?

The number of times an ad is broadcast is one of the most important strategic decisions made during the campaign. Professional ad buyers specialize in picking time slots and television shows advantageous for particular candidates. Whereas a candidate interested in appealing to senior citizens may air ads repeatedly during television shows catering to the elderly, youth-oriented politicians may run spots on Fox Network or MTV, and minority candidates may advertise on Black Entertainment Television. Obama, for example, advertised extensively on minority stations, whereas McCain broadcast ads on television shows with large older audiences, such as *NCIS*.

The content and timing of ads are crucial for candidates because of their link to overall success. Campaigns have become a blitz of competing ads, quick responses, and counter-responses. Ads have become serial in nature, with each ad building thematically on previous spots. Election campaigns feature strategic interactions as important as the individual ads themselves.

In the fast-changing dynamics of election campaigns, decisions to advance or delay particular messages can be quite important. Quick-response strategies require candidates to respond immediately when negative ads appear or political conditions are favorable. Candidates often play off each other's ads in an effort to gain the advantage with voters.

Advertising and the News Media

One of the developments of the contemporary period has been coverage of political advertising by reporters. Network news executive William Small described this as the most important news trend of recent years: "Commercials are now expected as part of news stories."[44] Many news outlets have even launched "ad watch" features. These segments, aired during the news and discussed in newspaper articles, present the ad, along with commentary on its accuracy and effectiveness. The most effective ads are those whose basic messages are reinforced by the news media.

Scholars traditionally distinguished the free from the paid media. Free media meant reports from newspapers, magazines, radio, and television that were not billed to candidates. The paid media encompassed commercials purchased by the candidate on behalf of the campaign effort. The two avenues of communications were thought to be independent in terms of effects on viewers because of the way viewers saw them.

But the increase in news coverage of advertising has blurred or even eliminated this earlier division between free and paid media. People who separate the effects of these communications channels need to recognize how intertwined the free and paid media have become. It is now quite common for network news programs to rebroadcast entertaining, provocative, or controversial ads. Even entertainment shows are filled with references to contemporary politics. Journalists and entertainers have begun to evaluate the effects of campaign commercials, and it has become clear that the free media provide significant audiences for television ads.

Ads broadcast for free during the news or discussed in major newspapers have several advantages over those aired purely as commercials. One strength is that viewers traditionally have trusted the news media—at least in comparison with paid ads—for fairness and objectivity. William McGuire has shown that the credibility of the source is one determinant of whether the message is believed.[45] The high credibility of the media gives ads aired during the news an important advantage over those seen as plain ads. Roger Ailes explained it this way: "You get a 30 or 40 percent bump out of [an ad] by getting it on the news. You get more viewers, you get credibility, you get it in a framework."[46]

The 2004 presidential election introduced a new category of advertisements—*phantom,* or *vapor, ads.* These are commercials produced and distributed to journalists but barely broadcast. Journalists complained that Kerry released half a dozen spots on topics such as health care, taxes, and the Iraq War that were never aired to the general public. This made the ads "video news releases purporting to be substantial paid advertising," according to reporters.[47]

In 2008, McCain and Obama did the same thing. One vapor ad by McCain attracted considerable media attention. Although it aired infrequently, it accused Obama of supporting comprehensive sex education for kindergarten children because of a law he had cosponsored while in the Illinois Senate. The ad was misleading because the intent of the legislation was to protect young kids from sexual predators, not to indoctrinate them with sexual content.

Commercials in the news guarantee campaigners a large audience and free air time. Opinion polls have documented that nearly two-thirds of Americans cite television as their primary source of news. This is particularly true for what is referred to as the "inadvertent audience"—those who are least interested in politics and among the most volatile in their opinions.[48]

But there can be disadvantages to having an ad aired during a newscast. When an ad is described as unfair to the opposition, media coverage undermines the sponsor's message. The advantages of airing an ad during the news can also be lost if reporters challenge the ad's factual accuracy.

During recent elections, though, journalists have tried in vain to keep up with the onslaught of negative and misleading appeals.[49] Both candidates in 2004 pushed the envelope of factual inaccuracy. For example, Kerry accused the Bush White House of having a secret plan to reintroduce a military draft and of wanting to privatize Social Security. Bush, meanwhile, complained that Kerry's health care program would create new federal bureaucracies and that Kerry thought terrorism was a nuisance like prostitution and gambling. In 2008, McCain broadcast a number of misleading ads, such as the sex education spot described above, and commercials saying Obama would raise taxes on middle-class families. This led to considerable media criticism alleging that these claims were misleading at best or downright inaccurate.[50]

Reporters write stories criticizing the candidates for misleading and inaccurate claims, but the sheer volume of ad expenditures and campaign trail rhetoric overwhelms press oversight.[51] Journalists simply cannot compete with the hundreds of times ads are broadcast by the candidates. Campaigners are very adroit at communicating directly with the public and ignoring critical press stories about their advertisements.

Changes in Public Opinion

Public opinion and voting behavior have undergone significant changes that are relevant to advertising. Voters are less trusting of government officials today than they were in the past. Whereas 23 percent of voters in 1958 agreed that you cannot trust the government to do what is right most of the time, 84 percent were untrusting at the turn of the twenty-first century. A significant bloc of voters does not identify with either one of the major parties.[52] These citizens are often the kind of voters who swing back and forth between the parties.

The independence of American voters and the volatility in American politics unleashed by corporate downsizing and the end of the Cold War have uprooted some parts of citizen attitudes. People's impressions of short-term political events can be fluid, and the issues or leadership qualities seen as most important at any given time can change.[53]

Each of these developments has altered the tenor of electoral campaigns and led to extensive efforts to appeal to undecided voters. Writing in the 1830s, Alexis de Tocqueville worried that the great masses would make "hasty judgments" based on the "charlatans of every sort [who] so well understand the secret of pleasing them."[54] The prominence today of an open electoral system filled with mistrusting voters and fast-paced ads has done nothing to alleviate this concern.

Conclusion

In short, there are many different things that affect the use, interpretation, and impact of campaign ads. No single perspective can explain why an ad works well at a particular time but may backfire in a different context. One must look at the political environment, the nature of public opinion, how reporters cover the ads, the way in which ads are edited and financed, and the strategies of stereotyping, association, demonization, and code words used by campaigners.

NOTES

1. Ira Chinoy, "In Presidential Race, TV Ads Were Biggest '96 Cost by Far," *Washington Post,* March 31, 1997, A19.

2. Michael Franz, Paul Freedman, Kenneth Goldstein, and Travis Ridout, *Campaign Advertising and American Democracy* (Philadelphia: Temple University Press, 2007).

3. Kathleen Jamieson, *Packaging the Presidency,* 2nd ed. (New York: Oxford University Press, 1992), 6–7.

4. "Ads for a Web Generation," *New York Times,* August 24, 1998, D7.

5. Jamieson, *Packaging the Presidency,* 50.

6. Quoted in Jamieson, *Packaging the Presidency,* 195. For a description of Johnson's strategy, see Edwin Diamond and Stephen Bates, *The Spot* (Cambridge: MIT Press, 1984), 127–140.

7. "How Bush Won," *Newsweek,* November 21, 1988, 117. Also see Paul Taylor and David Broder, "Early Volley of Bush Ads Exceeded Expectations," *Washington Post,* October 28, 1988.

8. Richard Berke, "Democrats See, and Smell, Rats in G.O.P. Ad," *New York Times,* September 12, 2000, A1.

9. Howard Kurtz, "Presidential Attack Ads Move from Land to Water—and Back," *Washington Post,* September 23, 2004, A9.

10. Jim Rutenberg, "Kerry Ads Draw on Saudis for New Attack on Bushes," *New York Times,* October 5, 2004, A16.

11. Elizabeth Kolbert, "Secrecy over TV Ads, or, the Peculiar Logic of Political Combat," *New York Times,* September 17, 1992, A21.

12. Emmett Buell and Lee Sigelman, *Attack Politics: Negativity in Presidential Campaigns since 1960* (Lawrence: University Press of Kansas, 2008).

13. Paul Farhi, "Ad Says Kerry 'Secretly' Met with Enemy; but He Told Congress of It," *Washington Post,* September 22, 2004, A8.

14. Ken Dilanian, "Defenders Say Wright Has Love, Righteous Anger for USA," *USA Today,* March 19, 2008.

15. Darrell M. West and John Orman, *Celebrity Politics* (Upper Saddle River, N.J.: Prentice Hall, 2003).

16. "Anti-Bush Ad Contest Includes Hitler Images," *Washington Post,* January 6, 2004, A4.

17. Howard Kurtz, "Ads Aiming Straight for the Heart," *Washington Post,* October 27, 2004, A1.

18. Darrell M. West, *Patrick Kennedy: The Rise to Power* (Upper Saddle River, N.J.: Prentice Hall, 2000).

19. Harry Berkowitz, "Campaigns Aim at Economy," *Newsday,* September 28, 1996, A13.

20. Marjorie Connelly, "A 'Conservative' Is (Fill in the Blank)," *New York Times,* November 3, 1996, E5.

21. Howard Kurtz, "Bush's Health Care Ads Not Entirely Accurate," *Washington Post,* October 13, 2004, A8.

22. David Kirkpatrick, "Republicans Admit Mailing Campaign Literature Saying Liberals Will Ban the Bible," *New York Times,* September 24, 2004, A20.

23. Paul Begala, "A Good Dirty Fight," *New York Times,* November 4, 2004, A25.

24. Glen Justice, "In Final Days, Attacks Are in the Mail and below the Radar," *New York Times,* October 31, 2004, A30.

25. Sandra Maler, "'French' Becomes Campaign Slur," *Seattle Times,* October 27, 2004, A5.

26. "Today on the Presidential Campaign Trail," *Washington Post,* October 30, 2008.

27. Wisconsin Advertising Project, "Presidential TV Advertising Battle Narrows to Just Ten Battleground States," October 12, 2004, press release.

28. Graeme Zielinski, "Michels Makes Case with Images from 9–11," *Milwaukee Journal Sentinel,* October 19, 2004, A1.

29. Martin Schram, *The Great American Video Game* (New York: William Morrow, 1987), 25–26. For a reassessment of the differential impact of radio and television viewers on the 1960 debates, see David Vancil and Sue Pendell, "The Myth of Viewer-Listener Disagreement in the First Kennedy-Nixon Debate," *Central States Speech Journal* 38 (Spring 1987): 16–27.

30. Kathleen Hall Jamieson, *Everything You Think You Know about Politics . . . and Why You're Wrong* (New York: Basic Books, 2000).

31. Daniel Stevens, "Separate and Unequal Effects: Information, Political Sophistication and Negative Advertising in American Elections," *Political Research Quarterly* 58, no. 3 (September 2005): 413–425; and Ted Brader, "Striking a Responsive Chord: How Political Ads

Motivate and Persuade Voters by Appealing to Emotions," *American Journal of Political Science* 49, no. 2 (April 2005): 388–405.

32. The Media Studies Center poll is reported in *Providence Journal*, "Hype Swells as First Presidential Debate Approaches," September 29, 1996, A7. The CBS News/*New York Times* numbers come from Richard Berke, "Should Dole Risk Tough Image? Poll Says He Already Has One," *New York Times*, October 16, 1996, A1.

33. Kathleen Hall Jamieson, "Context and the Creation of Meaning in the Advertising of the 1988 Presidential Campaign," *American Behavioral Scientist* 32 (1989): 415–424. Also see Marion Just et al., *Cross Talk: Citizens, Candidates, and the Media in a Presidential Campaign* (Chicago: University of Chicago Press, 1996).

34. James Ceaser, *Presidential Selection* (Princeton: Princeton University Press, 1979).

35. Karen DeWitt, "Tsongas Pitches Economic Austerity Mixed with Patriotism," *New York Times*, January 1, 1992, A10.

36. Ken Goldstein and Paul Freedman, "New Evidence for New Arguments: Money and Advertising in the 1996 Senate Elections," *Journal of Politics* 62 (2000): 1087–1108.

37. Daron Shaw, "The Methods behind the Madness: Presidential Electoral College Strategies, 1988–1996," *Journal of Politics* 61 (1999): 893–913. Also see his "The Effect of TV Ads and Candidate Appearances on Statewide Presidential Votes, 1988–96," *American Political Science Review* 93 (1999): 345–361.

38. Thomas Patterson and Robert McClure, *The Unseeing Eye* (New York: Putnam's, 1976). Also see Martin Wattenberg, *The Rise of Candidate-Centered Politics* (Cambridge: Harvard University Press, 1991); and Richard M. Perloff, *Political Communication: Press, Politics, and Policy in America* (Mahwah, N.J.: Erlbaum, 1998).

39. The Harold Mendelsohn and Irving Crespi quote comes from their book, *Polls, Television, and the New Politics* (Scranton, Penn.: Chandler, 1970), 248.

40. Craig Leonard Brians and Martin Wattenberg, "Campaign Issue Knowledge and Salience: Comparing Reception from TV Commercials, TV News, and Newspapers," *American Journal of Political Science* 40 (February 1996): 172–193; and Xinshu Zhao and Steven Chaffee, "Campaign Advertisements versus Television News as Sources of Political Issue Information," *Public Opinion Quarterly* 59 (Spring 1995): 41–65.

41. Lynn Vavreck, Constantine Spiliotes, and Linda Fowler, "The Effects of Retail Politics in the New Hampshire Primary," *American Journal of Political Science* 46 (2002): 595–610.

42. Alliance for Better Campaigns, "Spot Comparison," *The Political Standard* 3 (June 2000): 1. See also Jonathan Krasno and Daniel Seltz, "Buying Time: Television Advertising in the 1998 Congressional Elections," Brennan Center for Justice, undated.

43. Elizabeth Kolbert, "Test-Marketing a President: How Focus Groups Pervade Campaign Politics," *New York Times Magazine*, August 30, 1992, 18–21, 60, 68, 72.

44. Quoted in John Foley, Dennis Britton, and Eugene Everett Jr., eds., *Nominating a President: The Process and the Press* (New York: Praeger, 1980), 79.

45. William McGuire, "Persuasion, Resistance, and Attitude Change," in *Handbook of Communication*, ed. Ithiel de Sola Pool (Chicago: Rand McNally, 1973), 216–252; and "The Nature of Attitudes and Attitude Change," in *Handbook of Social Psychology*, 2nd ed., vol. 3, ed. Gardner Lindzey and Elliot Aronson (Reading, Mass.: Addison-Wesley, 1969), 136–314.

46. Quote taken from David Runkel, ed., *Campaign for President: The Managers Look at '88* (Dover, Mass.: Auburn House, 1989), 142.

47. Howard Kurtz, "Some Kerry Spots Never Make the Air," *Washington Post,* October 20, 2004, A6.

48. Michael Robinson, "Public Affairs Television and the Growth of Political Malaise," *American Political Science Review* 70 (1976): 409–432.

49. David Peterson and Paul Djupe, "When Primary Campaigns Go Negative," *Political Research Quarterly* 58, no. 1 (March 2005): 45–54.

50. Larry Rohter, "Ad on Sex Education Distorts Obama Policy," *New York Times,* September 11, 2008, A22.

51. Howard Kurtz, "Ads Push the Factual Envelope," *Washington Post,* October 20, 2004, A1.

52. Seymour Martin Lipset and William Schneider, *The Confidence Gap* (New York: Free Press, 1983), 17; Paul Abramson, John Aldrich, and David Rohde, *Change and Continuity in the 1996 Elections* (Washington, D.C.: CQ Press, 1997); James Campbell, *The Presidential Pulse of Congressional Elections,* 2nd ed. (Lexington: University Press of Kentucky, 1997); and Bruce Keith, *The Myth of the Independent Voter* (Berkeley: University of California Press, 1992).

53. Thomas Holbrook and Scott McClurg, "The Mobilization of Core Supporters: Campaigns, Turnout, and Electoral Composition in United States Presidential Elections," *American Journal of Political Science* 49, no. 4 (October 2005): 689–703.

54. Alexis de Tocqueville, *Democracy in America,* trans. George Lawrence (Garden City, N.J.: Doubleday, 1969), 198.

11-4

America's Ignorant Voters

Michael Schudson

The meagerness of the average American's political knowledge has dismayed observers for decades. But Michael Schudson asks whether the informed citizen—meaning one who knows basic facts about government and politics— is truly the foundation of effective democracy. Reviewing the evidence, Schudson argues, contrary to conventional wisdom, that the problem is not growing worse. Moreover, voters may not recall many facts but still be able to vote in a way that reflects reasonable evaluations of candidates and parties.

EVERY WEEK, the *Tonight Show's* Jay Leno takes to the streets of Los Angeles to quiz innocent passersby with some simple questions: On what bay is San Francisco located? Who was president of the United States during World War II? The audience roars as Leno's hapless victims fumble for answers. Was it Lincoln? Carter?

No pollster, let alone a college or high school history teacher, would be surprised by the poor showing of Leno's sample citizens. In a national assessment test in the late 1980s, only a third of American 17-year-olds could correctly locate the Civil War in the period 1850–1900; more than a quarter placed it in the 18th century. Two-thirds knew that Abraham Lincoln wrote the Emancipation Proclamation, which seems a respectable showing, but what about the 14 percent who said that Lincoln wrote the Bill of Rights, the 10 percent who checked the Missouri Compromise, and the nine percent who awarded Lincoln royalties for *Uncle Tom's Cabin?*

Asking questions about contemporary affairs doesn't yield any more encouraging results. In a 1996 national public opinion poll, only 10 percent of American adults could identify William Rehnquist as the chief justice of the Supreme Court. In the same survey, conducted at the height of Newt Gingrich's celebrity as Speaker of the House, only 59 percent could identify the job he held. Americans sometimes demonstrate deeper knowledge about a major issue before the nation, such as the Vietnam War, but most could not describe the thrust of the Clinton health care plan or tell whether the Reagan administration supported the Sandinistas or the contras during the conflict in Nicaragua (and only a third could place that country in Central America).

Source: Michael Schudson, "America's Ignorant Voters," *Wilson Quarterly,* Spring 2000, Vol. 24, Issue 2.

It can be misleading to make direct comparisons with other countries, but the general level of political awareness in leading liberal democracies overseas does seem to be much higher. While 58 percent of the Germans surveyed, 32 percent of the French, and 22 percent of the British were able to identify Boutros Boutros-Ghali as secretary general of the United Nations in 1994, only 13 percent of Americans could do so. Nearly all Germans polled could name Boris Yeltsin as Russia's leader, as could 63 percent of the British, 61 percent of the French, but only 50 percent of the Americans.

How can the United States claim to be [a] model democracy if its citizens know so little about political life? That question has aroused political reformers and preoccupied many political scientists since the early 20th century. It can't be answered without some historical perspective.

Today's mantra that the "informed citizen" is the foundation of effective democracy was not a central part of the nation's founding vision. It is largely the creation of late-19th-century Mugwump and Progressive reformers, who recoiled from the spectacle of powerful political parties using government as a job bank for their friends and a cornucopia of contracts for their relatives. (In those days before the National Endowment for the Arts, Nathaniel Hawthorne, Herman Melville, and Walt Whitman all subsidized their writing by holding down federal patronage appointments.) Voter turnout in the late 19th century was extraordinarily high by today's standards, routinely over 70 percent in presidential elections, and there is no doubt that parades, free whiskey, free-floating money, patronage jobs, and the pleasures of fraternity all played a big part in the political enthusiasm of ordinary Americans.

The reformers saw this kind of politics as a betrayal of democratic ideals. A democratic public, they believed, must reason together. That ideal was threatened by mindless enthusiasm, the wily maneuvers of political machines, and the vulnerability of the new immigrant masses in the nation's big cities, woefully ignorant of Anglo-Saxon traditions, to manipulation by party hacks. E. L. Godkin, founding editor of the *Nation* and a leading reformer, argued that "there is no corner of our system in which the hastily made and ignorant foreign voter may not be found eating away the political structure, like a white ant, with a group of natives standing over him and encouraging him."

This was in 1893, by which point a whole set of reforms had been put in place. Civil service reform reduced patronage. Ballot reform irrevocably altered the act of voting itself. For most of the 19th century, parties distributed at the polls their own "tickets," listing only their own candidates for office. A voter simply took a ticket from a party worker and deposited it in the ballot box, without needing to read it or mark it in any way. Voting was thus a public act of party affiliation. Beginning in 1888, however, and spreading across the country by 1896, this system was replaced with government-printed ballots that listed all the candidates from each eligible party. The voter marked the ballot in secret, as we do today, in an act that affirmed voting as an individual choice rather than a social act of party loyalty. Political parades and other public spectacles increasingly gave way to pamphlets in what reformers dubbed "educational" political campaigns. Leading newspapers, once little more than organs of the political parties, began to declare their independence and to portray themselves as nonpartisan commercial institutions of public enlightenment and public-minded criticism. Public secondary education began to spread.

These and other reforms enshrined the informed citizen as the foundation of democracy, but at a tremendous cost: Voter turnout plummeted. In the presidential election of 1920, it dropped to 49 percent, its lowest point in the 20th century—until it was matched in 1996. Ever since, political scientists and others have been plumbing the mystery created by the new model of an informed citizenry: How can so many, knowing so little, and voting in such small numbers, build a democracy that appears to be (relatively) successful?

There are several responses to that question. The first is that a certain amount of political ignorance is an inevitable byproduct of America's unique political environment. One reason Americans have so much difficulty grasping the political facts of life is that their political system is the world's most complex. Ask the next political science Ph.D. you meet to explain what government agencies at what level—federal, state, county, or city—take responsibility for the homeless. Or whom he or she voted for in the last election for municipal judge. The answers might make Jay Leno's victims seem less ridiculous. No European country has as many elections, as many elected offices, as complex a maze of overlapping governmental jurisdictions, as the American system. It is simply harder to "read" U.S. politics than the politics of most nations.

The hurdle of political comprehension is raised a notch higher by the ideological inconsistencies of American political parties. In Britain, a voter can confidently cast a vote without knowing a great deal about the particular candidates on the ballot. The Labor candidate generally can be counted on to follow the Labor line, the Conservative to follow the Tory line. An American voter casting a ballot for a Democrat or Republican has no such assurance. Citizens in other countries need only dog paddle to be in the political swim; in the United States they need the skills of a scuba diver.

If the complexity of U.S. political institutions helps explain American ignorance of domestic politics, geopolitical factors help explain American backwardness in foreign affairs. There is a kind of ecology of political ignorance at work. The United States is far from Europe and borders only two other countries. With a vast domestic market, most of its producers have relatively few dealings with customers in other countries, globalization notwithstanding. Americans, lacking the parliamentary form of government that prevails in most other democracies, are also likely to find much of what they read or hear about the wider world politically opaque. And the simple fact of America's political and cultural superpower status naturally limits citizens' political awareness. Just as employees gossip more about the boss than the boss gossips about them, so Italians and Brazilians know more about the United States than Americans know about their countries.

Consider a thought experiment. Imagine what would happen if you transported those relatively well-informed Germans or Britons to the United States with their cultural heritage, schools, and news media intact. If you checked on them again about a generation later, after long exposure to the distinctive American political environment—its geographic isolation, superpower status, complex political system, and weak parties—would they have the political knowledge levels of Europeans or Americans? Most likely, I think, they would have developed typically American levels of political ignorance.

Lending support to this notion of an ecology of political knowledge is the stability of American political ignorance over time. Since the 1940s, when social scientists began measuring it, political ignorance has remained virtually unchanged. It is hard to gauge the extent of political knowledge before that time, but there is little to suggest that there is some lost golden age in U.S. history. The storied 1858 debates between Senator Stephen Douglas and Abraham Lincoln, for example, though undoubtedly a high point in the nation's public discourse, were also an anomaly. Public debates were rare in 19th-century political campaigns, and campaign rhetoric was generally overblown and aggressively partisan.

Modern measurements of Americans' historical and political knowledge go back at least to 1943, when the *New York Times* surveyed college freshmen and found "a striking ignorance of even the most elementary aspects of United States history." Reviewing nearly a half-century of data (1945–89) in *What Americans Know about Politics and Why It Matters* (1996), political scientists Michael Delli Carpini and Scott Keeter conclude that, on balance, there has been a slight gain in Americans' political knowledge, but one so modest that it makes more sense to speak of a remarkable stability. In 1945, for example, 43 percent of a national sample could name neither of their U.S. senators; in 1989, the figure was essentially unchanged at 45 percent. In 1952, 67 percent could name the vice president; in 1989, 74 percent could do so. In 1945, 92 percent of Gallup poll respondents knew that the term of the president is four years, compared with 96 percent in 1989. Whatever the explanations for dwindling voter turnout since 1960 may be, rising ignorance is not one of them.

As Delli Carpini and Keeter suggest, there are two ways to view their findings. The optimist's view is that political ignorance has grown no worse despite the spread of television and video games, the decline of political parties, and a variety of other negative developments. The pessimist asks why so little has improved despite the vast increase in formal education during those years. But the main conclusion remains: no notable change over as long a period as data are available.

Low as American levels of political knowledge may be, a generally tolerable, sometimes admirable, political democracy survives. How? One explanation is provided by a school of political science that goes under the banner of "political heuristics." Public opinion polls and paper-and-pencil tests of political knowledge, argue researchers such as Arthur Lupia, Samuel Popkin, Paul Sniderman, and Philip Tetlock, presume that citizens require more knowledge than they actually need in order to cast votes that accurately reflect their preferences. People can and do get by with relatively little political information. What Popkin calls "low-information rationality" is sufficient for citizens to vote intelligently.

This works in two ways. First, people can use cognitive cues, or "heuristics." Instead of learning each of a candidate's issue positions, the voter may simply rely on the candidate's party affiliation as a cue. This works better in Europe than in America, but it still works reasonably well. Endorsements are another useful shortcut. A thumbs-up for a candidate from the Christian Coalition or Ralph Nader or the National Association for the Advancement of Colored People or the American Association of Retired Persons frequently provides enough information to enable one to cast a reasonable vote.

Second, as political scientist Milton Lodge points out, people often process information on the fly, without retaining details in memory. If you watch a debate on TV—and 46 million did watch the first presidential debate between President Bill Clinton and Robert Dole in 1996—you may learn enough about the candidates' ideas and personal styles to come to a judgment about each one. A month later, on election day, you may not be able to answer a pollster's detailed questions about where they stood on the issues, but you will remember which one you liked best—and that is enough information to let you vote intelligently.

The realism of the political heuristics school is an indispensable corrective to unwarranted bashing of the general public. Americans are not the political dolts they sometimes seem to be. Still, the political heuristics approach has a potentially fatal flaw: It subtly substitutes voting for citizenship. Cognitive shortcuts have their place, but what if a citizen wants to persuade someone else to vote for his or her chosen candidate? What may be sufficient in the voting booth is inadequate in the wider world of the democratic process: discussion, deliberation, and persuasion. It is possible to vote and still be disenfranchised.

Yet another response to the riddle of voter ignorance takes its cue from the Founders and other 18th-century political thinkers who emphasized the importance of a morally virtuous citizenry. Effective democracy, in this view, depends more on the "democratic character" of citizens than on their aptitude for quiz show knowledge of political facts. Character, in this sense, is demonstrated all the time in everyday life, not in the voting booth every two years. From Amitai Etzioni, William Galston, and Michael Sandel on the liberal side of the political spectrum to William J. Bennett and James Q. Wilson on the conservative side, these writers emphasize the importance of what Alexis de Tocqueville called "habits of the heart." These theorists, along with politicians of every stripe, point to the importance of civil society as a foundation of democracy. They emphasize instilling moral virtue through families and civic participation through churches and other voluntary associations; they stress the necessity for civility and democratic behavior in daily life. They would not deny that it is important for citizens to be informed, but neither would they put information at the center of their vision of what makes democracy tick.

Brown University's Nancy Rosenblum, for example, lists two essential traits of democratic character. "Easy spontaneity" is the disposition to treat others identically, without deference, and with an easy grace. This capacity to act as if many social differences are of no account in public settings is one of the things that make[s] democracy happen on the streets. This is the disposition that foreign visitors have regularly labeled "American" for 200 years, at least since 1818, when the British reformer and journalist William Cobbett remarked upon Americans' "universal civility." Tocqueville observed in 1840 that strangers in America who meet "find neither danger nor advantage in telling each other freely what they think. Meeting by chance, they neither seek nor avoid each other. Their manner is therefore natural, frank, and open."

Rosenblum's second trait is "speaking up," which she describes as "a willingness to respond at least minimally to ordinary injustice." This does not involve anything so impressive as organizing a demonstration, but something more like objecting when an adult cuts ahead of a kid in a line at a movie theater, or politely rebuking a coworker who slurs a racial or religious group. It is hard to define "speaking up" precisely, but we all recognize it, without necessarily giving it the honor it deserves as an element of self-government. . . .

The Founding Fathers were certainly more concerned about instilling moral virtues than disseminating information about candidates and issues. Although they valued civic engagement more than their contemporaries in Europe did, and cared enough about promoting the wide circulation of ideas to establish a post office and adopt the First Amendment, they were ambivalent about, even suspicious of, a politically savvy populace. They did not urge voters to "know the issues"; at most they hoped that voters would choose wise and prudent legislators to consider issues on their behalf. On the one hand, they agreed that "the diffusion of knowledge is productive of virtue, and the best security for our civil rights," as a North Carolina congressman put it in 1792. On the other hand, as George Washington cautioned, "however necessary it may be to keep a watchful eye over public servants and public measures, yet there ought to be limits to it, for suspicions unfounded and jealousies too lively are irritating to honest feelings, and oftentimes are productive of more evil than good."

If men were angels, well and good—but they were not, and few of the Founders were as extravagant as Benjamin Rush in his rather scary vision of an education that would "convert men into republican machines." In theory, many shared Rush's emphasis on education; in practice, the states made little provision for public schooling in the early years of the Republic. Where schools did develop, they were defended more as tutors of obedience and organs of national unity than as means to create a watchful citizenry. The Founders placed trust less in education than in a political system designed to insulate decision making in the legislatures from the direct influence of the emotional, fractious, and too easily swayed electorate.

All of these arguments—about America's political environment, the value of political heuristics, and civil society—do not add up to a prescription for resignation or complacency about civic education. Nothing I have said suggests that the League of Women Voters should shut its doors or that newspaper editors should stop putting politics on page one. People may be able to vote intelligently with very little information—even well educated people do exactly that on most of the ballot issues they face—but democratic citizenship means more than voting. It means discussing and debating the questions before the political community— and sometimes raising new questions. Without a framework of information in which to place them, it is hard to understand even the simple slogans and catchwords of the day. People with scant political knowledge, as research by political scientists Samuel Popkin and Michael Dimock suggests, have more difficulty than others in perceiving differences between candidates and parties. Ignorance also tends to breed more ignorance; it inhibits people from venturing into situations that make them feel uncomfortable or inadequate, from the voting booth to the community forum to the town hall.

What is to be done? First, it is important to put the problem in perspective. American political ignorance is not growing worse. There is even an "up" side to Americans' relative indifference to political and historical facts: their characteristic openness to experiment, their pragmatic willingness to judge ideas and practices by their results rather than their pedigree.

Second, it pays to examine more closely the ways in which people do get measurably more knowledgeable. One of the greatest changes Delli Carpini and Keeter found in their study, for example, was in the percentage of Americans who could identify the first 10 amendments to the Constitution as the Bill of Rights. In 1954, the year the U.S. Supreme Court declared school segregation unconstitutional in *Brown v. Board of Education,* only 31 percent of Americans could do so. In 1989, the number had moved up to 46 percent.

Why the change? I think the answer is clear: The civil rights movement, along with the rights-oriented Warren Court, helped bring rights to the forefront of the American political agenda and thus to public consciousness. Because they dominated the political agenda, rights became a familiar topic in the press and on TV dramas, sitcoms, and talk shows, also finding their way into school curricula and textbooks. Political change, this experience shows, can influence public knowledge.

This is not to say that only a social revolution can bring about such an improvement. A lot of revolutions are small, one person at a time, one classroom at a time. But it does mean that there is no magic bullet. Indeed, imparting political knowledge has only become more difficult as the dimensions of what is considered political have expanded into what were once nonpolitical domains (such as gender relations and tobacco use), as one historical narrative has become many, each of them contentious, and as the relatively simple framework of world politics (the Cold War) has disappeared.

In this world, the ability to name the three branches of government or describe the New Deal does not make a citizen, but it is at least a token of membership in a society dedicated to the ideal of self-government. Civic education is an imperative we must pursue with the full recognition that a high level of ignorance is likely to prevail—even if that fact does not flatter our faith in rationalism, our pleasure in moralizing, or our confidence in reform.

11-5

Super PACs and Secret Money

Paul Blumenthal

In 2010, the U.S. Supreme Court ruled, in a 5–4 decision, that the First Amendment's guarantee of free speech prohibits government from barring political broadcasts in candidate elections when those broadcasts are funded by corporations or unions. The ruling served as the basis for the creation of independent groups, now called Super PACs, which can be used to field campaigns for and against candidates for federal office. They differ from regular political action committees (PACs) in that they cannot contribute directly to candidates' campaigns, but they may raise unlimited sums from individuals, corporations, and unions for advertising campaigns of their own. In this article, journalist Paul Blumenthal describes how Super PACs raise and spend hundreds of millions of dollars and have invented ways to make it difficult to trace the sources of their funding.

IN THE SPAN of a week in September [2011], two independent political committees announced unheard-of fundraising plans for the coming campaign season. The Karl Rove–linked American Crossroads, along with its sister nonprofit, Crossroads GPS, announced a plan to raise and spend $240 million in 2012. Make Us Great Again, a group solely dedicated to electing Texas Gov. Rick Perry the 45th President of the United States, revealed a plan to spend $55 million in the Republican primary alone. Both of these multimillion dollar plans would break all reported records for spending by an independent political committee, and offer a sign of how campaign finance rules have been upended.

The federal system of campaign finance is in the midst of a sea change following the Supreme Court's decision in *Citizens United v. Federal Election Commission (FEC)*, which undid a host of regulations covering the use of corporate and union money by independent groups in elections. Those independent groups are forming a shadow campaign apparatus fueled by unlimited and often undisclosed contributions, without the same accountability required of political parties or candidates' own political action committees.

American Crossroads and Make Us Great Again represent one of the two new kinds of groups playing in the shadow campaign: super PACs, independent

Source: Paul Blumenthal, "Super PACs and Secret Money," *Huffington Post*, September 26, 2011. http://www.huffingtonpost.com/2011/09/26/super-pacs-secret-money-campaign-finance_n_977699.html

political committees filed with the FEC that can accept unlimited funds from corporations, unions and individuals.

In their debut election cycle in 2010, super PACs, like American Crossroads, spent a combined $65.3 million, according to the Center for Responsive Politics. This was part of a huge surge in spending by non-party groups, whose spending hit $304 million in 2010, a record for any election cycle—presidential or midterm.

If the fundraising goals of American Crossroads and Make Us Great Again are any indication, the 2012 elections will shatter this record.

Super PACs weren't solely responsible for the surge in outside spending in 2010. Nonprofit groups organized under section 501(c)(4) of the tax code were also finally allowed to spend money on express advocacy—calling for the election or defeat of a candidate—thanks to the *Citizens United* ruling. Unlike super PACs, these nonprofits, including Crossroads GPS, are not required to disclose the source of their funds.

While overall outside spending surged, undisclosed spending by nonprofits, or "dark money," exploded. According to the Center for Responsive Politics, the source of only 51 percent of non-party outside spending was disclosed to the public in 2010.

"In the case of the tax-exempt groups, citizens have absolutely no idea what's going on here," Democracy 21 President Fred Wertheimer, a long-time campaign finance watchdog, explained to HuffPost. "They have no way of knowing how groups are trying to influence their votes."

The explosion of unlimited money and secret money is expected to continue unabated in 2012. It is already taking different forms and creating new headaches for those concerned about the increasing role of money in politics. The new campaign finance system is now a two-tiered one: candidates and parties governed by tight regulations and shadow groups that operate with little to no rules.

* * * * *

Justice Anthony Kennedy wrote the majority opinion in the *Citizens United* ruling, offering the main argument underlying the decision. "Independent expenditures, including those made by corporations, do not give rise to corruption or the appearance of corruption," he wrote.

That statement led to an immediate trickle-down effect on a lower court case, *SpeechNow.org v. FEC*. Months after the *Citizens United* ruling, the U.S. Court of Appeals for the District of Columbia Circuit ruled that SpeechNow.org, a nonprofit, could accept not only the unlimited individual contributions that it had requested, but also unlimited contributions from corporations and unions. The end result, after the FEC approved the ruling, was the creation of super PACs.

SpeechNow.org was founded by David Keating, the executive director of the Club for Growth, a free-market conservative group that has long played a role as an independent spender in elections.

"I really believe in the First Amendment and I wanted to start a PAC that supported candidates who supported the First Amendment," Keating told HuffPost. "Part of the inspiration I got for this is that it's perfectly okay for someone who's rich to speak out all they want, and there have been cases where rich individuals have run their own independent expenditures. If it's John Doe funding the independent expenditure, it says, 'Paid for by John Doe.' If it's okay for one person to spend $1 million, I thought, 'Why can't a few of us get together to pool our money.' It turned out that was illegal."

The changes to the existing structure of the campaign finance system happened almost instantaneously following the *SpeechNow.org* ruling. Before the 2010 midterms even happened, just five months after ruling, there were 65 super PACs registered with the FEC. Now, more than a year later these groups are emerging with the sole intent of backing presidential candidates, and they are raising huge sums to do so.

Make Us Great Again is one of 11 super PACs backing a specific candidate in the Republican presidential primary. Another super PAC, Priorities USA Action, supports President Barack Obama's reelection bid. These groups are routinely run by former staffers or close associates of the candidates they're supporting and have been targeted by campaign finance watchdogs who consider them a means to subvert the campaign finance system's limits on contributions to candidates.

"The reason why supporters of a particular candidate start a super PAC is pretty obvious," said Bill Allison, editorial director of the Sunlight Foundation, a pro-transparency nonprofit that tracks outside spending in elections. "You can raise tons of money without campaign finance limitation and then support or attack in the same way as traditional committees."

Paul S. Ryan, a lawyer with the campaign finance watchdog Campaign Legal Center, concurred. "As long as contribution limits have been in existence, specifically since the 1970s, candidates have felt inconvenienced by them and would like to run without them," he said. "It's easier to raise money in $1 million chunks than in $2,500 chunks."

Super PACs are technically not allowed to coordinate with campaigns or parties, but candidates can get involved in the fundraising. The FEC ruled in July that candidates can appear at a fundraiser for a super PAC, with just one restriction: They personally cannot solicit money in excess of the federally-mandated candidate contribution limit of $2,500 per election or $5,000 per election cycle.

"It's fully permissible for the candidates to go to a fundraising event for these super PACs and have a super PAC spokesperson ask the crowd for money before introducing the candidate, who then speaks about the campaign strategy," said Ryan.

According to iWatch News, former Massachusetts Gov. Mitt Romney appeared at a fundraiser for the super PAC supporting his presidential bid,

Restore Our Future, to address the crowd, but left promptly before organizers asked the audience for donations.

Romney's appearance at the Restore Our Future fundraiser was made possible by the super PAC's three co-founders, who all worked on Romney's 2008 presidential campaign. The other candidate-centric super PACs could get their favored candidate to their fundraisers thanks to similar relationships between those running the super PACs and the candidates.

Like Restore Our Future, other candidates' super PACs are helmed by former staffers. Make Us Great Again, a pro–Rick Perry super PAC is led by Mike Toomey, Perry's former chief of staff and longtime friend; both Veterans for Rick Perry and Jobs for Vets were started by Dan Shelley, a former Perry legislative director; Rep. Michele Bachmann's former top media aide, Ed Brookover, is the co-chairman of Citizens for a Working America; the pro–Ron Paul Revolution PAC was started with the help of two former aides to the congressman; and Our Destiny, the pro–Jon Huntsman group, was started by Thomas Muir, a vice president at Hunstman Corp., Huntsman's father's company, and listed in filings for two charities run by Huntsman's parents. The Obama-supporting Priorities USA is run by Bill Burton, a former White House aide and Obama campaign adviser.

In the past month candidate super PACs and the candidates' campaigns have been drifting even closer. On Aug. 30, Fred Davis, the ad man for Huntsman's campaign, jumped ship and immediately joined Our Destiny PAC. On Aug. 24, iWatch reported that Romney's top campaign fundraiser was leaving the campaign to raise money for Restore Our Future.

"The idea that this is some independent disconnected operation is a farce," said Wertheimer. The candidate super PACs are "undermining and in the process of eviscerating the contribution limits that exist for candidates in order to protect against corruption."

Priorities USA Action's Burton disputed suggestions that his group was not independent. "Priorities USA and Priorities USA Action are independent committees and we are operating well within prescribed guidelines," he told HuffPost.

Candidate super PACs are even popping up on the congressional level. On Sept. 21, Utah political consultant Kelly Casady announced the formation of the Strong Utah PAC, a super PAC backing the reelection of Sen. Orrin Hatch (R-Utah). The super PAC aims to counter the weight of the conservative nonprofit FreedomWorks, which has targeted Hatch for defeat as a "Republican in name only" (RINO).

* * * * *

The decrease in campaign finance disclosure comes after Kennedy's *Citizens United* opinion provided one of the strongest affirmations of transparency and disclosure issued by the Court. Kennedy wrote, "With the advent of the Internet, prompt disclosure of expenditures can provide shareholders and citizens with the information needed to hold corporations and elected officials accountable for their positions." The new spending that Kennedy's opinion would allow he believed, would be transparent and, thus, limit public concerns that could arise about the corporate or union spending.

That hasn't panned out. In 2010 the number of non-disclosing groups, including nonprofits, jumped dramatically. Spending hidden from the public went from $79.8 million in 2008 to $137.5 in 2010, according to the Center for Responsive Politics. Nonprofits accounted for $90 million of that total in 2010.

"[The Supreme Court isn't] supposed to be designing our campaign finance system," Trevor Potter, the president and general counsel of the Campaign Legal Center and a former FEC Chairman and counsel to the 2008 presidential campaign of Sen. John McCain (R-Ariz.), explained to HuffPost. The result has been "the opposite of what the Supreme Court predicted would happen."

Nonprofit spending increased as the groups were freed to spend money on express advocacy advertisements. While more than half the money spent by non-disclosing groups went to so-called electioneering communications, issue ads that had previously been allowed, almost the entire growth in spending by non-disclosing groups came from the newly-allowed express advocacy, which grew from $6.9 million in 2008 to $62 million in 2010.

Super PACs have even gotten in on the secret money act. While Super PACs are required to disclose their donors, they can accept contributions from nonprofits that do not disclose their donors and from corporations, some of which either do not identify their owners or dissolve upon making a large donation. This has already caused controversy for the Romney-backing Restore Our Future, which received three $1 million contributions from corporations that appear to do no business, one of which dissolved a few months after making the donation.

"The money has shifted to the fringes and it's become less and less transparent," said Center for Responsive Politics Executive Director Sheila Krumholz. "It's shifting away from the parties, the candidates, the PACs, and shifting to these unregulated groups and becoming much and much more secret."

The decrease in disclosure was aided by a 2007 ruling by the FEC that gutted a provision of the McCain-Feingold campaign finance reform law requiring the disclosure of donors to groups spending money on election ads, whether they be issue ads or express advocacy.

"We had 100 percent disclosure for nonprofit spending on electioneering communications in 2004," explained Craig Holman, the lobbyist for the watchdog group Public Citizen. "The FEC changed the disclosure rule in 2007 to only require disclosure for contributors who earmark their donations for [express advocacy and issue] spending, which no one does. Now, everyone has figured out that they don't have to disclose at all."

Rep. Chris Van Hollen (D-Md.) filed suit in April against the FEC for failing to enforce this disclosure provision properly.

During the 2010 elections one of the non-disclosing groups cited in Van Hollen's lawsuit, Americans for Job Security (AJS), supported North Carolina Republican candidate Renee Ellmers with $350,000 in attack ads against her opponent. Ellmers won the race and went to Washington as part of the giant Tea Party class joining the 112th Congress. But that outside spending would come back to haunt Ellmers.

A previous HuffPost article documented how Ellmers attached her support to a bill that would have blocked a new rule regulating swipe fees for debit cards. This seemed obvious—the conservative blog RedState was for the bill, as was the Republican caucus. And Bank of America, a major supporter of the legislation, is one of the dominant businesses in North Carolina.

But AJS was running ads in Republican districts against the bill and in support of the swipe fee rule at the behest of a client. Ellmers had her name taken off of the bill as the bill's path slowed in the Senate. Her office chalked up the bill sponsorship to a staff error.

Reformers worries about influence exerted on the legislative process by outside groups are not limited to this one case.

Public Citizen's Holman told HuffPost a story highlighting that concern: "I talked to a Capitol Hill staffer and he told me, 'How do I say no to a corporate lobbyist with deep pockets knowing that the corporate client can spend unlimited money to unseat my boss?'" Whether these fears are well-founded remains to be seen.

By empowering corporations to donate to groups that can sway elections, Potter said, the court has empowered organizations that have very different incentives than actual human beings. "Corporations do not behave in the same way people do. They think about the best way to get an advantage over their competitor, either through the government or the marketplace. The whole country is going to see a situation where corporate interests are going to be electing members of Congress for that purpose."

Chapter 12

Political Parties

————•••————

12-1

from *Why Parties?*

John H. Aldrich

American political parties were created by politicians and committed citizens who sought to win elections and control legislatures, executives, and even the courts. The parties exist at local, state, and national levels—wherever elections are held for coveted offices. The system of political parties that has evolved over time is fragmented and multilayered. In the following essay, John H. Aldrich describes the nature of the political problems that parties solve for candidates and voters. As much as we may dislike partisanship, modern democracies could not, Aldrich explains, function without it.

Is the Contemporary Political Party Strong or in Decline?

The Case for the Importance of Political Parties

THE PATH TO OFFICE for nearly every major politician begins today, as it has for over 150 years, with the party. Many candidates emerge initially from the ranks of party activists, all serious candidates seek their party's nomination, and they become serious candidates in the general election only because they have won their party's endorsement. Today most partisan nominations are decided in

Source: John H. Aldrich, *Why Parties? The Origin and Transformation of Political Parties in America* (Chicago: University of Chicago Press, 1995), 14–27. Notes appearing in the original have been deleted.

primary elections—that is, based on votes cast by self-designated partisans in the mass electorate. Successful nominees count on the continued support of these partisans in the general election, and for good reason. At least since surveys have provided firm evidence, all presidential nominees have won the support of no less than a majority of their party in the electorate, no matter how overwhelming their defeat may have been.

This is an age of so-called partisan dealignment in the electorate. Even so, a substantial majority today consider themselves partisans. The lowest percentage of self-professed (i.e., "strong" and "weak") partisans yet recorded in National Election Studies (NES) surveys was 61 percent in 1974, and another 22 percent expressed partisan leanings that year. Evidence from panel surveys demonstrates that partisanship has remained as stable and enduring for most adults after dealignment as it did before it, and it is often the single strongest predictor of candidate choice in the public.

If parties have declined recently, the decline has not occurred in their formal organizations. Party organizations are if anything stronger, better financed, and more professional at all levels now. Although its importance to candidates may be less than in the past, the party provides more support—more money, workers, and resources of all kinds—than any other organization for all but a very few candidates for national and state offices.

Once elected, officeholders remain partisans. Congress is organized by parties. Party-line votes elect its leadership, determine what its committees will be, assign members to them, and select their chairs. Party caucuses remain a staple of congressional life, and they and other forms of party organizations in Congress have become stronger in recent years. Party voting in committee and on the floor of both houses, though far less common in the United States than in many democracies, nonetheless remains the first and most important standard for understanding congressional voting behavior, and it too has grown stronger, in this case much stronger, in recent years.

Relationships among the elected branches of government are also heavily partisan. Conference committees to resolve discrepancies between House and Senate versions of legislation reflect partisan as well as interchamber rivalries. The president is the party's leader, and his agenda is introduced, fought for, and supported on the floor by his congressional party. His agenda becomes his party's congressional agenda, and much of it finds its way into law.

The Case for Weak and Weakening Parties

As impressive as the scenario above may be, not all agree that parties lie at the heart of American politics, at least not anymore. The literature on parties over the past two decades is replete with accounts of the decline of the political party. Even the choice of titles clearly reflects the arguments. David Broder perhaps began this stream of literature with *The Party's Over* (1972). Since then, political scientists have written extensively on this theme: for example, Crotty's *American Political Parties in Decline* (1984), Kirkpatrick's *Dismantling the Parties* (1978), Polsby's *Consequences of Party Reform* (1983) . . . , Ranney's thoughtful *Curing the Mischiefs of Faction* (1975), and Wattenberg's *The Decline of American Political Parties* (1990).

Those who see larger ills in the contemporary political scene often attribute them to the failure of parties to be stronger and more effective. In "The Decline of Collective Responsibility" (1980), Fiorina argued that such responsibility was possible only through the agency of the political party. Jacobson concluded his study of congressional elections (1992) by arguing that contemporary elections induce "responsiveness" of individual incumbents to their districts but do so "without [inducing] responsibility" in incumbents for what Congress does. As a result, the electorate can find no one to hold accountable for congressional failings. He too looked to a revitalized party for redress. These themes reflect the responsible party thesis, if not in being a call for such parties, at least in using that as the standard for measuring how short the contemporary party falls.

The literature on the presidency is not immune to this concern for decaying parties. Kernell's account of the strategy of "going public" (1986)—that is, generating power by marshaling public opinion—is that it became more common as the older strategy of striking bargains with a small set of congressional (and partisan) power brokers grew increasingly futile. The earlier use of the president's power to persuade (Neustadt 1960, 1990) failed as power centers became more diverse and fragmented and brokers could no longer deliver. Lowi argued this case even more strongly in *The Personal President* (1985). America, he claimed, has come to invest too much power in the office of the president, with the result that the promise of the presidency and the promises of individual presidents go unfulfilled. Why? Because the rest of government has become too unwieldy, complicated, and fragmented for the president to use that power effectively. His solution? Revitalize political parties.

Divided partisan control over government, once an occasional aberration, has become the ordinary course of affairs. Many of the same themes in this literature are those sounded above—fragmented, decentralized power, lack of coordination and control over what the government does, and absence of collective responsibility. Strong political parties are, among other things, those that can deliver the vote for most or all of their candidates. Thus another symptom of weakened parties is regularized divided government, in the states as well as in the nation.

If divided government is due to weakened parties, that condition must be due in turn to weakened partisan loyalties in the electorate. Here the evidence is clear. The proportions and strength of party attachments in the electorate declined in the mid-1960s. There was a resurgence in affiliation twenty years later, but to a lower level than before 1966. The behavioral consequences of these changes are if anything even clearer. Defection from party lines and split-ticket voting are far more common for all major offices at national, state, and local levels today than before the mid-1960s. Elections are more candidate centered and less party centered, and those who come to office have played a greater role in shaping their own more highly personalized electoral coalitions. Incumbents, less dependent on the party for winning office, are less disposed to vote the party line in Congress or to follow the wishes of their party's president. Power becomes decentralized toward the individual incumbent and, as Jacobson argues, individual incumbents respond to their constituents. If that means defecting from the party, so be it.

Is the Debate Genuine?

Some believe that parties have actually grown stronger over the past few decades. This position has been put most starkly by Schlesinger: "It should be clear by now that the grab bag of assumptions, inferences, and half-truths that have fed the decline-of-parties thesis is simply wrong" (1985, p. 1152). Rather, he maintains, "Thanks to increasing levels of competition between the parties, then, American political parties are stronger than before" (p. 1168). More common is the claim that parties were weakened in the 1960s but have been revitalized since then. Rohde pointed out that "in the last decade, however, the decline of partisanship in the House has been reversed. Party voting, which had been as low as 27 percent in 1972, peaked at 64 percent in 1987" (1989, p. 1). Changes in party voting in the Senate have been only slightly less dramatic, and Rohde has also demonstrated that party institutions in the House strengthened substantially in the same period (1991). If, as Rohde says, parties in the government are stronger, and if . . . others are correct that party organizations are stronger, a thesis of decline with resurgence must be taken seriously. The electorate's partisan affiliations may be a lagging rather than a leading indicator, and even they have rebounded slightly.

A Theory of Political Parties

As diverse as are the conclusions reached by these and other astute observers, all agree that the political party is—or should be—central to the American political system. Parties are—or should be—integral parts of all political life, from structuring the reasoning and choice of the electorate, through all facets of campaigns and seemingly all facets of the government, to the very possibility of effective governance in a democracy.

How is it that such astute observers of American politics and parties, writing at virtually the same time and looking at much the same evidence, come to such diametrically opposed conclusions about the strength of parties? Eldersveld . . . wrote that "political parties are complex institutions and processes, and as such they are difficult to understand and evaluate" (1982, p. 407). As proof, he went on to consider the decline of parties thesis. At one point he wrote, "The decline in our parties, therefore, is difficult to demonstrate, empirically or in terms of historical perspective" (p. 417). And yet he then turned to signs of party decline and concluded his book with the statement: "Despite their defects they continue today to be the major instruments for democratic government in this nation. With necessary reforms we can make them even more central to the governmental process and to the lives of American citizens. Eighty years ago, Lord James Bryce, after studying our party system, said, 'In America the great moving forces are the parties. The government counts for less than in Europe, the parties count for more. . . .' If our citizens and their leaders wish it, American parties will still be the 'great moving forces' of our system" (1982, pp. 432–33).

The "Fundamental Equation" of the New Institutionalism Applied to Parties

That parties are complex does not mean they are incomprehensible. Indeed complexity is, if not an intentional outcome, at least an anticipated result of those who shape the political parties. Moreover, they are so deeply woven into the fabric of American politics that they cannot be understood apart from either their own historical context and dynamics or those of the political system as a whole. Parties, that is, can be understood only in relation to the polity, to the government and its institutions, and to the historical context of the times.

The study of political parties, second, is necessarily a study of a major pair of political *institutions.* Indeed, the institutions that define the political party are unique, and as it happens they are unique in ways that make an institutional account especially useful. Their establishment and nature are fundamentally extralegal; they are nongovernmental political institutions. Instead of statute, their basis lies in the actions of ambitious politicians that created and maintain them. They are, in the parlance of the new institutionalism, *endogenous institutions*—in fact, the most highly endogenous institutions of any substantial and sustained political importance in American history.

By endogenous, I mean it was the actions of political actors that created political parties in the first place, and it is the actions of political actors that have shaped and altered them over time. And political actors have chosen to alter their parties dramatically at several times in our history, reformed them often, and tinkered with them constantly. Of all major political bodies in the United States, the political party is the most variable in its rules, regulations, and procedures—that is to say, in its formal organization—and in its informal methods and traditions. It is often the same set of actors who write the party's rules and then choose the party's outcomes, sometimes at nearly the same time and by the same method. Thus, for example, one night national party conventions debate, consider any proposed amendments, and then adopt their rules by a majority vote of credentialed delegates. The next night these same delegates debate, consider any proposed amendments, and then adopt their platform by majority vote, and they choose their presidential nominee by majority vote the following night.

Who, then, are these critical political actors? Many see the party-in-the-electorate as comprising major actors. To be sure, mobilizing the electorate to capture office is a central task of the political party. But America is a republican democracy. All power flows directly or indirectly from the great body of the people, to paraphrase Madison's definition. The public elects its political leaders, but it is that leadership that legislates, executes, and adjudicates policy. The parties are defined in relation to this republican democracy. Thus it is political leaders, those Schlesinger (1975) has called "office-seekers"—*those who seek and those who hold elective office*—who are the central actors in the party.

Ambitious office seekers and holders are thus the first and most important actors in the political party. A second set of important figures in party politics comprises those who hold, or have access to, critical resources that office seekers need to realize their ambitions. It is expensive to build and maintain the party and campaign organizations necessary to compete effectively in the electoral arena. Thomas Ferguson, for example, has made an extended argument for the "primary and constitutive role large investors play in American politics" (1983, p. 3). Much of his research emphasizes this primary and constitutive role in party politics in particular, such as in partisan realignments. The study of the role of money in congressional elections has also focused in part on concentrations of such sources of funding, such as from political action committees which political parties are coming to take advantage of. Elections are also fought over the flow of information to the public. The electoral arm of political parties in the eighteenth century was made up of "committees of correspondence," which were primarily lines of communication among political elites and between them and potential voters, and one of the first signs of organizing of the Jeffersonian Republican party was the hiring of a newspaper editor. The press was first a partisan press, and editors and publishers from Thomas Ritchie to Horace Greeley long were critical players in party politics. Today those with specialized knowledge relevant to communication, such as pollsters, media and advertising experts, and computerized fund-raising specialists, enjoy influence in party, campaign, and even government councils that greatly exceeds their mere technical expertise.

In more theoretical terms, this second set of party actors include those Schlesinger (1975) has called "benefit seekers," those for whom realization of their goals depends on the party's success in capturing office. Party activists shade from those powerful figures with concentrations of, or access to, money and information described above to the legions of volunteer campaign activists who ring doorbells and stuff envelopes and are, individually and collectively, critical to the first level of the party—its office seekers. All are critical because they command the resources, whether money, expertise, and information or merely time and labor, that office seekers need to realize their ambitions. As a result, activists' motivations shape and constrain the behavior of office seekers, as their own roles are, in turn, shaped and constrained by the office seekers. The changed incentives of party activists have played a significant role in the fundamentally altered nature of the contemporary party, but the impact of benefit seekers will be seen scattered throughout this account.

Voters, however, are neither office seekers nor benefit seekers and thus are not a part of the political party at all, even if they identify strongly with a party and consistently support its candidates. Voters are indeed critical, but they are critical as the targets of party activities. Parties "produce" candidates, platforms, and policies. Voters "consume" by exchanging their votes for the party's product (see Popkin et al. 1976). Some voters, of course, become partisans by becoming activists, whether as occasional volunteers, as sustained contributors, or even as candidates. But until they do so, they may be faithful consumers, "brand name" loyalists as it were, but they are still only the targets of partisans' efforts to sell their wares in the political marketplace.

Why, then, do politicians create and recreate the party, exploit its features, or ignore its dictates? The simple answer is that it has been in their interests to do so. That is, this is a *rational choice* account of the party, an account that presumes that rational, elective office seekers and holders use the party to achieve their ends.

I do not assume that politicians are invariably self-interested in a narrow sense. This is not a theory in which elective office seekers simply maximize their chances of election or reelection, at least not for its own sake. They may well have fundamental values and principles, and they may have preferences over policies as means to those ends. They also care about office, both for its own sake and for the opportunities to achieve other ends that election and reelection make possible. . . . Just as winning elections is a means to other ends for politicians (whether career or policy ends), so too is the political party a means to these other ends.

Why, then, do politicians turn to create or reform, to use or abuse, partisan institutions? The answer is that parties are designed as attempts to solve problems that current institutional arrangements do not solve and that politicians have come to believe they cannot solve. These problems fall into three general and recurring categories.

The Problem of Ambition and Elective Office Seeking

Elective office seekers, as that label says, want to win election to office. Parties regulate access to those offices. If elective office is indeed valuable, there will be more aspirants than offices, and the political party and the two-party system are means of regulating that competition and channeling those ambitions. Major party nomination is necessary for election, and partisan institutions have been developed—and have been reformed and re-reformed—for regulating competition. Intra-institutional leadership positions are also highly valued and therefore potentially competitive. There is, for example, a fairly well institutionalized path to the office of Speaker of the House. It is, however, a Democratic party institution. Elective politicians, of course, ordinarily desire election more than once. They are typically careerists who want a long and productive career in politics. Schlesinger's ambition theory (1966) . . . is precisely about this general problem. Underlying this theory, though typically not fully developed, is a problem. The problem is that if office is desirable, there will be more, usually many more, aspirants than there are offices to go around. When stated in rigorous form, it can be proved that in fact there is no permanent solution to this problem. And it is a problem that can adversely affect the fortunes of a party. In 1912 the Republican vote was split between William Howard Taft and Theodore Roosevelt. This split enabled Woodrow Wilson to win with 42 percent of the popular vote. Not only was Wilson the only break in Republican hegemony of the White House in this period, but in that year Democrats increased their House majority by sixty-five additional seats and captured majority control of the Senate. Thus failure to regulate intraparty competition cost Republicans dearly.

For elective office seekers, regulating conflict over who holds those offices is clearly of major concern. It is ever present. And it is not just a problem of access to government offices but is also a problem internal to each party as soon as the party becomes an important gateway to office.

The Problem of Making Decisions for the Party and for the Polity

Once in office, partisans determine outcomes for the polity. They propose alternatives, shape the agenda, pass (or reject) legislation, and implement what they enact. The policy formation and execution process, that is, is highly partisan. The parties-in-government are more than mere coalitions of like-minded individuals, however; they are enduring institutions. Very few incumbents change their partisan affiliations. Most retain their partisanship throughout their career, even though they often disagree (i.e., are not uniformly like-minded) with some of their partisan peers. When the rare incumbent does change parties, it is invariably to join the party more consonant with that switcher's policy interests. This implies that there are differences between the two parties at some fundamental and enduring level on policy positions, values, and beliefs. Thus, parties are institutions designed to promote the achievement of collective choices—choices on which the parties differ and choices reached by majority rule. As with access to office and ambition theory, there is a well-developed theory for this problem: *social choice theory.* Underlying this theory is the well-known problem that no method of choice can solve the elective officeholders' problem of combining the interests, concerns, or values of a polity that remains faithful to democratic values, as shown by the consequences flowing from Arrow's theorem (Arrow 1951). Thus, in a republican democracy politicians may turn to partisan institutions to solve the problem of collective choice. In the language of politics, parties may help achieve the goal of attaining policy majorities in the first place, as well as the often more difficult goal of maintaining such majorities.

The Problem of Collective Action

The third problem is the most pervasive and thus the furthest-ranging in substantive content. The clearest example, however, is also the most important. To win office, candidates need more than a party's nomination. Election requires persuading members of the public to support that candidacy and mobilizing as many of those supporters as possible. This is a problem of collective action. How do candidates get supporters to vote for them—at least in greater numbers than vote for the opposition—as well as get them to provide the cadre of workers and contribute the resources needed to win election? The political party has long been the solution.

As important as wooing and mobilizing supporters are, collective action problems arise in a wide range of circumstances facing elective office seekers. Party action invariably requires the concerted action of many partisans to achieve collectively desirable outcomes. Jimmy Carter was the only president in the 1970s and 1980s to enjoy unified party control of government. Democrats in Congress, it might well be argued, shared an interest in achieving policy outcomes. And yet Carter was all too often unable to get them to act in their shared collective interests. In 1980 not only he but the Democratic congressional parties paid a heavy price for failed cooperation. The theory here, of course, is the *theory of public goods* and its consequence, the *theory of collective action*.

The Elective Office Seekers' and Holders' Interests Are to Win

Why should this crucial set of actors, the elective office seekers and officeholders, care about these three classes of problems? The short answer is that these concerns become practical problems to politicians when they adversely affect their chances of winning. Put differently, politicians turn to their political party— that is, use its powers, resources, and institutional forms—when they believe doing so increases their prospects for winning desired outcomes, and they turn from it if it does not.

Ambition theory is about winning per se. The breakdown of orderly access to office risks unfettered and unregulated competition. The inability of a party to develop effective means of nomination and support for election therefore directly influences the chances of victory for the candidates and thus for their parties. The standard example of the problem of social choice theory, the "paradox of voting," is paradoxical precisely because all are voting to win desired outcomes, and yet there is no majority-preferred outcome. Even if there happens to be a majority-preferred policy, the conditions under which it is truly a stable equilibrium are extremely fragile and thus all too amenable to defeat. In other words, majorities in Congress are hard to attain and at least as hard to maintain. And the only reason to employ scarce campaign resources to mobilize supporters is that such mobilization increases the odds of victory. Its opposite, the failure to act when there are broadly shared interests—the problem of collective action— reduces the prospects of victory, whether at the ballot box or in government. Scholars may recognize these as manifestations of theoretical problems and call them "impossibility results" to emphasize their generic importance. Politicians recognize the consequences of these impossibility results by their adverse effects on their chances of winning—of securing what it is in their interests to secure.

So why have politicians so often turned to political parties for solutions to these problems? Their existence creates incentives for their use. It is, for example, incredibly difficult to win election to major office without the backing of a major party. It is only a little less certain that legislators who seek to lead a policy proposal through the congressional labyrinth will first turn to their party for assistance. But such incentives tell us only that an ongoing political institution is used when it is useful. Why form political parties in the first place? . . .

First, parties are institutions. This means, among other things, that they have some durability. They may be endogenous institutions, yet party reforms are meant not as short-term fixes but as alterations to last for years, even decades.

Thus, for example, legislators might create a party rather than a temporary majority coalition to increase their chances of winning not just today but into the future. Similarly, a long and successful political career means winning office today, but it also requires winning elections throughout that career. A standing, enduring organization makes that goal more likely.

Second, American democracy chooses by plurality or majority rule. Election to office therefore requires broad-based support wherever and from whomever it can be found. So strong are the resulting incentives for a two-party system to emerge that the effect is called Duverger's law (Duverger 1954). It is in part the need to win vast and diverse support that has led politicians to create political parties.

Third, parties may help officeholders win more, and more often, than alternatives. Consider the usual stylized model of pork barrel politics. All winners get a piece of the pork for their districts. All funded projects are paid for by tax revenues, so each district pays an equal share of the costs of each project adopted, whether or not that district receives a project. Several writers have argued that this kind of legislation leads to "universalism," that is, adoption of a "norm" that every such bill yields a project to every district and thus passes with a "universal" or unanimous coalition. Thus everyone "wins." . . . As a result, expecting to win only a bit more than half the time and lose the rest of the time, all legislators prefer consistent use of the norm of universalism. But consider an alternative. Suppose some majority agree to form a more permanent coalition, to control outcomes now and into the future, and develop institutional means to encourage fealty to this agreement. If they successfully accomplish this, they will win regularly. Members of this institutionalized coalition would prefer it to universalism, since they always win a project in either case, but they get their projects at lower cost under the institutionalized majority coalition, which passes fewer projects. Thus, even in this case with no shared substantive interests at all, there are nonetheless incentives to form an enduring voting coalition—to form a political party. And those in the excluded minority have incentives to counterorganize. United, they may be more able to woo defectors to their side. If not, they can campaign to throw those rascals in the majority party out of office.

In sum, these theoretical problems affect elective office seekers and officeholders by reducing their chances of winning. Politicians therefore may turn to political parties as institutions designed to ameliorate them. In solving these theoretical problems, however, from the politicians' perspective parties are affecting who wins and loses and what is won or lost. And it is to parties that politicians often turn, because of their durability as institutionalized solutions, because of the need to orchestrate large and diverse groups of people to form winning majorities, and because often more can be won through parties. Note that this argument rests on the implicit assumption that winning and losing hang in the balance. Politicians may be expected to give up some of their personal autonomy only when they face an imminent threat of defeat without doing so or only when doing so can block opponents' ability to build the strength necessary to win.

This is, of course, the positive case for parties, for it specifies conditions under which politicians find them useful. Not all problems are best solved, perhaps even solved at all, by political parties. Other arrangements, perhaps interest groups, issue networks, or personal electoral coalitions, may be superior at different times and under different conditions. The party may even be part of the problem. In such cases politicians turn elsewhere to seek the means to win. Thus this theory is at base a theory of ambitious politicians seeking to achieve their goals. Often they have done so through the agency of the party, but sometimes, this theory implies, they will seek to realize their goals in other ways.

The political party has regularly proved useful. Their permanence suggests that the appropriate question is not When parties? but How much parties and how much other means? That parties are endogenous implies that there is no single, consistent account of the political party—nor should we expect one. Instead, parties are but a (major) part of the institutional context in which current historical conditions—the problems—are set, and solutions are sought with permanence only by changing that web of institutional arrangements. Of these the political party is by design the most malleable, and thus it is intended to change in important ways and with relatively great frequency. But it changes in ways that have, for most of American history, retained major political parties and, indeed, retained two major parties.

REFERENCES

Arrow, Kenneth J. 1951. *Social Choice and Individual Values.* New York: Wiley.

Broder, David S. 1972. *The Party's Over: The Failure of Politics in America.* New York: Harper and Row.

Crotty, William. 1984. *American Political Parties in Decline.* 2d ed. Boston: Little, Brown.

Duverger, Maurice. 1954. *Political Parties: Their Organization and Activities in the Modern State.* New York: Wiley.

Eldersveld, Samuel J. 1982. *Political Parties in American Society.* New York: Basic Books.

Ferguson, Thomas. 1983. "Party Realignment and American Industrial Structures: The Investment Theory of Political Parties in Historical Perspective". In *Research in Political Economy,* vol. 6, ed. Paul Zarembka, pp. 1–82. Greenwich, Conn.: JAI Press.

Fiorina, Morris P. 1980. "The Decline of Collective Responsibility in American Politics". *Daedalus* 109 (summer): 25–45.

Jacobson, Gary C. 1992. *The Politics of Congressional Elections.* 3d ed. New York: Harper-Collins.

Kernell, Samuel. 1986. *Going Public: New Strategies of Presidential Leadership.* Washington, D.C.: CQ Press.

Kirkpatrick, Jeane J. 1978. *Dismantling the Parties: Reflections on Party Reform and Party Decomposition.* Washington, D.C.: American Enterprise Institute of Public Policy Research.

Lowi, Theodore. 1985. *The Personal President: Power Invested, Promise Unfulfilled.* Ithaca, N.Y.: Cornell University Press.

Neustadt, Richard E. 1960. *Presidential Power: The Politics of Leadership.* New York: Wiley.

_____. 1990. *Presidential Power and the Modern Presidents: The Politics of Leadership from Roosevelt to Reagan.* New York: Free Press.

Polsby, Nelson W. 1983. *Consequences of Party Reform.* Oxford: Oxford University Press.

Popkin, Samuel, John W. Gorman, Charles Phillips, and Jeffrey A. Smith. 1976. Comment: What Have You Done for Me Lately? Toward an Investment Theory of Voting. *American Political Science Review* 70 (September): 779–805.

Ranney, Austin. 1975. *Curing the Mischiefs of Faction: Party Reform in America.* Berkeley and Los Angeles: University of California Press.

Rohde, David W. 1989. "Something's Happening Here: What It is Ain't Exactly Clear": Southern Democrats in the House of Representatives. In *Home Style and Washington Work: Studies of Congressional Politics,* ed. Morris P. Fiorina and David W. Rohde, pp. 137–163. Ann Arbor: University of Michigan Press.

_____. 1991. *Parties and Leaders in the Postreform House.* Chicago: University of Chicago Press.

Schlesinger, Joseph A. 1966. *Ambition and Politics: Political Careers in the United States.* Chicago: Rand McNally.

_____. 1975. The Primary Goals of Political Parties: A Clarification of Positive Theory. *American Political Science Review* 69 (September): 840–49.

_____. 1985. The New American Political Party. *American Political Science Review* 79 (December): 1152–69.

Wattenberg, Martin P. 1990. *The Decline of American Political Parties: 1952–1988.* Cambridge: Harvard University Press.

12-2

Partisanship and Voting Behavior, 1952–1996

Larry M. Bartels

Many Americans consider themselves to be Democrats or Republicans, and a few identify with some other party. In the late 1960s and 1970s the number of Americans willing to call themselves Democrats or Republicans declined, leading political scientists to speak of a dealignment and worry about the declining importance of parties. Then partisanship appeared to rebound in the 1990s. In this essay political scientist Larry M. Bartels describes these trends and explains the importance of partisanship for the voting behavior of Americans. He argues that party identification increased in the 1980s and 1990s and that the correlation between party identification and presidential voting increased even more. He concludes by observing that changes in the behavior of elected partisans—greater partisanship among presidents and members of Congress—may have contributed to resurgent partisanship in voting in the electorate.

THE "DECLINE OF PARTIES" is one of the most familiar themes in popular and scholarly discourse about contemporary American politics. One influential journalist has asserted that "the most important phenomenon of American politics in the past quarter century has been the rise of independent voters." . . . The most persistent academic analyst of partisan decline has argued that "For over four decades the American public has been drifting away from the two major political parties," while another prominent scholar has referred to a "massive decay of partisan electoral linkages" and to "the ruins of the traditional partisan regime."

I shall argue here that this conventional wisdom regarding the "decline of parties" is both exaggerated and outdated. Partisan loyalties in the American public have rebounded significantly since the mid-1970s, especially among those who actually turn out to vote. Meanwhile, the impact of partisanship on voting behavior has increased markedly in recent years, both at the presidential level (where the overall impact of partisanship in 1996 was almost 80 percent greater than in 1972) and at the congressional level (where the overall impact of

Source: Larry Bartels, "Partisanship and Voting Behavior, 1952–1996," *American Journal of Political Science* 44, no. 1 (January 2000): 35–50. Notes and bibliographic references appearing in the original have been deleted.

partisanship in 1996 was almost 60 percent greater than in 1978). . . . My analysis suggests that "partisan loyalties had at least as much impact on voting behavior at the presidential level in the 1980s as in the 1950s"—and even more in the 1990s than in the 1980s.

The Thesis of Partisan Decline

Almost forty years ago, the authors of *The American Voter* asserted that

> Few factors are of greater importance for our national elections than the lasting attachment of tens of millions of Americans to one of the parties. These loyalties establish a basic division of electoral strength within which the competition of particular campaigns takes place. . . . Most Americans have this sense of attachment with one party or the other. And for the individual who does, the strength and direction of party identification are facts of central importance in accounting for attitude and behavior.

The so-called "Michigan model," with its emphasis on the fundamental importance of long-standing partisan loyalties, dominated the subsequent decade of academic research on voting behavior. However, over the same decade, changes in the political environment seemed to be rendering the "Michigan model" increasingly obsolete. By the early 1970s, political observers were pointing to the increasing proportion of "independents" in opinion surveys and the increasing prevalence of split-ticket voting as indications of significant partisan decline. By the mid-1970s, some political scientists were extrapolating from a decade-long trend to project a permanent demise of partisan politics. . . .

The "increase in the number of independents" in the 1960s and early '70s . . . —and the corresponding decrease in the proportion of the public who identified themselves as Democrats or Republicans—constitute the single most important piece of evidence in support of the thesis of partisan decline. These and subsequent trends are displayed in the two panels of Figure 1, which show the proportions of party identifiers (including "strong" and "weak" identifiers) and independents (including "pure" independents and "leaners"), respectively, in each of the biennial American National Election Studies from 1952 through 1996.

. . . The proportion of "strong" identifiers in the population increased from 24 percent in 1976 to 31 percent in 1996, while the proportion of "pure" independents—those who neither identified themselves as Democrats or Republicans nor "leaned" to either party in response to the traditional Michigan follow-up question—declined from 16 percent in 1976 to only 9 percent in 1996.

Figure 1. The Distribution of Party Identification, 1952–1996

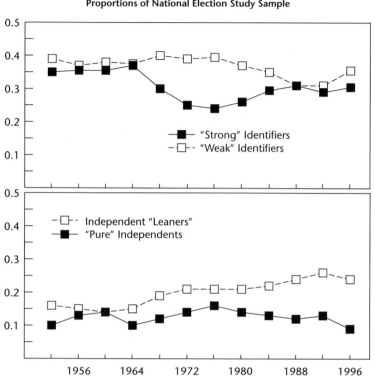

A Summary Measure of Partisan Voting

What significance should we attach to the shifts in the distribution of party iden-tification documented in Figure 1? . . . To the extent that our interest in partisan loyalties is motivated by an interest in voting behavior, we would seem to need (at least) two kinds of additional information to interpret the electoral implica-tions of changing levels of partisanship. First, are the shifts documented in Figure 1 concentrated among voters or among nonvoters? Declining partisanship among nonvoters may leave the distribution of party identification in the voting booth unchanged. And second, has the electoral *impact* of a given level of partisanship declined or increased over time? Declining *levels* of partisanship might be either reinforced or counteracted by changes in the *impact* of partisanship on electoral choices.

The first of these two questions is addressed by Figure 2, which shows sepa-rate trend lines for the proportion of ("strong" or "weak") party identifiers among voters and nonvoters in presidential elections since 1952. Not surpris-ingly, nonvoters are less partisan than voters in every year. But what is more

Figure 2. Party Identification among Presidential Voters and Nonvoters

Proportions of (Strong or Weak) Identifiers in National Election Study Sample

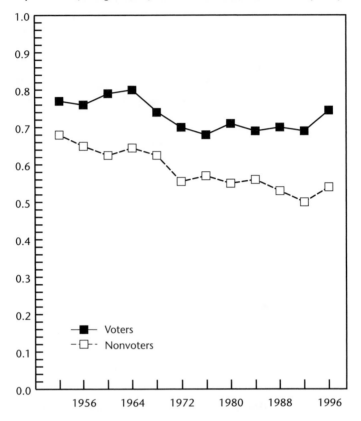

important to note here is that the gap in partisanship between voters and non-voters has widened noticeably over time, from about ten percentage points in the 1950s to about twenty percentage points by the 1990s. Indeed, it appears from these results that the decline in partisanship evident in Figure 1 has been almost entirely reversed among voters: the proportion of party identifiers in the presidential electorate was 77 percent in 1952, 76 percent in 1956, and 75 percent in 1996, while the proportion among nonvoters was almost fifteen points lower in 1996 than in the 1950s. Thus, while the trend lines shown in Figure 1 suggest that the erosion of party loyalties underlying the "partisan decline" thesis has ended and probably even reversed in the last two decades, the results presented in Figure 2 suggest that these developments have been especially pronounced among actual voters.

The erosion of party loyalties among nonvoters evident in Figure 2 is of importance for any general account of the role of partisanship in contemporary

American politics. It is especially important in view of evidence suggesting that declining partisanship is, at least in modest part, *responsible* for the substantial decline in turnout over the period covered by Figure 2, and that individual turnout decisions are increasingly sensitive to the strength of prospective voters' preferences for one candidate or the other, which derive in significant part from long-term partisan attachments. However, given my narrower aim here of documenting changes in the impact of partisanship *on voting behavior,* the most important implication of Figure 2 is that the distribution of partisan attachments *among those citizens who actually got to the polls* was not much different in the 1990s from what it had been in the 1950s.

Of course, the significance of partisanship in the electoral process depends not only upon the level of partisanship in the electorate, but also upon the extent to which partisanship influences voting behavior. How, if at all, has that influence changed over the four and a half decades covered by the NES data? . . . . [Editors: Bartels estimates the impact of party identification on voting by taking advantage of the survey from which respondents are coded as strong Republican, weak Republican, leaning Republican, independent, leaning Democrat, weak Democrat, and strong Democrat. For each category, a statistical estimate is calculated for the effect of being in that category on voting for the alternative presidential or congressional candidates. The statistical estimate, called a probit coefficient, is averaged for the partisan categories to yield an overall measure "partisan voting." Figure 3 presents the result for elections in the 1952–1996 period.]

The Revival of Partisan Voting in Presidential Elections

. . . Figure 3 shows noticeable declines in the level of partisan voting in the presidential elections of 1964 and, especially, 1972. These declines primarily reflect the fact that Republican identifiers in 1964 and Democratic identifiers in 1972 abandoned their parties' unpopular presidential candidates by the millions, depressing the estimated effects of partisan loyalties on the presidential vote in those years. However, an even more striking pattern in Figure 3 is the monotonic increase in partisan voting in every presidential election since 1972. By 1996, this trend had produced a level of partisan voting 77 percent higher than in 1972—an average increase of 10 percent in each election, compounded over six election cycles—and 15 to 20 percent higher than in the supposed glory days of the 1950s that spawned *The American Voter.*

. . . One possible explanation for the revival of partisan voting evident in Figure 3 is the sorting out of partisan attachments of southerners following the civil rights upheavals of the early and middle 1960s. As national party elites took

Figure 3. Partisan Voting in Presidential Elections

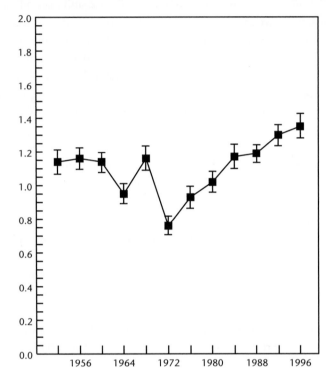

Estimated Impact of Party Identification on Presidential Vote Propensity

Note: Average probit coefficients, major-party voters only, with jackknife standard error bars.

increasingly distinct stands on racial issues, black voters moved overwhelmingly into the Democratic column, while white southerners defected to conservative Republican presidential candidates. What is important here is that many of these conservative white southerners only gradually shed their traditional Democratic identifications—and Democratic voting behavior at the subpresidential level—through the 1980s and '90s. Thus, it may be tempting to interpret the revival of partisan voting at the presidential level largely as a reflection of the gradual reequilibration of presidential votes and more general partisan attachments among white southerners in the wake of a regional partisan realignment.

As it happens, however, the steady and substantial increases in partisan voting over the past quarter-century evident in Figure 3 are by no means confined to the South. This fact is evident from Figure 4, which displays separate patterns of partisan voting for white southerners and white nonsoutherners. The trend lines are somewhat more ragged for these subgroups than for the electorate as a whole, especially in the South (where the year-by-year estimates are based on an average of fewer than 300 southern white voters in each election); nevertheless, the general pattern in Figure 3 is replicated almost identically in both subgroups in Figure 4. The absolute level of partisan voting in the 1964 and 1972 elections is only slightly lower among southern whites than among nonsouthern whites, and the substantial increase in partisan voting since 1972 appears clearly (indeed, nearly monotonically) in both subgroups.

It should be evident from Figure 4 that the revival of partisan voting in presidential elections documented in Figure 3 is a national rather than a regional phenomenon. Indeed, additional analysis along these lines suggests that the same pattern is evident in a wide variety of subgroups of the electorate, including voters under 40 and those over 50 years of age, those with college educations and those without high school diplomas, and so on. Thus, any convincing explanation

Figure 4. Partisan Voting in Presidential Elections,
White Southerners and White Nonsoutherners

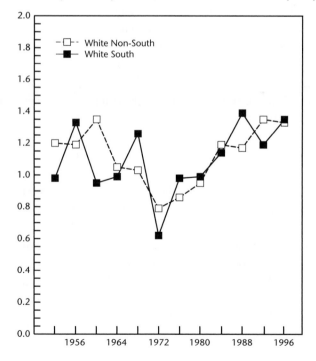

Estimated Impact of Party Identification on Presidential Vote Propensity

Note: Average probit coefficients, major-party voters only.

of this partisan revival will presumably have to be based upon broad changes in the national political environment, rather than upon narrower demographic or generational developments.

Partisan Voting in Congressional Elections

My analysis so far has focused solely on the impact of partisan loyalties on voting behavior in presidential elections. However, there are a variety of reasons to suppose that the trends evident in presidential voting might not appear at other electoral levels. For one thing, I have already argued that the significant dips in partisanship at the presidential level evident in Figure 3 are attributable primarily to the parties' specific presidential candidates in 1964 and 1972. If that is so, there is little reason to expect those dips—or the subsequent rebounds—in levels of partisan voting to appear at other electoral levels.

In any case, analysts of congressional voting behavior since the 1970s have been more impressed by the advantages of incumbency than by any strong connections between presidential and congressional votes—except insofar as voters may go out of their way to split their tickets in order to produce divided government. Thus, it would not be surprising to find a longer, more substantial decline in the level of partisan voting in congressional elections than in the analysis of presidential voting summarized in Figure 3.

. . . Figure 5 clearly shows a substantial decline in partisan voting in congressional elections from the early 1960s through the late 1970s. Indeed, the level of partisan voting declined in seven of the eight congressional elections between 1964 and 1978; by 1978, the average impact of partisanship on congressional voting was only a bit more than half what it had been before 1964. Although the overall impact of partisanship at the presidential and congressional levels was generally similar for much of this period, the declines at the congressional level were less episodic and longer lasting than those at the presidential level.

What is more surprising is that the revival of partisanship evident in presidential voting patterns since 1972 is also evident in congressional voting patterns since 1978. While the trend is later and less regular at the congressional level than at the presidential level, the absolute increases in partisan voting since 1980 have been of quite similar magnitude in presidential and congressional elections. While partisan voting remains noticeably less powerful in recent congressional elections than it was before 1964—or than it has been in recent presidential elections—the impact of partisanship on congressional votes in 1996 was almost 60 percent greater than in 1978.

An interesting feature of the resurgence of partisan voting in congressional elections documented in Figure 5 is that it appears to be concentrated disproportionately among younger and better-educated voters. For example, voters under

Figure 5. Partisan Voting in Presidential and Congressional Elections

Estimated Impact of Party Identification on Presidential and Congressional Vote Propensities

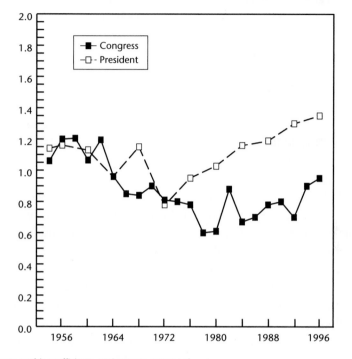

Note: Average probit coefficients, major-party voters only.

the age of 40 were noticeably less partisan in their voting behavior than those over the age of 50 in almost every election from 1952 through 1984, but virtually indistinguishable from the older voters in the late 1980s and 1990s. Similarly, levels of partisan voting were distinctly lower among voters with some college education than among those without high school diplomas before 1982, but not thereafter. These patterns suggest that the resurgence of partisan voting reflects some positive reaction by younger and better-educated voters to the political developments of the past two decades, rather than simply a "wearing off" of the political stimuli of the 1960s and 1970s.

Discussion

If the analysis presented here is correct, the American political system has slipped, with remarkably little fanfare, into an era of increasingly vibrant partisanship in the electorate, especially at the presidential level but also at the congressional level. How might we account for this apparent revival of partisan voting?

One plausible hypothesis is that increasing partisanship in the electorate represents a response at the mass level to increasing partisanship at the elite level. "If parties in government are weakened," [political scientist Martin] Wattenberg argued, "the public will naturally have less of a stimulus to think of themselves politically in partisan terms." But then the converse may also be true: in an era in which parties in government seem increasingly consequential, the public may increasingly come to develop and apply partisan predispositions of exactly the sort described by the authors of *The American Voter*.

Why might parties in government seem more relevant in the late 1990s than they had a quarter-century earlier? The ascensions of two highly partisan political leaders—Ronald Reagan in 1981 and Newt Gingrich in 1995—may provide part of the explanation. So too may the increasing prominence of the Religious Right in Republican party nominating politics over this period. At a more structural level, the realignment of partisan loyalties in the South in the wake of the civil rights movement of the 1960s may be important, despite the evidence presented in Figure 4 suggesting that the revival of partisan voting has been a national rather than a regional phenomenon.

Regional realignment in the South and the influence of ideological extremists in both parties' nominating politics have combined to produce a marked polarization of the national parties at the elite level. By a variety of measures . . . votes on the floor of Congress have become increasingly partisan since the 1970s. . . . These changes in the composition of the parties' congressional delegations have been "reinforced by the operation of those reform provisions that were intended to enhance collective control" by party leaders in Congress, including a strengthened Democratic caucus and whip system. The new Republican congressional majority in 1995 produced further procedural reforms "delegating more power to party leaders than any House majority since the revolt against Joe Cannon in 1910."

We know less than we should about the nature and extent of mass-level reactions to these elite-level developments. However, the plausibility of a causal link between recent increases in partisanship at the elite and mass levels is reinforced by the fact that the decline in partisan voting in the electorate in the 1960s and 1970s was itself preceded by a noticeable decline in party voting in Congress from the 1950s through the early 1970s. Moreover, some more direct evidence suggests that citizens have taken note of the increasing strength of partisan cues from Washington. For example, the proportion of NES survey respondents perceiving "important differences" between the Democratic and Republican parties increased noticeably in 1980 and again in 1984 and reached a new all-time high (for the period since 1952) in 1996.

Even more intriguingly, [political scientist John] Coleman has documented a systematic temporal relationship between the strength of partisanship in government and the strength of partisanship in the electorate. Analyzing data from 1952 through 1990, Coleman found a strong positive correlation across election years (.60) between the strength of partisanship in NES surveys and the proportion of House budget votes with opposing party majorities—and an even stronger correlation (.66) between mass partisanship and opposing party majorities on budget authorization votes. While the detailed processes underlying this aggregate relationship are by no means clear, the strength of the correlation at least suggests that students of party politics would do well to examine more closely the interrelationship of mass-level and elite-level trends. . . .

12-3

Parties as Problem Solvers

Morris P. Fiorina

Political parties receive conflicting reviews. Some people view parties as self-serving entities that generate unnecessary conflict, make essential compromise more difficult, and serve as obstacles to solving important national problems. Others view party competition as the means for aggregating a variety of interests, generating policy alternatives, coordinating action across branches of government, and holding elected officials accountable. In this essay, political scientist Morris Fiorina evaluates the role of parties in addressing the nation's problems in the first decade of the new millennium.

SOME TWENTY-FIVE YEARS AGO I wrote an article entitled "The Decline of Collective Responsibility in American Politics." In that article (henceforth referenced as DOCR), I updated the classic arguments for party responsibility in light of which the politics of the 1970s looked seriously deficient. . . . . [I] noted that in the 1970s party cohesion had dropped to a level not seen since before the Civil War. As a result, national politics had degenerated into a free-for-all of unprincipled bargaining in which participants blithely sacrificed general interests in their pursuit of particularistic constituency interests. The unified Democratic government of President Jimmy Carter that failed to deal with national problems such as runaway inflation and successive energy crises exemplified the sorry state of national politics. Moreover, not only had policy failure become more likely, but because voting for members of Congress increasingly reflected the particularistic activities and personal records of incumbents, members had little fear of being held accountable for their contribution to the failures of national politics. In that light, I sympathetically resurrected the arguments of early to midcentury political scientists who advocated more responsible parties. Although not all problems were amenable to government solution, unified political parties led by strong presidents were more likely to act decisively to meet the challenges facing the country, and when they took their collective performance records to the electorate for ratification or rejection, the voters at least had a good idea of whom to reward or blame.

Source: Morris P. Fiorina, "Parties as Problem Solvers," in *Promoting the General Welfare: New Perspectives on Government Performance,* eds. Alan S. Gerber and Eric M. Patashnik (Washington, D.C.: Brookings Institution Press, 2006), 237–253. Notes appearing in the original have been deleted.

Looking back at these essays, the 1980s clearly was the decade of party responsibility for me. But . . . . the prevalence of divided government in the late twentieth century had raised doubts in my mind about the arguments articulated a decade earlier. These doubts cumulated into a change of position explicated at length in *Divided Government* and later writings. In brief, as the parties became more distinct and cohesive during the 1980s, voters seemed to show little appreciation for the changes. Rather than entrust control of government to one unified party, Americans were increasingly voting to split control of government—at the state as well as the national level. And whether that was their actual goal or not—a matter of continuing debate—polls showed that majorities were happy enough with the situation, whatever political scientists thought of the supposed programmatic inefficiency and electoral irresponsibility of divided government. By the early 1990s, I had come to appreciate the electorate's point of view.

Moving from one side of an argument to the other in a decade suggests that the protagonist either was wrong earlier or (worse!) wrong later. But there is another less uncomplimentary possibility—namely, that the shift in stance did not reflect blatant error in the earlier argument so much as changes in one or more unrecognized but important empirical premises, which vitiate the larger argument. . . . . By 1990 I had come to believe that in important respects the parties we were observing in the contemporary era were different in composition and behavior from the ones described in the political science literature we had studied in graduate school. Parties organized to solve the governance problems of one era do not necessarily operate in the same way as parties organized to solve the problems of later eras.

This chapter considers the capacity of the contemporary party system to solve societal problems and meet contemporary challenges. I do so by revisiting DOCR and reconsidering it against the realities of contemporary politics. I begin by briefly contrasting American politics in the 1970s and the 2000s.

Politics Then and Now

DOCR reflected the politics of the 1970s, a decade that began with divided government (then still regarded as something of an anomaly), proceeded through the resignations of a vice president and president followed by the brief administration of an unelected president, then saw the restoration of the "normal order"—unified Democratic government—in 1976, only to see it collapse at the end of the decade in the landslide rejection of a presidency mortally wounded by international humiliation, stagflation, and energy crises. Contemporary critics placed much of the responsibility for the "failed" Carter presidency at the feet of Carter himself—his obsession with detail, his inability to delegate, his political tin ear, and so forth—but I felt then that the critics were giving insufficient attention to larger developments and more general circumstances that would have posed serious obstacles for presidents who possessed much stronger executive and political skills than Carter.

Political Conditions in the 1970s

Not only did Jimmy Carter's 1976 victory restore the presidency to the Democrats, but large Democratic majorities also controlled both the House and Senate. It seemed that the great era of government activism that had been derailed by the war in Vietnam would resume. Such was not to be. After four years of political frustration Carter was soundly defeated, the Republicans captured the Senate with a remarkable gain of twelve seats, and the Democrats lost thirty-three seats in the House. What happened?

Basically, the country faced a series of new problems, and the Democratic Party failed to deal with them in a manner satisfactory to electoral majorities in the nation as a whole and in many states and districts. Gas lines in particular, and the energy crisis in general, were something new in modern American experience, as were double-digit inflation and interest rates near 20 percent. Middle-class tax revolts were a startling development that frightened Democrats and energized Republicans, and a succession of foreign policy setbacks led many to fear that the United States was ill prepared to deal with new challenges around the world. In the face of such developments Democratic majorities in Congress failed to deliver. Indeed, they seemed fixated on old, ineffective solutions like public works spending and trade restrictions. The honeymoon between Carter and congressional Democrats ended fairly quickly, and the partnership was under strain for most of Carter's administration. Members worked to protect their constituencies from the negative effects of the new developments and worried much less about the fate of Carter or the party as a whole. As Figure 1 shows, this was a period of low party cohesion, and although cross-party majorities were not as common as in the late 1960s, Figure 2 shows that they still were common.

The generation of congressional scholars who contributed to the literature of the 1950s and 1960s had defended the decentralized Congresses of the period against the centralizing impulses of presidential scholars and policy wonks. True, Congress did not move fast or efficiently, nor did it defer to presidential leadership, but most scholars would have characterized this as pragmatic incrementalism rather than the "deadlock of democracy." Congress reflected and was responsive to the heterogeneity of interests in the country. . . .

To a younger generation of scholars, however, the failings of the decentralized Congresses and disorganized parties were cause for concern. Serious problems

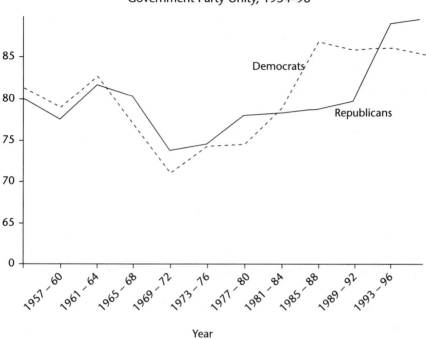

Figure 1. The Decline and Resurgence of Party in
Government Party Unity, 1954–98

Source: Harold W. Stanley and Richard G. Niemi, eds., *Vital Statistics on American Politics, 2005–2006* (Washington, DC: CQ Press, 2005), Table 5.8.

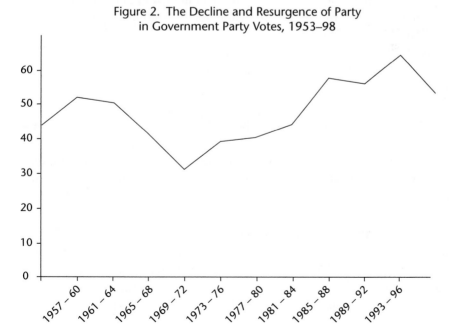

Figure 2. The Decline and Resurgence of Party
in Government Party Votes, 1953–98

Source: Harold W. Stanley and Richard G. Niemi, eds., *Vital Statistics on American Politics, 2005–2006* (Washington, DC: CQ Press, 2005), Table 5.7.

faced the country, presidents were held responsible for solving these problems, but incumbent members of Congress seemingly could win reelection by abandoning their presidents and parties in favor of protecting parochial constituency interests. By emphasizing their individual records, members of Congress had adapted to an era of candidate-centered politics. Historically speaking, they had far less to gain or lose from the effects of presidential coattails, nor need they be very concerned about midterm swings against their president's party. Collective responsibility traditionally provided by the political parties was at a low ebb. *Pluribus* was running rampant, leaving *unum* in the electoral dust.

Political Conditions Now

In retrospect, the trends decried in DOCR had already bottomed out by the Carter presidency. The cross-party majorities that passed President Reagan's budget and tax cuts may have obscured the fact, but party unity and party differences already were on the rise and continued rising in succeeding years (Figures 1 and 2). In a related development, the electoral advantages accruing to incumbency already were beginning to recede as national influences in voting reasserted themselves. And a new breed of congressional leaders emerged to focus the efforts of their parties in support of or opposition to presidential proposals. In 1993 President Clinton's initial budget passed without a single Republican vote in the House or Senate, and unified Republican opposition contributed greatly to the demise of the administration's signature health care plan.

And then came 1994, when the Republicans finally had success in an undertaking they had sporadically attempted for a generation—nationalizing the congressional elections. In the 1994 elections, personal opposition to gun control or various other liberal policies no longer sufficed to save Democrats in conservative districts whose party label overwhelmed their personal positions. The new Republican majorities in Congress seized the initiative from President Clinton to the extent that he was asked at a press conference whether he was "still relevant." When congressional Republicans overreached, Clinton reasserted his relevance, beating back Republican attempts to cut entitlement programs and saddling them with the blame for the government shutdowns of 1995–96.

At the time, the Republican attempt to govern as a responsible party struck many political scientists as unprecedented in the modern era, but, as Baer and Bositis pointed out, politics had been moving in that direction for several decades. Indeed, a great deal of what the 1950 APSA [American Political Science Association] report called for already had come to pass (Table 1). Now, a decade

Table 1. APSA Report after Forty Years

Fate of proposal	Democrats	Republicans	System
Full implementation	13	6	5
Partial implementation	7	5	5
De facto movement	8	9	5
No change	3	10	3
Negative movement	2	3	2

Source: Grossly adapted from Denise Baer and David Bositis, *Politics and Linkage in a Democratic Society* (Upper Saddle River, N.J.: Prentice-Hall, 1993), appendix.

later, it is apparent that the Congress elected in 1994 was only the leading edge of a new period in national politics. Party unity and presidential support among Republicans hit fifty-year highs during the first term of President George W. Bush, and in 2002 the president pulled off the rare feat of leading his party to seat gains in a midterm election. After his reelection in 2004, President Bush spoke in terms clearly reminiscent of those used by responsible party theorists. On the basis of a 51 percent popular majority, he claimed a mandate to make his tax cuts permanent and transform Social Security. Moreover, early in 2005 when the president was asked why no one in his administration had been held accountable for mistakes and miscalculations about Iraq, he replied in words that should have warmed the hearts of responsible party theorists: "We had an accountability moment, and that's called the 2004 election. And the American people listened to different assessments made about what was taking place in Iraq, and they looked at the two candidates, and chose me, for which I'm grateful." No president in living memory had articulated such clear statements of collective party responsibility legitimized by electoral victory.

In sum, the collective responsibility DOCR found wanting in the 1970s seems clearly present in the 2000s. Why, then, am I troubled by the operation of something I fervently wished for in the 1970s?

The Problems with Today's Responsible Parties

In 2002 a Republican administration ostensibly committed to free enterprise endorsed tariffs to protect the U.S. steel industry, a policy condemned by economists across the ideological spectrum. Also in 2002 Congress passed and President Bush signed an agricultural subsidy bill that the left-leaning *New York Times* decried as an "orgy of pandering to special interest groups," the centrist *USA Today* called "a congressional atrocity," and the right-leaning *Economist* characterized as "monstrous." In 2003 Congress passed and the president signed a special interest–riddled prescription drug plan that was the largest entitlement program adopted since Medicare itself in 1965, a fiscal commitment that immediately put the larger Medicare program on a steep slide toward bankruptcy. In 2004 congressional Republicans proposed and President Bush supported a constitutional amendment to ban gay marriage, a divisive proposal that had no chance of passing. After his reelection, President Bush declared his highest priority was to avert a crisis in a Social Security system he insisted was bankrupt, by establishing a system of personal accounts, while disinterested observers generally pronounced the situation far from crisis and in need of relatively moderate reform—especially compared to Medicare. In 2005 the Republican Congress passed and President Bush signed a pork-filled transportation bill that contained 6,371 congressional earmarks, forty times as many as contained in a bill vetoed by an earlier Republican president in 1987. Meanwhile, at the time of this writing Americans continue to die in a war of choice launched on the basis of ambiguous intelligence that appears to have been systematically interpreted to support a previously adopted position.

The preceding are only some of the more noteworthy lowlights of public policies adopted or proposed under the responsible party government of 2000–05. All things considered, if someone wished to argue that politics in the 1970s was better than today, I would find it hard to rebut them. Why? Are today's problems and challenges so much more difficult than those of the 1970s that the decentralized, irresponsible parties of that time would have done an even poorer job of meeting them than the more responsible parties of today? Or are today's responsible parties operating in a manner that was not anticipated by those of us who wished for more responsible parties? In the remainder of this chapter, I will focus on the latter possibility.

What Didn't DOCR Anticipate?

With the benefit of hindsight, one potentially negative effect of political competition by cohesive, differentiated parties is to raise the stakes of politics. Certainly, majority control of institutions always is valuable; committee chairs, agenda control, staff budgets, and numerous other benefits go to the majority. But if majority control of the House or Senate means relatively little for policymaking because moderate Republicans and Democrats hold the balance of power, which party formally holds control means less than when policy is decided within each party caucus. Similarly, the knowledge that the president's program either will be rubber-stamped by a supportive congressional majority or killed by an opposition majority makes unified control of all three institutions that much more valuable. The fact that the parties have been so closely matched in the past decade makes the competition that much more intense.

With the political stakes ratcheted upward, politics naturally becomes more conflictual. The benefits of winning and the costs of losing both increase. Informal norms and even formal rules come under pressure as the legislative majority strives to eliminate obstacles to its agenda. Meanwhile, the minority is first ignored, then abused. House Democrats under Jim Wright marginalized House Republicans in the 1980s, and the Republicans have enthusiastically returned the favor since taking control in 1994. Meanwhile Senate Majority Leader Bill Frist threatens the minority Democrats with the "nuclear option"—a rules change that effectively eliminates the filibuster on presidential appointments. In sum, the increasing disparity between majority and minority status further raises the electoral stakes and makes politics more conflictual.

In retrospect, it is probable that the development of more responsible parties was a factor—certainly not the only one—that contributed to the rise of the permanent campaign. With majority status that much more valuable, and minority status that much more intolerable, the parties are less able to afford a hiatus between elections in which governing takes precedence over electioneering. All else now is subordinated to party positioning for the next election. Free trade principles? Forget about them if Pennsylvania and Ohio steel workers are needed to win the next election. Budget deficits? Ignore them if a budget-busting prescription drug plan is needed to keep the opposition from scoring points with senior citizens. Politics always has affected policies, of course, but today the linkage is closer and stronger than ever before.

A second problem with cohesive parties that offer voters a clear choice is that voters may not like clear choices. The APSA report asserted that responsible parties would offer voters "a proper range of choice." But what is "proper"? Voters may not want a clear choice between repeal of *Roe v. Wade* and unregulated abortion, between private Social Security accounts and ignoring inevitable problems, between launching wars of choice and ignoring developing threats. Despite much popular commentary to the contrary, the issue positions of the electorate as a whole are not polarized; voters today remain, as always, generally moderate, or, at least, ambivalent. But candidates and their parties are polarized, and the consequence is candidate evaluations and votes that are highly polarized, which is what we have seen in recent elections.

Even if voters *were* polarized on issues and wished the parties to offer clear choices, they would still be dissatisfied if there were more than one issue and the opinion divisions across issues were not the same. For example, contemporary Republicans are basically an alliance between economic and social conservatives, and Democrats an alliance between economic and social liberals. So, in which party does someone who is an economic conservative and a social liberal belong? An economic liberal and a social conservative? Such people might well prefer moderate positions on both dimensions to issue packages consisting of one position they like a great deal and another they dislike a great deal.

The bottom line is that the majoritarianism that accompanies responsible parties may be ill suited for a heterogeneous society. With only one dimension of conflict a victory by one party can reasonably be interpreted to mean that a majority prefers its program to that of the other party. But with more than one dimension a victory by one party by no means guarantees majority support for its program(s). Indeed, . . . given variations in voter intensity on different issues, a party can win by constructing a coalition of minorities—taking the minority position on each issue.

American politics probably appeared to have a simpler and clearer structure at the time the APSA report was written. Race was not on the agenda. Social and cultural issues were largely dormant in the midcentury decades, their importance diminished by the end of immigration in the 1920s, the Great Depression, and World War II. A bipartisan consensus surrounded foreign and defense policy. Under such conditions it is understandable that a midcentury political scientist could have felt that all the country needed was two parties that advocated alternative economic programs. For example, in 1962 political historian James McGregor Burns wrote, "It is curious that majoritarian politics has won such a reputation for radicalism in this country. Actually it is moderate politics; it looks radical only in relation to the snail-like progress of Madisonian politics. The Jeffersonian strategy is essentially moderate because it is essentially competitive; in a homogeneous society it must appeal to the moderate, middle-class independent voters who hold the balance of power."

To most contemporary observers the United States looks rather less homogeneous than it apparently did to observers of Burns's era. Compared to 1950, our present situation is more complex with a more elaborate political issue space and less of a tendency to appeal to the moderate voter, as we discuss below.

Burns's contention that majoritarian politics is moderate politics is quite interesting in light of the contemporary discussion of the polarization of American politics. Although the electorate is not polarized, there is no question that the political class—the variegated collection of candidates, activists, interest group spokespersons, and infotainment media—is polarized. And, where we can measure it well, there is little doubt that the political class has become increasingly polarized over the past several decades. Figure 3 illustrates the oft-noted fact that moderates have disappeared from Congress: the area of overlap where conservative Democrats and liberal Republicans meet has shrunk to almost nothing, and

Figure 3. Polarization of Congress since the 1960s

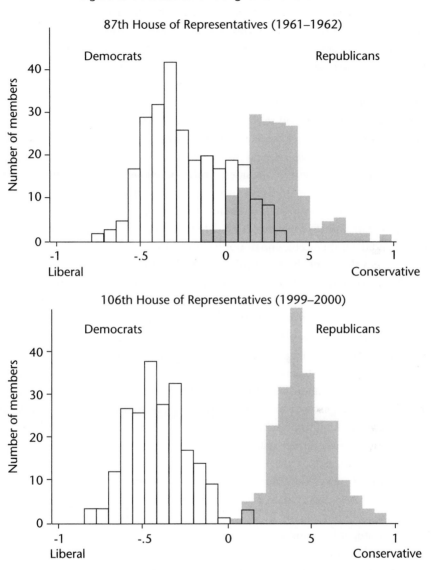

Source: Keith Poole, http://voteview.com/dwnomin.htm.

it has done so at the same time as the parties were becoming more responsible—indeed, figures like these often are cited as indicators of party responsibility.

Why would polarization accompany party responsibility? Logically it need not. Indeed, the APSA report asserted that "[n]eeded clarification of party policy in itself will not cause the parties to differ more fundamentally or more sharply than they have in the past." But as I have argued elsewhere, today's parties are not the same as the parties described in midcentury textbooks. The old distinctions between "amateurs" and "professionals" or "purists" and "professionals" no longer have the same conceptual value because the amateurs have won, or perhaps more accurately, the professionals now are purists. At the time the responsible party theorists wrote, parties nominated candidates on the basis of their service to the party and their connections to party leaders, or, in more competitive areas, their electability. Aside from times when a party was bitterly divided, issue positions were seldom a litmus test of a candidate's suitability. Material motivations—control of offices, patronage—were dominant, but civil service, public sector unionization, conflict of interest laws, social welfare programs, and other developments have lessened the personal material rewards that once motivated many of those active in politics. Today, ideological motivations are relatively more important than previously. Candidates must have the right set of issue stances to attract support, and many of the potential supporters would prefer to lose with a pure ideological candidate than to win with a mushy moderate. Some candidates themselves no doubt feel the same.

These developments have contributed to a basic shift in party electoral strategy in the contemporary United States. At midcentury, the conventional wisdom expressed by Burns was in accord with political science theory—that two-party competition induces parties to move toward the center to capture the median voter. But in the last decade of the century we saw a shift to what now seems to be the prevailing strategy of concentrating on the party base—doing whatever is necessary to maximize loyalty and turnout by core party constituencies. Thus, the aforementioned forcing of a Senate vote on gay marriage was an entirely symbolic gesture toward the evangelical Christian base of the Republican Party. It had nothing to do with governing; it was a costly signal that the Bush administration was on their side.

Seemingly, today's parties no longer strive to maximize their vote, only to suffice—to get more votes than the other party. At one time a maximal victory was desirable because it would add credibility to the victors' claim that the voters had given them a mandate. But as the previously quoted remarks of President Bush indicate, at least some of today's politicians consider any victory, narrow or not, a mandate.

Parties composed of issue activists and ideologues behave differently from the parties that occupied the political science literature of the mid-twentieth century. At midcentury, each party appealed to a different swath of the American public, Democrats primarily to blue-collar workers and Republicans to middle-class-professionals and managers. Because such large social groupings were far from homogeneous internally, the party platform had to tolerate internal heterogeneity to maintain itself and compete across a reasonably broad portion of the country. As Turner put it, "[Y]ou cannot give Hubert Humphrey [liberal Democratic

Senator from Minnesota] a banjo and expect him to carry Kansas. Only a Democrat who rejects part of the Fair Deal can carry Kansas, and only a Republican who moderates the Republican platform can carry Massachusetts."

Although both parties continue to have support in broad social groupings like blue-collar workers and white-collar professionals, their bases now consist of much more specifically defined groups. Democrats rely on public-sector unions, environmentalists, prochoice and other liberal cause groups. Republicans rely on evangelicals, small business organizations, prolife and other conservative cause groups. Rather than compromise on a single major issue such as economics, a process that midcentury political scientists correctly saw as inherently moderating, parties can now compromise across issues by adding up constituency groups' most preferred positions on a series of independent issues. Why should conservative mean prolife, low taxes, procapital punishment, and preemptive war, and liberal mean just the opposite? What is the underlying principle that ties such disparate issues together? The underlying principle is political, not logical or moral. Collections of positions like these happen to be the preferred positions of groups that now constitute important parts of the party bases.

At one time political scientists saw strong political parties as a means of controlling interest groups. Parties and groups were viewed as competing ways of organizing political life. If parties were weak, groups would fill the vacuum; if parties were strong, they would harness group efforts in support of more general party goals. Two decades ago, I was persuaded by this argument, but time has proved it suspect. Modern parties and their associated groups now overlap so closely that it is often hard to make the distinction between a party activist and an issue activist. As noted above, the difference between party professionals and purists does not look nearly so wide as it once did.

Although more speculative, I believe that unbiased information and policy effectiveness are additional casualties of the preceding developments. The APSA report asserts, "As a means of achieving responsibility, the clarification of party policy also tends to keep public debate on a more realistic level, restraining the inclination of party spokesmen to make unsubstantiated statements and charges." Recent experience shows just the opposite. Policies are proposed and opposed relatively more on the basis of ideology and the demands of the base, and relatively less on the basis of their likelihood of solving problems. Disinformation and outright lies become common as dissenting voices in each party leave or are silenced. The most disturbing example comes out of congressional passage of the 2003 Medicare prescription drug add-on bill. Political superiors threatened to fire Medicare's chief actuary if he informed Congress that the add-on would be 25–50 percent more costly than the administration publicly claimed. The administration apparently was willing to lie to members of its own party to assure passage

of a bill whose basis was mostly political. More recently, President Bush introduced his campaign to add personal accounts to Social Security by claiming that
Social Security was bankrupt and that personal accounts were a means of restoring the system to fiscal solvency. Although many experts see merit in the idea of
personal savings accounts, most agreed that implementing them would increase
Social Security's fiscal deficits in the coming decades. Even greater agreement
surrounded rejection of the claim that Social Security was bankrupt. Although
politically difficult, straightforward programmatic changes in the retirement age,
the tax base, or the method of indexing future benefits would make Social
Security solvent for as long as actuaries can reasonably predict.

Moreover, because parties today focus on their ability to mobilize the already
committed, the importance of performance for voting declines in importance relative to ideology and political identity. It was telling that in 2004 John Kerry frequently was criticized for not having a plan to end the war in Iraq that was
appreciably different from President Bush's. This seems like a new requirement. In
1952 did Dwight Eisenhower have a specific plan to end the war in Korea that differed from President Truman's? "I will go to Korea" is not exactly a plan. In 1968
did Richard Nixon have a specific plan to end the war in Vietnam that differed from
President Johnson's? A "secret plan" to end the war is not exactly a precise blue-
print that voters could compare to the Johnson policy. Some decades ago voters
apparently felt that an unpopular war was sufficient reason to punish an incumbent, regardless of whether the challenger offered a persuasive "exit strategy."

A final consideration relates to the preceding ones. Because today's parties are
composed relatively more of issue activists than of broad demographic groupings, they are not as deeply rooted in the mass of the population as was the case
for much of our history. The United States pioneered the mass party, but, as
Steven Schier has argued, in recent decades the parties have practiced a kind of
exclusive politics. The mass-mobilization campaigns that historically characterized American elections gave way to the high-tech media campaigns of the late
twentieth century. Voter mobilization by the political parties correspondingly
fell. Late-century campaigns increasingly relied on television commercials, and
there is some evidence that such ads demobilize the electorate. In a kind of "back
to the future" development, the two most recent presidential elections have seen
renewed party effort to get out the vote, with a significant impact, at least in
2004. But modern computing capabilities and rich databases enable the parties to
practice a kind of targeted mobilization based on specific issues that was more
difficult to do in earlier periods. It is not clear that such activities make the parties
more like those of yesteryear, or whether they only reinforce the trends I have
previously discussed. One-third of the voting age population continues to eschew
a party identification, a figure that has not appreciably changed in three decades.

Discussion

In sum, the parties today are far closer to the responsible party model than those of the 1970s, a development that some of us wished for some decades ago, but it would be difficult to argue that today's party system is more effective at solving problems than the disorganized decentralized party system that it replaced. Rather than seek power on the basis of coherent programs, the parties at times throw fundamental principles to the wind when electoral considerations dictate, just as the decentralized parties of the mid-twentieth century did. At other times they hold fast to divisive positions that have only symbolic importance— President Bush reiterated his support for a constitutional amendment to ban gay marriage in his 2005 State of the Union address—for fear of alienating ideologically committed base elements. On issues like Social Security and the war in Iraq, facts are distorted and subordinated to ideology. Mandates for major policy changes are claimed on the basis of narrow electoral victories.

To be sure, I have painted with a broad brush, and my interpretations of recent political history may prove as partial and inaccurate as some of those advanced in DOCR. In particular, I am sensitive to the possibility that unified Democratic government under present conditions might be significantly different from the unified Republican government we have experienced—Nils Gilman argues that the features of responsible parties discussed above are really Republican features. But even if true, this implies that an earlier generation of political scientists failed to appreciate that Republican and Democratic responsible party government would be significantly different, let alone identify the empirical bases for such differences. What this reconsideration has demonstrated to me is the difficulty of making broad recommendations to improve American politics, even when seemingly solid research and argument underlie many of the component parts, which is the reason I will venture no such recommendations here. It is possible that this paper is as much a product of its temporal context as DOCR was. As Aldrich argues, the political parties periodically reinvent themselves better to deal with the problems they face. That, in fact, is my hope—that the next reinvention of the parties results in organizations that are better than the current models at dealing with the problems our society faces.

Chapter 13

Interest Groups

———•◦•———

13-1

The Scope and Bias of the Pressure System

E. E. Schattschneider

In the mid-twentieth century, many observers believed that James Madison's vision of America—as a multitude of groups or factions, none of which dominated the government—had been realized. E. E. Schattschneider provided an alternative view. In the following essay, which was originally published in 1960, Schattschneider argued that moneyed interests dominated mid-twentieth-century politics. In his view the dominance of moneyed interests limited the scope of government action and created a bias in the pressures placed on policymakers. Early in the twenty-first century, the issues raised by Schattschneider remain relevant to debates over the influence of organized and moneyed interests in American government and politics.

THE SCOPE OF CONFLICT is an aspect of the scale of political organization and the extent of political competition. The size of the constituencies being mobilized, the inclusiveness or exclusiveness of the conflicts people expect to develop leave a bearing on all theories about how politics is or should be organized. In other words, nearly all theories about politics have something to do with the question of who can get into the fight and who is to be excluded. . . .

Source: E. E. Schattschneider, "The Scope and Bias of the Pressure System," in *The Semi-Sovereign People* (New York: Holt, Rinehart, Winston, 1960), 20–45. Some notes appearing in the original have been deleted.

If we are able . . . to distinguish between public and private interests and between organized and unorganized groups we have marked out the major boundaries of the subject; *we have given the subject shape and scope.* . . . [W]e can now appropriate the piece we want and leave the rest to someone else. For a multitude of reasons *the most likely field of study is that of the organized, special-interest groups.* The advantage of concentrating on organized groups is that they are known, identifiable, and recognizable. The advantage of concentrating on special-interest groups is that they have one important characteristic in common; they are all exclusive. This piece of the pie (the organized special-interest groups) we shall call the *pressure system.* The pressure system has boundaries we can define; we can fix its scope and make an attempt to estimate its bias.

It may be assumed at the outset that all organized special-interest groups have some kind of impact on politics. A sample survey of organizations made by the Trade Associations Division of the United States Department of Commerce in 1942 concluded that "From 70 to 100 percent (of these associations) are planning activities in the field of government relations, trade promotion, trade practices, public relations, annual conventions, cooperation with other organizations, and information services."

The subject of our analysis can be reduced to manageable proportions and brought under control if we restrict ourselves to the groups whose interests in politics are sufficient to have led them to unite in formal organizations having memberships, bylaws, and officers. A further advantage of this kind of definition is, we may assume, that the organized special-interest groups are the most self-conscious, best developed, most intense and active groups. Whatever claims can be made for a group theory of politics ought to be sustained by the evidence concerning these groups, if the claims have any validity at all.

The organized groups listed in the various directories (such as *National Associations of the United States,* published at intervals by the United States Department of Commerce) and specialty yearbooks, registers, etc., and the *Lobby Index,* published by the United States House of Representatives, probably include the bulk of the organizations in the pressure system. All compilations are incomplete, but these are extensive enough to provide us with some basis for estimating the scope of the system.

By the time a group has developed the kind of interest that leads it to organize, it may be assumed that it has also developed some kind of political bias because *organization is itself a mobilization of bias in preparation for action.* Since these groups can be identified and since they have memberships (i.e., they include and exclude people), it is possible to think of the *scope* of the system.

When lists of these organizations are examined, the fact that strikes the student most forcibly is that *the system is very small.* The range of organized, identifiable, known groups is amazingly narrow; there is nothing remotely universal about it. There is a tendency on the part of the publishers of directories of associations to place an undue emphasis on business organizations, an emphasis that is almost inevitable because the business community is by a wide margin the most highly organized segment of society. Publishers doubtless tend also to reflect public demand for information. Nevertheless, the dominance of business groups in the pressure system is so marked that it probably cannot be explained away as an accident of the publishing industry.

The business character of the pressure system is shown by almost every list available. *National Associations of the United States* lists 1,860 business associations out of a total of 4,000 in the volume, though it refers without listing to 16,000 organizations of businessmen. One cannot be certain what the total content of the unknown associational universe may be, but, taken with the evidence found in other compilations, it is obvious that business is remarkably well represented. Some evidence of the overall scope of the system is to be seen in the estimate that 15,000 national trade associations have a gross membership of about one million business firms. The data are incomplete, but even if we do not have a detailed map this is the shore dimly seen.

Much more directly related to pressure politics is the *Lobby Index, 1946–1949* (an index of organizations and individuals registering or filing quarterly reports under the Federal Lobbying Act), published as a report of the House Select Committee on Lobbying Activities. In this compilation, 825 out of a total of 1,247 entries (exclusive of individuals and Indian tribes) represented business. A selected list of the most important of the groups listed in the *Index* (the groups spending the largest sums of money on lobbying) published in the *Congressional Quarterly Log* shows 149 business organizations in a total of 265 listed.

The business or upper-class bias of the pressure system shows up everywhere. Businessmen are four or five times as likely to write to their congressmen as manual laborers are. College graduates are far more apt to write to their congressmen than people in the lowest educational category are.

The limited scope of the business pressure system is indicated by all available statistics. Among business organizations, the National Association of Manufacturers (with about 20,000 corporate members) and the Chamber of Commerce of the United States (about as large as the N.A.M.) are giants. Usually business associations are much smaller. Of 421 trade associations in the metal-products industry listed in *National Associations of the United States,* 153 have a membership of less than 20. The median membership was somewhere between 24 and 50. Approximately the same scale of memberships is to be found in the lumber, furniture, and paper industries, where 37.3 percent of the associations listed had a membership of less than 20 and the median membership was in the 25 to 50 range.

The statistics in these cases are representative of nearly all other classifications of industry.

Data drawn from other sources support this thesis. Broadly, the pressure system has an upper-class bias. There is overwhelming evidence that participation in voluntary organizations is related to upper social and economic status; the rate of participation is much higher in the upper strata than it is elsewhere. The general proposition is well stated by [political scientist Paul] Lazarsfeld:

> People on the lower SES levels are less likely to belong to any organizations than the people on high SES (Social and Economic Status) levels. (On an A and B level, we find 72 percent of these respondents who belong to one or more organizations. The proportion of respondents who are members of formal organizations decreases steadily as SES level descends until, on the D level only 35 percent of the respondents belong to any associations.)[1]

The bias of the system is shown by the fact that even non-business organizations reflect an upper-class tendency.

Lazarsfeld's generalization seems to apply equally well to urban and rural populations. The obverse side of the coin is that large areas of the population appear to be wholly outside the system of private organization. A study made by Ira Reid of a Philadelphia area showed that in a sample of 963 persons, 85 percent belonged to no civic or charitable organization and 74 percent belonged to no occupational, business, or professional associations, while another Philadelphia study of 1,154 women showed that 55 percent belonged to no associations of any kind.[2]

A *Fortune* farm poll taken some years ago found that 70.5 percent of farmers belonged to no agricultural organizations. A similar conclusion was reached by two Gallup polls showing that perhaps no more than one third of the farmers of the country belonged to farm organizations, while another *Fortune* poll showed that 86.8 percent of the low-income farmers belonged to no farm organizations. All available data support the generalization that the farmers who do not participate in rural organizations are largely the poorer ones. . . .

The class bias of associational activity gives meaning to the limited scope of the pressure system, because *scope and bias are aspects of the same tendency.* The data raise a serious question about the validity of the proposition that special-interest groups are a universal form of political organization reflecting *all* interests. As a matter of fact, to suppose that everyone participates in pressure-group activity and that all interests get themselves organized in the pressure system is to destroy the meaning of this form of politics. The pressure system makes sense only as the political instrument of a segment of the community. It gets results by being selective and biased; *if everybody got into the act, the unique advantages of this form of organization would be destroyed, for it is possible that if all interests could be mobilized the result would be a stalemate.*

Special-interest organizations are most easily formed when they deal with small numbers of individuals who are acutely aware of their exclusive interests. To describe the conditions of pressure-group organization in this way is, however, to say that it is primarily a business phenomenon. Aside from a few very large organizations (the churches, organized labor, farm organizations, and veterans' organizations) the residue is a small segment of the population. *Pressure politics is essentially the politics of small groups.*

The vice of the groupist theory is that it conceals the most significant aspects of the system. The flaw in the pluralist heaven is that the heavenly chorus sings with a strong upper-class accent. Probably about 90 percent of the people cannot get into the pressure system.

The notion that the pressure system is automatically representative of the whole community is a myth fostered by the universalizing tendency of modern group theories. *Pressure politics is a selective process* ill designed to serve diffuse interests. The system is skewed, loaded, and unbalanced in favor of a fraction of a minority.

On the other hand, pressure tactics are not remarkably successful in mobilizing general interests. When pressure-group organizations attempt to represent the interests of large numbers of people, they are usually able to reach only a small segment of their constituencies. Only a chemical trace of the fifteen million Negroes in the United States belong to the National Association for the Advancement of Colored People. Only one five-hundredth of 1 percent of American women belong to the League of Women Voters, only one sixteen-hundredth of 1 percent of the consumers belong to the National Consumers' League, and only 6 percent of American automobile drivers belong to the American Automobile Association, while about 15 percent of the veterans belong to the American Legion.

The competing claims of pressure groups and political parties for the loyalty of the American public revolve about the difference between the results likely to be achieved by small-scale and large-scale political organization. Inevitably, the outcome of pressure politics and party politics will be vastly different. . . .

. . . Everything we know about politics suggests that a conflict is likely to change profoundly as it becomes political. It is a rare individual who can confront his antagonists without changing his opinions to some degree. Everything changes once a conflict gets into the political arena—*who* is involved, *what* the conflict is about, the resources available, etc. It is extremely difficult to predict the outcome of a fight by watching its beginning because we do not even know who else is going to get into the conflict. The logical consequence of the exclusive emphasis on the determinism of the private origins of conflict is to assign zero value to the political process.

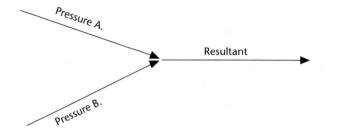

The very expression "pressure politics" invites us to misconceive the role of special-interest groups in politics. The word "pressure" implies the use of some kind of force, a form of intimidation, something other than reason and information, to induce public authorities to act against their own best judgment. [This is reflected in the famous statement by political scientist Earl Latham, in his 1952 book *The Group Basis of Politics,* that] the legislature is a "referee" who "ratifies" and "records" the "balance of power" among the contending groups.[3]

It is hard to imagine a more effective way of saying that Congress has no mind or force of its own or that Congress is unable to invoke new forces that might alter the equation.

Actually the outcome of political conflict is not like the "resultant" of opposing forces in physics. To assume that the forces in a political situation could be diagramed as a physicist might diagram the resultant of opposing physical forces is to wipe the slate clean of all remote, general, and public considerations for the protection of which civil societies have been instituted.

Moreover, the notion of "pressure" distorts the image of the power relations involved. Private conflicts are taken into the public arena precisely because someone wants to make certain that the power ratio among the private interests most immediately involved shall not prevail. To treat a conflict as a mere test of the strength of the private interests is to leave out the most significant factors. This is so true that it might indeed be said that the only way to preserve private power ratios is to keep conflicts out of the public arena.

The assumption that it is only the "interested" who count ought to be reexamined in view of the foregoing discussion. The tendency of the literature of pressure politics has been to neglect the low-tension force of large numbers because it *assumes that the equation of forces is fixed at the outset.*

Given the assumptions made by the group theorists, the attack on the idea of the majority is completely logical. The assumption is that conflict is monopolized narrowly by the parties immediately concerned. There is no room for a majority when conflict is defined so narrowly. It is a great deficiency of the group theory that it has found no place in the political system for the majority. The force of the majority is of an entirely different order of magnitude, something not to be measured by pressure-group standards.

Instead of attempting to exterminate all political forms, organizations, and alignments that do not qualify as pressure groups, would it not be better to attempt to make a synthesis, covering the whole political system and finding a place for all kinds of political life?

One possible synthesis of pressure politics and party politics might be produced by *describing politics as the socialization of conflict*. That is to say, the political process is a sequence: conflicts are initiated by highly motivated, high-tension groups so directly and immediately involved that it is difficult for them to see the justice of competing claims. As long as the conflicts of these groups remain *private* (carried on in terms of economic competition, reciprocal denial of goods and services, private negotiations and bargaining, struggles for corporate control or competition for membership), no political process is initiated. Conflicts become political only when an attempt is made to involve the wider public. Pressure politics might be described as a stage in the socialization of conflict. This analysis makes pressure politics an integral part of all politics, including party politics.

One of the characteristic points of origin of pressure politics is a breakdown of the discipline of the business community. The flight to government is perpetual. Something like this is likely to happen wherever there is a point of contact between competing power systems. It is the *losers in intrabusiness conflict who seek redress from public authority. The dominant business interests resist appeals to the government*. The role of the government as the patron of the defeated private interest sheds light on its function as the critic of private power relations.

Since the contestants in private conflicts are apt to be unequal in strength, it follows that *the most powerful special interests want private settlements* because they are able to dictate the outcome as long as the conflict remains private. If A is a hundred times as strong as B he does not welcome the intervention of a third party because he expects to impose his own terms on B; he wants to isolate B. He is especially opposed to the intervention of public authority, because public authority represents the most overwhelming form of outside intervention. Thus, if $A/B = 100/1$, it is obviously not to A's advantage to involve a third party a million times as strong as A and B combined. Therefore, it is the weak, not the strong, who appeal to public authority for relief. It is the weak who want to socialize conflict, i.e., to involve more and more people in the conflict until the balance of forces is changed. In the schoolyard it is not the bully but the defenseless smaller boys who "tell the teacher." When the teacher intervenes, the balance of power in the schoolyard is apt to change drastically. It is the function of public authority to *modify private power relations by enlarging the scope of conflict*.

Nothing could be more mistaken than to suppose that public authority merely registers the dominance of the strong over the weak. The mere existence of public order has already ruled out a great variety of forms of private pressure. Nothing could be more confusing than to suppose that the refugees from the business community who come to Congress for relief and protection *force* Congress to do their bidding.

Evidence of the truth of this analysis may be seen in the fact that the big private interests do not necessarily win if they are involved in public conflicts with petty interests. The image of the lobbyists as primarily the agents of big business is not easy to support on the face of the record of congressional hearings, for example. The biggest corporations in the country tend to avoid the arena in which pressure groups and lobbyists fight it out before congressional committees. To describe this process exclusively in terms of an effort of business to intimidate congressmen is to misconceive what is actually going on.

It is probably a mistake to assume that pressure politics is the typical or even the most important relation between government and business. The pressure group is by no means the perfect instrument of the business community. What does big business want? The *winners* in intrabusiness strife want (1) to be let alone (they want autonomy) and (2) to preserve the solidarity of the business community. For these purposes pressure politics is not a wholly satisfactory device. The most elementary considerations of strategy call for the business community to develop some kind of common policy more broadly based than any special-interest group is likely to be.

The political influence of business depends on the kind of solidarity that, on the one hand, leads all business to rally to the support of *any* businessman in trouble with the government and, on the other hand, keeps internal business disputes out of the public arena. In this system businessmen resist the impulse to attack each other in public and discourage the efforts of individual members of the business community to take intrabusiness conflicts into politics.

The attempt to mobilize a united front of the whole business community does not resemble the classical concept of pressure politics. The logic of business politics is to keep peace within the business community by supporting as far as possible all claims that business groups make for themselves. The tendency is to support all businessmen who have conflicts with the government and support all businessmen in conflict with labor. In this way *special-interest politics can be converted into party policy.* The search is for a broad base of political mobilization grounded on the strategic need for political organization on a wider scale than is possible in the case of the historical pressure group. Once the business community begins to think in terms of a larger scale of political organization the Republican party looms large in business politics.

It is a great achievement of American democracy that business has been forced to form a political organization designed to win elections, i.e., has been forced to compete for power in the widest arena in the political system. On the other hand, *the power of the Republican party to make terms with business rests on the fact that business cannot afford to be isolated.*

The Republican party has played a major role in *the political organization of the business community,* a far greater role than many students of politics seem to have realized. The influence of business in the Republican party is great, but it is never absolute because business is remarkably dependent on the party. The business community is too small, it arouses too much antagonism, and its aims are too narrow to win the support of a popular majority. The political education of business is a function of the Republican party that can never be done so well by anyone else.

In the management of the political relations of the business community, the Republican party is much more important than any combination of pressure groups ever could be. The success of special interests in Congress is due less to the "pressure" exerted by these groups than it is due to the fact that Republican members of Congress are committed in advance to a general probusiness attitude. The notion that business groups coerce Republican congressmen into voting for their bills underestimates the whole Republican posture in American politics.

It is not easy to manage the political interests of the business community because there is a perpetual stream of losers in intrabusiness conflicts who go to the government for relief and protection. It has not been possible therefore to maintain perfect solidarity, and when solidarity is breached the government is involved almost automatically. The fact that business has not become hopelessly divided and that it has retained great influence in American politics has been due chiefly to the overall mediating role played by the Republican party. There has never been a pressure group or a combination of pressure groups capable of performing this function.

NOTES

1. Paul F. Lazarsfeld, Bernard Berelson, and Hazel Gaudet. *The People's Choice* (New York: Columbia University Press, 1948), p. 145.

2. Ira Reid and Emily Ehle, "Leadership Selection in the Urban Locality Areas," *Public Opinion Quarterly* (1950), 14:262–284. See also Norman Powell, *Anatomy of Public Opinion* (New York: Prentice Hall, 1951), pp. 180–181.

3. Earl Latham, *The Group Basis of Politics* (Ithaca: Cornell University Press, 1952), pp. 35–36.

13-2

The Evolution of Interest Groups

John R. Wright

In the following essay John R. Wright provides an overview of the develop-
ment of interest groups in America. Interest groups form, Wright explains, as
a net result of two factors—societal disturbances and collective action prob-
lems. Societal disturbances create common interests for groups of individuals,
who then join forces to pursue those interests. All groups then face the collec-
tive action problem known as free riding—the tendency for group members to
benefit from others' contributions to the provision of a public good without
contributing themselves. Interest groups must find a way to encourage people
to join and contribute in order to achieve their political goals.

THE RAPID ECONOMIC and social development in the United States immediately
following the Civil War created a new and uncertain political environment for
members of Congress. Congress emerged as the dominant force in national policy making, and members' electoral constituencies became far more heterogeneous and complex than ever before. In this new and uncertain political
environment, the informational needs of members of Congress were greater
than at any previous time, and it was in this environment that the American
interest group system evolved.

Although the evolution of interest groups in the United States did not begin in
earnest until after the Civil War, the groundwork for their development was laid
much earlier in several key provisions of the U.S. Constitution. These constitutional provisions have had a profound effect on the American political party system, which in turn has had a major impact on the interest group system.

Constitutional Underpinnings

The place of special interests in American politics today is largely a consequence
of two competing political values expressed in the U.S. Constitution: a concern
for liberty and freedom of political expression on the one hand, and the desire to
prevent tyranny on the other. James Madison's *Federalist* No. 10 is the classic

Source: John R. Wright, "The Evolution of Interest Groups," in *Interest Groups and Congress,* John R. Wright
(Boston: Allyn & Bacon, 1996), 11–22. Some notes appearing in the original have been deleted.

justification for the various constitutional checks and balances, which disperse power and make it difficult for any single group of citizens to control the entire government. Madison, whose thinking was strongly influenced by the English philosopher David Hume, believed that it is natural for people to differ, and in differing, to form into factions, or parties. The problem with factions, according to Madison and his contemporaries Jefferson and Hamilton, is their potential for subverting government and the public good. Factions, in Madison's words, are mischievous.

Madison's primary concern in *Federalist* No. 10 was with *majority* factions—typically, but not exclusively, political parties as we know them today—not minority factions such as contemporary interest groups. Although he recognized that minority factions could lead to disorder and conflict, Madison believed that it is the possibility of tyranny by the majority that poses the greatest threat to individual liberties. Madison did not recommend that factions be forbidden or repressed, a practice that would conflict with the fundamental values of liberty and freedom of expression, but instead that their negative tendencies be held in check and controlled through explicit constitutional safeguards.

Formal mechanisms in the U.S. Constitution for controlling majority factions include the requirements that the president be elected separately from members of Congress and that members of Congress reside in the states from which they are elected. These provisions disperse power horizontally—across national institutions of government—and vertically—from national to local political jurisdictions. Separation of the executive and legislative branches eased fears among the smaller states in 1787 that large states, which presumably would control the Congress, would also control the presidency; and geographic representation ensured that control over elected representatives would rest with local rather than national interests, thereby lessening the influence of the national government over state decisions.

These basic constitutional provisions have had a profound effect on the abilities of modern political parties to control and manage American government. Historically, control of the government has frequently been divided between the two major political parties, neither of which has been capable of exerting much discipline over its members. A single party has controlled the presidency and a majority in the U.S. House and Senate in just 43 of the 70 Congresses—61 percent—that have convened from 1855 to 1993. Even in times of single-party control of the government, voting defections within both major parties have been common. Since World War II, a majority of Democrats has voted against a majority of Republicans only 44 percent of the time on average in the U.S. House of Representatives and only 45 percent of the time on average in the U.S. Senate. American legislators have little incentive to toe the party line for the simple reason that a cohesive majority is not required to maintain control of the government or to preclude calling new elections, as is the case in parliamentary regimes. In the absence of party discipline, American legislators look to their geographic constituencies rather than to their parties for voting cues.

Madison and his contemporaries succeeded brilliantly in designing a constitutional system to attenuate the power of majority factions, but in doing so, they also created unanticipated opportunities for minority factions to be influential. When political parties are unable to take clear responsibility for governing, and when they cannot maintain cohesion and discipline among those elected under their labels, special interests have opportunities to gain access to the key points of decision within the government. David Truman explains that when a single party succeeds regularly in electing both an executive and a majority in the legislature, channels of access "will be predominantly those within the party leadership, and the pattern will be relatively stable and orderly."[1] He notes, however, that when "the party is merely an abstract term referring to an aggregation of relatively independent factions," as in the case of the United States, then the channels of access "will be numerous, and the patterns of influence within the legislature will be diverse, constantly shifting, and more openly in conflict."[2]

One important consequence of this "diffusion of access" is that legislators will be much more accessible to interests within their local constituencies, especially *organized* interests. Simply put, interest groups will thrive in an environment in which legislators take their behavioral cues from heterogeneous constituencies rather than from cohesive political parties. E. E. Schattschneider has summed up the situation succinctly:

> If the parties exercised the power to govern effectively, *they would shut out the pressure groups.* The fact that American parties govern only spasmodically and fitfully amid a multitude of lapses of control provides the opportunity for the cheap and easy use of pressure tactics.[3]

Although the constitution makes no specific mention of interest groups, or even political parties for that matter, it has influenced the evolution of both. The weakness of the political parties in their ability to control and manage the government is an intended consequence of the efforts by the founding fathers to inhibit majority factions; the prevalence of special interests, however, is an unintended consequence of weak parties. The U.S. Constitution indirectly laid the groundwork for a strong interest group system, but that system, unlike the political party system, did not evolve right away. It took nearly 70 years from the development of the first party system in 1800 until groups began to form and proliferate at a significant rate.

652   INTEREST GROUPS

The Formation and Maintenance of Interest Groups

Although trade unions and associations have historical roots dating to the beginning of the republic, interest groups of regional or national scope as we know
them today did not develop significantly until after the Civil War, and even then,
pronounced growth did not really begin to take place until the late 1800s. Table 1
lists a few of the early organizations and their founding dates.

In what is known as the "disturbance theory" of interest group formation, David
Truman argued that organizations will form when the interests common to unorganized groups of individuals are disturbed by economic, social, political, or technological change.[4] As society becomes increasingly complex and interconnected,
Truman argued that individuals have greater difficulty resolving their differences
and grievances on their own and instead must seek intervention from the government. It is at this time that political organizations will begin to take shape. Once
interest groups begin to form, they will then tend to form in "wavelike" fashion,
according to Truman, because policies designed to address one group's needs typically disturb the interests of other unorganized citizens, who then form groups to
seek governmental intervention to protect and advance their particular interests.

The period from 1870 to 1900 was rife with disturbances favorable to the formation of interest groups in the United States. The economic, social, and political

Table 1. Selected Organizations and Their Founding Dates

American Medical Association	1847
National Grange	1867
National Rifle Association	1871
American Bankers Association	1875
American Federation of Labor	1886
Sierra Club	1892
National Association of Manufacturers	1895
National Audubon Society	1905
National Association for the Advancement of Colored People	1909
U.S. Chamber of Commerce	1912
American Jewish Congress	1918
American Farm Bureau Federation	1919
National League of Cities	1924

upheaval following the Civil War destabilized relationships within and between numerous groups of individuals. The completion of the railroads and the introduction of the telegraph dramatically altered communication and transportation patterns; immigration and population growth gave rise to new economic and social relationships; and commercial and territorial expansion in the West, combined with the task of maintaining order and rebuilding the infrastructure in the South, increased demands for routine services such as post offices, law enforcement, internal improvements, customs agents, and so forth. The process of industrialization created further economic and political tensions and uncertainties. The period 1870 to 1900 witnessed three economic depressions: a major one from 1873 to 1879, a minor one in the mid-1880s, and the collapse of 1893. Overall, the period from 1870 to 1900 was one when conditions were finally right for the widespread growth of organized interests in the United States.

Margaret Susan Thompson points out that in addition to the unprecedented economic and social upheaval at the end of the Civil War, political conditions in the 1870s were also favorable to the formation of groups and, in particular, the lobbying of Congress.[5] Two factors—the ascendancy of congressional power associated with the impeachment proceedings against Andrew Johnson and the growing heterogeneity of congressional constituencies—were instrumental in the growth of congressional lobbying and interest group activity. Congress, by enacting a comprehensive program on reconstruction in 1865 over the determined opposition of the president, established political preeminence over federal policy making and, as a consequence, became the focal institution for receiving and processing the conflicting demands of many newly recognized interests. Then, as congressional constituencies diversified economically and socially, the presence of multiple and competing interests began to force legislators to develop "representational priorities."[6] Thompson notes that legislators at this time had to determine which were their "meaningful" constituencies, and organization was the critical means by which interests achieved such designation. Thompson refers to the nascent organization of interests during the 1870s as "clienteles" rather than interest groups, for even though numerous subgroups of the population began making significant demands on the government during the 1870s, there was not a great deal of formal organization then as we know it today. Still, even these nascent groups began to provide important information to members of Congress about the interests and priorities of their constituents.

One example of how interest groups formed in response to economic and political disturbances during the post–Civil War period is provided by the organization of postal workers. Even before the Civil War, the volume of mail had grown tremendously in response to the development of railroads and the resulting decrease in the costs of postage. But in 1863, another significant increase in the volume of mail occurred when Congress lowered the long-distance postage rates.

This created additional strains for letter carriers and postal clerks who already were greatly overworked. Then, in 1868, the Post Office Department refused to apply the "eight-hour" law—a law enacted that same year by Congress stipulating that eight hours constituted a day's work for laborers, workmen, and mechanics—to letter carriers on the grounds that they were government employees, not laborers, workmen, or mechanics. Finally, implementation of civil service following passage of the Pendleton Act in 1883 eliminated what little political clout the letter carriers had enjoyed. Once the patronage system was eliminated, politicians lost interest in the letter carriers and no longer intervened on their behalf.

In response to these deteriorating circumstances, the letter carriers organized into the National Association of Letter Carriers in 1889. Once organized, the letter carriers had a significant advantage over the unorganized postal clerks in the competition for wages. At the time, wages for all postal workers, letter carriers and clerks alike, were provided through a single congressional appropriation to the Post Office Department, and the letter carriers used their organizational clout to claim a disproportionate share of the annual appropriation. Thus, the postal workers came under pressure to organize as well, and so in predictable "wavelike" fashion, the National Association of Post Office Clerks was established in 1894.

Changing economic, social, and political conditions are necessary but not sufficient circumstances for the formation and development of organized interests. Even when environmental conditions are favorable to the formation of groups, there is still a natural proclivity for individuals *not* to join political interest groups. The reason is that individuals do not always have to belong to political groups in order to enjoy the benefits they provide. Wheat farmers, for example, benefit from the price supports that Congress establishes for wheat even though they do not belong to the National Association of Wheat Growers (NAWG), which lobbies for price supports. Similarly, individuals do not have to belong to environmental groups in order to reap the benefits of a cleaner environment brought about by the lobbying efforts of groups such as the Sierra Club and the National Wildlife Federation. More generally, the lobbying benefits provided by groups such as the wheat growers and the environmentalists are consumed *jointly* by all citizens affected; that is, Congress does not guarantee a higher price for wheat only to farmers who have paid dues to the National Association of Wheat Growers, and it does not and cannot restrict the benefit of a clean environment only to individuals who have paid their dues to environmental groups.

Unlike lobbying benefits, which are available even to those who do not contribute to lobbying efforts, the costs of lobbying are borne only by those who actually pay their dues to political groups or otherwise participate in lobbying activities. This creates a major organizational problem, for when it is possible to get something for nothing, many individuals will rationally choose to free ride on the efforts of others. When there are thousands of wheat farmers, for example, and the annual dues to the National Association of Wheat Growers are $100 or less, individual wheat farmers might very well conclude that their single contributions are not very important, that the NAWG will manage quite nicely without their money because there are so many other wheat farmers paying dues, and that there are much better uses for the $100 in light of the fact that the government will still provide price supports for their crop. The problem for the NAWG is that if every wheat farmer reasoned this way there would be no national association, and thus probably no price supports for wheat.

Given the natural proclivity for individuals to be free riders, all organizations must provide incentives of one sort or another to induce individuals to pay dues and otherwise contribute to the collective efforts of the organization. Generally speaking, individuals do not join interest groups because of benefits that can be consumed jointly; they join because of benefits that can by enjoyed *selectively* only by those individuals who pay dues to political groups. There are three main types of selective benefits. A selective *material* benefit includes such things as insurance and travel discounts and subscriptions to professional journals and other specialized information. A second type of selective benefit is what Peter Clark and James Q. Wilson have labeled *solidary* incentives. These, too, derive only from group membership and involve benefits such as "socializing, congeniality, the sense of group membership and identification, the status resulting from membership, fun and conviviality, the maintenance of social distinctions, and so on."[7] The third basic type of selective benefit is an *expressive* incentive. Expressive incentives are those that individuals attach to the act of expressing ideological or moral values such as free speech, civil rights, economic justice, or political equality. Individuals obtain these benefits when they pay dues or contribute money or time to an organization that espouses these values. What is important in receiving these benefits is the feeling of satisfaction that results from expressing political values, not necessarily the actual achievement of the values themselves.

Most organizations provide a mix of these various benefits, although different kinds of organizations typically rely more heavily on one type of benefit than another. Professional and trade associations, for example, are more likely to offer selective material benefits than purposive benefits, whereas environmental groups and other organizations claiming to lobby for the public interest rely more heavily on expressive benefits. Expressive benefits are also common in organizations relying heavily on mass mailings to attract and maintain members. Many direct mail approaches use negatively worded messages to instill feelings of guilt and fear in individuals, with the hope that people will contribute money to a cause as a means of expressing their support for certain values or else assuaging their guilt and fear.

That individuals are not drawn naturally to interest groups and must instead be enticed to join makes it very difficult for groups to get started. Organizations often need outside support in the form of a patron—perhaps a wealthy individual, a nonprofit foundation, or a government agency—to get over the initial hurdle of organizing collective action. In one of the leading studies on the origins and maintenance of interest groups, Jack Walker discovered that 89 percent of all citizen groups and 60 percent of all nonprofit occupational groups (e.g., the National Association of State Alcohol and Drug Abuse Directors) received financial assistance from an outside source at the time of their founding.[8] Many of these organizations continued to draw heavily from outside sources of support to maintain themselves once they were launched. Walker concluded that "the number of interest groups in operation, the mixture of group types, and the level and direction of political mobilization in the United States at any point in the country's history will be determined by the composition and accessibility of the system's major patrons of political action."[9]

In summary, the proficiency that contemporary interest groups have achieved in attracting and maintaining members has evolved from a combination of factors. Most fundamental to their evolution has been a constitutional arrangement that has not only encouraged their participation but also created unanticipated opportunities for them to exert influence. Changing economic, social, and political circumstances have also played critical roles at various times throughout American history. However, even under conditions favorable to their development, the formation and maintenance of interest groups requires leadership and creative approaches for dealing with the natural inertia that individuals exhibit toward collective activities. The number of groups continues to grow each year, however, as does the diversity of the issues and viewpoints they represent.

NOTES

1. David B. Truman, *The Governmental Process: Political Interests and Public Opinion* (New York: Knopf, 1951), p. 325.

2. Ibid., p. 325.

3. E. E. Schattschneider, *Party Government* (New York: Holt, Rinehart and Winston, 1941), p. 192.

4. David B. Truman, *The Governmental Process,* Chapters 3 and 4.

5. Margaret Susan Thompson, *The Spider Web: Congress and Lobbying in the Age of Grant* (Ithaca, N.Y.: Cornell University Press, 1985).

6. Thompson, *The Spider Web,* pp. 130–131.

7. Peter B. Clark and James Q. Wilson, "Incentive Systems: A Theory of Organizations," *Administrative Science Quarterly* 6 (1961): 134–135.

8. Jack L. Walker, "The Origins and Maintenance of Interest Groups in America," *American Political Science Review* 77 (1983): 390–406.

9. Ibid., p. 406.

13-3

Buying Time: Moneyed Interests and the Mobilization of Bias in Congressional Committees

Richard L. Hall and Frank W. Wayman

Lobbyists often are thought to be in the business of influencing legislators' votes by offering campaign contributions. Richard Hall and Frank Wayman argue that lobbying is more likely to influence legislators' participation, particularly in the committee setting, than their voting behavior.

AT LEAST SINCE Madison railed about the mischiefs of faction, critics of U.S. political institutions have worried about the influence of organized interests in national policy making. In this century, one of the most eloquent critics of the interest group system was E.E. Schattschneider, who warned of the inequalities between private, organized, and upper-class groups on the one hand and public, unorganized, and lower-class groups on the other. The pressure system, he argued in *The Semisovereign People*, "mobilized bias" in national policy making in favor of the former, against the interests of the latter, and hence against the interests of U.S. democracy. Such concerns have hardly abated thirty years since the publication of Schattschneider's essay. In particular, the precipitous growth in the number and financial strength of political action committees has refueled the charge that moneyed interests dominate the policy making process. The current Congress is *The Best Congress Money Can Buy* according to one critic, one where *Honest Graft* is an institutional imperative. "The rising tide of special-interest money," one close observer concludes, "is changing the balance of power between voters and donors, between lawmakers' constitutional constituents and their cash constituents."

Despite the claims of the institutional critics and the growing public concern over PACs during the last decade, the scientific evidence that political money matters in legislative decision making is surprisingly weak. Considerable research on members' voting decisions offers little support for the popular view that PAC money permits interests to buy or rent votes on matters that affect them. Based on an examination of 120 PACs in 10 issue areas over four congresses, one recent

Source: Richard L. Hall and Frank W. Wayman, "Buying Time: Moneyed Interests and the Mobilization of Bias in Congressional Committees," *American Political Science Review* 84, no. 3 (September 1990): 797–805, 809–815. Notes appearing in the original have been deleted.

study concludes flatly that PAC contributions do not affect members' voting patterns. Another study, designed to explore the "upper bounds" of PAC influence on House roll calls, emphasizes "the relative inability of PACs to determine congressional voting." . . . Does money matter?

. . . We revisit the question by developing a theoretical account of the constrained exchange between legislator and donor quite different from the one evident in the substantial literature cited above. In particular, we adopt the premise that PACs are rational actors, seeking to maximize their influence on the legislative outcomes that affect their affiliates; but we take issue with the standard account of PAC rationality. Our approach does not lead us to predict a strong causal relationship between PAC money and floor votes. House members and interest group representatives are viewed as parties to an implicit cooperative agreement, but the constraints on member behavior and the rational calculations of group representatives limit the extent to which votes become the currency of exchange. Instead, we advance two hypotheses about the effect of money on congressional decision making.

First, we suggest that in looking for the effects of money in Congress, one must look more to the politics of committee decision making than those of the floor. . . .

Second, and more importantly, our account of the member-donor exchange leads us to focus on the *participation* of particular members, not on their votes. This variable, we believe, is a crucial but largely neglected element of congressional decision making. It is especially important in any analysis of interest group influence in a decentralized Congress. In their famous study of lobbying on foreign trade policy, for instance, Bauer, Pool, and Dexter concluded that a member's principal problem is "not how to vote but what to do with his time, how to allocate his resources, and where to put his energy." . . . If money does not necessarily buy votes or change minds, in other words, it can buy members' time. The intended effect is to mobilize bias in congressional committee decision making.

[We seek to determine whether moneyed interests mobilize bias in committee decision making.] Analyzing data from three House committees on three distinct issues, we find that they do. In the final section we briefly discuss the implications of the findings for our understanding of money, interest groups, and representation in Congress. . . .

The Rational PAC Revised

The literature on PAC contribution strategies and members' roll call voting behavior . . . suggests two puzzles. First, if group strategists are reasonably rational, why would they continue to allocate scarce resources to efforts where the expected political benefits are so low? Second, if PAC allocation strategies are designed to influence members' votes, why do they contribute so heavily to their strongest supporters and occasionally to their strongest opponents? Is it the case that PACs are systematically irrational and, by extension, that claims about the influence of money on legislative process almost certainly exaggerated? We believe that the premise of rationality need not be rejected but that theoretical work in this area requires a more complete account of rational PAC behavior. . . . Simply put, interest group resources are intended to accomplish something different from, and more than, influencing elections or buying votes. Specifically, we argue that PAC money should be allocated in order to *mobilize* legislative support and *demobilize* opposition, particularly at the most important points in the legislative process.

This argument turns directly on what we already know about the nature of legislators' voting decisions from a very rich literature. The simple but important point is that a number of powerful factors exist that predispose a member to vote a certain way, among them party leaders, ideology, constituency, and the position of the administration. Kingdon notes, moreover, that members' votes on particular issues are also constrained by their past voting histories. Members attach some value to consistency, independent of the other factors that influence their voting behavior. A third and related point is that the public, recorded nature of the vote may itself limit the member's discretion: a risk-averse member may fear the appearance of impropriety in supporting major campaign contributors in the absence of some other, legitimate force pushing her in the same direction. Finally, the dichotomous nature of the vote acts as a constraint. Money must not only affect members' attitudes at the margin but do so enough to push them over the threshold between *nay* and *yea*. In short, the limits on member responsiveness to messages wrapped in money are substantial, perhaps overwhelming, at least insofar as floor voting is concerned.

. . . The rational PAC should expect little in the way of marginal benefits in votes bought for dollars spent, especially when individual PAC contributions are limited by the Federal Election Campaign Act to ten thousand dollars—a slight fraction of the cost of the average House race. Individual votes, that is, simply aren't easy to change; and even if some are changed, the utility of the votes purchased depends on their net cumulative effect in turning a potentially losing coalition into a winning one. For the rational PAC manager, the expected marginal utility approximates zero in most every case. All other things being equal, scarce resources should be allocated heavily elsewhere and to other purposes.

How, then, should the strategic PAC distribute its resources? The first principle derives from the larger literature on interest group influence in Congress. Well aware of the decentralized nature of congressional decision making, interest groups recognize that resources allocated at the committee stage are more efficiently spent. Interest group preferences incorporated there have a strong chance of surviving as the bill moves through subsequent stages in the sequence, while provisions not in the committee vehicle are difficult to attach later. Second, the nature of the committee assignment process increases the probability that organized interests will find a sympathetic audience at the committee or subcommittee stage. Members seek and often receive positions that will permit them to promote the interests that, in turn, help them to get reelected. Finally, the less public, often informal nature of committee decision making suggests that members' responsiveness to campaign donors will receive less scrutiny. Indeed, a long tradition of research on subgovernments emphasizes that such clientelism flourishes at the committee stage. In short, groups will strategically allocate their resources with the knowledge that investments in the politics of the appropriate committee or subcommittee are likely to pay higher dividends than investments made elsewhere. Indeed, this principle is especially important in the House, where the sheer size of the chamber's membership, the greater importance of the committee stage, and the frequent restrictions on floor participation recommend a more targeted strategy.

If PACs concentrate at the committee level, what, specifically, do they hope to gain there? Purchasing votes is one possibility; and, in fact, the rationale for allocating campaign money to buy votes in committee is somewhat stronger than for vote-buying on the floor. But even within committee, PACs still tend to give to their strongest supporters. In addition, committee votes, like floor votes, are dichotomous decisions. And despite the lower visibility of committee decision making, the factors of constituency, ideology, party, and administration are almost certainly at work. In fact, . . . there is little evidence that contributions influence voting in committee any more than they do voting on the floor.

The alternative hypothesis that we test here is that political money alters members' patterns of legislative involvement, a point that emerges from an older literature on interest group influence in Congress. Stated somewhat differently, the object of a rational PAC allocation strategy is not simply the *direction* of legislators' preferences but the *vigor* with which those preferences are promoted in the decision making process. Such strategies should take the form of inducing sympathetic members to get actively involved in a variety of activities that directly affect the shape of committee legislation: authoring or blocking a legislative vehicle; negotiating compromises behind the scenes, especially at the staff level; offering friendly amendments or actively opposing unfriendly ones; lobbying colleagues; planning strategy; and last and sometimes least, showing up to vote in favor of the interest group's position. . . .

Several arguments support this view. First, participation is crucial to determining legislative outcomes; and voting is perhaps the least important of the various ways in which committee members participate. Second, while members' voting choices are highly constrained, how they allocate their time, staff, and political capital is much more discretionary. . . . The member's level of involvement is something that a strategic PAC can reasonably expect to affect. The contribution need not weigh so heavily in a member's mind that it changes his or her position in any material way; it need only weigh heavily enough to command some increment of legislative resources. The minimum threshold that must be passed is thus a fairly modest one, and the potential effect of contributions on behavior is one of degree. Specifically, the member will allocate scarce legislative resources on the group's behalf so long as the marginal utility of the contribution to the member exceeds the expected marginal utility of the most valuable remaining use of the member's resources.

A third advantage of this view is that it explains the ostensibly anomalous tendency of PACs to contribute so heavily to members who are almost certain to win reelection and almost certain to support the group's point of view. Such behavior now appears quite rational. It is precisely one's supporters that one wants to mobilize: the more likely certain members are to support the group, the more active it should want them to be. Furthermore, this view of purposive PACs makes sense of the evidence that PACs sometimes contribute to members who will almost certainly oppose them and whose involvement in an issue stands to do the group harm. The PAC may have no hope of changing the opponent's mind, but it may, at the margin at least, diminish the intensity with which the member pursues policies that the organization does not like. The intent of the money, then, is not persuasion but demobilization: "We know you can't support us, but please don't actively oppose us." However, we should not expect the demobilizing effect of money to be nearly so strong as the mobilizing effect. The message provided through contributions to one's supporters is widely perceived as a legitimate one: in asking for help, the group is encouraging members to do precisely what they would do were resources plentiful. In contrast, contributions to opponents are meant to encourage them to go against their predispositions: the implicit message is to "take a walk" on an issue that they may care about. In short, the expected effects are not symmetric; the mobilization hypothesis is on stronger theoretical ground. . . .

The Data: Money and Mobilization on Three Committees

The data for this investigation are drawn from staff interviews and markup records of three House committees on three issues: (1) the Dairy Stabilization Act, considered by the Agriculture Committee in 1982; (2) the Job Training

Partnership Act (JTPA), considered by Education and Labor in 1982; and (3) the Natural Gas Market Policy Act, considered by Energy and Commerce during 1983–84.

Several features of these cases make them particularly appropriate for exploring the effects of money on the participation of committee members. First, all were highly significant pieces of legislation, the stakes of each measuring in the billions of dollars. At issue in the Natural Gas Market Policy Act was the deregulation of natural gas prices, a proposal that would transfer billions of dollars from one region to another, from consumer to industry, and within the industry from interstate pipelines and distributors to the major natural gas producers. Annual spending on the Job Training Partnership Act was expected at the time of its passage to be in the four-to-five-billion-dollar range, and it replaced one of the most important domestic programs of the 1970s. While more narrow than these in scope, the Dairy Stabilization Act also entailed significant economic effects. The principal purpose of the act was to adjust the scheduled support price for milk downward by as much as a dollar per hundredweight over two years, creating budget savings of 4.2 billion dollars for fiscal years 1983–85 and decreasing the profitability of milk production by as much as 30% for the typical dairy farmer. In each case, then, evidence of the influence of PAC money on congressional decision making can hardly be counted narrow or trivial. The deliberations in each case bore in significant ways on major interests, both public and private.

A second feature relevant to this investigation follows from the economic importance attached to these issues. All three were salient among actors other than the private groups immediately affected, a feature that the considerable research on roll call voting suggests should depress the effect of PAC contributions on congressional decision making. . . .

At two levels, then, past research indicates that our selection of cases is biased against our argument. It suggests that high salience issues should exhibit little PAC influence on legislative behavior, yet each of the cases here commanded the attention of a wide range of political actors. Second, past research suggests that we will find little PAC influence in precisely these three policy areas. Should we find support for the hypothesis that money mobilizes support (or demobilizes opposition) at the committee level, we should be on reasonably solid ground to conclude that (1) the results of this exploration are apt to generalize to other committees and other issues and (2) the null results of past research are more likely to be artifacts of the legislative behavior and the legislative stage studied than evidence that moneyed interests do not matter in congressional decision making. . . .

Results and Interpretations

In estimating [a] model of participation, we explicitly account for the possibility that contributions are effectively endogenous, that is, that in allocating contributions to committee members during the previous election cycle, a group may attempt to anticipate who the principal players will be on issues it cares about. . . . In each of the three cases, the model performs quite well, explaining over 55% of the variance in participation. More importantly, the analysis provides solid support for the principal hypothesis of this study, that moneyed interests mobilize bias in committee decision making.

This finding is clear for all three cases. The campaign contributions that dairy industry PACs gave to their likely supporters significantly increased their participation, even when we controlled for the importance of the issue to individual members' districts, whether they sat on the subcommittee of jurisdiction, and whether they held a leadership position (Table 1). . . .

The results of the job training case are also clear, and the specific estimates are striking in their similarity to the dairy stabilization case. As Table 2 shows, the contributions that labor groups made to their supporters had a substantial, statistically significant effect on participation during Education and Labor deliberations. Remarkably, the unstandardized coefficient for the money support variable

Table 1. PAC Money and Committee Participation: 1982 Dairy Stabilization Act

Independent Variables	Unstandardized 2SLS Coefficient	t-statistic
Intercept	.01	.05
Number of dairy cows in district	.27**	2.21
Dairy PAC contributions to supporters	.26**	2.42
Dairy PAC contributions to opponents	−.11	−.61
Membership on reporting subcommittee	.17**	3.54
Committee or subcommittee leadership position	.35**	4.50
Freshman status	−.02	-.31

Note: Adjusted R-squared = .60; number of observations = 41. All variables are measured on a 0–1 scale. The contributions term is the predicted value from the first-stage equation.
**Statistically significant at .05 level, one-tailed test.

Table 2. PAC Money and Committee
Participation: 1982 Job Training Partnership Act

Independent Variables	Unstandardized 2SLS Coefficient	t-statistic
Intercept	.13	.77
CETA expenditures in district	.03	.23
Labor union net contributions to supporters	.25*	1.62
Labor union net contributions to opponents	−.18	−.80
Membership on reporting subcommittee	.19**	2.61
Committee or subcommittee leadership position	.47**	4.55
Freshman status	−.05	−.51

Note: Adjusted R-squared = .56; number of observations = 32. All variables are measured on a 0–1 scale. The net contributions term is the predicted value from the first-stage equation.
*Statistically significant at .10 level, one-tailed test.
**Statistically significant at .05 level, one-tailed test.

is almost identical in size to the analogous coefficient in the dairy stabilization model despite the fact that the two cases are drawn from different committees with qualitatively different jurisdictions and policy environments. In each case, a change in the money support variable from its minimum to its maximum value moves a member approximately one-fourth of the way along the participation scale, almost exactly one standard deviation. In both cases, likewise, this coefficient is greater than that for subcommittee membership, a variable generally considered central to understanding participation in the postreform House. As in the dairy stabilization case, finally, the Education and Labor bill provides some support for the demobilization hypothesis. While it fails to meet conventional levels of statistical significance, the size of the money-opposition term proves negative and substantively significant, nearly matching the size of subcommittee membership.

The results regarding moneyed interests and mobilization are only slightly less compelling in the natural gas case, a case complicated both by divisions within the industry and the apparent importance of both organized and unorganized interests. As we note[d] above, such conditions are likely to mitigate the efficacy of interest group efforts, and they complicate the measurement of anticipated support and opposition. Still, the mobilization hypothesis finds strong support in the behavior of Energy and Commerce members. . . .

A change in the money support variable from its minimum to its maximum moves a Commerce Committee member approximately one-sixth of the way along the participation scale. . . .

As Table 3 shows, finally, the demobilization hypothesis is not supported in the natural gas case. While the coefficient on the money opponents interaction is slight, its positive sign is inconsistent with our prediction. The foundation for the demobilization hypothesis being theoretically weaker, however, the null result here, as well as the weak results in the dairy and job training cases, are not altogether surprising. The theoretically stronger hypothesis, that money mobilizes a pro-PAC bias at the committee level, is confirmed in all three. . . .

Finally, most of the variables that tap members' institutional positions prove to be strong determinants of committee participation. While the coefficients on freshman status differ in sign, both subcommittee membership and leadership position are positive, statistically significant, and substantiv[e]ly large in all three cases. Even on issues that are widely perceived among the committee membership to be important, issues where the organized interests in the policy environment are themselves active, the opportunities and resources provided by formal

Table 3. PAC Money and Committee Participation:
1984 Natural Gas Market Policy Act

Independent Variables	Unstandardized 2SLS Coefficient	t-statistic
Intercept	.08	.40
Natural gas production in district	.32*	1.65
Natural gas price increase effect on district	.17*	1.35
High production/high inflation interaction	−.18	−1.28
Producer-intrastate net contributions to supporters	.17**	1.69
Producer-intrastate net contributions to opponents	.01	.06
Membership reporting subcommittee	.23**	3.17
Committee or subcommittee leadership position	.54**	4.77
Freshman status	.13*	1.31

Note: Adjusted R-squared = .57; number of observations = 42. All variables are measured on a 0–1 scale. The net contributions term is the predicted value from the first stage equation.
*Statistically significant at .10 level, one-tailed test.
**Statistically significant at .05 level, one-tailed test.

institutional position are major factors in determining who makes the laws at the committee stage. Such findings are generally consistent with findings from other committees and larger samples of issues and reinforce the assumption that the model of participation employed here is specified correctly.

Conclusion

We have elaborated a theory of the member-group exchange relationship that comprehends the general patterns of PAC contributions reported in the literature. House members and interest group representatives are parties to an implicit cooperative agreement, but the constraints on member behavior and the rational calculations of group strategists limit the extent to which votes become the basis for exchange. This view suggests expectations about the effects of money on congressional decision making quite different from the ones that motivate the substantial research on the subject. We should find little causal connection between contributions and votes, especially on the floor—an expectation generally supported, although not adequately explained, in the literature. We should expect to find an important connection between contributions and the legislative involvement of sympathetic members, especially in committee—a relationship that empirical research to date has altogether ignored.

In order to test this view of moneyed interests and congressional decision making, we investigated the participation of House members on three issues in three committees. In each case, we found solid support for our principal hypothesis: moneyed interests are able to mobilize legislators already predisposed to support the group's position. Conversely, money that a group contributes to its likely opponents has either a negligible or negative effect on their participation. While previous research on these same issues provided little evidence that PAC money purchased members' votes, it apparently did buy the marginal time, energy, and legislative resources that committee participation requires. Moreover, we found evidence that (organized) producer interests figured more prominently than (unorganized) consumer interests in the participation decisions of House committee members—both for a case in which the issue at stake evoked high district salience and one where it did not. And we found little evidence that committee members respond to the interests of unemployed workers except insofar as those interests might be represented in the activities of well-financed and well-organized labor unions. Such findings suggest several implications for our understanding of political money, interest groups, and the legislative process.

The first and most important implication is that moneyed interests *do* affect the decision-making processes of Congress, an implication that one does not easily derive from the existing political science literature on contributions. In fact, it matters most at that stage of the legislative process that matters most and for a form of legislative behavior likely to have a direct bearing on outcomes. . . . Parliamentary suffrage gives a member relatively little leverage over the shape of legislation, especially at the committee stage. Only a small fraction of the decisions that shape a bill ever go to a vote, either in committee or on the floor. The vast majority are made in authoring a legislative vehicle, formulating amendments, negotiating specific provisions or report language behind the scenes, developing legislative strategy, and in other activities that require substantial time, information, and energy on the part of member and staff. While such efforts by no means guarantee that a particular member will influence the final outcome, they are usually a precondition for such influence.

A second and related implication of this investigation, then, is that empirical research should expand its view of the legislative purposes of political money and the other group resources that may accompany it. We focus here on committee participation; but the more general implication is that group expenditures may do much more than buy votes, or they may buy votes under certain conditions and affect other forms of legislative behavior under others. Such a suggestion, of course, usually appears in the various studies that examine the relationship between contributions and floor roll calls, but it needs to be elevated from the status of footnote or parenthetic remark to a central element of future research designs. Even for a small set of issues and a single group, the legislative strategies available are several, sometimes mixed. To speculate beyond the research reported here, for instance, we believe groups allocate their various resources (1) to mobilize strong supporters not only in House committees but also on the Senate floor, in dealings with executive agencies, and in various other decision-making forum[s] relevant to the group's interests; (2) to demobilize strong opponents; and (3) to effect the support of swing legislators. We require greater knowledge of the frequency and efficacy of such strategies, in any case, before we denigrate the role of moneyed interests in Congress, especially when the overwhelming weight of the evidence provided by Washington journalists and political insiders suggests that they matter a great deal.

Finally, the argument presented here provides a very different slant on the role of interest groups as purveyors of information in the deliberations of representative assemblies. A common defense of group lobbying activity, in fact, is that it provides ideas and information although its effect on member preferences is slight. Members (and their staffs) tend to consume information selectively, relying on sources with whom they already agree and discounting sources with whom they usually disagree. The view that we have advanced here suggests that while this may in fact describe how such information is used, it does not render it inconsequential. In light of the extraordinary demands on each congressional office, information—gathering it; analyzing it; turning it into speeches, amendments, and bills; using it to develop legislative strategy—can be very costly. Such costs, more than anything, limit the extent to which a nominal member will be a meaningful player in the decision-making process on a particular bill. At the very least, then, money-induced activity will distort the "representativeness of deliberations," a standard that democratic theorists since John Stuart Mill have used to evaluate the legitimacy of legislative assemblies. But it may also affect the "representativeness of decisions." By selectively subsidizing the information costs associated with participation, groups affect the *intensity* with which their positions are promoted by their legislative agents. In short, not all preferences weigh equally in legislative deliberations; and the resources of moneyed interests at least partly determine the weights.

The extent to which such efforts are damaging to representative government, as Schattschneider claimed, depends in part on the balance of interests and resources apparent in the relevant set of groups that are organized for political action. On any given issue, the efforts of one interest to mobilize supporters in Congress may be at least partially offset by the efforts of some competing group to mobilize its own supporters; indeed, there is some evidence that such countervailing efforts occurred in the natural gas case. But for those who believe that money is an illegitimate resource in such efforts—that pluralism requires something more than a competition among moneyed interests—the results of this study can only be disturbing.

Chapter 14

News Media

───◆◆───

14-1

The Market and the Media

James T. Hamilton

With good reason, the news media have long been called the "fourth branch" of government. In a democracy citizens need news to monitor the performance of their representatives. Conversely, officeholders and those who wish to replace them need to be able to communicate with their constituencies. Moreover, with officeholders needing to coordinate with one another across the institutions that divide them, "news," as Woodrow Wilson aptly observed, "is the atmosphere of politics." The First Amendment to the Constitution recognizes the news media's special role by placing freedom of the press alongside freedoms of speech and religion as deserving categorical protection from government infringement. More than in any other Western democracy, the news media developed in America as private business enterprises virtually free of government regulation or investment. Modern news, James Hamilton reminds us, is as much a product of business as it ever was. As technology creates new audiences and products, the business of news has undergone significant market adjustment.

SINCE MARKET FORCES have played the most decisive role in transforming the delivery of news, the history of the American press from the 1970s to the present is economic history. Although journalists may not explicitly consider economics

Source: James T. Hamilton, "The Market and the Media," in *The Press*, by Geneva Overholser and Kathleen Hall Jamieson, eds. (Oxford University Press: 2005), 351–371. Some notes appearing in the original have been deleted.

as they cover the day's events, the stories, reporters, firms, and media that ultimately survive in the marketplace depend on economic factors. The decisions of producers and editors are driven by supply and demand: Who cares about a particular piece of information? What is an audience willing to pay for the news, or what are advertisers willing to pay for the attention of readers, listeners, or viewers? How many consumers share particular interests in a topic? How many competitors are vying for readers' or viewers' attention, and what are these competitors offering as news? What are the costs of generating and transmitting a story? Who owns the outlet? What are the owners' goals? What are the property rights that govern how news is produced, distributed, and sold? News is a commercial product.

News outlets that cover public affairs have always struggled with the tension between giving people what they want to know and giving them what they need to know. The low probability that any reader has of influencing the outcome of a policy debate leaves many readers "rationally ignorant" about the details of governing.[1] From an investment perspective, why learn about global warming if your actions have little chance of affecting policy? News outlets do face strong demand for entertaining news, or information that helps people in their role as consumers or workers. Some people may also express a demand for news about politics, though the set of viewers that prefers politics covered as a sport or drama may exceed that which prefers detailed analysis.

In this essay I argue that since the 1970s news coverage has shifted to an increasing emphasis on what people want to know and away from information that they may need as voters. I identify three economic factors that help account for this shift: changes in technology, product definition and differentiation, and media ownership. I will examine in detail how each has affected news content over time. I then focus on network evening news programs in a case study that demonstrates how these economic factors have shaped news coverage. After providing a snapshot of current media coverage, I conclude with a section analyzing the implications of these alterations in the ways in which news is defined, distributed, and consumed.

What's Different: Technology, Products, and Owners

Three technological changes have affected the way in which images and information have entered households since 1970: the growth of cable television; the advent of the Internet; and the increased use of satellite technology to transmit news across continents and into homes. The spread of cable television in the 1980s and 1990s and introduction of direct-broadcast satellite delivery meant that by 2003 at least 85 percent of television households subscribed to multichannel delivery systems. The average number of channels per home went from 7.1 in 1970 to 71.2 in 2001. The average number of channels viewed weekly for at least ten minutes went from 4.5 to 13.5 channels per television household.[2] This proliferation of channels meant that news on cable could focus on specific niches. Rather than attempting to garner 10 million viewers (the audience attracted by the *NBC Nightly News* in 2003), a cable news program could be successful by attracting less than 1 million viewers. The result is that cable channels can focus their products on particular types of news: sports stories on ESPN; business news on CNBC; storm data on the Weather Channel; and news that appeals to a conservative audience on FOX News Channel. Both the network evening news programs and daily newspapers have broader audiences than cable channels. If survey respondents are asked to rate themselves on an ideological scale of liberalism and conservatism, the average rating for consumers of the network evening news programs and daily newspapers is the same as the national sample average. The regular consumers of the FOX News Channel, however, have the most conservative ideological rating in the survey. Cable political shows such as *Crossfire* and *Hardball*, in contrast, attract audiences more likely to rate themselves as liberal.

The relatively small audiences of some cable news programs yield profits because of low production budgets. Since talk can be cheap, cable news programs often feature journalists acting as political pundits. Political pundits, who offer a mixture of fact and opinion, face many market constraints. Since readers have the freedom to sample and ignore stories across the portfolio of topics covered in a paper, those writing for newspapers can aim for a relatively educated audience and afford to write about topics that may not be of interest to many. Television pundits, in contrast, operate in a medium where viewers of a particular program all consume the same story. If these pundits pick topics of little interest, they risk losing viewers, who may be less educated (than newspaper readers) and more likely to search for entertainment than enlightenment from television. The result is that pundits choose different languages to talk about politics, depending on the avenue of expression.

To see these differences, consider the case of George Will, who writes a syndicated column and appears as a commentator on ABC News programming.[3] As I demonstrate in my book *All the News That's Fit to Sell*, the print George Will uses a greater variety of terms and longer words than the television George Will. When composing for a print audience, Will uses more abstract terms such as those relating to inspiration, as well as more numeric terms. He writes about groups rather than individuals, as reflected in a greater focus on core values and institutions. In television appearances, Will changes expression to comply with the greater demands for entertainment. He uses more human-interest language. He makes more self-references. He simplifies and summarizes, and at the same time hedges his bets through qualifications (higher use of ambivalent language). His statements on television focus more on the present and emphasize motion. On television, Will offers opinions that are marked by greater activity and realism. Although George Will has developed a brand name for expression, he changes the delivery of his product to suit the audience demands and cost constraints of the medium. . . .

A second technological change affecting news markets is the spread of the Internet. Competition for attention across sites has driven the price of news on nearly all Internet sites to zero (the marginal delivery cost of the information). This explosion of free information has many ramifications. Consumption of high-quality newspapers, for example, is now possible around the world. If one looks at the top one hundred newspapers in the United States, the circulation of the top five (the *Wall Street Journal, USA Today,* the *New York Times, Los Angeles Times,* and *Washington Post*) accounted for 21.5 percent of the total newspaper circulation in 1999.[4] If you look at the links generated on the Internet by these top one hundred newspapers, however, the top five papers in terms of links (which included *USA Today,* the *New York Times,* and the *Washington Post*) accounted for 41.4 percent of the total links. In part this reflects the advantages of established brands on the Internet, since familiarity with a product's existence and reputation can lead to its consumption. . . .

The low cost of entry to placing information on the Internet has had many effects on news. The ability of news outlets, and columnists such as Matt Drudge, to post instantly during any time of the day has extended news cycles and created additional pressure on traditional news outlets to run with breaking news.[5] The lack of large investment in sites means that news provided may not be heavily edited or screened, which can give rise to a spread of rumor and gossip. The archiving of data on the Internet and easy accessibility make it easier for errors in reporting to propagate, as journalists access information collected by others and incorporate it into stories. The widespread existence of government and nonprofit Web sites lowers the cost of information generation and analysis for reporters. Journalists writing about campaign finance, for example, can readily locate data at the individual contributor level at the Federal Election Commission Web site or at Opensecrets.org. Similarly, reporters writing about the environment can use government data aggregated by the nonprofit Environmental Defense, which posts detailed pollution data by the zip code level at Scorecard.org.

Widespread use of satellite technology to beam images across the country and the world marks a third change in news reporting. During the 1970s the three evening network news programs had an "oligopoly of image," where viewers tuned in the programs in part to see the first pictures of the day's breaking stories.

The deployment of satellite technology across the country, however, soon meant that local television stations had the ability to import stories quickly from other parts of the country and to go live to events in their own city. The ability of local stations to share in network feeds or tap into other sources of pictures meant that local news programs began to offer viewers images of national or international stories, which in turn put pressure on the evening news to offer a differentiated product (including more interpretative or contextual material). The existence of satellite technology also meant that international coverage could take place in real time, including the coverage of the Iraq War by embedded reporters.

These technological changes have put increased pressures on traditional news outlets to compete for readers and viewers. The growth in cable channels and cable / direct broadcast satellite subscription has eroded the market share of the network evening news programs and focused attention on retaining viewers. The network evening news programs have a core audience of faithful viewers and a set of marginal viewers, those who may tune in to the news or choose another program depending on what has happened in the world or what types of news the networks choose to focus on. News directors will select a mix of stories aimed at capturing the marginal viewers while not alienating the average or regular viewers. The result of competition from cable is a mix of stories that leaves average viewers somewhat frustrated and marginal viewers somewhat placated.

Survey data from the Pew Center for the People and the Press in 2000 show the tension between the interests of the average (i.e., regularly view) and marginal (i.e., sometimes view) consumers of the network nightly news programs.[6] A majority of the regular viewers are over fifty (54.8 percent) and female (53.9 percent). The marginal viewers are much younger. Females aged eighteen to thirty-four account for 20.6 percent of those who sometimes view the national news, and males aged eighteen to thirty-four account for 17.5 percent of these sometime viewers. In contrast, eighteen-to-thirty-four-year-old females are only 9.1 percent of the regular audience, and males of that age group only 9.2 percent of the regular viewers. These demographic differences translate into predictable and sharp differences between the interests of marginal and average viewers. Marginal viewers are not as attached to the news. When asked whether they enjoyed keeping up with the news, 68.1 percent of average viewers responded that they did "a lot" versus only 37.0 percent for the marginal viewers. A majority of marginal viewers said that they followed national or international news closely "only when something important or interesting is happening." Marginal viewers also were more likely to report that they watched the news with "my remote in hand" and switched channels when they were not interested in a topic.

What captures the interests of occasional viewers differs from the type of news favored by loyal viewers. The marginal and average viewers have the same top two news interests, crime and health, which may explain the prevalence of these news categories on the network evening news. The two sets of viewers differ markedly, however, in their interest in politics. For the average viewer of network news, news about political figures and events in Washington ranked fifth out of thirteen news types. This same category of news ranked tenth among marginal viewers. Political news about Washington was followed very closely by 28.4 percent of the average viewers, versus 12.3 percent of the marginals. Sports ranked sixth and entertainment news ranked twelfth among the regular viewers. These topics ranked much more highly among marginal viewers, who ranked them third and eighth among the thirteen news topics.

Viewers who are younger than fifty may also merit attention for another reason—they are more highly valued by advertisers. Reasons offered for why advertisers pay more for viewers under fifty include a belief that their brand preferences are not as fixed and the fact that they watch less television and hence are harder to reach. The rewards for capturing relatively younger viewers offer another reason for news directors to pay less attention to the (older) loyal watchers. One way to forge a compromise between the interests of average and marginal viewers is to cover the political issues of interest to younger viewers. The January 2000 Pew survey asked respondents to indicate the priority they attached to twenty political issues. When I examined the number of minutes or number of stories devoted on each network to these issues in 2000, I found that the higher the priority attached to an issue at the start of the year by the eighteen-to-thirty-four set, the more attention devoted over the year by the network news. The priorities of older viewers had no impact or a negative effect on coverage devoted by the networks. The survey data indicate that females in the [above] age range care relatively more about issues such as dealing with the problems of families with children and strengthening gun control laws. Searching for marginal viewers and those valued by advertisers may thus lead the networks to talk about issues often associated with the Democratic Party. The competition generated by technology, and the influence of advertiser values, thus generate pressure to provide network stories that may give rise to perceptions of media bias. Among those identifying themselves as very conservative, 37.4 percent reported in 2000 that they viewed the national nightly network news as very biased. Among survey respondents who labeled themselves as very liberal, only 16.6 percent saw network news programs the same way.

Product Changes

In print and broadcast, there has been a substantial change in the content and style of news coverage since 1970. These product changes are numerous: a decrease in hard news (e.g., public-affairs coverage) and an increase in soft news (e.g., entertainment, human-interest stories); an increase in negative tone to cover elections; less focus on watchdog stories (e.g., those dealing with the operation of government); and an increase in the mix of opinion and interpretation in news coverage. These product changes also have many origins. Emphasis on cost cutting and profits has led to declines in international coverage. Competition across media and the pressure for product differentiation within a market have led some outlets to specialize in soft news. The drive to entertain can transform political coverage into horse-race coverage, with a focus on who is ahead in the polls and a tone that is often critical of candidates and events. In publicly traded companies, pressures to meet market earnings expectations can mean more focus on pleasing readers and viewers and less room for journalists to exercise their own news judgment. Changes in rules by the Federal Communications Commission (FCC) have reduced station worries about whether views expressed on air are "fair" and removed specific requirements that broadcasters provide a minimum amount of public-affairs coverage. In this section I describe the dimensions of news product changes since 1970. These changes in product attributes result from an interplay of demand and supply factors, though I do not attempt here to specify which factors generate particular product alterations.

Content analysis by the Committee of Concerned Journalists (CCJ) in 1998 captured broad changes in the media by examining for 1977, 1987, and 1997 one month of coverage on the three network evening news programs, each cover story during the year for *Time* and *Newsweek*, and each front-page story for the *New York Times* and *Los Angeles Times*. For this sample of 3,760 stories, the CCJ found that straight news accounts (e.g., what happened yesterday) went from 52 percent of stories in 1977 to only 32 percent in 1997. Story topics in traditional hard-news areas (i.e., government, military, and domestic and foreign affairs) went from 66.3 percent of all reports to 48.9 percent. Feature stories such as those about entertainment, celebrities, lifestyle, and celebrity crime grew from 5.1 percent in 1977 to 11.1 percent in 1997. Crime stories went from 8.4 percent to 11.4 percent and personal health from 0.7 percent to 3.5 percent. Attention also grew for stories about science (2.7 percent to 5.9 percent) and religion (0.5 percent to 3.7 percent).[7] . . .

As hard-news coverage declined, the tone of many stories about elections grew more critical. Assessing coverage of major-party presidential nominees in *Time* and *Newsweek* from 1960 to 1992, [Thomas] Patterson found that unfavorable references to the candidates grew from approximately 25 percent in 1960 to 60 percent in 1992. Studying front-page election stories in the *New York Times*, he found that in the 1960s the candidates and other partisan sources set the tone of nearly 70 percent of the articles. By 1992, journalists set the tone for the reports about 80 percent of the time. Kiku Adatto documented similar patterns of a shrinking role for the candidate and increasing role for the reporter on network television coverage of presidential campaigns. She found that in 1968 the average sound bite for a presidential candidate on the network evening news was 42.3 seconds. By the 1988 campaign this figure dropped to 9.8 seconds (and decreased further to 8.4 seconds in the 1992 general election). What replaced the words of the candidates was strategy coverage provided by reporters, who gave viewers their assessment of why the candidate was engaged in a particular strategy and how the candidate was faring in the horse race. Critical coverage also greeted the eventual winners. A study for the Council for Excellence in Government found that in the first year of the presidencies of Ronald Reagan (1981), Bill Clinton (1993), and George W. Bush (2001), coverage of the administration on network television news was negative in tone by a ratio of nearly two to one. The critical eye reporters used in covering government emerged in part from journalists' experience with government deception during both the Vietnam War and Watergate.[8] . . .

Product changes are evident too in the percentage of journalists saying that a particular media role was extremely important. In 1971 76 percent of journalists said investigating government claims was an extremely important mass media role, 61 percent said the same for providing analysis of complex problems, and 55 percent for discussing national policy. These figures dropped in 1992 to 67 percent for investigating government, 48 percent for analysis of complex problems, and 39 percent for national problems. Journalists in 1992 were much more likely (69 percent) to say that getting information to the public quickly was an extremely important role, versus 56 percent in 1971.[9]

In extended interviews with journalists, Howard Gardner, Mihaly Csikszentmihalyi, and William Damon also found that journalists were frustrated: 51 percent said changes in the media were negative, versus 24 percent indicating that the changes were positive. Sixty-four percent of the journalists they interviewed said the demands to comply with business goals in journalism were increasing, and 63 percent said there was a perceived drop in ethics and values in the media. Many of those interviewed pointed to the drive for market share as a prime force undercutting the performance of journalists.[10]

Changes in government regulation also affected the extent and kind of information provided. Prior to 1987, the FCC's fairness doctrine required broadcasters to provide free and equal time to parties that dissented from controversial views that stations chose to air. While the policy may have promoted perceptions of fairness, empirical evidence indicates that the policy may have chilled speech by discouraging stations from presenting viewpoints that might trigger demands for free response time on air.[11] Once the fairness doctrine was abolished by the FCC, the genre of informational programming immediately expanded on radio. This radio genre, which includes news programming and the talk-radio format made famous by Rush Limbaugh, became both a popular and controversial force in public-affairs debates in the 1990s.

Ownership

Change in ownership of news media outlets is a third factor affecting content. There are many theories about why ownership matters: publicly traded firms could be more likely to focus on profits than journalism properties (e.g., newspapers) owned by individuals or families; outlets owned by groups, whether a newspaper in a chain or a broadcast station owned by a network may be less likely to identify with the problems of a specific city; and the concentration of ownership in a small number of firms may crowd out a diverse set of views.

Calculating how ownership has changed over time requires defining a medium and a market. Between 1970 and 1998, the number of daily newspapers declined from 1,748 to 1,489 and average circulation dropped from 62,202 to 56,183. The number of weekly newspapers, however, grew from 7,612 to 8,193 and average circulation jumped from 3,660 to 9,067. The number of cities with two or more fully competing dailies with different ownership declined from 37 in 1973 to 19 in 1996. The number of newspaper groups dropped from 157 in 1970 to 129 in 1996. In the same period, the percentage of dailies owned by chains grew from 50.3 percent to 76.2 percent and the percentage of daily circulation accounted for by these group-owned papers increased from 63.0 percent to 81.5 percent. The fifteen largest newspaper chains generated slightly more than half of the daily circulation of newspapers in the United States in 1998.[12]

At a broad level, the media have not become significantly more concentrated (in terms of the concentration of sales in a specific number of firms) over this time period. It is estimated that in terms of revenues, the top fifty media firms (which include newspaper, broadcast, cable, publishing, music, and film companies) accounted for 79.7 percent of all media industry revenues in 1986 and 81.8 percent in 1997; the share of the top four firms grew from 18.8 percent to 24.1 percent.[13] . . . One study looked at how ownership had changed between 1960 and 2000 for ten local media markets in the United States. After counting for each local market the number of broadcast outlets, cable systems, direct-broadcast satellite systems, and daily newspapers available, the study found that the percentage growth in the total number of media outlets available averaged more than 200 percent between 1960 and 2000. The percentage increase in the number of owners in the market averaged 140 percent.[14]

The actual impact of group or chain ownership in media outlets is a topic of spirited empirical debate. Reviewing the social science evidence on the impact of chain ownership on newspaper operation in 1994, Edwin Baker concluded, "Chain ownership's primary documented effects are negative. However, the findings seem tepid, hardly motivating any strong critique of chain ownership or prompting any significant policy interventions." Lisa George found that as the number of owners in a local newspaper market goes down, product differentiation between newspapers increases and the number of topical reporting beats covered in the market overall goes up. The Project for Excellence in Journalism found that in local television markets, stations affiliated with networks produced higher-quality news programs than those actually owned and operated by the networks, that stations owned by a company also operating a newspaper in the market generated higher-quality local television news programs, and that locally owned stations were not obviously superior to other stations in news production.[15]

The Changing Nature of Network News

The transformation of the network evening news programs since 1970 offers a case study of the impact of changes in technology, news definitions, and ownership.[16] In 1969 the daily debates among network news executives and reporters about what stories to include in the evening news broadcasts centered around which domestic politics and foreign policy stories to cover. Each television network was part of a media company. For each of the three networks, the founder or an early leader was still involved and identified with the operation of the organization. Network news operations were expected to generate prestige, part of which reflected back on the owners and broadcasters. The FCC routinely examined the number of hours of public-affairs programming provided when stations had their licenses renewed. A reputation for covering public affairs well in the news provided added security when licenses were up for renewal. If viewers did not enjoy the hard-news stories provided in the evening news programs, they had few other options on the dial. The average television household received seven channels. At the dinner hour more than one-third of all television households watched the network evening news. The stories they saw were news to most viewers. National news programs were not on earlier in the afternoon, and local news programs lacked the technology and time to cover national events on their own. Decision makers on network news programs felt a responsibility to provide viewers with information they needed as citizens. The large audience share and focus on politics attracted significant scrutiny of the programs, which were a frequent target of criticism from the White House.[17]

In 2000 the daily debates in network story conferences centered on whether to include domestic political stories or softer news items about health and entertainment topics. Foreign coverage was not often on the agenda, except in cases of military action. Each network was part of a publicly traded conglomerate. Network news operations were expected by corporate managers and Wall Street analysts to generate profits. The FCC no longer scrutinized public affairs coverage and license renewals were virtually assured. Television households received an average of sixty-three channels. Viewers at the dinner hour could watch sitcoms, entertainment news, sports news, and news on PBS. The three major network news programs combined captured only 23 percent of all television households. Viewers often came to the network news programs with a sense of the day's headline stories, after watching news on cable channels or local television programs containing stories and footage from around the nation. Network decision-makers felt pressure to gain ratings, which translated into a competition to discover and serve viewers' interests. Anchors and reporters were promoted as celebrities. Political criticisms of news coverage focused more on the content of cable news programs, though press critics faulted the network evening news shows for an increasing shift to soft-news stories.

To see the shift in news content, consider how the network evening news treated a consistent set of stories over time. Each year, *People* magazine selects its "25 Most Intriguing People" of the year, which consist of a set of soft-news personalities (i.e., television stars, movie actors, sports figures, persons involved in famous crimes, and royalty) and a set of famous figures from business and politics. In 1974–78, 40 percent of the soft-news personalities on the *People* list were covered in stories on at least one of the three major network evening news programs. In 1994–98, this figure rose to 52 percent. For those soft-news personalities that generated coverage over the course of the year they were listed by *People*, on ABC the "Intriguing" person averaged 9.9 stories and 1,275 seconds in coverage per year in 1974–78. This grew to 17.2 stories and 2,141 seconds of annual average coverage by 1994–98. NBC's reputation of providing more soft news than the other two networks is confirmed by its average of 25.6 stories and 3,238 seconds of coverage in 1994–98.

By many measures hard-news coverage dropped over this period. Each year, *Congressional Quarterly* identifies the key votes that take place in the U.S. Senate and House. In 1969–73, 82 percent of these major votes were covered on at least one of the network evening news programs on the day of or day after the congressional action. Yet for the period 1994–98, only 62 percent of the *CQ* votes generated network stories. A similar pattern holds for the key legislative votes identified each year by two ideological interest groups, the Americans for Democratic Action (ADA) and the American Conservative Union (ACU). The percentage of key interest-group votes in Congress that generated stories on the nightly news dropped from 64 percent in 1969–73 to 44 percent in 1994–98. The shift on the network news away from a headline service toward more background reporting is evident in the fact that those bills that were covered got more time on the evening news programs. On ABC, for example, the mean overage length for *CQ* bills went from 117 seconds in 1969–73 to 211 seconds in 1994–98.

Statistical analysis shows that many factors contributed to these changes in coverage. *People's* intriguing personalities were more likely to be covered over the course of a year on the network evening news in the era (i.e., 1984 or later) when the FCC had deregulated much of broadcast television. Coverage of *CQ* votes declined in election years (when they were probably crowded out by campaign stories) and dropped as cost cutting became more prominent in network news operations. Interest-group vote coverage declined on each network as the percentage of households with cable increased, indicating how broadcast television shifted away from some forms of hard news as competition increased from cable. In the period 1969 to 1999, the number of network evening news stories mentioning soft-news terms such as *actor, sex*, or *movie* increased along with the percentage of households with cable. In the post-deregulation era, stories about hard-news topics such as education or Medicaid or NATO declined.

Network evening news anchors not only covered celebrities, they became them. News products have always been what economists call experience goods, which means that companies have always sought ways to signal to potential customers what today's version of events will look like in their papers or programs. The pressure for journalists to become part of the news product, however, is increasing as the number of news outlets expands. In a world of four broadcast television channels, a consumer can easily switch among viewing options to sample content. In a world where channels can number in the hundreds, sampling becomes more time-consuming.[18] If viewers recognize and enjoy watching a particular journalist on television, they may be more likely to watch a given channel because of this familiarity. The personalities of those who present the information become shortcuts for viewers to find their news niche. The changing salary rewards in network evening news programs provide evidence of how journalists have become part of the product in news.

Although network anchors deliver the news, they are rewarded in the marketplace for delivering viewers to advertisers. The salary patterns for network evening news anchors suggest that the value attached to the personal ability of these stars to deliver viewers increased markedly during the 1990s. . . . When consumers have many more choices, the value of a known commodity can increase. Network anchors become a way for channels to create a brand image in viewers' minds. If anchors become more important in drawing viewers to programs, this may translate into higher returns for anchors in salary negotiations. . . . The amount in salary that an anchor received for attracting a thousand viewing households increased from a range of $0.13 to $0.31 (in 1999 dollars) in 1976 to a range of $0.86 to $1.07 in 1999. Another way to view this is to look at the ratio of the anchor's salary to the ad price on the evening news programs. In 1976 anchors such as Walter Cronkite and John Chancellor were paid the equivalent of 28 ads per year, while in 1999 this had grown to 149 ads for Dan Rather and Tom Brokaw. The marked increase in the amount paid per viewing household, salary expressed in ad revenues, and the absolute magnitude of the salary took place in the 1990s. This was a time of declining absolute audiences, but rising importance of anchors in attracting viewers. The increased value placed on anchors is consistent with these personalities playing a growing role in attracting viewers in a multichannel universe.

Current News Markets

The expanding opportunities for individuals to consume media products has meant declining market shares for most traditional news media outlets. The percentage of survey respondents saying that they were regular consumers of a specific news outlet dropped substantially between May 1993 and April 2002 in Pew surveys: from 77 percent to 57 percent for local television news; 60 percent to 32 percent for nightly network news; and 52 percent to 24 percent for network television news magazines. Between 1994 and 2002, Pew surveys indicated drops in regular consumption from 47 percent to 41 percent for radio and 58 percent to 41 percent for newspapers. Respondents reporting regular consumption of online news grew from 2 percent in April 1996 to 25 percent in April 2002; NPR's figures also increased during that period, from 13 percent to 16 percent. In April 2002, 33 percent of survey respondents reported that they were regular consumers of cable television news. . . .

   The multiplication of news outlets on cable and the Internet means [also] that an individual is more likely today than in the 1970s or 1980s to find a news outlet closer to his or her ideal news source. The creation of niche programming and content means that individuals may be more likely to find what they want. But the division of the audience into smaller groups also means that any one channel may be less likely to attract viewers, less likely to amass advertiser revenue, and hence less able to devote resources to programming. There may be a trade-off between cable channels' catering to individual topical interests and the quality of programming that can be supported by the audience size. On the Internet, the drive of competition means that price eventually equals marginal costs (zero), so sites are searching for ways to generate revenue. This means that breaking news becomes a commodity essentially offered for free. The lack of revenue may mean that sites simply repeat readily available information rather than generate their own coverage. In a study of Internet content during the 2000 presidential primaries, the Committee of Concerned Journalists found that one-quarter of the political front pages on Internet sites they studied had no original reporting.[19] The time pressure to provide news generated by the Internet and the lack of resources to do original reporting may increase the likelihood that information cascades occur. When initial news reports get facts wrong, the tendency of reporters to rely on the work of others and the quick multiplication effects can mean that bad information propagates. . . .

An additional dilemma for hard-news consumers is the economic pressures that may push some outlets away from offering the type of news they prefer. If advertisers value younger viewers and younger viewers demonstrate a higher willingness to switch channels, then broadcast programs may end up at the margins, putting more soft-news topics into previously hard-news programs. This explains in part the increased emphasis on entertainment and human-interest stories on the network news broadcasts. Media bias can also emerge as a commercial product, in at least two forms. If networks are targeting relatively younger female viewers, and these viewers express more interest in issues such as gun control and the problems of families with children, the network news programs may focus on traditionally Democratic (liberal) issues out of economic necessity. The development of niche programs on cable can also generate programs targeted at viewers with a particular ideology. The FOX News Channel. for example, attracts a relatively conservative audience and offers the cable news program with the largest audience—*The O'Reilly Factor*. The added variety arising from the expansion of cable programming means that viewers uninterested in politics can more readily avoid it. In 1996 viewers with cable who had low levels of political interest (i.e., had low levels of political information) were much less likely to watch presidential debates than viewers who had broadcast channels.[20] Those who were not interested in politics but had only broadcast television did end up watching these debates, since their options were limited. The greater entertainment options provided by cable television also appear to affect who votes. Among viewers with high interest in entertainment programming, those with cable are much less likely to vote (perhaps because they are able to avoid political programming by watching the many entertainment channels offered on cable). . . .

Changes in news markets from 1970 to today have brought new media, generated more diverse offerings, and added opportunities to find both hard and soft news. In pushing for the deregulation of broadcast television in the 1980s, FCC chairman Mark Fowler declared famously, "The public's interest . . . defines the public interest." [21] The competition for interested audiences has clearly driven many of the recent changes in journalism. Whether the aggregation of individuals pursuing the stories they want to know about yields the type of information they need to know about as citizens and voters is a question pursued further in other chapters in this volume.

NOTES

1. Anthony Downs, *An Economic Theory of Democracy* (New York: Harper Books, 1957). Downs coined the term *rational ignorance* to refer to the fact that the small probability that an individual has of influencing public policy decisions means that it may be rational to remain ignorant of current affairs, if one views information only as an instrument in making decisions and calculates the personal payoffs from keeping up with public affairs. There may still be a demand expressed for political coverage, from those who feel a duty to be informed, people who find the details of politics and policies inherently interesting, or people who derive entertainment from politics as drama, horse race, or scandal. The logic of rational ignorance may help explain why Delli Carpini and Keeter find that "despite the numerous political, economic, and social changes that have occurred since World War II, overall political knowledge levels in the United States are about the same today as they were forty to fifty years ago" (*What Americans Know about Politics and Why It Matters*. New Haven, Conn.: Yale University Press, 1996, 270).

2. For data on channel availability and consumption, see Ed Papazian, ed., *TV Dimensions 2002* (New York: Media Dynamics, 2002).

3. To study the market for pundits, I analyzed a sample of the print offerings and broadcast transcripts of fifty-six pundits in 1999 using the text analysis software DICTION. See chapter 8 in Hamilton, *All the News That's Fit to Sell,* (Princeton, N.J.: Princeton University Press, 2004).

4. For analysis of news markets on the Internet, see chapter 7 in Hamilton, *All the News That's Fit to Sell.*

5. See Kovach and Rosenstiel, *Warp Speed* (New York: Century Foundation Press, 1999), and Kalb, *One Scandalous Story* (New York: Free Press, 2001), for discussions of the time pressures on journalists created by the speed of information transmission and the Internet.

6. See chapter 3 in Hamilton, *All the News That's Fit to Sell*, for an analysis of the network news audience.

7. Committee of Concerned Journalists, *Changing Definitions of News* (Washington, D.C.: Committee of Concerned Journalists, 1998), available from www.journalism.org.

8. Patterson, *Out of Order* (New York: Knopf, 1993); Adatto, *Picture Perfect* (New York: Basic Books, 1993); Council for Excellence in Government, *Government: In and Out of the News*, study by the Center for Media and Public Affairs, 2003, available at http://www.excelgov.org/displaycontent.asp?keyword=prnHomePage. Patterson's *Out of Order* also includes a discussion of distrust between reporters and politicians.

9. Weaver and Wilhoit, *The American Journalist in the 1990s* (Mahwah, N.J.: Lawrence Erlbaum, 1996).

10. Gardner, Csikszentmihalyi, and Damon, *Good Work* (New York: Basic Books, 2001).

11. Thomas W. Hazlett and David W. Sosa, "Was the Fairness Doctrine a 'Chilling Effect'?: Evidence from the Post-Deregulation Radio Market," *Journal of Legal Studies* 26, no. 1 (1997): 279–301.

12. For data on newspaper markets, see Compaine and Gomery, *Who Owns the Media?* 3rd ed. (Mahwah, N.J.: Lawrence Erlbaum, 2000).

13. Ibid.

14. Scott Roberts, Jane Frenette, and Dione Stearns, "A Comparison of Media Outlets and Owners for Ten Selected Markets: 1960, 1980, 2000" (working paper, Media Ownership Working Group, Federal Communications Commission, Washington, D.C., 2002).

15. For discussion of the impact of media ownership and concentration on content, see Peter O. Steiner, "Program Patterns and Preferences, and the Workability of Competition in Radio Broadcasting," *Quarterly Journal of Economics* 66 (1952): 194-223; Demers, *The Menace of the Corporate Newspaper* (Ames: Iowa State University Press, 1996); Bagdikian, *The Media Monopoly* (Boston: Beacon Press, 1997); McChesney, *Rich Man, Poor Democracy* (Urbana: University of Illinois Press, 2000); Jeff Chester, "Strict Scrutiny: Why Journalists Should Be Concerned about New Federal and Industry Media Deregulation Proposals," *Harvard International Journal of Press/Politics* 7, no. 2 (2002): 105–15; and Roberts and Kunkel, eds., *Breach of Faith* (Fayetteville: University of Arkansas Press, 2002). The quotation on ownership studies comes from C. Edwin Baker, "Ownership of Newspapers: The View from Positivist Social Science" (research paper, Joan Shorenstein Center on the Press, Politics and Public Policy, Kennedy School of Government, Harvard University, Cambridge, Mass., 1994), 19. See also Lisa George, "What's Fit to Print: The Effect of Ownership Concentration on Product Variety in Daily Newspaper Markets" (working paper, Michigan State University, East Lansing, Mich., 2001), and Project for Excellence in Journalism, *Does Ownership Matter in Local Television News? A Five-Year Study of Ownership and Quality,* updated April 29, 2003, http://www.journalism. org/resources/research/reports/ownership/default.asp.

16. This section excerpts and summarizes analysis from chapters 6 and 8 of Hamilton, *All the News That's Fit to Sell.*

17. In 1969 the founders or early leaders of each network still served as the chairman of the board: William S. Paley (CBS); David Sarnoff (RCA, which owned NBC); and Leonard Goldenson (ABC). For an overview of the networks that focuses on the 1980s, see Auletta, *Three Blind Mice* (New York: Random House, 1992). Data on channels per television household come from Ed Papazian, ed., *TV Dimensions 2001* (New York: Media Dynamics, 2001), which indicates (on p. 22) that averages were 7.1 for 1970 and 63.4 for 2000. Larry M. Bartels and Wendy M. Rahn, in "Political Attitudes in the Post-Network Era" (paper prepared for the Annual Meeting of the American Political Science Association, Washington, D.C., September, 2000), report that the sum of the Nielsen ratings for the three network evening news programs was close to 36 in 1970–71 and 23 in 1999–2000. For the text of Vice President Spiro Agnew's speech attacking network television news on November 13, 1969, see James Keogh, *President Nixon and the Press* (New York: Funk & Wagnalls, 1972).

18. In summer 2001 DirecTV, a digital satellite service, offered subscribers more than 225 channels (see www.directv.com). The average number of channels received in U.S. television households grew from 28 in 1988 to 49 in 1997. Households clearly have favorites among these channels. The average number of channels viewed per household, where viewing is defined as "10 or more continuous minutes per channel," was 12 in 1997. See Nielsen Media Research, *1998 Report on Television* (New York: Nielsen Media Research, 1998), 19.

19. Committee of Concerned Journalists, *ePolitics: A Study of the 2000 Presidential Campaign on the Internet* (Washington, D.C.: Committee of Concerned Journalists, 2000), available from www.journalism.org.

20. See Matthew A. Baum and Samuel Kernell, "Has Cable Ended the Golden Age of Presidential Television?" *American Political Science Review* 93, no. 1 (1999): 99–114.

21. See Hamilton, *All the News That's Fit to Sell,* 1.

14-2

from *War Stories*

Matthew A. Baum and Tim J. Groeling

The authors begin with the basic proposition that both reporters and Washington politicians contribute to news to serve their separate goals. Politicians seek influence with voters and fellow politicians; reporters need stories that will make the front page or lead the newscast. The result of their exchange becomes the news we consume. It is not likely to be wholly objective reporting, Baum and Groeling explain, because reporters prefer a fresh "man bites dog" perspective. In politics, this takes the form of members of the same party criticizing each other or their party's president. This essay explores the kinds of biases in reporting our military policies that result from the strategic exchange between reporters and politicians.

SPEAKING IN ST. LOUIS on July 5, 2008, then-Democratic presidential candidate Barack Obama outlined his plans for withdrawing U.S. troops from Iraq: "The tactics of how we ensure our troops are safe as we pull out, how we execute the withdrawal, those are things that are all based on facts and conditions. I am not somebody—unlike George Bush—who is willing to ignore facts on the basis of my preconceived notions." In his statement, Obama accused President Bush, in effect, of ignoring reality in his Iraq policies, and implied that his own promised timetable for withdrawal might be adapted to reflect the actual situation there.

Obama's statement drew heavy coverage throughout the news media and exposed the presumptive Democratic presidential nominee to sharp criticism from both the Left and the Right for his apparent "flip-flop" regarding withdrawal, especially among online commentators. Upon calling another press conference to refine his stance mere hours after making his initial statement, Obama confessed that he was "a little puzzled by the frenzy that I set off with what I thought was a pretty innocuous statement." The campaign of Republican candidate John McCain in turn attacked Obama both for his initial speech and for his subsequent puzzlement about the furor. "What's really puzzling is that Barack Obama still doesn't understand that his words matter," said McCain spokesman Tucker Bounds.

Source: Matthew A. Baum and Tim J. Groeling, *War Stories: The Causes and Consequences of Public Views of War* (Princeton, NJ: Princeton University Press, 2010), 17–36, 45. Notes and some bibliographic references appearing in the original have been deleted.

This incident brings into focus several vital components of public opinion and foreign policy in the modern American context. First, it illustrates that the statements of politicians, which studies of politics often dismiss as "cheap talk," can be consequential. Second, it highlights the importance of events on the ground in a conflict even as it demonstrates the degree to which politicians can politicize and manipulate public perceptions of such "reality." Third, Obama's puzzlement regarding why this particular statement provoked such massive media comment draws attention to the news choices of journalists, who generally stand between politicians and the public they hope to persuade, and new media actors, who helped stoke the fires of the controversy online. Finally, Obama's accusation that Bush would "ignore facts" because of "preconceived notions" about Iraq calls into question the degree to which prior opinions, political rhetoric, and reality can alter public opinion over the course of a conflict.

. . . [W]e seek to explain how various partisan messages emanating from different sources and media outlets influence public opinion, particularly with respect to foreign policy crises and wars. In addition, we seek to explain how these effects on news content and public opinion might systematically change with time and the flow of events. Finally, we seek to determine exactly *which* elite messages are likely to make it into the news under different circumstances, and how new media actors might alter those patterns. . . .

What Politicians Want from the Media

We begin by examining the incentives of politicians. Politicians expend considerable effort in shaping their messages and images in the news media. The most universally accepted assumption in U.S. electoral politics is that politicians seek, first and foremost, reelection. . . . [P]oliticians seek reelection both for themselves and for their fellow partisans. After all, winning an election holds dramatically different implications, with respect to both resources available for subsequent election campaigns and a party member's ability to influence public policy, if one is a member of the majority party in Congress, and particularly when that party also controls the executive branch. Winning election or control of government in turn requires making one's self and one's fellow partisans took good, while casting members of the opposition party in a negative light. The implication for politicians' preferences regarding media coverage is straightforward: typical politicians prefer stories that praise themselves and fellow partisans, or criticize their opponents and the opposition party.

In the context of interbranch relations, this further implies that . . . members of the presidential party (PP) in Congress are likely to express rhetorical support for the president, while members of the opposition party, or nonpresidential party (NPP), should be more likely to oppose him. While periodically there are incentives for individual members to depart from these strategies, particularly if they are running for president or wish to gain press coverage by taking "maverick" stances, the perceived novelty of such instances highlights the prevailing baseline from which they depart.

Senator John McCain's (R-AZ) campaigns for the 2000 and 2008 Republican presidential nominations provide perhaps the most famous recent example of this tendency. In both elections, McCain ran campaigns that initially challenged the Republican Party leadership, instead relying heavily on what he jokingly referred to as "my base"—the national news media. While this close relationship was undoubtedly attributable in part to McCain's comparatively open access to members of the press, reporters viewed his "defiant character" in the Senate, in which he broke with his own party over campaign finance reform and other key issues, as "delightfully subversive" (Weisberg 1999). Even before McCain's candidacy, Republicans had complained that journalists granted conservatives who took liberal positions fawning press coverage . . . .

If journalists do consistently report discord among the president's fellow partisans more frequently than affirmation, . . . there can be only two explanations. Either such coverage must reflect journalists' preferences, or elites from the president's own party must be routinely criticizing the president more often than they praise him during times of foreign crises. . . . We consider the latter possibility highly improbable, especially given that in the most public of all representations, votes for or against presidential legislative initiatives, recent presidents have typically received overwhelming support from members of their own party and similarly strong opposition from the opposing party. . . .

What Journalists Want from Politicians

Despite politicians' best efforts to control their public communication, journalists and news organizations have historically maintained ultimate control over the content of their news programs because of their function as gatekeepers of political news content. In deciding what political material is or is not news, certain characteristics of stories or sources make them more (or less) desirable for journalists. In particular, professional journalists generally prefer stories that are novel, conflictual, balanced, and involve authoritative political actors. Below, we consider exactly how each of these characteristics applies to news about politics.

The most obvious characteristic of newsworthiness is that it places a premium on stories that are actually new. Informing readers or viewers of unexpected, inconsistent, or novel information is the core value provided by news organizations. In fact, without novelty, it makes very little sense to speak of news organizations at all. This preference leads reporters to strongly resist attempts by politicians to deliver scripted, consistent messages to the public. As Andrew Rosenthal (2007), *New York Times* editorial page editor, put it, "We like to be surprised, and to surprise our readers." CBS's chief White House correspondent noted when covering the 2004 Republican National Convention that journalists want "to find the inconsistency here, to find the people who aren't quite agreeing with the script that's going on any given convention night, to get behind the story" (Kurtz 2004). Journalists participating in Bush press conferences have tellingly described their interactions with the president as a "contest between Bush's desire to repeat his previously articulated views ('sticking a tape in the VCR,' as one frequent Bush questioner puts it), and the reporters' quest to elicit something that will contribute to democracy, not to mention getting them on television or the front page" (Allen 2005). Along these lines, Robin Sproul, Washington Bureau Chief for ABC News, commented in an interview with one of the authors that she prefers stories "that are counterintuitive or present a point of view that we haven't focused on as much." In brief, *journalists prefer stories that contain new or unexpected information to stories presenting old or expected information.*

A second characteristic of "good" news is, ironically, a preference for bad news. Numerous scholars have observed that while negativity and conflict have long been staples of American journalism, the news media have increasingly embraced "attack journalism" and cynicism since the 1960s. Indeed, there seems to be a consensus within the scholarly literature that negativity is pervasive and dominant in modern news coverage.

While not all politicians go so far as former Vice President Spiro Agnew in characterizing the media as "nattering nabobs of negativism," recent politicians appear to share the view that the press favors negativity and conflict in its story choices. Early in his first year in office, President Bill Clinton had already concluded that, for the media, "success and lack of discord are not as noteworthy as failure." As one prominent journalist bluntly observed, "Well, journalists are always looking for conflict. That's what we do" (Saunders, in Kurtz 2004). Therefore, we argue that *journalists prefer stories in which political figures attack each other to stories in which political figures praise each other.*

. . . Gaye Tuchman (1972) famously argued that, in part to counter . . . bias accusations, journalists have a strong incentive to use procedures or strategic "rituals" of objectivity in doing their jobs. The main ritual Tuchman and others discuss is presenting *both sides of the story*. News organizations, particularly broadcasters, have long practiced this balancing. For most of the twentieth century, FCC regulations held broadcast stations and networks to an exceptionally high standard of fairness (the so-called fairness doctrine).

Journalists have also internalized these standards through professional ethics and norms, which require them to make every effort "to assure that the news content is accurate, free from bias and in context, and that all sides are presented fairly" (American Society of Newspaper Editors [ASNE] 2002). Indeed, Robin Sproul commented that, in her judgment, "there would be a professional price to pay" for a professional journalist who consistently privileged one political perspective over others, adding, with respect to covering the Iraq conflict, "My expectation for ABC is that we would put a balanced story on the air." We thus assume *journalists prefer stories that include both parties' views to stories that present only the views of members of a single party.*

Finally, journalists place a premium on including the most authoritative and high-ranking sources in their stories. . . . Sigal (1986, 20) adds that "by convention, reporters choose authoritative sources over other potential sources," and that "the higher up an official's position in government, the more authoritative a source he or she [is] presumed to be, and the better his or her prospects for making the news." . . . Finally, Rosenthal (2007) concurs, noting, "When an editorial page comments on the government, it makes a lot more sense to comment on the party in power than the party in opposition. . . . The focus of all news-gathering tends to be on the party in power." In other words, *journalists prefer to include sources with greater authority in their stories over less authoritative sources.* . . . Because we are primarily concerned with coverage and opinion related to foreign policy, we focus our attention here on party messages about the executive branch, especially the president. . . . [T]able 1 applies the aforementioned assumed story preferences to four types of partisan evaluations of the president, allowing us to determine which types of stories are most likely to gain airtime. Table 1 shows that evaluations of the president by the opposition party (that is, the NPP) tend to be at least somewhat newsworthy, regardless of which party controls Congress, although they are somewhat more so in divided government, when NPP rhetoric has greater authority by virtue of a legislative majority. Such comments are always either novel, if they support the president, or conflictual, if they criticize him. Airing NPP comments also adds balance to stories about the president and his policies.

In contrast, praise of the president by his own party (or PP praise) has little novelty, balance, or conflict, and thus is of little interest to journalists. As Sproul observed, "[PP praise is] like the plane took off and flew safely. . . . [I]t's not really news unless that were a big change." During divided government, PP praise of the president is even less interesting to journalists than in unified government because the PP does not control Congress. This makes all PP rhetoric less authoritative

Table 1. Newsworthiness, Novelty, and Credibility of Rhetoric Regarding President from Presidential Party (PP) and Nonpresidential Party (NPP) Elites

	PP Praise	PP Criticism	NPP Praise	NPP Criticism
Newsworthiness of Partisan Evaluations of the President				
Novelty	Low	High	High	Low
Conflict	Low	High	Lew	High
Balance	Low	Low	High	High
Authority (unified government)	High	High	Low	Low
Authority (divided government)	Low	Low	High	High
Partisan Credibility				
Presidential partisans	High	High	Low	Low
Independents	Low	Low	Low	Low
Nonpresidential partisans	Low	Low	High	High

than in unified government. Thus, as Table 1 shows, PP praise is especially uninteresting, particularly in divided government, where it lacks appeal for journalists on all four dimensions.

Conversely, PP criticism of the president is particularly attractive to journalists, especially during unified government, because it is highly novel, conflictual, and in unified government authoritative (again, because the PP controls both branches). In her interview, Sproul rated PP criticism the most appealing type of story, commenting that during the Republican Bush administration, "[The] number one [most appealing story] would be [a] Republican breaking from the President." Sproul further explained that part of the reason she ranked Republican criticism of President Bush as the most appealing type of story was "because it's the president's policy. With Clinton I would have led with the Democrat breaking away. . . . In this case, it's which party is in the White House." Along these lines, in a question-and-answer session with *New York Times* readers, Rosenthal (2007) observed, "An Op-Ed by a Republican criticizing the Democrats, or vice versa, is easy to come by and not that interesting. But a Democrat who takes issue with his or her party, or a Republican who does that, is more valuable." A hypothesis follows. (Here and in each subsequent hypothesis specifying certain conditions or states of the world, we assume that other such conditions are held constant or remain unchanged—in other words, ceteris paribus). . . .

. . . [I]f members of either party choose to criticize the president, they should find journalists even more eager to air their comments than during other times. . . .

Partisan Media

The rise of new media, and particularly the Internet, has challenged and begun to redefine the business of news. As media have fragmented and some news outlets have begun to cater to partisan audience niches, the underlying preferences and routines of news organizations have shifted markedly. . . . [T]hese changes have widened the gap between the true nature and extent of elite rhetoric and public perceptions of such rhetoric. Whereas traditional journalistic norms and preferences have for the most part persevered, their applicability clearly varies across media outlets, particularly for the norm of offering balanced coverage. Indeed, sophisticated and motivated consumers are increasingly able to seek out news sources, from cable news to partisan web sites to political talk radio, that reflect their own ideological preferences.

One clear manner in which the Internet appears to differ from other mass media is the degree of niche targeting by political web sites. To be sure, some Internet outlets seek mass audiences. But these sites tend to represent the online versions of traditional mainstream news media, such as the *New York Times* or CBS News. Many other Internet outlets, including but not limited to weblogs, or "blogs," are overtly niche-oriented, aimed at attracting a smaller but more loyal segment of the overall audience. While political partisanship is by no means the only dimension on which niche marketing strategies might be based, in the realm of political information, partisanship is one of the key lines of demarcation allowing web sites to attract a relatively loyal audience. It is therefore not surprising that many of the most widely visited political blogs, and certainly those with the most loyal audiences, tend to be overtly partisan, ranging from sites like MoveOn.org and DailyKos.com on the left to FreeRepublic.com and Instapundit.com on the right. . . .

The Mediating Effect of the Outlet Reputation on Opinion

Recent research suggests that media outlet labels, and the ideological reputations their brand names carry, serve as important judgmental heuristic cues, which consumers employ to help interpret both the meanings and implications of partisan messages in the media. As a consequence, we argue that the nature of the media's influence on policy has evolved from what scholars often refer to as the "CNN effect," which emphasized the importance of the 24-hour news cycle and live coverage of events, to what we refer to as an emerging "Fox effect." The latter effect concerns the implications of perceived partisan favoritism by news outlets, combined with the effects of audience self-selection (that is, audiences sorting into ideologically "friendly" news environments) and credibility-based discounting of information from outlets perceived as ideologically hostile. . . .

Rhetoric and Reality

. . . The information advantage of government officials, especially those from the administration and majority party in Congress, makes them appealing to journalists seeking authoritative sources. This advantage is particularly acute in the early stages of an overseas conflict or crisis, when an administration possesses a near monopoly on high-quality information about the event. Speaking with respect to the early stages of the 2003 Iraq invasion, Sproul explained the dominance of the Bush administration's preferred framing of war coverage as follows:

> Number one is the relative dearth of information that would allow you to [challenge the President's claims]. . . . Number two would be [that] . . . we usually have in the political universe of Washington a very powerful opposing point of view or opposition party or interest groups that speak out with powerful opposition and/or evidence and/or something that is independent. . . . That really wasn't there to the extent that certainly [it] is now [in 2007].

Over time, as information diffuses, journalists will both gather an increasing store of information about the event and develop alternative information sources. Hence, while an administration conducting a war will always have *some* informational advantage, its extent is almost certain to recede with time.

Regardless of how events on the ground actually unfold, any administration has a powerful incentive to cast them in the most favorable light. Journalists in turn can he expected to challenge this attempt at framing and to seek to highlight any evaluations that depart from the party line. However, in the early stages of a conflict, the administration's substantial informational advantage will likely limit the ability of journalists to effectively challenge the administration's preferred frame. Over time, as journalists are better able to discern for themselves what is actually happening on the ground, and as any prior discrepancies between administration framing and reality come to light, the administration's advantage recedes, and the discrepancy between reality and coverage should diminish. In the case of the Iraq War, for instance, Sproul commented that

> [T]he tone of the story changed as the facts on the ground changed. . . . It wasn't that we had the same set of facts and we suddenly looked at it through a different prism. It was that it became a more transparent view of what the facts actually were, had been all along. . . . Some of the inspectors started speaking out and then Colin Powell. Over a period of time it became clear that. . . there weren't people celebrating in the streets and this wasn't hailed as a great victory, and that it wasn't as billed, that the things they said would happen didn't happen, and then it started to get worse and worse.

Stated differently, in the words of one political blogger, "Reality asserted itself." If things are, in fact, going well, then an administration may be able to continue framing the conflict as a success. Such was mostly the case in the first Persian Gulf War in 1991. However, if the state of the conflict is more ambiguous, or if events are not going well, a negative frame becomes increasingly likely to predominate. Either way, media coverage seems likely to converge on the actual valence of events over time. The greater the initial gap between reality and the administration's frame, the larger the likely change, over time, in the tenor of coverage. . . .

Of course, over time, as reporters settle on a particular narrative for a conflict that is continually reinforced by subsequent events and reporting of those events, the narrative frame should become increasingly resistant to change. Scholars have long recognized that journalists tend to cue off one another in their coverage, producing "pack journalism" and "meta-narratives." Once the media settle on a particular narrative regarding a candidate, such as "Al Gore is dishonest" or "George W. Bush is unintelligent," this meta-narrative tends to be continually referenced and thereby reinforced. Over time, it becomes increasingly resistant to challenges, even if it is based on faulty assumptions (as many believe is the case with both of the aforementioned examples from the 2000 presidential campaign). In the context of a military conflict, once a given narrative frame becomes entrenched, only large and sustained changes in events on the ground are likely to influence it.

Such dominant frames in turn can take hold fairly rapidly, as the media repeatedly exposes citizens to them. In the context of the Iraq War, retired U.S. Army Lieutenant General Ricardo S. Sanchez complained to military reporters and editors, "Once reported, your assessments become conventional wisdom and nearly impossible to change. . . . [I]n your business 'the first report' gives Americans who rely on the snippets of CNN . . . their 'truths' and perspectives on an issue" (Sanchez 2007). . . .

The dynamics in public opinion over time are likely to track those in the media, although at different rates among different partisan groups. After all, typical individuals largely depend on the news media—either directly, through their own consumption, or indirectly, by talking to individuals who have gained *their* information through the media—for their information about an overseas conflict. As one newspaper reporter observed with respect to the relationship between media reporting on Iraq and public attitudes regarding the conflict, "War reporting and public opinion entered an echo chamber: one rebounded off the other." . . .

Conclusion

The following excerpt from a 2007 report on trends in public opinion regarding Iraq, appearing on pollster.com, summarizes several core aspects of our argument:

> [C]itizens don't shift their opinion based on quantified measures of progress. . . . For most citizens, opinions are driven more by the messages they hear from partisan leaders, with some sifting for credibility of the claims and filtering by predispositions. And, it must be added, by some effects of "reality," whatever that is. (Franklin 2007) . . .

REFERENCES

Allen, Mike. "Pelosi Calls Iraq a 'Failure.'" *Politico*, February 10, 2008. http://www.politico.com/news/stories/0208/8422.html (accessed December 1, 2008).

American Society of Newspaper Editors (ASNE). *ASNE Statement of Principles*. Revised August 28, 2002. http://www.asne.org/kiosk/archive/principl.htm (accessed September 7, 2005).

Franklin, Charles. "Ten Months of Opinion Change on War and More." *Pollster.com*, November 6, 2007. http://www.pollster.com/blogs/ten_months_of_opinion_change_o.php

Kurtz, Howard. "Republican Convention Gets Under Way; Kerry Interviewed on 'The Daily Show.'" *CNN's Reliable Sources*, August 29, 2004. http://transcripts.cnn.com/TRANSCRIPTS/0408/29/rs.00.html

Rosenthal, Andrew. "Talk to the Times: Editorial Page Editor Andrew Rosenthal." *New York Times Online*, September 17, 2007. http://www.nytimes.com/2007/09/17/business/media/24askthetimes.html.

Sanchez, Ricardo S. "Military Reporters and Editors Luncheon Address," Washington, DC, October 12, 2007. http://www.militaryreporters.org/sanchez_101207.html

Sigal, Leon V. "Sources Make the News," in *Reading the News: A Pantheon Guide to Popular Culture*, ed. R. K. Manoff and M. Schudson. New York: Pantheon Books, 1986.

Tuchman, Gaye. *Making News: A Study in the Construction of Reality*. New York: Macmillan, 1972.

Weisberg, Jacob. "Ballot Box: Why the Press Loves John McCain." *Slate.com*. October 4, 1999. http://www.slate.com/?id=1003748 (accessed December 1, 2008).

14-3

Understanding the Participatory News Consumer

Kristen Purcell, Lee Rainie, Amy Mitchell, Tom Rosenstiel, and Kenny Olmstead

American politics is being transformed by technological changes in how Americans receive news about government and politics. In this survey report from the Pew Research Center's Project for Excellence in Journalism, we discover that news consumption has become very personalized. There are important generational, class, racial, and partisan differences in the use of online news and in their attitudes about the quality of major news sources. Social networks, such as Twitter, are increasing in their importance as a source of news and may radically change how news is acquired in the future.

The News Environment in America

AMERICANS' RELATIONSHIP with news is changing in dramatic and irreversible ways due to changes in the "ecology" of how news is available. Traditional news organizations are still very important to their consumers, but technology has scrambled every aspect of the relationship between news producers and the people who consume news. That change starts with the fact that those consumers now have the tools to be active participants in news creation, dissemination, and even the "editing" process.

This report is aimed at describing the extent of the transformation and the ways in which news serves a variety of practical and civic needs in people's lives. It focuses on those who receive and react to news and asks questions that are rarely asked about how people use the news in their lives, especially by exploiting the internet and cell phones. The report draws from a national phone survey of adults (those 18 and older) that documents how people's use of new technologies has disrupted the traditional flow of news to consumers and in communities.

The overarching narrative here is tied to technological change, generational differences, and the rise of a new kind of hybrid news consumer/participator. These shifts affect how people treat the news, relate to news organizations, and think of themselves as news makers and commentators in their own right.

Source: Excerpted from "Understanding the Participatory News Consumer," Pew Internet & American Life Project, March 1, 2010. pp. 8–48. http://www.pewinternet.org/Reports/2010/Online-News.aspx.

People's Daily News Attention Is High, But Varies Considerably by Age

A bit more than half of American adults (56%) say they follow the news "all or most of the time." Another 25% say they follow the news "some of the time"; 12% say they do so "now and then" and 7% say they follow news "hardly ever" or "never." . . . Those who are well-educated, relatively well-off financially, and older are more likely than others to say they follow the news all or most of the time. [See Figure 1.] The generational story is particularly striking. Younger adults are the least likely to say they follow the news avidly and the most likely to say they hardly ever or never get news:

Most People Use Several Platforms as They Search for News

When asked about their routines for getting news on a typical day, and specifically which news platforms individuals turn to daily, the results are striking. Almost all American adults (99%) say that on a typical day, they get news from

Figure 1. The Young Are Least Likely to Be Avid News Consumers

The percentage of adults in each age group who say they follow the news all or most of the time

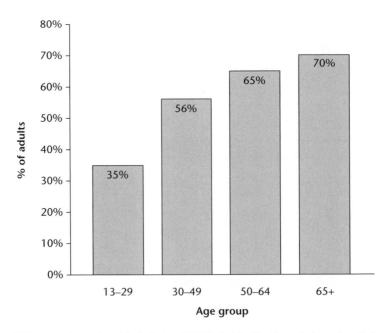

Source: PRC-Internet & American Life Project and PRC-Project for Excellence in Journalism Online News Survey—December 28, 2008–January 19, 2010. N = 2.259. margin of error is +/–2 percentage points.

at least one news platform (local or national newspapers, local or national television news broadcasts, radio, or the internet), including 92% who follow the news on multiple platforms on a typical day.

On a typical day:

- 78% of Americans get news from a local TV station

- 73% get news from a national television network such as CBS or a cable TV station such as CNN or FoxNews

- 61% get some kind of news online

- 54% listen to a radio news program at home or in the car

- 50% read news in the print version of a local newspaper

- 17% read news in the print version national newspaper such as the *New York Times* or *USA Today.*

. . . Six in ten Americans (59%) get news from a combination of online and offline sources on a typical day, and the internet is now the third most popular news platform, behind local television news and national television news. While 61% of Americans get news online on a typical day, some 71% get news online at least occasionally. . . .

. . . Who uses multiple platforms? As would be expected, those with the highest educational attainment and annual household incomes are more likely than other adults to use multiple news platforms. Among college graduates, half (52%) get news from at least four news platforms on a typical day. Overall, single platform users tend to be younger, less educated, and have lower household incomes than adults who use multiple news platforms. An individual's race/ethnicity is not related to the number of news platforms he or she uses on a regular basis. . . .

. . . When it comes to the quality of coverage itself, respondents give . . . mixed signals. Just under two-thirds (63%) agree with statement that "Major news organizations do a good job covering all of the important news stories and subjects that matter to me." Yet 72% also back the idea that, "Most news sources today are biased in their coverage." Some of the explanation for this dichotomy seems to be rooted in the views of partisans. Liberals and Democrats are more likely to say the big news organizations do a good job on subjects that matter to them, while conservatives and Republicans are the group most likely to see coverage as biased.

. . . Americans do not approach the news with a unified set of expectations and norms. Only half say their preference is for objective, straight news: 49% say they prefer getting news from sources that do not have a particular point of view; 31% prefer sources that share their point of view; and 11% say they prefer sources whose point of view differs with theirs. The rest say they don't know their preference or don't want to declare it.

The people who are more likely than others to prefer sources with no point of view include: internet users who get news online, whites, and those with higher levels of educational attainment. Those without strong partisan ties (i.e. Independents) or ideological connections (i.e. moderates) are also more likely than partisans to want their news straight. Those who are disproportionately likely to seek out news sources that match their own views include Republicans and conservatives. Democrats, in contrast, are more likely than other groups to seek out news that either supports their own views or differs from their own views (as opposed to seeking out news coverage that has no particular point of view). . . .

News and the Internet

Six in ten American adults (61%) get news online on a typical day, placing it third among the six major news platforms asked about in the survey, behind local television news and national or cable television news. While the internet is growing as a news platform, it has not displaced completely offline news sources for most American adults: A majority of Americans (59%) get news from a combination of online and offline sources on a typical day. Just over a third (38%) rely solely on offline sources, while just 2% rely exclusively on the internet for their daily news. Asked more generally if they ever get news online, and if they ever get news online about 12 specific topics (such as weather, sports, national news, and business or finance), 71% of American adults say they get news online at least occasionally. This equates to 94% of all internet users.

Who Gets Their News Online?

Online news users skew younger than the general adult population. About two-thirds of online news users (68%) are under age 50, including 29% who are under age 30. Given their younger age profile, it is not surprising that this group is also more likely than other Americans to have never been married (24% v. 9%) and/or to have young children (36% v. 17%). Online news users tend to be employed full-time (50%), two-thirds (67%) have at least some college education (including 22% with a bachelor's degree and 15% with advanced degrees), and their annual household income trends higher than American adults in general. Racially, this group skews toward Hispanics and whites; while 50% of non-Hispanic African-Americans get their news entirely offline, the same is true of just 38% of non-Hispanic whites and 32% of Hispanics.

Because they represent such a large segment of internet users, the demographic profile of online news users mirrors that of the online population as a whole, and it reflects the same characteristics that drive both broadband and wireless use. Yet even among internet users, those who get news online stand out in terms of their high income and education levels, their young age, their racial/ethnic identity, and their use of broadband and wireless (see Table 1). . . .

Table 1. Who Are Online News Users?

How online news users compare to other internet users and other adults

	Online news users	Other internet users	Total other adults
Age			
18–29	29%*	16%	9%
30–49	39*	29	24
50+	31	63*	66*
Median Age	40	50	58*
Education			
Less than a HS degree	6%	10%	24%*
High School Grad	SB	80*	65
College Grad+	36*	11	10
Income			
Less than $30,000	24%	26%	46%*
$30,000–$49,999	19	26*	16
$50,000–$74,999	15	13	7
$75,000+	29*	16	7
Race/Ethnicity			
White, non-Hispanic	71 %*	72%	66%
Black, non-Hispanic	9	19*	18*
Hispanic	12*	6	11
Home internet connection			
Broadband	84%*	48%	2%
Premium broadband	34*	11	1
Dial-up	6	11	2
Wireless internet use	69	42	15

* indicates a statistically significant difference.
Source: PRC-Internet & American Life Project and PRC-Project for Excellence in Journalism Online News Survey—December 23. 2009–January 19. 2010. N = 2.259. Margin of error is +./−2 percentage points.

Most Individuals Use Just a Handful of Online News Sources and Do Not Have a Favorite

While internet users who get news online tend to explore a wide variety of news topics, they are fairly modest in the number of internet sites they use to gather that information. One in five online news users (21%) say they routinely rely on just one website for their news and information, and another 57% rely on between two and five websites. Surprisingly, asked whether they have a favorite online news source, the majority of online news users (65%) say they do not. Among those who do, the most popular sites are those of major news organizations such as such as CNN and Fox.

To get a sense of their daily online news consumption, we asked online news consumers if, on a typical day, they used a number of different online sources, ranging from the websites of major newspapers and TV news organizations to posts from journalists and news organizations on sites like Facebook and Twitter.

Portal websites like GoogleNews, AOL and Topix are the most commonly used online news sources, visited by over half of online news users on a typical day. Also faring well are the sites of traditional news organizations with an offline presence, such as CNN, BBC and local or national newspapers. Twitter updates, either from either journalists and news organizations or from other individuals and organizations (including friends and family), were the least commonly used news sources of those asked about. The vast majority of online news users (84%) use five or fewer of the 14 news sources asked about on a typical day, including 14% who do not use any and another 34% who use just one or two.

While overall, most individuals who get news online use just a handful of internet sources on a typical day, younger online news users tend to frequent more sites on a daily basis. The youngest online news users, those under age 30, are particularly likely to use portal news sites and to get news from journalists, news organizations, and others on Facebook. Online news users age 30–49 are more likely than both older and younger news users to make a daily visit to the website of a local or national newspaper or a website that offers a mix of news and commentary.

In addition to these distinct preferences for certain online news sources across different age groups, it is not surprising that affinities for online news sources also reflect a user's political party and ideology. In general, Democrats and those who describe themselves as liberal are most likely to get news on a typical day from:

- A news organization or individual journalist they follow on a social networking site such as Facebook

- The Twitter posts of individuals who are not journalists, or organizations other than the major news organizations

- The websites of international news organizations

- The websites of radio news organizations such as NPR

- News podcasts from organizations such as NPR or the New York Times

In contrast, Republicans and those who describe themselves as conservative are more likely to make a daily visit to the website of a major TV news organization, and are also more likely than other online news users to utilize just 1–2 internet news sources on a typical day. . . .

"Serendipitous News Discovery" and "Hunting and Gathering" Top "News Reception" as Methods for Getting News Online

One major concern about the internet is that people would use new technology to retreat into their narrow interests and that accidental news discovery, according to some scholars, is essential to forming public opinion and creating informed consensus and stable cohesion around public policy that makes governing possible. So, the prospect that technology might reduce the likelihood of that happening is a major civic concern.

To get a sense of the different approaches employed by online news users, and how active or passive online news consumption is, we asked how often online news users:

- Go online specifically to get news?

- Come across news while they are online doing other things?

- Get news forwarded to them through email, automatic alerts and updates, or posts on social networking sites

The answers to these questions reveal that it is most common for online news users to chance upon news while they are online doing other things—what could be called "serendipitous" news consumption. Eight in ten online news users (80%) say this happens at least a few times a week, including 59% who say this happens everyday or almost everyday. Only slightly less common, however, is the hunting and gathering approach to online news consumption. About seven in ten online news users (71%) say they go online specifically to get news at least a few times a week, including almost half (48%) who say they do this every day or almost every day.

Meanwhile, a smaller segment of online news users say that news finds them—44% get news forwarded to them through email, automatic updates and alerts, or posts on social networking sites at least a few times a week, which includes 28% who receive news everyday or almost everyday. One quarter of online news users (25%) say they never have news forwarded to them.

Demographic groups who tend to be daily internet users—including younger adults, the more educated, those with higher incomes, and broadband and wireless users—report more frequent chance encounters with news as well as more frequent hunting and gathering experiences. The youngest adults (those under age 30) and cell phone users are most likely to have news forwarded to them.

News Gets Personal, Social, and Participatory

Americans' relationship to the news is being transformed in several directions thanks to the new tools and affordances of technology. Encounters with news are becoming more personal as users customize their experience and take charge of the flow of news into their lives. News is becoming a shared social experience as people exchange links and recommendations as a form of cultural currency in their social networks. And news is becoming a participatory activity, as people contribute their own stories and experiences and post their reactions to events.

Getting the News Is a Social Activity for Many Users

Recall that earlier in this report we noted the evidence in this survey that people's connection to the news is a social activity equally as much as it is a learning activity and productivity enhancer. Some 72% of Americans who follow the news at least now and then say they enjoy talking with friends, family, and colleagues about what is happening in the world and 69% feel that keeping up with the news is a social or civic obligation. Moreover, in the age of technological social networking, some now say they rely on the people around them to tell them when there is news they need to know. Half of Americans (50%) say that describes them very well or somewhat well.

How does this play out online? The act of sharing of news and conversation about news is an integral part of email exchanges and social media activity. Of the 71% of the adult population who get news online, 75% of them say they get news forwarded to them through email or posts on social networking sites. That amounts to 71% of all internet users. When news is passed along to them, 38% of this cohort read the material all or most of the time; 37% read it some of the time, and 23% say they hardly have time to read it.

Of these internet users who get news online, 50% say they pass along email links to news stories or videos to others. (That represents 48% of all internet users.) Those who follow the news avidly, who are on-the-go consumers, who use social networking sites or Twitter or have a blog are much more likely than others to send along links to news in their emails than other internet users are. . . .

Beyond the chatter about news that takes place in email exchanges, a notable number of internet users are beginning to treat news organizations, particular journalists, and other news mavens as nodes in their social networks. In this survey we found that 57% of online Americans use social networking sites such as Facebook, MySpace or LinkedIn—and 97% of them are online news consumers. Some 51% of the social networking users who are in the online-news population say that on a typical day they get news from people they follow on sites like Facebook. That amounts to 28% of all internet users who get news via social networking with friends.

In addition 23% of the social networking users who get news online say they specifically get news from news organizations and individual journalists they follow in the social networking space. In other words, they have friended or become a fan of a journalist or news organization and they catch up on news through this relatively new channel of news dissemination. That amounts to 13% of all internet users. Overall, 30% of internet users get news from friends, journalists or news organizations they follow on social networking sites on a typical day.

In addition, we found that in the general internet population, 19% of online Americans use Twitter or other status update functions. Of those Twitter users, virtually all (99%) are online news consumers. And 28% of those who are in the online news consumer cohort say they get Twitter updates about news from friends and colleagues they follow on Twitter and 18% follow the Twitter feeds of news organizations or individual journalists. Combined, that amounts to 6% of all internet users who get news via Twitter feeds.

The importance of news to social experiences online also shows up in one other way in our survey. A significant portion of online news consumers judge news organization websites by the degree to which they facilitate the social sharing of news. Some 44% of these online news consumers say that one of the factors they use in choosing where to get news online is whether it is easy to share the site's content with others through emails or postings on social networking sites. A quarter of these online news consumers (25%) say an important factor for them is being able to follow the news organization through social networking sites like Facebook or Twitter. As Table 2 shows, young online news users have substantially stronger attachments to the social features of websites than older users.

The "Daily Me" and the "Daily Us" Are Taking Shape for Many Users

We noted earlier that 67% of Americans say they only follow specific subjects that are of particular interest to them. Online tools like news filtering and aggregator sites allow people to apply different kinds of customization to their news experiences.

Table 2. The Young Are Most Interested in Many Features

% of online news users who say these features are important

	All online news users	Age 18–29	Age 30–49	Age 50–4	Age 65+
Links to related material	68%	72%*	72%*	63%*	50%
Multi-media content like photo essays or video clips	48%	57%*	51%*	39%*	22%
Being a portal site or news aggregator that gathers news from all over the internet	48%	55%*	49%*	43%*	31%
Being able to easily share the sites news content with others, through emails or posting to other websites like Facebook	44%	57%*	45%	35%	24%
Being able to customize the news you get at the site	42%	48%*	46%*	34%*	25%
Interactive material like charts, quizzes, graphics, and maps that you can manipulate yourself	38%	45%*	39%*	31%	28%
Opportunities to comment on stories	37%	51%*	33%	33%	25%
Being able to follow the news site through social networking sites like Facebook or Twitter	25%	39%*	25%*	14%*	7%

*indicates a statistically significant differences.

Source: PRC-Internet & American Life Project and PRC-Project for Excellence in Journalism Online News Survey–December 23. 2009–January 19. 2010. N = 1.5B2. Margin of error is +/− 3 percentage points.

In this survey we found that 28% of all internet users say they have customized the home page on their browser to include their favorite news sources or topics. Interestingly, this does not seem to be a strategy of those who are trying to narrow the flow of news in their lives or as a coping mechanism for information overload. Instead, customization is used by the most voracious and wide-ranging news consumers. Those who use the most news media platforms on a typical day (4–6) and those who have the widest range of online sources (6–14) are far more likely than others to have customized their home page. Those who are involved with social media such as Facebook, Twitter, and blogging are also more likely to have tweaked their home page towards news that interests them.

This preference among online news consumers also translates into a priority when they are picking news websites to visit. Some 42% of the internet users who get news online—or 30% of all internet users—say that it is important to them when choosing news sites to be able to customize the news they get at that site. It is fascinating to note that this feature applies equally as much to those who say they prefer to follow specific topics (51% of them like being able to customize news on a site) and those who say they rely on others to keep them abreast of news (52% of them like this feature on a news website). At the same time, disproportionate numbers of those under age 50, blacks, wide-ranging platform users and browsers for online news, and social media users say this is a preference for them on a news website.

Another way that people personalize the news is by getting alerts about news developments. Some 71% of internet users say they get news forwarded to them through email and automatic alerts and updates and 11% of cell phone owners have alerts sent to their phones via text or email.

Yet another way that people connect in a personal way with news is through interactive material. Some 36% of internet users (38% of online news users) say an important part of the news websites they choose is whether it has interactive content like charts, quizzes, graphics and maps they can manipulate themselves. Those who use a large number of news media platforms on a typical day (4–6), those who use a wide range of online news sources (6–14), and those who are interested in a diverse set of online topics are more likely than others to cite this preference for interactive material.

Finally, there are several other ways that people can customize their online news experiences. In effect, they can create a kind of news "playlist" by using the internet to look at news events at the time of their choosing and to the level of depth that matters to them. In this survey we asked questions about people's use of video content on news sites and found that 68% of internet users have watched a video online of a news story or event that happened in the past and 62% have watched a video feed of a live or breaking events. Those who use a lot of media platforms on a typical day, who have a diverse set of news interests, and who visit a relatively high number of online news sites are more likely than others to have used news sites this way. In effect, they are reallocating their attention to news to fit their own needs and schedule.

News Creation, Commentary and Dissemination Is Now a Participatory Activity for a Sizable Group of Americans

Some 37% of internet users have actively contributed to the creation, commentary, or dissemination of news. We arrived at that figure by adding up the number of internet users who said they did any of the following activities:

- 25% of internet users have commented on an online news story or blog item about news that they read

- 17% of internet users have posted links and thoughts about news on a social networking site like Facebook. That translates into 30% of social network site users.

- 11% of internet users have tagged or categorized content online

- 9% of internet users have contributed their own article, opinion piece, picture, or video to an online news site

- 3% of internet users have used Twitter to post or re-Tweet a link to a news story or blog. That amounts to 18% of Twitter users.

News participators are information omnivores and technophiles. They stand out from the pack in the same way as those who have set up their cell phones to be "on alert." In fact, among news participators, 19% have news alerts sent to their cell phones. News participators are fond of social media: 76% of news participators use social networking sites; 34% of news participators use Twitter, and 26% of news participators are bloggers. The average participator uses 4–6 media platforms on a typical day; seeks out nine or more news topics online; and surfs 3–5 different kinds of news websites on a typical day.

The typical online news participator is white, 36 years old, politically moderate and Independent, employed full-time with a college degree and an annual income of $50,000 or more. Interestingly, while white adults make up the bulk of the online news participator population, black internet users are significantly more likely to be news participators than their white and Hispanic counterparts. Almost half of black internet users (47%) are news participators, compared with just 36% of white internet users and 33% of Hispanic internet users. Not surprisingly, the youngest internet users (18–29 year-olds) are more likely than their older counterparts to be online news participators, with just under half of that age group (46%) contributing to the creation, commentary, or dissemination of news online. Men and women are equally likely to participate in online news production.

. . . And what kinds of stories would participators like to get more often from news organizations? They disproportionately say they would like more news about science and technology, state government, health and medicine, and their local community. When it comes to their news wish list, the biggest gap between participators and other Americans involves international affairs. Some 42% of news participators say they would like more coverage of this topic by news organizations, compared with 28% of all other adults who desire more content of this nature.

Constitution of the United States

We the People of the United States, in Order to form a more perfect Union, establish Justice, insure domestic Tranquility, provide for the common defence, promote the general Welfare, and secure the Blessings of Liberty to ourselves and our Posterity, do ordain and establish this Constitution for the United States of America.

ARTICLE I

Section 1. All legislative Powers herein granted shall be vested in a Congress of the United States, which shall consist of a Senate and House of Representatives.

Section 2. The House of Representatives shall be composed of Members chosen every second Year by the People of the several States, and the Electors in each State shall have the Qualifications requisite for Electors of the most numerous Branch of the State Legislature.

No Person shall be a Representative who shall not have attained to the age of twenty five Years, and been seven Years a Citizen of the United States, and who shall not, when elected, be an Inhabitant of that State in which he shall be chosen.

[Representatives and direct Taxes shall be apportioned among the several States which may be included within this Union, according to their respective Numbers, which shall be determined by adding to the whole Number of free Persons, including those bound to Service for a Term of Years, and excluding Indians not taxed, three fifths of all other Persons.][1] The actual Enumeration shall be made within three Years after the first Meeting of the Congress of the United States, and within every subsequent Term of ten Years, in such Manner as they shall by Law direct. The Number of Representatives shall not exceed one for every thirty Thousand, but each State shall have at Least one Representative;

Source: U.S. Congress, House, Committee on the Judiciary, *The Constitution of the United States of America, as Amended,* 100th Cong., 1st sess., 1987, H Doc 100-94.

and until such enumeration shall be made, the State of New Hampshire shall be entitled to chuse three, Massachusetts eight, Rhode-Island and Providence Plantations one, Connecticut five, New-York six, New Jersey four, Pennsylvania eight, Delaware one, Maryland six, Virginia ten, North Carolina five, South Carolina five, and Georgia three.

When vacancies happen in the Representation from any State, the Executive Authority thereof shall issue Writs of Election to fill such Vacancies.

The House of Representatives shall chuse their Speaker and other Officers; and shall have the sole Power of Impeachment.

Section 3. The Senate of the United States shall be composed of two Senators from each State, [chosen by the Legislature thereof,][2] for six Years; and each Senator shall have one Vote.

Immediately after they shall be assembled in Consequence of the first Election, they shall be divided as equally as may be into three Classes. The Seats of the Senators of the first Class shall be vacated at the Expiration of the second Year, of the second Class at the Expiration of the fourth Year, and of the third Class at the Expiration of the sixth Year, so that one third may be chosen every second Year; [and if Vacancies happen by Resignation, or otherwise, during the Recess of the Legislature of any State, the Executive thereof may make temporary Appointments until the next Meeting of the Legislature, which shall then fill such Vacancies.][3]

No Person shall be a Senator who shall not have attained to the Age of thirty Years, and been nine Years a Citizen of the United States, and who shall not, when elected, be an Inhabitant of that State for which he shall be chosen.

The Vice President of the United States shall be President of the Senate, but shall have no Vote, unless they be equally divided.

The Senate shall chuse their other Officers, and also a President pro tempore, in the Absence of the Vice President, or when he shall exercise the Office of President of the United States.

The Senate shall have the sole Power to try all Impeachments. When sitting for that Purpose, they shall be on Oath or Affirmation. When the President of the United States is tried, the Chief Justice shall preside: And no Person shall be convicted without the Concurrence of two thirds of the Members present.

Judgment in Cases of Impeachment shall not extend further than to removal from Office, and disqualification to hold and enjoy any Office of honor, Trust or Profit under the United States: but the Party convicted shall nevertheless be liable and subject to Indictment, Trial, Judgment and Punishment, according to Law.

Section 4. The Times, Places and Manner of holding Elections for Senators and Representatives, shall be prescribed in each State by the Legislature thereof; but the Congress may at any time by Law make or alter such Regulations, except as to the Places of chusing Senators.

The Congress shall assemble at least once in every Year, and such Meeting shall [be on the first Monday in December],[4] unless they shall by Law appoint a different Day.

Section 5. Each House shall be the Judge of the Elections, Returns and Qualifications of its own Members, and a Majority of each shall constitute a Quorum to do Business; but a smaller Number may adjourn from day to day, and may be authorized to compel the Attendance of absent Members, in such Manner, and under such Penalties as each House may provide.

Each House may determine the Rules of its Proceedings, punish its Members for disorderly Behaviour, and, with the Concurrence of two thirds, expel a Member.

Each House shall keep a Journal of its Proceedings, and from time to time publish the same, excepting such Parts as may in their Judgment require Secrecy; and the Yeas and Nays of the Members of either House on any question shall, at the Desire of one fifth of those Present, be entered on the Journal.

Neither House, during the Session of Congress, shall, without the Consent of the other, adjourn for more than three days, nor to any other Place than that in which the two Houses shall be sitting.

Section 6. The Senators and Representatives shall receive a Compensation for their Services, to be ascertained by Law, and paid out of the Treasury of the United States. They shall in all Cases, except Treason, Felony and Breach of the Peace, be privileged from Arrest during their Attendance at the Session of their respective Houses, and in going to and returning from the same; and for any Speech or Debate in either House, they shall not be questioned in any other Place.

No Senator or Representative shall, during the Time for which he was elected, be appointed to any civil Office under the Authority of the United States, which shall have been created, or the Emoluments whereof shall have been encreased during such time; and no Person holding any Office under the United States, shall be a Member of either House during his Continuance in Office.

Section 7. All Bills for raising Revenue shall originate in the House of Representatives; but the Senate may propose or concur with Amendments as on other Bills.

Every Bill which shall have passed the House of Representatives and the Senate, shall, before it become a Law, be presented to the President of the United States; If he approve he shall sign it, but if not he shall return it, with his Objections to that House in which it shall have originated, who shall enter the Objections at large on their Journal, and proceed to reconsider it. If after such

Reconsideration two thirds of that House shall agree to pass the Bill, it shall be sent, together with the Objections, to the other House, by which it shall likewise be reconsidered, and if approved by two thirds of that House, it shall become a Law. But in all such Cases the Votes of both Houses shall be determined by yeas and Nays, and the Names of the Persons voting for and against the Bill shall be entered on the Journal of each House respectively. If any Bill shall not be returned by the President within ten Days (Sundays excepted) after it shall have been presented to him, the Same shall be a Law, in like Manner as if he had signed it, unless the Congress by their Adjournment prevent its Return, in which Case it shall not be a Law.

Every Order, Resolution, or Vote to which the Concurrence of the Senate and House of Representatives may be necessary (except on a question of Adjournment) shall be presented to the President of the United States; and before the Same shall take Effect, shall be approved by him, or being disapproved by him, shall be repassed by two thirds of the Senate and House of Representatives, according to the Rules and Limitations prescribed in the Case of a Bill.

Section 8. The Congress shall have Power To lay and collect Taxes, Duties, Imposts and Excises, to pay the Debts and provide for the common Defence and general Welfare of the United States; but all Duties, Imposts and Excises shall be uniform throughout the United States;

To borrow Money on the credit of the United States;

To regulate Commerce with foreign Nations, and among the several States, and with the Indian Tribes;

To establish an uniform Rule of Naturalization, and uniform Laws on the subject of Bankruptcies throughout the United States;

To coin Money, regulate the Value thereof, and of foreign Coin, and fix the Standard of Weights and Measures;

To provide for the Punishment of counterfeiting the Securities and current Coin of the United States;

To establish Post Offices and post Roads;

To promote the Progress of Science and useful Arts, by securing for limited Times to Authors and Inventors the exclusive Right to their respective Writings and Discoveries;

To constitute Tribunals inferior to the supreme Court;

To define and punish Piracies and Felonies committed on the high Seas, and Offences against the Law of Nations;

To declare War, grant Letters of Marque and Reprisal, and make Rules concerning Captures on Land and Water;

To raise and support Armies, but no Appropriation of Money to that Use shall be for a longer Term than two Years;

To provide and maintain a Navy;

To make Rules for the Government and Regulation of the land and naval Forces;

To provide for calling forth the Militia to execute the Laws of the Union, suppress Insurrections and repel Invasions;

To provide for organizing, arming, and disciplining, the Militia, and for governing such Part of them as may be employed in the Service of the United States, reserving to the States respectively, the Appointment of the Officers, and the Authority of training the Militia according to the discipline prescribed by Congress;

To exercise exclusive Legislation in all Cases whatsoever, over such District (not exceeding ten Miles square) as may, by Cession of particular States, and the Acceptance of Congress, become the Seat of the Government of the United States, and to exercise like Authority over all Places purchased by the Consent of the Legislature of the State in which the Same shall be, for the Erection of Forts, Magazines, Arsenals, dock-Yards, and other needful Buildings;—And

To make all Laws which shall be necessary and proper for carrying into Execution the foregoing Powers, and all other Powers vested by this Constitution in the Government of the United States, or in any Department or Officer thereof.

Section 9. The Migration or Importation of such Persons as any of the States now existing shall think proper to admit, shall not be prohibited by the Congress prior to the Year one thousand eight hundred and eight, but a Tax or duty may be imposed on such Importation, not exceeding ten dollars for each Person.

The Privilege of the Writ of Habeas Corpus shall not be suspended, unless when in Cases of Rebellion or Invasion the public Safety may require it.

No Bill of Attainder or ex post facto Law shall be passed.

No Capitation, or other direct, Tax shall be laid, unless in Proportion to the Census or Enumeration herein before directed to be taken.[5]

No Tax or Duty shall be laid on Articles exported from any State.

No Preference shall be given by any Regulation of Commerce or Revenue to the Ports of one State over those of another; nor shall Vessels bound to, or from, one State, be obliged to enter, clear, or pay Duties in another.

No Money shall be drawn from the Treasury, but in Consequence of Appropriations made by Law; and a regular Statement and Account of the Receipts and Expenditures of all public Money shall be published from time to time.

No Title of Nobility shall be granted by the United States: And no Person holding any Office of Profit or Trust under them, shall, without the Consent of the

Congress, accept of any present, Emolument, Office, or Title, of any kind whatever, from any King, Prince, or foreign State.

Section 10. No State shall enter into any Treaty, Alliance, or Confederation;
grant Letters of Marque and Reprisal; coin Money; emit Bills of Credit; make any
Thing but gold and silver Coin a Tender in Payment of Debts; pass any Bill of
Attainder, ex post facto Law, or Law impairing the Obligation of Contracts, or
grant any Title of Nobility.

No State shall, without the Consent of the Congress, lay any Imposts or Duties
on Imports or Exports, except what may be absolutely necessary for executing
it's inspection Laws: and the net Produce of all Duties and Imposts, laid by any
State on Imports or Exports, shall be for the Use of the Treasury of the United
States; and all such Laws shall be subject to the Revision and Controul of the
Congress.

No State shall, without the Consent of Congress, lay any Duty of Tonnage,
keep Troops, or Ships of War in time of Peace, enter into any Agreement or
Compact with another State, or with a foreign Power, or engage in War, unless
actually invaded, or in such imminent Danger as will not admit of delay.

ARTICLE II

Section 1. The executive Power shall be vested in a President of the United States
of America. He shall hold his Office during the Term of four Years, and, together
with the Vice President, chosen for the same Term, be elected, as follows

Each State shall appoint, in such Manner as the Legislature thereof may direct,
a Number of Electors, equal to the whole Number of Senators and Representatives
to which the State may be entitled in the Congress: but no Senator or
Representative, or Person holding an Office of Trust or Profit under the United
States, shall be appointed an Elector.

[The Electors shall meet in their respective States, and vote by Ballot for two
Persons, of whom one at least shall not be an Inhabitant of the same State with
themselves. And they shall make a List of all the Persons voted for, and of the
Number of Votes for each; which List they shall sign and certify, and transmit
sealed to the Seat of the Government of the United States, directed to the
President of the Senate. The President of the Senate shall, in the Presence of the
Senate and House of Representatives, open all the Certificates, and the Votes
shall then be counted. The Person having the greatest Number of Votes shall be
the President, if such Number be a Majority of the whole Number of Electors
appointed; and if there be more than one who have such Majority, and have an

equal Number of Votes, then the House of Representatives shall immediately chuse by Ballot one of them for President; and if no Person have a Majority, then from the five highest on the list the said House shall in like Manner chuse the President. But in chusing the President, the Votes shall be taken by States, the Representation from each State having one Vote; A quorum for this Purpose shall consist of a Member or Members from two thirds of the States, and a Majority of all the States shall be necessary to a Choice. In every Case, after the Choice of the President, the Person having the greatest Number of Votes of the Electors shall be the Vice President. But if there should remain two or more who have equal Votes, the Senate shall chuse from them by Ballot the Vice President.]⁶

The Congress may determine the Time of chusing the Electors, and the Day on which they shall give their Votes; which Day shall be the same throughout the United States.

No Person except a natural born Citizen, or a Citizen of the United States, at the time of the Adoption of this Constitution, shall be eligible to the Office of President; neither shall any Person be eligible to that Office who shall not have attained to the Age of thirty five Years, and been fourteen Years a Resident within the United States.

In Case of the Removal of the President from Office, or of his Death, Resignation, or Inability to discharge the Powers and Duties of the said Office,⁷ the Same shall devolve on the Vice President, and the Congress may by Law provide for the Case of Removal, Death, Resignation or Inability, both of the President and Vice President, declaring what Officer shall then act as President, and such Officer shall act accordingly, until the Disability be removed, or a President shall be elected.

The President shall, at stated Times, receive for his Services, a Compensation, which shall neither be encreased nor diminished during the Period for which he shall have been elected, and he shall not receive within that Period any other Emolument from the United States, or any of them.

Before he enter on the Execution of his Office, he shall take the following Oath or Affirmation:—"I do solemnly swear (or affirm) that I will faithfully execute the Office of President of the United States, and will to the best of my Ability, preserve, protect and defend the Constitution of the United States."

Section 2. The President shall be Commander in Chief of the Army and Navy of the United States, and of the Militia of the several States, when called into the actual Service of the United States; he may require the Opinion, in writing, of the principal Officer in each of the executive Departments, upon any Subject relating to the Duties of their respective Offices, and he shall have Power to grant Reprieves and Pardons for Offences against the United States, except in Cases of Impeachment.

He shall have Power, by and with the Advice and Consent of the Senate, to make Treaties, provided two thirds of the Senators present concur; and he shall nominate, and by and with the Advice and Consent of the Senate, shall appoint Ambassadors, other public Ministers and Consuls, Judges of the supreme Court, and all other Officers of the United States, whose Appointments are not herein otherwise provided for, and which shall be established by Law: but the Congress may by Law vest the Appointment of such inferior Officers, as they think proper, in the President alone, in the Courts of Law, or in the Heads of Departments.

The President shall have Power to fill up all Vacancies that may happen during the Recess of the Senate, by granting Commissions which shall expire at the End of their next Session.

Section 3. He shall from time to time give to the Congress Information of the State of the Union, and recommend to their Consideration such Measures as he shall judge necessary and expedient; he may, on extraordinary Occasions, convene both Houses, or either of them, and in Case of Disagreement between them, with Respect to the Time of Adjournment, he may adjourn them to such Time as he shall think proper; he shall receive Ambassadors and other public Ministers; he shall take Care that the Laws be faithfully executed, and shall Commission all the Officers of the United States.

Section 4. The President, Vice President and all civil Officers of the United States, shall be removed from Office on Impeachment for, and Conviction of, Treason, Bribery, or other high Crimes and Misdemeanors.

ARTICLE III

Section 1. The judicial Power of the United States, shall be vested in one supreme Court, and in such inferior Courts as the Congress may from time to time ordain and establish. The Judges, both of the supreme and inferior Courts, shall hold their Offices during good Behaviour, and shall, at stated Times, receive for their Services, a Compensation, which shall not be diminished during their Continuance in Office.

Section 2. The judicial Power shall extend to all Cases, in Law and Equity, arising under this Constitution, the Laws of the United States, and Treaties made, or which shall be made, under their Authority;—to all Cases affecting Ambassadors, other public Ministers and Consuls;—to all Cases of admiralty and maritime Jurisdiction;—to Controversies to which the United States shall be a Party;—to

Controversies between two or more States;—between a State and Citizens of another State;[8]—between Citizens of different States;—between Citizens of the same State claiming Lands under Grants of different States, and between a State, or the Citizens thereof, and foreign States, Citizens or Subjects.

In all Cases affecting Ambassadors, other public Ministers and Consuls, and those in which a State shall be Party, the supreme Court shall have original Jurisdiction. In all the other Cases before mentioned, the supreme Court shall have appellate Jurisdiction, both as to Law and Fact, with such Exceptions, and under such Regulations as the Congress shall make.

The Trial of all Crimes, except in Cases of Impeachment, shall be by Jury; and such Trial shall be held in the State where the said Crimes shall have been committed; but when not committed within any State, the Trial shall be at such Place or Places as the Congress may by Law have directed.

Section 3. Treason against the United States, shall consist only in levying War against them, or in adhering to their Enemies, giving them Aid and Comfort. No Person shall be convicted of Treason unless on the Testimony of two Witnesses to the same overt Act, or on Confession in open Court.

The Congress shall have Power to declare the Punishment of Treason, but no Attainder of Treason shall work Corruption of Blood, or Forfeiture except during the Life of the Person attainted.

ARTICLE IV

Section 1. Full Faith and Credit shall be given in each State to the public Acts, Records, and judicial Proceedings of every other State. And the Congress may by general Laws prescribe the Manner in which such Acts, Records and Proceedings shall be proved, and the Effect thereof.

Section 2. The Citizens of each State shall be entitled to all Privileges and Immunities of Citizens in the several States.

A Person charged in any State with Treason, Felony, or other Crime, who shall flee from Justice, and be found in another State, shall on Demand of the executive Authority of the State from which he fled, be delivered up, to be removed to the State having Jurisdiction of the Crime.

[No Person held to Service or Labour in one State, under the Laws thereof, escaping into another, shall, in Consequence of any Law or Regulation therein, be discharged from such Service or Labour, but shall be delivered up on Claim of the Party to whom such Service or Labour may be due.][9]

Section 3. New States may be admitted by the Congress into this Union; but no new State shall be formed or erected within the Jurisdiction of any other State; nor any State be formed by the Junction of two or more States, or Parts of States, without the Consent of the Legislatures of the States concerned as well as of the Congress.

The Congress shall have Power to dispose of and make all needful Rules and Regulations respecting the Territory or other Property belonging to the United States; and nothing in this Constitution shall be so construed as to Prejudice any Claims of the United States, or of any particular State.

Section 4. The United States shall guarantee to every State in this Union a Republican Form of Government, and shall protect each of them against Invasion; and on Application of the Legislature, or of the Executive (when the Legislature cannot be convened) against domestic Violence.

ARTICLE V

The Congress, whenever two thirds of both Houses shall deem it necessary, shall propose Amendments to this Constitution, or, on the Application of the Legislatures of two thirds of the several States, shall call a Convention for proposing Amendments, which, in either Case, shall be valid to all Intents and Purposes, as Part of this Constitution, when ratified by the Legislatures of three fourths of the several States, or by Conventions in three fourths thereof, as the one or the other Mode of Ratification may be proposed by the Congress; Provided [that no Amendment which may be made prior to the Year One thousand eight hundred and eight shall in any Manner affect the first and fourth Clauses in the Ninth Section of the first Article; and][10] that no State, without its Consent, shall be deprived of its equal Suffrage in the Senate.

ARTICLE VI

All Debts contracted and Engagements entered into, before the Adoption of this Constitution, shall be as valid against the United States under this Constitution, as under the Confederation.

This Constitution, and the Laws of the United States which shall be made in Pursuance thereof; and all Treaties made, or which shall be made, under the Authority of the United States, shall be the supreme Law of the Land; and the Judges in every State shall be bound thereby, any Thing in the Constitution or Laws of any State to the Contrary notwithstanding.

The Senators and Representatives before mentioned, and the Members of the several State Legislatures, and all executive and judicial Officers, both of the United States and of the several States, shall be bound by Oath or Affirmation, to support this Constitution; but no religious Test shall ever be required as a Qualification to any Office or public Trust under the United States.

ARTICLE VII

The Ratification of the Conventions of nine States, shall be sufficient for the Establishment of this Constitution between the States so ratifying the Same.

Done in Convention by the Unanimous Consent of the States present the Seventeenth Day of September in the Year of our Lord one thousand seven hundred and Eighty seven and of the Independence of the United States of America the Twelfth. IN WITNESS whereof We have hereunto subscribed our Names,

George Washington,
President and
deputy from Virginia.

New Hampshire:	John Langdon,
	Nicholas Gilman.
Massachusetts:	Nathaniel Gorham,
	Rufus King.
Connecticut:	William Samuel Johnson,
	Roger Sherman.
New York:	Alexander Hamilton.
New Jersey:	William Livingston,
	David Brearley,
	William Paterson,
	Jonathan Dayton.
Pennsylvania:	Benjamin Franklin,
	Thomas Mifflin,
	Robert Morris,
	George Clymer,
	Thomas FitzSimons,
	Jared Ingersoll,

(Continued)

(Continued)

	James Wilson,
	Gouverneur Morris.
Delaware:	George Read,
	Gunning Bedford Jr.,
	John Dickinson,
	Richard Bassett,
	Jacob Broom.
Maryland:	James McHenry,
	Daniel of St. Thomas Jenifer,
	Daniel Carroll.
Virginia:	John Blair,
	James Madison Jr.
North Carolina:	William Blount,
	Richard Dobbs Spaight,
	Hugh Williamson.
South Carolina:	John Rutledge,
	Charles Cotesworth Pinckney,
	Charles Pinckney,
	Pierce Butler.
Georgia:	William Few,
	Abraham Baldwin.

[The language of the original Constitution, not including the Amendments, was adopted by a convention of the states on September 17, 1787, and was subsequently ratified by the states on the following dates: Delaware, December 7, 1787; Pennsylvania, December 12, 1787; New Jersey, December 18, 1787; Georgia, January 2, 1788; Connecticut, January 9, 1788; Massachusetts, February 6, 1788; Maryland, April 28, 1788; South Carolina, May 23, 1788; New Hampshire, June 21, 1788.

Ratification was completed on June 21, 1788.

The Constitution subsequently was ratified by Virginia, June 25, 1788; New York, July 26, 1788; North Carolina, November 21, 1789; Rhode Island, May 29, 1790; and Vermont, January 10, 1791.]

Amendments

Amendment I

(First ten amendments ratified December 15, 1791.)

Congress shall make no law respecting an establishment of religion, or prohibiting the free exercise thereof; or abridging the freedom of speech, or of the press; or the right of the people peaceably to assemble, and to petition the Government for a redress of grievances.

Amendment II

A well regulated Militia, being necessary to the security of a free State, the right of the people to keep and bear Arms, shall not be infringed.

Amendment III

No Soldier shall, in time of peace be quartered in any house, without the consent of the Owner, nor in time of war, but in a manner to be prescribed by law.

Amendment IV

The right of the people to be secure in their persons, houses, papers, and effects, against unreasonable searches and seizures, shall not be violated, and no Warrants shall issue, but upon probable cause, supported by Oath or affirmation, and particularly describing the place to be searched, and the persons or things to be seized.

Amendment V

No person shall be held to answer for a capital, or otherwise infamous crime, unless on a presentment or indictment of a Grand Jury, except in cases arising in the land or naval forces, or in the Militia, when in actual service in time of War or public danger; nor shall any person be subject for the same offence to be twice put in jeopardy of life or limb; nor shall be compelled in any criminal case to be a witness against himself, nor be deprived of life, liberty, or property, without due process of law; nor shall private property be taken for public use, without just compensation.

Amendment VI

In all criminal prosecutions, the accused shall enjoy the right to a speedy and public trial, by an impartial jury of the State and district wherein the crime shall have been committed, which district shall have been previously ascertained by law, and to be informed of the nature and cause of the accusation; to be confronted with the witnesses against him; to have compulsory process for obtaining witnesses in his favor, and to have the Assistance of Counsel for his defence.

Amendment VII

In Suits at common law, where the value in controversy shall exceed twenty dollars, the right of trial by jury shall be preserved, and no fact tried by a jury, shall be otherwise re-examined in any Court of the United States, than according to the rules of the common law.

Amendment VIII

Excessive bail shall not be required, nor excessive fines imposed, nor cruel and unusual punishments inflicted.

Amendment IX

The enumeration in the Constitution, of certain rights, shall not be construed to deny or disparage others retained by the people.

Amendment X

The powers not delegated to the United States by the Constitution, nor prohibited by it to the States, are reserved to the States respectively, or to the people.

Amendment XI (Ratified February 7, 1795)

The Judicial power of the United States shall not be construed to extend to any suit in law or equity, commenced or prosecuted against one of the United States by Citizens of another State, or by Citizens or Subjects of any Foreign State.

Amendment XII (Ratified June 15, 1804)

The Electors shall meet in their respective states and vote by ballot for President and Vice-President, one of whom, at least, shall not be an inhabitant of the same state with themselves; they shall name in their ballots the person voted for as President, and in distinct ballots the person voted for as Vice-President, and they shall make distinct lists of all persons voted for as President, and of all persons voted for as Vice-President, and of the number of votes for each, which lists they shall sign and certify, and transmit sealed to the seat of the government of the United States, directed to the President of the Senate;—The President of the Senate shall, in the presence of the Senate and House of Representatives, open all the certificates and the votes shall then be counted;—The person having the greatest number of votes for President, shall be the President, if such number be a majority of the whole number of Electors appointed; and if no person have such majority, then from the persons having the highest numbers not exceeding three on the list of those voted for as President, the House of Representatives shall choose immediately, by ballot, the President. But in choosing the President, the votes shall be taken by states, the representation from each state having one vote; a quorum for this purpose shall consist of a member or members from two-thirds of the states, and a majority of all the states shall be necessary to a choice. [And if the House of Representatives shall not choose a President whenever the right of choice shall devolve upon them, before the fourth day of March next following, then the Vice-President shall act as President, as in the case of the death or other constitutional disability of the President.—][11] The person having the greatest number of votes as Vice-President, shall be the Vice-President, if such number be a majority of the whole number of Electors appointed, and if no person have a majority, then from the two highest numbers on the list, the Senate shall choose the Vice-President; a quorum for the purpose shall consist of two-thirds of the whole number of Senators, and a majority of the whole number shall be necessary to a choice. But no person constitutionally ineligible to the office of President shall be eligible to that of Vice-President of the United States.

Amendment XIII (Ratified December 6, 1865)

Section 1. Neither slavery nor involuntary servitude, except as a punishment for crime whereof the party shall have been duly convicted, shall exist within the United States, or any place subject to their jurisdiction.

Section 2. Congress shall have power to enforce this article by appropriate legislation.

Amendment XIV (Ratified July 9, 1868)

Section 1. All persons born or naturalized in the United States, and subject to the jurisdiction thereof, are citizens of the United States and of the State wherein they reside. No State shall make or enforce any law which shall abridge the privileges or immunities of citizens of the United States; nor shall any State deprive any person of life, liberty, or property, without due process of law; nor deny to any person within its jurisdiction the equal protection of the laws.

Section 2. Representatives shall be apportioned among the several States according to their respective numbers, counting the whole number of persons in each State, excluding Indians not taxed. But when the right to vote at any election for the choice of electors for President and Vice President of the United States, Representatives in Congress, the Executive and Judicial officers of a State, or the members of the Legislature thereof, is denied to any of the male inhabitants of such State, being twenty-one years of age,[12] and citizens of the United States, or in any way abridged, except for participation in rebellion, or other crime, the basis of representation therein shall be reduced in the proportion which the number of such male citizens shall bear to the whole number of male citizens twenty-one years of age in such State.

Section 3. No person shall be a Senator or Representative in Congress, or elector of President and Vice President, or hold any office, civil or military, under the United States, or under any State, who, having previously taken an oath, as a member of Congress, or as an officer of the United States, or as a member of any State legislature, or as an executive or judicial officer of any State, to support the Constitution of the United States, shall have engaged in insurrection or rebellion against the same, or given aid or comfort to the enemies thereof. But Congress may by a vote of two-thirds of each House, remove such disability.

Section 4. The validity of the public debt of the United States, authorized by law, including debts incurred for payment of pensions and bounties for services in suppressing insurrection or rebellion, shall not be questioned. But neither the United States nor any State shall assume or pay any debt or obligation incurred in aid of insurrection or rebellion against the United States, or any claim for the loss or emancipation of any slave; but all such debts, obligations and claims shall be held illegal and void.

Section 5. The Congress shall have power to enforce, by appropriate legislation, the provisions of this article.

Amendment XV (Ratified February 3, 1870)

Section 1. The right of citizens of the United States to vote shall not be denied or abridged by the United States or by any State on account of race, color, or previous condition of servitude.

Section 2. The Congress shall have power to enforce this article by appropriate legislation.

Amendment XVI (Ratified February 3, 1913)

The Congress shall have power to lay and collect taxes on incomes, from whatever source derived, without apportionment among the several States, and without regard to any census or enumeration.

Amendment XVII (Ratified April 8, 1913)

The Senate of the United States shall be composed of two Senators from each State, elected by the people thereof, for six years; and each Senator shall have one vote. The electors in each State shall have the qualifications requisite for electors of the most numerous branch of the State legislatures.

When vacancies happen in the representation of any State in the Senate, the executive authority of such State shall issue writs of election to fill such vacancies: *Provided,* That the legislature of any State may empower the executive thereof to make temporary appointments until the people fill the vacancies by election as the legislature may direct.

This amendment shall not be so construed as to affect the election or term of any Senator chosen before it becomes valid as part of the Constitution.

Amendment XVIII (Ratified January 16, 1919)[13]

Section 1. After one year from the ratification of this article the manufacture, sale, or transportation of intoxicating liquors within, the importation thereof into, or the exportation thereof from the United States and all territory subject to the jurisdiction thereof for beverage purposes is hereby prohibited.

Section 2. The Congress and the several States shall have concurrent power to enforce this article by appropriate legislation.

Section 3. This article shall be inoperative unless it shall have been ratified as an amendment to the Constitution by the legislatures of the several States, as provided in the Constitution, within seven years from the date of the submission hereof to the States by the Congress.

Amendment XIX (Ratified August 18, 1920)

The right of citizens of the United States to vote shall not be denied or abridged by the United States or by any State on account of sex.

Congress shall have power to enforce this article by appropriate legislation.

Amendment XX (Ratified January 23, 1933)

Section 1. The terms of the President and Vice President shall end at noon on the 20th day of January, and the terms of Senators and Representatives at noon on the 3d day of January, of the years in which such terms would have ended if this article had not been ratified; and the terms of their successors shall then begin.

Section 2. The Congress shall assemble at least once in every year, and such meeting shall begin at noon on the 3d day of January, unless they shall by law appoint a different day.

Section 3.[14] If, at the time fixed for the beginning of the term of the President, the President elect shall have died, the Vice President elect shall become President. If a President shall not have been chosen before the time fixed for the beginning of his term, or if the President elect shall have failed to qualify, then the Vice President elect shall act as President until a President shall have qualified; and the Congress may by law provide for the case wherein neither a President elect nor a Vice President elect shall have qualified, declaring who shall then act as President, or the manner in which one who is to act shall be selected, and such person shall act accordingly until a President or Vice President shall have qualified.

Section 4. The Congress may by law provide for the case of the death of any of the persons from whom the House of Representatives may choose a President whenever the right of choice shall have devolved upon them, and for the case of the death of any of the persons from whom the Senate may choose a Vice President whenever the right of choice shall have devolved upon them.

Section 5. Sections 1 and 2 shall take effect on the 15th day of October following the ratification of this article.

Section 6. This article shall be inoperative unless it shall have been ratified as an amendment to the Constitution by the legislatures of three-fourths of the several States within seven years from the date of its submission.

Amendment XXI (Ratified December 5, 1933)

Section 1. The eighteenth article of amendment to the Constitution of the United States is hereby repealed.

Section 2. The transportation or importation into any State, Territory, or possession of the United States for delivery or use therein of intoxicating liquors, in violation of the laws thereof, is hereby prohibited.

Section 3. This article shall be inoperative unless it shall have been ratified as an amendment to the Constitution by conventions in the several States, as provided in the Constitution, within seven years from the date of the submission hereof to the States by the Congress.

Amendment XXII (Ratified February 27, 1951)

Section 1. No person shall be elected to the office of the President more than twice, and no person who has held the office of President, or acted as President, for more than two years of a term to which some other person was elected President shall be elected to the office of the President more than once. But this Article shall not apply to any person holding the office of President when this Article was proposed by the Congress, and shall not prevent any person who may be holding the office of President, or acting as President, during the term within which this Article become operative from holding the office of President or acting as President during the remainder of such term.

Section 2. This article shall be inoperative unless it shall have been ratified as an amendment to the Constitution by the legislatures of three-fourths of the several States within seven years from the date of its submission to the States by the Congress.

Amendment XXIII (Ratified March 29, 1961)

Section 1. The District constituting the seat of Government of the United States shall appoint in such manner as the Congress may direct:

A number of electors of President and Vice President equal to the whole number of Senators and Representatives in Congress to which the District would be entitled if it were a State, but in no event more than the least populous State; they shall be in addition to those appointed by the States, but they shall be considered, for the purposes of the election of President and Vice President, to be electors appointed by a State; and they shall meet in the District and perform such duties as provided by the twelfth article of amendment.

Section 2. The Congress shall have power to enforce this article by appropriate legislation.

Amendment XXIV (Ratified January 23, 1964)

Section 1. The right of citizens of the United States to vote in any primary or other election for President or Vice President, for electors for President or Vice

President, or for Senator or Representative in Congress, shall not be denied or abridged by the United States or any State by reason of failure to pay any poll tax or other tax.

Section 2. The Congress shall have power to enforce this article by appropriate legislation.

Amendment XXV (Ratified February 10, 1967)

Section 1. In case of the removal of the President from office or of his death or resignation, the Vice President shall become President.

Section 2. Whenever there is a vacancy in the office of the Vice President, the President shall nominate a Vice President who shall take office upon confirmation by a majority vote of both Houses of Congress.

Section 3. Whenever the President transmits to the President pro tempore of the Senate and the Speaker of the House of Representatives his written declaration that he is unable to discharge the powers and duties of his office, and until he transmits to them a written declaration to the contrary, such powers and duties shall be discharged by the Vice President as Acting President.

Section 4. Whenever the Vice President and a majority of either the principal officers of the executive departments or of such other body as Congress may by law provide, transmit to the President pro tempore of the Senate and the Speaker of the House of Representatives their written declaration that the President is unable to discharge the powers and duties of his office, the Vice President shall immediately assume the powers and duties of the office as Acting President.

Thereafter, when the President transmits to the President pro tempore of the Senate and the Speaker of the House of Representatives his written declaration that no inability exists, he shall resume the powers and duties of his office unless the Vice President and a majority of either the principal officers of the executive department or of such other body as Congress may by law provide, transmit within four days to the President pro tempore of the Senate and the Speaker of the House of Representatives their written declaration that the President is unable to discharge the powers and duties of his office. Thereupon Congress shall decide the issue, assembling within forty-eight hours for that purpose if not in session. If the Congress, within twenty-one days after receipt of the latter written declaration, or, if Congress is not in session, within twenty-one days after Congress is required to assemble, determines by two-thirds vote of both Houses that the President is unable to discharge the powers and duties of his office, the Vice President shall continue to discharge the same as Acting President; otherwise, the President shall resume the powers and duties of his office.

Amendment XXVI (Ratified July 1, 1971)

Section 1. The right of citizens of the United States, who are eighteen years of age or older, to vote shall not be denied or abridged by the United States or by any State on account of age.

Section 2. The Congress shall have power to enforce this article by appropriate legislation.

Amendment XXVII (Ratified May 7, 1992)

No law varying the compensation for the services of the Senators and Representatives shall take effect, until an election of Representatives shall have intervened.

NOTES

1. The part in brackets was changed by section 2 of the Fourteenth Amendment.
2. The part in brackets was changed by the first paragraph of the Seventeenth Amendment.
3. The part in brackets was changed by the second paragraph of the Seventeenth Amendment.
4. The part in brackets was changed by section 2 of the Twentieth Amendment.
5. The Sixteenth Amendment gave Congress the power to tax incomes.
6. The material in brackets has been superseded by the Twelfth Amendment.
7. This provision has been affected by the Twenty-fifth Amendment.
8. These clauses were affected by the Eleventh Amendment.
9. This paragraph has been superseded by the Thirteenth Amendment.
10. Obsolete.
11. The part in brackets has been superseded by section 3 of the Twentieth Amendment.
12. See the Nineteenth and Twenty-sixth Amendments.
13. This Amendment was repealed by section 1 of the Twenty-first Amendment.
14. See the Twenty-fifth Amendment.

Credits

Chapter 1. Designing Institutions

1-1: Reprinted by permission of the publisher from *The Logic of Collective Action: Public Goods and the Theory of Groups* by Mancur Olson, pp. 1–3, 5–19, Cambridge, Mass.: Harvard University Press, Copyright © 1965, 1971 by the President and Fellows of Harvard College.

1-2: Excerpted from *Science*, Vol. 162, December 13, 1968, pp. 1243–1248. Copyright 1968 AAAS. Reprinted with permission from AAAS.

1-3: Reprinted by permission of the author.

Chapter 2. The Constitutional Framework

2-1: Excerpted from the article originally appearing in the *American Political Science Review 55*, no. 4 (December 1961): 799–816. Copyright © 1961 American Political Science Association. Reprinted with the permission of Cambridge University Press.

Chapter 3. Federalism

3-3: *The Atlantic Monthly.* Copyright 2007 by *The Atlantic Monthly.* Reproduced with permission of *The Atlantic Monthly* in the format Textbook via Copyright Clearance Center.

3-4: Reprinted by permission of the author.

Chapter 4. Civil Rights

4-1: Excerpts from "Introduction: Playing the Race Card" from *The Race Card* by Richard Thompson Ford. Copyright © 2008 by Richard Thompson Ford. Reprinted by permission of Farrar, Straus and Giroux, LLC.

4-2: Prewitt, Kenneth. "Immigrants and the Changing Categories of Race," in *Transforming Politics, Transforming America: The Political and Civic Incorporation of Immigrants in the United States.* Taeku Lee, S. Karthick Ramakrishnan, and Ricardo Ramírez, eds. pp. 19–31. © 2006 by the Rector and Visitors of the University of Virginia. Reprinted by permission of the University of Virginia Press.

Chapter 5. Civil Liberties

5-1: Sunstein, Cass R.; *Republic.com 2.0.* © 2007 by Princeton University Press. Reprinted by permission of Princeton University Press.

5-2: William N. Eskridge, Jr., "A Liberal Vision of U.S. Family Law in 2020," ch 22 in Jack M. Balkin and Reva B. Siegel, eds., *The Constitution in 2020* (New York: Oxford University Press, 2009), p. 245–254. Published by permission of William N. Eskridge, Jr. in c/o Writers Representatives LLC, New York, NY 10011, www.writersreps.com. All rights reserved.

5-4: Excerpted from Lee Epstein, ed., *Contemplating Courts* (Washington, D.C.: CQ Press, 1995), pp. 390–419.

Chapter 7. The Presidency

7-1: Reprinted by permission of the estate of Richard E. Neustadt.

Chapter 8. The Bureaucracy

8-1: Excerpted from John E. Chubb and Paul E. Peterson, eds. *Can the Government Govern?* (Washington, D.C.: Brookings Institution Press, 1989), 267–285. Reprinted by permission.

8-2: *National Journal* by Government Research Corporation Copyright 2005 Reproduced with permission of National Journal Group, Inc. in the format Textbook via Copyright Clearance Center.

8-3: Lewis, David E.; *The Politics of Presidential Appointments.* © 2008 by Princeton University Press. Reprinted by permission of Princeton University Press.

8-4: Excerpted from Mathew D. McCubbins, Roger G. Noll, and Barry R. Weingast, "Administrative Procedures as Instruments of Political Control," *Journal of Law, Economics, and Organization* 3(2), Fall 1987, p. 243–277. © 1987 by Yale University. By permission of Oxford University Press.

Chapter 9. The Judiciary

9-1: Scalia, Antonin; *A Matter of Interpretation.* © 1997 Princeton University Press. Reprinted by permission of Princeton University Press.

9-2: From *Active Liberty: Interpreting Our Democratic Constitution* by Stephen Breyer, copyright © 2005 by Stephen Breyer. Used by permission of Alfred A. Knopf, a division of Random House, Inc.

Chapter 10. Public Opinion

10-1: Originally published in Herbert Asher, *Polling and the Public: What Every Citizen Should Know,* 4th edition (Washington, D.C.: CQ Press, 1998), pp. 141–169.

10-2: Excerpted from the article originally published in *American Political Science Review 89,* no. 3 (September 1995): 543–564. Copyright © 1995 American Political Science Association. Reprinted with the permission of Cambridge University Press.

10-3: Fiorina, Morris P.; *Culture War? The Myth of a Polarized America,* 1st Edition, © 2005. Reprinted by permission of Pearson Education, Inc., Upper Saddle River, NJ.

10-4: Reprinted from *Commentary,* February 2006, by permission; copyright © 2006 by Commentary, Inc.

10-5: *From American Grace: How Religion Divides and Unites Us* by Robert D. Putnam and David E. Campbell. Copyright © 2010 Robert D. Putnam and David E. Campbell. Reprinted with the permission of Simon & Schuster, Inc. and the authors, Robert D. Putnam and David E. Campbell.

Chapter 11. Voting, Campaigns, and Elections

11-1: Excerpted from Samuel L. Popkin, *The Reasoning Voter: Communication and Persuasion in Presidential Campaigns,* 2nd ed. (Chicago: University of Chicago Press, 1994), pp. 212–219. Copyright © 1991, 1994 by the University of Chicago. All rights reserved. Reprinted by permission.

11-3: Darrell M. West, from "Overview of Ads" in *Air Wars,* by Darrell M. West (CQ Press: 2010), 1–24. Notes appearing in the original have been deleted.

11-4: Michael Schudson is Professor of Communication at the University of California, San Diego and author of *The Good Citizen: A History of American Civic Life* (1998) and *The Sociology of News* (2003). Reprinted with permission.

11-5: "Content by Paul Blumenthal © 2012 AOL Inc. Used with permission." Paul Blumenthal is a reporter covering money-in-politics for *The Huffington Post* and the editor of the *HuffPost Fundrace* newsletter.

Chapter 12. Political Parties

12-1: Originally published in John H. Aldrich, *Why Parties?: The Origin and Transformation of Political Parties in America* (Chicago: University of Chicago

Press, 1995), pp. 14–27. Copyright © 1995 by the University of Chicago. All rights reserved. Reprinted by permission.

12-2: Excerpted from Larry Bartels, "Partisanship and Voting Behavior, 1952–1996," *American Journal of Political Science, Vol. 44* (1), 2000, pp.35–50. Reproduced with permission of Blackwell Publishing, Ltd.

12-3: Morris P. Fiorina, "Parties as Problem Solvers" in *Promoting General Welfare: New Perspectives on Government Performance,* eds. Alan S. Gerber and Eric M. Patashnik (Washington, D.C.: Brookings Institution Press, 2006), 237–253. Reprinted by permission.

Chapter 13. Interest Groups

13-1: From Schattschneider. *Semi-sovereign People Re-Issue,* 1E. © 1975 Wadsworth, a part of Cengage Learning, Inc. Reproduced by permission. www.cengage .com/permissions.

13-2: Wright, John R.; *Interest Groups and Congress: Lobbying, Contributions and Influence,* 1st Edition, © 2003. Reprinted by permission of Pearson Education, Inc., Upper Saddle River, NJ.

13-3: Richard L. Hall and Frank W. Wayman, "Buying Time: Moneyed Interests and the Mobilization of Bias in Congressional Committees," *American Political Science Review 84*, n0.3 (September 1990): 797–820. Copyright (c) 1990 American Political Science Association. Reprinted with the permission of Cambridge University Press.

Chapter 14. News Media

14-1: James T. Hamilton, "The Market and the Media," in *The Institutions of American Democracy: The Press,* edited by Geneva Overholser and Kathleen Hall Jamieson, pp. 351–370. Copyright © 2005 Oxford University Press, Inc. By permission of Oxford University Press, Inc.

14-2: Baum, Matthew A.; *War Stories.* © 2010 by Princeton University Press. Reprinted by permission of Princeton University Press.

14-3: Excerpted from Kristen Purcell, Lee Rainie, Amy Mitchell, Tom Rosenstiel, and Kenny Olmstead, "Understanding the Participatory News Consumer," Pew Internet & American Life Project, March 1, 2010. p. 8–48. http://www.pew internet.org/Reports/2010/Online-News.aspx. Reprinted by permission.

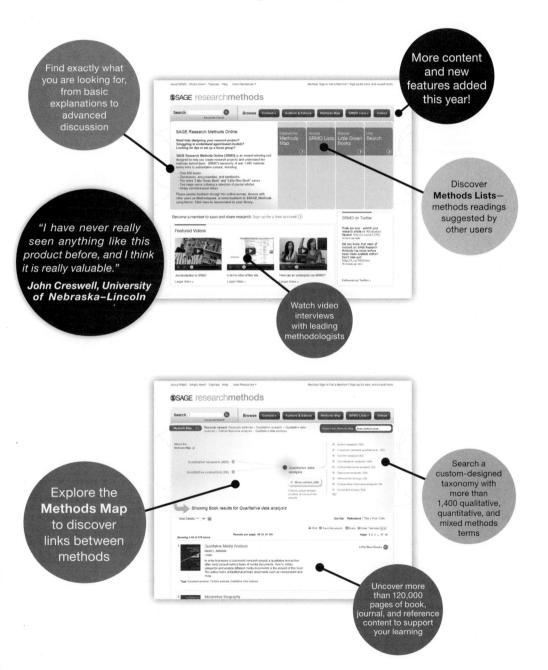

⑤SAGE research**methods**

The essential online tool for researchers from the world's leading methods publisher

Find exactly what you are looking for, from basic explanations to advanced discussion

More content and new features added this year!

Discover **Methods Lists**— methods readings suggested by other users

"*I have never really seen anything like this product before, and I think it is really valuable.*"
John Creswell, University of Nebraska–Lincoln

Watch video interviews with leading methodologists

Explore the **Methods Map** to discover links between methods

Search a custom-designed taxonomy with more than 1,400 qualitative, quantitative, and mixed methods terms

Uncover more than 120,000 pages of book, journal, and reference content to support your learning

Find out more at
www.sageresearchmethods.com